Politics and P

MW00810806

Strategic Actors and Policy Domains

FOR

Polly, Maggie, Ben and Cory Baumer
Christy, Evan and Ross Van Horn
whose support and encouragement made this work possible

Politics and Public Policy

Strategic Actors and Policy Domains

Fourth Edition

Donald C. Baumer
Smith College

Carl E. Van Horn
Rutgers University

Los Angeles | London | New Delhi
Singapore | Washington DC

Los Angeles | London | New Delhi
Singapore | Washington DC

FOR INFORMATION:

CQ Press

An Imprint of SAGE Publications, Inc.

2455 Teller Road

Thousand Oaks, California 91320

E-mail: order@sagepub.com

SAGE Publications Ltd.

1 Oliver's Yard

55 City Road

London EC1Y 1SP

United Kingdom

SAGE Publications India Pvt. Ltd.

B 1/I 1 Mohan Cooperative Industrial Area

Mathura Road, New Delhi 110 044

India

SAGE Publications Asia-Pacific Pte. Ltd.

3 Church Street

#10-04 Samsung Hub

Singapore 049483

Printed in the United States of America

A catalog record of this book is available from the Library of Congress.

ISBN 978-1-4522-2017-8

This book is printed on acid-free paper.

Acquisitions Editor: Charisse Kiino

Production Editor: Laura Barrett

Copy Editor: Jim Kelly

Typesetter: C&M Digitals (P) Ltd.

Proofreader: Sarah J. Duffy

Indexer: Kathy Paparchontis

Cover Designer: Anupama Krishan

Marketing Manager: Erica DeLuca

Permissions Editor: Jennifer Barron

Certified Chain of Custody
Promoting Sustainable Forestry
www.sfiprogram.org
SFI-01268

SFI label applies to text stock

13 14 15 16 10 9 8 7 6 5 4 3 2 1

CONTENTS

TABLES, FIGURES, AND BOXES

W hy do policymakers select certain problems for attention and ignore others? Why do some policy ideas fail and others succeed? In addition to the president, Congress, and the Supreme Court, what other institutions are influential in shaping public policies? How do policymakers design and implement policies? How do those policies ultimately influence the nation? Providing answers to these and other questions is the focus of this book. The practice of politics and policymaking is complicated, involving thousands of people in government institutions and the private sector. Although each public law and public policy has a unique history, *Politics and Public Policy* is designed to help students understand the larger patterns of the policymaking process.

In *Politics and Public Policy*, we go beyond conventional analyses that focus narrowly and exclusively on presidents and members of Congress to offer a more comprehensive and realistic view of policymaking in the United States. The judicial rulings, regulations, administrative rulings, and corporate decisions of judges, bureaucrats, corporate officials, journalists, and voters determine government policy and its results just as much as the decisions of legislators and chief executives. Moreover, state and local governments play an increasingly important and expanding role in the design and conduct of public policies.

In *Politics and Public Policy*, we use a unique framework to examine the policymakers and institutions that make public policy. Differences in the politics within these arenas produce different policies and outcomes. To help students understand such variations, we describe six domains of public policy:

1. *Boardroom politics:* decisions by business leaders and professionals that have important public consequences

2. *Bureaucratic politics:* rulemaking and adjudication by administrators who consider the interests of clients, legislators, and the chief executive, in addition to using their own professional judgment

3. *Cloakroom politics:* lawmaking by legislators who weigh the competing demands of constituents, interest groups, and presidents or governors

4. *Chief executive politics:* decision making dominated by presidents, governors, mayors, and their advisers

5. *Courtroom politics:* court orders by judges, influenced by the Constitution, laws, and competing adversaries in judicial proceedings

6. *Living room politics:* the consequences of public opinions expressed by and through grassroots movements, political activists, voters, and social and mass media

We prefer the "policy domain" approach to the traditional "policy process" approach, with its focus on the stages of agenda setting, policy formulation, implementation, and evaluation. However, the two approaches are not incompatible. Although this book was designed to stand on its own in public policy and American government courses, many of our colleagues use our book in conjunction with a more traditional policy process text to broaden students' perspectives on the politics of policymaking in the United States.

What we offer is a road map for negotiating the twists and turns of the public policy landscape. We hope readers will come away with a better understanding of how policies are made and implemented, who is powerful and who is not and why, and how public policies influence American citizens and the nation. We also hope readers will be better equipped to assess the performance of the nation's political institutions and their leaders.

The book integrates discussions of policymaking with a focus on real policies and their effects. How policies are chosen and implemented is important, but so are what is decided and what those decisions mean for citizens and society. Policymakers are often forced to make difficult and unpleasant choices. Tax and budget policies, global warming, natural disasters, terrorism, international conflicts, and a plethora of other problems pose severe tests for political institutions. Understanding more about how institutions process decisions and make policy will help readers better evaluate their leaders' performance on the issues that matter most to them.

This fourth edition of *Politics and Public Policy* incorporates new scholarship, and the entire book has been updated to reflect conflicts and controversies facing political institutions and policy leaders in the early years of the twenty-first century. The first two chapters introduce the actors and institutions that shape policies and the distinctively American context in which public solutions to problems are demanded. These chapters also identify for students some of the normative concerns to which we return in the concluding chapters. In chapters 3 through 8, we apply our unique approach to understanding public policy through the perspective of the six policy domains; each domain has different power centers, different arenas for struggle, different participants, and often different outcomes. After describing and analyzing the policy domains, we turn to more normative and evaluative concerns in chapters 9 and 10. These chapters assess American political institutions and evaluate progress on broad goals of public policy.

We appreciate the support and encouragement we received from many people in the production of this fourth edition of *Politics and Public Policy*. We especially want to express our gratitude to Professor William Gormley of Georgetown University for the major contributions he made as our coauthor on the first three editions of this book. Because of other obligations, Professor Gormley was not available to join us on the fourth edition.

Others who helped with earlier editions have been acknowledged in those editions. We are pleased to recognize the reviewers of this edition, Christine DeGregorio (American University), Steve Sheppard (University of Arkansas), Chuck Cushman (Georgetown University), Scot Schraufnagel (Northern Illinois University), and Greg McAvoy (University of North Carolina at Greensboro), and colleagues who have used our book in their classes for their helpful and insightful suggestions for this edition. Cecilia Kaltz, a master of public policy student in the Edward J. Bloustein School of Planning and Public Policy at Rutgers University, provided outstanding research assistance.

We are very appreciative of CQ Press and SAGE Publications for their continuing support of this book. Charisse Kiino encouraged us to undertake another edition, as did several professors at other colleges and universities who have regularly used earlier versions of our book in their classes. This edition also reflects the careful attentions of Robb Sewell of Rutgers University's John J. Heldrich Center for Workforce Development, Christine Jenter, Jade McClain, and the CQ Press manuscript editor who saw the book through the editing process.

Finally, we are most grateful to our families for their continued support and encouragement.

chapter 1

American Politics and Public Policy

H ouse Speaker John Boehner was not a happy camper. He was preparing his chamber for a vote on a deal to step back from the "fiscal cliff," which had been created eighteen months earlier by another deal that
was necessary to avoid having the federal government default on its debt obligations. It was New Year's Day, January 1, 2013, and the 112th Congress had yet
to finish its business because it had postponed solving the fiscal cliff problem
until almost the last possible hour (the 113th Congress was scheduled to start
on January 3). Boehner and his Republican caucus had been outflanked by the
White House and the Senate, and they alone stood between the president and
a compromise package that had been negotiated by Senate leaders and Vice
President Joe Biden. The Senate had acted the day before, passing legislation
with an 89-8 vote that would allow tax rates to rise on American families earning more than $450,000 per year, but avoiding income tax increases for every-
one else. Under normal circumstances, Boehner and House Republicans would
have voted as a majority bloc to keep the legislation off the floor, but with tax
increases for all Americans looming, could he and his party explain to the
public why important legislation passed by the Senate (and supported by the
president) didn't deserve a vote in the people's chamber?

Boehner didn't think so; therefore, despite protests from his Tea Party
colleagues, he was bringing the bill to the floor. As he did this, he knew that
with the support of some Republicans, and virtually all of the House
Democrats, the measure would pass and would be viewed as a victory for
President Obama, who would finally realize his long-held goal of overcoming
Republican opposition to increasing taxes on the wealthy. To add insult to
injury, Boehner, who had remarked in the fall of 2011 that most Americans
would prefer to watch football rather than hear a speech by the president
about his latest job creation proposal, was missing the Rose Bowl. At one
point, he was quoted as saying, "Am I having a nightmare or what?" Around
11 p.m., the House finally voted 257-167 to approve the deal.[1] (Stanford beat
Wisconsin in the Rose Bowl 20-14.)

To observers of American politics and public policy, the bitter, drawn-out
battles between Democrats and Republicans, the president and Congress, over
fiscal policy (taxes and spending), which were fought almost continuously

from 2010 to 2013, offered another striking example of the public policy process in the United States. It is a process, established by the U.S. Constitution more than 200 years ago, that divides power across legislative, executive, and judicial institutions and operates in a similar way at the federal, state, and local levels. Some of the important lessons about the political and policy process that were brought into sharp relief by these events are as follows:

- Presidents can exhort, but they cannot dictate policy. Presidents command media and public attention, but the legislature must approve all tax and spending policies.
- Elections matter. President Obama had just been reelected, and even his first-term archnemesis, Senate minority leader Mitch McConnell, had come around to the view that compromise was necessary to avoid greater economic harm to the country.
- The government and the economy are closely connected. The large cuts in government spending and the large increases in taxes on all Americans that lay beyond the fiscal cliff had grave economic implications, not only for the United States but for the entire world.
- The mass media play an important role in communicating information about unfolding events and helping shape public views about desirable policy steps. In this case, the public remained divided, Democrats versus Republicans, on the merits of the legislation, but most people agreed with President Obama that the wealthy could and should pay more to keep the government solvent and the economy healthy.[2]
- Wealthy Americans do not always get what they want out of the policy process.

In this book, we attempt to explain public policy by focusing on political institutions as critical but changing elements of the policymaking process. As shown in Table 1-1, American public policy and politics have undergone significant changes in the past two decades. Helping the reader understand those changes and, more important, how they came about is a core objective of this book. We stress the importance of the interaction between political institutions and the larger political culture and political economy in creating both constraints and opportunities for policymakers. In addition, we extend our analysis beyond the traditional branches of government—the executive, legislative, and judicial—to encompass corporate executives at one end and ordinary citizens and the mass media at the other. In doing so, we advance a broader view of what constitutes public policy.

Our approach confirms E. E. Schattschneider's observation that the choice of conflicts is critical to the determination of political success or failure.[3] American policymaking institutions, and the policy domains associated with them, differ significantly in terms of the scope of conflict that occurs within them, how settled or unsettled they are, and how they shape the choices we, as a society, face.

TABLE 1-1 The Changing Context of Politics and the American Economy, 1990, 2000, and 2010

Factor	1990	2000	2010
Unemployment	5.6% (decade high of 7.5% in 1992)	4%	9.6%
Deficit (−) or surplus (+)	−$290 billion (1992)	+$124 billion	−$1.29 trillion
Cost of congressional campaigns	House and Senate candidates spent a total of $408 million in 1990	House and Senate candidates spent a total of $900 million in 2000	House and Senate candidates spent a total of $1.6 billion in 2010
Divided government: composition of Congress	Republican president, Democratic majority in Congress	Republican president, Republican majority in House, Senate split evenly between parties	Democratic president, Democratic Senate, Republican majority in House (2011)
Internet access	11% (1994)	41.5%, broadband 5%	Internet (use) 77%, broadband 69%
Number of welfare cases	11,460,382	6,603,607 (September 1999)	4,505,089 (July 2011)
Gross domestic product	$5,738.4 billion	$9,571.9 billion	$14,526.5 billion

Sources: Unemployment: Bureau of Labor Statistics, "Labor Statistics from the Current Population Survey: Household Data: Annual Averages: 1. Employment Status of the Civilian Noninstitutional Population, 1942 to Date," February 5, 2013, www.stats.bls.gov/cps/cpsaat01.htm, and http://data.bls.gov/timeseries/LNS14000000; deficit or surplus: *Economic Report of the President* (Washington, D.C.: U.S. Government Printing Office, 2000), and Paul Krawzak, "Budget Proposal Avoids Making Tough Choices," *CQ Weekly*, February 21, 2011, 686; cost of congressional campaigns: The Campaign Finance Institute, "Data," www.cfinst.org/data.aspx; Internet access: Department of Commerce, U.S. Census Bureau, "Publications about Computer and Internet Use," www.census.gov/hhes/computer/publications/, Internet World Stats, "United States of America: Internet Usage and Broadband Usage Report," www.internetworldstats.com/am/us.htm, and Samuel Kernell, Gary Jacobson, and Thad Kousser, *The Logic of American Politics*, 5th ed. (Washington, D.C.: CQ Press, 2012), 642; welfare cases: Department of Health and Human Services and Administration for Children and Families, Office of Family Assistance, "July 2011-SSP-MOE Caseload: TANF Caseload Data," April 3, 2012, www.acf.hhs.gov/programs/ofa/resource/2011-07-tanssp-0; gross domestic product: Executive Office of the President, Office of Management and Budget, *Budget of the United States Government, Fiscal Year 2001* (Washington, D.C.: U.S. Government Printing Office, 2000), 170–171, and Department of Commerce, Bureau of Economic Analysis, "National Economic Accounts," www.bea.gov/national/index.htm#gdp.

Our primary aim in this book is to develop a conceptual framework for thinking about the relationship between politics and public policy. That framework stresses the importance of political institutions, which we have defined broadly to include structures and norms associated with different policymaking settings. Such a perspective yields six policy domains that form the core of the discussion in this book. Although we generalize about the patterns of behavior within different political institutions, we also emphasize that political institutions can be changed. We cite examples of such changes and spell out their implications for public policy. We have tried to move away from the view that policymaking is a sequential, linear process. We have also eschewed the perspective that voters and public officials are profit maximizers whose behavior can be predicted on the basis of rational expectations. Thus, our approach is to stress the importance of political institutions without reducing them to quantities in abstract mathematical formulas. The world of politics is messier than all of that, but it is not so chaotic as to preclude some generalizations.

This book is organized so that the connection between politics and public policy remains in view. It is important to be able to see the forest *and* the trees. To that end, this chapter introduces several important themes and perspectives. We begin with a discussion of the public officials authorized by the national and state constitutions to make policy. Next, we turn to the subject of how different kinds of governments interact with one another in a federal system. After that, the influence of lobbyists and journalists on public policy is examined. We then illustrate the remarkable elasticity of policymaking in the United States by focusing on the two ends of the policymaking spectrum: private decision making, which features a limited scope of conflict, and public decision making, with a wide scope of conflict. Last, we introduce the six policy domains and attempt to show how complex and interdependent the process is. The six policy domains are explored in depth in chapters 3 through 8.

POLICYMAKERS

At all levels of American government, power over public policy is shared by different institutions—legislatures, chief executives, and courts. The U.S. Constitution gives Congress the authority to make laws, the president the responsibility to administer them, and the Supreme Court the right to interpret and enforce them. The separation of powers is designed to make each institution independent of the others. However, each delegation of authority is qualified by other constitutional provisions so that legislative, executive, and judicial powers are shared to some extent. The same phenomenon is apparent at the state and local levels. Government institutions are as interdependent as they are independent.

The functioning of these institutions over time has accentuated this sharing and interdependence, although a considerable degree of separateness and independence still exists. In addition, a variety of bureaucratic institutions has been created that, independently, wield substantial power over public policy. In this and subsequent chapters, we demonstrate that there is much more to public policy than public officials. Our initial focus is on legislators, chief executives, bureaucrats, and judges.

Legislators

Under the Constitution and its state-level counterparts, legislators are the principal lawmakers in the political system. To become a law, a proposal, in the form of a bill, must be approved by Congress, a state legislature, or a city council. Approval depends on coalition building, the aim of which is to obtain the support of a legislative majority. Without legislative approval, no taxes can be raised, no money can be spent, and no new programs can be launched. The constitutional assumption is that the people's elected representatives should play the leading role in making public policy.

To ensure a high degree of responsiveness, legislators are accountable to the electorate every two, four, or six years. In practice, however, electoral accountability does not always result in the adoption of policies favored by the voters. One reason is that individual legislators can often escape responsibility for policies adopted or not adopted by the legislature as a whole. Through casework, or constituency service, legislators can cultivate a core of grateful constituents who will support their legislators because they have performed some useful service for them, such as expediting the delivery of a Social Security check or arranging a tour of the White House or the Capitol building. These norms and practices enable legislators to pursue their own preferred policies, subject, of course, to certain constraints. A senator from a ranching state probably would not tempt fate by leading the fight to raise fees for grazing cattle on federal lands.

Service to constituents, coupled with decentralized and fragmented policymaking systems (centered around legislative committees), and high incumbent reelection rates characterized legislative bodies in the United States from the 1950s to the 1990s. During this period, legislative observers often compared American legislatures with those in Western Europe, where it was common to find parliamentary systems, in which the chief executive was also the leader of the parliament or legislative body, and "responsible party" systems, in which legislative members of the same party voted together on major issues. U.S. legislative bodies were typically found lacking in these comparisons because broad, party-based agendas were not the central focus of policy debates and conflicts. In recent years, however, party-centric behavior has become more prominent in legislatures in the United States. Legislators still pursue constituency services and personal political priorities, but party-based policies and party discipline have become increasingly important parts of the legislative process.

Even though parties and party leaders now exercise considerable centralized power in U.S. legislatures, legislative committees continue to be significant countervailing forces, especially in the U.S. Congress. Often referred to as "little legislatures," committees are the legislative workshops, where bills are hammered out, amendments are drafted, and deals are struck. But here, too, many ideas are condemned to the dustbin of history. For that reason, committees are known as legislative graveyards; most bills die in committee without coming to the floor for a vote.

Despite these obstacles, legislators pass an amazing number of measures. In 2010, for example, state legislatures in the United States approved over 25,000 bills and resolutions.[4] In general, legislative bodies prefer to pass bills that distribute benefits, rather than bills that impose penalties, or bills that redistribute the wealth across social classes.[5] Many legislative bodies also prefer bills that delegate authority to the chief executive or the bureaucracy, even though they may complain about executive "usurpation." By delegating authority to others, legislators escape responsibility for difficult policy problems and for solutions that upset people. Delegation has become rampant since Franklin Roosevelt's New Deal, when the Supreme Court, after some initial resistance, eventually allowed Congress to delegate considerable authority to the executive branch. This has led some observers to wonder whether our system of checks and balances has in fact become a system of blank checks.

Chief Executives

With individual legislators marching to their own drumbeats, chief executives face a formidable task when they engage in the politics of lawmaking. Legislative deference to chief executives is far from automatic. Legislative resistance is especially likely when the legislative and executive branches are controlled by different political parties. During the past twenty-five years, more than half of the states have had divided control of government, with at least one chamber of the legislature controlled by the opposite party of the governor. After the 2011 elections, divided control in state government stood at seventeen states, but 2012 brought about a change as thirty-seven states moved to one-party control of the governorship and the legislature (twenty-four Republican and thirteen Democratic), the highest level of unified government in sixty years.[6] At the national level, at least one chamber of Congress has been controlled by a party different from the president's for thirty-two of the past fifty-two years.[7] The 2012 national elections kept this trend intact, as Democrats held the presidency and the Senate and Republicans retained control of the House of Representatives.

Regardless of which party controls the legislative branch, chief executives cannot take legislative cooperation for granted. Even under the best of circumstances, the chief executive's power is the "power to persuade."[8] Members of Congress may be hostile to presidents who try to exert influence over the decisions of a separate and coequal branch of government. In short, chief executives cannot tell legislators what to do. Rather, they must wheedle and cajole, relying on good ideas, political pressure, personal charm, public support, and a touch of blarney. Some chief executives, such as Lyndon Johnson and Ronald Reagan, have made the most of their power to persuade, at least for a time. Others, such as Jimmy Carter, were far less effective at speech making and personal appeals. Bill Clinton was quite adept at mobilizing public opinion to advance his initiatives in the face of an opposing Congress. In advancing their legislative agendas, George W. Bush and Barack Obama focused most of their persuasive efforts on fellow partisans in Congress; few members of the opposition parties were even willing to listen.

If wit and wisdom facilitate persuasion, chief executives also possess other important resources that come with the office. Perhaps the most important of these resources is visibility. When the president of the United States catches a cold, it makes national news. A gubernatorial runny nose is less newsworthy, but governors and mayors have no difficulty making headlines. Because of this visibility, chief executives have emerged as the leading agenda setters within the government. Along with the mass media, they help determine which issues the public thinks about and which issues the government will address. Some formal vehicles for this agenda-setting role are the president's State of the Union address and a governor's State of the State address. But chief executives can command an audience at almost any time, especially during a crisis.[9]

Despite their best efforts, chief executives lose many legislative battles, or get less than they wanted out of them. For example, the legislature may adopt a bill, as requested by the chief executive, but one with so many amendments that it is unacceptable. When this happens, the chief executive may veto the bill, in which case the legislature may vote to override (although successful overrides are fairly rare). In most cases, vetoes result in a new round of negotiation between chief executives and legislators. In many states, governors have what is known as the line-item veto for budget bills. This enables governors to delete particular line items or programs from the budget without vetoing the entire bill—a formidable power that many presidents have coveted. Even line-item vetoes may be overridden, however.

When chief executives get sufficiently frustrated with the legislative branch, they may resort to other means to pursue their policy goals. One tool that is often used is the executive order. Although such orders are supposed to be restricted to the operations of the executive branch of government and be pursuant to powers delegated to the chief executive by the legislature, the size of modern governments and the extensive delegation that has occurred can make this tool quite formidable. For example, President Truman integrated the military via executive order; President George W. Bush allowed the Central Intelligence Agency to ignore the Geneva Conventions in its interrogations through an executive order, which was rescinded by President Obama almost immediately after he took office.[10] To the dismay of congressional Republicans, President Clinton issued more than 360 executive orders while in office, nearly matching President Reagan's total of 380. Clinton was especially well known for the orders he issued upon leaving office that, among other things, expanded environmental protection of federal lands in several western states and imposed inspections and gun-tracing requirements on gun dealers.[11] Despite his frequent assertions of presidential power, President George W. Bush issued fewer executive orders (290) in his eight years in office than Clinton.

Another tool chief executives commonly use to pursue their policy objectives in the face of an uncooperative legislature is their appointment power. By appointing loyal, capable cabinet and subcabinet officials, they can influence bureaucratic policymaking and advance their policy goals. Presidents Reagan, Clinton, and George W. Bush were known for pursuing policy by aggressive appointments to key executive branch positions. In 2013, President Obama tried to send a message to Wall Street about tough regulation ahead by nominating a former federal prosecutor (Mary Jo White), rather than someone with a background in finance (banking), to head the U.S. Securities and Exchange Commission.[12] Even when the appointment requires confirmation by the Senate, presidents have sometimes worked around this restriction by placing people in office through so-called recess appointments that take place while Congress is not officially in session. This power, which has been used by many presidents over the past fifty years, was called into question by a federal appeals court panel in January 2013, when it ruled that the only real recesses occur between Congresses, which would restrict the period for recess appointments to a few days every two years.[13]

Battles over appointments illustrate the point that presidents and governors spend a good deal of time managing their governments. President Nixon attempted to create an "administrative presidency," with high-level bureaucrats who followed the president's lead on all major issues. Nixon's administrative presidency was derailed by the Watergate affair, but a similar strategy was used with reasonable effectiveness by Presidents Reagan and George H. W. Bush.[14] President George W. Bush was even more determined to centralize executive power than Reagan and his father, following a model called the "unitary executive," which held that the president had unchecked power over all actions of executive agencies and officials. In partial contrast, Democratic presidents Clinton and Obama arranged their administrations with somewhat less rigidity; however, they also stressed the importance of having all executive officials support the president's policies and present a unified front in the face of legislative attempts to curb executive prerogatives.

Bureaucrats

The bureaucracy's size, power, and discretion to make decisions have grown enormously in the past several decades. Since 1972, both state and local bureaucracies have increased by about 55 percent, with 5.3 million people now employed by the states and 14.3 million by local governments.[15] Although the size of the federal bureaucracy has been more stable in recent years (ranging between 2.7 million and 3.1 million), its influence has grown as it dispenses ever larger amounts of federal money (see Table 1-1). Federal officials have ample opportunities to structure the behavior of state and local governments by awarding or withholding federal grants-in-aid. Bureaucrats at all levels of government also award contracts to private sector firms for goods or services supplied to the government. There can be little doubt that the bureaucracy constitutes a "fourth branch of government."

One of the bureaucracy's jobs is to implement policy by designing programs to carry out laws. The Internal Revenue Service implements policy when it designs tax forms to conform with congressional intent. Similarly, the U.S. Citizenship and Immigration Services implements policy when it warns employers not to hire illegal immigrants. If statutes were clear and airtight, the implementation of policy would be fairly routine, but few statutes fit that description.

The importance of the bureaucracy in policy implementation sometimes distracts attention from the role the bureaucracy plays in the creation and shaping of public policies. Many laws are in fact drafted by bureaucrats, or by legislative aides with substantial assistance from bureaucrats. In addition, bureaucrats make policy openly and directly through what is known as administrative rulemaking. For example, in 2011, the Department of Education changed the rules of the federal government's elementary and secondary education law, called No Child Left Behind, to relieve states of requirements ensuring that all students would achieve "proficiency" in reading and mathematics by 2014.[16] This action was provoked in part by five years of legislative deadlock in Congress over how to revise this law.

High-profile enactments of rules and regulations are often the products of independent regulatory commissions—multimember bodies that operate relatively independently of the chief executive. The president appoints the regulatory commissioners, but they serve until their terms expire. Independent regulatory commissions are responsible for regulating radio and television networks, licensing nuclear power plants, resolving labor relations disputes, protecting consumers from unsafe products, regulating the money supply and stock markets, and setting the rates charged by public utilities.

In contrast to independent regulatory commissions, most bureaucracies are nominally accountable to the chief executive, who has the power to appoint and to fire the top officials. Working beneath the thin layer of officials who are appointed by the president, most bureaucrats are civil servants with considerable job security. As a general rule, they are less committed to the president's policies than are cabinet and subcabinet officials. Moreover, agencies develop strong symbiotic relationships with constituents and client groups. The Department of Agriculture may be more sympathetic to farmers and the agricultural industry than to a president who wants to reduce farm price supports. In addition, chief executives do not appoint all agency heads. In state government, citizens elect some top officials, which may include the attorney general, the treasurer, the secretary of state, the auditor, and the superintendent of education. Finally, bureaucrats are accountable to other public officials, including legislators and judges. It is fair to say that the bureaucracy has many masters.

Judges

When legislators, chief executives, and bureaucrats cannot agree on appropriate public policies, the controversies are frequently settled in the courts. In the American system of government, judges are often the ultimate arbiters of policy disputes. They decide whether a law is constitutional and whether an administrative rule is legal. They decide when the federal government may tell state and local governments what to do. They decide the meaning of phrases such as "equal protection," "freedom of speech," "separation of powers," and "due process of law."

Judges, particularly federal judges, play a central role in the policy process. Federal judges are not passive arbiters of narrowly defined disputes but rather active architects of public policy. Certain cases force them to immerse themselves in the details of technology, methodology, and administration. Increasingly, they have moved from procedural reasoning to substantive reasoning, at times functioning as legislators and managers. In specific cases, federal judges have seized control of state prisons, mental health facilities, and public schools. They have also directed state legislatures to spend more money on underfunded programs, and challenged the military's "don't ask, don't tell" policy.

Decisions by federal district court judges may be reversed by U.S. circuit courts of appeals or by the U.S. Supreme Court. However, appellate judges, as they are sometimes called, generally defer to trial (district court) judges. They also defer to judges who preceded them on the bench. It is rare for the Supreme Court to reverse an earlier Supreme Court decision, even if today's justices would have decided the case differently. This informal norm is known as the doctrine of stare decisis, or adherence to precedent, from the Latin phrase meaning "to stand by things decided."

Despite stare decisis, courts move in new directions as new problems, such as domestic terrorism, arise, and as society takes note of systemic changes, such as the growing number of working women. Indeed, in many policy domains, judges have been the principal trailblazers in government. The Supreme Court under Chief Justice Earl Warren took the lead in advancing the civil rights of African Americans and in securing rights for persons accused of a crime.[17] The Court under Chief Justice William H. Rehnquist, although widely viewed as conservative, took steps to limit sexual harassment at the workplace and to ensure privacy rights for homosexual couples. The Rehnquist Court was also continuously innovative (in a conservative direction) in the area of federalism. During the 1990s, a majority of justices overruled federal law in favor of state statutes on several occasions. For example, the Rehnquist Court declared unconstitutional a federal law that would have required state and local officials to do background checks of gun dealers in *Printz v. United States* (1997).[18]

Both the Rehnquist Court and the current Court under Chief Justice John G. Roberts have been characterized by fairly sharp ideological divisions. Many high-profile cases have been decided by 5-4 votes, making the justice in the middle of the ideological spectrum key to liberal and to conservative rulings. Sandra Day O'Connor was the swing judge during most of the Rehnquist Court, giving way to Anthony Kennedy on the Roberts Court. Kennedy's mostly conservative tendencies have been exhibited in several major cases in recent years, including one that interpreted the Second Amendment as giving individuals the right to bear arms, *District of Columbia v. Heller* (2008), and another granting corporations and unions the right to speak (spend) independently in federal elections, *Citizens United v. Federal Election Commission* (2010). In a somewhat surprising and very nuanced ruling, Chief Justice Roberts joined the liberal wing of the Supreme Court (Justices Stephen Breyer, Ruth Bader Ginsburg, Elena Kagan, and Sonia Sotomayor) in upholding most of the key provisions of President Obama's health care reform law (the Patient Protection and Affordable Care Act) in June 2012.[19]

When the Supreme Court interprets the Constitution, that interpretation is binding on other courts; however, state supreme courts usually are the ultimate arbiters of disputes covered by state constitutions. If the Supreme Court allows searches and seizures under certain circumstances favorable to law enforcement officials, a state supreme court may strike down the same kinds of searches and seizures, on the basis of its reading of the state constitution.[20] State supreme courts may also find new kinds of civil rights, such as the right of same-sex couples to marry, on the basis of their readings of state constitutions.

The vagueness of phrases such as "equal protection" and "due process of law" permits courts wide leeway and discretion. Constitutions constrain the behavior of judges but do not determine their behavior. Richard Neely, chief justice of the West Virginia Supreme Court, wrote:

> Since there is hardly any question which cannot be framed in such a way as to assume "constitutional" dimensions, for all intents and purposes every conceivable question of public policy is up for review by the courts. Vested with this power to determine what is and what is not within the purview of their authority, courts can at will substitute their judgment for that of all the other agencies of government.[21]

Judges, however, cannot act unless a case is brought before them by litigants. Furthermore, appellate judges must reach a consensus before they can speak. But this process is far less complex for a panel of three judges (circuit courts of appeals) or nine justices (the Supreme Court) than it is for a legislative body consisting of dozens or hundreds of individuals who represent diverse constituencies. As a result, when legislators reach an impasse on controversies such as abortion, affirmative action, and capital punishment, judges are often in a position to fill this power vacuum.

A FEDERAL SYSTEM

Federalism

Washington, D.C., has no monopoly over the making of public policy in the United States. State and local governments are policy institutions within the federal system of government, and in their own right. They are responsible for implementing most federal domestic programs, which typically leave many basic aspects of policy to the discretion of state and local decision makers.

The United States has a truly multigovernmental system. For many issues, state governments are virtually immune from federal supervision and control. Many aspects of banking regulation, insurance regulation, and occupational licensing remain firmly in the hands of state administrative agencies. Questions concerning marriage, divorce, and child custody are handled almost exclusively by state courts. Public utility regulation is controlled largely by the states, as are most aspects of drilling for natural gas on nonfederal lands.

Considerable autonomy is also exercised at the local level. Most zoning decisions, which shape the character of neighborhoods and the quality of everyday life, are made by local governments, without so much as a raised eyebrow from state government officials or federal court judges. Inspections of housing, restaurants, and buildings, all of which are necessary for public health, are controlled by local governments, with little input from other levels of government.

Intergovernmental Relations

Despite the considerable discretion exercised by state and local governments, the federal government has extended its influence over them by offering the "carrot" of federal grants-in-aid in return for certain concessions. Federal grants-in-aid come in two basic forms: categorical programs and block grants. Categorical programs have narrowly defined objectives, distinct statutory and budget identities, detailed planning and operational requirements, and defined target populations. Head Start, which provides preschool education to children from poor families, is a classic example of a categorical program. Block grant programs give states and localities money for broad purposes, such as health, housing, education, and employment, but do not require that all recipient states offer a specific set of programs and services. An example would be the Community Development Block Grant program, whereby mayors, governors, and their staffs may select a mix of housing services that seems well suited to the particular needs of their communities.

President Johnson's War on Poverty relied heavily on categorical grants. President Nixon used a different approach, which he called the "new federalism," that called for the conversion of many categorical programs into block grants. Under Nixon, the flow of federal dollars continued to increase, but federal restrictions were loosened somewhat. President Reagan also voiced support for a new federalism, but his version combined sharp cutbacks in federal support with new responsibilities for state governments. President George H. W. Bush continued the Reagan approach. President Clinton did not try to reduce grant-in-aid funding but, as a former governor, he did lean in the direction of giving states more discretion in implementing federal programs. During the Clinton years, and in the years since, several categorical programs have been modified to take on some of the characteristics of block grants, in particular giving states more flexibility in choosing the specific services they offer to target populations. In the twenty-first century, Republicans in Congress, and President George W. Bush, proposed changing many federal aid (categorical) programs to block grants, but most of these efforts were rebuffed by Democrats. Thus, since the 1990s, the general trend has been gradually increasing federal grant-in-aid spending, despite Republican efforts to rein it in, with more discretion and responsibility being placed on states.[22]

The enactment of welfare reform during the Clinton presidency is a good example of the trends in federalism. The 1996 law converted the long-standing categorical welfare program (Aid to Families with Dependent Children [AFDC]) to a block grant program (Temporary Assistance for Needy Families [TANF]), continued funding to states for welfare programs at the previous fiscal year's level, but empowered states to decide how those funds would be spent. States submitted their individual plans to the federal government for approval but had relatively few and very broad federal guidelines to follow.

Presently, over 80 percent of the federal aid to state and local governments still comes in the form of categorical programs.[23] Many of the most important categorical programs, such as Medicaid and Food Stamps (now the Supplemental Nutrition Assistance Program), are also entitlement programs, which give qualifying individuals a legal right to benefits. Thus, the conversion of categorical entitlement programs to block grants is importantly about constraining spending. The change from AFDC to TANF meant that Congress had to appropriate a certain amount of money for cash assistance for poor families each year, rather than having that amount determined by eligibility. Thus, the transformation of welfare from a categorical grant into a block grant removed the guarantee of cash assistance to low-income parents caring for young children. States now have wide discretion in determining eligibility and allocating aid. When a state's block grant runs dry, it has the option to fund assistance out of the state budget, but there are few federal requirements to do so. Not surprisingly, annual federal spending on TANF has remained more or less the same (in nominal dollars; it has declined in real dollars) since 1997, whereas federal spending on Medicaid, the primary national health insurance program for the needy, has more than doubled (in nominal terms) over this same time period.[24] As shown in Table 1-1, the welfare caseload in 2011 was less than half of the 1990 level.

As the federal government has moved to giving states more flexibility in grant-in-aid programs over the past thirty years, it has made a similar accommodation with regard to federal regulations. It now issues fewer direct orders and universal mandates and relies more on indirect forms of federal control, such as partial preemptions and crossover sanctions. An example of a partial preemption is the Surface Mining Control and Reclamation Act of 1977, which grants states the option of running their own strip-mining regulation programs, provided that federal standards are accepted. If a state refuses the option, the federal government exercises full preemption, running the program out of a regional office. Many environmental programs operate in this way. Examples of crossover sanctions include the federal government's ability to withhold highway funds from states that refuse to set the drinking age at twenty-one years or to conform to a certain maximum highway speed limit. In many regulatory arenas, the federal government usually bargains with the states over disputed matters in the hope of achieving federal objectives rather than imposing sanctions.

POLICY INFLUENCES OUTSIDE GOVERNMENT

Interest Groups and Political Parties

The multilayered policy system described so far is highly permeable to groups outside of government. Private interest group involvement in public policy is a widely recognized and long-standing fact of American government. Interest groups work closely with legislators and bureaucrats to develop mutually beneficial policies. The specialized committee structure of Congress, which is mirrored in most state legislatures, enables interest groups to focus their efforts on the individuals and groups with power over the issues of greatest concern to them.

Clusters of people interested in the same issue—members of legislative committees and subcommittees, bureaucratic agencies that administer the policies formulated by a committee, and the groups that are most directly affected by such policies—are often called subgovernments or issue networks. These networks wield considerable influence over many policy domains, such as the financial industry, agriculture, public works, and defense contracting. Interest groups are full-fledged partners in major policymaking circles.[25]

The number and variety of interest groups in the United States are enormous. Although no one has been able to count all of them, various sources provide a rough estimate of the size of the interest group population, which has grown rapidly since the 1960s. A study of interest groups in 1991 found that the number of lobbying groups grew by over 300 percent between the 1960s and the 1990s; this number then doubled between 2000 and 2005.[26] Consider these facts:

- The number of registered lobbyists grew by 37 percent between September 1997 and June 1999, from 14,946 lobbyists to 20,512, and then increased to over 27,000 by 2010.
- In 1998, there were more than nineteen registered lobbyists and $2.7 million in lobbying expenditures for every member of Congress; by 2010, the comparable figures were twenty-six and $6.5 million.
- Between 1998 and 2012, the top-spending lobby groups included the U.S. Chamber of Commerce ($926 million), the American Medical Association ($278 million), the American Hospital Association ($229 million), the Pharmaceutical Research and Manufacturers of America ($228 million), and the AARP ($220 million), which advocates on behalf of older Americans.[27]

Given the strong representation of private economic interests (roughly 70 percent of all Washington lobbyists), it is not surprising that citizen groups have gotten into the act.[28] More than 1,200 citizen groups are represented in Washington. Environmental groups, civil rights organizations, women's groups, and gun owners' organizations are all examples of such groups. Thousands of additional groups may be found in state capitals and other communities.

State and local government officials also hire staffs to represent them in Washington. The National Governors Association, National Conference of State Legislatures, National League of Cities, U.S. Conference of Mayors, National Association of Counties, and other organizations actively lobby the national government on matters of concern to states and localities. They also press legislators and administrators to act favorably on requests for financial assistance and regulatory decisions.

There is tremendous diversity in the size, resources, leadership, cohesiveness, and prestige of interest groups that participate in the policy process. Those with substantial money, committed members, strong leadership, and favorable reputations exert considerable influence. All other things being equal, having a large membership is desirable because a group's political clout is enhanced if it speaks for many voters. But large groups have difficulty maintaining unified memberships and directing their activities toward policy goals that excite members. Therefore, small, intense, single-issue groups are sometimes more successful than large groups. An interest group with few members, but a good deal of clout, is the Business Roundtable, an organization of a few hundred top corporate executives. Although its membership is small, the enormous wealth it represents enables it to compete effectively in policy arenas with labor unions, including the American Federation of Labor and Congress of Industrial Organizations, which represents over 11 million workers.

When interest groups approach elected officials and government administrators, they are lobbying for help either to get something done to benefit them or to stop something from happening that adversely affects them. Many people equate lobbying with corrupt contributions or pressure tactics of one sort or another. Although some of these practices do go on, the normal situation is considerably more complicated than that.

Effective lobbying rests on the use of information and money. When lobbyists meet with members of Congress, they supply facts about issues and political intelligence about the positions and strategies of others in Congress and the executive branch. Lobbyists testify at congressional hearings, observe committee deliberations, and perform other services for their members. Groups sponsor professional and social gatherings to which elected officials are invited to cement relationships. Interest groups may conduct public relations campaigns to persuade voters in a member's district to support their causes. Advertising, press releases, and letter-writing campaigns are all used to build a climate of support for their positions and to secure favorable treatment from legislators. And, of course, groups contribute to presidential and congressional election campaigns—nearly $220 million in 1998, rising to almost $415 million in 2008 and $450 million in 2012.[29] As discussed below, contributions to candidates are just one facet of interest groups spending during elections.

Given all the attention paid to group spending in the 2012 election, it is important to understand the evolution of this kind of political activity. The modern American election process was initiated with the passage of the Federal Election Campaign Act (FECA) of 1971, with important amendments added in 1974. Further changes were made with the enactment of the Bipartisan Campaign Reform Act (BCRA) of 2002, also known as the McCain-Feingold act. FECA established a clear path for interest groups to participate in the election process, which was to form a political action committee (PAC). Such committees had to be registered with the Federal Election Commission, which was created by FECA to oversee election donations and spending, and the primary purpose of PACs was to donate money in limited amounts ($5,000 per election) to candidates. The number of PACs grew rapidly from 1975 to 1985, reaching the level of 4,000 or so, where it leveled off and remains today. As described above, contributions by PACs have risen steadily, even when adjusted for inflation.[30]

In addition to donating money to candidates, PACs could also spend money independently of candidates, which many of them did, sometimes to support candidates they liked but most often to attack candidates they didn't like. By the late 1990s, new, more shadowy groups called 527 committees were forming with the goal of speaking in elections. These groups did not donate to candidates but engaged in what they called "issue advocacy." Following the passage of BCRA, which banned "soft money" contributions to political parties, these 527 committees and various nonprofit groups (501[c] organizations) became important players in American elections. Soft money, or funds acquired by these groups that could be given and spent in unlimited amounts, provide their financial base. Spending by such groups exceeded $400 million in the 2004 election cycle, declining to $258 million in 2008 and rising to over $300 million in 2012.[31] However, are these organizations actually interest groups, or simply legal entities created by one, or a few, wealthy individuals?

The presence of these independent, semiregulated organizations that purported to be in the business of political education continued to churn the waters of campaign finance when, in 2010, the Supreme Court took up the case of *Citizens United v. Federal Election Commission*. In this now famous ruling, the Court eliminated all restrictions on groups speaking (spending) independently of candidates in elections, and declared that corporations and unions had the same rights as individuals when it came to independent spending, meaning that they could spend on politics from their own coffers rather than relying on donations from their employees and members. This gave rise to so-called super PACs, which could accept donations in unlimited amounts (soft money) and spend as much as they wanted, as long as they were not acting in concert with the campaigns of candidates. By the end of 2012, almost 13,000 super PACs had been formed (one by comedian Stephen Colbert), and they had spent over $730 million to influence elections.[32] If one looks at all outside group spending (super PACs, 527s, 501[c] groups, and party committees), nearly $1.5 billion was spent, almost $1 billion by conservative groups and nearly $500 million by liberal groups.[33]

Interest groups also lobby executive agencies. Bureaucratic agencies are responsive to interest groups because they need political allies to advance their policy goals and to protect them from legislators or chief executives who may dislike their programs and policies.[34] Lobbying bureaucratic agencies generally entails using the same techniques used with legislators, except that campaign contributions apply only to elected officials. All major agencies have one or more constituent groups with which they maintain close and mutually beneficial alliances.

Interest groups are active within the judicial arena, although there they are less visible. The direct contribution of money is rare because it is illegal to bribe judicial officials. But interest group budgets can be used to back legal cases that have policy significance. Suits seeking to overturn legislative or administrative decisions are a common part of practically all important policy disputes. These challenges come not just from businesses trying to protect their financial interests; civil rights groups and environmentalists have successfully pursued legal strategies that have advanced their causes. Even the selection of judges is not beyond the reach of interest groups. They lobby executives and legislators on behalf of certain court nominees, and in some states and localities, interest groups try to influence election contests between candidates for the bench.

As interest groups have become more numerous and influential, political parties have become somewhat less important as "linkage mechanisms" between citizens and government. Party organizations lack the technical expertise that some interest groups possess—a key weakness in complex policy debates. Still, political parties continue to play a vital role in recruiting candidates for office, providing easily understood cues to voters and supporting their candidates directly and indirectly through polling, campaign ads, and other services. From 1980 to 2002, campaign finance law allowed political parties to raise soft money donations from wealthy individuals for so-called party-building activities, which bolstered party organizations around the country. They have continued to thrive in the post-BCRA era through limited "hard money" donations. Both major parties have well-staffed organizations at the national and state levels and in most localities. And, like interest groups, they can make contributions to candidates and spend (in unlimited amounts) independently of candidates. In the 2012 national elections, both the Democratic and Republican national party organizations raised and spent very close to $1 billion.[35] The resurgence of political parties has been one of the most important developments in American politics since the 1980s. Still, candidates for office do not rely primarily on parties to bring their message to voters. Instead, they have turned increasingly to the mass media to play that important role.

The Mass Media

Perceptions of public officials, public policies, and governments are shaped significantly by the mass media, especially television and newspapers (now often accessed online). By focusing obsessively on the "horse race" aspects of presidential campaigns, the media do not give voters enough real help in their efforts to evaluate the candidates' issue positions. By devoting more attention to national and local politics than to state politics, the media limit public awareness of state politics. By oversimplifying and sensationalizing certain policy controversies, the media discourage rational decision making. On the positive side, the media can be credited with exposing public problems and errant public officials. Political scientists and other observers are devoting increased attention to the role of the media in politics, especially their impact on election campaigns. The outcomes of electoral contests often usher in new administrations, with new visions for the future. By influencing the outcomes of elections, the mass media indirectly influence public policy as well.

Clearly, media coverage influences public perceptions of the candidates' character traits and thereby shapes campaign issues. Election results frequently hinge on how well each side presents its case to the media or through the media. Jimmy Carter was unable to overcome a perceived lack of leadership ability in 1980, but Ronald Reagan did not seem to be hurt by reports that he invented or distorted facts in his political speeches. President Clinton continued to score high in public opinion polls even after unflattering portrayals of him in media coverage of various scandals during his term, as evidenced by his easy reelection in 1996 and the failure of the Republican impeachment effort in 1998. Presidents George W. Bush and Obama both passed their essential media tests by establishing themselves as plausible presidential material in the debates of 2000 and 2008. In his concession speech following an overwhelming defeat at the polls in 1984, Walter Mondale admitted that he was an anachronism—a candidate who felt uncomfortable on television in a television age.

The media have increasingly examined the private lives of political candidates. The presidential campaign of former senator Gary Hart in 1988 was abruptly interrupted when newspapers ran stories suggesting marital infidelity; a similar set of circumstances helped doom the presidential aspirations of Republican candidate Herman Cain in 2012. These days, few people remember that Senator Joseph Biden also withdrew from the 1988 presidential race following press accounts of plagiarism, but this issue failed to surface when he ran again in 2008 and eventually became vice president. During Clinton's campaigns in 1992 and 1996, as well as during his tenure in office, the American people were treated to frequent media investigations into his private financial, social, or marital life. The 2000 and 2004 presidential election campaigns produced the same phenomena. The private lives and pasts of George W. Bush and Al Gore, and then John Kerry, were featured prominently in the mass media's coverage of those campaigns. Kerry's candidacy was definitely hurt by media coverage of an ad sponsored by Swift Boat Vets and POWs for Truth (a 527 organization) that attacked Kerry's Vietnam War record. In 2008, it was Obama's birth certificate, his association with fiery minister Jeremiah Wright, and his middle name (Hussein) that garnered a good deal of media attention; his opponent, John McCain, was subject to frequent media innuendo regarding his age. In 2012, the media often featured stories about the extensive income and personal wealth of Republican nominee Mitt Romney.

The media's influence on politics and public policy extends well beyond the electoral arena. It is pervasive, reaching citizens in the nation's heartland and the powerful in Washington. Ironically, the media's influence is often so strong and ubiquitous that it is not noticed. The readers of the *Tri-City Herald* live near a nuclear power plant and a high-level nuclear waste disposal site in Hanford, Washington. In the 1970s and 1980s, this newspaper, which has long promoted nuclear power, ran numerous stories about the safety, reliability, and economy of nuclear power and few stories about the dangers and unanticipated costs of nuclear energy. Stories carried headlines such as "Radiation Linked to Good Health" and "A-Plants Don't Taint Environment." The paper's editors referred to nuclear "storage sites" rather than nuclear "dumps."[36] Exposure to such pronuclear sentiment on a regular basis meant that local citizens were primed to view nuclear power favorably. (Their views may also be affected by the fact that the federal government has poured billions of dollars into the Hanford community in an effort to clean up the nuclear waste stored there.[37]) Unless local newspapers fairly present both sides of an issue, citizens will lack one source of information they need to make intelligent decisions.

Many newspapers do encourage investigative reporting, much of it very thorough and effective. The *Washington Post*'s persistent investigation of the Watergate break-in helped bring about the resignation of President Nixon and ushered in a new era in campaign finance. A 1978 *Chicago Sun-Times* series on the bribes, kickbacks, and payoffs accepted by city building inspectors, health inspectors, and fire inspectors had a major impact on city practices. In its zeal to catch greedy inspectors, the *Sun-Times* purchased a tavern dubbed *The Mirage*, operated it for several months, and documented numerous instances of corruption. Following the publication of a series of articles based on this sting operation, major changes were made in fire, building, and health inspections in the city of Chicago.[38] Here we see an example of media directly affecting policy.

Traditional investigative reporting by newspaper journalists and television shows such as *60 Minutes* continues to be important; however, these days, the initial leads on matters of corruption or impropriety often come from bloggers. Bloggers enjoy a good deal more freedom to post stories as they see fit, and their stories often attract the attention of the more established media outlets, which then follow up on the leads and sometimes find juicy (and credible) material.[39] In 2009, two conservative activists used tactics similar to those used by the *Chicago Sun Times* to expose apparent corruption (advice on how to hide prostitution activities and avoid paying taxes) on the part of staff members in different offices of the Association of Community Organizations for Reform Now (ACORN), a liberal nonprofit group that received government money to conduct voter registration drives and engage in other community-based activities. The videos they made were soon shown on Fox News, and this sting led to the demise of ACORN, even though subsequent investigations by state and federal agencies suggested that the videos were very heavily edited and possibly misleading.[40]

The two most interesting and important developments in the media world over the past two decades are the rapid evolution of media technology and the balkanization of television, radio, and online media. Constantly evolving communication technology has caused important changes in the types of media the public relies on most. Newspapers, radio, and television network news have all seen their mass media dominance come and go. Presently, for example, the big news about newspapers is their declining number. With more and more advertising revenue going to online sources, traditional print media companies have had difficulty making a profit. The number of daily newspapers has declined steadily from its peak level in 1910 of more than 2,500 to 1,476 in 2012.[41] Media balkanization means that people can now read or listen to people who agree with them. Media outlets such as Fox News and MSNBC, not to mention talk show hosts such as Rush Limbaugh and Rachel Maddow, are openly partisan in their coverage and editorializing. These days, many people seek out news and information from the media sources that reinforce their partisan or ideological views, rather than using the increased number of news sources to form better developed and more nuanced policy views.[42] Thus it should come as no surprise that partisan polarization has become a dominant presence in the public policy debates in the United States in the twenty-first century.

Regardless of its source, the mass media's power to directly affect public policy is rooted in their ability to shape public opinion and gain the attention of policymakers. Public officials often react to widely covered investigative and other reports to get ahead of the firestorm of public criticism the stories are expected to trigger. In the process, media influence is magnified. Sometimes these reactions are accompanied by policy proposals or policy actions. The mere threat of a public outcry may be sufficient to alter public policy.

THE SCOPE OF CONFLICT

In most textbooks on American politics and public policy, the United States is described as a "representative democracy" in which citizens elect representatives—legislators and chief executives—who in turn make public policy. Elected representatives, taking the public's views into account, pass laws and make other authoritative decisions. They also appoint bureaucrats and judges, who adopt rules and adjudicate disputes. But representative democracy is only part of the picture. Many decisions of the utmost importance are made by corporate elites who do not have to answer to the American people. Although nominally accountable to boards of directors or stockholders (or both), corporate managers are in fact often free to make many decisions as they see fit. These decisions—concerning plant location, production, investments, marketing, jobs, and wages—are private.

| TABLE 1-2   **The Policymaking Spectrum: The Scope of Conflict** | | |

Narrow	Moderate	Broad
Private decision making (corporate governance, capitalism)	Representative democracy (candidate elections, conventional lawmaking)	Public decision making (issue elections, aroused public opinion)

At the other end of the policymaking spectrum, some decisions are made not by public officials but by the people. This is literally true when voters participate in "issue elections," such as initiatives and referendums. It is also true, for all intents and purposes, when public opinion becomes so aroused that public officials feel compelled to defer to citizens and their preferences.

What exists in the United States, therefore, is not representative democracy but "elastic" democracy. When the scope of conflict is exceedingly narrow, representative democracy gives way to private decision making, such as corporate governance. When the scope of conflict is exceedingly broad, representative democracy gives way to public decision making in the form of direct democracy or expressions of public opinion that can't be ignored (Table 1-2). The policymaking process can be thought of as a kind of rubber band, which stretches well beyond the original contours of representative democracy.

Private Decision Making

Although it is useful to view business groups as lobbyists or interveners in the policymaking process, it is necessary to view them as policymakers as well. If one considers only conventional politics, one misses the more worrisome side of business influence—namely, the private sector's capacity to make decisions that affect large numbers of people, and the private sector's lack of public accountability. Technically, such decisions are private policies; they are made by private actors such as corporate chief executive officers, vice presidents, chief financial officers, and board members. As a practical matter, however, such private decisions are sanctioned and legitimated by the government—for example, by court decisions upholding private property rights. On the basis of his observations going back to the 1960s and 1970s, Charles Lindblom argued that business enjoyed a "privileged position" in American politics.[43] The government, for better or for worse, has delegated to the private sector primary responsibility for mobilizing and organizing society's economic resources. As a result, decisions by "private governments" are often as far reaching as decisions by the government itself.

Large corporations, the private governments under consideration here, have distinctive decision-making processes. The focal point for corporate decision making is the board of directors, which typically consists of top company executives, prominent business leaders from other companies, and a few noncorporate outside representatives. At some companies, workers have representatives on the board; at many others, however, labor is not directly represented. According to close observers, corporate boards are usually dominated by top corporate executives. Even if outsiders constitute a majority of the board members, the strategic decisions are usually made by insiders and then ratified by the rest of the board.[44] This phenomenon has been referred to as "managerial capitalism."[45]

Most large corporations are free to make policy decisions as they wish, with a minimum of government control. If a steel or automobile company decides to shut down a factory and lay off 2,000 workers, it is free to do so. In most states, companies are not even required to give their workers advance notice if they make such a decision. Corporations are also free to set prices as they see fit. A privately owned monopoly, such as an investor-owned public utility, is not free to set prices. Under an arrangement that dates back to the early twentieth century, private monopolies, such as public utilities, must accept fairly close government regulation, including price controls, in return for their monopoly status. But public utilities are exceptional, and the number of private monopolies has declined in recent years as new technologies have injected competition into what were once monopoly markets. In general, government control over the private sector is weak, and corporate exercise of discretion is pervasive.

Corporate executives argue, with some justification, that they are accountable to the public through the workings of the market. If companies are mismanaged, or their prices are too high, or their products are inferior, consumers "vote with their pocketbooks" and spend their money elsewhere. But markets do not function that perfectly. Information about companies, their products, and their finances can be costly to obtain and may not be easy to understand. Consumers are handicapped by inadequate information. Moreover, markets fail to take into account the social costs of "externalities," such as air or water pollution. Where externalities are substantial, market prices grossly understate the underlying costs of producing services. Finally, government subsidies disguise the real costs of producing some goods and services. It is difficult to know, therefore, whether oil companies are operating efficiently, considering the generous subsidies they receive from the federal government (fewer now than in the past). Indeed, some industries, such as defense and aerospace, receive such huge subsidies that it is difficult to evaluate them at all.

Many companies, especially publicly held companies whose stock is traded in the various stock markets, are accountable to their stockholders, on whom they depend for capital. As a group, stockholders are becoming more aware and more astute. Mobilized by citizen activists, such as Ralph Nader, or social movements, such as the Occupy Wall Street protests of 2011 and 2012, and by "corporate raiders," such as Carl Icahn, stockholders have put pressure on corporate managers and corporate boards to eliminate certain investments, award higher dividends, pay attention to environmental concerns, rein in the salaries of top management, and change other practices. In 2013, for example, public and stockholder voices helped persuade Wal-Mart, the nation's largest retailer and employer, to announce programs to buy more American-made products and hire more veterans.[46] For the most part, however, stockholders routinely accept the policies of corporate managers. They also typically rubber-stamp the slate of corporate directors proposed by management.

If stockholders are relatively weak, workers are even weaker. Although some workers can bargain through their unions over wages, benefits, and working conditions, union workers constitute a small portion (just over 11 percent) of the American workforce. Workers, whether union or nonunion, have virtually nothing to say about major strategic decisions that affect a company's future and theirs. Private corporations are profoundly undemocratic in their governing arrangements. By accepting private ownership of corporate enterprises, the U.S. government precluded any sort of economic democracy and allowed corporate oligarchies to develop. As Robert Dahl observed, "a system of government [that] Americans view as intolerable in governing the state has come to be accepted as desirable in governing economic enterprises."[47]

Public Decision Making

If private decision making epitomizes one end of the policymaking spectrum—a narrow scope of conflict, limited accountability, and government deference to corporations—public decision making epitomizes the other end—a broad scope of conflict, high accountability, and government deference to the public at large. Some decisions are made in "the court of public opinion." When public officials sense that an issue is too controversial to be handled through normal channels, public opinion comes into play and the views of public officials recede into the background. In E. E. Schattschneider's words, the "scope of conflict" expands.[48]

Public opinion is like a slumbering giant, which, when aroused, becomes intimidating. The effects on public policy may thus be considerable. Public opinion has been credited with ending the war in Vietnam, sustaining the environmental movement, promoting tax relief, halting the spread of nuclear power plants, cracking down on drunk driving, and forcing Presidents Johnson and Nixon from office. Conversely, positive public opinion helped President Clinton remain in office despite his impeachment and trial in Congress, and public support for U.S. military personnel who were (or are) fighting in Iraq and Afghanistan has forced Congress to continue funding these wars. Public opinion also has jeopardized civil rights and civil liberties, encouraging local governments to "exclude" poor people from the suburbs and to undermine efforts to achieve meaningful school desegregation. Public opinion is the stuff of which dreams and nightmares are made.

Public decision making means, for the most part, that public officials defer to public opinion when an issue is highly salient and controversial. But the people also make policy more directly from time to time, at least at the state and local levels. They do so through mechanisms, including the initiative and the referendum, popularized by the Progressives early in the twentieth century.

A referendum is the practice by which a measure that has been passed by or proposed by a legislature is placed on a ballot for voter approval or disapproval. An initiative is the procedure by which a measure proposed by citizens becomes law if approved by a majority of voters or by the legislature. To get an initiative on the ballot, a significant number of state residents—usually 5 percent to 10 percent of those voting in the last statewide election—must sign petitions.

Forty-nine state constitutions authorize some form of referendums, and twenty-four state constitutions authorize initiatives. Referendums outnumber initiatives by approximately four to one, but initiatives carry more weight because they enable citizens to adopt policies opposed by elected officials. Initiatives and referendums were used sporadically in the early twentieth century, but they became very popular during the 1970s, as citizens, disenchanted with government, attempted to participate more directly in the policymaking process. They remain popular today; for example, in 2010, 183 propositions appeared on state ballots around the country, and in 2012, there were 174 propositions in thirty-eight states.[49]

Public decision making, whether through initiatives and referendums or through government deference to public opinion polls, is more controversial than it might seem. Many politicians believe that they were elected to make these decisions and that ordinary citizens lack the knowledge to make public policy directly. Politicians also worry about the growing influence of activist groups and the mass media, which contribute so significantly to the formation of public opinion. If public opinion mirrors the views of the most strident, or most sensationalistic, voices in society, then direct democracy cannot accomplish the "good government" goals the Progressives had in mind.[50]

POLITICS AND POLICY

Politics varies from one issue to another because politics reflects issue characteristics such as visibility and complexity. Differences in politics in turn result in different policies and outcomes. To understand such variations, it is useful to think of six policy domains in which political struggles take place. These domains reflect the highly elastic nature of American democracy. They run the gamut from highly private to highly public decision making.

Following are brief descriptions of the six policy domains that can be used as a framework for analyzing the policy process:

1. *Boardroom politics:* decision making by business elites (top management and board members) and professionals, but with important public consequences

2. *Bureaucratic politics:* rulemaking and adjudication by bureaucrats, with input from clients and professionals

3. *Cloakroom politics:* policymaking by legislators, constrained by various constituencies

4. *Chief executive politics:* the role of presidents, governors, mayors, and their advisers in policymaking and policy implementation

5. *Courtroom politics:* the issuance of court rulings in response to controversies (cases) involving interest groups, governments, and aggrieved individuals

6. *Living room politics:* the galvanization of public opinion, usually through the mass media and/or grassroots movements

Each of these domains implies a different arena of combat, a different set of participants, and different rules of conduct. Each also implies a different set of outcomes, ranging from maintenance of the status quo (no change in past policy), to incremental change, to genuine innovation and from limited responsiveness (to public demands), to symbolic responsiveness, to meaningful policy responsiveness (Table 1-3). In short, different institutions yield different sets of likely policy consequences. The six policy domains thus serve as convenient bridges between issue characteristics and policy outcomes or consequences. As shown in Table 1-3, each policy domain can be related to both common issue characteristics and common policy outcomes. The effects of issue characteristics such as salience, conflict, complexity, and costs on policymaking and the implications of various policy processes for change, responsiveness, and other outcomes are examined in the chapters that follow. The changes that occur in issue characteristics over time and the consequences of such changes are also highlighted.

The reason for integrating issue characteristics and policy processes is the close relationship that exists between the two of them. Consider the following propositions:

- Issues that concern large numbers of people are likely to stimulate intense public debate and draw more participants into the policy process than issues that concern only a small segment of the public.
- Complex policies and those that call for major changes in public or bureaucratic behavior are much more difficult to implement than policies that can be routinely carried out through established organizational networks.
- Issues involving hidden costs are handled by the private sector, whereas issues involving disputed costs or manifest costs require some governmental response.

Likewise, the reason for linking politics and policy is that substantive results flow from different policymaking processes. Consider, for example, the following:

- Decisions made within the private sector and ratified by government agencies legitimate self-regulation (and profit seeking), impose hidden costs on consumers, and have a powerful effect on the overall economy.

TABLE 1-3   **Domains of the Policy Process**

Domain	Principal actors	Common issue characteristics	Common policy outcomes
Boardroom politics	Business elites	Low salience	Status quo
	Professionals	High complexity	Limited responsiveness
		Hidden costs	Innovation
Bureaucratic politics	Bureaucrats	Low to moderate salience	Incrementalism
	Professionals	Low to moderate conflict	Limited responsiveness
	Clients	Disputed costs	
Cloakroom politics	Legislators	Moderate to high salience	Incrementalism
	Interest groups	Moderate to high conflict	Symbolic responsiveness
	Executive officials	Disputed costs	Gridlock (status quo)
			Policy responsiveness
Chief executive politics	Chief executives	High salience	Crisis management
	Top advisers	High conflict	Policy responsiveness
		Disputed costs	Symbolic responsiveness
Courtroom politics	Judges	Low to high salience	Incrementalism
	Interest groups, governments	High conflict	Policy responsiveness (to minorities)
	Aggrieved individuals	Manifest costs	Innovation
Living room politics	Mass media	High salience	Electoral change
	Public opinion	High conflict	Policy responsiveness, symbolic responsiveness
		Manifest costs	Innovation, status quo

- Decisions made by low-level or middle-level bureaucrats tend to reflect professional norms, organizational imperatives, and standard operating procedures. Incrementalism, policymaking that changes things only marginally, is the most likely result.
- Decisions made by politicians against a backdrop of public arousal occasionally provide opportunities for policy innovation. Highly conflictive issues that do not quite reach the crisis point often result in gridlock or stalemate, however.

- Politicians frequently make only symbolic responses to aroused citizens, or they may address the problems of only a few groups or individuals, instead of taking broad policy action.
- Decisions made by judges may differ significantly from decisions made by other public officials, in that little or no effort need be made to dilute or disguise policy change. The Constitution, job security, and strong professional values protect judges from politicians, although not from politics. The courts are capable of addressing problems that paralyze other institutions of government.

An approach to the study of policymaking that highlights different policy domains has several advantages. First, the policy process is dynamic but disorderly. Issues move from one arena to another over time, but they do not follow the same sequence. This observation is importantly different from a leading point of view in the public policy literature that assumes that issues proceed in a rather orderly fashion from the agenda-setting stage to the policy formulation stage to the policy adoption stage to the policy implementation stage, and, finally, to the policy impact stage. Second, institutional settings matter, and they matter in somewhat predictable ways. As illustrated in Table 1-3, different branches of government and different levels of government present their own special opportunities and pitfalls. Successful political strategists are attentive to both. Third, our examination of the policy domains will demonstrate that the nontraditional areas of policymaking deserve attention, for without them, the picture is incomplete. The discussions of boardroom politics and living room politics will shed light on actors outside government, including business people, journalists, and citizens.

Overall, we will establish that issue characteristics constrain policymakers in significant ways, that there is no single policy process but rather several, that controversies shift from one arena to another over time, and that politics is a significant determinant of policy outcomes.

Political Culture, the Economy, and Public Policy

A merican political institutions function as parts of the larger national cultural and socioeconomic system. The actions of political institutions and, therefore, the nature of public policy are greatly influenced by these cultural and economic forces, unique to the United States. The country, as a part of the global environment, is also affected by developments in other parts of the world. But the political agenda of U.S. policymakers is not the same as that of leaders in other industrial nations, and it is fundamentally different from those of less developed, socialist, or formerly socialist countries. The United States has the world's most powerful economy, which is greatly influenced by the actions of privately owned corporations. Government ownership of major industries is an important item of political debate in many countries around the world, but it is not even under consideration in the United States. Public discussions of nutrition and health in the United States often focus on whether Americans eat too much of the wrong kinds of foods and are thus becoming obese; in many other parts of the world, discussions of nutrition and health are about how to provide citizens with enough food to keep them alive.

In this chapter, we outline some of the underlying features and characteristics of the American cultural and economic environment. Before examining the specific arenas in which public policy is formulated and implemented, we should consider the broader context within which political institutions and policymakers, and those who try to influence them, operate.

A DURABLE POLITICAL CULTURE

Political culture can be defined as the attitudes and beliefs of citizens about how political institutions and processes ought to work, about fellow citizens and their place in the political process, and about the proper rules of the political game.[1] Several enduring values of the American political culture have shaped public policy from the beginning of the republic. Individualism, the right of people to pursue their self-interest and to be responsible for their own well-being, is a fundamental American cultural value. Personal freedom, which is closely linked to individualism, has meant the right to pursue self-improvement and protection from government interference. Along with individualism, the sanctity of contracts and the right to acquire and own property contribute to the free market ideology that prevails in the United States' political and economic system.[2]

Americans also believe in democracy—the right of every citizen to participate in the political process. Support is widespread for equal treatment under the law, political equality, and equality of opportunity. In addition to these core political values, cultural values, such as religious freedom and the centrality of the nuclear family, have significant political implications. It must be noted, however, that in many ways, the United States does not live up to its political ideals, that it is a society with racist and sexist elements. As recently as the 1950s and early 1960s, black Americans did not have equal access to public schools or the voting booth. Even today, although government officials repeatedly express their commitment to breaking down racial barriers, few truly racially integrated communities exist in the United States. Women did not have the right to vote in elections until early in the twentieth century, and they still earn considerably less money on average than men.

Conflicts and tensions between values and beliefs have frequently been the source of political struggle and debate in the United States. For example, southerners and midwesterners, who rallied around Andrew Jackson in the 1830s, triumphed over the eastern aristocratic cliques that controlled American government in the late eighteenth and early nineteenth centuries by appealing to the public's belief in individualism, pragmatism, and equality of opportunity. Franklin Roosevelt's New Deal in the 1930s, which substantially expanded government management of the economy and publicly funded social safety net programs, represented a victory for democratic egalitarian values over uncompromising individualism and capitalism. Ronald Reagan's policies of the 1980s represented a swing back toward individualism, capitalism, and traditional family values. Bill Clinton's reelection in 1996 marked the end of the Reagan era and ushered in a new era of pragmatism, defined by moderate economic policy (free markets), balanced federal budgets, and progressive social values (equality of opportunity). President George W. Bush and Congress lowered taxes on those earning the highest incomes, but also increased prescription drug benefit programs for elderly Americans. President Barack Obama and Democratic majorities in Congress pushed through new guidelines and a huge expansion of health care insurance. The dynamism of America's political culture stems in part from the inherent tensions between cherished, yet competing, cultural values. Political struggles that aim to change an existing balance between these values can have dramatic effects on the nature of public policy.

The Market Paradigm and Procedural Democracy

A towering presence in the American political culture is, and always has been, a worldview that regards the so-called free market as the best allocator of society's goods and services. This viewpoint holds that government's role is primarily one of protecting certain economic, social, and political norms, or rules of conduct, such as competitive markets, private property, and representative government. This worldview dominated the thinking of nearly all the Framers of the Constitution.

What is a free market? Or what is the market mechanism for allocating goods in a society? It is a system that relies on voluntary exchanges between autonomous individuals to allocate goods and services in an efficient manner. Efficiency can be defined as the maximum output technology can produce with the minimum use of resources. In free markets, producers compete with one another to satisfy consumer demand for goods and services. Consumers are assumed to be willing to give up a certain amount of what they have, usually in the form of money, for various quantities of other goods and services—what economists call a demand function. When voluntary exchanges occur between producers and consumers, both parties are viewed as better off. A producer has given away something (a chair, for example) for something (say, $100) he or she values more. The consumer has given away something, the $100, for something he or she values more, the chair. As long as no coercion is involved, there is no reason to believe that these exchanges are not mutually beneficial.

In such a system, those who provide the goods and services on the terms most consumers find attractive should naturally be involved in the most exchanges, whereas those who offer goods on unattractive terms should be involved in the least. Over time, the inefficient producers will fall out of the market. The efficiency of the system, the highest output at the lowest cost, is guaranteed by competition. Furthermore, many people benefit because their preferences ultimately determine what kinds of goods and services are provided and they buy them at the lowest possible cost.

This formulation was fully worked out in the eighteenth century and is usually credited to Adam Smith, who described his theory in his seminal work *The Wealth of Nations*.[3] The free market formulation was enormously influential because it provided the justification for laissez-faire capitalism and representative democracy, advocates of which were fighting to free societies from the remnants of feudalism and curtail the privileges of the aristocracy. The free market paradigm forms the basis of the individualist ethic so central to American life. The logic of the free market is compelling: give people a chance to produce what they can, and those who produce what is most wanted will obtain the greatest rewards. It is both democratic and meritocratic. This seems like a very desirable combination.

Before going further, however, we must carefully examine the free market paradigm. First, it is a theoretical construct, not an empirical reality. Often, a vast difference exists between actual markets and the free market ideal. Like any theoretical construct, it is based on many assumptions. One such assumption is that individuals and businesses behave on the basis of the rational pursuit of self-interest. Rationality requires knowledge; therefore, to work properly, a market must include consumers who have "perfect knowledge" of what the market has to offer. That is, people must be aware of the alternatives to make rational choices about exchanges into which to enter. Otherwise, inefficient producers might be rewarded, and various other market distortions could occur.

Other necessary conditions are open entry into a market and fair competition among producers. If potential producers are excluded from offering their products to consumers, then innovation becomes less likely and efficiency is jeopardized. Similarly, if certain companies are able to engage in unfair behavior—terrorizing competitors, producing at a loss for a long period of time, misrepresenting their products to consumers—the free market dynamic is upset, and both production efficiency and consumer utility are compromised. The nature of a free market is quite specific, and actual markets are easily distorted.

Another essential point about the free market paradigm is that it does not prescribe outcomes. One cannot predict the mix of goods and services that will be available in a society using such a model. One can only assume that people know what they want and attempt to establish rules and procedures that will give society as many of the desired goods and services as is possible within the limits imposed by resources, technology, and individual productive capacity. If markets are free and open and people know what is available, goods and services should be allocated in a way that creates the greatest happiness for the greatest number. The desired outcome, happiness, or what economists call "utility," is defined by the rules and procedures through which it is realized.

Under the free market paradigm, individual freedom is defined as the opportunity that each person has to produce valued commodities and trade them to others for items of value. Giving every individual an equal opportunity to engage in such exchanges is recognized as being necessary if markets are to work properly. Clearly, equality of opportunity was not a reality when the Constitution was first designed, but the free market paradigm convinced many political philosophers and politicians of the validity of the idea of equality of opportunity. If markets were to operate optimally, entry into them had to be free and open; if societies were to be properly ordered, opportunities had to be open to all. When Thomas Jefferson wrote in the Declaration of Independence that "all men are created equal," he meant that all men, except slaves and the indentured, should be free to compete in society for the benefits that were available.

The basic point is that the free market paradigm dominates far more than the discipline of economics and the business sector of American society; it dominates the political and legal spheres as well. American democracy is procedural—it is defined by rules according to which political leaders are chosen by citizens in elections.[4] Its bedrock values—equality of opportunity, freedom of expression, the right to vote, the sanctity of property—spring directly from the free market paradigm. The Constitution elevates these procedural values above all others. Its logic is that justice is defined by procedural guarantees, and that maintaining the integrity of procedures is the main task of government. Thus governments have an important but limited role to play in society. Other principal components of the Constitution—separation of powers, checks and balances, and federalism—were designed to limit governmental activity and are best understood as attempts to protect markets from majority power and minority privilege.[5]

Procedural democracy is complex, amoral, antitraditional, and vague about certain questions, such as what happens when property rights conflict with other rights. Therefore, it should not be surprising that procedural democracy is not always implemented perfectly. Equality of opportunity, in particular, has been extremely difficult to realize because capitalist societies have allowed accumulated wealth, and the advantages that go with it, to be passed from one generation to the next. Cultural biases also have been stubbornly persistent in the United States. Nevertheless, the commitment of political elites and citizens to the values of procedural democracy has led to a gradual recognition that obvious contradictions to ideals such as equality of opportunity have to be confronted and resolved. Still, the ultimate goals are procedural. American democracy does not stand for equality of condition, only equality of opportunity; it is decidedly nonegalitarian in this sense.

Participatory Democracy

Representative or procedural democracy does not place a great deal of value on direct citizen involvement in the making of policy decisions. To many democratic theorists, this is a critical shortcoming. Jean-Jacques Rousseau, one of Adam Smith's contemporaries and acquaintances, said about representative government in England, "The people of England regards itself as free, but is grossly mistaken; it is free only during the election of members of parliament. As soon as they are elected, slavery overtakes it, and it is nothing."[6] He prescribed a much more classical form of democracy, in which citizens would make societal laws directly, submerging their self-interest in pursuit of the collective interest or "general will." Participatory democracy is an alternative to procedural democracy.

Interest in participatory forms of democracy is very much alive among contemporary democratic theorists.[7] For example, Jane Mansbridge has written about what she calls "unitary" democracy, which envisions a common good that is separate and distinct from the outcome of the struggle between competitive interests in a political community.[8] Advocates of unitary democracy contend that community forums in which citizens meet face to face (possibly mediated by computer monitors and broadband cables) and work toward consensual solutions to their common problems are both feasible and highly desirable. In such settings, issues can be framed in such a way as not to be easily divisible into "we" versus "they" dichotomies, and citizens learn how to work toward commonly desired ends.

A classic example of unitary democracy at work is a town meeting in which a question such as whether to invest in a new water purification facility is discussed. The issue affects nearly everyone in more or less the same way; advocates on both sides debate the issue face to face; most participants are looking for a consensual solution; and preferences are registered publicly without behind-the-scenes maneuvering. This form of democracy is still practiced in some rural American communities, such as in Vermont and Maine, and holds considerable appeal for many Americans.

Participatory forms of democracy emphasize the importance of direct citizen involvement in the policymaking process. Such direct involvement, although without face-to-face debate, is present when citizens vote for initiatives and referendums in state and local elections. This form of public decision making is examined at length in chapter 8. The idea of participatory democracy is very much a part of American culture, albeit in a somewhat abstract and mythical form. Political reality is typically dominated by citizens voting for representatives in periodic elections, by the pursuit of private interests through affiliations with narrow interest groups, and by legal or adversarial processes and procedures.

Assessing Contemporary Political Culture

Debate about contemporary political culture usually centers on issues such as multiculturalism and diversity, political correctness, distrust of politics and politicians, and the status of so-called traditional values. All these issues partake of the core American political values—individualism, freedom, private property, democracy, and equality—discussed above. For example, those most in favor of making sure people from different backgrounds are treated fairly place primary importance on equality; their opponents commonly worry about the government providing entitlements for certain groups, which would violate their sense of individualism and fairness. What seems clear is that contemporary political culture is highly textured; many different combinations of values can be found among Americans. Despite this diversity, conflicts among core values are central components of most political debate and disagreement in the United States.

During the second half of the twentieth century in the United States, major changes in politics and policy were somewhat easier to identify than changes in political culture and values. In politics and policy, the principal eras were the conservative 1950s, symbolized by President Dwight Eisenhower, which gave way to the liberal 1960s and 1970s, a return to conservatism in the 1980s, and then to moderation and pragmatism by the mid-1990s and then greater partisan conflicts in the 2000s. Seminal events were the elections of John F. Kennedy and Lyndon Johnson in the 1960s, then the election and reelection of Ronald Reagan in the 1980s, and then the elections and reelections of Bill Clinton in 1990s, George W. Bush in the 2000s, and Barack Obama in 2008 and 2012.

The liberal social programs of Johnson's Great Society that dominated the political agenda in the 1960s and 1970s were augmented by the environmental movement in the 1970s. The Reagan era shifted the locus of political discussion to more conservative issues such as tax cuts, reduced domestic federal spending, and privatization of government service delivery. Clinton's elections seemed to confirm public support for moderate to conservative fiscal policy (deficit reduction) and moderate to liberal social policy (increased support for education, Social Security, Medicare, and environmental protection). Yet George W. Bush's terms brought about more tax cuts, higher deficits, greatly expanded defense and security spending, and much larger federal deficits. Barack Obama's election expanded government economic spending and expanded health care coverage for millions of uninsured Americans. The cultural changes that took place from the 1960s to the present did not exactly mirror the political eras just described; they were more subtle and complex.

A central political development in the second half of the twentieth century was the Democratic liberalism of the 1960s. Modern American liberalism is closely associated with the Democratic Party. Liberalism and the Democrats rose to power in the 1930s through New Deal legislation that expanded government involvement in social welfare and the economy. Uniting workers, intellectuals, southerners, and various ethnic minorities, the Democrats implemented unprecedented social welfare programs and policies. The most conspicuous and enduring law, the Social Security Act, guarantees financial assistance to elderly, poor, and disabled Americans. During the 1960s and early 1970s large Democratic majorities in Congress worked cooperatively with Lyndon Johnson, and combatively with Richard Nixon, to design new government programs in housing, education, welfare, health, employment, civil rights, and environmental regulation. This second wave of Democratic liberalism seemed to set a political course for the rest of the century.

Even most conservatives would agree that the Reagan era was largely a reaction to the Great Society programs. They would argue that the American people tried liberalism in the 1960s and 1970s, but found it wanting. During the 1980s, Americans sought to establish a new equilibrium among leading political values, an equilibrium that was more traditional and conservative than that prevailing in the late 1960s and the 1970s. Criticisms of the second-wave liberal Democratic policies were voiced by politicians, researchers, and citizens from the beginning of the Kennedy administration, and they eventually grew stronger. Academic studies of social welfare, civil rights, and regulatory programs revealed many serious flaws of theory, design, and execution. Politicians and intellectuals also questioned the morality of liberalism, especially as it applied to abortion, school prayer, sex education, criminal justice, and the threat of communism. By the 1980s, few politicians willingly identified themselves as liberals. Instead, they called themselves moderates, pragmatists, progressives, or neoliberals.

Although political leaders no longer labeled themselves liberal, Americans continued to support most liberal programs in the 1980s and 1990s. Public support for Social Security has been strong for a long time. In a 1979 poll, for example, nine Americans in ten could cite at least one advantage of the program.[9] Despite years of chronic federal deficits of $200 billion or more, 90 percent of the public thought that either too little or about the right amount of money was being spent on Social Security from 1985 to 2008.[10] In the early

2000s, a majority of the public favored the idea of allowing people to invest a portion of their Social Security payroll taxes in a personal retirement account, although this approach held little favor with those over sixty-five years of age. However, when George W. Bush attempted to reform Social Security in this manner in his second term, public support for this idea dropped from 58 percent to 46 percent, and Congress refused to support the changes.[11]

In 1990, a majority of Americans (56 percent) favored a national health insurance system, and even though support for national health insurance declined after 1994, the portion of the public that thought the government was spending too little to protect the nation's health rose from roughly 60 percent in the mid-1980s to 70 percent in the mid-1990s. The percentage of the public that believed government was spending too little to protect the nation's health remained fairly consistent with the mid-1990 figures from 2000 to 2008, with the public's agreement peaking in 2004 at 78 percent. The percentage of the public's agreement then slipped back to 60 percent in 2010. This may be attributable to the public's perception of the increased spending associated with the Patient Protection and Affordable Care Act passed in that same year.[12]

Of course, one should be cautious about interpreting these poll results as meaning that the public supports "bigger" government. Since the 1950s, public opinion polls consistently have found that Americans like government benefits, but do not like to pay for them. For example, in the summer of 1990, 60 percent thought that spending for domestic programs should increase, but 79 percent opposed raising federal income taxes.[13] In February 2011, more than 65 percent of Americans thought that state spending on roads and public transportation, public colleges and universities, health care services, and funding for K–12 public schools should not decrease, but at the same time, more than 65 percent were opposed to increases in sales or personal income taxes.[14]

In 2011, The Pew Research Center for the People & the Press asked this question of a national sample of Americans: "If you were making up the budget for the federal government this year, would you increase spending, decrease spending or keep spending the same," for a whole host of programs.[15] Large percentages said that they would either increase or continue to spend the same amounts on:

- Medicare (increase, 40 percent; increase or the same, 83 percent);
- government assistance for the unemployed (increase, 27 percent; increase or the same, 68 percent);
- Social Security (increase, 41 percent; increase or the same, 84 percent);
- economic assistance to needy people in the United States (increase, 42 percent; increase or the same, 76 percent);
- education (increase, 62 percent; increase or the same, 87 percent);
- public school systems (increase, 56 percent; increase or the same, 85 percent);
- health care (increase, 41 percent; increase or the same, 71 percent);

- rebuilding highways, bridges, and roads (increase, 38 percent; increase or the same, 75 percent); and
- financial aid for college students (increase, 44 percent; increase or the same, 81 percent).

Around the same time this survey was reported, a national CBS News poll asked Americans whether taxes should be increased on people such as themselves to reduce the federal budget deficit, and nearly six in ten said that this was "not necessary."[16] One clear change in public attitude that occurred between 1965 and 1975, and remains important today, is the decline in public trust in government institutions and public officials. Although the decline was steepest in the post-Watergate period, thus seemingly disadvantaging Republicans, its continuation is probably more detrimental to Democrats, because they are the ones who believe in active government. Ronald Reagan certainly tapped into this mistrust in his successful presidential campaigns. The percentage of Americans who believed that the government would do "what is right" (always or most of the time) slid from 80 percent to about 30 percent between 1964 and 1980. It did rise a bit (to about 42 percent) by 1986 to 1988 but then fell again to 20 percent in 2011.[17] A similar trend has occurred for all major institutions, public and private. That is, high levels of trust or confidence through the mid-1960s have been replaced by substantially lower levels of trust since then.

In government, Congress and the presidency inspired lower levels of confidence from the 1990s to the present (with 20 percent or fewer having "a great deal of confidence" in them) than the Supreme Court and the military.[18] This lack of trust and confidence in government also reveals itself in low voter turnout rates. In the 1960s, 60 percent or more of those eligible voted in presidential elections, and close to 50 percent voted in off-year congressional elections. Then, between 1970 and 2000, turnout in presidential elections exceeded 56 percent only twice (1972 and 1992), dipping to an all-time low of 52 percent in 1996. Turnout in off-year congressional elections has hovered around 40 percent since 1970. However in the twenty-first century, turnout in presidential elections has returned to levels close to those of the 1960s; in 2004 it was 60.7 percent, and in 2008 it was 62.2 percent.[19] Even in states such as Minnesota, with election day registration, voter turnout seldom exceeds 60 percent. In the 2002 midterm election turnout was 64.1 percent, but it was only 55.9 percent in the 2010 election cycle. In 2010, only nine states exceeded the 50 percent level for voter turnout.[20]

Some critics of modern liberalism argue that it is not the public's distaste for government spending that undermines liberal programs; rather, the public has become disillusioned with the social and moral values spawned by liberalism. If this argument is correct, it should be reflected in surveys about attitudes on abortion, school prayer, capital punishment, and racial integration. In fact, liberal attitudes have survived or prospered in most of these areas, except gun control. For example, public support for maintaining legal abortions under some circumstances, such as to protect the health of the mother, or if pregnancy is the result of rape or incest, has been above 70 percent since 1975; in the 1990s it was above 80 percent, and in the 2000s it averaged about 75 percent.[21] Americans overwhelmingly believe that black and white Americans should attend the same schools and be permitted to live in the same neighborhoods. Since the 1980s, more than 90 percent of Americans have supported integrated schools.[22] By 1996, 87 percent of white Americans did not think "Whites should be able to prevent Blacks from living in their neighborhoods"; in 1972, only 61 percent of whites held this view.[23]

There are several issues on which the American public did move away from liberal positions in the second half of the twentieth century. One was crime and criminals; the portion of the public endorsing capital punishment rose from about 50 percent in the late 1950s to more than 80 percent in 1994; however, it declined to 61 percent in 2011.[24] In the 1970s, more than 70 percent of the public thought the emphasis of prisons should be on the rehabilitation of criminals; by the mid-1990s, fewer than 20 percent believed this, and most believed the main purpose of prisons was to keep criminals out of society.[25] Although expressing strong support for integration, white Americans have shown increased levels of opposition over the past thirty years to government interventions such as school busing or affirmative action to assist minorities. By 2008, 51 percent of black Americans said that government should help minority groups, but only 16 percent of white Americans held this view.[26] Moreover, the public remains committed to certain traditional ideas. Despite the rulings of the Supreme Court, 69 percent of citizens polled in 2004 supported prayer in public schools—a level that has declined only slightly over several decades.[27] Although the proportion of the public that views religion as "very important" in their lives has remained below the 70 percent level of the mid-1960s, it rose from just over 50 percent in the late 1970s to just under 60 percent in 2000, declining a bit to 55 percent in 2011.[28]

Detailed studies of American values reveal some generational differences on issues of political culture that are closely tied to life experiences and economic conditions. Americans born after World War II are more likely to exhibit what have been labeled "postmaterialist" values. They are more apt than their elders to believe that giving people a say in government decisions, protecting freedom of speech, and improving the environment are more important than curbing inflation, fighting crime, and expanding the economy.[29] These values, linked to the baby boom generation, appeared to be somewhat less popular among American young adults in the late 1980s, who showed a great interest in pursuing lucrative careers in business, than they were among youth in the 1970s. However, responses in 2008 to a battery of questions about whether the government should spend more or less on Social Security, health, public schools, welfare, environment, and government-guaranteed jobs showed voters under thirty to be more liberal than other age cohorts in every area except health and Social Security.[30] This finding is not surprising in that Social Security and Medicare are very salient for older voters, and younger voters are typically more liberal in their political views than middle-aged and older voters. However, it also suggests that the baby boomers, now well into middle age, have become somewhat more concerned about the economy (they are still noticeably more liberal than the elder generation), and the younger generation has not eschewed postmaterialist values, although these values are perhaps not as prominent as they were twenty-five years ago (see Table 2-1).

TABLE 2-1   **Generational Differences within the Political Culture, 2011**

Topic	Millennial (aged 18–30 years)	Generation X (aged 31–46 years)	Baby boomers (aged 47–65 years)	Silent (aged 66–83 years)
Conservative ideology[a]	30%	36%	42%	46%
Liberal ideology[a]	26%	21%	19%	16%
Trust in government[a]	26%	19%	16%	16%
Anger with government[a]	13%	18%	26%	30%
Believe the United States is "the greatest country in the world"[b]	32%	48%	50%	64%
In favor of smaller government, fewer services[a]	35%	47%	54%	59%
Immigration: believe newcomers threaten customs and values[c]	27%	37%	46%	45%
Religious faith and values are very important[b]	46%	64%	69%	78%
In favor of same-sex marriage[a]	59%	50%	42%	33%
Agree that interracial dating is acceptable[a]	91%	92%	87%	76%
Believe stricter environmental laws and regulations are worth the cost[c]	57%	57%	54%	40%
Opposed to capital punishment for murderers[a]	46%	34%	33%	31%

Source: Pew Research Center for the People & the Press, "The Generation Gap and the 2012 Election," November 3, 2011, www.people-press.org/2011/11/03/the-generation-gap-and-the-2012-election-3/.

[a] Pew Research poll conducted September 22 to October 4, 2011.

[b] Pew Research poll conducted September 1 to 15, 2011.

[c] Pew Research poll conducted February 22 to March 14, 2011.

Americans' responses to direct questions about their ideological leanings reveal a very small conservative shift over the past three decades. Those who regard themselves as liberal (from slightly to extremely) declined from 26 percent in 1972 to 23 percent in 1988, rising slightly to 29 percent by 2008. Conservative self-identification (again, from slightly to extremely) rose from 37 percent in 1972 to 46 percent in 1988, and stood at 43 percent in 2008.[31] To return to the question of liberalism among young adults, in the 1980s those aged eighteen to twenty-nine were less inclined to describe themselves as liberals (30 percent) than the same age cohort in 1972 (39 percent) or 2008 (38 percent).[32] The most significant pattern is that most Americans place themselves near the center of the ideological spectrum. In 1972, 74 percent of those surveyed saw themselves as moderates, or slight liberals or conservatives; the percentages in these categories changed very little during the 1980s, 1990s, and 2000s.[33] As many public opinion specialists have pointed out, it is not at all clear that respondents have the same understanding of what the terms *liberal* and *conservative* mean when they answer questions about their ideological orientations, thus reinforcing the point that the principal finding is one of ideological moderation on the part of the American public.

Changes have occurred in the percentages of Americans calling themselves Republicans, Democrats, and independents over the past fifty years, and in the connection between ideology and partisanship. In the 1950s and 1960s, 45 percent to 50 percent of voters were affiliated with the Democratic Party, and 25 percent to 30 percent with the Republican Party, leaving 30 percent or fewer as independents. However, many of those who described themselves as Democrats considered themselves to be conservative. In the 1970s, Republican affiliation dipped below 25 percent, Democratic affiliation also declined to about 40 percent, and independents increased to 35 percent to 40 percent. From the 1980s to the present, identification with the Democratic Party has ranged from highs of 40 percent to 45 percent (in the early 1980s) to lows of just over 30 percent (in 2004). Over this same period, Republican identification has varied from lows of about 25 percent (in the early 1980s) to highs of about 30 percent (from the mid-1990s to the 2000s).[34] The primary cause of the uptick in Republican identification since the 1970s was the movement of southern white conservatives from the Democratic to the Republican Party. In 2012, the Pew Research Center reported that 32 percent of those polled identified as Democrats, 24 percent as Republicans, and 38 percent as independents.[35] The major patterns, therefore, are the decline, of roughly 10 percent, over the past forty to fifty years in the portion of the electorate that identifies with the Democratic Party; the increase in the number of independents, which is especially evident among younger voters; the rebound of 5 percent to 10 percent in the numbers of Americans identifying with the Republican Party from its nadir in the 1970s; and the hardening of party lines, with Republicans consisting of conservatives and Democrats of liberals and moderates.[36]

THE CHANGING AMERICAN ECONOMY

Over the past sixty years, the American economy has dominated the world's commerce. The U.S. economy, like most others in the world, was still sputtering from the Great Depression as the country entered World War II. But following the war, the economy experienced twenty to twenty-five years of unprecedented growth. During the 1970s and 1980s, the economy experienced a variety of painful problems, but in the 1990s, it rebounded and the country enjoyed record growth and prosperity again. The Great Recession hit in 2008.

The central economic objectives of U.S. policymakers are quite clear and have remained fairly constant for decades: to promote sustained economic growth without price inflation, to maintain low levels of unemployment and poverty, and to attempt to ensure a high standard of living for American citizens. When unemployment and inflation rise, people suffer and the cost of government goes up. But keeping unemployment and inflation low is very difficult. Since 1950, the United States has experienced ten recessions—periods of six months or more of negative economic growth (in gross domestic product [GDP]), which resulted in high levels of unemployment.[37]

The task of managing the American economy today is very challenging. Whether and how government should intervene in the economy has always been a matter of great controversy in American politics, a central dividing line between liberals and conservatives, Democrats and Republicans. Moreover, the economic realities since 1970 have shattered many of the old assumptions, increased the stakes of the game considerably, and multiplied the number and difficulty of choices policymakers face.

Government's Role in a Strong Economy: The 1950s and 1960s

Government economic policymaking was easier, and in some ways less critical, when the U.S. economy was expanding at a stable rate during the 1950s and 1960s. Consider the following indicators:

- The economy grew at a healthy rate of over 4 percent annually, and per capita income increased by 2.5 percent per year.
- Productivity growth—the measure of output per person per hour worked—was also impressive; the average annual increase was more than 3 percent.
- Unemployment averaged about 4 percent, and annual inflation rates were seldom more than 2 percent.
- The cost of borrowing money, although gradually rising from a 2 percent interest rate in 1950, did not exceed 4 percent until 1965.
- The economy was running smoothly, with slightly less than 60 percent of the adult population in the labor force—more than 85 percent of the men and 37 percent of the women.[38]

Government's role in the economy was fairly uncomplicated, by contemporary standards. When the economy slumped, the government enlarged the supply of money for investors and increased government spending to stimulate growth. Major recessions and accompanying unemployment were thus mitigated or avoided altogether. When a recession hit in 1957 and 1958, unemployment rose to a postwar high of nearly 7 percent; the federal government increased spending beyond revenues, resulting in a deficit of $13 billion at the end of 1958, also a postwar high. The unemployment rate had dropped to 5.5 percent by the following year.

The main purpose of macroeconomic policy—increasing or decreasing the money supply (monetary policy) and the extent of deficit spending or surplus revenue (fiscal policy)—was to maintain high levels of employment by stimulating demand for goods and services. With the economic depression of the 1930s and 1940s not far behind them, policymakers were preoccupied with the problem of unemployment. Joblessness was perceived as a problem that applied mainly to male "breadwinners" and was closely related to the condition of manufacturing firms, which employed one-third of the workforce (compared with about one-sixth in today's economy).

The absence of strong competition from other nations for consumer markets was another fact of economic life in the 1950s and 1960s, when practically all products sold in the United States were manufactured domestically. U.S. exports accounted for one-fourth of all world exports and far exceeded imports.[39]

The American standard of living was the highest of any nation. In 1960, the nation's per capita gross national product (GNP), the monetary value of all goods and services produced in a year, was roughly twice that of Western Europe and six times that of Japan.[40] The United States provided a model of economic strength and prosperity that the entire noncommunist world sought to emulate.

The 1950s and 1960s were not free of economic problems. Poverty was quite severe. For more than twenty years after World War II, roughly one American in five lived in poverty by U.S. government standards. In 1960, for example, 40 million Americans, 22 percent of the population, were poor. In the 1970s, the poverty rate was reduced to about half of the 1960 level.[41] Furthermore, the average American's standard of living was much lower in the 1950s and 1960s than in the 1980s and the present. Taking inflation into account, per capita income was roughly half the level achieved in the 1980s, and 40 percent of the present level.

By the 1960s, various sectors of society, especially blue-collar workers, elderly people, and the middle class, had begun to demand a larger slice of the economic pie. The federal government initiated policies aimed at improving the economic well-being of these and other segments of society. The domestic portion of the federal budget burgeoned as programs for elderly, poor, and unemployed Americans, students, veterans, military retirees, and many other groups were either created or enlarged. At the same time, billions of dollars were being spent to fight a war in Vietnam.

Expanding Government's Role

The late 1960s and early 1970s represent a watershed in American policymaking, for hundreds of new spending and regulatory programs were established in that period. It was taken for granted that the economy would grow and that sufficient revenues would be produced to sustain these new government endeavors. Policymakers were not spending money lavishly; indeed, many of the new programs had meager budgets. But the political climate in Washington accepted, and in many ways encouraged, the practice of defusing conflicts by creating programs or regulations to satisfy interest groups and voters. The substantial reduction in poverty during the late 1960s and 1970s can be attributed in large part to federal income transfer programs, particularly Social Security.[42]

This flurry of policy initiatives expanded government spending quite significantly. In 1965, federal spending was just under $120 billion, roughly double the 1952 level. Over the next twenty-one years, the federal budget doubled every six to eight years—in 1972, 1978, and 1986. As a percentage of GNP, federal spending rose from 14 percent in 1950 to 18 percent in 1960, to 20 percent in 1970, to 22 percent in 1980, and to 23.5 percent in 1985. Stimulated by the explosion of federal grant-in-aid programs, state and local government spending also shot up—from $52 billion in 1960 to $369 billion in 1980, to $908 billion in 1990. Government was spending more and relying more heavily on individuals to pay for it. Taxpayers began to feel the pinch. Personal income taxes and Social Security payroll taxes accounted for 60 percent of federal revenue in 1968, 70 percent in 1980, and 78 percent in 1990.

The growth in the Social Security program provides an excellent example of how spending can increase dramatically over time as policymakers adjust programs even in seemingly small ways. During the 1960s and 1970s, the basic program for elderly Americans, known as Old Age, Survivors, and Disability Insurance, was amended several times. More people were made eligible, benefits were increased, a cost-of-living adjustment was added to offset the erosion in income caused by inflation, and other income security programs, including Supplemental Security Income, were created for disadvantaged groups. At the time, these actions were not regarded as radical policy decisions. They were far less controversial than the creation of the Community Action Program, the passage of several civil rights acts, or the enactment of medical insurance programs for poor (Medicaid) and elderly (Medicare) people. The cumulative effect of these "modest" adjustments in Social Security became clear later on. The federal government allocated $17.5 billion to Social Security programs in 1965; by 1975 outlays for Social Security and Medicare had increased to nearly $78 billion. Social Security and Medicare expenditures had jumped to $150 billion by 1980 and were just under $350 billion in 1990.

exploding SSA & health care costs

Changing Political-Economic Problems: The 1970s and 1980s

Mounting public sector spending was only one dimension of the rapidly changing American economy in the 1970s and 1980s. More Americans were working than ever before. The labor force expanded from 70 million in 1960 to 107 million in 1980, to nearly 126 million in 1990, and women's participation in the labor force increased dramatically, from 38 percent in 1960 to 52 percent by 1980, to 58 percent by 1990. The economy shifted away from the manufacturing of steel, automobiles, and heavy equipment and toward services, such as insurance, banking, and information. Between 1960 and 1990, employment in manufacturing remained fairly stable (17 million in 1960, rising to 20 million by 1980, then falling to 19 million in 1990), but service sector employment jumped to 28 million in 1990 from 7 million in 1960.

Economic troubles emerged during the 1970s, and continued through the 1980s, as revealed by the following indicators:

- Economic growth slowed to an annual rate of 3 percent; per capita income growth slowed to an average rate of 2.1 percent.
- Annual productivity increases fell to just over 1.5 percent.
- Unemployment averaged 6.7 percent, and inflation averaged 6.3 percent, both well above the levels from 1950 to 1969.
- Interest rates were more than twice as high as in the 1950s and 1960s.
- Imports exceeded exports in seventeen of the twenty years.
- Economic growth and productivity in some Western European countries and Japan were higher than in the United States.
- The standard of living in several Western European countries edged ahead of the United States for the first time in thirty years.[43]

Various sectors of the economy reacted to the unfavorable economic developments of the 1970s by seeking to protect their vital interests. An ever-expanding number of interest groups pressed lawmakers for more government subsidies or protective regulations. By acceding to the demands of various interest groups, national policymakers shielded society from the negative effects of a sputtering, treadmill economy, but avoided confronting the real problems. Americans were running faster—more people working, more money in circulation, higher interest rates—but the economy was going nowhere. The Federal Reserve Board expanded the nation's money supply twice as fast in the 1970s as it had in the 1960s. Government spending consistently exceeded revenues, and the budget deficits mounted. The administrations of Richard Nixon, Gerald Ford, and Jimmy Carter adopted various government policies aimed at curbing spiraling inflation, including outright controls on wages and prices.

By the late 1970s, the unprecedented combination of high unemployment, rising prices, and mounting interest rates brought economic hardship to millions of Americans and gave rise to a new economic term: *stagflation.* Inflation became the most dreaded malady in this economy of sorrows, and for good reason. Prices increased by an average of 7.4 percent per year in the 1970s, compared with only 2.4 percent per year during the 1960s. Americans shifted their concern from unemployment to inflation and its effect on their standard of living. Everyone wanted to be protected from the negative effects of inflation: unions bargained for inflation-adjusted wages, senior citizens demanded cost-of-living increases in Social Security programs, management passed price increases along to consumers, and landlords raised rents to offset rising utility bills.

Conditions were ripe for change as the 1980 presidential election approached. The extent of the nation's economic deterioration was clear: inflation surpassed 13 percent, interest rates exceeded 15 percent, productivity was declining, and 7 percent of the labor force was jobless. In this economic climate, any president would have been hard-pressed to achieve reelection. Ronald Reagan and the Republicans proposed tax and expenditure reductions that the American middle class found understandable and appealing, and President Jimmy Carter was defeated easily.

Ironically, several of the building blocks in the Reagan administration's economic and government reform program had already been put in place during the last two years of the Carter administration. The Federal Reserve Board, under Chairman Paul Volcker, instituted a stricter monetary policy to choke off inflation. The Carter administration began to loosen government regulations in various sectors of the economy and shift spending priorities toward a larger defense budget, freezes or cuts in domestic programs, and a balanced federal budget. These moderate policies reflected a consensus among national policymakers that a new economic order was needed.

There can be no doubt, however, that Reagan's election and the adoption of his economic policies by Congress in 1981 brought about major changes in American politics and the American economy. These policies and their consequences dominated the nation's economic policy agenda in the 1980s. The pillars of Reagan's economic strategy were the Economic Recovery Tax Act, which slashed personal income taxes by one-quarter over three years, and the Omnibus Budget Reconciliation Act, which increased defense spending and cut social spending in areas such as government jobs and training, education, and programs for poor people.[44]

This economic strategy was nothing less than audacious. Senate Republican leader Howard Baker called it a "riverboat gamble." During the presidential primaries, rival candidate George W. Bush called it "voodoo economics." Reagan claimed that cutting taxes and domestic spending would invigorate the economy sufficiently to bring in the revenues needed for the continuation of other government programs and for the expansion in military spending.

These predictions were wrong, at least in the short term. The economy plunged into the deepest recession in forty years; unemployment exceeded 10 percent in 1982, and the federal deficit increased from $60 billion in 1981 to over $200 billion two years later. Annual deficits averaged almost $185 billion for the remainder of the decade. These large deficits caused the national debt to triple during the 1980s, and interest payments on the debt soared. By 1984, they reached $110 billion, or about 18 percent of all federal spending, climbing to $170 billion by 1989.

One positive result of the painful recession of 1981 to 1983 was that the inflation genie was put back in the bottle. Inflation fell from double digits from 1979 to 1981 to 6 percent in 1982 and averaged about 4 percent per year for the rest of the decade. By the end of 1983, an economic recovery was under way: productivity improved substantially (from 1984 to 1987) and unemployment fell steadily through the remainder of the decade. The American economy of the mid- to late 1980s looked reasonably healthy, but by 1990, another recession had set in. Furthermore, large federal deficits continued into the 1990s, imposing a tremendous long-term burden on American citizens and policymakers.

Other problems, less obvious than the deficits, also lurked in the economy of the 1980s. By 1985, as a result of the recession of 1982, the poverty rate had risen to 15 percent (from 11 percent in 1979), which meant that there were 35 million poor Americans. In the remainder of the decade, the poverty rate gradually declined, dipping just below 13 percent in 1989. But the gap between rich and poor widened during the 1980s, as the more affluent households (the top 20 percent) enjoyed a substantial increase in their share of personal income, whereas the shares of all others remained about the same or declined.[45] Wealth disparities also increased in the 1980s and were especially pronounced along racial lines; the median accumulation of property and other assets by white families in 1988 was more than $43,000, whereas the comparable figures for African Americans and Hispanics were $4,200 and $5,500, respectively.[46]

Another problem was high real interest rates (the difference between nominal interest rates and the rate of inflation) due, to some extent, to the deficits. When individuals and corporations wanted to borrow money, they had to pay more for it, in part because they were competing with the federal government, which was borrowing billions of dollars to pay for its activities. From 1981 to 1984, real interest rates in the United States were very high (more than 8 percent); by the middle of the decade, they had declined to about 5 percent, but this level was still substantially higher than real interest rates in the 1960s (2.75 percent) and comparable rates in many other countries. From 1984 to 1990, the economy grew at a healthy rate (just under 4 percent annually), but government borrowing continued to limit the Federal Reserve Board's flexibility in adjusting interest rates.

High real interest rates in the United States in the 1980s increased worldwide demand for the dollar and the value of the dollar relative to most other currencies. This led to high annual trade deficits, which averaged more than $110 billion per year between 1984 and 1990. Thus, at the end of the 1980s, the U.S. economy was no longer the unchallenged economic powerhouse of the industrial world. Many industrial nations, and several less developed nations, had become important economic competitors, including Japan, Germany, and Taiwan.[47] The diminished autonomy of the American economy revealed more clearly than ever the intimate connection between government policy and economic performance. What American policymakers decided about trade and tax matters had a direct bearing on the ability of U.S. corporations to compete in the world market against countries and corporations that were governed by different rules.

The debt of less developed countries added another dimension to U.S. economic difficulties. During the 1970s, American banks lent a great deal of money at interest rates ranging from 15 percent to 20 percent to many African and South American countries, whose main form of collateral was raw materials—in most cases, crude oil. At that time, oil prices were high and were projected to stay that way. But when the Organization of the Petroleum Exporting Countries lost its control over crude oil supplies in the 1980s, oil prices fell precipitously, putting debtor nations in a terrible position. Many of them could not even pay the interest on their loans, let alone the principal. Brazil and Mexico, for example, owed more than $100 billion each to foreign creditors by 1988, and many debt-dependent countries were spending more than 50 percent of their incomes from exports on debt repayment. Major U.S. banks had outstanding loans to developing countries of more than $43 billion in 1989 and looked to the government for help in finding a solution to this problem.

THE RISING TIDE OF THE 1990s

Much as the economic recovery of the mid- to late 1980s followed the recession of 1981 to 1982, the economic boom of the 1990s followed the recession of 1990 to 1991. In both cases, a significant number of jobs were lost. In the 1981–1982 recession, it was mainly well-paid blue-collar jobs that were lost, hundreds of thousands of them. According to one estimate, between 1979 and 1989, 4.1 million manufacturing jobs were lost permanently.[48] Blue-collar workers were hurt again by the recession of 1990 to 1991, but in this recession, a new twist was added: large numbers of white-collar, salaried employees lost their jobs. Between 1991 and 1993, roughly 9 million people lost jobs that they never regained.[49] Furthermore, large-scale job loss continued well after the recession had ended, as the "downsizing" movement swept the corporate world.[50] By 1995, almost every *Fortune* 500 company, America's largest corporations, either had gone through a downsizing or had plans to undertake one. As a result, job insecurity was widespread among American workers, which no doubt affected their propensity to demand higher wages when the economy improved. Real wages for industrial workers declined for most of the decade, not catching up to the level of the 1980s until 1998.

To be sure, millions of new jobs were created from 1992 to 2000. And even though many of these new jobs were temporary and did not carry employee benefits, there is no doubt that the economy as a whole was strong after the 1990–1991 recession. This is perhaps best illustrated by the fact that the unemployment rate reached a thirty-year low of 4 percent during 2000. To review the indicators we have used to assess previous periods: during the 1990s, the economy grew at a 3.1 percent annual rate, slightly above the 1970–1989 rate; per capita income increased by 2.7 percent annually, exceeding the increases of the 1950s and 1960s; productivity increases averaged 2.1 percent, midway between the 1950–1969 average and the 1970–1989 average; the average unemployment rate for the decade of 5.8 percent was well above the 4 percent level of the 1950s and 1960s, but the decade ended with the unemployment rate at 4.2 percent and heading downward; interest rates declined about 2 percent from the average levels of the 1970s and 1980s, but remained well above the rates of the 1950s and 1960s; the trade deficits fell markedly in the early portion of the decade, only to rise to record levels by the end of the decade; and economic growth in the United States exceeded that of Europe and Japan by some margin.[51]

The most remarkable and salutary political-economic development of the decade was the elimination of federal deficits. Many factors contributed to this development, most notably a strong economy accompanied by a booming stock market, but policy decisions at the national level also played an important role. President Clinton made deficit reduction a priority in 1993 with his first budget proposal to Congress, which passed the Senate by a single vote (Vice President Al Gore's). After winning a showdown with the new Republican Congress over the budget in 1995 (and winning reelection in 1996), he followed up with a historic tax and budget agreement with the Republican Congress in 1997. The basic course followed by Clinton and Congress was to restrain federal spending by sticking to the rules first laid out in budget legislation in 1990, which set caps on discretionary spending and subjected entitlement spending to a pay-as-you-go discipline that prohibited new spending programs or tax cuts unless they were offset by cuts in other programs or new taxes. Spending on defense actually declined in the 1990s, as did overall federal spending as a percentage of the GDP. The Federal Reserve kept inflation in check and real interest rates low, especially from 1992 to 1995, and in 1998 the federal government saw its first surplus in twenty-nine years.[52] The stock market reacted very positively to this development; thus government surpluses should be appreciated as both a cause and a symptom of economic strength.

The vitality of the economy of the 1990s appears to have been the result of the confluence of several favorable internal factors: a postrecession recovery, corporate downsizing that encouraged high stock values amid job insecurity, large supplies of funds for investment from the retirement accounts of the baby boom generation and other sources, reduced government spending and borrowing, low inflation, and stable currency values. The main problem with this economy was the inequity with which the benefits were distributed. This is manifested not only in the concentration of income and wealth among the very rich, but also in the great disparity in wages and earnings between highly skilled, well-educated workers and those who lacked education and skills. Workers in the latter category saw their real wages decline steadily in the 1980s and 1990s.[53] In addition, the poverty rate was stubbornly persistent during the 1980s and 1990s, hovering in the range of 13 percent to 15 percent, which was higher than it was in the 1970s. Income and wealth was distributed more unequally in the United States than in any country in Western Europe.[54]

Another very important set of economic developments in the 1990s was the finalization of key international trade agreements, which marked the era of so-called globalization. Despite their differences, President Clinton and Congress were able to agree on the need to implement the North American Free Trade Agreement and a new General Agreement on Tariffs and Trade, which created the World Trade Organization (WTO), in 1994. Both of these were designed to remove national barriers to trade and ultimately to promote economic growth. In 2000, Clinton and Congress reached another agreement to permanently lift all trade restrictions against China.[55] The WTO included 128 nations as original signatories, and it features a codified system, using international panels, for resolving trade disputes.[56] The WTO, along with the International Monetary Fund and the World Bank, form a powerful international triad that aims to promote economic growth and development through the expansion of free markets. These organizations have many critics in the United States and abroad who believe that their actions and policies often work to the disadvantage of poor countries and ignore human rights and environmental issues.[57] Such criticism, voiced in several visible protests around the world, along with strong world economic growth, led to a consensus between the United States and Europe in the fall of 2000 to forgive billions of dollars of debt to developing nations in Africa and Latin America to give them a better chance of fighting poverty and disease.[58]

THE VOLATILE ECONOMY OF THE 2000s

In the 1990s, the U.S. economy had achieved the proverbial sweet spot of sustained economic growth and low levels of unemployment. In the early twenty-first century, American workers have experienced an entirely different reality. During the past decade, employment has surged and plunged. Stock market fluctuations and the collapse of housing prices have rocked the U.S. economy. The hypergrowth bubbles of the late 1990s and early 2000s were spurred on by technological change, easy credit, government spending and tax cuts, and speculative gaming in the financial markets.[59]

The Great Recession, which officially began in December 2007 and ended in June 2009, had enormously negative impacts on the American economy and labor market that will linger for years. It was devastating for millions of working Americans and their families and unsettled policymakers in Washington and in state capitals throughout the United States. Nobel Prize–winning economist Paul Krugman labeled the first decade of the twenty-first century the "Big Zero . . . a decade in which nothing good happened and none of the optimistic things we were supposed to believe turned out to be true." He continued that there was "basically zero job creation . . . zero economic gains for the typical family . . . zero gains for home owners" and "zero gains for stocks."[60]

After a decade when average Americans experienced no wage or salary increases, and many saw their paychecks decline and benefits disappear, the Great Recession piled misery on top of anxiety. In the United States, no economic calamity of this magnitude had been experienced since the Great Depression of the 1930s. Except for a major recession in the early 1980s, the number of American jobs grew at consistent pace until the end of 2007. The Great Recession was entirely different in depth and duration. Among the key markers of the unprecedented economic crisis are the following:

- The Great Recession was the longest recession on record.
- The unemployment rate rose to over 10 percent, the highest in thirty years.
- The unemployment rate for African Americans reached 16.7 percent, the highest level since 1984.
- In 2010, over 20 million workers were unemployed, were working in part-time jobs but wanted full-time employment, or had dropped out of the workforce.
- Long-term unemployment for six or more months was at its highest level in more than sixty years.
- More private sector jobs were lost, nearly 9 million, than in the previous four economic recessions combined; by 2013, the United States (along with Italy, Spain, and Greece) had yet to restore the jobs lost, even though most of Europe had gained jobs since 2007.[61]
- The median family income fell from $49,600 in 2007 to $45,800 in 2010, and income inequality became greater.[62]
- Worker productivity climbed to all-time highs.[63]
- Family net worth declined from $126,400 in 2007 to $77,300 in 2010 because of the collapse of the real estate market.[64]

The initial policy responses to the economic crisis were swift and bold. In October 2008, Congress passed the Emergency Economic Stabilization Act of 2008 with strong support from President Bush and Democrats who controlled Congress. The law established the $700 billion Troubled Asset Relief Program (TARP) to buy back bad loans ("toxic assets") from banks and financial institutions. The law required that banks exchange the purchase amounts for "equity warrants" and pledge to repay the federal government in the future. This measure had been championed by President George W. Bush, Treasury Secretary Henry Paulson, and Federal Reserve Chairman Ben Bernanke, and supported by Democratic presidential candidate Barack Obama and Republican presidential candidate John McCain.

In the fall of 2008, previously profitable global financial institutions, such as Citigroup, Goldman Sachs, and Bank of America, received TARP monies, along with dozens of other financial firms. Automakers Chrysler and GM received over $84 billion in loans and equity investments from TARP, and U.S. government protection from creditors, to enable them to restructure and avoid bankruptcy and massive layoffs.[65]

The federal government's swift actions subsequently became known as a "bailout" of financial institutions that were deemed "too big to fail." Washington policymakers were desperate to prevent a meltdown of the global financial and banking system. By doing so, they hoped to protect deposits and savings, recapitalize banks, and create a firewall against catastrophic unemployment, which had already skyrocketed from 5 percent in January 2008 to 7.8 percent in January 2009.[66]

Shortly after the November elections, President-elect Barack Obama, his new economic team, and Democratic leaders in Congress began crafting additional policy responses to the economic and financial emergency. In February 2009, soon after the inauguration of President Obama, Congress passed an $840 billion stimulus package that was unprecedented in its size and scope. Titled the American Recovery and Reinvestment Act (ARRA), the law included provisions that:

ARRA

- provided $288 billion in tax cuts and benefits, principally by reducing wage taxes;
- increased federal funds for entitlement programs, such as extending unemployment benefits, by $224 billion; and
- made $275 billion available for construction projects, grants to state and local governments, and renewable energy investments.

The enactment of the Emergency Economic Stabilization Act of 2008 and ARRA demonstrated that policymakers in the White House, Congress, and the Federal Reserve could act decisively when urgent responses were needed. In a matter of months, two presidential administrations (one Republican, one Democratic), leaders from both parties in Congress, and independent financial regulators, such as the Federal Reserve, reached agreement on a rescue plan for the economy (Republicans did not support ARRA). Together, these laws allocated over $1.5 trillion in loans, grants, and tax reductions to combating the economic woes gripping the nation and damaging millions of Americans who were losing jobs, financial assets, and even their homes.

At the time these two landmark bills were under consideration and immediately after these laws took effect, progressive and conservative politicians, analysts, and commentators sharply criticized the government's actions. Progressive economists warned that the stimulus package was too anemic to cure the nation's economic ills.[67] Conservative members of Congress and analysts complained that President Obama's approach to reigniting economic growth was not only the wrong medicine but also a dangerous expansion of government power over the economy. Even though over 100 Republican members of Congress voted in favor of the TARP "bailouts" in 2008 when George W. Bush was president, no Republicans in the House of Representatives voted for the economic stimulus plan in early 2009. Republican presidential candidate and former Massachusetts governor Mitt Romney praised aspects of TARP in his book *No Apology*, but criticized its size and implementation during the 2012 campaign.[68]

Although TARP and ARRA generated plenty of criticism as either too small or too large, dispassionate analysts offered more nuanced assessments. Independent, nonpartisan agencies, such as the Congressional Budget Office (CBO) and the U.S. Government Accountability Office concluded that the TARP "bail-out," aggressive monetary policy by the Federal Reserve, and the economic stimulus package (ARRA) achieved their fundamental objectives: averting a cata-strophic global financial crisis and saving or creating millions of jobs.[69] For example, CBO concluded that TARP will eventually cost the federal government approximately $19 billion, dramatically less than original estimates that exceeded $700 billion.[70] By and large, the financial institutions that received assistance from TARP paid back their loans, the U.S. Treasury sold its equity shares at a profit, and improvements in the financial services industry meant less demand for TARP funds.

The initial criticisms from the left and right of the political spectrum were reinforced by the fact that the economy did not recover swiftly or fully: about 60 percent of the 9 million jobs lost during the Great Recession had returned by early 2013. Elected officials and commentators from the left of the ideo-logical spectrum argued that the slow economic recovery was caused in part by the government's timid response to the crisis.[71] For those on the right, weak economic performance had been caused by excessive government spending and borrowing, and regulations that would saddle future generations with unpaid bills. Republican presidential candidate Mitt Romney, commenting on the sustained high levels of unemployment, offered this sharp assessment of the Obama administration's policies: "Badly misguided policies have acted as a severe drag on growth." He further commented that the stimulus package included "a binge of borrowing and spending that set off worldwide alarms about the creditworthiness of the United States" and a "vast expansion of costly and cumbersome regulations of sectors of the economy."[72]

Ordinary Americans were also dissatisfied with the federal government's handling of the economy. After all, hardly anyone working in America during the Great Recession had ever experienced a labor market with widespread, high levels of long-term unemployment. During the Great Recession, eco-nomic misery was so pervasive that few individuals could reasonably be satis-fied with the pace of recovery. Given such widespread suffering and fear about the future, blame was bound to be directed at the nation's leaders. Asked by the Heldrich Center for Workforce Development at Rutgers University in 2010 whether the president or congressional Republicans could best manage the economy, 45 percent of American workers said they trusted neither. That same year, 31 percent blamed President George W. Bush's policies for high unem-ployment levels, and 33 percent blamed President Obama's policies.[73]

Throughout his entire first term, President Obama and Congress received low marks for their handling of the economy.[74] In April 2010, a national survey conducted by the Pew Research Center for the People & the Press found that "many Americans are dubious about the effectiveness of the government's prin-cipal economic programs. Just 33% say the economic stimulus passed by Congress last year has helped the job situation and only somewhat more (42%) say the loans the federal government provided to troubled financial institutions prevented a more severe financial crisis. Less than a third (31%) say that the government has made progress in fixing the problems that caused the 2008 financial crisis."[75] In exit polls conducted on election day in 2012, only 23 percent of voters said that they thought the condition of the economy was excellent or good, with the balance of 77 percent saying that it was not so good or poor, and only 39 percent said that it was getting better. Although most voters remained pessimistic about the economy, more of them (53 percent) blamed the conditions on President George W. Bush than on President Obama (38 percent).[76]

A COMPARATIVE PERSPECTIVE

The relationship between cultural values, economic conditions, and public policy is apparent when we compare the United States with other nations of the world. Western industrial nations have quite different governmental operations and public philosophies that reflect diverse cultural and economic experiences. Consider the difference between the United States and Western Europe 100 years ago. In Europe, desirable land had long been held by the wealthiest segments of society, economic mobility was minimal, and a large industrial working class had formed. In the United States, the government was practically giving away large tracts of land in the west, frontiers remained to be settled, and large fortunes were being made and lost quickly. An industrial working class, composed mostly of European immigrants, was beginning to form, but most parts of the country remained primarily agrarian. American economic development was greatly influenced by the existence of a large property-owning segment of the population and an expanding middle class. These factors help account for some of the distinctive aspects of American politics and the American economy today: its large, fairly autonomous private sector, its relatively modest government social welfare spending, and the widespread acceptance of the values of individualism and capitalism.

The social welfare state came relatively late to the United States. Programs to aid sick or injured workers, elderly and disabled individuals, unemployed workers, and new parents were established in Western Europe several decades before they appeared in this country.[77] Nearly all Western European countries have universal income support programs for poor and unemployed citizens, along with national health insurance systems; these have never taken hold in the United States. Although American social welfare spending expanded significantly in the late 1960s and 1970s, other Western democratic governments were considerably more generous in providing housing assistance, unemployment benefits, vacation and maternity leave, and income security for elderly individuals.[78] Over the past twenty years, the gap between social welfare expenditures in the United States and those of European countries has narrowed somewhat because of the steady spending growth in U.S. entitlement programs (Social Security, Medicare, and others). Still, the data presented in Table 2-2 demonstrate that the U.S. government taxes its citizens less and spends less money on social welfare purposes, in the form of transfer payments, than most other industrial nations. Because the private sector and free

TABLE 2-2   **Government Outlays and Revenues in Selected Countries**

Country	Government outlays as a percentage of GDP (2012)	Transfer payments as a percentage of GDP (2006)[a]	Tax and other revenues as a percentage of GDP (2012)
Canada	42	20	38
France	56	30	52
Germany	46	27	45
Italy	50	30	49
Japan	43	20	33
Sweden	52	27	52
United Kingdom	49	23	41
United States	41	21	32

Sources: Organisation for Economic Co-operation and Development, *OECD Economic Outlook*, vol. 2012, no. 1 (Paris, France: OECD Publishing, 2012): 257–258; Richard W. Tresch, *Public Sector Economics* (New York: Palgrave Macmillan, 2008).

[a] Transfer payments equal total general government expenditures less general government final consumption.

market ethic continues to dominate the political culture and economy of the United States, American policymakers face choices that are importantly different from those in other countries.

Although it is smaller than that of other industrial nations, the public sector in the United States influences nearly every aspect of the nation's social and economic life. Especially influential is the large body of federal, state, and local regulatory law that governs public and private behavior. Federal regulations burgeoned from the 1960s until the election of Ronald Reagan. Between 1960 and 1980, the number of federal regulatory agencies doubled, from twenty-eight to fifty-six; their workforce grew by 90,000; and their budgets increased threefold. The *Federal Register*, which is a compilation of all government regulations, grew from about 15,000 pages in 1946 to 87,000 pages in 1980. Reagan administration efforts at deregulation reduced the regulatory state somewhat, highlighted by budget and staff cuts in federal agencies, and symbolized by a reduction in the number of pages in the *Federal Register* to just over 50,000.[79] As noted in chapter 1, many industries were deregulated in the late 1970s and 1980s, including trucking, banking, broadcasting, and airlines, but in many areas, regulatory responsibilities were simply shifted from the government to private companies, or to states and localities.

Since the Reagan years, numerous regulatory laws have been strengthened, particularly in the areas of civil rights, air pollution, and the rights of disabled Americans. According to scholars Susan Dudley and Melinda Warren's analysis of the fiscal year 2012 federal budget, the government was slated to spend $57.3 billion on regulatory actions during the year, with regulatory agencies employing over 290,000 people, and these estimates did not take into account possible new regulatory spending connected to the implementation of the Affordable Care Act and the Dodd-Frank Wall Street Reform and Consumer Protection Act. In short, the federal regulatory state is alive and well.[80]

In the 1960s and 1970s, the government regulatory presence in most states increased in ways that mirrored the changes at the federal level. Spheres long regulated by the state and federal governments, such as transportation, food and drug quality, agriculture, occupational licensing, and banking, were joined by consumer product safety, air and water pollution, workplace health and safety, automobile safety, and civil rights. And, as noted above, the Reagan administration's efforts at deregulation often increased, rather than decreased, the regulatory duties of state governments. Furthermore, budgetary pressures at the national level between 1985 and 1995 produced a certain proclivity on the part of Congress to impose direct or indirect regulatory mandates on the states. In 1995, however, Congress made it more difficult for the federal government to impose mandates on the states by enacting the Unfunded Mandates Reform Act.[81] Nevertheless, uneasy relations between the federal government and state governments over spending responsibilities are still very much with us.

The sharing of policy responsibilities among different levels of government is characteristic of the American political system. Subnational governmental power is based on a tradition of local self-determination that is older than the country itself, protected by the Constitution, and sustained by individualistic cultural values. American state and local governments are stronger and more autonomous than their counterparts in most other countries, but it would be a mistake to believe that only in the United States are power and authority vested in subnational governments. Canadian provincial governments have considerable constitutional authority, which gives them a good measure of autonomy from the national government and superiority over the city governments. Many other countries, such as Britain and Sweden, have unitary, rather than federal, systems, and even though there are relatively few local chief executives, local governments are important political institutions. For example, some large cities have taxing power, and in nearly all countries central government leaders know that they must obtain the support of networks of local public officials to finance and implement education, health, housing, and welfare programs.[82]

Relationships between national and subnational governments undergo change. It is evident that over the past forty years, state governments have grown in stature within the federal system. States have demonstrated their willingness and ability to raise money for public services, and state governments have become more innovative in policymaking and in reforms aimed at improving management.[83] The Great Recession significantly damaged state budgets. Although ARRA brought federal assistance to the states to alleviate some of the financial hardships, the National Association of State Budget Officers concluded that the Great Recession brought about "one of the worst periods in state fiscal conditions since the great depression."[84]

SUMMARY

The purpose of this brief review has been to show how two broad forces in American society—political culture and the economy—influence politics, government, and public policy. Political culture determines what people expect of government and what role citizens and politicians play in politics. Economic well-being has been the most consistently important issue in American politics, and economic performance is both a cause and an effect of government policy. Political beliefs and expectations and the economy change over time, and these changes are reflected in the policy agenda of government.

Politics in the twenty-first century is markedly different from politics in earlier epochs in American history, and different politics means different policies. Most notably, the surpluses of the late 1990s have been replaced by huge deficits and a growing national debt. Interestingly, however, the positions of major players are not that different. Most Republicans still favor across-the-board tax cuts and increased spending on national defense; Democrats are wary of tax cuts for wealthy Americans (whom they describe as those who earn more than $250,000 annually) and want to spend more on domestic programs, such as health care and education. Nevertheless, macroeconomic policymaking continues to be complicated. If the government tries to control inflation using strict monetary policies, for example, it hurts the export market. Certain sectors of the economy, such as agriculture, feel the effects quickly and forcefully. If the government tries to alleviate the trade deficit by loosening monetary policies, American consumers pay higher prices for many imported products. If the government commits large sums of money to national defense or runs large deficits, less money is available for housing, education, medical care, and public works programs.

Americans have seen different priorities come and go. During the New Deal period, federal government spending was seen as the key to prosperity; the private sector reemerged during Dwight Eisenhower's administration. The government came back with more spending and regulation in the late 1960s and 1970s, then drew back from regulation in the 1980s. In the 1990s, despite intense partisan bickering, Democrats and Republicans (the Clinton administration and Congress) were able to agree on key economic policies, including limiting federal government spending, pursuing free trade agreements, and keeping Alan Greenspan in charge of the Federal Reserve. From the standpoint of the economy, these proved to be very important areas of agreement, indeed.

The Bush administration in the 2000s both limited and expanded federal government's power in different areas. The tax cuts passed in 2001 and 2003 limited government's taxing authority, yet the USA PATRIOT Act of 2001 (Uniting and Strengthening America by Providing Appropriate Tools Required to Intercept and Obstruct Terrorism) broadened government's authority over foreign financial transactions and law enforcement measures directed at suspected terrorists. Democratic president Barack Obama, first elected in 2008 as the Great Recession was under way, focused his administration on stabilizing and rebuilding the U.S. economy. During this era, multiple laws were enacted that substantially increased government spending to help boost the economy and improve health care coverage for more Americans.

The American government's response to the challenges of the present and the future will be shaped by cultural and economic developments, and by the actions of policymaking institutions. Understanding the peculiarities of, and the distinctions among, the different domains of politics is central to the study of American public policy. These domains and their policymaking processes are the subjects of chapters 3 through 8.

chapter 3

Boardroom Politics

S ocial scientist Harold Lasswell once defined politics as "who gets what, when, how."[1] By that definition, many private sector decisions are as political as those made by government officials. When an automobile company shuts down an assembly plant, the consequences for workers, their families, and the local community can be devastating. When a coal-fired power plant discharges poisonous chemicals into the atmosphere, the public health effects may be serious. When a hospital decides to invest in expensive lifesaving equipment, such as emergency helicopters, it may save many lives but may also raise hospital prices. When a business chooses to donate 5 percent of its pretax profits to charity, numerous nonprofit organizations may benefit, but the government may collect less tax money. In each of these cases, private organizations decide who gets what, when, and how.

To describe private decision making that has public consequences, we use the metaphor of "boardroom politics." At the core of boardroom politics are decisions made by private organizations, usually corporations, over which the government has limited control. Some of these decisions are literally made in corporate boardrooms; others are made at lower levels by corporate managers, subject to constraints imposed by a board of directors. The private sector is not monolithic in its structure, norms, or purposes. There are important differences between publicly held and privately held companies, nonprofit and for-profit organizations, big corporations and small businesses, monopolies and competitive entities. Despite these differences, one statement is true of private sector entities: they have an enormous impact on the daily lives of all Americans. Charles Lindblom wrote that the role of the private sector is vital not just in the United States but in all market-oriented societies: "Corporate executives in all private enterprise systems . . . decide a nation's industrial technology, the pattern of work organization, location of industry, market structure, resource allocation, and, of course, executive compensation and status."[2]

The role of the private sector is especially significant in the United States. We can conclude from Table 2-2 that by 2012, the private sector accounted for about 59 percent of the gross domestic product of the United States, whereas in the United Kingdom the figure was 51 percent, in Sweden it was 48 percent, and in France it was 44 percent. Presently, the overwhelming majority of Americans, approximately 84 percent, are employed by the private sector; Japan's private sector employs 95 percent of its population; in the United Kingdom, roughly 80 percent of all workers are privately employed; in Germany, 70 percent; in France, 66 percent; and in China 50 percent.[3] In the United States, most vital industries are controlled primarily or exclusively by the private sector. These include railroads, airlines, electric companies, telecommunications firms, oil producers, and automobile manufacturers. In Western Europe, more of these industries are controlled by government, but the trend has been toward greater privatization. In Great Britain, for example, publicly owned utilities, energy producers, and transportation firms were transferred to private ownership in the late 1980s and early 1990s.[4]

During the 1980s and 1990s, the private sector in the United States also grew as a result of privatization and deregulation. Privatization, the transfer of service delivery functions from the public sector to the private sector, spread rapidly at the state and local levels in the 1980s. A 1987 survey revealed that 99 percent of cities with populations over 5,000, and counties with populations over 25,000, contracted out for services; at this same time, approximately 35 percent of U.S. cities contracted with private companies for refuse collection.[5] Contracting for social services, usually with nonprofit organizations, also became widespread in the 1980s. By the mid-1980s, almost half of the states contracted for mental health services; other social services provided through contracts included employment services, child abuse centers, nursing homes, day care centers, drug abuse clinics, and halfway houses for parolees.[6] By 1997, seven states (California, Colorado, Florida, Iowa, Maryland, Michigan, and New Jersey) had privatized more than 100 programs and services; however, since then the extent of state contracting has leveled off nationwide.[7] Still, several states with Republican governors continue to expand their privatization programs, including New Jersey, led by Governor Chris Christie, and Louisiana, led by Governor Bobby Jindal.[8]

Privatization advanced more slowly at the federal level in the 1980s and 1990s, despite support from the administrations of Ronald Reagan and George H. W. Bush and, to a lesser degree, that of Bill Clinton. However, it did increase substantially during George W. Bush's administration, reaching an estimated 7.5 million employees in 2005.[9] With the expansion came much criticism, and one major study found that using contractors to carry out many types of public functions actually costs the government more money than using federal employees.[10]

Deregulation, the relaxation of government standards and requirements, has proceeded steadily at the federal level since about 1980. Beginning with the Carter administration, Congress took steps to deregulate the airline, trucking, and financial industries, and the prices of oil and natural gas. In the process, the Civil Aeronautics Board and the Interstate Commerce Commission were abolished, barriers to entry into the trucking industry were reduced, and much greater freedom was given to certain financial institutions (savings and loan banks) to engage in a variety of lending and investment activities. In the 1980s, the Federal Communications Commission (FCC) relaxed government regulation of the broadcasting industry by eliminating limits on commercial time and by issuing licenses for longer periods of time. The telecommunications industry changed rapidly in the 1980s and 1990s; an antitrust settlement involving AT&T in the early 1980s and legislation in 1996 deregulated the industry, allowing AT&T, cable providers, and local and regional telephone companies to compete in an open and expanded market.[11] (The FCC has retained an important role in reviewing mergers and acquisitions within the telecommunications industry to ensure that they serve "the public interest.") Legislation passed in 1999 further deregulated the financial services industry so that banks, brokerage houses, and insurance companies could all participate in a very wide range of investment and lending practices, which they pursued with vigor in the ensuing years until the financial "house of cards" came tumbling down in 2008.[12]

As noted in chapter 1, led by the Reagan and George H. W. Bush administrations, but continued in a very significant way during the Clinton and George W. Bush administrations, the federal government has generally stepped away from intrusive regulation of many areas of the private sector. In some cases, especially during Republican administrations, this was done by discouraging federal agencies from issuing new, restrictive rules and regulations, but, as highlighted above, the change has also been accomplished through the adoption and implementation of deregulatory legislation. There have been occasional reversals in this pattern. Following the collapse of the energy company Enron, for example, Congress passed the Sarbanes-Oxley Act (2002), which imposed new and stricter accounting standards on corporations.[13] And, of course, the financial industry was subjected to new restrictions starting in 2008 through government bailout legislation (the Emergency Economic Stabilization Act and its Troubled Asset Relief Program [TARP]), and then the Dodd-Frank Wall Street Reform and Consumer Protection Act in 2010.[14] The extent to which Dodd-Frank will change business as usual on Wall Street has yet to be determined.

In addition to its deregulatory posture, the government has been reluctant to interject itself into important new industries, including most varieties of Internet technology. The federal government has also prohibited state governments from taxing business done online, at least up to this point. As a result of these trends, the power of the private sector in American politics has grown. The American public seems to have mixed feelings about the private sector, particularly large corporations. In a 1999 study, roughly two-thirds of the public gave businesses credit for the prosperity of the 1990s, but over 70 percent thought corporations had too much power over too many aspects of American life. Although 68 percent of the public thought big companies made good products, over 70 percent thought corporate executives were paid too much and that corporations had too much political influence.[15] Little has changed since then. A 2010 poll found 64 percent of the public holding a negative view of large corporations, and 69 percent viewing banks and financial institutions negatively. Because of the Great Recession and its aftermath, there wasn't much credit given for prosperity by 2010.[16]

CORPORATE CONCERNS

An agenda, whether corporate or governmental, consists of items or issues thought to warrant serious attention. The building blocks of corporate agendas differ from those of government agendas. The question that faces a private corporation is not whether to make changes in health policy or energy policy or transportation policy, but whether to focus most of its efforts on finance, management, or public relations. Within these broad categories, further choices must be made: whether to concentrate on diversification, modernization, product quality, expansion, or labor relations in order to achieve profit objectives or to focus on advertising, customer relations, community relations, or government affairs. Although the typical corporation carries on all these activities at once, the emphasis given to one area or another varies considerably.

The Bottom Line

Corporate priorities can be inferred from a variety of sources, including corporate behavior, but when executives speak for themselves, they invariably say something about the proverbial "bottom line." As the editors of *Fortune* magazine discovered in their 1986 survey of 500 CEOs, the top priority for business leaders was improving profits or earnings.[17] The importance placed on profits is hardly surprising, since most companies cannot survive without them; thus profitability can be seen as an overriding objective for most corporate executives. But, as illustrated in Box 3-1, executives take many factors into account when they evaluate corporate success.

The fact that corporate executives view profits as a necessary condition for success does not make their decisions easy. They must make complicated choices about how to juggle priorities to achieve their profit objectives. It should come as no surprise, then, that the priorities established by some corporations do not adequately anticipate all the difficulties they face down the road. Consider the case of U.S. Steel. During the 1950s and 1960s, steel executives concentrated on profit margins and labor relations, instead of focusing on modern techniques for steel production. Over the years they lost out, first to the Japanese, but then to production facilities in other countries such as Korea and Mexico. Eventually, U.S. Steel's ability to compete decreased to such an extent that company executives decided to concentrate more on oil and gas production (merging with Marathon Oil to form USX) than on steel manufacturing. Then, in something of a turnaround, U.S. Steel separated from Marathon in 2001 and concentrated on producing steel. U.S. Steel, once the mightiest steel company in the world and a symbol of

BOX 3-1 *Fortune's* **Eight Key Attributes of Reputation and America's Most Admired Companies, 2000 and 2012**

Attributes (2000)	Attributes (2012)
Innovativeness	Innovation
Quality of management	People management
Employed talent	Use of corporate assets
Financial soundness	Social responsibility
Use of corporate assets	Quality of management
Long-term investment value	Financial soundness
Social responsibility	Long-term investment value
Quality of products/services	Quality of products/services

Top Ten Companies (2000)	Top Ten Companies (2012)
1. General Electric	1. Apple
2. Microsoft	2. Google
3. Dell Computer	3. Amazon.com
4. Cisco Systems	4. Coca-Cola
5. Wal-Mart Stores	5. IBM
6. Southwest Airlines	6. FedEx
7. Berkshire Hathaway	7. Berkshire Hathaway
8. Intel	8. Starbucks
9. Home Depot	9. Procter & Gamble
10. Lucent Technologies	10. Southwest Airlines

American know-how, now ranks eighth among steel producers in the world.[18] The ups and downs of U.S. Steel are not unusual among major corporations in the twenty-first century world economy, as a comparison of the most admired companies in 2000 and 2012 (Box 3-1) shows. Only two companies, Berkshire Hathaway and Southwest Airlines made the list in both years. Apple almost folded in the mid-1980s but had risen to the top by 2012; Google did not exist until 1998.

Some companies neglect certain issues because they are preoccupied with other matters; other companies neglect issues because they doubt their importance or see no advantage in dealing with them. For example, from the 1960s to the 1980s, it was common for companies to neglect the mental and physical health of their employees because they did not take seriously the connection between employee health and productivity. By the 1990s, and continuing to the present, awareness of this connection has increased significantly, largely because more commercial mental and physical health services sought to sell it, and more companies (and media) were listening. As union membership declined, from approximately 17.7 million in 1983 (20 percent of the workforce) to about 14.4 million (11.3 percent of the workforce) in 2012, the ability of organized labor to sensitize companies to employee concerns also diminished.[19] Some companies neglect the effect their activities have on the environment, despite laws aimed at regulating it, because they do not wish to incur cleanup costs. As punishment they may pay fines, but only if the government discovers the violations and vigorously enforces the law; even then, paying the fines, while avoiding cleanup costs, may still benefit these firms' bottom lines.

The mass media occasionally bring neglected issues to the public's attention because layoffs, environmental degradation, and threats to worker safety make good stories. For example, it was media attention that forced corporate officials, and members of Congress, to confront the problems of Enron in 2001 and of Wall Street investment practices leading up to and during the Great Recession (2007–2010). Still, in both of these cases, the bigger story was the fact that potentially dangerous practices had been taking place for some time, with little or no media attention being devoted to them. Clearly, some important issues will remain buried if companies find it convenient to ignore them and the media fail to shed light on them.

Agenda Determination

Corporate executives are the principal determiners of corporate agendas. As long as the company prospers, corporate managers are free to chart a course for the future. When earnings decline or a crisis erupts, board members intervene in an effort to get the company back on track. Board meetings can provide opportunities for members to establish new priorities, but this is often difficult, in part because top corporate executives usually sit on the board. A board meeting typically is the final step in a protracted process. Like a congressional debate, a board meeting is the culmination of a series of discussions, of maneuvers and countermaneuvers, bargains, and power plays. The meeting itself may be only a formality because the "decision" has been made. When the board of the Wall Street firm Bear Stearns & Company met in December 2007, the job of its CEO, Jimmy Cayne, was definitely on the line. Not only was the firm losing money, but Cayne had been featured in a *Wall Street Journal* article as having played in a bridge tournament during a crisis the firm faced that summer, and as being a regular marijuana smoker. By January 4, 2008, Cayne was out as the company's CEO.[20]

Prior to important board meetings, managers may attempt to mobilize support to stave off a policy change or a coup d'état. It seems hard to believe, but in 1985, Steve Jobs, then the chairman of Apple Computer, was fighting to retain his job. He threw a dinner party, with an influential board member as the guest of honor, hoping to persuade the board member to rally to his cause. When the board member merely picked at his whole wheat pizza, Jobs began to see the handwriting on the wall. Of course, his dismissal from Apple was by no means Jobs's corporate swan song. After some false starts, he scored several successes with computer-animated films and then enjoyed the ultimate vindication of being rehired as Apple's CEO in 1997. After he took over for the second time, Apple realized increased revenues, larger market shares, and higher stock values.[21] As shown in Box 3-1, Apple was the most admired firm in the world in 2012, and Jobs was given much of the credit. When he died in 2011, Steve Jobs was hailed as a genius; one biographer placed him "in the pantheon with Thomas Edison and Henry Ford."[22] Another retrospective stated, "Steve Jobs remade the world as completely as any single human being ever has."[23]

Corporate agendas are also influenced by the policies, schemes, and strategies of company rivals. Automobile companies frequently announce new sales strategies involving prices, warranties, and gas mileage. In the early 1980s, Ford Motor Company decided to offer a five-year, 50,000-mile warranty, and Chrysler responded by offering a seven-year, 70,000-mile warranty. A similar episode occurred in 2000 when Ford announced plans to improve the fuel economy of its sport utility vehicles. Within one week, General Motors announced that it would do the same, only better. GM's vice chairman said, "G.M. will be the leader [in fuel economy] in five years, and in 15 years for that matter."[24] When one company hits upon a successful marketing strategy, its competitors must react, thus putting marketing high on their agendas. Sometimes, however, marketing efforts can go too far and get companies in trouble. Drug giant GlaxoSmithKline had to pay the government $3 million in 2012 for aggressively promoting the sale of drugs (mostly antidepressants), on the basis of questionable data from clinical trials, for uses that were not approved by the U.S. Food and Drug Administration.[25]

Corporations have also thrown one another into a tizzy by staging takeover attempts. If unwelcome, these are referred to as "hostile" takeovers. In the 1980s, television mogul Ted Turner proposed to take over CBS, forcing a transformation in the network's agenda. For weeks CBS was preoccupied with preventing the takeover. CBS eventually prevailed, but later found it necessary to undertake a major management shake-up and massive layoffs. Many at CBS, particularly in the news division, never recovered from the shock of these actions. In the 1990s and 2000s, hostile takeovers became less frequent and salient in the corporate world, but mergers and acquisitions were on the agendas of numerous major corporations. Chrysler became DaimlerChrysler and more recently was acquired by Fiat, Exxon and Mobil merged, AT&T bought major cable companies such as MediaOne and Bell South, Time Warner bought Turner Broadcasting and then merged with AOL, Citibank became Citigroup, Lockheed joined with Martin Marietta to become the largest defense contractor, Procter & Gamble acquired Gillette in 2005, and Anheuser-Busch (the maker of Budweiser) was acquired by the Belgian firm InBev in 2008, to list just a few of the prominent mergers.[26]

Corporate agendas may also be shaped by government officials. President Lyndon Johnson famously issued Executive Order 11246 in 1965, placing affirmative action on the agendas of businesses throughout the nation. Johnson's order prohibited discrimination by government contractors and established a compliance office to ensure cooperation. Because most sizable companies did some business with the government, Johnson's executive order guaranteed that affirmative action would receive serious attention in corporate boardrooms across the land. By offering lucrative contracts to companies willing to design and develop new weapons systems, the Defense Department has long been successful in shaping corporate agendas and in influencing university agendas. Corporate scientists and academics throughout the United States are engaged in research on space, defense, agriculture, energy, and environmental projects funded by the federal government. During the wars in Iraq and Afghanistan, defense contracting for various war-related activities expanded to the point that personnel working for contractors outnumbered military personnel in Afghanistan in 2009.[27] The Justice Department's enforcement of antitrust law can become a dominant factor in corporate agendas, as Microsoft learned when the Justice Department sought to break it up in 1998; the Federal Trade Commission (FTC) undertook a similar antitrust investigation of Google in 2012, but after twenty-one months took no action against the company.[28]

Citizens can play a significant role in helping set corporate agendas. By mobilizing activist shareholders, concerned citizens have attempted to shape corporate agendas through proxy resolutions that address important social issues: civil rights, corporate transparency and accountability, apartheid in South Africa, child labor in poor countries, environmental sustainability, and most recently the salaries of top corporate management.[29] An early, highly publicized effort in the 1970s was Campaign GM, organized by Ralph Nader (the Green Party presidential candidate in 2000 and 2004), which fought, using shareholder proposals, for reforms aimed at increasing consumer influence at GM. The actual proposals were not adopted, but a new arena for activism was introduced. These days proxy battles are typically led by "institutional shareholders" (individuals, companies, or other entities that hold large portions of a target corporation's stock, also called institutional investors), and often aim to oust CEOs and board members because of poor performance.[30] Following allegations that Wal-Mart had been involved in a bribery scandal in Mexico, more than 12 percent of its shareholders voted against the reelection of the CEO and three other board members, including chairman S. Robson Walton.[31] Like most proxy efforts, this one did not succeed in its immediate goal, but it did capture the attention of the board and the public. Thus, even when shareholder reform proposals are voted down, concessions from management are often forthcoming. The boards of major corporations are very concerned about their companies' public images and discuss them frequently in meetings.

The Public-Private Spectrum

Thus far, corporations have been considered as a class. There are, however, differences among private sector entities, and these differences, present in policymaking, are also apparent in agenda setting. Some businesses "affected with a public interest" are more vulnerable to public pressure than most[32]; other businesses, whose stock is not publicly traded, are less vulnerable to outside pressures. In between are those corporations with which the public is most familiar: corporations whose stock is traded but that are free to set prices as they please (see Table 3-1). Another set of actors includes government corporations, which are creations of federal, state, or local governments but are supposed to operate like private, for-profit firms. They are highly susceptible to influence from elected officials and, to some extent, the public. A final type of private sector group (not categorized above) is nonprofit organizations, which vary greatly in the degree to which they are affected by government (from almost not at all to a great deal).

Public utilities are businesses definitely affected with a public interest. These are often what economists call "natural monopolies": an industry in which services can be supplied most efficiently by a single company. It is generally

TABLE 3-1   **The Public-Private Spectrum: Degree of Government Influence**

Very low	Fairly low	Fairly high	Very high
Privately held firms and foundations (e.g., SC Johnson, Cargill, the Ford Foundation or Gates Foundation)	Publicly held firms: firms in competitive industries and in oligopolies (the retail sales, drug, automobile, and airline industries)	Publicly held firms: firms providing monopoly or semimonopoly services (investor-owned public utilities)	Government corporations (e.g., the Tennessee Valley Authority, the U.S. Postal Service, municipal utilities)

accepted that the rates natural monopolies charge for their services should be set by government officials to keep prices at a reasonable level. A classic example of a natural monopoly is a regional electric utility company; in some parts of the country, the rates such companies charge customers are determined by state public utility commissions. Regulators decide whether to grant a utility company's rate hike request in full or in part. A "stingy" public utility commission, in effect, places revenue issues on a company's agenda; a "generous" commission enables a utility company to concentrate on other issues, such as expansion or diversification. In the late 1990s, almost half the states relaxed government controls on utilities, and the trend in electricity markets in the twenty-first century, as in so many other markets, has been toward pricing deregulation.[33]

New ideas (such as deregulation) and technologies have muddied the waters of so-called natural monopolies. By the late 1970s, Congress had decided that there was enough competition in the energy industry that natural gas companies should operate with less price regulation. As discussed earlier, the telecommunications industry was transformed by the breakup of AT&T in 1982 and deregulatory legislation in 1996. Meanwhile, cable television appeared and was treated like a public utility, with city councils setting rates, until 1984, when Congress decided that cable television companies should be allowed to set their own rates. Presently, former cable-only companies such as Comcast, and former regional telephone companies, such as Verizon and the current AT&T (the former Southwestern Bell) compete over multiple platforms and services, including cell phones, broadband Internet, television, and traditional telephone services.

At the private end of the public-private spectrum are companies whose stock is not traded publicly but rather is held by family members or employees. These companies have considerable discretion in what they do and when they do it. In contrast to other companies, privately held companies need not hold annual public meetings and need not submit extensive financial data to the Securities and Exchange Commission (SEC). Of course, most of these companies are quite small (fewer than twenty-five employees), but privately held companies employ a substantial portion of the workforce (roughly one-half) in the United States. Attention to the distinction between companies wholly or partially owned by stockholders, and privately held companies, has increased in recent years as relatively new and high-profile privately held firms such as Google and Facebook have held initial public offerings of their stock.

Foundations, which exist to dispense money to favored causes, constitute a small subset of private organizations that have extraordinary flexibility in setting their agendas. Although bequests sometimes impose constraints, foundations are usually free to set priorities and to change direction rapidly. The Ford Foundation, for example, announced in 1966 a major effort to promote equal opportunity for African Americans in politics, education, employment, and housing. Over the next two decades, Ford supported civil rights litigation through grants to the NAACP Legal Defense Fund and other legal advocacy groups. Its current agenda is quite broad, encompassing everything from democratic governance (here and abroad) and human rights to economic fairness and environmental sustainability. Many foundations, including the Andrew W. Mellon Foundation and the Howard Hughes Medical Institute, have played important roles in setting priorities for colleges and universities through their grant programs that support students and faculty members. As a result of the huge amount of wealth created in the 1990s and 2000s, many companies and individuals (Bill and Melinda Gates, and William and Flora Hewlett) have set up new foundations to direct their charitable giving, often in an effort to influence education reforms in the United States and to reduce hunger and poverty worldwide.

Many citizen groups owe their origins to seed money from foundations. In 1983, political scientist Jack Walker noted that 39 percent of citizen groups formed during the postwar era received foundation grants at the time of founding.[34] Without the timely support of leading foundations, many civil rights groups and environmental groups probably would not exist; others would have vanished by now. Many think tanks also depend on foundation support. Conservative think tanks such as the American Enterprise Institute, the Heritage Foundation, and the Reason Foundation helped place deregulation, privatization, and a variety of other conservative causes on the government's agenda beginning in the 1970s, and they continue to do so. Through grants to nonprofit organizations, foundations also have transformed the agendas of city councils, state legislatures, and Congress, as nonprofit groups have promoted long-neglected political causes, from gay rights to homelessness. Nonprofit groups that deliver social services are subject to extensive influence from government officials, both legislative and bureaucratic.

CORPORATE GOVERNANCE

Boardroom politics is more hierarchical than cloakroom politics, more competitive than bureaucratic politics, and more volatile than courtroom politics. It is less visible than chief executive politics and living room politics, but more pervasive than both. The scope of conflict—or the extent of public involvement—is typically rather narrow, not because the stakes are low but because many of the issues are regarded as being outside the government's jurisdiction and away from the public eye. As Donald Regan, the White House chief of staff in the Reagan administration, once put it, "Businessmen, for the most part, are not used to the glare of publicity."[35] In fact, there is an important gap between the importance of boardroom politics and the degree of public involvement in it. Although boardroom politics has become more visible and more controversial since the 1960s, particularly during and after the Great Recession of 2008, it is still largely private.

Who Has the Power?

American corporations wield considerable power and enjoy substantial autonomy. Nevertheless, no corporation is an island. Virtually all corporations operate under constraints imposed by government regulators (environmental, health and safety, and others). Publicly held corporations also take the interests and demands of their stockholders into account. All corporations and privately held companies must be sensitive to market forces. During times of upheaval, corporations find themselves responding to social movements, if only to deflect them. During times of crisis, corporations have responded to appeals by political leaders that the "national interest" or the "public interest" requires their cooperation. During World War II, for example, corporations stopped producing consumer goods and mobilized to build ships, tanks, and aircraft. In 2012, numerous corporate CEOs supported raising taxes on the wealthy, like themselves, to avoid the looming fiscal cliff.[36]

Increasingly, corporations must be sensitive to the wishes and machinations of certain investors, especially institutional investors. As mentioned previously, institutional investors include banks, insurance companies, holders of pension funds, colleges and universities, and other entities with substantial stock portfolios. These institutional investors, more aware and active than ever before, wield power by threatening to sell their stock unless corporate policies change. By 1996, institutional investors owned over 47 percent of all stock in American corporations; by 2006, the percentage of American stocks held by institutional investors had increased to 67 percent.[37] In the 1980s, corporate raiders, such as Carl Icahn and T. Boone Pickens, were powerful players, frequently creating waves within their target companies and throughout the stock market by letting it be known that they intended to take over. Icahn continues to be a force, using his enormous wealth to buy large portions of the stock in companies such as Time Warner, RJR Nabisco, and Chesapeake Energy to force reforms that would help shareholders against the wishes of management.[38] (Pickens's attention is now focused on energy production, particularly natural gas and wind.) As we have seen, corporations also pay a great deal of attention to other companies they might want to acquire, or with which they might want to merge. The globalization of the economy means that many of these companies might be foreign owned, and that the policies and actions of other governments must be considered.

Despite pressure from investors and public officials, corporations have considerable autonomy, in large part because they have legal rights that protect them from politicians, bureaucrats, and judges. Government laws and regulations frequently pose obstacles and challenges to corporate officials, but such leaders are usually well equipped (with lawyers, lobbyists, and money) to meet these challenges. Moreover, corporate power can be highly concentrated. A relatively small number of corporations control a relatively high percentage of many markets. Examples of highly concentrated industries include aircraft production, defense contracting, breakfast cereals, lighting and bulb manufacturing, computer operating systems, online search systems, and tobacco; many others could be cited.[39] Moreover, power within corporations tends to be concentrated in the hands of a few individuals, including the company's CEO, chief financial officer, president, and board chair.

The archetype for sociologist Max Weber's hierarchical model of organization was the government bureaucracy, but the modern corporation comes closer to his ideal type than the modern government bureaucracy. As discussed in the following chapter, the bureaucracy's chain of command is blurred by the fact that it has multiple sovereigns (chief executives, legislators, interest groups). In addition, the bureaucracy's top executives must bargain with career employees; they cannot simply issue an order and wait for it to be carried out. Top corporate officials can behave more autocratically if they wish to do so. Private corporations normally operate with a clear chain of command and fixed responsibilities.

Wizards and Whales

There is no such thing as a corporate leader for all seasons, because corporations differ in their dependence on sound management, creative experimentation, public favor, and government support. Some corporations require leaders who can play an "insider" game, that is, people who excel at organizational management. Others require leaders who can play an "outsider" game, that is, those who excel at public relations. If demand for a product or service is stable and a company's market share is secure, an insider game may be sufficient. A more volatile situation may require greater reliance on an outsider game.

There are different types of outsider games. In some instances, corporate leaders must win the support of customers; in others, they must curry the favor of investors or government officials. New technology firms, for example, generally need the help of venture capitalists to garner sufficient resources to perfect their products and gain a niche in their markets. Established public utilities, in contrast, must be mindful of their images in the regulatory community. Television stations, protected to some extent by the First Amendment, are subject to rather light-handed government regulation (except when it comes to profanity and nudity), but they must constantly be concerned about the popularity of their programming, because advertising revenue is directly dependent on market share or ratings.

Corporate leadership styles are highly diverse. Whitney MacMillan, former CEO and chairman of the board of Cargill, the largest grain company in the world, maintained a very low profile outside the company. He was, by choice, a rather mysterious figure, a sort of Wizard of Oz—one heard about his great deeds and accomplishments but seldom saw the man in the flesh. A twenty-first-century wizard is Jim Clark, who started Silicon Graphics in the 1980s, then Netscape in the 1990s. He then launched into the health care industry with a firm called Healtheon/WebMD (now WebMD Corporation). Clark, who was kicked out of his high school in Texas, but later managed to earn a Ph.D. in computer science, is a legendary figure in California's Silicon Valley. After Netscape, Clark eschewed day-to-day involvement in the companies he spawned; he became a "concept man." Concept people come up with the ideas; others implement their visions.[40] Henry Hillman, a reclusive president of his own, privately held company, once explained why he seldom granted interviews: "A whale is harpooned only when it spouts."[41]

Of course, other corporate executives spout all the time. In the 1980s, Lee Iacocca, Chrysler's chairman, personified the corporate executive as impresario. More visible than any other corporate leader in America, Iacocca routinely took to the airwaves with a direct message: "If you can find a better buy than Chrysler, buy it!" Iacocca's style was bold, direct, forceful, and flamboyant. In the 1990s, Iacocca's role (as visible corporate leader) was assumed by Michael Eisner, head of the Walt Disney Corporation, who frequently appeared on television to tout the various attractions of his company. After his return to the helm at Apple, Steve Jobs assumed a high profile over the next fourteen years (until his death in 2011), making frequent speeches to large crowds, and inviting all manner of media to the unveilings of his new products. By the late 1990s, Microsoft chairman Bill Gates could no longer maintain his preferred low profile. The richest man in the United States, whose company was on trial for antitrust violations, made increasing numbers of public appearances, including testifying before Congress, in an effort to keep his company from being split up by the government. Gates's foray into the public spotlight did not deter Judge Thomas Penfield Jackson from finding against Microsoft and ordering the breakup of the company.[42] In the end, however, Gates's efforts were not in vain; much of Judge Jackson's ruling was overturned on appeal, which led the government to enter into an agreement with Microsoft that did not call for the company to break up. Facebook CEO Mark Zuckerberg also appeared to prefer a low profile, but following the release of a movie about him in 2011, and the announcement that his company was going public in 2012, he made himself more available to the media.

Iacocca, Eisner, and Jobs may represent special cases; most corporate executives prefer to be less visible. For many top executives, public attention is unwelcome because scandals and corporate salaries are the typical lightning rods that attract attention from the press and the public. This was certainly the case for Lloyd Blankfein of Goldman Sachs and Jamie Dimon of JPMorgan Chase in 2012. Unflattering revelations about the business practices of both Goldman and Chase forced Blankfein and Dimon to appear before Congress to defend themselves and their companies, and to deal with all manner of questions from major media outlets.[43] Both agreed to television interviews, but neither seemed pleased to be in the public spotlight. In January 2013, after a well-publicized investment blunder that cost the company several billion dollars was made under his watch, Dimon was punished by his board in the form of a 50 percent pay cut (from $23 million to $11.5 million).[44]

The shunning of publicity by corporate CEOs and other top managers is also a reflection of the formidable responsibilities these jobs carry. The inside and outside games have become increasingly demanding in the era of e-commerce, rapid technological change, and globalization. Most CEOs have their hands full just trying to keep up with the competition. Furthermore, corporate boards seem less willing to tolerate questionable performance from their top executives. For example, technology giant Hewlett-Packard has been through four CEOs in the past thirteen years. Carly Fiorina was fired after six years at the helm in 2005 (and then ran for a California Senate seat in 2010, but lost), Mark Hurd lasted five years and was replaced by Léo Apotheker, who lasted only one year before he was replaced by Meg Whitman. Whitman, who had earlier amassed a fortune as a tech executive, no doubt needed a new job: she had just spent $144 million of her own money in an unsuccessful bid to become California's governor in 2010.[45]

Decision Making

As we have seen, normally most corporate decisions are made by managers, with limited input from boards of directors. However, there are times when key decisions are made by boards, despite opposition from managers. As a general rule, managers are free to make strategic decisions as long as the bottom line is favorable. When a corporation begins to flounder, board members intervene. In short, corporate boards are most active in times of crisis.

If boards are seldom dominant, they are nevertheless more important than they used to be. Corporate boards were once regarded as little more than rubber stamps; decisions were made by top managers and then were simply ratified by members of the board. The role of the board, it seemed, was to legitimate management decisions and to convince investors that the corporation was in fact being guided, or at least monitored, by a distinguished panel of leading citizens. Over the past thirty years, this has changed, not dramatically perhaps, but noticeably. First, boards are now more diverse demographically. Women and minorities in growing numbers now sit on boards, which means a greater variety of viewpoints and more lively debates on topics such as the diversity policies of corporations and the difficulties faced by women in corporations. A 1998 census of corporate boards found that women occupied 11 percent of the board seats of *Fortune* 500 companies; by 2010, that figure had risen to 18 percent, while minorities (African Americans, Hispanics, and Asians) held 13 percent of the board seats.[46] Of course, this means that 73 percent of *Fortune* 500 board members were white men. A lone African American on a corporate board may not be able to win a showdown vote, but, as most boards prefer to operate by consensus, the first response to a protest by a minority board member is likely to be a search for a compromise.

Second, boards have given greater representation to outsiders—bankers, lawyers, college and university presidents, and others who do not work for the companies. According to one estimate, by the 1980s, about 65 percent of corporate directors were outsiders, meaning that managers occupied fewer seats than before.[47] Although many of these outsiders are handpicked by the managers, the potential for dissent is greater than it used to be. Normally, one or more of these outside directors play a leadership role on the board. A third trend is to place limits on interlocking directorates in which board members are selected from institutions that have official dealings with the company, such as banks, insurance companies, or law firms. The goal of all these trends is to reduce conflicts of interest and biases that limit the vision and cloud the judgment of corporate boards.

The significance of these trends is that corporate boards are, more than ever before, in a position to voice vigorous dissent, to challenge management decisions, and to identify corporations' best interests without regard to personal circumstances. These trends increase the potential leverage of boards over managers. But an important limitation on board domination of decision making is time and knowledge; managers have a lot of time to devote to company business and considerable knowledge of it, whereas most nonmanagement board members have quite limited amounts of both. One approach to dealing with the time and knowledge limitations is division of labor. Like other important institutions in American politics, corporate boards have found it useful to delegate certain tasks to committees, which then make recommendations to the full boards. This practice conserves time and permits some board members to develop enough expertise to challenge managers. Corporate boards have established audit committees, compensation committees, and external relations and nominating committees, which exercise growing influence in decision making.

STRATEGIES AND POLICIES

Although achieving or maintaining profitability and increasing shareholder value are the predominant goals of corporate managers and boards, the strategies and policies for realizing these goals are not always obvious. These strategies and policies include everything from decisions about how much to pay employees to how to comply with government regulations, even whether to merge with another corporation or whether to divest the company of certain divisions.

Adaptability

If corporations are to prosper in a competitive environment, they must be able to adapt to changing circumstances and trends. This is, perhaps, more true today than ever before. The question is not whether corporations are capable of changing, but whether they are capable of changing in time. A business tottering on the edge of bankruptcy is desperate enough to try something drastic; a corporation whose strategic decisions will lead to trouble in five to ten years may not yet perceive the need for a new approach.

The history of the U.S. auto industry over the past fifty years is mostly a story of nonadaptability to changing market conditions, but it is also one of survival. In the late 1960s and early 1970s, the U.S. automakers (Ford, GM, and Chrysler) ignored the handwriting on the wall—the growing popularity of small, economical foreign cars—preferring instead to continue the old, familiar pattern of large cars and large inventories in the United States. Before and after the Organization of the Petroleum Exporting Countries' oil embargo of 1973 to 1974, voices from inside and outside the companies proposed a shift to smaller cars, but Henry Ford II (for one) rejected such suggestions, dismissing small cars as "little shitboxes."[48] The "big three" auto companies survived the 1980s (Chrysler needed a government bailout in the late 1970s) by diversifying their products to include several varieties of minivans and light trucks, but they more or less yielded the smaller car market to Honda and Toyota, with the partial exception of Ford, whose fuel-efficient Escort became its leading seller. By the 1990s, the big three were better informed, but not fully reformed, featuring sport utility vehicles that offered room and comfort, but not fuel economy. When the Great Recession hit in 2008, the big three were losing money, with no end in sight. The unthinkable loomed on the horizon: the end of American-owned automobile manufacturing.

The federal government came to the rescue, offering loans, government purchases of company stock, "cash for clunkers" programs, and other assistance.[49] Chrysler and GM had to go through structured bankruptcy proceedings in May and June 2009, but Ford survived without government money or bankruptcy. By 2012, all three appeared to be back on their feet. Chrysler (now owned by Italian automaker Fiat) had paid off its loans, Ford and GM were making profits, although the government still owned over a quarter of GM's stock in the summer of 2012 (down from 60 percent in 2009).[50] Part of their postrecession success was embracing new product lines, featuring fuel-efficient vehicles, but cost-cutting actions that involved plant closings, thousands of layoffs, and reductions in employee wages and benefits probably had a larger impact on the bottom line. New employees at auto plants in 2011 were paid half the wages of longtime employees and were no longer offered pensions.[51] In 2013, all three companies announced plans to expand domestic manufacturing and hire more workers.[52]

A basic problem with U.S. auto companies from the 1970s to the Great Recession was the unwillingness of top managers to take a long-term perspective. Many other companies suffer from the same affliction. Unable to demonstrate favorable returns on investment in a few years, they routinely reject proposals for risky innovations. Westinghouse, a large company that produced home appliances and other products, was more or less the peer of GE in the 1960s and early 1970s. But Westinghouse was unable to keep up with the changes in the industry—foreign competition, new product lines, and so forth—and suffered severe decline and eventual demise; meanwhile, GE continued to be one of America's most successful companies. Indeed, GE won *Fortune* magazine's Most Admired Companies competition in 2000 (see Box 3-1).[53] A big reason for GE's success has been its willingness to unload divisions within the company that were not performing at high levels. Former CEO Jack Welch followed a strategy by which "businesses" within the company had to be number 1 or 2 in their fields, or they would be sold off.[54] This is the kind of bold thinking GM's current CEO, Daniel Akerson, wants to bring to his company. He is openly critical of previous management: "They were all over the map. Where was the vision? Where do you want to take this company?"[55] Only time will tell if he can deliver.

Corporations differ in their inclination and their ability to shift gears quickly. According to economics professors Walter Adams and James Brock, size is a factor: big companies are more conservative and more bureaucratic than small companies.[56] Competition is another factor. Companies that face tough competition, such those in the computer and electronics industries, have to adapt quickly to changing circumstances. In the late 1990s, Xerox, a firm whose name was synonymous with copying machines in the 1970s and hugely successful at that time, was struggling to survive in a market that featured a continuous stream of new products and companies.[57] But the appointment of Anne Mulcahy as CEO in 2001, and her determination to return the company to profitability, revitalized the organization. Over the next several years, Xerox diversified and updated its product lines, in part by acquiring new high-tech firms, and reestablished itself in the office equipment industry. In 2009, Ursula Burns became the new CEO and the first African American woman to run a major U.S. corporation. Presently Xerox employs about 140,000 people and shows profits well above $1 billion per year.[58] Meanwhile, GE has fallen out of *Fortune*'s current top ten list (Box 3-1), another demonstration of the fact that staying at the top is not easy.

Symbols and the Corporate Image

A positive corporate image is a tremendous asset, and a negative image is a major liability. A drug company that symbolizes safety and reliability is likely to prosper; if the same company is suddenly seen as careless or dishonest, its sales may plummet. Clever company executives appreciate the close connection between symbols and their companies' images. They also recognize that symbols may reinforce or undermine company policy.

A corporate symbol may be a building, a press release, a charitable contribution, a logo, an advertisement, a year-end bonus, or an appointment. Apple, its Macintosh computer, and now its i- products (iPod, iPad, etc.) are instantly recognizable brands that the company has cultivated with great success over the years. Other efforts to create symbols are more defensive. When brewers started running television ads in the late 1990s emphasizing the need for designated drivers, they were trying to avoid the image of a socially irresponsible corporation. Of course, they had the benefit of watching the tobacco companies plumb new depths on the image front. Joe Camel, once viewed as a kind of innocent cartoon figure, had been definitively linked to efforts to sell cigarettes to children, and many states were running powerful antismoking ads on television. Cigarette manufacturers were in a public relations quandary from which there was no escape.[59]

There is no doubt that corporate executives pay attention to symbols. Often, however, they fail to recognize what kinds of symbols they are creating, or they have blind spots about the impact of certain symbols on important constituencies. When the management of the Mitsubishi auto assembly plant in Illinois faced a lawsuit filed by female employees alleging sexual harassment in 1994, they probably couldn't have imagined how bad things were going to get. Within a few years, the Equal Employment Opportunity Commission had also filed against them, Jesse Jackson and the National Organization for Women were calling for a boycott of their products, and they had to hire former secretary of labor Lynn Martin to give some credibility to a review of plant procedures. By 1998, after lurid details of harassment in the plant had been made public by the *Chicago Tribune* and the *New York Times*, the company agreed to pay $34 million in damages to women who had been harassed, and plant production levels were down by 25 percent.[60]

The earnings of top corporate executives, and/or their exit pay packages ("golden parachutes"), have contributed to an image problem for corporate America for some time, but the issue took on new salience after the financial crisis of 2007 to 2009, the Wall Street bailout, the Great Recession, and the Wall Street protest movement. In the 1980s, when corporate takeovers were common, golden parachutes gave top corporate executives generous severance payments if they lost their jobs because of a takeover. These days, golden parachutes are usually products of mergers, but many corporate CEOs who are fired for poor performance are also well compensated as they leave their firms. Robert Nardelli was fired by Home Depot in 2007 with a $210 million exit pay package; and, yes, he was later hired by Chrysler as their CEO, eventually leading them to bankruptcy in 2009. Carly Fiorina's 2005 exit pay from Hewlett-Packard of $29 million looks small in comparison.[61] In recent years, there have been numerous challenges to the pay packages of CEOs and top management, stimulated in part by rules passed by the SEC in 2011.[62] In the spring of 2012, Citigroup's shareholders voted down the $15 million pay proposal for CEO Vikram Pandit, along with those of four other top managers; later in the year, Pandit was fired by the Citigroup board.[63] Amid protests surrounding Bank of America's shareholder meeting, CEO Brian Moynihan's $7 million pay package was approved, but the bank's foreclosure practices were widely criticized by shareholders.[64] Currently, shareholder activism and proxy voting drives are supported not only by grassroots movements but also by citizen groups that employ well-connected lobbyists.[65]

Despite the image problem associated with executive compensation, the salaries of corporate CEOs continue to grow, but perhaps at a more modest pace than in previous decades. The salaries of top corporate executives in the 1990s grew at a rate that far exceeded that of workers, or even corporate profits. A 1998 survey of 365 of the largest companies in the United States found that the average annual compensation for CEOs was over $10 million, much of it in stock options.[66] Corporate pay fell in 2009 in the midst of the Great Recession, but rose in 2010 and 2011. In 2011, the average pay for the head of a public corporation was $9.6 million; for the top 200 corporations, the median CEO compensation was $14.5 million.[67] For the average American, compensation at these high levels is difficult to understand as anything other than an example of corporate greed. Thus it is not surprising that most Americans think big corporations have too much power over too many aspects of American life, including the political system. These negative perceptions are acknowledged within corporate boardrooms, but as long as shareholders are satisfied with a company's performance, there is limited pressure to curb corporate salaries.

Two Views of Profitability

All corporations pursue higher profits, but a recurring question is how to balance short-term costs and long-term benefits. Johnson & Johnson decided to recall Tylenol products after several people died from ingesting poisoned capsules in 1982. The recall, and subsequent design and production of tamper-proof packaging, was very costly. In the long run, however, the decision enhanced Johnson & Johnson's credibility in a market that depends on consumer confidence, and the company regained its pre-recall market share within a few years. In 1991, when two people died in the state of Washington after taking Sudafed capsules laced with cyanide, the maker of the product, the Burroughs Wellcome Company, seemed to take a lesson from Johnson & Johnson, because it wasted no time taking Sudafed capsules off the market. More recently, after its settlement with the government for illegally promoting certain drugs, mentioned earlier in this chapter, GlaxoSmithKline went public with a commitment to open up most of its research data to the public in an effort to restore its credibility.[68]

Corporations do not always take enlightened, decisive action in times of emergency, however. In the late 1970s, the Firestone Tire and Rubber Company, whose steel-belted radial tires were prone to blowouts, tread separations, and other dangerous defects, continued to manufacture and sell these tires to unsuspecting customers despite considerable evidence that the tires were hazardous. When pressed by the National Highway Traffic Safety Administration for performance data, Firestone refused and went to court to prevent the agency from releasing to the press the results of a consumer survey. In October 1978, after months of controversy, Firestone agreed to a massive recall. By that time, however, the company's reputation for safety had been badly damaged by hundreds of accidents resulting in at least thirty-four deaths, and the company had a public image of greed and defiance.[69] In a somewhat more nuanced example, drug giant Pfizer promoted its arthritis drug Celebrex as more stomach friendly than rival drugs by presenting only some of the results of a study under way in 2000. As one Pfizer scientist put it, they were "cherry-picking the data."[70] In the next several years, Pfizer made billions of dollars with Celebrex. When safety concerns about Vioxx, a drug very similar to Celebrex, came to light in 2004, Pfizer ordered a new study, one that will not be completed until 2014, the year Celebrex's patent runs out.

Most people would applaud Johnson & Johnson, condemn Firestone, and scold Pfizer. Confronted by evidence that a product is unsafe, it would seem that a company should act swiftly to withdraw the product or improve it. But the issue is not always so clear-cut. When does a product become unsafe? All automobiles are unsafe to some extent and could be made safer. Should companies make their products as safe as they can be? Should companies make some products safer, and others cheaper, so that consumers have a choice?

Should consumers be free to place cost above safety? And who should define safety, the companies or the government? At a minimum, the public might insist that companies be honest about their products' virtues and vices. But does this require that they go out of their way to reveal flaws and problems? Finally, there are questions about relative risk. Do certain pesticides and preservatives serve a public health function by controlling or eliminating harmful organisms in food, or are their own toxic qualities more of a risk than a benefit to the average consumer? These are questions government regulators are constantly trying to answer, but their answers are often challenged in court by affected companies.

In the contemporary economy, questions of long-term benefits, and profitability, are continually at issue in new and emerging industries. In 2000, most everyone was certain that companies selling products and services on the Internet (e-commerce) would eventually make money, even though none of them had at the time; the question was when and which ones. One of the founders of e-commerce, Jeff Bezos, was confident that his company, Amazon .com, would be the first to return real profits to investors, and he was right. As Bezos predicted, his company made a profit (of $5 million) for the first time in 2001, with a customer base of 23 million and revenues over $1.5 billion.[71] Since then Amazon's profits have been up and down, but new investments and innovation have been constant features of the company. In 2011, Amazon sold about $10 billion worth of products (books, Kindle Fire tablets, videos, etc.), with a profit of about $322 million, and in 2012, Bezos was named *Fortune* magazine's Business Person of the Year.[72] Meanwhile, e-commerce has grown enormously, with old companies joining new ones in selling their wares on the Internet. The commercial value of Internet sales activity in 2011, as reported by the Commerce Department, was $194 billion, up over 16 percent from the previous year.[73]

AFTER THE BOARD HAS MET

After corporate strategies and policies have been established, they must be implemented, and their impact must be assessed. In many cases, the impacts reach far beyond the boardroom, affecting many citizens and even entire communities.

Implementation Problems

The implementation of corporate policies is seldom automatic. Just as governments depend on corporate cooperation to implement a variety of environmental protection policies (the Clean Air Act, the Clean Water Act, etc.), corporations depend on government cooperation to carry out policies such as plant construction. Many businesses have been unable to expand because of antipollution laws that forbid new plants in "nonattainment" areas if new plants would degrade air quality. Federal agencies such as the FTC and the Justice Department have to decide whether they will allow an Internet giant such as Google to purchase Motorola Mobility because of the control the new company might exert over the communications industry.[74] For many large corporations and public utilities, the implementation of a policy involves a number of steps in a long chain of problematic events.

The implementation of corporate policies is especially tricky in an intergovernmental setting. In the 1980s, many electric utility companies were unable to build nuclear power plants because of government disapproval, either from the Nuclear Regulatory Commission (NRC) or from a state agency. For example, the Pacific Gas & Electric Company (PG&E) needed the approval of the NRC and the California Energy Conservation Commission (CECC) to build a nuclear plant. Although the approval of the NRC was assured, that of the CECC was not. Citing a California statute banning new nuclear power plants in the state until a safe means of nuclear waste disposal had been found, the CECC rejected PG&E's request. The decision was subsequently upheld by the U.S. Supreme Court.[75] In 2012, the NRC and state officials approved the construction of two new nuclear power plants in Georgia; they are the first such plants approved in the United States since 1978.[76] Meanwhile, the federal government still has not found a solution to the nuclear waste disposal problem.

Implementation is also highly problematic for corporations characterized by a high degree of decentralization, strong professionalism, or both. When a newspaper or magazine owner tries to pressure a reporter or editor, the journalist may resign rather than submit to censorship. When a hospital administrator instructs doctors to cut costs to improve the hospital's financial picture, doctors may cite the Hippocratic oath—and utter a few other oaths as well—as grounds for refusal. Multinational corporations face special challenges in implementing policies across a far-flung empire. Indeed, this was Union Carbide's defense when it tried to explain a poisonous gas leak that killed an estimated 2,000 people in Bhopal, India, in 1984. According to Union Carbide headquarters, its foreign subsidiary failed to conform to company safety policies, with catastrophic results.

Despite these difficulties, there are several reasons why corporate policies are less difficult to implement than government rules and regulations. First, in the private sector, it is easier to fire people who are not performing well than it is in the public sector. Although white-collar corporate employees may take their employers to court if they believe they have been fired without just cause, most of the time corporations can make a convincing case that their actions were not arbitrary, capricious, or reckless. In comparison, government regulations controlling civil service employment include procedures and appeal rights that provide more protection to employees. Second, the private sector has access to considerable financial resources that help remove obstacles. Corporate lobbyists, or trade association lobbyists representing smaller businesses, intervene directly to prevent government agencies from spoiling the plans of private sector firms. And, of course, corporate and trade association political action committees remind politicians that reelection is easier if business interests are on their side. Third, the private sector can use talented public relations professionals when mass persuasion is necessary. Many of the leading media experts—the advertising wizards of Madison Avenue and others—are known to politicians, who also make use of their services to win elections. Corporations, like government bureaucracies, face obstacles when they propose controversial policies, but they have a good deal of power to remove such obstacles from their path.

In Search of Golden Eggs

To many politicians, corporations are geese that lay golden eggs. This observation is especially true at the state and local levels, where politicians perceive corporations as sources of jobs, taxes, economic development, and prosperity. To persuade corporations to settle within their boundaries, state and local politicians offer special subsidies and tax breaks, and if these overtures are successful, the politicians can take credit for a coup. The embattled Mitsubishi plant mentioned previously has been considered a great prize by political officials in the twin cities of Normal and Bloomington, Illinois, since it opened in 1988. Recently, Mitsubishi invested $45 million in plant renovations, so that it can produce its newest product, the Outlander Sport crossover utility vehicle, in the United States. Governor Pat Quinn of Illinois joined company officials for the public announcement of this venture in July 2012.[77]

Many communities owe their revitalization to public-spirited corporate leaders. During the 1950s, the Mellon family joined forces with Democratic politicians to clean up the air in Pittsburgh; in addition, they spearheaded a Pittsburgh renaissance, which included the construction of picturesque skyscrapers and public parks in the city's Golden Triangle. Following a second renaissance in 1988, Rand McNally hailed Pittsburgh as the most livable city in America; it won the award again (this time from *Forbes* magazine) in 2010.[78] In Minneapolis, the Downtown Council, a business coalition, supported an extensive downtown revitalization program in the 1950s, including the building of pedestrian skywalks that protect shoppers from Minnesota's harsh winters. Since then, Minneapolis has been praised for its favorable business climate, progressive government, and cultural amenities. In addition, corporations in the Twin Cities (Minneapolis and St. Paul) have established a tradition of donating generously to local charities, thus demonstrating their commitment to the community.

Pioneering corporations offer benefits not just to particular states and communities, but also to society at large. Consider, for example, the history of Bell Laboratories. Among its many achievements were the development of high-fidelity sound recording (1925), direct long-distance dialing (1951), communication satellites (1960), and digital cellular phones (1980). Bell Labs also developed the transistor (1947), which laid the groundwork for portable radios, space flight, and computers. From 1925 to 1975, scientists at Bell Labs acquired an astonishing 18,000 patents.[79] Bell's accomplishments, and those of IBM's Thomas J. Watson Laboratory and Xerox's Palo Alto Research Center, inspired Microsoft to build nine research facilities, including four in the United States and five abroad in England, India, China, Egypt, and Israel.[80]

In recent years, the development of innovative technologies with far-reaching implications has become an almost daily occurrence. Breakthroughs in personal computers, software, the Internet, electronic transmission (broadband), and mobile devices have not only changed communities (Silicon Valley in California; Redmond, Washington, home of Microsoft; and Cambridge, Massachusetts) but have also brought the world closer together. Still, these new technologies give rise to many questions and concerns. To what extent should the Internet be regulated to prevent fraud? Should e-commerce be subject to taxation? Should we be concerned that most e-commerce is conducted by individuals and families with above-average incomes?[81] How far should governments go to make sure all citizens have Internet access and, more generally, in addressing issues associated with the digital divide?

Corporations also demonstrate a sense of social responsibility by donating money to charity, but they differ greatly in their generosity. Many corporations give less than 1 percent of their pretax profits to charity (the median percentage in 2010 was just below 1 percent), whereas others give up to 10 percent, which is the maximum tax-deductible contribution allowed by the Internal Revenue Service.[82] Some of the charitable programs set up by corporations have produced compelling results. For example, Merrill Lynch set up a program in 1988 whereby it promised to pay full college expenses for 251 first graders from some of the worst neighborhoods in ten cities around the United States if they graduated from high school in 2000. With the help of the Urban League, over 90 percent of the students included in this program went to college in the fall of 2000.[83] Prominent corporate individuals also give to charitable and humanitarian causes by donating their own money to organizations or by setting up foundations to support worthy causes. Much like the corporate barons of 100 years ago (Ford, Mellon, Carnegie, etc.), the new breed of very rich, including Bill and Melinda Gates, the Hewletts, and many others, have established foundations and/or pledged to give away half of what they have earned to charity.[84] (Warren Buffett made the largest charitable contribution on record of $37 billion to the Gates Foundation in 2006.[85]) Much of the foundation money goes to education, but other popular causes include poverty, hunger, disease prevention and treatment, and affordable housing.[86] Interestingly, gifts to the arts are not as popular among contemporary philanthropists as gifts to education and aiding poor individuals.

Decisions regarding charitable contributions, although they are significant expenditures, pale in comparison to such big-ticket corporate decisions as those concerning wage settlements, plant modernization, diversification, dividend payouts, and compliance with government regulations. Moreover, these decisions often resemble a zero-sum game in which one party's gain is another's loss. Corporations often must choose between higher profits or higher wages, expansion or environmental protection, higher dividends, or secure futures for the companies. The natural instinct of all corporations is to pursue higher profits and stock values; today's managers tend to share this goal because much of their compensation is in the form of stocks or stock options. And mid- and entry-level employees are sometimes shareholders, as many corporations have extended stock ownership opportunities to employees at all levels. Still, despite the added complication of large-scale employee stock ownership, it is safe to say that the most significant beneficiaries of corporate decisions are the investors and managers.

Shattered Dreams

Corporate policies can have devastating consequences for workers, taxpayers, and consumers. Unemployment is perhaps the most common negative conse-quence of corporate policies. For most people, unemployment is a bitter pill to swallow. Unemployed workers experience self-doubt, guilt, shame, depression, and despair, which often affect their physical and mental health. Alcoholism, child abuse, spousal abuse, and suicide are occasional side effects. In American society, as in many others, a person's self-image is intimately connected to his or her job. Moreover, unemployment almost always has serious consequences for a family's economic well-being. Even if another member of the household works during the period of unemployment, that one income may not be suf-ficient, and finding a new job at comparable pay is often difficult. Since 2008, unemployment has become a highly salient issue for all Americans, as nearly everyone has been affected by it either directly or indirectly.[87]

The effects of unemployment are especially harsh in certain communities and certain segments of society. Small towns, long dependent on particular industries, may have difficulty coping when companies decide to mothball plants. Restaurants and shops may close their doors forever, and city services may decline as a city's tax revenue drops. A virtual ghost town may result. African Americans are disproportionately affected by unemployment, and the black community suffers acutely when unemployment increases. In 1983 and again in 2009, at the end of recessions, black teenage unemployment reached nearly 50 percent, an alarmingly high level; even in the booming economy of 1999 the black teenage unemployment rate was nearly 30 percent; the current level is about 40 percent.[88] These conditions are breeding grounds for crime and drug abuse. A society that suffers high unemployment pays a high price in many ways.

Unemployment need not be tragic if it is temporary and if it leads to a new, better job. In fact, when workers are laid off from relatively unproductive jobs and find more productive ones, society benefits. Many Western countries have retraining programs that facilitate the transition from one job to another by paying for the unemployed, in some cases for as long as two years, to receive training in schools or on the job. In contrast, job training programs in the United States are severely limited in scope and focus. Most private job training is geared to a particular job rather than to acquisition of a broader set of mar-ketable skills. The U.S. government conducts job training programs, most of them through the Workforce Investment Act, but they are generally restricted to job placement assistance and short-term programs for unskilled workers and welfare recipients; there are few programs that provide longer term retraining for people with obsolete skills or those who wish to improve their skills. Moreover, government outlays for job training have declined in real terms since the early 1980s. For all these reasons, the consequences of unemployment in the United States are worse than they need be.

Bankruptcy is another possible consequence of corporate policies. From a societal point of view, the occasional bankruptcy is not alarming if it is caused by changing market conditions or technological advances in related industries. But the collapse of a pivotal company can be disturbing, especially if the company is part of a complex web of other companies. Society can ill afford the bankruptcies of major companies in industries that are heavily concentrated or that are central to commerce or national security. Even more disastrous is the collapse of an entire industry. When such catastrophes occur, taxpayers are often asked to mop up the mess. In the 1980s, the savings and loan industry collapsed, and the federal government had to step in to salvage the situation as best it could. Although this debacle had many causes, including shortsighted government deregulatory policy and a recessionary economy, poor investment choices and extravagant spending by savings and loan executives contributed greatly to the problem.[89] The whole mess ended up costing national taxpayers $124 billion.[90] The cost of a bailout can be very high indeed. Unfortunately, the savings and loan fiasco was just a miniature of the financial industry collapse of 2008 (with the same causes). TARP, authorized in 2008, cost the federal government $700 billion in initial outlays; however, by the end of 2012, almost all of this had been repaid.[91]

Taxpayers pay in still another way for corporate mistakes. Many industries, especially defense and aerospace, receive large amounts of their revenue from public funds. When these industries are wasteful and inefficient, the costs ultimately are borne by taxpayers. Although the government is partly to blame for awarding these contracts in the first place, or for tolerating cost overruns, corporations bear primary responsibility.[92]

If taxpayers pay for some corporate mistakes, consumers pay for others. There have been numerous instances in which products were sold to millions of consumers and later determined to be unsafe, causing thousands of injuries and hundreds of deaths: to name just a few, the Dalkon Shield, an intrauterine birth control device marketed by the A. H. Robins Company in the early 1970s; Eli Lilly's arthritis drug Oraflex; Ford's Pinto, which had an exploding gas tank; Manville's asbestos; and Dow Corning's silicone breast implants. It is impossible to calculate the costs of these disasters in shattered dreams and shattered lives.

A prolonged spectacle of corporate misdeeds, mistakes, and blame casting took place in the summer of 2010. The main players were British Petroleum (BP) and two other companies (Transocean and Halliburton Energy Services), the Department of the Interior (DOI), the White House, Congress, the U.S. Coast Guard, and the media. The episode began with a blast on an oil rig in the

Gulf of Mexico that killed eleven people, and left an uncapped well leaking millions of gallons of crude oil into the waters of the gulf. The Deepwater Horizon rig was owned by BP, but the drilling operations were conducted by Transocean, with help from Halliburton. Following the explosion, a somewhat predictable series of events took place, starting with constant media attention featuring live pictures of oil spewing into the Gulf of Mexico from a wellhead deep underwater, and followed by congressional hearings, the appointment of a presidential commission, the announcement of a victim's compensation fund, and litigation. Two of the early prominent players, S. Elizabeth Birnbaum, the head of the federal agency (Minerals Management Service of the DOI, later changed to the Bureau of Ocean Energy Management) responsible for regulating offshore drilling, and BP CEO Tony Hayward, were pressured into resigning their positions; she roughly a month after the spill, he about six months later.[93] Meanwhile, there was drama and dread every day for more than three months as some 5 million barrels of oil leaked into the gulf, and the company and the government scrambled to find ways to plug the leak. The main cause of the rig explosion was later found to be a poor mixture of cement foam, made by Halliburton, which is used to seal the area around the casing pipe of a well once it is drilled. Apparently, BP was told of the cement problem before the rig exploded, but neither BP nor Halliburton acted to correct the problem.[94] The environmental damage from the spill was somewhere between very high and incalculable.

By January 2011, the Presidential Commission on the BP Deepwater Horizon Oil Spill and Offshore Drilling, led by former Florida senator Bob Graham and former Environmental Protection Agency (EPA) administrator William Reilly, produced a report with two principal and somewhat contradictory findings: the spill was preventable, but no one involved had "made a conscious decision to favor dollars over safety."[95] Meanwhile, under intense pressure from President Obama, BP put up $20 billion in a compensation fund for disaster victims, mostly fishermen and tourism-related businesses, and hired super bureaucrat turned private sector lawyer Kenneth Feinberg (of post-9/11 victims' compensation fund fame) to administer it. As expected, Feinberg's decisions were attacked by local businesses for being too stingy, by BP for being too generous, and by members of Congress for being both.[96] To date, hundreds of thousands of claims have been filed, billions have been paid out, and controversy continues.[97] Not surprisingly, BP, Transocean, and Halliburton all sued one another.

In the months following the spill, the Obama administration acted to restrict drilling activities in the Gulf of Mexico, but less than a year after the disaster, they were approving new drilling permits, thanks in part to an order by a federal judge in Louisiana.[98] However, the Justice Department assured the public that it was pursuing criminal charges related to the spill, and by November 2012, a settlement had been reached that cost BP $4 billion. But the settlement was not the end of the government's criminal case; two Deepwater Horizon supervisors were indicted on manslaughter charges, and a deepwater oil and gas specialist was charged for misleading Congress about the magnitude of the releases during the spill.[99] A few weeks later, the EPA announced that it was banning BP from any government contracts, and the Justice Department announced that it had settled criminal claims with Transocean for $1.4 billion.[100] Finally, the government was pursuing civil actions against BP, hoping to collect $16 billion in fines and penalties that would be used to pay for the cleanup and restoration of areas affected by the spill.[101] Meanwhile, throughout 2012 and 2013, television watchers were being treated to numerous commercials extolling the pleasures of the postspill gulf region, ads paid for and proudly promoted by BP.

Redemption

Corporations do learn from their mistakes. Despite a rather grim future outlook in the early 1980s and then again in 2008, U.S. automobile companies did rather well in the 1990s and are making money today. Many U.S. manufacturing firms whose products are environmentally damaging for reasons ranging from plastic packaging to toxic chemicals have begun to change their processes to make them more environmentally friendly and to develop recycling and waste management programs to stave off criticism by citizens and politicians, and to make money. Presently the idea of "sustainable production" is emerging, with manufacturing firms in the United States placing great emphasis on the use of recycled products such as paper, glass, aluminum, and steel to produce new goods.[102] Even the banks are getting into the green technology business by making loans and investments in renewable energy and low-carbon transportation projects.[103] As mentioned in chapter 1, in early 2013, Wal-Mart got into the redemption game by first pledging to hire 100,000 veterans over five years and then committing to buy more American-made products.[104]

If companies learn from their mistakes, they also learn from the successes of risk-taking pioneers; a "diffusion of innovations" often occurs in the private sector.[105] From some of their early applications, such as editing and production in newsrooms, manufacturing assembly lines, and grocery store checkout lines, computers, particularly personal computers, have transformed how Americans work and businesses operate. Indeed, the personal computer has penetrated almost all workplaces in the United States; it is hard to believe that there were few personal computers in use thirty years ago. The telecommunications industry deserves a great deal of credit for multiplying the ways we communicate with one another and the educational and commercial value of that communication. At this point, it is hard to remember when Americans didn't rely on cell phones for everything from instant communication (texting) to browsing the Internet. With the great advances that have been made in biotechnology over the past thirty years, including the decoding of various genomes, major pharmaceutical companies around the world are exploring the potential applications for treating diseases and other maladies. A relatively new kid on the block, nanotechnology, along with further advances in robotics, may well revolutionize manufacturing in the years to come.

During the 1980s and 1990s, many U.S. corporations followed exhortations from academics and market analysts to undertake a management approach, commonly attributed to Japanese corporations, that emphasizes teamwork between management and labor, inventory control, customer satisfaction, and demonstrable results for investors.[106] So-called total quality management (TQM) was widely credited with having turned around many stumbling corporations in the United States. However, it now seems that the most significant component of this new approach to management was probably the downsizing of corporate workforces in the early 1990s, which affected both blue- and white-collar employees. Such downsizing has continued, and conflicts between corporate management and labor, especially labor unions, have become very intense. Some companies have even resorted to tactics commonly used in the early twentieth century, including lockouts of union employees.[107] Although TQM and, more generally, corporate learning have produced positive results for many companies, there is a very real danger that the unrelenting drive of corporations to reduce employee-related costs will result in high levels of unemployment for the foreseeable future.

Corporations and smaller businesses have also learned that joint ventures with government (public-private partnerships) can be successful, even profitable. During the 1990s, and continuing to the present, some of the worst areas of major cities, including Boston, Chicago, Cleveland, New York, Philadelphia, and San Francisco, were turned into functioning neighborhoods through the combined efforts of community development corporations, local governments, and private companies. Aided by national legislation such as the Community Reinvestment Act and by a national public-private partnership called the National Community Development Initiative, cities have been able to attract businesses back to depressed neighborhoods, such as New York's South Bronx, which had been all but abandoned previously. A big part of the community revitalization picture has been the willingness of cities and community-based organizations to take on the problems of crime and deteriorating schools. Dealing with these problems was a necessary condition for private sector investment. Another major piece was the emergence of intermediaries, such as the Enterprise Foundation and the Local Initiatives Support Corporation (LISC), which connect major corporate and foundation capital to local community development corporations and other grassroots groups. Together, LISC and Enterprise have channeled over $23 billion to thousands of community development corporations, enough to leverage about $75 billion in development spending, which has led to the construction of almost 600,000 housing units and millions of square feet of commercial and industrial space in major cities throughout the country over the past thirty years.[108]

SUMMARY

The distinction between public policy and private policy is in many ways a cultural artifact. Many Western democracies regard industrial policy as public policy; in the United States, industrial policy is private, with some governmental oversight and supervision. Many Western democracies view rail transportation, steel production, electricity, and telecommunications as public enterprises; in the United States, these are, for the most part, private. Some Western democracies rely on the government to employ a substantial number of people and to retrain employees when necessary; in the United States, public sector employment is relatively small, and government-assisted training and retraining is minimal. Here, most people pay for their own education beyond high school, which the private sector supplements with more specific training after people are hired. The United States does not have anything that would qualify as a national employment policy.

To use E. E. Schattschneider's terms, we have "privatized" conflict by removing certain issues from public debate.[109] The privatization of conflict limits participation in the policymaking process, but it does not limit policy effects. As a result, there is a mismatch between the importance of many private decisions and the degree of public involvement in them. Most citizens are bystanders and spectators when these critical decisions are made. Although ordinary people are not completely powerless, their ability to affect corporate decisions is quite limited.

The trend in the 1960s and 1970s was toward greater government intervention in the private sector to promote goals such as racial integration and affirmative action, affordable housing, environmental protection, and consumer protection. From the 1980s to 2008, government intervention, particularly that of the federal government, diminished somewhat as a result of deregulation and privatization. Some see great advantages in a reduced government role because privatizing conflicts reduces the number of issues on which public policymakers must achieve consensus and thus makes governing less difficult. Regardless of how one assesses its merits, less government intervention leaves more decisions in the hands of corporate managers and corporate boards. After taking office in 2009, President Obama and his administration took some steps in the direction of stricter regulation of some private sector industries and activities, but the changes were modest overall.

In making strategic decisions, managers and board members of publicly held corporations are influenced by investors and their perceived interests. But it is often difficult to discern the course of action that will yield maximum benefits for a corporation and its investors. There is the issue of short-term versus long-term profitability, the need to stay on a par with the competition, and the desire to blunt criticisms from consumers and the government. Privately held corporations have greater flexibility in making decisions than government agencies and legislative bodies, but they have similar difficulty in determining what will produce the most favorable bottom line.

Not surprisingly, corporations have made some spectacular mistakes. Employees are the most obvious victims of corporate mistakes; layoffs inflict economic and psychological damage. Moreover, neither the government nor the private sector goes very far to ensure that displaced workers will land on their feet. From the standpoint of most of those without jobs, the U.S. government does little to cushion the blow of unemployment or to prepare them for new jobs. Needless to say, five years (starting in 2008) of consistently high unemployment have caused ripple effects throughout society. Median family incomes have fallen, cities have gone bankrupt, and states are facing very tough decisions, especially when it comes to the wages and benefits of public employees.[110]

Consumers also suffer when corporations make mistakes. Despite the work of government agencies such as the Consumer Product Safety Commission, the Food and Drug Administration, the National Highway Traffic Safety Administration, the Occupational Safety and Health Administration, and the new Consumer Financial Protection Bureau, companies still produce defective automobiles, tires, birth control devices, drugs, toys, and power plants. Finally, taxpayers are harmed by poor corporate judgment. Cost overruns on government contracts and bailouts of failed corporations or industries are the most obvious examples. Companies do learn from their mistakes, but they learn slowly. In the meantime, the nation pays a heavy price for their errors.

Our intention in evaluating boardroom politics is not to be overly harsh. The government bears partial responsibility for many corporate mistakes. In appraising boardroom politics, we must ask not whether it is perfect, but whether it is superior or inferior to other political processes where the scope of conflict is broader. By examining these other political processes in the chapters that follow, we will be able to make useful comparisons.

Bureaucratic Politics

The federal government employs just over 2.8 million civilians. State and local governments account for just under 20 million additional public employees.[1] Congress, the presidency, and the courts, with their supporting coterie of staff members, advisers, and patronage appointees, make up about 2 percent of the federal total, and their institutional counterparts at the state and local levels claim similarly small shares of their public workforces. Most government employees work in executive branch agencies administering programs or providing services to citizens; these workers are referred to as bureaucrats. The American bureaucracy, or the "administrative state," is often said to constitute a fourth branch of government.[2]

These bureaucrats work in the Internal Revenue Service (IRS) office in Philadelphia sorting tax returns, entering information into computers, and sending electronic files to an IRS center in West Virginia. They work for the Nuclear Regulatory Commission (NRC) as field investigators reviewing plant construction plans with engineers from the Duke Energy Corporation and negotiating agreements on contested issues having to do with power plant construction or operating standards. They are highway patrol officers enforcing speed limit laws and bans on driving while intoxicated.

Sometimes bureaucrats have to make controversial decisions. In 2012, amid public outcries about distracted drivers, the Federal Motor Carrier Safety Administration (of the Department of Transportation [DOT]) issued new rules prohibiting commercial drivers from texting while driving. To do this, the agency had to define texting—"manually entering text into, or reading text from, an electronic device"—and set fines for violators: $2,750 for drivers and $11,000 for employers who allow drivers to text. Whether these penalties are hefty enough to discourage the behavior the DOT is trying stop remains to be seen.[3]

Central to the political world of bureaucratic agencies are the statutes authorizing their existence and specifying their structures, activities, and budgets. Also central are the relevant legislative committees, interest groups, and citizens whose lives are affected by the particular bureaucracy. Many agencies carry out policies on the basis of broad, vague statutes. The federal

Communications Act of 1934, for example, instructed the Federal Communications Commission (FCC) to regulate the broadcasting industry in accordance with "the public interest, convenience, and necessity." The Wagner Act of 1935 created the National Labor Relations Board (NLRB) and instructed it to control "unfair labor practices."[4] Even more detailed statutes, such as environmental laws or those creating social service programs, give agencies significant discretion in determining how a policy will be implemented. After all, legislators cannot anticipate all the contingencies of policy implementation, and in some cases they may not even be sure of what they want out of policies. Policymakers often agree on general principles, but cannot agree on the details that would give government officials clear direction. The discretionary power delegated to administrative agencies, whether intentional or not, is a vital component of bureaucratic politics.

The size, structure, and resources of an agency are also essential to its identity. Large staffs and budgets generally carry a certain measure of power and influence, and consume the time of the legislatures that debate how agencies should be organized, to whom they should report, and how much money they should receive. The range of variation in staffing and resources is enormous (see Table 4-1). Figure 4-1 shows the organizational structure of a typical bureaucratic agency, in this case the Department of Health and Human Services (HHS).

Contrary to popular belief, most bureaucrats do not try to be obstructionist or unpleasant. Indeed, they are very attentive to the concerns and preferences of certain noteworthy individuals and groups: the occupational or categorical groups they serve, the industries they regulate, and the ideological groups with whom they share an affinity. These private sector groups are often referred to as an agency's "clientele." Bureaucrats are also particularly attentive to legislative committees and high-ranking executive branch officials. They usually respond very quickly to requests or inquiries from members of congressional committees and subcommittees that have jurisdiction over their agencies: they are somewhat slower in responding to inquiries from private citizens.[5] Having and maintaining supporting coalitions both within and outside government is often the key to agency strength and survival. To put it more emphatically, bureaucrats must have the support of various groups and political elites in order to succeed.[6]

Internal forces are another aspect of bureaucratic politics. Government agencies typically put many knowledgeable and well-trained individuals to work on highly complex problems; these individuals soon acquire additional expertise and develop preferred ways of dealing with such problems. Expert knowledge and standard operating procedures simplify daily decisions and help protect an agency from outside criticism and legal challenges. In addition, skillful leadership within the bureaucracy is necessary because an agency's success depends in part on its positive relationships with other government officials.

TABLE 4-1 **Outlays and Employees of Federal Departments and Selected Agencies, 2011**		
Agency	Outlays (in millions)	Full-time employees
Health and Human Services	$889,290	83,745
Social Security Administration	$784,535	70,270
Defense	$691,471	771,614
Treasury	$492,180	112,541
Agriculture	$140,677	98,235
Labor	$130,168	16,554
Veterans Affairs	$122,798	312,878
Transportation	$70,512	58,189
Housing and Urban Development	$48,528	9,818
Education	$43,628	4,611
Homeland Security	$41,648	191,197
Justice	$29,184	118,104
State	$26,879	12,086
Energy	$22,631	16,651
National Aeronautics and Space Administration	$18,432	18,732
Interior	$12,279	72,168
Environmental Protection Agency	$8,565	18,737
Commerce	$5,704	45,348

Sources: Office of Management and Budget, as presented in *CQ Weekly,* February 20, 2012; Curtis W. Copeland, "The Federal Workforce: Characteristics and Trends," April 19, 2011, www.digital.library.unt .edu/ark:/67531/metadc40238/m1/1/high_res_d/RL34685_2011Apr19.pdf.

CIVIL SERVANTS AT WORK

What is it that bureaucrats do? How much discretion do they enjoy? To whom are they accountable? To answer these questions, we must first discuss the functions that bureaucracies, and the civil servants who work in them, are expected to perform.

Executing Tasks

American bureaucracies have two major functions—regulation and service delivery—and the issues of bureaucratic politics fall into these categories.

FIGURE 4-1   The U.S. Department of Health and Human Services

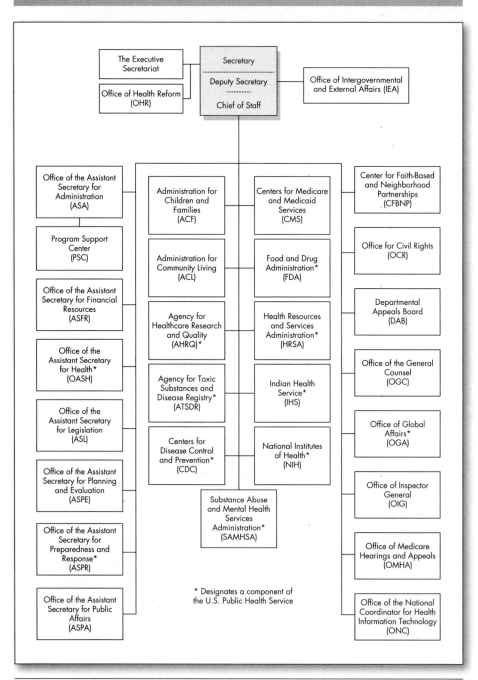

Source: Department of Health and Human Services, "HHS Organizational Chart," www.hhs.gov/about/orgchart/.

Virtually every administrative agency was created either to regulate private sector industries or to provide services to citizens, including the monthly cash payments made by the Social Security Administration and preschool education provided by the Head Start program, which is managed by the Administration for Children and Families of HHS. Many large agencies or departments perform both functions. The distinction between the two is obvious when we contrast, for example, the regulation of food and drug quality with the provision of college loans or medical care. But it is also obvious that all government service delivery and cash transfer programs must have regulatory components that identify eligible recipients, outline procedures, and prohibit certain actions. The distinction between regulatory and service delivery policy is not hard and fast.

Regulatory policy occupies an important place in American history. Federal laws passed in the late nineteenth century to regulate railroad pricing and corporate mergers were a central part of the Populist and Progressive reaction to the arbitrary practices of big business. These precedent-setting government interventions into the private sector were quite controversial at the time. The present scope of government regulation is enormous, encompassing such areas of private sector activity as advertising, agriculture, air and water pollution, aviation safety, banking, consumer products, corporate mergers, food and drug quality, hospitals and medical practice, nuclear energy, radio and television, transportation, and utility pricing. And regulation is still a controversial enterprise. Regulatory statutes provide aggrieved parties with the right to appeal agency decisions, which means that many of these issues are resolved through formal judicial procedures either within the agency or in the court system (discussed in chapter 7). Therefore, two characteristics of regulatory issues are their focus on the actions of private industry and their highly legalistic nature.

Service delivery issues typically involve categorical groups of citizens and public sector organizations: veterans and the Department of Veterans Affairs, welfare recipients and state departments of social services, state and local governments and the Department of Housing and Urban Development. The issues are usually distributive or redistributive in nature. Should education grants received by welfare recipients be counted as income when determining future benefits? Should local in-kind contributions be counted as meeting matching-funds requirements in federal urban development programs? How should garbage pickups be scheduled in different city neighborhoods? How many people should Postal Service offices serve? The appeals of agency decisions on such matters are likely to be directed at legislators or chief executives, not the courts. Service delivery issues can be contrasted with regulatory issues in that they are confined largely to the public sector and are usually resolved through political rather than legal channels.

Because regulatory policy is aimed at private sector organizations such as businesses and unions, regulatory issues often reflect the concerns of these groups. Utilities and energy companies are usually the first to react to Environmental Protection Agency (EPA) emission rules; the same is true of radio and television stations and FCC decisions, meat packers and drug companies and decisions of the Food and Drug Administration (FDA), and unions and regulations of the NLRB. The rules promulgated by regulatory agencies and the adjudicative decisions they make also provoke questions and criticisms from many other quarters. Citizen groups, legislative committees, other agencies, the media, and citizens all contribute to the ongoing chorus of commentary about regulatory actions or the need for them. Regulatory issues spring largely from this commentary.

Most conflict about service delivery issues originates in much the same way. Services are delivered, and various individuals and groups react. The commentary and subsequent bureaucratic response to it lead to the definition of problems for which solutions must be sought. Like regulatory policy, government-sponsored social service programs in the United States had a slow, halting start, but they are now extensive.[7] The government provides a vast array of cash and in-kind assistance programs to poor, elderly, unemployed, disabled, and handicapped Americans, as well as to veterans, farmers, migrant workers, and many other categories of needy individuals. In 2013, the federal government will spend approximately $1.3 trillion on Social Security and Medicare, and another $900 billion on various social programs to help low and moderate income Americans. In addition, many people and private firms benefit from "tax expenditures," such as the earned income tax credit for low wage earners, and tax credits or deductions for health and pension benefits or for using renewable energy sources.[8] Governments at all levels also supply traditional public services such as highway construction and maintenance, water and sewers, police and fire protection, and parks and recreational facilities. The programs through which all these services are provided are subject to varying degrees of scrutiny, as are the agencies that administer them, and issues arise among those who are watching, such as congressional committees, and those who are receiving—the intended beneficiaries.

Shaping Agendas

Administrative agencies have an instinctive reaction when issues are raised about their performance, and that is to try to define them in nonthreatening ways and to process complaints through established channels. If advocates for poor individuals are complaining about bureaucratic insensitivity, contradictory and self-defeating regulations, and meager budgets, the likely response by federal or state agencies will be to define the issues in very specific terms. Should caseloads be decreased by a certain percentage? Should day care allowances be increased to $100 from $75 per week? In the regulatory realm, complaints about testing requirements for chemical pesticides, for example, would be whittled down to very specific questions about the number and kinds of tests that must be completed, the time allowed for test results to be released, and the physical and procedural safeguards that should accompany the use of the chemicals. These are the kinds of questions and issues bureaucratic agencies can deal with effectively. Broad questions about fairness, equity, sensitivity, and the like are usually matters of statutory law and, therefore, are more likely to be debated and decided by legislative and executive authorities, or judges.

Bureaucrats normally play what Laurence Lynn calls "the low game." This means that deep within the bureaucracy, issues are narrowly framed and focused. In Lynn's words, "Low games involve the fine-resolution, small-motor processes of government and reflect the concerns of those with operating responsibilities."[9] Thus, within the federal Administration for Children and Families, the question is not whether to require welfare recipients to work (a high-game decision already made by Congress and the president) but rather how to induce state governments to structure the programs in such a way as to make "workfare" effective.

Despite the operational specificity of bureaucratic agendas, they are by no means unaffected by the "high games" of politicians. Bureaucratic agendas reflect and change with the politics of the administration. An especially good example of this is the recent history of the Civil Rights Division of the Justice Department. During the Carter administration, the Justice Department actively pursued affirmative action by arguing on behalf of numerical hiring goals for blacks, women, and Hispanics in cases involving public agencies, most notably police and fire departments that were being sued for discrimination. Its position on affirmative action changed dramatically under the Reagan administration. The Justice Department began entering employment discrimination cases on the other side, arguing against numerical hiring systems that earlier federal efforts had helped establish.[10] The Clinton administration reversed the Reagan course by making a stronger effort to enforce civil rights laws through the Justice Department and the Equal Employment Opportunity Commission (EEOC), and President Clinton expressed strong support for the concept of affirmative action despite U.S. Supreme Court decisions that questioned its legitimacy.[11] Not surprisingly, the priorities of both agencies changed during George W. Bush's administration; for example, the staff of the EEOC was cut by 25 percent, and Justice Department hires in the Civil Rights Division were screened to prevent liberal civil rights lawyers from being employed.[12] And, of course, the Obama administration reestablished Democratic priorities in the Justice Department and the EEOC.

The argument put forth here is that the agenda of bureaucratic politics is determined by the interaction of the major "process streams"—problem identification, the formation of policy proposals, and politics—that run through government.[13] Problems are being identified all the time by individuals and groups affected by bureaucratic actions, by legislators, by the media, by agency personnel, and by other levels of government. Problems for which politically and bureaucratically acceptable solutions are available receive attention, and the rest are postponed and often ignored. Agendas change when these major process streams, particularly the political ones, change. Long lists of identified problems and potential solutions for them are continually circulating around legislative, bureaucratic, and academic communities; those that dominate the agendas of bureaucracies at any given time are those that fit best with the prevailing political climate.[14] Because the chief executive is the most powerful agenda setter, agencies such as the Office of Management and Budget (OMB), and its state-level counterparts, which perform the central clearinghouse and oversight functions for the presidents and governors, play a central role in determining what does or does not conform with an administration's politics and policies. Internal bureaucratic forces, such as standard procedures, expertise, and control of information, can offer considerable resistance to changing political winds, but they cannot completely shield an agency's agenda from the effects of political forces generated at the top.

THE CROSS-PRESSURED BUREAUCRACY

Bureaucrats live in a highly political world where politics and administration are inextricably intertwined. In administering programs and enforcing regulations, bureaucrats are making public policy. Even low-game decisions are laden with policy content. Recognizing this, politicians, interest groups, and judges have stepped up their efforts to influence and control the bureaucracy. As a result, the bureaucracy is more cross pressured than ever before.[15] Power struggles abound, and the bureaucracy's power resources, so impressive during the days of Lyndon Johnson's Great Society (1965–1968), now seem finite and stretched.

Power

Power in the world of bureaucratic politics comes in a variety of forms. Career bureaucrats, especially professionals and administrators, have power because of what they know and what they do. Their expertise is based in part on access to and control over specialized information that their organizational superiors may not be able to acquire and process on their own.[16] Engineers for the Army Corps of Engineers or the National Aeronautics and Space Administration (NASA), for example, help shape the practices and policies of those agencies with their specialized training and knowledge. The same is true, but to a lesser extent, of program analysts and managers in agencies such as the Department of Labor and HHS. Clearly, the rarer the expertise, the greater the power that goes with it.[17]

In addition to power based on expertise, there is power conferred by authority. The political executives who are placed at the tops of bureaucratic hierarchies have a certain amount of formal authority to impose their will on an agency or a department. Independent regulatory commissioners have the authority, as specified by Congress, to promulgate rules and adjudicate cases involving the industry practices they regulate. Secretaries of state, attorneys general, and local fire chiefs have a great deal of formal authority over the procedures and policies of their organizations. This power is not always as straightforward as it might first appear, however. There are many areas of overlapping jurisdiction and numerous conflicting claims to authority within the administrative state. This is especially true in the intergovernmental arena, where local, state, and federal agencies frequently compete for power over policy.

A third kind of bureaucratic power comes from outside political alliances, affiliations, and connections. Strong agencies usually have strong constituencies: the politicians and client groups they serve, and other groups that identify with the agency. Reciprocal relationships between bureaucratic organizations and outside interest groups, in which the groups try to protect the agencies from hostile citizens or elected officials in exchange for favorable policies, are common at all levels of government. Notable examples include veterans' groups and the Department of Veterans Affairs, and farmers' organizations and the agricultural industry and the Department of Agriculture. How a policy option affects client groups is a very important consideration in agency policymaking, a consideration that can both guide and constrain action. Courting interest groups is not as easy as it once was, however; the number of groups an agency must be concerned about has proliferated, and they often strongly disagree about policy.[18] For example, the EPA is constantly trying to keep environmental groups satisfied without alienating business groups.

Power Struggles

Policymaking is a continuous enterprise in most bureaucracies. Line bureaucrats (those in direct contact with clients and problems), investigators, and policy analysts supply a steady stream of policy ideas to legislative staffs within an agency for drafting into agency regulations or statutory language. These policy proposals move up through the organizational hierarchy, and high-level officials either accept them or reject them.[19] Top administrators play a pivotal role in the bureaucratic policymaking process because they stand between agency personnel and the central administration—the White House or governors' offices—and have alliances on both sides. They try to satisfy politicians and career staff members by making sure the careerists see some of their ideas put into practice, while preventing conflicts with the chief executive's preferences. Central administrative units—budget and policy offices—are now used by nearly all chief executives to review agency regulations before they are presented for public comment, and legislative proposals before they go to the legislature, as a further check on policy entrepreneurs or renegades within the bureaucracy.

The most common form of power struggle within an agency occurs between the careerists, who have standard routines, turf, and interests to preserve and protect, and agency heads, who seek to promote partisan or ideological agendas. Normally, outright conflict is avoided through "mutual accommodation."[20] Agency heads often have considerable substantive knowledge of the policy issues they confront and experience with the organizations they direct, and they try, for the most part, not to threaten bureaucratic values. On the other side, careerists are accustomed to seeing leaders come and go— the average term of office for presidential appointees is less than three years[21]—and are willing to make certain concessions to appease the leadership of the moment.

When internal bargaining and accommodation procedures break down, which occurs most often when a markedly new policy direction is being imposed from above, bureaucratic conflict ensues. This situation is generally unpleasant; conflicts attract outsiders—interest groups, the media, legislators, and chief executives—and their entry fundamentally changes a bureaucratic political struggle. The power of these outsiders usually overwhelms the bureaucratic combatants and shifts the dispute into the larger political arena. Such a development represents a failure of administrative politics. In this larger arena, almost anything can happen; indeed, it is likely that unusual actions will take place: firings, resignations, or dramatic policy changes or reversals. Shifting policy disagreements to this level is very risky, yet it is sometimes seen as necessary by threatened bureaucratic actors.

A typical scenario of bureaucratic conflict occurs when careerists work through interest groups, legislative committees, the mass media, or the courts to bring to light unwelcome actions or policies of agency heads. A well-publicized example is the controversy over the EPA during Ronald Reagan's first term. Reagan appointed Anne Gorsuch to head the agency, and she and her top staffers, who had little knowledge of or experience with agency procedures or practices, began making major changes, such as new regulations along with personnel and budget alterations. Before long, congressional committees, at the prodding of environmental groups and veteran agency employees, began looking into the EPA's activities. They discovered what appeared to be overt attempts to circumvent environmental statutes.[22] Several resignations resulted, including Gorsuch's, and the president replaced the agency's leadership with a group of experienced EPA administrators headed by William Ruckelshaus.

Conflicts also arise between political executives and their superiors, including the president. In 1996, for example, President Clinton upset several top officials at HHS when he signed a welfare reform law eliminating welfare as an entitlement for poor Americans. Although Secretary Donna Shalala, who urged the president to veto the law, stayed on, several top HHS officials resigned in protest, including Assistant Secretary Mary Jo Bane, Assistant Secretary Peter Edelman, and Deputy Assistant Secretary Wendell Primus.[23] These resignations highlighted policy differences within the Clinton administration. A similar episode occurred in 2003 when EPA administrator Christine Todd Whitman resigned after her efforts to do something about climate change and harmful power plant emissions were repeatedly rejected by President George W. Bush and Vice President Cheney.[24]

The normal state of a bureaucratic agency is low-visibility politics, unchallenged authority over a certain policy and program domain, and support from outside groups and legislative committees. Under these circumstances, internal administrative norms, tempered by statutes and the policy preferences of agency heads, determine policy. Bureaucratic conflict disrupts normal procedures and relationships. When an agency's authority to make certain decisions is challenged, control can be lost to outside institutions—the legislature, the chief executive, or the courts. This situation is obviously one that agencies try to avoid.

Leadership

Leadership in bureaucratic politics consists of strategies and tactics for gaining and maintaining a powerful and autonomous role for bureaucratic actors in the policy process. Bureaucratic officials exercise influence over a certain realm of policy in large part because they are able to use organizational tools to mask the extent of their power. Plainly, certain administrative officials are more successful in this endeavor than others. Robert Moses, who planned and saw through to completion much of New York City's present infrastructure of highways, bridges, tunnels, and parks, was a strong leader. Another was Admiral Hyman Rickover, who, despite the misgivings of most other navy leaders, led the navy into the nuclear era by showing that nuclear reactors could be designed to power submarines. J. Edgar Hoover, who shaped the Federal Bureau of Investigation (FBI) to his own specifications and became powerful enough to challenge presidents, was a leader of almost mythic strength.[25] More recently, James Lee Witt transformed the Federal Emergency Management Agency from (in the words of one senator) the "sorriest bunch of bureaucratic jackasses I've ever encountered" to a highly effective agency during the Clinton administration.[26] Analyses of the careers of these and other bureaucratic leaders suggest that leadership in the administrative state has three basic determinants: motivation, context, and personal ability.

In his classic study of bureaucracy, Anthony Downs developed an excellent typology for understanding the motivations of bureaucratic leaders. He described **climbers**, who are interested only in power, money, and prestige; **conservers**, who seek "convenience and security" above all else; **zealots**, who vigorously promote certain ideas and policies and seek power to advance these ideas; **advocates**, who promote somewhat broader organizational interests and policies and seek power as a way of advancing or elevating their organizational functions; and **statesmen**, who promote the public interest, and seek power to steer government in a direction that is advantageous to the society as a whole.[27]

Using Downs's framework, it becomes apparent that effective bureaucratic leadership depends on the political context an agency faces. Young agencies, for example, usually need advocates, and maybe a few zealots, to establish a reputation and power base in policymaking circles. Sargent Shriver's vigorous promotion of the Peace Corps in the early 1960s is often cited as a classic example of effective advocacy on behalf of a fledgling agency. Admiral Rickover was essentially a nuclear power zealot, and he fought to establish his own organizational domain within the navy's Bureau of Ships to get his projects under way. There is no guarantee, however, that zealots will promote the best interests of their organizations. If a zealot's worldview conflicts with an organization's basic goals, "sabotage" is a distinct possibility.[28]

Advocates, but also conservers, can be effective defenders of agencies during periods of budget stringency, a time when more statesmanlike behavior might result in dramatic agency losses. Of course, these days budget stringency is more or less a constant in governmental settings. Zealots come to the fore when functional crises hit—when dams break, hurricanes strike, power plants or electrical grids fail, satellites explode, or reserve stockpiles of toxic wastes overflow—because such circumstances put a premium on ideas and people who are sure of their ideas. Robert Moses, Admiral Rickover, and J. Edgar Hoover were always sure of their ideas, and they rose to prominence during crises—the Great Depression, World War II, and the Cold War. In quieter times, their aggressive brand of leadership may be both less necessary and less acceptable.

Many effective bureaucratic leaders are entrepreneurs who extend their organizational domain and become more powerful. Moses used his base as president of the Long Island State Park Commission and chairman of the New York State Council of Parks during the early 1920s to become the head of more than ten city, state, and metropolitan commissions and authorities at the peak of his career in the late 1950s.[29] Entrepreneurs such as Moses exhibit the characteristics of advocates and climbers; they aggressively promote their organization and themselves. Bureaucratic imperialism is not always possible or even desirable, however. When the climate of opinion, elite and public, regarding an agency is unfavorable, bureaucratic leaders often try to consolidate rather than extend their authority.[30] At times, bureaucratic leaders even ask that their agencies' jurisdictions be narrowed. For example, in the late 1990s, the head of the Bureau of Indian Affairs (BIA) asked Congress to transfer responsibility for recognizing Native American tribes to another agency. Facing a surge of recognition applications by groups hoping to cash in on the benefits offered by tribal casinos, the BIA's leader concluded that this task was distracting his agency from other, more important duties.[31]

The need for statesmanlike leadership is most evident in mature administrative organizations and during times of national crisis, when it is important to offset the myopic inclinations of advocates, zealots, climbers, and conservers. Hoover was discredited in part because his zealous leadership was no longer appropriate in a mature and established FBI. One of the most serious problems in the administrative state is not having a leadership that is flexible enough to adapt to changing political environments, and one of the major impediments to flexible leadership is that some of the most consistently rewarded bureaucratic motives—those of advocates, zealots, and conservers—are not particularly conducive to flexible leadership.

Having examined motivation and context, we now turn to individual ability. Studies of bureaucratic organizations have identified a consistent set of attributes, behavioral patterns, and outlooks associated with successful leaders. Leadership in administrative politics demands intelligence, especially the ability to acquire substantive knowledge and to use organizational processes; the will to achieve or succeed; highly developed interpersonal skills; the willingness and ability to listen and learn from others; and the inclination to enjoy organizational and political work and the exercise of power.[32] Leaders are quick to identify the wielders of power and know how to deal with them in various situations. They are capable of thinking creatively, of solving difficult problems, and of resolving internal conflicts. They appreciate the normative and symbolic aspects of their decisions and actions, and take seriously their role as teachers and promoters of esprit de corps. They must also know how to make effective use of the media when circumstances require it or when opportunities present themselves. A new framework for understanding bureaucratic leadership emphasizes three factors, all of which are consistent with those described above. Bureaucratic leaders are more likely to succeed if they have expertise and experience relevant to the agency they are leading, make commitments that are perceived as credible and follow through on them, and have a flair for publicity that is used to cast the agency in a favorable light.[33]

Although personal ability is sometimes enhanced by charisma, the two are not synonymous. For example, the head of the Forest Service during the Clinton administration, Mike Dombeck, proved remarkably adept as a bureaucratic leader despite a tendency to speak in a monotone and having an image of being a bit of a "square." Ultimately, those traits proved less important than an enormous reservoir of patience, a good sense of humor, and a strong commitment to wilderness preservation. During his tenure at the Forest Service, Dombeck changed agency policies and incentives to make concrete progress on environmental goals such as forest preservation and the protection of watersheds and wildlife.[34]

Another example of exceptional bureaucratic leadership is former Secretary of Defense Robert Gates. Not only did he have to manage the largest department in the federal government, but he also had to do so with two wars (in Iraq and Afghanistan) in progress. He performed well enough that something rarely seen in contemporary Washington occurred: he served for two years under conservative Republican George W. Bush and then for two more under liberal Democrat Barack Obama. Gates, a former Central Intelligence Agency (CIA) head and university president, who was not particularly charismatic, succeeded by being knowledgeable, experienced, politically and organizationally astute, flexible, creative, and straightforward in his dealings with members of Congress and the media.

Like most analysts, we have stressed the role of high-profile political executives as bureaucratic leaders. But civil servants also provide leadership on numerous occasions. Consider, for example, the role of David Edie, a civil servant with the Wisconsin Department of Health and Social Services in the 1980s. Edie, the department's child care coordinator, spearheaded over a three-year period a departmental effort to craft a new set of rules that would be more acceptable and less costly to providers, and that would be easier for the department to enforce. The result was a substantial improvement over the status quo.[35] Edie's initiative and perseverance were essential, but it is important to add that his efforts ultimately succeeded because he won the tacit support of political executives within his agency and key members of the Wisconsin state legislature.

How Bureaucracies Decide

The literature on political and organizational decision making is emphatic about the tendency of public bureaucracies to make only marginal changes in existing policies in any given round of decision making, a practice known as incrementalism.[36] Administrative decision makers rarely consider problems in their entirety. They restrict themselves to a specialized slice of the problem, react to feedback about the success or failure of current policy by considering a limited number of alternative approaches, and choose options that seem to satisfy all or most of the major interests in their political environment.[37] Past policy decisions serve as the highly valued base for subsequent decisions precisely because of their political character: they represent the best compromises decision makers could devise in the past, and in the absence of overwhelming evidence to the contrary, there is no reason to believe that the problems or the attendant politics have changed enough to require a radically new approach.

Incremental decision making is in many ways a result of bureaucratic inertia (the adherence to standard operating procedures or professional norms, and the presence of internal support for long-standing policies), which has a powerful conservative effect on administrative decisions.[38] The specialized knowledge and information that exist in the middle and lower levels of the bureaucracy are often used effectively to protect internal interests. From his study of information transmission in the military, Morton Halperin identified eleven different ways information can be packaged to influence decisions.[39] The following are some of them: report only those facts that support the stand you are taking; structure the reporting so that senior participants will see what you want them to see and not other information; request a study from those who will give you the desired conclusions; advise other participants on what to say; direct the facts toward a desired conclusion if necessary and if you can get away with it.[40] In his study of police and other "street-level" bureaucratic behavior, Michael Lipsky notes that police officers often exaggerate the danger connected with their jobs to reduce the likelihood that superiors will impose sanctions on those who take certain "threat-reducing" actions—in other words, engage in tough treatment of suspected criminals.[41]

The link between bureaucratic politics and incrementalism does not entirely eliminate the importance of rational or analytic factors in bureaucratic decision making. The so-called rational model of decision making would have administrators look at problems comprehensively and use certain analytic techniques to evaluate policy options with precision. Rational decision making can be distinguished from incremental or political decision making in that a wider range of alternatives for achieving policy objectives can be considered (nonincremental options are not ruled out automatically), and because decision makers search for solutions that provide the most benefits at the lowest cost, rather than for solutions that satisfy as many interests as possible.[42] Rational decision makers use techniques such as cost-benefit analysis in identifying the best solutions to policy problems. Increasingly, they also use various kinds of performance measurement to evaluate programs already in place and the organizations responsible for them.[43]

The Army Corps of Engineers was probably the first government agency to make consistent use of cost-benefit analysis in determining the best water projects to undertake, and in justifying the projects to Congress. For example, a proposal to build a dam on a particular river to create a lake would be evaluated by listing all the costs and benefits of the project and then attaching dollar values to them. The costs would include items such as the value of the land that would be flooded, the cost of relocating families whose homes would be destroyed, the value of lost recreational opportunities, and the cost of construction. The benefits would include new hydroelectric power, irrigation water for farmers, new recreational opportunities, and reduced damage from floods.[44] (Retrospective examinations of the Army Corps cost-benefit analyses revealed that many of them were "cooked" to support projects favored by members of Congress.[45])

Market prices are commonly used in assigning dollar amounts to costs and benefits. Where no market values apply, as with questions regarding the preservation of natural habitats or the psychological and social turmoil associated with destroying communities, imagination and creativity must be put to use. Some recent innovations on this score include "revealed preferences," in which analysts use behavior to measure the value people place on environmental amenities (how much people pay to visit a virgin forest, for example), or "stated preferences," in which such values are measured through surveys.[46] The basic rule of cost-benefit analysis is that projects whose benefits are larger than their costs should be pursued, with the proviso that future costs and benefits must be discounted to their present value to make this determination. When there are many potential projects from which to choose and there is a limited amount of money that can be spent, as is the case in any real-world setting, the projects offering the largest net benefits, often expressed by benefit-to-cost ratios, are preferred. As this brief discussion of cost-benefit analysis illustrates, the technique can provide decision makers with fairly clear-cut choices. But many assumptions—that market prices accurately reflect the social value of different outcomes, for example—and a good deal of guesswork, especially in projecting future costs and benefits, go into the final calculations.

Although related to cost-benefit analysis, performance measurement differs from it in its focus on whether existing programs or strategies are working as intended. In the past, performance measurement efforts within government were fairly crude, focusing on agency "outputs" such as the number of people served, the number of inspections conducted, the number of checks written, or the number of penalties imposed. The Government Performance and Results Act (GPRA) of 1993 tried to change all that by requiring federal agencies to shift their attention to "outcomes" or results, such as improvements in air quality, workplace safety, or public health. By 2000, all federal agencies were required to prepare annual strategic plans and annual performance plans, to compare stated goals with actual results. In 1997, the General Accounting Office (now the Government Accountability Office [GAO]) and key members of Congress expressed "disappointment" at "uneven" progress toward implementing GPRA.[47] Two years later, the GAO noted that some improvements had occurred, but numerous weaknesses remained. A key problem was that many agencies had great difficulty finding good outcome measures supported by solid data, and that Congress did not seem to pay much attention to performance reports. The GPRA was revamped by Congress in 2010 in an effort to fine-tune performance-based reporting.[48]

George W. Bush's administration instituted a performance-based evaluation system within the OMB to rate federal programs as effective, moderately effective, adequate, ineffective, or "results not yet demonstrated," and then used the scores in making agency budget decisions. This system did achieve some success in encouraging agencies to come up with credible performance measures. The Obama administration modified the Bush program performance system a bit to emphasize "high-priority performance goals" within federal departments and agencies. The idea is to encourage bureaucratic officials to identify outcomes that would yield important benefits for American society, and then do what is necessary to achieve them.[49]

One problem with rational approaches to decision making is that most administrators find them difficult to use because of the cognitive demands they impose, such as evaluating long lists of alternatives and sorting through highly technical analyses, and because of the economic pressure caused by the amount of staff time needed to complete all the analytic chores. In the case of performance measurement, administrators must wrestle with a more specific dilemma: They have a good deal of control over agency outputs, but the connection between outputs and outcomes may be weak. Also, outcomes matter more, but they depend on many factors that are beyond the control of agency officials. If agency officials truly measure outcomes, they may be blamed for statistics that reflect the vicissitudes of economic activity, the weather, and other forces well outside their jurisdiction and control. Not surprisingly, many administrators have viewed performance measurement requirements with nervousness and suspicion.

Overall, the influence that analytic procedures have on administrative decisions varies according to the nature of the problem and the dispositions of decision makers. Highly technical matters invite analytic solutions, but most of the questions administrators confront are too political to be answered wholly by analysis. Richard Zerbe puts it nicely when he argues that "the role of benefit-cost analysis is to provide information relevant to the decision, not to provide the decision."[50] The same is true of performance measurement. If the numbers reveal that a particular strategy isn't working, they do not necessarily indicate whether the solution is to spend more, spend less, fine-tune the strategy, or abandon it altogether. Among bureaucratic officials there are many who dislike and distrust analysis, but a growing number are comfortable with it.[51] Many see mastery of policy planning and analytic activities as a path to greater power and influence in decision-making circles because analysis has become an accepted part of the process by which most high-level bureaucratic decisions are made. Unless the interests associated with policy decisions have numbers to back up their views, they operate at a disadvantage.

RULES AND REGULATIONS

Bureaucratic policies come in many different forms. First, there are written rules and regulations that have wide applicability and carry the force of law. Second, there are adjudicatory decisions that settle, through quasi-judicial procedures, disputes between antagonistic parties, usually an agency and a business accused of violating an administrative rule or regulation. Third, there are guidelines, policy statements, and advisory opinions that convey to interested parties an agency's thinking or intentions about various matters, but do not have the full legal force of formal rules and regulations. Fourth, there are informal means of settling disputes that do not entail full adjudication. Finally, there are the actions that line bureaucrats take that define the meaning of regulatory or service delivery policy in practice.

Administrative agencies have developed a mountain of rules and regulations that specify the meaning of legislative statutes. These are published in the *Federal Register* and the *Code of Federal Regulations* and in comparable documents in the states and localities. The adoption of such rules and regulations at the federal level takes place in accordance with procedures spelled out in the Administrative Procedure Act of 1946 (APA); similar statutes exist in most states. When an agency wants to develop rules to enforce provisions of statutes, which Congress has authorized agencies to do, the APA requires that (1) a public notice be entered in the *Federal Register* specifying the time, place, and nature of the rule-making proceedings; (2) interested parties be given the opportunity to submit written, and in some cases oral, arguments and facts relevant to the rule; and (3) the statutory basis and purpose of the rule be indicated. After rules are promulgated, thirty days' notice is required before they take effect.[52] These procedures, known as "notice and comment" or "informal" rulemaking, are designed to give everyone (citizens and interest groups) a chance to participate in this essentially legislative activity.

Two relatively new wrinkles in the informal rule-making arena are electronic rulemaking and negotiated rulemaking (reg-neg). Beginning with the Clinton administration, and expanding during George W. Bush's administration, agencies can post rule-making information on an electronic platform and allow individuals and groups to submit comments via e-mail. Many federal departments and agencies now do this. When agencies use the reg-neg process, they invite those parties that will be most directly affected by a new rule they are contemplating to meet with agency officials, or to be part of an agency advisory committee, to negotiate the details and final form of the rule. The Clinton administration supported and promoted reg-neg, and some recent statutes require it.[53]

The APA rule-making procedures can be much more formal and cumbersome when a statute requires rulemaking "on the record after a formal hearing." Under such circumstances, agencies must conduct proceedings that resemble trials; witnesses present testimony and submit data or other evidence, there are opportunities for cross-examination of witnesses, and interested parties are prohibited from contacting agency officials during the proceedings. After the hearings, time is set aside for further evidence to be submitted, and agency officials must go over the entire record and carefully document their reasons for issuing a rule. Such hearings often last for weeks or even months. Although agencies are seldom enthusiastic about this degree of formality, they may use this procedure even when they are not required to do so by statute as a means to blunt criticism of the rules, and perhaps more important, to bolster their position with the courts, whose reviews of contested agency rules typically focus on the adequacy of the procedures used in rulemaking.

Administrative adjudication has a narrower focus than rulemaking. When there is a disagreement between a company and a union about labor standards, or between the Social Security Administration and a recipient about eligibility for certain benefits, or between a utility company and the NRC about a plant safety issue, a settlement can be reached through adjudication. The procedures are similar to those in a court of law: formal notifications to appear are given to all parties, public records are kept, only certain kinds of evidence are admissible, and each party gets a chance to cross-examine adverse witnesses.[54]

To conduct these proceedings, the bureaucracy employs specially trained personnel, called administrative law judges, who bring with them impartiality and legal and substantive knowledge.[55] The judges interpret administrative law as it applies to the particular case and either issue "orders" (in other words, make decisions) or submit recommendations for decisions to commissioners or chief administrators. In many instances, adjudicated cases are appealed to federal courts. Adjudicated decisions provide a clear indication of agency policies with regard to the specific issues raised in particular cases, but unlike rules and regulations, they do not establish policy that can be applied with confidence to similar cases.

Bureaucratic agencies also make policy statements and issue advisory opinions, but these pronouncements, usually made informally, are not as authoritative as rules and regulations. Statements and advisory opinions enable an agency to tell individuals or companies how it intends to react to certain actions or conditions, or what that agency's operating policy is, with the understanding that such statements do not bind the agency and are subject to full review by the courts, which regard such guidelines as less deserving of deference than formal rules or adjudicatory decisions. An example of a policy statement is a 2010 announcement by the Federal Reserve and other federal banking agencies reminding banks that they should maintain "sound funding and liquidity risk management practices" by taking various steps such as having diversified funding sources, conducting stress tests, and maintaining a cushion of liquid assets.[56] Businesses of all sorts seek advisory opinions from agencies such as the Federal Trade Commission (FTC), the Securities and Exchange Commission, the Labor Department, and the EPA on matters ranging from whether certain employees are subject to provisions of the Fair Labor Standards Act to whether certain air pollution devices will satisfy Clean Air Act requirements.

Advisory opinions often are issued to head off litigation. In fact, most of the disputes about policy enforcement that could lead to litigation or to formal adjudication are resolved through informal agreements between agency personnel and the other parties involved. For example, the Labor Department and a company agree that an outside arbiter should meet with company employees to discuss their grievances, or a drug company promises the FDA that it will conduct additional tests on a medical device under scrutiny. These informal agreements are another attempt to cope with reality because agencies cannot possibly use formal adjudication to resolve all the disagreements they encounter about matters of fact and policy application.

The day-to-day actions taken by bureaucratic officials in their efforts to administer statutory law represent a final large piece of the policy picture. As incredible as it may seem, despite the thousands and thousands of pages of administrative rules and regulations, many real-life situations are still ambiguous, and on-the-spot bureaucratic discretion is needed. Street-level bureaucrats, such as police officers and welfare caseworkers, are continually faced with the need to make judgments in ambiguous situations—when to make arrests for certain crimes, when to waive certain evidentiary requirements for benefits or special assistance.[57] Although the use of such discretion may seem inevitable, many argue that the police and others who engage in selective enforcement should establish more rules and follow them in more situations.[58] Policy that is determined through direct action or informal agreement tends to be unsystematic and inconsistent; but there are limits to what can be specified, and in certain circumstances, there are advantages to be gained for an agency and its clients from acting informally.

Symbolism

At first glance, bureaucratic politics would not seem to provide fertile ground for symbolism. After all, it is the bureaucracy that has to translate the often ambiguous and symbolic statutes enacted by legislatures into concrete rules and activities. Bureaucrats cannot fudge the details; they have to make decisions about who gets what, where, and how. When an individual is granted public assistance, or a firm is fined for polluting a river, that means the administrative state has acted in a tangible, substantive manner. Rules, regulations, and adjudicative decisions allocate benefits, specify administrative procedures, and prescribe certain public sector or private sector behaviors; none of these would seem to be symbolic exercises. Furthermore, most administrative officials do not conceive of their activity as symbolic. They see themselves as executing the will of the legislature—defining problems, designing solutions, and evaluating the effectiveness of past actions.

Several scholars who have written about bureaucracy have emphasized its symbolic aspects, however. At one extreme, some argue that the administrative state exists largely to carry out symbolic functions.[59] Regulatory policy is said to provide reassurance to the citizens that certain decisions (concerning transportation and banking regulation, for example) are being made with regard for their interests, even though the results of the decisions may not benefit them. Regulatory policy also serves notice to the regulated industries that punitive steps may be taken if they engage in excessively selfish behavior, even though such steps are rarely taken. The administrative policies of social welfare agencies are designed to indicate to the lower classes that they are not entitled to government assistance, even though many of them are, while suggesting to the middle class that assistance is available to anyone who really needs it, even though it is not, and finally to reassure the upper classes that traditional values of individualism and self-reliance are not being abandoned.[60] The thrust of such arguments is that administrative policies, either purposefully or unwittingly, are designed not to solve problems but rather to appease or legitimate certain interests, and to provide an institutional forum in which recognized interests can compete for influence over policy.

One can find symbolism in other administrative behaviors. Federal and state commissions may hold hearings to obtain citizen input or to grant agenda status to issues raised by grassroots groups, but then continue to formulate policies in accordance with bureaucratic or industry preferences, thereby revealing the symbolic nature of their public actions.[61] Highway patrol officers send a symbolic message when they allow motorists to exceed the speed limit by ten miles per hour. Social workers also send symbolic messages if they keep welfare clients waiting in their outer office for long periods of time. Whether bureaucratic officials recognize it in their actions or not, symbolism is an unavoidable aspect of policy implementation and enforcement.

Change

Bureaucracies depend on continuity. Most agencies prefer to build up a solid base of effective policies and then work carefully and patiently to extend that base as they confront new problems. This way of working is the incrementalism described in several of the previous sections. However, administrative agencies are capable of change and innovation. This observation applies not only to recently established agencies, where one might expect some novelty, but also to older ones. Politics, not incrementalism, is the constant in bureaucratic life. When political developments convince bureaucratic leaders that change and innovation are necessary, they can bring them about.

During the 1970s, significant changes took place in administrative policies, especially in the area of regulation. These changes can be traced to the growing consumer and environmental movements that brought together previously unorganized interests to exert pressure at all levels of govern-ment.[62] Regulatory agencies and policies, which were notorious for favoring the industries being regulated, were a primary target of consumer and environ-mental groups. Over time these reformers were able to achieve an impressive number of victories over the regulatory dragons. Ralph Nader's breakthroughs on automobile safety regulations helped pave the way for many other reform efforts.[63] State public utility commissions all over the country began eliminat-ing reduced rates for high-volume industrial users after citizen groups armed with the analyses of economists argued convincingly that such pricing schemes discouraged conservation, caused unnecessary strain on generating facilities, and penalized homeowners and poor individuals. The solutions they proposed—peak-load and marginal cost pricing and lifeline rates—were widely adopted.[64] New leadership and supportive political environments also led to the reinvigoration of the FTC as a protector of consumers in the early 1970s and even to a major change to a more environmentally sensitive philosophy within the Army Corps of Engineers.[65] New forces were pushing their way into the political environments of government agencies and were stimulating policy change.

The bureaucracy changed far less in the 1980s, especially at the federal level. Because he viewed the federal bureaucracy as a threat to a market economy, President Reagan sought to tame it rather than to utilize it.[66] But Reagan's policies contributed in interesting ways to a revival of bureaucratic reform initiatives in the 1990s. By stimulating enormous budget deficits, Reagan made it difficult for politicians to endorse new spending programs or increases in the size of the federal bureaucracy. By lambasting the bureau-cracy relentlessly, Reagan helped ensure that the bureaucracy would be an issue in future presidential campaigns. These and other developments, such as the growing professionalism of state bureaucracies, encouraged a new wave of reforms in the 1990s. President Clinton and Vice President Gore vowed to create a leaner, more efficient federal bureaucracy. Under the ban-ner of "reinventing government," they championed numerous reforms, including quicker procurement processes, a sharp reduction in the size of the federal bureaucracy, and greater emphasis on customer service.[67] Both the Clinton administration and Congress supported devolution initiatives that granted greater discretion to state governments and that substituted intergov-ernmental "partnerships" for direct mandates.[68] Both the federal government and many state governments enacted performance measurement legislation that required bureaucracies to measure the results of their activities.[69] If the reforms of the 1970s reflected interest group politics, the reforms of the 1990s exemplified managerial politics. Politicians at all levels of government pro-moted a more efficient, more effective bureaucracy through management reform. By the end of the decade, the federal bureaucracy was 17 percent smaller, state bureaucracies enjoyed greater discretion and respect, and greater attention was being paid to what bureaucracies achieve rather than how they achieve it.

In the twenty-first century, bureaucratic politics and change have taken on a more partisan flavor. Interest in government efficiency and effectiveness continues, as have innovations at the state level, but both regulation and service delivery are very much at the center of partisan battles. Thus, George W. Bush drew directly from the Reagan playbook, using appointments, such as making pro–energy industry advocate Gail Norton the head of the Interior Department, to advance his proindustry agenda; relaxing federal regulatory efforts pretty much across the board of industries, from power plants to banks; and cutting, or trying to cut, regulatory agency and social service program funding.

The Great Recession gave the Obama administration an opening to reestablish credible regulation, and passage of the Dodd-Frank financial regulatory law added some statutory authority to this effort, but the election of 2010 brought much of the re-regulatory movement to a halt as Republicans regained control the House of Representatives. The Dodd-Frank law enabled President Obama to create a new federal agency, the Consumer Financial Protection Bureau, which was intended to protect ordinary citizens from abusive actions by banks and other financial institutions. One of its first actions was to get Capital One to pay its customers over $150 million in rebates for selling credit card products in misleading ways.[70] This was followed by the issuance of new rules that were designed to protect consumers from deceptive mortgage packaging, such as those involving low initial payments and subsequent balloon payments.[71] Two other agencies (the Office of the Comptroller of the Currency, in the Treasury Department, and the Federal Reserve) started a review of banking practices regarding foreclosures during and after the Great Recession in 2011, and by early 2013 had announced a settlement involving ten banks and $8.5 billion, much of which would be paid to households that were victimized by the banks.[72]

Because of the sharpness of partisanship, change and innovation in the administrative state are often short lived. What one administration may "giveth" (in the way of innovation or reform), another may "taketh" away. This is particularly true of key regulatory departments and agencies such as the Justice Department, the Interior Department, the Department of Labor, the Energy Department, the EPA, the FTC, and others.

One entity that has seemed for many years to stand above the partisan fray is the Board of Governors of the Federal Reserve. It is without doubt the most powerful and independent of all the federal independent regulatory commissions. And, going back to the Carter administration, its leadership (chair) has managed to obtain a good deal of bipartisan support. Carter's chairman, Paul Volker, was retained by President Reagan; his successor, Alan Greenspan, was retained by Clinton; and the current chairman, Ben Bernanke, was appointed by George W. Bush and retained by Barack Obama. Since the Great Recession, the Federal Reserve has drawn a good deal of attention with steps it has taken to help the economy recover, which have produced both internal and external critics.[73] In 2012, Republican presidential candidate

Mitt Romney made a point of promising to replace Ben Bernanke if elected, and the Board of Governors was often divided over key decisions.

Winners and Losers

It is commonly alleged that regulatory policies primarily benefit the regulated industries and that social service policies primarily benefit the bureaucrats who administer them. These rather cynical observations can serve as a useful starting point for a discussion of who benefits from administrative politics.

In the regulatory realm, the so-called capture theory is often put forward.[74] The basic argument is that over time, regulated industries come to dominate regulatory agencies. This capture takes place because the fervor for reform, usually stimulated by callous industry behavior that results in the creation of a regulatory entity, recedes over time. Meanwhile, it becomes apparent that the expertise, interest, and dependable political support a regulatory agency needs to sustain itself reside mainly in the regulated industry. As time passes, a symbiotic relationship—the movement of personnel back and forth and shared interest in each other's priorities and policies—develops between the two, and the capture process is well under way. This analysis has been applied fairly convincingly to the former Interstate Commerce Commission and the railroad industry, the former Federal Power Commission and the natural gas industry, the Civil Aeronautics Board (also former) and the airlines, and several other pairs.[75] According to economist George Stigler, some industries come to see regulation as a benefit, mainly because most forms of regulation restrict entry into regulated markets, thereby reducing competition.[76]

There is no doubt that the capture concept is apt for many different regulatory situations past and present, but it is also true that not all regulatory agencies are captured, that captured agencies do not necessarily stay captured, and that some regulatory legislation is intended to promote and protect industry. There are also important differences in regulatory realms that need to be taken into account. The capture theory was typically applied to regulatory agencies that focused on a single industry, or on a limited number of companies, and to situations in which regulatory objectives were primarily economic. Many current regulatory agencies oversee more than one industry and have social objectives, such as environmental protection, health and safety in the workplace, and civil rights. The multifaceted political environments these agencies face make any simple influence model implausible. One would expect these agencies to pursue various objectives—serving the public, accommodating industry, ensuring their own survival—with the emphasis given to each changing over time in accordance with external and internal pressures. As law professor Jonathan Macey has noted, "The interest group that is regulated by a single regulatory agency will be able to influence that agency to a far greater extent than the interest groups that must share their agency with a variety of other interest groups."[77]

Gormley's differentiation of regulatory policies according to complexity and conflict provides a useful framework for sorting out expectations about beneficiaries.[78] Regulations that are not terribly complex, such as seatbelt rules, procedures to cut off service by public utilities for nonpayment of bills, or smoking bans in public facilities, give various groups some say in policy because unusual expertise is not required to exert influence. If citizen advocacy groups are active and skillful, there is a good chance the public will benefit from the policies, or at least that some conception of the public interest will be considered in policymaking. If public advocacy groups are not present, self-interested groups will dominate. When policies are technically complex (for example, the use of genetically altered material, securities fraud, or banking regulations), a proxy advocate (an agency that advocates for the public) is usually needed to secure policies beneficial to the public. In such cases, the specialized expertise and political muscle needed for an effective challenge to objectionable industry behavior may not be available except in a government agency.

In their efforts to influence bureaucratic decision making, interest groups engage in a variety of behaviors. In addition to submitting comments on proposed regulations, they attend hearings sponsored by agencies as part of the rule-making process, they form coalitions with like-minded groups to augment their voice, they meet informally with agency officials before and after rules and regulations have been proposed, and they sometimes try to mobilize grassroots support for their positions to give them more of a public-spirited appearance.[79] In addition, they may contact members of Congress, or congressional committees, to express their views on a proposed agency action with the expectation that legislators will intervene on their behalf. Although the political environments of many agencies are reasonably well balanced, with citizen or public interest groups countering the efforts of business groups (corporations and trade associations), the latter would appear to have an influence advantage overall. To some extent, this advantage boils down to greater resources, which translate into more expertise, greater credibility, and better connections. Business groups are especially effective when agency rules affect them directly, but do not affect many others as directly, and when the agency is operating in a low visibility environment. Media attention tends to reduce the clout of business groups, while increasing the influence of citizen groups.[80] Finally, it should come as no surprise that partisanship matters: business groups do well with many regulatory agencies under Republican administrations; they do less well under Democratic administrations.

The argument linking bureaucrats and social service policies is similar in some ways to capture theory. Concern about poverty in the 1960s brought into being some hastily designed programs that were not nearly strong enough to solve the problem, but they did create a certain number of jobs for those interested in administering social services. Some alleged that black community organizers were the primary beneficiaries of many War on Poverty programs because community groups were enlisted to implement programs, and known minority leaders were hired to administer them. The actual subsidies and services provided by the programs were said to be too meager or too difficult to obtain for the truly needy to benefit, and unnecessary or even harmful for many of those who did receive them.[81]

The systematic research that has been done on social service programs does not completely refute the arguments just presented, but it suggests that they are simplistic and misleading. Food assistance programs, such as the one formerly known as Food Stamps, have helped reduce malnutrition among poor Americans; Medicaid has allowed many low-income people to receive medical treatment previously unavailable to them; job-training programs have helped people find jobs; and Head Start, Upward Bound, and Pell Grants have enabled many minority students to complete high school and college.[82] It is also true, however, that Medicaid has resulted in expensive and in some cases unnecessary treatment, that some of those who benefited most from job-training programs were not especially disadvantaged, and that the largest welfare programs— Temporary Assistance to Needy Families, Food Stamps (now the Supplemental Nutrition Assistance Program), Medicaid, and housing subsidies—do not always encourage self-sufficiency or reward industry and entrepreneurship. A more accurate appraisal of the beneficiaries of social service programs, therefore, would be that recipients of services, as well as bureaucrats, benefit from the programs, but there is clearly a need for ongoing programmatic reform.

Distinctions among service delivery programs should also be noted. The War on Poverty programs are often referred to as "social welfare" programs. As the term suggests, these programs aim to improve the lives and aspirations of poor and disadvantaged citizens. But many American social service programs are not aimed at poor individuals; they have a middle-class clientele. Veterans' benefits and farm subsidies are prime examples, as are Social Security and Medicare (sometimes referred to as "social insurance" programs). Another category of service programs, infrastructure improvements—highways, mass transportation, water and sewer construction projects—benefit the public as a whole, as well as contractors and their employees. Overall, more money is spent on these nontargeted, middle-class programs than on programs designed to help poor individuals. In fiscal year 1996, for example, means-tested human services programs, such as Medicaid, Food Stamps, Supplemental Security Income, and public housing, amounted to $261.3 billion. Although a substantial amount of money, this represented only 16.8 percent of the federal budget.[83] In 2011, the comparable figures were $650 billion and 18 percent.[84]

THE QUEST FOR RESULTS

Implementing policies and programs is the central task of bureaucratic agencies. The goal of these implementation efforts, of course, is to correct or treat the problems that policies and programs were created to address. Yet too often, the results of bureaucratic actions, regulatory and service delivery, are disappointing. The principal reasons for the disappointing results are long standing and fairly well known: programs and policies often have multiple and conflicting goals, implementing agencies are given inadequate resources to

achieve statutory goals, there is a lack of cooperation among various implementation actors and stakeholders, and political officials, legislative and
executive, often intervene during the course of implementation in unhelpful
ways. If programs and policies are not implemented properly, it is highly unlikely
that they will have the impact on society that lawmakers and citizens desire.

Implementation

The EPA is the largest and perhaps the most important federal *regulatory*
entity. As described in Table 4-1, it has over 18,000 employees and an annual
budget of over $8 billion. Still, most experts would argue that the EPA is hope-
lessly unstaffed and underfunded relative to the tasks Congress has asked it to
perform. It has primary responsibility for implementing thirteen major environmental laws, including the Clean Air Act, the Clean Water Act, the Toxic
Substances Control Act, and the Comprehensive Environmental Response,
Compensation, and Liability Act (Superfund), which deals with hazardous
waste sites. Thus air and water quality, the regulation of a vast array of chemicals and pesticides, and the management of all sorts of wastes fall to the EPA.[85]
Not surprisingly their success has been mixed. Air pollution in the United
States has been greatly reduced since the original Clean Air Act was passed in
1970, yet about one-third of all Americans live in areas that do not meet the
EPA's air quality standards. Although many rivers, streams, and lakes have been
cleaned up since the passage of the Clean Water Act in 1972, over a quarter of
the streams in the country are highly polluted.[86]

A somewhat more detailed look at some of the issues the EPA has faced in
implementing the Superfund program offers a glimpse into the challenges it
faces in many of its regulatory efforts. Passed originally in 1980, Superfund has
been amended several times, most recently in 2002. Its principal purpose is to
identify, and then clean up, hazardous substances wherever they may appear
(air, water, and soil), but many of its activities have focused on abandoned
hazardous waste sites. The first step is to find the sites where hazardous wastes
reside. As of 2011, the EPA had identified nearly 90,000 potential contamination sites, and placed 1,652 of them on its National Priorities List (NPL).[87] Full
cleanup has been achieved for about 30 percent of these, but substantial cleanups have occurred for just over 1,100.[88] Cleaning up an NPL site includes two
basic steps: removal and remediation. The former involves making sure the site
is no longer releasing hazardous materials in a way that endangers the public,
while the latter consists of finding and implementing a permanent solution to
the problems posed by the site. Remediation, which is the core of the program,
requires a series of planning and operational actions, several of which are subject to public commentary (notice and comment); the average time that elapses
between listing a site and cleaning it up fully is eight to eleven years, with the
average cost being $2.1 million.[89]

When Superfund was first enacted, following the discovery of a massive
hazardous waste dump in Love Canal, New York, a tax was placed on the oil and
chemical industries to create a trust fund to pay for cleanups when a "potentially

responsible party" (PRP) could not be identified. When PRPs can be found, the law makes them responsible for paying the cleanup costs. The legislative authority for the Superfund tax expired in 1995 (during a Republican Congress) and has not been reinstated since. Therefore, Congress must appropriate funds for Superfund activities annually, and it has, at a level of $1.25 billion.[90] For roughly 30 percent of the NPL sites, the EPA has been unable to identify PRPs, or the PRPs have gone out of business, and the appropriated funds are spent on these sites. For the other 70 percent, the cleanup operations have been paid for by PRPs, at over $3 billion per year in recent years.[91] States are also required to put up 10 percent of the cleanup costs at most sites.

Given the disappearance of the tax-based trust fund (which inspired the program's name), the number of potential and actual sites, the complexity of most remediation plans, and the involvement of multiple actors, the slow and halting progress the EPA has made in cleaning up hazardous waste sites should come as no surprise. Deciding which sites should have highest priority for cleanup, given limited resources, has been a major challenge for the EPA. Disagreements between the EPA and state and local officials over the appropriate cleanup standards have contributed greatly to delays. Litigation is rampant as the federal and state governments sue PRPs, which then sue others they claim are responsible for hazardous wastes and/or their insurance companies. A comprehensive study by the environmental research group Resources for the Future, completed in 2001, found that the $1.2 billion Congress was appropriating for the Superfund program was 25 percent below the level necessary for the EPA to achieve its own goals.[92] Despite all of this, in 2007 the EPA stated that it was making "significant progress" in meeting its Superfund goals.[93]

The first *service delivery* agency of the federal government was the Post Office Department, which George Washington added to his cabinet in 1792. The Post Office, headed by the postmaster general, remained a cabinet-level department until 1971, when it became an independent "establishment" of the federal government as a result of the Postal Reorganization Act of 1970. After 1971, the Postal Service (as it was renamed) operated as a government corporation, which meant that it was supposed to sell its mail services in such a way as to cover its operating expenses (or make a profit), and thus not require annual appropriations from Congress. In fact, the Postal Reorganization Act gave the Postal Service even more independence than other government corporations, like the Tennessee Valley Authority, by exempting it from the provisions of the Government Corporation Control Act. Writing in 1975, bureaucracy scholar Harold Seidman described the Postal Service as "the most independent of the independent agencies," and "practically a law unto itself."[94] It was governed by the postmaster general and a nine-member Board of Governors, all appointed by the president with Senate confirmation, and it operated successfully for many years with increasing volumes of mail delivered, and the cost of postage not growing faster than inflation.[95] However, the image of the Postal Service did take a hit in the 1980s and 1990s, when several shooting incidents involving employees or former employees led to the popularization of the term "going postal," which was a far cry from previous flattering images of heroic Pony Express riders or friendly neighborhood mail carriers.

By the beginning of the twenty-first century, there were growing signs of trouble for the Postal Service. Many of them stemmed from the organization's core model. Congress has long granted the Postal Service a monopoly on the delivery of first- and third-class mail (which includes business advertising) and exclusive access to mailboxes around the country. However, it also tied the Postal Service's hands in many ways, such as requiring mail delivery to all locations in the country six days a week, forcing it to pay for the retirement pensions of its employees at the level mandated for federal employees, and limiting its rate-setting power. By 2001, the Postal Service's problems were being described as a "crisis" by the GAO, and many members of Congress were taking notice. The causes of the crisis included declining revenues from advertising mail because of the recession of 2000 to 2001; a rate-changing process (imposed by Congress) that required excessive negotiation (and time) between the Postal Service and the Postal Rate Commission; competition from other providers of package and express mail delivery service, such as United Parcel Service and FedEx; growing substitution of other media, especially e-mail and online bill-paying services, for traditional mail; and high labor costs and excessive numbers of facilities, especially in rural areas. After several years of haggling, Congress finally passed, and President George W. Bush signed, the Postal Accountability and Enhancement Act of 2006, which among other things replaced the Postal Rate Commission with the Postal Regulatory Commission that had expanded rate-setting powers; created the Postal Service Retiree Health Benefits Fund, into which the Postal Service had to make large ($5.5 billion) prepayments annually; and charged the postmaster general with evaluating the Postal Service's business model and making recommendations for change to Congress.[96]

Not long after this overhaul legislation passed, the Great Recession hit, and the Postal Service was again in trouble; indeed, in deeper trouble than before. Between 2007 and 2011, the Postal Service lost $25 billion. Some of these losses were covered by borrowing from the Treasury Department, which the law allowed up to $15 billion, but clearly the borrowing could not go on forever. Mail volume dropped precipitously, from 212 billion pieces delivered in 2006 to just under 170 billion pieces in 2011, while revenue fell from $75 billion in 2008 to $65.7 billion in 2011.[97] A new major issue was the size of the mandated retiree health benefits payments, which Postal Service officials and other experts argued were too large. At $5.5 billion per year, these payments would more or less account for the $25 billion in losses over the four-year period, except for the fact that only three of the five annual payments during this period were made in full, with Congress providing the Postal Service with temporary and partial relief from this obligation.[98]

The postmaster general, Patrick Donahoe, has offered a plan for correcting the Postal Service's deficit problems, but most of the proposed actions will require legislation from Congress. He has proposed to cut the workforce by 120,000 employees (this is in addition to 250,000 positions that were eliminated between 2001 and 2011), to close nearly 4,000 post offices and 300 of 500 sorting facilities, to eliminate Saturday mail delivery, and to reduce health benefits fund payments by $3 billion per year.[99] In April 2012, the Senate passed a bill that would defer taking most of these steps; a House bill would allow for the cuts and closures, but it never made it to the floor during the 112th Congress of 2012.[100] Thus the once great U.S. Postal Service was looking at default—owing two years worth ($11 billion) of health benefit payments, nearing the end of its borrowing capacity, and continuing to lose money on its operations. On September 30, 2012, the Postal Service defaulted on a $5.6 billion payment that was due.[101] By the end of the year, it reported a $15.9 billion loss, and in the Spring of 2013, the postmaster general first announced and then cancelled plans to suspend Saturday regular mail delivery beginning in August.[102]

Impact

It is hard to imagine the impact of a Postal Service default that threatened the continued operation of its services. Presumably, Congress would act to prevent a stoppage of mail delivery, because the Constitution specifies (Article 1, section 8) that establishing post offices is one of Congress's responsibilities. But as usual, Republicans and Democrats have very different views on what should happen to the Postal Service. Many Republicans are prepared to make extensive changes, such as the large layoffs and the closing of postal facilities the postmaster general has proposed. Democrats generally oppose radical changes.

The struggles of the Postal Service are not unique. The government had to bail out and take over the operations of mortgage lenders Fannie Mae (the Federal National Mortgage Association) and Freddie Mac (the Federal Home Loan Mortgage Corporation) in 2008, and has yet to figure out what to do with them. These two "government-sponsored enterprises" (started by the government, but owned by stockholders) had operated successfully for many years, helping provide home loans to millions of Americans. They were major victims of the collapse of the housing and financial markets in 2008. At the time, Fannie and Freddie either owned or guaranteed about half the home mortgages in the country, so it was pretty much inconceivable that the government would let them default. As of 2012, the Treasury had put up about $150 billion to keep Fannie and Freddie afloat, but by the end of the year, both organizations had regained solvency. Much like the Postal Service situation, the parties differ on the approach they would take. Democrats want to keep Fannie and Freddie in business, and have them help homeowners who are struggling to pay their mortgages. Many Republicans would like to eliminate Fannie and Freddie.[103]

As described in the previous section, the regulatory actions taken by the EPA have had a positive impact on air and water quality in the United States, and in protecting Americans from hazardous and toxic substances. However, there are many parts of the country with significant air pollution problems;

large numbers of contaminated lakes, rivers, and streams; numerous wetlands that are being lost; and widespread groundwater contamination.[104] As we have seen, cleaning up waste sites is expensive and takes a lot of time; therefore, much remains to be done. An interesting new development is that even though the United States is not part of the Kyoto Treaty covering greenhouse gas emissions, carbon dioxide emissions in the United States are declining.[105] This is partly attributable to stricter EPA regulations regarding emissions from coal-fired power plants, including the first regulations to limit carbon dioxide emissions, but equally important have been the explosion in natural gas production in the United States and the low prices of that fuel. Abundant and inexpensive gas has led many utilities to switch from coal to natural gas, thus reducing the percentage of U.S. electricity generated from coal from 50 percent in 2007 to 32 percent in 2012.[106] Of course, no one seems to be happy. Many environmentalists think that much more can and should be done to protect our air, water, natural resources, and wildlife, while many business interests (and Republicans) are convinced that the costs of current regulations are too high and that the EPA represents a clear and present danger to the U.S. economy.

Learning

When bureaucracies and their overseers make mistakes, or fail to perform as expected, a key question is whether they can learn from their past shortcomings and institute appropriate reforms. After the passage of the Clean Air Act of 1990, the EPA was charged with implementing an important new approach to regulation: a market-based "cap and trade" program to limit sulfur dioxide emissions that cause acid rain. The basic idea is simple: the government sets a national cap on annual sulfur dioxide emissions and provides allowances (of one ton each) to established utilities on the basis of their sizes and past levels of emissions, and then the actual emissions are measured and reported to the EPA. The allowances can be used by the utilities that receive them, or sold in a market at the Chicago Board of Trade. Utilities that invest in cleaning technologies may not need their allowances and can make some money selling them; older utilities (those that face closure in five to ten years) often decide that the cost of cleanup technology is too high, and buy allowances. This is a much more flexible system of regulation than traditional "command and control," and it has been quite successful.[107] Since the program started, annual sulfur dioxide emissions have been well below the cap, declining by nearly 50 percent overall; the cost of the reduction has been less than anticipated, with savings estimated at $1.8 billion per year compared with what they would have been had more rigid command and control regulations been used.[108] The program's success is widely acknowledged, and it has provided the model for legislation aimed at reducing greenhouse gases (which cause global warming); however, so far no legislation has passed (partisan polarization again). The EPA has undertaken several other initiatives aimed at making regulation more cooperative (between government and industry), collaborative (involving all stakeholders), and efficient, especially during the Clinton years. Many of these have produced some successes, such as voluntary efforts by some companies to reduce their pollution by more than what was required by law.[109]

Gauging the effectiveness of bureaucratic entities is a difficult enterprise, but in 1999, a research effort called the Federal Performance Project rated eighteen different federal agencies, using thirty-four criteria, over a four-year period (1999–2002). The EPA was included in the 1999 study and received a grade of B–. This placed it above the Immigration and Naturalization Service, the Customs Service, and the Health Care Financing Administration (all of which got grades of C), but below the Social Security Administration, which received an A. The 2001 study included the Postal Service, which received an impressive A–, below the National Weather Service (A), but above the BIA (D), the Bureau of Consular Affairs (C), and NASA (B).[110] As noted above, this was the same year the GAO described the Postal Service as being in a state of crisis. A 2009 Gallup Poll asked respondents to rate nine federal agencies; the EPA finished sixth, with 42 percent saying that the EPA did an "excellent" or "good" job, while the Centers for Disease Control and Prevention received the highest rating (61 percent) and the Federal Reserve the lowest (30 percent).[111] (Recessions must not be good for the popularity of central banks.) Another rating system uses feedback from individuals and groups served by federal agencies to assign scores, on a 100-point scale, to over thirty different agencies. In this system, the Pension Benefit Guaranty Corporation received a 90, the Office of Disaster Assistance an 85, and the Federal Aviation Administration a 54. The aggregate score for all the federal agencies included in the survey was 66.9.[112]

SUMMARY

The Constitution has very little to say about the administrative state. The president is given primary authority over the executive branch, and therefore the bureaucracy, but Congress has the power to create, abolish, organize, and reorganize executive agencies. Congress also can specify authority relationships between the administrative entities it creates and the other branches of government. Any bureaucratic agency can be rendered powerless by Congress, and most of them can be severely crippled, if not paralyzed, by the president or the courts. For bureaucratic agencies, the exercise of power is mostly a matter of having the backing and support of interest groups and other branches of government that have the political influence or constitutional authority they lack.

This support is by no means automatic. Chief executives frequently try to reshape agencies whose policies they oppose. When an attack of this sort occurs, career bureaucrats may fight back by using sympathetic interest groups, the legislature, and the courts to help them protect their domain. If the assault comes from the legislature, a different coalition must be assembled. Agencies can sometimes compete effectively in the high-stakes, high-visibility arenas of politics by playing one branch of government off against another. These skills are part of what has enabled the bureaucracy to become a fourth institutional force in American government.

Clearly more important than their ability to resist incursions from other institutions is the fact that administrative agencies generally remain outside the political limelight. Their influence over policy is greatest when other institutional powers are not watching too closely. Because their policymaking power is derivative, it is always subject to review and alteration: Legislatures can abolish agency rules, adjudicative decisions can be overturned by the courts, and administrative regulations can be changed in the offices of chief executives. But these kinds of checks are used sparingly; the normal environment of bureaucratic agencies permits them to exercise considerable power over public policy precisely because the other branches want the bureaucracy to make the tough, unpopular decisions. The bureaucracy is one of the places in government where "the rubber meets the road."

Cloakroom Politics

M uch of American politics and policymaking takes place in the cloakrooms, committee rooms, and chambers of state legislatures and the U.S. Congress. Legislative institutions are often perplexing and frustrating to members and ordinary citizens alike. Describing and assessing the way legislatures operate is a little like retelling the story of the blind men who try to say what an elephant is by describing what they feel. The impression one gets depends on where one is standing.

Legislatures embody many political paradoxes. They are highly democratic, open institutions, yet they are also responsive to narrow, specialized interest groups and individuals who finance campaigns. Legislatures are powerful actors in the policy process, but they delegate responsibility for many significant decisions to other political institutions. Legislatures are the most responsive political institutions and, in some ways, the least responsible. It is not surprising that legislative policymaking may be both appealing and appalling to citizens and seasoned observers.

Compared with other domains of politics, cloakroom politics is perhaps the most open, chaotic, and human. Only chief executives command more public attention; only living room politics is more accessible to citizen participation. Legislatures embody a fundamental urge in the American democratic tradition—to have a place where the conflicts of public life are debated, deliberated, and decided, often in full view.

Legislatures are a focal point for the inside players. Government administrators, lobbyists, and journalists have ready access to legislative chambers, committee rooms, and offices. Legislators do not always dominate the policy process, but they do get deeply involved in all aspects of public policy. They discuss important societal issues, allocate public services, and set tax policy through government budgets. Legislatures influence public and private behavior even though they delegate the detailed administration of public programs and policies to chief executives and the bureaucracy.

Although Americans approve of what Alexis de Tocqueville called "the great political agitation of American legislative bodies," citizens often are confused and frustrated by the chaos of legislative life.[1] In 2012, only 10 percent of Americans approved of Congress's handling of its responsibilities in a Gallup poll, coming in below telemarketers! This was the lowest approval rating of Congress in the thirty-eight years the Gallup organization has measured public attitudes about government institutions.[2]

Legislatures reflect not only democratic impulses but also the interests of the wealthy and powerful. Sometimes legislatures courageously tackle the tough issues of the day; at other times, they seem to cower before the challenges that face them. Sometimes legislative actions make the situation worse; when legislatures do nothing, things sometimes get better. Legislatures mirror the conflicts that exist in American society; consensus is achieved slowly, and it can evaporate quickly.

THE CROWDED AGENDA

The scope of cloakroom politics is incredibly broad. It includes economic policy, defense and foreign policy, health care, education, the environment, and more. Every year, members of legislatures cast hundreds of votes on public laws and resolutions. Countless issues receive attention from committees, subcommittees, and individual members. The scope of cloakroom politics is illustrated by the issues considered at the outset of the 113th Congress (2013–2014). The list in Box 5-1 is incomplete, but it conveys the breadth of Congress's responsibilities and public policy interests. As American legislatures go, Congress is not unusual in having a far-reaching policy agenda. State legislatures also have extremely varied agendas. During recent sessions, the New Jersey legislature held hearings and passed legislation covering such topics as the structure of public higher education, same-sex marriage rights, economic development incentives, public pension policies, and the minimum wage.

One might at first conclude that legislatures, their committees, and their members consider practically everything imaginable. Open as they are, however, legislatures do not respond to everyone who knocks on their doors or sends them an e-mail. Legislatures are collections of many smaller organizations—the offices of the senators and representatives, and legislative committees. Most public policy issues are handled initially by subcommittees and committees, especially in Congress, and are given scant attention by legislators other than committee members. Committees and subcommittees have wide latitude to conduct hearings, investigate, and review legislation within their jurisdictions. Even with the ascent of party leaders, committee chairs are still able to formulate bills that go to the floor for action by the entire chamber.[3]

Most legislative activity consists of debate and discussions rather than lawmaking, and legislatures can influence policy without making laws. Legislatures often engage in protracted considerations of issues without making decisions because they are important democratic and political forums, where symbolism can be just as important as substance. A great deal of time and energy is spent raising issues, seeking publicity, educating the public, helping political supporters, and embarrassing opponents.

BOX 5-1   **Some Policies Considered in 2013, in the 113th Congress's First Session**

Gun control: assault weapons ban and background checks for firearms sales

Campaign finance disclosure requirements

Debt limit of the U.S. government

Military and Veterans Affairs appropriations

Hurricane Sandy relief efforts

Minimum wage increases

Pay for members of Congress held in escrow until the adoption of a budget resolution

Pay freeze for federal employees

Trafficking Victims Protection Act

Violence Against Women Act reauthorization

Temporary Assistance for Needy Families (welfare) reauthorization

Source: U.S. Senate, "Active Legislation: 113th Congress (2013–2014)," March 13, 2013, www .senate.gov/pagelayout/legislative/b_three_sections_with_teasers/active_leg_page.htm.

If a problem is not already on an institution's agenda, it can be difficult to get it there. One scholar noted that the bulk of Congress's time is consumed considering matters that recur each year.[4] The struggles to get a vote on the floor of the House of Representatives or Senate are often intense because the time these institutions can spend in collective deliberation is scarce, and there are many claimants to it. It is not unusual for sponsors to have to wait several years after committees have finished work on a bill to get it on the floor. Legislatures frequently must revisit past policy actions or deal with unfinished business from previous Congresses. Many of the issue areas listed in Box 5-1 cover bills that were passed by Congress five, ten, or even forty years ago, but in different forms.

Another large chunk of legislatures' limited time is consumed by crises. Wars in the Middle East, economic recessions, the federal budget, tornados and drought in the American Midwest, the status of Iranian nuclear arms development, the murder of an American ambassador in Libya, an oil spill in the Gulf of Mexico, the slaughter of schoolchildren in Connecticut, and other problems command the immediate attention of elected representatives. In rare cases, their response is quick and significant legislative action. But in most circumstances, legislatures do a lot of talking about whether and how to respond, pass minor bills while looking to the chief executive for direction, or criticize the chief executive's responses to the crisis.

For example, after Iraq invaded Kuwait in 1990, Congress waited several months before voting on resolutions to either give or withhold authorization for President Bush to use military force against Iraq (they gave him wide authorization). However, in December 1998, when President Clinton ordered air strikes against Iraq, just as the House prepared to discuss his impeachment, many Republicans in Congress openly questioned his motives.[5] By 1999, Congress was content to let President Clinton conduct air strikes in Kosovo for nearly three months, but they asserted their "power of the purse" very quickly after the air strikes succeeded in driving the Serbian military out of Kosovo, and the issue became who would pay for ground troops in the area.[6] When the United States was attacked in September 2001, Congress acted swiftly to authorize military action in Afghanistan and to give the executive branch more authority to investigate and prosecute suspected terrorists.

Many features of cloakroom politics keep the legislature's doors open to a broad range of views. Because power is widely dispersed, there are many ways to gain access to the institution's agenda. Legislatures respond to the concerns of their leaders, ordinary members, and a wide range of outsiders, including presidents and governors, executive agencies, interest groups, and citizens, but the response is not always the same in kind or degree. In general, getting the attention of a single member of the House or Senate is relatively easy, but it is very difficult to get the entire institution and its leadership to pay attention to an issue or proposed solution.

Members

The issue agendas of individual representatives and senators are strongly influenced by the concerns of citizens, businesses, and other organizations from their districts or states. Dealing with constituency problems consumes much of the time of members and their personal staffs. Representatives use their influence to speed up approval of grants for sewer projects, obtain funds for the building of research laboratories, obtain tax breaks for a new sports arena, or fight for more financial aid for college students. Collectively, the concerns of constituents play a strong part in shaping the policy activity of legislatures. In 1998, legislative scholar Alan Rosenthal estimated that "anywhere from one-third to two-thirds [of state legislators] would now cite constituency service as an important, or even *the* most important, part of the job of being a legislator."[7] The impulse to consider one's constituency helps shape many aspects of legislative behavior, from staff organization to voting on legislation.

When legislators stand for reelection every two, four, or six years, they must account, however loosely, for their action or inaction on important matters. Voters, interest groups, and journalists, who shape evaluations of legislators, like to ask, "What have you done for us lately?" Despite the fact that nine members of Congress in ten who seek reelection win their contests, most "run scared" even in districts that appear safe for the incumbents. Indeed, one reason so many seats are safe is that members work so hard at reelection.[8] The uncanny ability of Democratic incumbents to secure reelection in the 1970s and 1980s led President George H. W. Bush in 1991 to endorse a constitutional amendment to limit the number of terms members of Congress can serve. Support for this amendment became part of the Republicans' Contract with America, and the GOP scored a huge victory in the 1994 congressional elections, gaining majorities in both houses of Congress. The 1994 elections were notable in that thirty-four House Democratic incumbents (15 percent of those running) were defeated, and the Republicans won virtually all the open races (those that did not have incumbents running).[9] This result was widely viewed as a rejection of the Democratically controlled 103rd Congress and the policies, in particular health care reform, of President Clinton. However, in the congressional elections of 1996, 1998, and 2000, high rates of incumbent reelection prevailed, which, along with a 1995 Supreme Court ruling that state-imposed congressional term limits were unconstitutional, led to the disappearance of Republican interest in term limits.

Over the past decade, more than 90 percent of members of Congress and over 80 percent of U.S. senators who decided to seek reelection were successful. Even in 2010, when the Democrats lost control of the U.S. House of Representatives to the Republicans, 85 percent of the members seeking reelection were returned to office.[10] Both political parties have become very adept at constructing legislative districts for House members that nearly guarantee that one party or the other will be able to hold on to that district. In these cases, the primary campaigns that decide who will be the standard bearer for the dominant political party are more important than the general election.

Some legislators develop reputations as "policy entrepreneurs" because they exhibit keen interest in advancing a cause, an idea, or a new program. That interest, combined with ambition, makes them very influential. As they seek legislative accomplishments or perhaps higher office, they push new items onto committee or subcommittee agendas. They respond quickly to national and international events and mass media reports. Policy entrepreneurs do not necessarily want to expand government spending programs. For example, Representative Paul Ryan, R-Wis., who led the charge for reductions in federal spending in the 2000s, is no less an entrepreneur than former Democratic speaker Nancy Pelosi of California, a longtime advocate of expanded health care programs.

Legislators also use their committee and subcommittee positions to focus attention on scandals or government mismanagement and fraud. Investigations throw light on the members as well as the issues. For example, a congressional probe was launched in 1999 after newspaper reports of an alleged spy ring created by the Chinese government to obtain military and other technology secrets from Los Alamos National Laboratory captured national attention. A bipartisan

House investigative committee, headed by Christopher Cox, R-Calif., issued a report that largely confirmed the allegations and contained numerous recommendations for improving security at Los Alamos and other nuclear facilities run by the Energy Department. The most significant of the recommendations called for the establishment of a separate National Nuclear Security Administration (NNSA) within the Energy Department. Energy secretary Bill Richardson opposed this recommendation, calling it a dangerous congressional encroachment into his department's jurisdiction. Later that year, when President Clinton signed the fiscal year 2000 defense authorization bill that included the new agency, he appointed Secretary Richardson to head the NNSA. When they learned about this maneuver, angry House Republicans created a special panel to oversee nuclear security within the Energy Department and threatened, among other things, to cut Richardson's travel budget.[11]

Richardson's argument that he, not Congress, should be in charge of nuclear security was undermined when two computer hard drives containing nuclear weapons data turned up missing from a Los Alamos secure laboratory in June 2000. Richardson's critics on Capitol Hill didn't hold back. Senator Jon Kyl, R-Ariz., said,

> You could not blame someone who was in charge and doing his best to cooperate. But it's hard to give any slack to someone who said, "Don't interfere in my domain—this is my deal, I'm going to take care of it, and I'm going to assume full responsibility for whatever occurs." It's like the candidate who campaigns on some grand reform theme, and then you find out he himself is guilty of the same thing. He's dead.

Even some Democrats joined in the criticism. At a Senate Intelligence Committee hearing, Robert Byrd, D-W.Va., told Richardson point blank, "You will never again receive the support of the Senate of the United States for any office to which you might be appointed. It's gone. You've squandered your treasure, and I'm sorry."[12] Similar dramas, although not necessarily of the same level of visibility and intensity, occur dozens of times each year and help set Congress's agenda, while enabling members to increase their influence over the executive branch—and their visibility back home.

The agendas of legislators are shaped by many factors; constituency pressures are always important, but pressures from outside groups also figure prominently. Executive branch agencies and interest groups generally focus their concerns on the committees and subcommittees that develop the policies and programs that affect them most directly. Indeed, many of the issues considered by legislative committees originate in administrative agencies. Outside interest groups influence legislators because these groups supply the milk and honey of politics—money and grateful voters. Running for office costs a great deal of money. In the 2010 elections, the average cost for a winning Senate campaign totaled nearly $9 million; the average successful House race cost $1.4 million.[13]

The quest for campaign funds compels legislators to at least listen to the concerns of their contributors. Organizations with money use several methods to get the attention of subcommittees and committees. They hire lobbyists to monitor legislation, meet with members and staff, and invite legislators to speak at group meetings. Organizations that cannot deliver money or votes have a much tougher time gaining attention.[14]

Although committee chairs and other influential committee members, as well as party leaders, exercise a great deal of independent power, they are all very responsive to concerns expressed by the president or a governor from their political party because concerted action by these powerful elected officials is often necessary to elect as many fellow partisans as possible.

The Institution

Issues that dominate the attention of the entire legislature are broad societal concerns and issues advanced by presidents, governors, or legislative leaders. An especially good example was the legislation that created a new prescription drug benefit for older Americans in 2003. In that year, President George W. Bush and House speaker Dennis Hastert, R-Ill., announced that this was a top legislative priority. Congress had tried unsuccessfully over a nearly forty-year period to expand the Medicare program to provide prescription drug coverage. With both Bush and Hastert pushing for action, Republicans—and a few Democrats—were able to agree on compromise legislation. Despite considerable opposition from conservative Republicans and many Democrats, the Medicare Prescription Drug, Improvement, and Modernization Act passed both houses of Congress and was signed by President Bush.[15]

Legislatures listen to outsiders, especially chief executives, but the partisan and entrepreneurial instincts of members and committees also bring new ideas to the agenda that chief executives would prefer to ignore. During the last two years of the Reagan administration (1986–1988), Congress made sweeping changes in national immigration policy, passed a massive highway building and rehabilitation program, revised the Clean Water Act, and imposed economic sanctions on the South African government. None of these policies was promoted by President Reagan; some he actively opposed, but the Democratic majorities in both houses, with help from numerous Republicans, enacted them anyway.

Another dramatic example of partisan agenda setting occurred during the 104th Congress, when Speaker of the House Newt Gingrich, R-Ga., attempted to steer the Republican Contract with America through the Congress. The contract covered a variety of topics, including anticrime legislation, welfare reform, increased penalties for child pornography, tort reform, so-called unfunded mandates the federal government placed on states, term limits for members of Congress, and the line-item veto for presidents. Gingrich and his leadership team revamped the committee system, appointed party loyalists to head all the major committees, and succeeded in getting the House to pass ten bills and three resolutions that embodied the contract. Very little in the contract, other than the line-item veto, was favored by President Clinton, but it definitely dominated the congressional agenda in 1995. Although several of the bills became law (legal reforms, penalties for child pornography, paperwork reductions, limits on unfunded mandates, the line-item veto), most were either rebuffed by presidential vetoes or delayed and reformulated in the Senate.[16]

The intense partisanship in Congress exhibited in the mid-1990s continued during the presidencies of George W. Bush and Barack Obama; thus, sharp partisan conflicts have been evident in Congress for nearly twenty years. Republicans in Congress, especially in the House of Representatives, where they had a continuous majority, supported President George W. Bush with great loyalty from 2001 to 2006. When they lost control of the House and Senate in 2006, Democrats acted in a disciplined way to oppose Bush, and then to support Obama. After Republicans took back control of the House of Representatives and gained Senate seats in the 2010 election, Republican congressional leaders went to great lengths within and outside their chambers to thwart the president's legislative agenda. In one infamous moment, Congressman Joe Wilson, R-S.C., shouted "you lie" during a speech by President Obama to the nation held in the chamber of the House of Representatives, after the president had asserted that his health care reform would not offer coverage to illegal immigrants.[17] Senate minority leader Mitch McConnell declared in early 2011 that the focus of Republican senators during the 112th Congress would be to make sure President Obama did not receive a second term. Because of their control in the House of Representatives, and enough Senate votes to filibuster the Democrats proposals, Republicans were able to sideline most of Obama's legislative agenda.

Legislative staff members are another fertile source of policy proposals. Congress employs an army of professional analysts, lawyers, and political advisers—a personal and committee staff estimated to total about 13,000.[18] Additionally, approximately 6,000 employees work for support agencies, including the Congressional Research Service, the Government Accountability Office (GAO), the Congressional Budget Office, and the Government Printing Office.[19] These agencies provide general and specific research assistance to legislative members and committees, conduct studies either on their own initiative or in response to requests by members or committees, and review and investigate the actions of executive agencies.

State legislatures used to rely almost entirely on centralized staffs (offices of legislative councils and reference bureaus) that served entire chambers, but they have now "congressionalized" by greatly increasing the number of staff and assigning them to work for committees, legislative parties, and individual members. Nationally, there are over 20,000 full-time state legislative staffers.[20]

Entrepreneurial Politics

Although legislatures can engage in policy debates and focus public attention on social and economic problems, it is much harder for them to take decisive action. When legislators want to make policy, they must deal, bargain, and compromise in order to develop the several majorities required to enact legislation.

This majority-building enterprise is difficult and complicated, in large part because cloakroom politics is molded by the complex contemporary political and economic environment. Legislatures do not function in hermetically sealed chambers; deliberation and debate within them reflect societal differences about public problems and solutions.

Suppose someone asked for an explanation of why a landmark health care reform law was enacted in 2010 under President Obama, but not in 1993 when reform was pushed by President Clinton. Many of the basic features of the political landscape in 2009 and 2010 were similar to those in 1993. Both houses of Congress were controlled by Democrats, and there was a Democrat in the White House. Public opinion polls were revealing widespread support for broadening health care coverage. Surveys revealed widespread displeasure with insurance company practices of denying benefits to people who had what is known as "preexisting conditions," such as chronic disease, or terminating insurance coverage as soon as individuals became ill. Candidates Clinton and Obama had pledged to expand health care coverage for uninsured Americans during their campaigns. With more than 30 million people standing to benefit directly, and millions more indirectly, Democrats were eager to add this new program to their list of accomplishments for low- and moderate-income Americans during a tough economic period.

None of this explains why it passed in 2010 and not 1993, however. One would have to dig deeper to find an explanation. House speaker Nancy Pelosi was strongly committed to pushing the legislation through the House of Representatives, and she was willing to overrule the misgiving of some liberal members in her caucus who preferred a more expansive program. She insisted that the president's plan (and then the Senate plan) was the best alternative because it would be supported by the Democratic majority in the Senate, and thus was capable of becoming law. She used the full power of the speakership and obtained the support of her party caucus. Senate majority leader Harry Reid, D-Nev., also used the full array of persuasion with the members of his caucus and a variety of parliamentary strategies to push the legislation through the Senate. In the end, the key to passage was the policy cohesion of the Democrats, which was not present in 1994. After passage, the president held a signing celebration at the White House on March 23, 2010, designed to emphasize the historic accomplishment and to praise the Democrats who supported the bill. No Republican legislators voted for the Patient Protection and Affordable Care Act.[21] Similar politics molds hundreds of bills that do not make headlines. In the halls of every capitol, cloakroom politics is characterized by partisanship, fragmented power, bargaining and compromise, and deadlines. But it is also, as noted with health care reform, a by-product of strong legislative leadership.

wielding influence

Fragmented Power

Despite the prominence of legislative leaders in Congress, it is also true that no one controls or commands legislatures. At times, it seems that there are 535 leaders on Capitol Hill and no followers. House and Senate elected leaders retain their positions only as long as the members support them. Unlike bureaucracies, in which there is a hierarchy of authority, legislatures are collections of "independent contractors," each with his or her own priorities and positions on the issues of the day. Environmental Protection Agency (EPA) regulations governing auto emission standards are issued by the administrator, who may seek advice from staff members, industry, and the public, but the final decision on many matters rests with the administrator. When Congress writes laws affecting education, or health care, or housing, 535 members may have some say in the outcome.

Legislatures are not without organization. Committees and subcommittees are the heart and soul of legislative policymaking. Writing about Congress in 1885, political scientist (later president) Woodrow Wilson referred to its committees as "little legislatures."[22] What Wilson observed then is no less true today. Committees are powerful vehicles for policy deliberation and action. In fact, a legislature's ability to shape public policy is vastly expanded by the division of labor and development of expertise made possible by the committee and subcommittee system.

Congress is divided into dozens of these little legislatures, each with significant influence over the timing and shape of legislation. In the 113th Congress, there were twenty permanent (or "standing") committees in the House of Representatives and sixteen in the Senate.[23] Each of these in turn has its own subcommittees, which are chaired by members of the majority party. Most Republicans in the House chair subcommittees, and every majority party senator chairs one subcommittee and many chair two. The subcommittees of the Senate Finance Committee and the House Transportation and Infrastructure Committee are listed in Box 5-2.

In fact, power is so widely dispersed in legislatures that the mass media and the public have trouble keeping track of the key players in each legislative ball game. Even powerful groups, such as the House Ways and Means Committee, which handles such matters as taxation, trade policy, Social Security, and Medicare and Medicaid, are practically invisible to the public. Most committees and subcommittees are even more obscure. Few people outside Washington know that the House Appropriations Committee's Subcommittee on Labor, Health and Human Services, Education and Related Agencies appropriates roughly one-third of all federal spending, excluding Social Security and interest payments on the national debt. Fewer still have heard of the Subcommittee on Highways and Transit or the Subcommittee on Water Resources and the Environment (of the Transportation and Infrastructure Committee)—two of the largest subcommittees in the House—let alone have the foggiest idea what they do.

The policy issues handled by each subcommittee give rise to "issue networks" that include members of Congress and their staffs, executive agencies, interest groups, journalists, and academics.[24] Many important policy decisions that go unnoticed by the public are made within this subcommittee-centered power structure. The fragmented system satisfies legislators because

BOX 5-2   **Subcommittees of Two Congressional Committees, 113th Congress, 2013–2014**

Senate Finance Committee

Health Care

International Trade, Customs, and Global Competiveness

Fiscal Responsibility and Economic Growth

Social Security, Pensions, and Family Policy

Taxation and IRS Oversight

Energy, Natural Resources, and Infrastructure

House Transportation and Infrastructure Committee

Aviation

Coast Guard and Maritime Transportation

Highways and Transit

Railroads, Pipelines and Hazardous Materials

Economic Development, Public Buildings and Emergency Management

Water Resources and Environment

Sources: U.S. Senate Committee on Finance, "Subcommittees," www.finance.senate.gov/about/subcommittees/; U.S. House of Representatives, Committee on Transportation and Infrastructure, "Subcommittees," http://transportation.house.gov/subcommittees.

it permits more of them to exercise power. Interest groups are pleased because they gain access to the process and attention to their concerns. If the fishing industry is feeling threatened by environmental regulations, industry representatives know that they can go to the Subcommittee on Fisheries, Wildlife, Oceans and Insular Affairs of the House Natural Resources Committee or the Subcommittee on Water and Wildlife of the Senate Environment and Public Works Committee, where they will have an opportunity to press their case in a public forum. Executive agencies also recognize some benefit from the convenience and familiarity of dealing with a limited number of legislators who are knowledgeable about a particular agency's programs and policies.

Committees and subcommittees also create power bases for promoting innovative policies or stopping reforms that members do not support. In the 1970s and 1980s, the chairman of the House Energy and Commerce Committee,

John D. Dingell, D-Mich., and the chairman of the Health and Environment Subcommittee, Henry A. Waxman, D-Calif., used the Energy and Commerce Committee as their platform for launching investigations and formulating sweeping changes in health policy, environmental protection, and telecommunications. Although frequently at odds, especially over environmental policy matters such as auto emission standards and acid rain, both Dingell (representing Detroit's auto interests) and Waxman were very effective issue entrepreneurs, compiling impressive records of legislative accomplishments.

In the 1990s, the chairman of the Senate Health, Education, Labor and Pensions Committee, James M. Jeffords, a moderate Republican from Vermont, parlayed his ability to communicate with Democrats and groups typically affiliated with Democrats (teachers unions) to craft many successful policy innovations. (In 2001, he left the Republican Party and declared himself an independent, but "caucused" with the Democrats and generally voted with them.) One example of Senator Jeffords's leadership was legislation to consolidate virtually all federal job-training programs (the Workforce Investment Act, Public Law No. 105-220), which was enacted by the 105th Congress in 1998.

In 2011 and 2012, House Budget Committee chair Paul Ryan seized the spotlight, advancing federal budget proposals, gaining support from his Republican colleagues, and pleasing the conservative wing of the Republican party, known as the Tea Party.[25] His visibility with conservatives helped convince Republican presidential nominee Mitt Romney to put him on his ticket as the vice presidential candidate in 2012. Republican Darrell Issa of California used his Committee on Oversight and Government Reform in 2011 and 2012 to probe Obama administration policies ranging from drug- and crime-fighting policies on the U.S. border with Mexico to security problems at the U.S. consulate in Benghazi, Libya, where the U.S. ambassador and three other Americans perished in a terrorist attack.[26]

Bargaining and Compromise

Because power is widely dispersed, bargaining and compromise are central to legislative politics. Fragmentation enhances the power of members and subcommittee leaders, but it makes reaching consensus more difficult; a few determined individuals can stall the process. Legislatures may fail to make progress on important policy issues for months or even years. Typically, the legislative process moves at a snail's pace. Yet in rare circumstances, such as the months immediately following the attacks in New York and Washington in 2001, agreement can be reached and deals can be struck. Then, legislatures move with blinding speed.

A majority of legislators must support a bill repeatedly before it reaches a chief executive's desk for signature. Majorities must be obtained in subcommittees and committees, and in the entire House and Senate. If there are disagreements between the House and Senate—and there usually are—a temporary conference committee may be appointed to iron out the differences and then seek yet another majority in each chamber.

Deference to the legislative handiwork of committees can simplify the majority-building process. Until the late 1960s, members approved most of the committee proposals that came to the floor, making few or no amendments. By the mid-1970s, however, floor debates had changed dramatically; members insisted on introducing large numbers of amendments after committee bills reached the floor. By the mid-1980s, floor amending activity had produced so much frustration in the House that the Democratic leadership, working through the Rules Committee, took action to place significant new restrictions on the making of floor amendments.[27]

House Republicans, who had often felt silenced by the Rules Committee restrictions of Democratic leaders, promised to open the floor to amendments if they gained power over the chamber. However, when the Republicans took control of the House after the 1994 elections, the leadership quickly learned the advantages of using restrictive rules and made frequent use of them. Moreover, House Republican leaders frequently ignored or bypassed committees in order to advance the versions of legislation they preferred.[28]

In the Senate, the rules governing floor debates give policy-active senators ample opportunity to amend legislation and engage in a variety of delaying tactics on the floor.[29] The most important tool available to the minority party in the Senate is the rule permitting any group of at least forty-one senators to block consideration of a proposed bill. The use of this technique—the threat to filibuster a law and hold up action—has grown in frequency in the past two decades. For example, in 1991 and 1992, sixty motions were filed to place a limit on debate, so as to enable a bill to come to the floor for a vote. By 2009 and 2010, the practice had more than doubled to 137.[30] When the filibuster route is chosen by opponents of legislation, the practical implication is that majority rule, 50 percent plus one, is no longer sufficient to pass legislation; instead it often requires a supermajority of sixty senators to get things done. The routine use of filibusters, threatened or real, for partisan purposes is perhaps the biggest legislative development in Congress over the past twenty years because it has, for most purposes, turned the Senate into a supermajoritarian institution. Even the Framers of the Constitution, who created the Senate to serve as a restraining force on the popularly elected House of Representatives, might be troubled by this development.

Although members of Congress often take cues from party leaders and the president, majorities assembled to pass one law may not stick together for the next battle. As new issues arise, majorities must be put together at all stages of the legislative process, often one vote at a time. Building coalitions is painstaking work that involves difficult negotiations. David Stockman, President Reagan's first budget director, called the task of pulling coalitions together in Congress the "politics of giving":

> An actual majority for any specific bill had to be reconstructed from scratch every time. It had to be cobbled out of the patchwork of raw, parochial deals that set off a political billiard game of counter-reactions and corresponding demands. The last ten or twenty percent of the votes needed for a majority in both houses had to be bought, period.[31]

If presidents, governors, and some party leaders prefer "wholesale" politics—sweeping, popular ideas—most legislators prefer "retail" politics—rewards for their districts or states. A House leadership aide put it simply: "No matter how members ask the question it always comes down to one issue—how will it affect me?"[32] Crafting laws requires many different types of agreements. Deals may involve one member agreeing to vote yes on a bill with the understanding that the favor will be returned when that member has a bill that needs support. Or legislation may be modified to include a higher appropriation, lower taxes, or favorable treatment for an industry in a member's district as the price for a positive vote.

Nineteenth-century German chancellor Otto von Bismarck once remarked, "Politics is like sausage. Neither should be viewed in the making." Senator Robert Byrd, one of the longest-serving senators in U.S. history, once remarked, "Now someone said . . . that making legislation is like making sausage. Don't kid yourself. I have made sausage, and I can tell you that what we did this year is significantly more sloppy."[33] To some observers, the American political process, with its bargaining, compromise, and vote swapping, is distinctly unsavory. But the nature of representative democratic institutions makes it unlikely, and even undesirable, that they would operate without these kinds of transactions taking place. To fashion laws in an open democratic institution, a broad consensus must be achieved and sustained. "Good" policy benefits, or at least does not harm, the people and interests represented by elected officials.

Deadlines

The presence of annual deadlines helps explain why the members of legislatures often procrastinate until the last possible moment before reaching a decision. Just before adjournment or an election, legislatures often rush through bills, or combine a large number of bills into "omnibus" legislation. For example, after the 2010 midterm elections, during a very active lame-duck session, Democrats in the House and Senate advanced several major bills that had languished for years. In less than two months, Congress ratified a strategic arms treaty on nuclear weapons with Russia, adopted major reforms in food safety laws, provided health care insurance for 9/11 "first responders," repealed the "don't ask, don't tell" rule that prohibited homosexuals from serving openly in the military, and extended unemployment insurance and tax cuts for high-income Americans.[34]

Why does a legislature facing a deadline act like a football team executing a two-minute drill—quickly and efficiently moving the ball down the field for a touchdown, when at first they seemed unable to move it two feet? Why does a legislature not always act as if the deadline is fast approaching? Action is postponed primarily because savvy legislators often wait until the last minute in order to get the best deal possible. Knowing that decisions on major legislative initiatives and tax and spending bills may not be made until the eleventh hour encourages everyone to hold back on their commitments. There was no better illustration of this than the 2012 fiscal cliff showdown that would have resulted in automatic spending cuts and tax increases on

January 1, 2013 (see chapter 1). The U.S. Senate was able to reach the deal that was brokered on New Year's Eve. It was then approved in the House of Representatives near midnight on New Year's Day 2013, just before the expiration of the 112th Congress.

Legislators also delay action in the hope that unfavorable political conditions will improve. Perhaps public opposition to a controversial policy will soften; maybe the governor will take a different position; perhaps the next election will bring more like-minded individuals to the legislature. Without deadlines, legislatures find it difficult to make decisions. The end of a fiscal year, the expiration of a law's authorization, an impending election, or an adjournment can force legislatures to act, whether they are ready or not.

Leadership

Fragmented power and the need for compromise increase the importance of leadership in putting things together. Legislative leaders assemble coalitions and set priorities for the institution.[35] But leaders derive their power from the members and often must defer to their wishes to keep their support. The positions that legislative leaders take on policy issues are heavily influenced by the views of other legislators in their party. Thus, the power of leaders tends to increase when members of a party caucus have similar views about policy priorities and policy substance. This condition has become increasingly common in the U.S. Congress since the 1990s as Republicans have stood united in favor of tax cuts and high military spending, and against spending for social welfare programs, while Democrats have unified in opposition to these policy preferences.

According to Randall Ripley, a perceptive scholar of American politics, congressional leaders perform five policy-related tasks:

1. They help determine who sits on and chairs the most powerful committees.
2. They help decide when and in what form legislative business will come to the floors of the House and Senate.
3. They help organize votes on the floors of the House and Senate by contacting—whipping—members to attend and vote.
4. They communicate leadership preferences and collect information on member needs and preferences.
5. They serve as focal points for contact with the White House, the leaders of the other chamber, and the media.[36]

A leader's most important power is the ability to persuade his or her colleagues to follow. Majority and minority leaders generally exercise more influence on procedural matters—when a bill is considered or how an issue is framed for a vote—than they do on the substance of legislation, its policy objectives and strategies.[37] Leaders often package issues so that fellow party members can cast votes that help them satisfy their constituents or favorite interest groups. For example, in 2011 and 2012, Senate majority leader Harry Reid arranged for Democratic senators seeking reelection to introduce budget amendments restoring proposed cuts in popular programs in their states. Senators from states with large cities called for increases in aid to hire teachers and police officers. Senators from agricultural states proposed budget increases to provide higher crop price supports, and so on. Nearly all of these proposals were approved by the Senate.

Members are willing to play "follow the leader" if it advances their electoral goals. But members have a compelling excuse for ignoring a leader's requests: "I can't vote with you because it could cost me reelection." Even the party leaders sometimes support this defense. Senate majority leader Harry Reid, for example, refused to post several bills on the Senate calendar that were a priority for President Obama because he thought that Senate Democrats up for reelection in 2012 might lose support in their home states if he did so.

Congressional leaders are the essential glue for holding coalitions together, but in most cases, their work does not receive a great deal of media attention. An exception to their traditional role of working the "inside game" of legislating came in the mid-1990s when Representative Newt Gingrich and Republicans seized control of the House of Representatives in 1994 after forty years of uninterrupted Democratic control. With President Clinton in the White House, Speaker Gingrich not only handpicked the committee chairs, but also appointed several task forces to oversee the work of committees to make sure the legislation they reported conformed to the letter and spirit of the Contract with America, a set of campaign proposals for policy and government reform. If, despite all this, committees reported legislation at odds with the wishes of the leadership, Gingrich and his leadership team (including Majority Leader Dick Armey, R-Tex., and Majority Whip Tom DeLay, R-Tex.) would simply change the bills before they reached the floor. As promised by Gingrich, nearly the entire Contract with America had passed the House during the first 100 days of the 104th Congress. Senate Republicans under Robert Dole's leadership also made an effort to advance the House proposals, but much of the legislation passed in the House did not make it through the Senate.[38]

The main goal of this exercise was to challenge President Clinton for national leadership after the 1994 elections. By the end of the 104th Congress, it seemed clear that this experiment in party-based legislative governance was not working. This was confirmed in the way that speaks the loudest on Capitol Hill: the Republicans lost three House seats in the 1996 elections. House Republican rule changes then restored some of the power over policy formulation to committees.[39] Nevertheless, the pattern of strong centralized party leadership in the House of Representatives continued under Gingrich's successor, Dennis Hastert of Illinois; his successor, Democrat Nancy Pelosi of California; and her successor, Republican John Boehner of Ohio.[40]

In the 1970s and 1980s, party leaders in state legislatures were generally more influential than congressional leaders. They appointed the members and

chairs of standing committees, decided which committees considered legislation, determined when bills would be "posted" for a vote, and closely monitored and managed deliberations on the floors of the chambers. They also
promoted substantive programs and persuaded standing committees to enact
them. But even though these leaders wielded enormous influence, policymaking power in state legislatures was far from centralized. Alan Rosenthal, a leading authority on state legislatures, wrote, "Aggressive policy leadership is
probably the exception rather than the rule."[41]

Beginning in the 1990s, Rosenthal observed a decline in the power of state
legislative leaders. This decline appears to have been the result of more partisan
politics, which augmented the strength and importance of party caucuses, and
term limits, which brought in more rebellious newcomers, who were not content to have the legislatures governed by entrenched leaders. According to
Rosenthal, legislatures in states with term limits were losing their ability to
control their own affairs. In addition to having weak internal leadership, they
have been beset by all sorts of restrictions and requirements by the public,
speaking through ballot initiatives. These include rules by which legislation
will be considered, the timing of legislative sessions, and the salaries and working conditions of legislators.[42]

Ironically, legislators may be more readily led by presidents and governors
than by internal leaders. Presidents and governors can go directly to interest
groups, and to the public, upon whom legislators depend for support and campaign contributions. They have the wherewithal not only to set the legislative
agendas, but also to formulate policies and then push them through to final
adoption. "Whatever the precise sources of policy formulation," Rosenthal
observed, "the processes by which proposals make the agenda, receive serious
consideration, and get adopted may depend considerably on executive leadership."[43] Although divided government very significantly diminishes the possibilities for legislative leadership by chief executives, presidents and governors
have political powers that are unavailable to members of Congress and state
legislatures (see chapter 6). Chief among them is the ability to be heard above
the clamor of voices. As former Representative David Obey, D-Wis., said, "The
President has the only megaphone in Washington."[44]

RITES OF PASSAGE

The characteristics of cloakroom politics profoundly influence what legislatures do. What does this mixture of individual needs, fragmented power, compromise, and party-based leadership produce in the way of public policies?

Symbols over Substance

Symbols often triumph over substance in cloakroom politics. Much legislative
activity involves talk, not action. Hearings are held, bills are introduced,
speeches are delivered, but no legislation passes. Significant policy results are
often hard to achieve because they may require legislatures to wield the coercive

power of government (to regulate public or private behavior, or to impose taxes), and unpopular action of this type can cost members their jobs. A popular alternative to decisive action is symbolic policy. Laws that are primarily symbolic are often passed to reassure politically aroused groups.[45] Without offering tangible benefits, the legislature addresses the concerns of aggrieved parties with policy pronouncements that mollify them. Disadvantaged groups, such as unemployed and poor individuals, seldom have sufficient political clout to hold elected officials accountable.[46]

A variation on the symbolic policy theme is the tendency of legislatures to adopt policies that are long on goals, but short on the means for carrying them out. Such policies may strike only a glancing blow at the problem. The gulf between rhetoric and reality is frequently exposed by the difference between the authorizing language and the spending levels specified in actual appropriations bills. Authorizations set out the objectives and strategies for ameliorating a problem; appropriations bills supply money for programs and benefits to people. The Head Start program, which provides preschool education and other support to low-income children, is a rarity among domestic social service programs in that it has long been popular among both Democrats and Republicans (although more popular among Democrats). Despite its popularity, funding levels authorized by Congress are rarely provided in the appropriations process. According to an analysis by the Center on Budget and Policy Priorities:

> Head Start was repeatedly funded below the level needed just to keep pace with inflation. *In 2008, funding for Head Start is 11 percent—or $893 million—below the 2002 funding level, adjusted for inflation.*
>
> Head Start did not suddenly fall from favor on Capitol Hill. Instead, under Administration pressure to reduce the overall level of funding for appropriated programs or face certain vetoes of appropriations bills, Congress cut funding for numerous programs across the budget, including Head Start. The final omnibus appropriations bill provided $164 million less in Head Start funding than Congress had provided in the Labor-HHS appropriations bill that it passed earlier but that the President then vetoed. This funding difference is equivalent to the cost of serving more than 20,000 children in Head Start this year.[47]

Actions taken for largely symbolic reasons may still have important consequences. Early public concern over the degradation of the environment was met with the National Environmental Policy Act of 1969, which announced the government's intention to protect the environment, but did not specify many enforcement mechanisms. Among its seemingly innocuous provisions was a requirement that federal agencies prepare environmental impact statements for federally funded projects. Working through the courts, environmental activists have used this requirement on numerous occasions to block projects whose effects are perceived as detrimental to the environment.

Incremental Change

The drawn-out policy process often yields only minor policy changes. The stabilizing forces holding back substantial change are very powerful indeed. Agendas are crowded with proposals; only a few receive serious attention. Legislators opposing change have abundant opportunities to veto or water down proposals. When legislatures finally act, problems are addressed in small, manageable steps—modest departures from past practice.

Policy issues are rarely considered comprehensively. Legislatures slice up broad policy areas into many parts so that a large number of members serving on committees and subcommittees can participate. Rather than structure a government-wide policy on pollution, for example, Congress divides pollution issues into discrete programs and policies such as the Clean Air Act, Clean Water Act, Toxic Substance Control Act, Superfund, and so on.

It is not just the process but also fear of the unknown that inhibits rapid and radical change. In contrast to business leaders, many of whom are risk takers, legislators tend to be risk averse. When they vote for a law, they want to be reassured that the new law will not make things worse for their constituents—and thus for their chances for reelection. Under these circumstances, they may prefer to tweak existing laws and proceed through trial and error, rather than to embrace sweeping innovative approaches that have the potential for disastrous consequences. Reconsiderations of laws are practically guaranteed, as most laws are authorized only for three- to five-year periods, and others have built-in "sunset" provisions, both of which create opportunities or requirements for the legislature to examine the issue again and make changes.

Future policy directions are often molded by past decisions and experiences. Legislators find that the compromises reached by their predecessors serve as useful guides. Because lawmakers want to avoid controversy and conflict during a drawn-out process, they find it politically feasible and prudent to seek modest changes in current policy. Opposition is less likely when changes in the status quo are minor and therefore less threatening to various vested interests.

Congressional policymaking regarding the federal budget demonstrates incrementalism at work. Major changes are rare and take place only if accompanied by strong presidential and legislative leadership. In budgetary decision making, the budget levels under consideration usually equal last year's budget, plus or minus a small percentage.[48] Battles occur over what seem like inches of territory to the outside observer. Will spending increase by 1 percent or 2 percent? Will formulas governing grant-in-aid programs benefit smaller or larger cities? The competition is fierce, but the public rarely understands what, if anything, is at stake. To insiders, these battles are critical because they are, quite literally, the principal policy issues before the legislature.

During most of the 1990s, budget legislation more or less guaranteed incremental results because annual spending caps were imposed on most key areas of the budget, such as defense and domestic discretionary programs. Strict caps were not placed on entitlement programs such as Social Security and Medicare, and these programs accounted for most of the growth in federal spending during the decade. In 2001, after the 9/11 attacks, budget rules were loosened or suspended. Large increases in military spending occurred to support the wars in Afghanistan and Iraq. Deficits grew throughout the first decade of the twenty-first century as military spending remained high, and President George W. Bush's 2001 tax cuts were renewed. Incrementalism remained the norm in most areas of the budget because of the revenue squeeze from the tax cuts, and continuing demands to support troops in the field as well as those returning home. The huge spending increases authorized during the Great Recession (the Troubled Asset Relief Program and the American Recovery and Reinvestment Act, sometimes referred to as the economic stimulus package or law) were remarkable not only for their size, but also because such large increases occur so infrequently.

During the first term of the Obama administration, the budget fights between Democrats and Republicans essentially made a shambles out of the congressional budget process. Two central elements of that process are the passage of budget resolutions in both chambers and the enactment of twelve appropriations bills (each managed by a subcommittee of the House and Senate Appropriations Committees), which determine the spending levels for federal programs and agencies. In 2010, neither chamber approved a budget resolution, while in 2011 and 2012, highly partisan (Republican) resolutions were passed in the House but ignored by the Senate. Of the thirty-six appropriations bills that should have passed in this three-year period, exactly three (all in 2011) actually made it through the process. This means that the government (agencies and programs) had to run on "continuing resolutions," which are supposed to be temporary, short-term measures. The entire government ran on continuing resolutions in fiscal year 2011, and many of the showdowns between President Obama and Congress between 2010 and 2012 were over continuing resolutions rather than "normal" or full-blown budget legislation.[49]

Pork Barrel Policies

Legislators want to deliver benefits, sometimes known as "pork barrel programs" or "earmarks," to people, businesses, and communities in their states and districts. The desire to parcel out "particularized benefits" produces what are called distributive policies.[50] Members of Congress are not the only ones who want to participate in the politics of giving and credit claiming; ample supplies of pork are available to many state legislators. For example, in the 1990s, Florida legislative leaders allocated generous amounts for each member's local pork projects, which were referred to as "turkeys." Media attention to this practice led to reforms that have greatly limited the number of "turkeys."[51]

Pork barrel politics is perhaps most evident in the contemporary Congress when highway and mass transit bills are being formulated. Bud Shuster, R-Pa., was a widely acknowledged "king of pork" in the House of Representatives when he was the chairman of the Transportation and Infrastructure Committee, which develops such legislation (1995–2001). Shuster ruled the largest commit-tee in the House and used a system of earmarks to make sure members of his committee and others could have local projects included in the highway and mass transit bills. Shuster's rule of thumb was that roughly 5 percent of the fund-ing authorized in these bills would be devoted to earmarks; the 1998 highway bill authorized $218 billion in federal spending for a six-year period. Despite the antipork reform rhetoric of the Republican House leadership, Shuster not only survived, but flourished. His committee, all seventy-five Republicans and Democrats, pledged to vote as a bloc to protect his and its power. Shuster defended his earmarking system with vigor: "Are there bad projects? Certainly there are some bad projects. But 99 percent of the 5 percent are good projects. And if a member doesn't know what is good for his district, he isn't going to be a member for very long."[52] As federal deficits soared in the 2000s, the House and Senate voted to cut back, but not eliminate, the practice of district earmarks in transportation and other bills.[53] For example, in fiscal year 2010, according to the Office of Management and Budget, Congress approved over 9,000 district- or state-specific appropriations worth over $11 billion.[54] In 2011, a moratorium on earmarks was proclaimed by congressional leaders of both parties, but a clear definition of what constituted an earmark was not provided.[55]

Innovation

Occasionally, public policy undergoes radical change. Landmark laws may increase government involvement in matters previously left to the private sec-tor, such as health insurance for elderly and poor Americans (Medicare and Medicaid). The Social Security Act of 1935, which guaranteed government support for senior citizens; the Civil Rights Act of 1964, which forbade dis-crimination against minorities and other groups; the Bush tax cuts enacted in 2001; and the Affordable Care Act of 2010 represent fundamental innovations in public policy.

Certain conditions foster innovation by legislatures. According to political scientist Charles O. Jones, significant policy shifts may happen when a well-organized and vocal group of citizens unites and demands government action, or when policymakers achieve a temporary consensus on innovative propos-als.[56] Strong political leadership, often from the president or governor, and economic and political conditions that make the need for change apparent are also powerful agents of policy innovation. In the 1970s, for example, Senator Edmund Muskie, D-Me., who chaired the Senate Committee on Environment and Public Works, took advantage of growing bipartisan consensus on the need to protect the environment in the early 1970s and promoted passage of the Clean Air Act of 1970 and a number of other environmental laws that Presidents Nixon and Ford signed into law. Bipartisan consensus and presiden-tial support enabled Congress to pass landmark welfare reform in 1996 during President Clinton's term. Strong legislative leadership from House speaker Nancy Pelosi and Senate majority leader Harry Reid enabled President Obama to push his health care reform through Congress in 2009 and 2010.

Events, political conditions, and the state of the economy all affect the degree of innovation. Opportunities for new and expansive spending programs, such as adding prescription drug coverage to Medicare, as George W. Bush and Congress accomplished in 2003, or the 2009 economic stimulus package passed by Congress at the urging of Barak Obama, are rare, but other strategies, such as revising regulatory policy, provide other paths to innovative policy that may not cost as much money. When government revenues come close to or exceed projected expenditures—something that happens infrequently—new programs may be born. President Johnson's Great Society programs came about in an era of small annual deficits; President George W. Bush's tax cuts of 2001 came after several years of surplus. When state governments realized a revenue bonanza in the late 1990s, major reforms in education and economic development strategies were quickly initiated. The Great Recession and widespread public disapproval of the actions of Wall Street investment firms allowed the passage of the Dodd-Frank Wall Street Reform and Consumer Protection Act in 2010.

Significant policy breakthroughs inevitably create problems, but once new government initiatives are established, the fundamental questions are discussed less frequently. Instead, legislators try to fix and refine—to "rationalize" breakthrough policies. Political scientist Lawrence Brown makes a useful distinction: Breakthrough policies are normally highly partisan, ideological, contentious, and visible; rationalizing policies are less partisan and contentious and concern relatively fewer citizens or interest groups. Debates about how to rationalize breakthrough policies generally revolve around proposed incremental changes that reflect perceptions of what has worked and what has not, rather than ideological preferences.[57] Still, some breakthrough policies never seem to take hold.

The history of federal programs dealing with unemployment provides examples of breakthrough policies that became accepted and some that did not.[58] During President Franklin Roosevelt's administration, a major breakthrough in unemployment policy occurred when the government provided assistance to jobless Americans through unemployment insurance and job creation programs. Since then, the unemployment insurance program has been slightly modified dozens of times—increasing or decreasing benefit payments, expanding categories of program recipients—but it has never been seriously threatened with elimination. It is the largest and most durable government program for helping unemployed workers; annual expenditures for this program averaged $8.6 billion in the 1970s, $16.6 billion in the 1980s, and $22.4 billion in the 1990s. During the first three years of the Great Recession, from 2008 to 2010, unemployed workers collected over $314 billion in jobless benefits.[59] Congress voted to extend unemployment benefits several times between 2008 and 2013, with some unemployed workers being eligible for as many as ninety-nine weeks of coverage.[60] An extension of unemployment insurance, with a seventy-three-week maximum period of payments, was part of the fiscal cliff deal passed on January 1, 2013.[61]

In contrast, federal job creation programs have been alternately embraced and rejected by U.S. politicians over the years. The Depression-era public works programs vanished during World War II when unemployment declined. During the 1970s, federal job programs employed as many as 700,000 people at an annual cost of $3 billion, but they were completely eliminated as a result of President Reagan's budget-cutting initiative in 1981.[62] Even during the Great Recession, direct public employment programs of unemployed workers did not make it to the national agenda. Instead, President Obama and Democrats in Congress supported programs that resulted in more jobs for construction workers and state and local government employees, including teachers, police officers, and firefighters.

Gridlock

When legislatures deal with extremely controversial policies, the policy process sometimes gets stuck in a gridlock of opposing viewpoints and power plays. Representative David E. Price, D-N.C., has observed, "Congress is often difficult to mobilize, particularly on high-conflict issues of broad scope."[63] Legislatures have ground to a halt over civil rights policy, aid to education, environmental policy, and other issues in the past, but the long-running "battle of the budget" that began in the 1980s and continued into the twenty-first century deadlocked Congress repeatedly, thus severely curtailing its ability to act. Congressional budget scholar Allen Schick's observation of the early 1980s remains apt today: "Congress now has difficulty legislating because the role demanded of it by economic conditions is not congruent with the type of legislation encouraged by its organizations and behavior."[64]

The central problem of budget policymaking is that each party has chosen to stick resolutely to its core principles and views of the proper role of government. Republicans believe that keeping taxes low and reducing government spending will promote economic growth. Democrats believe that government spending on education, scientific research, and the nation's infrastructure will grow the economy and that higher income earners should pay a greater share in taxes. Their inability to compromise has led to higher deficits and debt. Annual deficits increased to $1.5 trillion in fiscal year 2009, declining slightly to $1.4 trillion in fiscal year 2011, which compares very unfavorably with ten years earlier, when there was a modest surplus. Over the same period, the debt problem also worsened: by the end of fiscal 2011, the national debt had risen above $14.7 trillion, which represented 67 percent of the nation's gross domestic product (GDP). This meant that the debt had nearly tripled, and debt as a percentage of GDP had nearly doubled, since fiscal 2000.[65]

These figures were well known to policymakers in Congress by the beginning of 2011. Earlier congressional legislation had set a ceiling on the national debt of $14.3 trillion, and all the estimates agreed that this level would be exceeded during the year. The president and Republicans in Congress battled along familiar lines (Republicans insisting on spending cuts, Obama wanting to raise revenues by taxing the wealthy) all spring until a last-minute deal was reached in August. But the deal was really a continuation of fiscal policy dead-lock. The debt ceiling was lifted and a special "super committee" was created to find $1.5 trillion in savings over ten years, with the proviso that if they failed to reach such an agreement, there would be "automatic" or across-the-board spending cuts (divided equally between defense and domestic spending) that would take effect in January 2013 (after the 2012 election).[66] The super com-mittee failed to reach an agreement, which, along with the fact that the Bush tax cuts that had been extended since 2001 were also scheduled to expire at the end of 2012, set up the "fiscal cliff" that occupied lawmakers in the aftermath of the 2012 election. In addition to illustrating the depth of partisan disagree-ment over taxes and spending, the debt limit fight in 2011 also showed how directly budget battles in Washington could affect the economy as the Standard & Poor's credit rating on U.S. Treasury bonds fell a notch (from AAA to AA+) on August 5, 2011, and the stock market plunged during the summer.

As noted above, the so-called fiscal cliff of automatic spending cuts and tax increases was averted at the last possible moment by the 112th Congress. The Senate and House agreed to raise income tax rates on individuals earning $400,000 or more and couples earning $450,000 or more. Tax rates were also increased on the interest from investments (dividends and capital gains), as were estate taxes for these upper income earners, about 1 percent of taxpayers, and the payroll tax cuts were allowed to expire and rates returned to their nor-mal level of 6.2 percent.[67] However, automatic spending cuts were postponed, ensuring that the issue of debt and deficit reduction would be revisited early in the 113th Congress, in 2013.

The automatic spending cuts were implemented in March 2013, and the prospects for breakthroughs in the 113th Congress do not look particularly good. Partisan polarization reigns, and bipartisan compromise on a broad plan that addresses both taxes and spending does not seem likely. Congressional Quarterly measures partisan voting in Congress by counting the number of votes on which a majority of Democrats opposed a majority of Republicans, which they call party unity votes, and then determines how frequently each member voted with his or her party on the party unity votes. They then calculate an aver-age for each party for each session of Congress. They have been doing this since late 1961, and, not surprisingly, the highest party unity scores for both parties in both houses of Congress have occurred in recent years. In 2012 (second session of the 112th Congress), the Democratic scores were 87 percent in the House and 92 percent in the Senate (the highest on record). The corresponding Republican scores were 90 percent and 80 percent (the lowest since 1994). By way of com-parison, in 1992, the average score for Republicans (House and Senate) was 79 percent; House and Senate Democrats also had an average score of 79 percent.[68]

SHAKY GROUND RULES, UNRELIABLE WATCHDOGS

Legislative lawmaking is often a blunt instrument for addressing public prob-lems. The precision with which courts and the executive branch can sometimes perform is rarely evident in the legislative arena. Broad, vague, and sometimes

contradictory policies are a direct by-product of the need to reconcile competing claims and preferences and the requirement to build majority support from
people with widely different interests. Consequently, many public laws contain
ambiguous statements that a majority of the legislature can endorse. The task of
translating aspirations into programs and services is delegated to government
administrators, other levels of government, courts, private businesses, and citizens. Indeed, the more controversial the policy, the more likely legislatures will
ask others to make the tough choices.[69]

When legislators delegate hard decisions to others, they can garner political rewards while shifting the wrath of aggrieved parties elsewhere. Delegating
authority also gives legislators leeway to blame federal agencies or other levels
of government for failing to fulfill legislative intent and to take credit for correcting the faults in legislative acts by conducting oversight hearings and
investigations, as well as by undertaking constituent casework.[70]

The most common form of policy delegation occurs when Congress or a
state legislature defines a problem in legislation and then mandates federal or
state agencies to solve it. Recognizing and defining a problem are important,
but the task of deciding precisely how to cope with it is likely to be much more
difficult. Consider the problem of hazardous waste management. State legislatures around the country have required the construction of safe facilities for
the storage and disposal of dangerous wastes generated by chemical and other
industrial plants. The choice of where to locate these facilities is up to state
environmental protection agencies or special commissions, and their decisions have frequently outraged citizens, leading to threats of civil disobedience, violence, and lawsuits and, in some cases, to passage of legislation to
block implementation of the decisions.[71]

Legislators also impose difficult policy tasks on individuals and businesses.
Laws such as the Americans with Disabilities Act impose potentially expensive
demands on private organizations, which must then decide whether to follow
the letter and spirit of the law or to evade it. Responsibility for enforcing immigration laws rests in part with private employers, who must verify an individual's citizenship or permit to work in the United States. Failure to do so can result
in a substantial fine. Often the courts must rule on whether congressional
intent has been followed by private firms.

Congress frequently hands complicated problems to state and local governments, and state legislatures pass tough issues on to local governments.
Legislatures also mandate changes in policies and programs at other levels of
government, without providing adequate resources, and then hold them
accountable, which is particularly irksome for those on the receiving end.
Congress has ordered state and local governments to upgrade the education of
young children, enhance air and water quality, and improve highway safety, but
many state and local officials believe that the funds appropriated for these purposes are insufficient to permit the realization of policy goals and expectations.

The nature of cloakroom politics influences not only the shape of laws
and policy objectives, but also the results. Even when legislatures delegate
authority, they establish the ground rules for who gets what, when, and how

from government. Legislatures are often the final arbiters of how much government spends on important societal goals and how money will be raised to pay for those commitments. Few individuals, institutions, and organizations are untouched by legislative action or inaction.

Policy Implementation

Laws are seldom written with potential implementation problems in mind. Because it is so difficult to reconcile competing interests, legislators expect administrative agencies and others to figure out how to put laws into effect. Furthermore, ambitious legislative goals are often regarded as an effective method for stimulating change. The authors of the Clean Air Act of 1970 insisted on including tough air quality standards in the legislation, even though it was obvious to most of those involved that the standards would not be met.[72] They reasoned that setting high standards would force the automobile industry to work harder to reduce pollution. In fact, this forcing method, which was also used in the 1977 and 1990 reauthorizations of the Clean Air Act, worked; the deterioration of air quality in the United States has decreased, and there have been some significant improvements.[73]

Nevertheless, a disregard for potential implementation difficulties can reduce the likelihood of achieving positive results. Public laws are sometimes endorsed without legislators' ever carefully defining the problems the laws are supposed to address. Policy entrepreneurs who perceive a need for government programs may not be sure how to translate their aspirations into workable laws. The know-how to "solve" problems such as minority youth unemployment or drug abuse may not yet be available, but legislators sometimes seize opportunities to advance innovative policies concerning these issues when they arise.

Legislators tend to be concerned about the distribution of program benefits provided by law and about the efficient application of administrative regulations, rather than whether the ultimate impacts of a policy are what was intended. Generally, they assume that programs or policies will be helpful to people if implemented properly, even though this view may be highly inaccurate. For example, suppose a member of the House Committee on Education and the Workforce believes that mandating student testing and requiring teacher performance evaluations is an end in itself. Such a committee member's basic goal may be to "reform" education and teaching, but he or she may be largely oblivious to the ultimate results of education programs, because such results will not show up for years, and will be difficult to gauge definitively. This perspective on policy impacts not only influences lawmaking, it also has consequences for the distribution of benefits in society.

Government benefits come in many different forms: tax breaks for companies; grants to fund social service programs or to build bridges; regulations that protect domestic industries from foreign competition; and income-support payments for unemployed, poor, and retired individuals. Underlying all tax and expenditure decisions, regulations, and policies is the struggle over who benefits and who does not. In general, legislative policy tends to favor the haves over the have-nots, the organized over the unorganized, and the middle and upper income classes over the lower class because poor and unorganized groups have great difficulty making a case for themselves to legislators, who view most decisions through electoral lenses.

When government programs try to serve poor Americans exclusively, they often have difficulty surviving. From the Resettlement Administration of the 1930s, which aimed to increase black land ownership in the South, to the public service employment programs of the 1970s, which provided jobs for long-term unemployed workers and poor individuals, to welfare (formerly known as Aid to Families with Dependent Children and now called Temporary Assistance for Needy Families), programs that help only poor Americans have been vulnerable to attack. Charges of mismanagement or corruption make headlines and lead legislators to withdraw support. Effective lawmaking depends upon finding the delicate balance of benefits that holds the majority together long enough for passage, and can maintain majority support when negative claims about program implementation are aired.

Ignoring implementation issues when laws are crafted may erode respect for government. To get laws enacted, legislators (and chief executives) may exaggerate not only the problem, but also the potential effectiveness of the remedy under consideration. Then, if the problem fails to go away, the public and many legislators may falsely conclude that it cannot be remedied with government programs or that the policy approach was misguided. Repeated rounds of hyperbole and rising expectations, followed by disappointment and condemnation, undermine public support for governmental solutions.

Policy Impacts

Sometimes laws are written so as to have clear and immediate impacts. This usually occurs after several earlier legislative attempts to solve a problem have failed, and the problem and a solution become well defined. The Voting Rights Act of 1965 is a good example. Previous civil rights laws (in 1957, 1960, and 1964) had attempted to solve the problem of low black voter registration in counties in the Deep South by encouraging citizens who had been intimidated, or otherwise discouraged by local registration officials, to go to federal courts with their grievances. This approach resulted in only marginal increases in black voter registration, and by 1965, Congress was ready for more decisive action. This time it simply declared that federal officials would be sent to any county where black registration was below 50 percent of the black population to make sure black citizens could register without interference. Black voter registration in the seven states of the Deep South covered by the law increased by more than 1 million between 1964 and 1972, an increase to 64 percent from 29 percent of eligible black voters.[74] By 2008 the regional average was just below 70 percent.[75] Effective implementation of the law depended on federal officials and the courts, but congressional initiative was critical to making progress.

Still, legislatures are probably more notable for their delays or failures to act than for their willingness to grapple with difficult problems. And legislative inaction can have serious consequences. The problems created by harmful chemicals in the nation's water supply and by worldwide air pollution can be traced to careless and unregulated industry practices. Strong federal regulations were not legislated until the 1970s, and decades of neglect meant slow progress in improving environmental quality. The failure of state legislatures to take strong action against drunk drivers until the mid-1980s probably resulted in thousands of unnecessary deaths. Congress's inability to contain the growth of federal debt during the past decade, and its unwillingness to address the mounting problems of global warming, could have serious consequences for future generations.

Oversight and Learning

As elected representatives grope for solutions to difficult problems, such as ameliorating poverty or controlling immigration, they often adopt politically appealing but poorly designed policies. Legislators typically do not concern themselves with the details of program administration unless bureaucrats and private citizens run into trouble and people start complaining. But political institutions can and do learn from experience. Feeble and misguided attempts can be reshaped through trial and error. After several attempts, Congress successfully revised and strengthened education programs for disadvantaged children. It took more than a decade, but by the mid-1980s, compensatory education programs could be shown to have narrowed the gap in test scores between disadvantaged and nondisadvantaged students.[76]

Legislators form their impressions of program performance from what they hear from constituents, from interest groups and their lobbyists, from reports in the news media, from testimony at hearings, and from evaluations conducted by government agencies and others. Over time, members acquire pictures of success or failure that become the basis for intervening in program administration and for major legislative reforms.[77]

Objective evaluations of how well programs work may be difficult to accomplish and expensive to conduct, and their results are sometimes distrusted or ignored by legislators.[78] Many systematic studies do not yield unequivocal answers because it may not be possible to establish cause-and-effect relationships for government programs or policies. Suppose, for example, that we needed to determine whether the multibillion-dollar Supplemental Nutrition Assistance Program (formerly known as Food Stamps) improves the nutrition and health of the eligible population. We would have to monitor the health and eating habits of people before and after they received aid, track similar groups of people who did not receive it, and compare the results. Most likely, large numbers of the people we tried to track would drop out of our study before it was completed, and this would give rise to questions about the validity of our findings. Furthermore, such attrition would be only one of many problems that make definitive policy impact studies difficult (see chapter 10).

Nevertheless, when evaluations provide clear evidence that a program works or does not work, they can be quite persuasive. For example, despite repeated attempts, the Reagan administration could not persuade Congress to eliminate education and training programs for the disadvantaged run by the Job Corps because strong evidence, gathered through numerous systematic evaluations, indicated that the program worked.[79]

As an institution, Congress pays a good deal of attention to oversight for many reasons. First, limited resources due to chronic deficits severely constrict the possibilities for creating new programs, and committees and subcommittees have therefore devoted more of their attention to overseeing the programs that are in place. Second, public displeasure at government performance, especially revelations of fraud, waste, and abuse, motivates congressional interest. Third, partisan conflict and competition between presidents and congressional majorities have raised the stakes in oversight. Fourth, the staff resources available to Congress—especially at the GAO and the Congressional Research Service—are substantial. The GAO, with a budget of over $500 million alone, produces hundreds of reports annually (most of which are responses to congressional requests for information), and its representatives testified at more than 170 hearings in 2011.[80] Thus, Congress today has both the capability and the incentive to conduct more oversight.[81]

Increased interest in oversight does not necessarily translate into systematic, comprehensive, or even rational oversight activity.[82] Indeed, like most other congressional activities, oversight has a decidedly partisan flavor to it. In the 1980s, congressional Democrats often suspected that the Reagan and George H. W. Bush administrations were not implementing programs in good faith and conducted oversight hearings to show this. They also used oversight hearings to defend programs the White House had targeted for cuts or elimination. From 2007 to 2009, Democrats focused similar scrutiny on the actions and inactions of George W. Bush's administration. In 2010 and 2011, the Republicans in the House of Representatives used the oversight function to bash agencies for adhering to Obama White House directives in carrying out certain laws, rather than following what they argued were the wishes of Congress. As we have seen in many areas of congressional policymaking, partisan gridlock has characterized much of the effort to use oversight in the improvement of programs.

In making up their minds about programs, legislators use whatever information they can get. The problem is that unsystematic and anecdotal information is often more available and influential than careful, systematic evaluations. Impressions about policy success or failure enter the policy process through many channels. Senior citizens write members of Congress to complain about exorbitant fees for routine visits to the doctor, or Fox News reports about alleged fraud in the awarding of loans to solar panel manufacturing companies, or the *New York Times* reports alarming increases in airline safety violations. Such evidence may be inconclusive or unrepresentative, but it exerts a powerful influence on a legislator's judgments about government programs.

Legislative oversight of public policies can be harmful, especially if the legislators reach inaccurate conclusions. The resulting criticism heaped on administrators can be demoralizing, and more important, reacting to the criticism may distract public officials from essential tasks. Because members of Congress and of state legislatures engage in oversight activities with an eye to possible electoral payoffs, it should come as no surprise that such activities are greeted by experienced administrators with a mixture of alarm and cynicism.

When the policy process is competitive, and diverse points of view are fully expressed, legislatures are best able to learn from their mistakes. For example, careful scrutiny of environmental laws has been ensured by continuing public health fears and the high degree of controversy involving industry and environmental groups about proposed solutions to environmental problems. The Superfund toxic waste cleanup law, which was first passed in late 1980, turned out to be anything but super during its early years of implementation. Congress, during intense oversight efforts focused on toxic dumps in members' districts, discovered from the EPA that only about 30 of the nation's 950 toxic waste dumps had been cleaned up. This discovery led to the passage of a much stronger cleanup law in 1986.[83]

There is an interesting paradox in legislative politics and policy. Widespread consensus is usually required to properly implement innovative policies, but some amount of disagreement and conflict is necessary to refine them. Too much consensus in the policy environment either supports the status quo—however effective or ineffective it may be—or fosters large, experimental policy initiatives that have little chance of achieving success.[84] Severe conflict and disagreement, however, may deadlock efforts to revise policy. Thus, institutional learning is most likely when parties and interest groups not only advance diverse policy remedies for the problems of program implementation, but also approach the oversight process with a willingness to compromise. Unfortunately, this type of approach has not been seen very often at the national level in recent years.

SUMMARY

No major government activity can be undertaken without the consent of legislatures, whether federal or state. No money can be borrowed or spent, and no taxes can be levied, unless the elected representatives willingly consent to the request of the president or a governor. No executive agency or top administrator can function for long without legislative support. The ground rules for the distribution of public goods, services, and regulations are established by legislatures, which may also influence the details of program implementation.

Congress and the state legislatures are responsive to the changing mood of public opinion and to the views expressed by constituents, interest groups, and chief executives. But the desire of legislators to serve the public and curry favor with potential voters and supporters can create problems. Legislative institutions are subject to fads and whims, and they tend to respond to the loudest, best financed, and most persistent demands. Legislators can be manipulated by outsiders who can stir up public support for a position or raise campaign contributions. Groups that are already powerful tend to get what they want, or at least avoid harmful legislative action.[85]

The desire to be responsive and democratic also shapes the organization and practices of American legislatures. The dispersal of power across committees and subcommittees creates opportunities for legislators to influence public policy and gain the gratitude of potential supporters who will help keep them in office. But because legislatures operate by consensus and compromise, they do not always speak with a clear and consistent voice when making public policy. The need to accommodate diverse political interests often produces confusing public policies or no policy at all. Legislatures sometimes are unable to look ahead or to address controversial issues decisively.

Legislative indecision reflects not only uncertainty about how to ameliorate public problems, but also deep partisan cleavages. If public demand for action is strong and clear enough, legislatures have little trouble moving swiftly to crack down on drug dealers or increase the legal drinking age. But major issues about which the parties disagree—taxes, military spending, social welfare spending, and others—have deadlocked legislatures at the national and state levels. The partisan conflict between presidents and Congress, or governors and state legislatures, has also led to stalemate and gridlock. Indeed, Congress has even tried to set the nation's agenda and wrest policy leadership from presidents of the opposite party, but this is an unusual posture for American legislatures to assume. The greatest strength of legislatures lies in acting as a forum where state and national controversies are debated in public. Legislatures are at their best when they educate the public, provide an outlet for the expression of diverse viewpoints, and forge consensus on new directions for public policy.

Chief Executive Politics

Americans have always preferred politics with a personal touch, making heroes and villains out of public figures and evaluating politicians on the basis of human qualities such as integrity, leadership ability, and physical attractiveness. It is rare for the American public to be mobilized by ideological debate or to be interested for very long in institutional deliberations and actions. Political interest typically focuses on individuals, and in most cases this means chief executives—presidents and governors. Chief executives are the most visible, and in many ways the most important, actors in American government.

The prominence of chief executives in American politics today is commonly attributed to the media. The modern media, especially television, find that covering powerful individuals in government is much more appealing and manageable than following complex and often slow-developing processes in legislative, judicial, or bureaucratic institutions. The visibility of chief executives contributes to the public perception that politics and government are principally about what they do.

But media attention is only part of the reason that American politics centers on chief executives. The system of governance set up by the federal and state constitutions also helps explain the phenomenon. The United States is notable in the world for the number of independent, elected chief executives in government. Presidents have an exclusive claim to a national electoral constituency, and unlike prime ministers in parliamentary governments, they are independent of the national legislature. Governors have a somewhat less distinctive electoral position, but they are also independent of the legislatures in their states and independent of elected officials who serve at the national level.[1] Politics centered on the chief executive is not simply a cultural oddity encouraged by media seeking to sell more beer and snack food; rather, it reflects in many ways the intentions of writers of the national and state constitutions.

The term *chief executive politics*, as used here, does not encompass the full range of policymaking activity of American chief executives; it includes only those aspects that are most exclusively attributable to these elected officials. In this chapter, we explore the more visible and important positions taken, decisions made, and policies whose enactment is secured by chief executives—the public record by which they are judged. These records have two main components. First are decisions made by chief executives during crises, such as wars or natural disasters. Second are policy initiatives and innovations advocated by chief executives, such as path-breaking legislation. Chief executives are also involved in a great many routine policy actions, most of which are covered in chapter 4.

RULERS OF THE AGENDA

Chief executives dominate the agenda-setting process in the United States. More often than not, they are able to transform policy ideas from items of discussion among a few to items of discussion among the many, including not only legislators but also citizens. Because they have the public's attention, they force other politicians to pay attention to the matters they think are important. This gives them a tremendous advantage over any rivals in defining the issues for the public and, ultimately, for other politicians. In short, chief executives typically set the terms of debate about political issues at the national, state, and local levels. This is not to say that chief executives are always, or even usually, successful in securing enactment of the policies they prefer. Indeed, it must be understood that chief executives are more impressive in the issue creation and agenda-setting process than in policy formulation and adoption.[2]

Presidents are opinion and policy leaders. Their unique relationship with the national electorate gives them a great deal of flexibility in choosing issues and policies that other national policymakers do not have. Franklin D. Roosevelt pushed the New Deal, Lyndon B. Johnson began the Great Society, Richard M. Nixon made diplomatic breakthroughs with China, Ronald Reagan launched an antigovernment crusade, George H. W. Bush forged a new relationship with the former Soviet Union, Bill Clinton tackled the federal deficit and balanced the budget, George W. Bush convinced Congress to enact major tax cuts, and Barack Obama successfully championed a major expansion of health care insurance. Chief executive politics encompasses the entire spectrum of policies, including distributive, redistributive, regulatory, social, intergovernmental, economic, foreign, defense, and national security.

Chief executives dominate certain issue domains more than others. At the national level, presidents traditionally have dictated American foreign and military policy. This power enables them to shape public opinion about America's proper role in the world. Although presidents cannot control what happens in other nations, the international scene provides "opportunities" for improving their standing and popularity at home, especially around election time. Nixon was an adept exploiter of these international opportunities, presenting the Strategic Arms Limitation Talks I agreement and Henry Kissinger's pledge that "peace was at hand" in Vietnam as he approached reelection in 1972, and taking trips to the Middle East and the Soviet Union as the Watergate scandal heated up.[3] Civil war in Kosovo and Bosnia awarded Clinton the opportunity to position himself as a concerned protector of victimized peoples. President Obama frequently reminded voters during the 2012 election campaign that he authorized the daring raid in Pakistan that resulted in the death of Osama bin Laden, the mastermind of the attacks on the World Trade Center and the Pentagon in 2001.

International crises and foreign and military interventions also pose huge problems for presidents. Since the Vietnam War, negative responses by the national media, Congress, and the public have become a more common reaction to statements presidents have made and actions they have taken in the international arena. Jimmy Carter's and Ronald Reagan's presidencies were damaged by festering foreign policy problems (the Carter administration's handling of the hostage crisis in Iran and the Reagan administration's trading of arms for hostages with Iran and support of Nicaraguan contras). George H. W. Bush's management of the Persian Gulf War in the early 1990s demonstrated his leadership in wartime, but also tested his skill in bringing stability to the troubled Middle East. Bill Clinton also tried to bring peace and stability to the Middle East, but he could not convince Israeli and Palestinian leaders of the need to resolve their differences. George W. Bush was severely criticized for the invasion of Iraq and the inability of the United States to bring about a stable democracy that is friendly to American interests in that country. President Obama endured criticism for expanding the war in Afghanistan, rather than winding it down, after he was elected in 2008. International affairs continue to offer opportunities for presidents to mold public opinion, but there are limits to what presidents can achieve and to what Americans will believe about what presidents say about the world and America's place in it.

Within their respective jurisdictions, most governors take the lead on issues and policies. As is true of presidents, the combination of the media attention and their formal powers makes them substantially more visible and influential than other state and local politicians. The public and other policymakers look to them for new ideas and new proposals, and they have flexibility in articulating policy concerns and proposing remedies that elected officials with narrower constituencies do not share. For example, in 2011, newly elected Republican governor Scott Walker of Wisconsin focused his administration's efforts on rolling back collective bargaining rights for public employees. Republican governor Arnold Schwarzenegger promoted huge investments in stem cell research at California universities during his time in office (2003–2011).

Issue Choice and Definition

Although chief executives have a good deal of freedom to choose their issues, there are limits to this freedom. Occasionally, an issue in the form of a crisis is thrust upon the chief executive. Iraq's invasion of Kuwait in 1990 was a crisis that demanded an immediate and sustained response from President George H. W. Bush. Stability in the Middle East and the world's oil supply were threatened, and a policy needed to be formulated at once. Serbian escalations of the civil war in Bosnia and demands from European allies provoked President Clinton to take action and deploy peacekeeping troops. Uprisings in Tunisia, Egypt, and Libya in 2011 (the so-called Arab Spring) forced President Obama to take various actions, including the formation of a North Atlantic Treaty Organization force to conduct air strikes in Libya. The Supreme Court's decision that upheld most of the provisions of the Patient Protection and Affordable Care Act in 2012 placed immediate demands on governors to reassess their positions on the state role in reforming health care programs and insurance policies in their states.

Not all crises are as compelling as the examples just cited, and chief executives therefore have considerable latitude in labeling an event a crisis. For example, many climate scientists regard increases in world temperatures as a crisis demanding immediate and forceful responses from the president, but neither Bill Clinton nor George W. Bush applied the crisis label to this problem. During his campaigns, and his administration, Barack Obama has emphasized the seriousness of the climate crisis, but he has been unable to get Congress to act on the problem. In part, crises exist in the eyes of their beholders, and presidents have important but limited influence over whether eyes are open or closed.

Table 6-1 shows some of the relationships between issues, stages in the agenda-setting process, and chief executive discretion or range of choice. Crisis situations tend to involve problems that are very difficult for chief executives to ignore, but they usually give chief executives a good deal of flexibility in defining the problem for other policymakers and the public, and in choosing a response. For issues that chief executives choose to promote, what happens at the different agenda-setting stages follows the opposite pattern. Chief executives have wide choice in the selection of problems to address, and they have a strong position from which to define these problems; but their ability to impose their preferred response is limited because they must take into account the preferences of the many other actors in the policymaking process, most of whom defer to chief executives during crises.

Governors may have somewhat less discretion than presidents in choosing issues to emphasize. For these politicians, there are certain perennial issues, reflecting the basic services that state governments provide—education, health care for poor and disabled individuals, highways, law enforcement and prisons, and state tax policy—and these issues are nearly always addressed by leading candidates and officeholders. There are exceptions to this pattern; for example, natural disasters, such as hurricanes or floods, or gun violence, demand immediate responses from governors.

For decades, tax and spending policy debates have dominated all other issues at the state level, sometimes to the point of ensuring the end of the political careers of incumbents who raised taxes and giving other candidates no real choice about how to position themselves.[4] Caught between the constitutional requirement to balance budgets and the reduction in revenues due to economic recessions, many governors are forced to urge their legislatures to raise taxes and cut program spending—actions that often lead to electoral defeat.

| TABLE 6-1 | **Issues, Agendas, and Chief Executive Discretion** |

	Agenda stage		
	Problem/issue	**Problem definition**	**Specification of policy alternatives**
Crisis situation	Violence in Syria	Corrupt regime	Military aid to "insurgents" or direct military action
		American humanitarian responsibility	Finance aid and assistance to refugees
	Inmates riot at state prison	Prisoners take hostages and threaten lives	Address prisoners' demands
		Prison conditions cause violent responses	Negotiation
		Lax security creates crisis	Use of force
Level of chief executive discretion	Low	Moderate	Moderate/high
Noncrisis situation	Health care	Millions uninsured	National insurance plan
		Rising health care costs	Regulation of insurance companies
		Quality of care concerns	Regulation of health care providers
	Education reform	Declining literacy in society	Improve educational facilities
		Underperforming teachers	Adopt performance-based pay system
		Teachers faced with too many students who require special attention	Increase resources available to teachers and schools
Level of chief executive discretion	Moderate/high	Moderate	Moderate/low

Decisions made in Washington also have a huge impact on state budgets because federal aid to the states represents about 25 percent of state and local revenue.[5] During the Great Recession that began in late 2007, state budget making became extremely difficult for state leaders. High unemployment and decreased revenues from income taxes and sales taxes created giant holes in state budgets. Many chief executives faced difficult choices: cutting government spending, laying off government employees, or raising taxes and fees to plug holes in their budgets. In 2009, at the urging of President Obama, Congress passed an economic stimulus program that sent billions of additional federal revenues to state governments to help them plug the budget gaps caused by the weak economy. However, when the stimulus funds ran out in 2011, states were forced to cut spending on education and other programs and lay off thousands of state and local employees.

Presidents and other chief executives are rarely, if ever, whimsical or free-wheeling in their choices about what issues to emphasize; too much is at stake for decisions to be made haphazardly. Presidential scholar Paul Light stated, "All presidential decisions are purposive. Presidents select issues on the basis of their goals."[6] He listed the principal goals as reelection, historical achievement, and good policy.[7]

Most chief executives want to be reelected or leave office with good reputations and, therefore, choose issues they think will help them garner votes and gratitude. In general, they believe their positions on issues matter—indeed, that their own success or failure can hinge on issue stances and policy pledges.[8] This belief does not mean that chief executives are always aggressive in taking positions on a wide range of issues. It means that most perceive a need to address some important issues and to act in a way that is consistent with what they have said, even if vigorous follow-up is lacking. With all the media hype and money that go into contemporary campaigns, chief executives with reelection in mind are likely to be listening to their political advisers, media consultants, and public opinion pollsters as much as to their policy specialists. President Obama prepared for his reelection campaign by "going to the people." Through focus groups and public opinion polls, Obama sought to determine the concerns of the average American and to discover effective language to communicate with potential voters. He even installed David Plouffe, his 2008 campaign manager, next to the Oval Office in the White House to serve as his senior adviser in 2011 and 2012.

Policy agendas are often formed around issues that are evocative and remedies that are thought to be popular, rather than being based on a serious effort to diagnose what is wrong and to find viable solutions. For example, in the 1990s, governors and presidents often took strong stands in favor of tougher criminal penalties for drug use, including capital punishment for so-called drug kingpins. In taking on drug users and drug pushers, chief executives were clearly addressing a popular cause with a popular remedy that never had much of a chance of actually ameliorating the problem. Chief executives sometimes advocate for an appealing remedy so that they can say they have addressed an issue of concern to most Americans, while not really dealing with the deeper problems of American society.

Not all chief executives are concerned with reelection. In fact, some of them—presidents in their second terms, governors who have reached the legal limit of their tenure in office, or others who decide they do not wish to run again—do not have to think about it at all. For most presidents and governors, an election is a means to some larger and more substantive end, such as initiating good public policies, not an end in itself. Chief executives want to leave favorable historical legacies, and most of them recognize that sponsoring noteworthy and effective public policies is the best way to achieve this goal.

The goals of historical recognition and good policies typically blend into one effort. Fortunate chief executives have knowledgeable advisers with ideas that are worthy of consideration. Chief executives who succeed in getting these ideas translated into policy are recognized and remembered, just as those who do not succeed in convincing the Congress or legislature to go along may be labeled as "failures."

Sometimes chief executives use their positions to promote particular ideologies, and ideological expression cannot be neatly subsumed under the categories of reelection, historical recognition, or good public policy. Chief executives emphasize certain issues that have strong ideological content, even though some of them are not particularly popular, as part of a larger effort to build, maintain, or repudiate a dominant ideological coalition. Lyndon Johnson, who had not been a strong supporter of civil rights policies, became in the mid-1960s a champion of programs for poor and minority citizens in an effort to defend and expand the liberal Democratic ideology and build his legacy. Ronald Reagan led an effort to divide this coalition and replace it with one built around conservative causes. He attacked all of the most ideologically loaded policy legacies of the Johnson era, such as public school busing, affirmative action, social welfare programs, and greater federal regulations.[9] President Clinton championed the idea of a "new Democrat" to reposition the Democratic Party in the mainstream of American politics. Clinton eschewed the liberal ideologies of the past and incorporated more centrist policies, such as debt reduction and balanced budgets, welfare reform, and anticrime measures, including support for capital punishment.

President George W. Bush had ambitious foreign and domestic policy agendas—and was able to convince Congress to go along with many of his priorities in his first term. After his reelection in 2004, however, political and public opinion turned against him, and most of his proposals were sidelined as the wars in Iraq and Afghanistan and the economy turned sour.

President Barack Obama was forced by economic circumstances to spend most of his first term dealing with the economic crisis created by the Great Recession and with managing the continuing wars in the Middle East. He was able to convince Democrats in Congress to enact a major economic stimulus program to combat the recession, and to pass a significant health care reform law that would bring health care insurance to 30 million Americans who did not have it.

In presidential administrations, there are often tensions among those who are concerned about issues that contribute to short-term popularity, those who seek to promote ideological principles, and those who are interested in establishing policies of long-term effectiveness. Achieving a balance between these forces is one of the main tasks of chief executives, and some are better at it than others. Franklin Roosevelt offered ideas that brought not only electoral success, but also historical recognition for his policy accomplishments and his ideological leadership. No president since has matched this record. Of the six presidents since Roosevelt who have achieved reelection (Eisenhower, Nixon, Reagan, Clinton, George W. Bush, and Obama), Reagan provided ideological leadership, but had relatively few policy accomplishments; Clinton oversaw unprecedented economic prosperity and achieved several important policy breakthroughs, but his efforts at centrist leadership seemed to inflame rather than cool partisan differences. The domestic policy agenda of President George W. Bush—cutting taxes and reforming education— were popular for a time, but the resulting budget deficits and troublesome wars undermined his legacy.

In 2008, President Obama campaigned on the promise of ending partisan strife and finding a new middle in American politics. He did achieve a major health care insurance overhaul, with little or no help from Republicans, but the backlash against government spending to rescue the struggling U.S. economy and health care reform ("Obamacare") in 2009 and 2010 brought about huge gains for Republican candidates in the 2010 elections, and turned control of the House of Representatives over to a Republican majority. That majority was determined not to cooperate with the president, and in 2011, policymaking ground to a halt, almost to the point at which the federal government defaulted on its debt obligations. In 2012, however, President Obama was reelected by a substantial majority in the Electoral College.

Chief executives, particularly presidents, are rarely at the cutting edge of new issues or policy ideas. In a strict sense, they do not initiate agenda issues or lead the way to innovative approaches to problems. The real initiators are likely to be political activists, interest groups, researchers, members of Congress, or bureaucrats. Most new issues and policy ideas have humble beginnings, with only a small number of people interested in them. Some of these ideas, however, attract the attention of more visible spokespersons, become widely discussed, and eventually attract coalitions of supporters.[10] At any given time, there are streams of acknowledged problems and potential solutions—policy proposals—flowing around and through policymaking institutions.[11] Chief executives and their policy advisers pick out those that fit with their philosophies and directions and promote them. For example, "Megan's law" originated from a small group of concerned New Jersey parents following the murder of a four-year-old girl by a convicted sex offender. Clinton moved this issue to the national agenda by including it in his anti-crime platform. Megan's law, requiring convicted sex offenders to register with local officials, became part of federal anticrime legislation in 1996.

Obviously, many considerations are factored in when choosing issues to promote, among them the political costs associated with certain ideas and the fit between the new idea and the other positions taken by a chief executive.[12] Political parties add another voice to the process of selecting issues. Every four years, the parties' platforms give various advocates the opportunity to debate policy ideas, thereby helping chief executives determine those that have broad support.[13] Typically, chief executive policy leadership does not consist of a flash of inspiration and a headlong rush to legislative action; most often it consists of a set of cautious, purposive decisions made by chief executives and their advisers after surveying the ideas and proposals circulating among the politically active and aware.

Chief executives' agendas frequently follow a predictable pattern dictated by their economic and political environments. For example, in times of economic recession, governors and presidents emphasize government support for unemployment insurance, public works projects, and helping private sector firms expand through tax credits or loan guarantees. When the economy is strong, the attention of chief executives is more likely to shift to other issues, such as education or environmental protection. Governors and presidents just taking office are likely to promote bolder ideas and plans for "cleaning up" the mess of the previous administration, especially if it was left by a different political party. Chief executives seeking reelection are more likely to cling to mainstream proposals and to highlight recent accomplishments, or to argue that they need another four years to complete their agenda, as President Obama did in the 2012 election campaign.

Neglected Matters

Compared with other American policymakers, chief executives deal with an exceptionally wide variety of issues. As tribunes of the people, they are free to discuss just about any policy question they wish. Still, certain kinds of issues are systematically neglected or excluded from their policy agendas; the spectrum of chief executive politics may be wide, but it is far from unlimited. Despite rising partisan polarization, the two major parties still have to assemble majority coalitions, which creates a centrist tendency in American politics. Candidates often stake out very conservative or liberal positions during primary campaigns, but they then "reboot" their positions during the general election. For example, Republican candidate Mitt Romney offered a tough line about illegal immigrants during the 2012 primary campaign, but tacked toward a more moderate position in the general election. His statements during the primaries about the need for illegal immigrants to "self-deport" came back to haunt him in the general election, in which he received few votes (less than 30 percent) from Latino and Asian voters.[14]

Chief executives, as candidates and officeholders, need majorities to support them if they are to succeed in advancing their policy agendas. Therefore, they aim most of their political pitches at the largest sector of the electorate. Because most Americans belong to the middle class—or think they do—U.S. politics tends to revolve around issues that most directly affect the middle class. Immediately after the election in 2012, President Obama asserted that his only mandate was to protect and advance the interests of the middle class. A radical expansion of government, such as a socialist agenda, is consequently irrelevant, and until recently, Republican leaders in Congress and Republican presidential candidates were reluctant to propose any major reductions in the New Deal programs, such as Social Security and unemployment insurance, or in the core entitlement programs of the 1960s, such as Medicare.

A striking example of this tactic was President Clinton's cooptation of portions of the traditional Republican agenda to position himself, and the Democratic Party, at the center of American politics. For example, strict work requirements for welfare recipients had traditionally been a part of the Republican agenda for welfare reform. Clinton championed an "end to welfare as we know it" by requiring a transition from welfare to work when he signed the Personal Responsibility and Work Opportunity Reconciliation Act of 1996. Although it may be difficult to pin down, a kind of majority consensus defines the acceptable range of political discourse in the United States, and successful chief executives remain within this range.[15] For example, George W. Bush strayed outside of this range when he called for changes in Social Security that would give people the option of establishing investment accounts that they would manage themselves, because this change introduced the possibility of reduced retirement income for those who made poor investment choices. The reactions of Democrats, the public, and eventually many Republicans in Congress were overwhelmingly negative.

Generalizations such as the one just offered are deliberately imprecise and can be easily misinterpreted. Our emphasis on middle class or centrist politics does not mean that minorities and poor Americans are neglected altogether. The political history of African Americans or Hispanics—neglected by the white majority for many years, followed by selective attention as their political significance was recognized—confirms the basic thrust of the claim about the forces that dominate agendas, but it also demonstrates that the trends can change. Significant events, media attention, and effective advocacy coalitions can turn a neglected issue into a salient issue in a fairly short time. By the same token, an issue may remain submerged indefinitely if no one with political muscle chooses to promote it. This is often the case for issues that concern poor or disadvantaged Americans. Groups without money to contribute to political campaigns have a harder time getting politicians to pay attention to their concerns. For example, the plight of homeless Americans rarely is addressed by national political leaders because neither homeless people themselves, nor their advocates, have sufficient resources to push their concerns on to the national agenda.

There are no absolutes in the issue creation process. Societies change, sometimes rapidly, and policy ideas that seemed outlandish at one time can become serious agenda items at another. For example, the issue of the digital divide—the disparity between the technological haves and have-nots in the United States—and policies to address the issue, such as Clinton's multibillion dollar proposal to increase access to computers and the Internet through funding technology infrastructure, did not attract widespread attention until the late 1990s.[16] (A follow-up program was part of President Obama's stimulus package.) Economic, technological, and environmental developments are not the only causes of these societal changes; human beings may also be the agents of social and political change. Chief executives can and do change the nature of political discourse by daring to explore new directions. President Obama's insistence on expanding health care insurance for previously uncovered Americans brought about proposals for a national health care program that had not been seriously considered since the first Clinton administration (1993–1994).

THE POWER TO PERSUADE

The presence or absence of crisis conditions is of overarching significance in explaining the politics associated with chief executive policymaking. During crises, normal politics is suspended, and the power to decide comes to rest with chief executives and those they choose to advise them. Policy is determined in a centralized, hierarchical manner. This is one of those matters about which there is nearly universal consensus among legislators and other policymakers. Presidents are expected to lead during times of crisis, and other political elites recognize that presidents need room to maneuver if they are to do this effectively. With this unilateral power comes the responsibility for the decisions that are made. Crises test a chief executive's leadership and decision-making ability in an arena where the stakes are very high. For example, George W. Bush was widely criticized for his handling of the devastating effects of Hurricane Katrina in New Orleans. He even prematurely praised his administration's emergency response to the disaster, even though more than 1,000 people perished and thousands of others were huddled in the Superdome with little or no assistance. In contrast, President Obama won high marks in 2012 for his quick and compassionate response to the victims of Hurricane Sandy, which devastated large areas of New York, New Jersey, and Connecticut just a week before the presidential election.

In other situations, chief executives must employ different political skills. Their ability to act unilaterally is greatly diminished, and their most important asset becomes the capacity to persuade the public and members of Congress that their policy ideas deserve not just consideration but also action. One aspect of this political skill is working with advisers and executive officials to put together an attractive program of policies. The other is selling the program to the legislature or the bureaucracy. In general, the government apparatus is stacked against chief executives who seek to innovate. There are many competing power centers that can frustrate the designs of chief executives if those centers are ignored or dealt with improperly. To be successful in normal politics, a chief executive must demonstrate the ability to be a leader among equals.

The failure of President Clinton's health care reform effort in 1993 is a classic example of the limits of presidential power. President Clinton made health care reform the top domestic policy objective of his first term. If successful, the reform would have made history by completely restructuring the health care insurance industry and the government's role in it. Although the president's party was in charge of both the Senate and House of Representatives, his proposal encountered intense opposition from the health insurance industry, which invested millions of dollars in advertising campaigns to convince the American people that greater government involvement in health care would be a disaster.[17]

Although health care was considered a top concern of more than half of the American people in public opinion polls of the early 1990s, most were confused by Clinton's technically laden proposals and easily swayed by the television advertisements.[18] Furthermore, Clinton's handling of the task force on health care was questioned by Republicans on Capitol Hill and ordinary citizens alike. The appointment of his wife, Hillary Clinton, to head the task force was controversial, as was the task force's reliance on closed-door meetings. The task force produced a thick document detailing a complicated national health plan that failed to muster the support of Congress and the public. The health care reforms that Clinton was eventually able to achieve included improvements in existing programs, such as Medicare and Medicaid, and the creation of a federal and state insurance program for low- and moderate-income children (the State Children's Health Insurance Program), but fell far short of his original grand vision.

Tools of the Trade

Richard Neustadt's influential book *Presidential Power* provides a useful framework for understanding how chief executives exercise power.[19] Neustadt points out that executive power in American government is both protected and restricted by the Constitution. Presidents have a great deal of authority over the implementation of laws passed by Congress and over foreign affairs and military matters, but their domestic policymaking authority is limited. Certain presidents, however—Franklin Roosevelt was always uppermost in Neustadt's mind—have exerted tremendous influence over both foreign and domestic policy.

This observation leads to one of Neustadt's major points: Executive power is largely potential. Actual power depends on the ability of chief executives to leverage their formal powers and to stretch their influence over as many aspects of government as possible. Success implies that chief executives have convinced other government actors that going along with the plans and policies of the chief executive will be in their best interest. Because this kind of governing entails extensive bargaining, Neustadt's primary and best-known conclusion is that presidential power lies mainly in the ability to persuade. Political scientist Alan Rosenthal elaborates on Neustadt's observation, pointing to the various tools that governors have at their disposal to practice the art of persuasion. They include several important powers, such as the power to initiate legislation, to reject legislation passed by the legislature, to provide services, to attract publicity, and to achieve popularity.[20]

The line-item veto is an especially useful weapon that governors can use in political battles. Whereas the Constitution does not afford the president the authority to strike out individual sections of bills, governors in most states can veto parts of bills that offend them, or even revise sentences in legislation to make them more to their liking. If legislators try to graft unrelated language onto a bill, or attempt to insert projects to benefit particular legislative districts, a governor can strike whatever he or she wants from the bill without rejecting the entire law.

Line-item vetoes can be particularly effective under conditions of divided government. When the legislature is controlled by one party and the chief executive is from another party, the veto (normal and line item) allows the chief executive to have much more control over legislative outcomes than would otherwise be the case. Because it is highly unlikely that a president or governor could continually veto whole bills and stay politically popular or viable, the line-item veto becomes an especially powerful tool. Presidents of both parties have been aware of this for some time and have argued for line-item veto power. Congress granted a form of this power to the president in the Line Item Veto Act, passed in 1996, but the veto provisions of this law were revoked by the U.S. Supreme Court two years later.[21]

The governorships in most states have evolved in a way that closely parallels the evolution of the presidency; the once largely ceremonial offices are now the engines of state politics. Governors operate in smaller arenas than presidents, which reduces somewhat the number of powerful political actors with whom they must contend. But the formal powers of governors are constrained in many important ways, which makes bargaining skills even more necessary. Governors may face tougher persuasive tasks than presidents because in most states, certain cabinet officers, such as the state treasurer or attorney general, are elected by the voters, not appointed by the governor. It is not unusual for these officials to be political rivals of the governor. In any case, their political independence is a virtual certainty.[22]

Chief executive power is "elastic" in that governors and presidents with similar or identical formal powers exert widely varying degrees of influence within their governments. Part of this variation can be attributed to political or economic factors, such as the presence or absence of crises, which affect the degree of centralized leadership. There can be no doubt, however, that the aspirations and abilities of chief executives also influence how much power they wield. As governors, Andrew Cuomo of New York and Chris Christie of New Jersey exert more influence on the national political scene than their predecessors, in part because their ambitions for higher office are well known, and they have become nationally prominent as a result. At the national level, President Carter's inability to master the political process during his administration, despite the presence of solid Democratic majorities in both houses of Congress, reveals him to have been considerably less adept at the use of his potential power than Lyndon Johnson or Ronald Reagan. President Clinton had difficulty managing Congress during the early years of his first term, when he enjoyed a Democratic majority there. He then squared off against House Republicans, who had gained control of that chamber in 1994, over budget legislation, which eventually led to a government shutdown in 1995. But during his second term, Clinton was able to work cooperatively with congressional Republicans on several matters, including welfare reform and a budget agreement in 1997. George W. Bush and Barack Obama were successful while their fellow party members were running Congress, but much less so when the opposition party gained in midterm elections.

Comparisons between the most recent presidents and those who served in the 1940s, 1950s, or 1960s should leave the student of contemporary politics somewhat uneasy. In the days of Franklin Roosevelt, Dwight D. Eisenhower, and Lyndon Johnson, there was a limited number of truly powerful interest groups, and like-minded groups often worked together so that deals could be struck with the leaders who represented broad segments of society, such as business, labor, and agriculture. Party leaders exercised a great deal of influence over their ranks, which simplified presidential negotiations with Congress. There were some strong and independent executive branch officials and military leaders who had to be taken into account, but as Neustadt emphasized, one man with sound management ability, good interpersonal skills, knowledge of politics, and a clear sense of direction could hold the various pieces of government together throughout the bargaining process.

By the 1970s many presidential scholars had begun to doubt whether anyone could do what Roosevelt and Johnson had done (and, in fact, none of the modern presidents have).[23] Political conditions had changed, and these changes were affecting the ways chief executives exercised power. Probably the most important changes from the 1970s to the present have been in the number of active participants in the political process, the relationship between politicians and their constituents, and, most recently, the expansion of media coverage through the Internet and around-the-clock cable television coverage. (For a discussion of the role of the media in contemporary politics, see chapter 8.) The increasing number and variety of interest groups, the staunch independence of elected officials, the persistent institutional conflict and competition, and the pervasive media have produced what many observers view as an unmanageable pluralism.

It was and is unmanageable if the chief executive uses traditional bargaining strategies. Presidents Reagan and Clinton demonstrated that power can be amassed in a significant new way. They did not rely exclusively on bargaining with political elites; instead they took their messages directly to the people, using weekly radio broadcasts and speeches on television to persuade them to pressure political officials to endorse the president's initiatives. The mass media emerged as the most potent weapon in a president's arsenal, and Reagan, Clinton, and Obama used it to their advantage. In the mass media age, it may not matter very much whether political power brokers admire a chief executive's political acumen, as long as they have sufficient respect for, or fear of, the chief executive's ability to arouse the public through direct appeals.[24]

Increased use of direct appeals to the public as a way of enhancing chief executive power is well suited to contemporary politics, just as "inside the beltway" bargaining was more appropriate strategy to pursue in the political environment of the 1950s. The independence of other elected officials comes from their certainty that they have established, and can maintain, favorable images with voters. These relationships hinge more and more on money and the use of advanced communication technology. To the extent that chief executives can disrupt these relationships, the independence of other political actors is threatened. Legislators pay close attention to constituent opinions and to the people who finance their costly political campaigns; chief executives who use the media effectively can influence these opinions.[25] When this kind of influence occurs, or when politicians think it is occurring, resistance to a chief executive's policy preferences dissipates, and persuasive power has been exercised.

Clinton's response to proposed Republican tax cuts provides a good example. During the balanced budget deliberations of the mid- and late 1990s, Republicans proposed tax cuts that could be covered only by reducing funding for many social programs, such as Medicare, Medicaid, education, and the environment.[26] Facing opposition from the Republican-controlled Congress, Clinton went directly to the public to preserve the funding levels for these programs. Through his weekly radio address and other media outlets, the president continually repeated his commitment to those programs. By arousing public concern and support, Clinton pressured the Republicans in Congress to forgo the proposed tax cuts and preserve more funding for his priorities.[27]

The ability to persuade is still the major determinant of chief executive power. Political persuasion is a multifaceted enterprise, however; it can be accomplished through traditional political bargaining among self-interested parties, through momentum-building appeals to the public, or through some combination of the two. When opportunities for "going public" are plentiful, as they are in contemporary national politics, one should expect extensive use of this tactic by telegenic politicians.[28] But bargaining and other customary political skills will continue to dominate when direct appeals to voters are difficult, when chief executives lack media appeal, or when there are a manageable number of high-ranking participants in the policy process. In most circumstances, chief executives must find the right mix of wholesale (public) and retail (private) politics to achieve their objectives.

Leaders and Followers

Most of those who have written on the subject seem to agree that the acquisition of power is the sine qua non of executive leadership.[29] Without power, leadership is virtually impossible. The fragmented nature of American government at all levels makes swift action difficult; therefore, the essence of chief executive leadership is providing government with a direction or purpose. Implied in this conception of leadership is change. Leaders need to produce tangible results, and typically these take the form of identifiable changes in government organization or policy.[30] Planned changes that are effective and long lasting, and decisive action in crises, are the hallmarks of effective leadership.

The essential ingredients of chief executive leadership are both personal and institutional. Judgments about personality or character are highly subjective; therefore, it is difficult to generalize, but personality seems more important than ever in the age of media politics. James David Barber, who made a career of studying the role of personality in politics, pointed out that some chief executives derive positive feelings, such as satisfaction, exhilaration, and joy, from their political activity, whereas others experience mostly negative feelings, such as paranoia, resentment, and sadness.[31] Exhibiting some sort of positive disposition is part of effective leadership. Advisers, subordinates, and even rivals and opponents are at their best when they are driven by a forceful and inspiring personality.

The institutional side of executive leadership is concerned with the selection of advisers, analysts, political operatives, communications specialists, and the others who are part of an administration. Most chief executives are able to surround themselves with a sizable cadre of loyalists, and their success at channeling the energies and skills of these individuals on behalf of their objectives is critical in determining their ultimate effectiveness as political leaders. The Executive Office of the President is the collection of individuals and groups that presidents use to direct the rest of the executive branch. It contains several important advisory bodies, such as the Council of Economic Advisers and the National Security Council and Homeland Security Council, as well as more operational units, such as the Office of Management and Budget (OMB) and the Office of the Trade Representative, and the White House staff. All told, almost 1,900 positions are included, with the OMB and the White House staff being the largest at 525 and 450, respectively.[32]

Once the appointees are in place, the chief executives make the most critical choices: whose advice to take and when. And their range of options is quite large. They can rely on many advisers or a few; they can make frequent or little use of cabinet officials, outside specialists, or members of their personal staff or families; or they can establish hierarchical, competitive, or collegial relationships among their advisers. There are no proven formulas for success, but the experiences of several presidents provide useful insights into this aspect of chief executive politics.

Having many close and able advisers who represent various perspectives is widely regarded as a prudent practice, although relatively few presidents have followed it. Franklin Roosevelt and John Kennedy usually get the highest marks on this score. Nixon's complete reliance on three or four advisers during his second term is regarded as a reason for his downfall and served as a warning to other presidents of the dangers of inaccessibility.[33] Despite the Nixon precedent, concerns about leaks of politically sensitive information to the press and the natural unpleasantness associated with hearing unfavorable reports about their administration limited the openness of the Ford, Carter, Reagan, and George H. W. Bush presidencies. President Clinton set out to assemble a cabinet that "looked like America" and achieved greater diversity in race and gender than any of his predecessors.[34] He also received good marks for openness.

George W. Bush organized his staff hierarchically and relied on a narrow range of advisers, which featured Dick Cheney, his vice president, but also included Condoleezza Rice, his first-term national security adviser and second-term secretary of state; Andrew Card, his chief of staff (until 2006); Donald Rumsfeld, his defense secretary (until 2006); and of course political adviser Karl Rove. President Obama followed many of Clinton's leads, and in fact hired many of Clinton's former advisers, such as Rahm Emanuel, his first chief of staff. Both Clinton and Obama organized their advisers in such a way that several senior staffers had direct access to the president, and both encouraged wide-ranging discussion among top advisers and cabinet officials. This may have broadened the range of advice, but it also contributed to hours of deliberation and leaks to the news media.[35] In an interesting twist, Obama was criticized at the beginning of his second term for having a top staff dominated by white men, and for exhibiting a tendency to be somewhat withdrawn and aloof.[36]

Governors have very different needs from those of presidents and organize their staffs accordingly. Governors have an average of 63 staff members; governors of small states such as Nebraska have only 9 staff members, whereas the governors of New York and Florida have 180 and 325 staff members, respectively.[37] Nearly all governors employ political advisers, legislative liaisons, bureaucratic liaisons, press secretaries or communications specialists, legal advisers, and budget experts.[38] The use of teams of agency officials and political advisers to develop policy initiatives is common. Most governors regard selling their policy ideas to the legislature as one of their most difficult tasks, a true test of their leadership ability.[39]

Making a distinction between decision making in crisis situations and that in normal, "noncrisis" situations helps simplify the enormous variation in the way presidents and governors go about carrying out their responsibilities. At one end of the spectrum are visible and threatening crises in which the number of participants is small, advice consists mainly of substantive information and analysis, and chief executive decisions are authoritative. At the other end are controversies over domestic initiatives in which the number of active participants is large, political advice and calculations are usually more important than analytical information, and chief executives and legislatures battle with one another over the ultimate outcomes. The power of chief executives is obviously greatest during crises, but some aspects of these situations are dangerous, in that they create political risks, and unpleasant, because difficult choices must be made.

Presidents and governors often try to achieve greater control over policymaking by defining problems in crisis terms and then demanding that legislatures comply with their suggestions. President George W. Bush declared a national crisis in education and persuaded Congress to enact a major education policy reform, known as the No Child Left Behind Act. President Obama emphasized the crisis in the lack of health care insurance for more than 30 million Americans and convinced Congress to pass the Affordable Care Act. At the state level, many governors have argued that their states' schools were performing so poorly that rapid and substantial change was required to remedy the situation. They have called special legislative sessions and introduced far-reaching reforms. By taking this approach, they have hoped to put additional pressure on the legislatures and on interest groups to act swiftly and in accordance with the governors' objectives.

The chief executive sets the basic outline of policy action in campaign promises and other statements, such as during annual State of the Union speeches for presidents or State of the State addresses by governors. Translating these ideas into concrete policy proposals is the job of advisers and policy development groups. The personal involvement of chief executives in the formulation process varies with their personalities and preferences. Some try to master most of the details, whereas others content themselves with sketching the big picture; some are rigid and doctrinaire, and others are flexible and accommodating. Clinton and Obama, and Bush and Reagan, offer illustrative contrasts. Obama and Clinton impressed other politicians with their command of the details of policies and policy options. They immersed themselves in the development and technical details of virtually every proposal. Reagan's knowledge of policy was quite general, in some cases mostly anecdotal, but many of his pronouncements inspired successful and significant policy actions that reflected the conservative philosophy he championed. George W. Bush, a self-styled "chairman of the board," also preferred to set a general course of action and then delegate the details to Vice President Dick Cheney, senior staff members, and cabinet members.

Once preferred policy approaches have been devised, chief executives and their staffs turn their attention to eliminating the many barriers to enactment. The outcome of this effort is determined largely by their ability to persuade others to follow their lead. If those with a stake in a decision can be herded into a few identifiable groups and agree to be bound by the bargains their leaders strike, policy change is likely. Unless competing interests are brought together, initiatives get shredded in the fragmented governmental machinery.

Chief executives have an array of persuasive devices that can be deployed on behalf of their initiatives. These include direct appeals to the public, the dispensation of special favors such as helping a member of Congress raise campaign funds, promises to key players of appointments to prestigious positions, and the threat or use of a veto. All of these strategies and more are commonly used in this high-stakes arena of power and politics.

The enactment of the nation's toughest laws governing the purchase and ownership of assault weapons in New Jersey is a case of strong gubernatorial leadership against entrenched opponents. During his campaign for the New Jersey statehouse in 1989, Governor Jim Florio announced that if elected, he would seek a ban on the sale and ownership of the assault weapons often used by drug dealers in street fighting against police officers. Within a month of his inauguration, he called upon the legislature to pass a tough ban on assault weapons. With the public opinion polls showing overwhelming public support, he pushed for action and lined up backing from gun control and law enforcement organizations.

The National Rifle Association (NRA), sportsmen's organizations, and hunting groups quickly organized to stop or water down Florio's proposal. Knowing that broad public support would not be forthcoming, they focused their fire on legislators and the governor. Thousands of letters poured into legislators' offices, and phone lines were jammed with calls from irate gun owners. Most effective were the weekend visits made by anti–gun control advocates to legislators at their homes and local offices to engage in face-to-face lobbying. A week before the vote, more than 5,000 gun enthusiasts rallied in the state capital and cheered as their leaders denounced Governor Florio and warned legislators that they would pay a price at the polls if they supported the ban on assault weapons. On the day of the vote, hundreds of NRA members chanted threatening slogans in the court-yard outside the legislative chambers while their leaders tracked individual legis-lators and reminded them of the consequences of voting against the NRA.

As the vote neared, the staff in the governor's office became fearful that the NRA tactics were working. Several Democrats were threatening to vote against the governor's plan. Wavering or uncommitted legislators were brought to the "front office" (the governor's office in Trenton) and reminded that they would need the governor's support for future measures. The ban finally passed both the state senate and the assembly, with no votes to spare. Governor Florio had succeeded in the art of persuasion, but not without putting maximum pressure on some of his supporters. As one senior New Jersey legislator described the experience, "I never want to be put through that kind of vote again. I am not cut out for suicide missions."[40]

More than twenty years later, President Obama also faced off against the NRA and Republicans over the issue of gun control following the massacre of twenty children and six adults in Newtown, Connecticut, in late 2012. He made speeches to national audiences several times just after the incident, stressed its importance in his second inaugural address, and put gun control measures (assault weapons ban and background checks for all gun purchases) at the top of his legislative agenda. Although the public had been more or less evenly divided for several years on whether stricter gun control laws were needed, public opinion was moving in the president's direction in early 2013, but his success in Congress was by no means ensured.[41]

THE BUCK STOPS HERE

Harry Truman, in characterizing his presidency, was fond of saying that "the buck stops here." Indeed, chief executives are involved in a staggering list of issues because the ultimate authority to carry out governmental policy nearly always rests with them. It is helpful to think of this vast range of issues as falling into three categories: (1) international and intergovernmental policies and actions, (2) economic and budgetary policies, and (3) domestic policies, such as health care and education.[42]

As the international economy becomes more extensively interwoven, states are having more frequent direct dealings with foreign nations, but for-eign policy is still reserved mainly for presidents. Modern presidents usually make foreign policy their highest priority because they have more power to determine policy in this area, and they cannot ignore international crises, such as international terrorism or humanitarian tragedies. Economic and budget-ary policies come next; presidents recognize that perceptions about the suc-cess or failure of their administrations hinge on the state of the economy. Domestic policies often come in third on the list of presidential priorities because significant breakthroughs in this area are almost entirely dependent on the willingness of Congress to go along with the president's proposals and are therefore difficult to achieve.[43]

President Clinton was an exception to the general rule of putting foreign policy first. With the end of the Cold War, issues that had demanded the greatest attention of previous presidents practically disappeared. Clinton focused on domestic policy issues. Unlike George H. W. Bush, who was well prepared as a foreign policy leader, Clinton's lack of military service and experience on the international stage made him less qualified to build his presidency on foreign policy accomplishments. Clinton's experience in state government prepared him to deal with the domestic issues he tackled, such as welfare and education reform, balancing the budget, and downsizing the government bureaucracy.

For governors, budgetary and social policy matters dominate. Budgets are particularly important; they represent the ultimate expression of the chief executive's priorities and are a principal means of exercising control over the legislature, the courts, and the bureaucracy.[44] Budget preparation affords chief executives at the state level the opportunity to assert their preferences on nearly every aspect of policy, from the cost of college tuition to the cost of a bus ride.

Budget decisions may be especially difficult for governors because, unlike the president and the federal government, they are typically unable to borrow money to operate government programs. Instead they must cut programs, raise revenues, or both to get through tough times. The Great Recession propelled the states into one of the worst fiscal periods in decades. The years following the Great Recession were especially troubling for states because the ability to obtain added state revenues usually lags behind the national economic recovery. Despite the $135 billion in temporary financial assistance from the federal American Recovery and Reinvestment Act passed in 2009, forty-three states reduced their 2009 budgets by $31.3 billion compared with only thirteen states reducing their budgets in fiscal 2008, and only three in fiscal 2007.[45] A total of $1.5 billion in revenue increases occurred in fiscal 2009, as fourteen states increased their taxes and fees. On the other hand, twenty states enacted net decreases in revenues from taxes and fees.[46]

For decades, budget decisions have overshadowed nearly all others at the national level as Congress scrambled to cope with huge and rising deficits. Washington insiders spoke of the "budget driving the policy process," by which they meant that substantive policy questions were subordinated to budgetary considerations, such as not exceeding the spending levels specified in budget resolutions when new programs were authorized or, more commonly, when old programs were reauthorized.

When the economy boomed in the late 1990s and revenues poured into the U.S. Treasury, there was a brief shift from "deficit politics" to "surplus politics." Government surpluses became the center of a debate: should they be used to overhaul the Social Security system to ensure its future viability, or should they be used to pay off the national debt or reduce taxes? After his election in 2000, George W. Bush answered that question by convincing Congress to lower tax rates, beginning in 2001. The Bush-era tax cuts, combined with rising costs for entitlement programs and wars in Afghanistan and Iraq meant that deficit and debt politics quickly returned, and continued to dominate policymaking in Washington in the early decades of the twenty-first century. During the last two years of President Obama's first term, he battled with Republican members of the House and Senate over how, and when, to increase taxes and cut spending to reduce the nation's annual deficit and long-term debt.

Slogans and Symbols

Presidents and governors inhabit worlds filled with symbolism. Aside from the many ceremonial functions associated with these offices, symbolic rhetoric is used to build consensus on matters of general principle or for specific policies. For example, President Clinton continually invoked certain themes and slogans in relation to his politics. Education and tax credits were ways to help the middle class, which had been "losing ground," and welfare reform, which emphasized work to "end welfare as we know it" and to "break the cycle of dependency." When the policies of a chief executive are announced, they are often described in highly symbolic terms, typically portraying the chief executive as being above parochial politics and working in the larger interest of the nation, state, or city.

All modern presidents have been attentive to symbolic rhetoric. In 1963, President Kennedy made a famous speech in Berlin in which he declared himself to be a citizen of Berlin ("Ich bin ein Berliner"), which received great applause from the German audience, and great attention from world leaders. President Johnson tried to reassure the country about the progress of the Vietnam War with periodic television addresses to the nation, but most of them fell flat. President Nixon emphasized the importance of "law and order" in nearly all of his speeches. President Reagan famously implored Soviet leader Mikhail Gorbachev to "tear down this wall" in Berlin in 1987. And George W. Bush used a bullhorn to assure the crowd at Ground Zero that he could hear them, and that the rest of the world could hear them, following the 9/11 terrorist attacks.

Nonrhetorical symbols also contribute to the leadership mystique of chief executives. President Kennedy played a lot of touch football and did a lot of sailing with his brothers and family. By jogging and playing golf, Bill Clinton sought to reinforce the image of a vigorous man who was strong enough to handle the job and who shared the average American's love of recreation and sports. By playing jazz saxophone, he positioned himself as an admirer of an important component of American culture. President George W. Bush also was often seen jogging or clearing brush at his ranch in west Texas. President Obama had a basketball court built on the White House lawn and was occasionally seen in regular games with staff members, cabinet members, and the occasional National Basketball Association professional. Projecting a compelling, vigorous image can be useful to effective political leadership.

It is not uncommon for political observers to point out that many chief executive policies are merely symbolic. This charge has often been leveled against policies in such areas as civil rights, welfare, environmental protection, and foreign policy, where rhetoric usually exceeds action by a large margin. The civil rights statutes of 1957 and 1960, and executive orders dating back to 1950, did little to reduce the various forms of discrimination at which they were directed. Eventually, however, they led to stronger and more effective statutes—the Civil Rights Act of 1964 and the Voting Rights Act of 1965 and executive orders in 1965 and 1969—that produced significant changes in black employment and voting.[47] Given the nature of American policymaking, initial steps that are high on symbolism and low on substance are often necessary to pave the way for policies that produce real change.

Symbolism also plays a major role in crisis decision making. The conduct of the Persian Gulf War was, in effect, a series of carefully orchestrated symbols. Before launching a war against Iraq in 1990, President George H. W. Bush visited the troops at Thanksgiving, consulted with world leaders at the White House, and summoned congressional leaders to his office for private briefings. The purpose of all this was to demonstrate that the president was carefully and deliberately weighing the options before risking American lives. President Obama regularly made unannounced visits to the troops serving in Afghanistan to show support and respect for their service, which sent a powerful message not only to them but also to Americans back home and to other world leaders.

These examples point up how difficult it is to make definitive judgments about symbolism and substance, particularly with regard to the high-visibility policies of chief executive politics. Chief executives sponsor policies for both symbolic and substantive reasons; the balance between the two is probably best judged with the benefit of historical perspective.

Opportunities for Innovation

The conservative inclinations of American government are likely to be embodied in chief executive policies. Nevertheless, the elective institutions of American government can make innovative decisions, and when they do, it is almost always chief executives who provide the driving force. Presidential scholar James Ceaser pointed out that "presidents have an important role to play in covering the struggle of self-interest [that pervades American politics] with a veneer of poetry and calling at certain moments for sacrifice for the common good."[48]

A crisis creates an opportunity for a chief executive to pursue innovative policies. Wars permit all sorts of unusual measures—industry seizures, rationing, strict wage and price controls, and plans for world government. The Great Depression brought forth the New Deal programs such as Social Security, unemployment insurance, and many more that had direct and tangible effects on citizens throughout the country. It is difficult to overstate the significance of agencies such as the Rural Electrification Administration or the Tennessee Valley Authority for the millions of rural Americans who lived in primitive conditions until the New Deal brought them electrical power, or of minimum wage and labor relations laws for the millions of blue-collar workers of that era. Policies that produce changes of such magnitude have long-standing political force and enshrine the leaders who sponsored them. They also encourage other chief executives to aspire to similar accomplishments.

It would be a mistake, however, to equate crises and innovation in American politics. One of the most significant revelations of a crisis like the Great Depression of the 1930s or the Great Recession of the 2000s is that centralized policy action is possible when the president gains support from Congress. President Johnson worked with a huge Democratic majority in Congress, which shared his view that poverty should be reduced and that health care should be guaranteed for older Americans and for those in poverty. They worked together to create innovative policies. President Reagan successfully sponsored major income tax legislation in his first year in office, as did President George W. Bush. Most recently, President Obama championed health care reform.

However, as described in chapter 1, from the 1950s to the 2000s, the presidency was often in the hands of one party while Congress was controlled by another. During most of the 1990s, the presidency was held by Clinton, a Democrat, whereas Congress was under the control of the Republicans. During half of President Obama's first term, Republicans held enough seats in the Senate to block action and controlled the House of Representatives. Such divided government frequently results in stalemate or compromise, but seldom expansive policy innovation. Presidents George W. Bush and Obama achieved most of their important accomplishments when members of their own parties were in charge on Capitol Hill.

Conditions favoring change in governmental programs also exist in state capitals as governors and legislatures of the same party have tackled such difficult problems as education and welfare reform, environmental concerns, and economic development. Welfare reform is an especially good example of state leadership eventually pushing the federal government to act. Beginning in the 1950s, federal policymakers bemoaned the dismal performance of welfare programs, but failed to effect significant change. Then, in the late 1980s and early 1990s, governors in various states forged a new consensus. Put simply, welfare programs had to be redefined; entitlements that were said to encourage dependency were replaced by welfare-to-work programs, such as Florida's GAIN program, to foster self-sufficiency. A strong emphasis on work activity was implemented through the use of work requirements as a condition for receiving assistance. By the time the federal government enacted its version of welfare reform, many states had already adopted similar programs.

Working majorities in legislatures do not simply appear out of the blue. They come about because popular chief executives make an effort to assemble them. Policies and politics are inseparable. Innovative policies are most often the product of an evolutionary process that includes an awareness among politicians of widespread public concern about certain problems, the selection of popular solutions, and the use of persuasive techniques to build a policy majority among legislators. Chief executives can easily stumble in any of these steps, but they can also succeed; their successes are policies that produce change.

Benefits for Whom?

Chief executives are fond of claiming that their policies benefit all members of society. In a sense, this is true. To the extent that macroeconomic policies contribute to overall economic growth, there are widely shared gains. When threats to national security are effectively rebuffed, everyone is more secure. When bureaucracies are reorganized to function more efficiently or law enforcement is improved to reduce crime, the whole society is better off. A more nuanced analysis, however, reveals variations in the benefits policies convey to different population segments or geographical areas. And, not surprisingly, these variations have political roots.

Like most elected officials, chief executives pursue policies that benefit their principal political supporters, or those they wish to cultivate in the next election. This support of constituent interests is not always a matter of narrow partisanship or cynicism about doing what is best for the country. For most chief executives, there is a natural merging, over time, of their views about what is best for society and their preference for policies that disproportionately benefit their supporters. New Deal Democrats, for example, tended to view the world as the struggle of workers and other ordinary citizens to use government to curb the abuses of big business. The policies of Franklin Roosevelt and Harry Truman were aimed primarily at helping white male workers, who became the core of the Democratic Party as the quality of their lives improved during the 1940s and 1950s.

In the early 1960s, John Kennedy presided over an increasingly fragile Democratic majority coalition that needed the votes not only of blue-collar whites but also of African Americans to control national elections.[49] This need led to the serious pursuit of civil rights policies and programs to aid poor individuals, but always with an eye toward not alienating white, middle-class Democrats. Since the 1960s, African Americans have been the most cohesive Democratic voting bloc.[50] Reagan's desire to shrink some government programs was aimed at pleasing the middle and upper classes, from which the Republican Party draws its strength.

Clinton's centrist platform was an attempt to win back many of the conservative Democrats, independents, and moderate Republicans who had stopped voting for Democratic presidential candidates in the 1980s. His emphasis on issues such as Medicaid, Medicare, education, and the environment during his 1996 reelection campaign, and at the beginning of his second term, was an attempt to put these issues on the national agenda and help Democrats get elected in future congressional elections. George W. Bush's program to lower capital gains and other taxes was designed to hold on to hard-core Republican supporters. His education reform legislation and expansion of prescription drug programs that emphasized "compassionate conservatism" were designed to broaden the appeal of the Republican Party, especially with older Americans who had often voted for Democratic presidents. President Obama's focus on health care reform, acceptance of gays in the military, support for equal pay for women, and support for the young children of illegal immigrants hoping to become U.S. citizens were also designed to build support with traditional and emerging constituent groups in the Democratic coalition.

The meshing of chief executive policies and constituent preferences is never by any means complete. The policy universe is too crowded and complicated for chief executives always to help their friends and hurt their enemies. Carter lost the support of organized labor because he did not push minimum wage and national health insurance legislation hard enough to suit union leaders.[51] Clinton left many of his most liberal supporters disillusioned because he did not push for policy changes such as allowing homosexuals to serve openly in the military, and preventing state restrictions on abortion. George W. Bush angered many fiscal conservatives when he persuaded Congress to expand prescription drug coverage for older Americans, which contributed to growing the federal deficit. Obama disappointed many liberals in his party when he expanded the war in Afghanistan, and did not push hard enough for a "single-payer" health care insurance, which would have greatly expanded the government's role in providing health care services.

It is not uncommon for chief executives to contradict one of their publicly stated positions, rather than to pursue policies that displease important voting blocs. For much of his public career, George H. W. Bush supported a woman's right to choose an abortion, but he shifted positions 180 degrees in order to fit comfortably on the Republican ticket in 1980. By 1988, when he sought the presidency on his own, Bush had become an ardent advocate of restrictions on abortion. Reagan often changed his mind at politically opportune moments, making adept adjustments in his positions on Social Security, farm subsidies, public works programs, and import restrictions. For much of his public career, Clinton supported policies aligned with liberal ideologies. He shifted his position somewhat in order to garner enough mainstream support to defeat Bush in the 1992 presidential election. During both his first and second terms, it was sometimes difficult to tell the difference between Clinton's policy proposals and those of Republicans in Congress, the passage of North American Free Trade Agreement (NAFTA) in 1993 and welfare reform in 1996 being two important cases in point. Political leaders sometimes have to follow changes in the political wind in order to stay in charge. Candidate Obama promised to close the prison at Guantanamo Bay, Cuba, that held accused terrorists, but changed his mind when he assumed the presidency.

PROMISES AND PERFORMANCE

Chief executive policies are born of grand promises and often generate great expectations about societal change. President Obama's campaign in 2008 was built around the simple themes of hope and change. Invariably, the results fall short of what was promised, but what is accomplished may be quite significant nonetheless. The true results of chief executive policies are realized over an extended period of time as programs and procedures become institutionalized and policies are modified. Studying the consequences of such policies reveals many examples that confirm the essentially political nature of the implementation process and underscore how difficult it is to make precise judgments about the effects of public policies.

In 1967, Lyndon Johnson came up with an idea for helping poor Americans with one of their most pressing problems, the lack of decent, affordable housing. The deplorable conditions in many cities had led to rioting, and no one seemed to know how to improve matters. Johnson remembered that the federal government owned land in most cities and could more or less give the land to builders, who would construct low-cost housing. With federal help, the cities could build "new towns in-town."[52] Johnson brought together the relevant agency heads and a program was launched. Four years later, the program had produced almost no new housing in the seven cities chosen to demonstrate its viability. Why?

The problems encountered during the implementation of the new towns program are familiar to experienced observers of public policy: local political opposition; inadequate federal resources, incentives, and guidance; poor communication between federal and local implementers; and a faulty program design.[53] What struck Johnson as a great idea made many community groups irate, left local elected officials cold, and kept bureaucrats confused.

Similar effects occurred in the welfare reforms enacted in 1996. Fueled by the idea that local and state governments are better equipped to determine the needs of the poor populations of their state, welfare reform devolved much of the implementation responsibility to states. Five years later, most states were still struggling with the implications of reform provisions, such as term limits for recipients. Should recipients with families who have emotional problems or addictions be terminated after two to five years on welfare if they have few realistic job prospects? If so, what happens to them after that? Much like Johnson's housing program, welfare reform has been plagued by inadequate resources for support services such as child care, a strange mix of regulation and flexibility, and a poor communication system between federal and local implementers.

The more general lesson is that pluralism and federalism make chief executive initiatives in domestic policy extremely difficult to implement. Many well-intentioned programs have floundered because of the difficulties associated with getting bureaucratic agencies, elected officials, and citizen groups to cooperate.

Implementation problems are by no means limited to domestic policies; they also occur in foreign policy, even during crises. The most common difficulties are the same as in the domestic area: presidential intentions may be poorly communicated, implementers lack the resources necessary to carry out directives, and implementers sometimes resist doing what they are told.[54] The State Department and the military are notorious for their adherence to standard procedures—perhaps the most common form of bureaucratic resistance to orders from above. At critical times during the Cuban missile crisis of 1962, President Kennedy ordered the navy to move its blockade closer to Cuba, and not to act belligerently toward the first few Soviet ships it encountered after the quarantine had been declared. Evidence indicates that the navy did not move its quarantine line as the president ordered, and a long argument ensued between Secretary of Defense Robert McNamara and Admiral George Anderson about how intercepted Soviet ships would be treated. It ended with Anderson waving the *Manual of Navy Regulations* at McNamara and remarking, "Now Mr. Secretary, if you and your Deputy will go back to your offices, the Navy will run the blockade."[55] The navy's reluctance to depart from standard operating procedures in the midst of this type of crisis shows that even when the president is directly involved, and the need for effective action is obvious, implementation is by no means automatic.

The existence of problems should not obscure the fact that some policies are effectively implemented with little apparent difficulty. Social Security, for example, is mainly a matter of eligibility determination and the issuance of checks, and government agencies are capable of executing these tasks quite well.

The chances of encountering major problems during the implementation of chief executive policies are largely dependent upon (1) the amount of societal or organizational change the policy seeks to generate; (2) the complexity of the implementation process—how many different bureaucratic agencies and elected officials are involved; and (3) the level of consensus among the principal implementation actors about the desirability and feasibility of making planned changes.[56]

Policies that seek to bring about fundamental change are difficult to implement successfully because they call for widespread modification in behavior, and the government usually has only limited resources for encouraging it. The degree of difficulty associated with implementing policies of fundamental change is also affected by the complexity of the implementation process and the level of consensus among the implementers. A major innovation such as tax reform, carried out by a simple organizational network in which those involved understand and support programmatic goals, has a good chance of succeeding. Complex implementation arrangements, such as those required to carry out the Affordable Care Act, and competing priorities among implementers, including governors and health care provides, are almost certain to distort the original goals of innovative policies.

For policies aimed at producing limited change, the expectations are quite different. In general, such policies are likely to be implemented with reasonable effectiveness. They can be derailed by a cumbersome implementation process or fundamental disagreement among implementers, however. Johnson's new towns program was not dramatically new in what it sought to accomplish, but the organizational network required to implement it was complex and clumsy, and the consensus among implementation actors was decidedly narrow. These two factors accounted for the program's minimal success.

INTENDED AND UNINTENDED CONSEQUENCES

Ambitious and innovative programs often have effects that can be clearly identified only many years after they are implemented. In an interesting and revealing study, political scientist Lester Salamon examined the effects of a New Deal program thirty years after it had been terminated. The Resettlement Administration of 1934 authorized the federal government to purchase nearly 2 million acres of land in 200 different locations and to supervise specially designed agricultural or industrial communities that would make use of the land.[57] A common way of implementing the agricultural program was for the government to break large former plantations up into family-size parcels and sell them under lenient terms to tenant farmers, regardless of their race. Because black land ownership in the South was uncommon, and black poverty was pervasive, this program, although small in scale, represented a "bold experiment in social reform."[58] Not surprisingly, the program had many critics, primarily white southern legislators, and it was killed in 1943, nine years after it began. The fact that it was terminated led to the general view that the program had been a failure. Salamon's analysis of the effects of the program in 1973, however, documented a solid record of land retention by the black families it had assisted. These families had moved out of poverty into the middle class. They now owned cars, television sets, and refrigerators. Their children had obtained white-collar jobs, and as a group they were active in political and community organizations and promoted causes. The effects, which Salamon called "sleepers," took many years to emerge in a discernible form.[59]

Head Start, a product of Lyndon Johnson's War on Poverty, did not seem an unqualified success in its first major evaluation, which was conducted in 1969, four years after the program's inception; but more recent studies have documented long-term positive effects for the participants, and funding was substantially increased in the 1990s.[60] Much the same pattern of delayed effects has held for other major social welfare programs like job training and Food Stamps (now the Supplemental Nutrition Assistance Program).[61]

The main problem with sleeper effects is that they do nothing to relieve the pressure chief executives feel to produce visible, short-term results from the policies they sponsor. Because of this, chief executives favor programs that have more immediate payoffs. Policies that cannot survive by demonstrating quick positive results must maintain a certain level of political popularity during the time it takes for definitive effects to emerge.

Chief executive policies often produce unintended results, and these, like latent or sleeper effects, must be considered if the full impact of a policy is to be accurately assessed. The iron curtain was an unanticipated result of Truman's effort, known as the Marshall Plan, to rebuild the economies of Western Europe after World War II. Kennedy's determination to land a man on the moon by 1970 resulted in many technological breakthroughs that have had a tremendous influence on the commercial electronics industry and the way of life in the United States. Acid rain in New England and Canada is widely believed to be caused in part by coal burned in the Midwest, a practice furthered by the Carter administration's energy program, which sought, through subsidies for coal conversion, to reduce the industrial use of crude oil and natural gas. More generous financial aid for students, championed by Presidents Clinton and Obama, has helped millions of students attend college, but it has also resulted in mounting debt for them and their families. It should be clear that chief executives do not always get the results they expect from the policies they sponsor, and many are no longer in office when the full consequences of their actions become apparent.

Even more basic than the uncertainties introduced by time and unanticipated results is the problem of establishing cause-and-effect relationships between policies and outcomes. This is particularly true of chief executive policies because they are often aimed at making significant changes in society, but such changes almost always have complex causes. The Reagan administration's monetary and fiscal policies—the tax cut and stricter control of the money supply— are frequently credited with reducing inflation during the 1980s. Similarly, Clinton's balanced-budget policies are given credit for reducing, then eliminating, the federal deficit. Clinton also took credit for the booming economy Americans enjoyed during most of his administration. However, in both cases, factors such as global markets and increasing foreign competition in certain core industries, lower energy costs, and natural economic cycles may have had as much to do with economic outcomes as did government monetary and fiscal policy. Consider, for example, the experiences of President Obama and gas prices. Whenever economic conditions were bad and gas prices rose, Obama pointed to forces beyond his control, such as rising worldwide demand. When conditions improved and gas prices fell, he pointed to his policies of increasing automobiles' fuel efficiency and pursuing the development of alternative energy sources.

State reforms of education have been praised, but linking changes in teaching techniques, approaches to discipline, or working conditions in the schools with student aptitude and achievement test scores is a notoriously complex task.[62] Nevertheless, studies with rigorous evaluation designs have shown clear connections between some specially designed teaching programs, such as the Success for All program, and positive student results.[63]

Foreign policies and subsequent developments are also difficult to connect. Did Clinton's free trade policy, in particular NAFTA, contribute to or detract from the economic well-being of citizens in Mexico and the United States? How about its effect on environmental conditions in the two countries? How much did the aggressive foreign policy of the Bush administration encourage or help prevent belligerent and violent actions by Middle Eastern nations and insurgent groups? Did President Obama's military expansion, and then exit strategy, regarding Afghanistan undermine American interests in the Middle East or improve them? As we have noted, politicians show little reluctance to assert that positive cause-and-effect relationships exist between policies they support and favorable outcomes, and that the opposite is true of policies they oppose.

Some chief executive policies and results have fairly straightforward relationships. One can readily determine the amount of money elderly recipients receive from Social Security and then measure the impact of such payments on poverty, defined as a monetary threshold, among elderly Americans.[64] Decisions about the sizes, accessibility, and locations of state highways have undeniable effects, such as changes in populations, property values, and commercial sales. Precise, carefully defined relationships can be established between certain policies and their effects, but many chief executive policies are so broad that the results and their causes are unclear.

THE MANAGEMENT PUZZLE

Organizational management and policy administration are core responsibilities of chief executives. But because of the pressures and incentives to take the lead in setting the policy agenda and pushing for the enactment of policies, few chief executives have the time or the inclination to carefully oversee the implementation of the policies they have championed. Therefore, most of the institutional learning that results from the implementation of chief executive policies takes place in bureaucracies or specialized legislative committees. At this point, chief executive politics gives way to bureaucratic or legislative politics.

Efforts to reorganize the executive branch are perhaps the most common form of chief executive activity that reflects institutional learning. Bureaucratic resistance to chief executive initiatives has been recognized as a problem at least since the turn of the twentieth century. Presidents Roosevelt, Truman, Nixon, Carter, Reagan, Clinton, and George W. Bush all sponsored executive branch reorganizations aimed at establishing more rational bureaucratic structures and enhancing central control. The results usually fell short of expectations, mainly because Congress and the interest groups that were tied to the existing subgovernmental networks effectively opposed the changes these presidents sought.[65] Through the Civil Service Reform Act of 1978, President Carter tried to shake up the bureaucracy, starting with individual employees. The act provided incentives for high-ranking civil servants to take on special tasks at the request of the president or cabinet officer, and it made the hiring, firing, and transfer of civil servants somewhat easier. During his 1992 presidential campaign, Clinton promised to cut his White House staff by 25 percent, and he achieved that goal in the spring of 1993.[66] Clinton and Vice President Al Gore also promised to reinvent government through downsizing the federal bureaucracy so that it could work better and cost less. However, studies by independent scholars argue that such promises were only partially fulfilled; some agencies did become more efficient and customer friendly, but these advances were often accompanied by reductions in services provided to citizens.

Although the federal government has employed about 2.8 million full-time salaried government workers for the past thirty years, several reports argue that this number is misleading.[67] In reality, almost 15 million people work for the government, providing goods and services directly or indirectly.[68]

As these figures make clear, contracting has become a major feature of federal policy implementation, one that was used with great frequency during George W. Bush's administration. Nevertheless, there has been a significant increase in the federal workforce since 9/11, with more than 350,000 positions being added between 2000 and 2010. This increase was due mainly to expansions in the number of employees working in the Defense Department, the Department of Homeland Security, and the Department of Health and Human Services.[69] Effectively managing nearly 3 million direct employees is difficult enough for presidents, OMB, and cabinet officials; accurately accounting for the actions of millions more who work for private sector firms on government business is simply impossible.

In state government, reorganizations have been common. Over the past several decades, more than half of the state governments have undergone comprehensive reorganizations, and nearly all states have reorganized at least part of their government operations.[70] Many governors have also pushed for higher standards in the hiring and retention of government employees, the inclusion of more jobs in civil service or merit systems, and the improvement of in-service training. The goals of these reforms are basically the same as those of federal reforms: establishing clear chains of command and making public service delivery more economical and responsive to central control.

Chief executives are not reluctant to get involved with implementation problems if questionable results become public concerns. In fact, chief executives who sponsor policy innovations that are adopted—either their own or those inherited from their immediate predecessor—are likely to assign a high priority to certain matters of program delivery. A common reaction to implementation problems is to propose program reform. Many of the War on Poverty programs were designed to avoid reliance on entrenched federal and state bureaucracies and to restrict state discretion, because the policy formulators in the Kennedy and Johnson administrations doubted the commitment of those bureaucratic and political officials to the programs' goals. Not surprisingly, these policies generated their own implementation problems, such as duplication of service, lack of coordination among related programs, and state and local political resistance, which Republican presidents Nixon, Reagan, and Bush used to justify proposals for a "new federalism." As discussed in chapter 1, the result of new federalism reforms is a modified intergovernmental program delivery system, fewer separate programs, and a larger state role in implementation decisions. President George W. Bush's expansion of the military, and use of military contractors, to fight wars in Afghanistan and Iraq resulted in calls for reductions in military spending, and reforms to make the military more focused and effective by the Obama administration.

SUMMARY

Chief executive politics commands the attention of almost every American. More than any other politicians, presidents and governors define and articulate the leading issues of the day and propose policy solutions. Much of what they say and do is covered by the media and becomes the focus of discussion among citizens. Their visibility and their formal powers give chief executives enormous political influence.

Their political strength is clearly evident in their ability to define issues and set agendas. The concerns they choose to address become issues for the entire political community. They can force others to pay attention to their priorities and, in many cases, to accept their definitions of issues. Their domination of the political agenda gives them a tremendous advantage in policy development.

Many chief executive proposals fail to gain the approval needed to become policy, which diminishes the political strength of the leaders who offer them. Chief executive power and policy effectiveness, therefore, depend for their success on the ability of the individuals who occupy high office to convince the public and other political elites of the merit of their proposals. When the quality of a chief executive's leadership is widely questioned, his or her political muscles atrophy. The ability of chief executives to overcome the many hurdles that confront them on the path to policy change may justifiably earn them legendary reputations.

All chief executives have long lists of important policy proposals they hope to have enacted. If they are successful, the public has a tangible basis for evaluating chief executive performance. Concrete policy accomplishments are a valuable form of political currency. Established politicians display a strong allegiance to the status quo, but the values of the public are continually changing. Chief executives, taking advantage of their unique relationship with the public, frequently have acted as agents for change in American politics.

All the time and energy chief executives devote to voicing public concerns and securing adoption of new policies naturally limits the attention they can devote to matters of administration and policy implementation. Still, because new policies tend to breed implementation problems, issues of program design and delivery frequently command the interest and concern of chief executives.

When crises occur, nearly all aspects of chief executive politics change. Media and public attention become a hindrance rather than an asset, and other political actors become much more cooperative and deferential. The power to act usually belongs unambiguously to chief executives, but the repercussions of ill-advised action can be severe. Effective crisis management is the way many chief executives build their reputations as effective leaders.

chapter 7

Courtroom Politics

I t is sometimes said that courts implement policies made by other branches of government. But for many issues—such as abortion, affirmative action, capital punishment, search and seizure, school prayer, and school desegregation—the opposite is true: the courts make policy, and other political institutions respond to their lead. When politicians are silent or ambiguous, judicial action involves more than just policy implementation; in fact, there may be no policy to implement until the courts act. For a wide variety of other issues, such as the environment, welfare, campaign finance, communications, and health care, the courts, although their powers are somewhat circumscribed, have considerable discretion in determining what is legal and what is not. Judges do more than resolve disputes in accordance with the law. Through their decisions, they create law every bit as much as legislators do.

The policymaking role of U.S. courts arouses considerable controversy because it is unique. In Great Britain, judges are more accurately described as technicians than as policymakers. With a few exceptions, their role is to dot *i*'s and cross *t*'s.[1] U.S. courts are more powerful than other courts in the Western world, and their power continues to grow. Law professor Donald Horowitz observed, "The courts have tended to move from the byways onto the highways of policymaking."[2] Although from time to time, politicians object to the growing power of the courts, the main reasons for judicial policymaking are the abdication of responsibility by elected officials, and the efforts of aggrieved parties to find another route to achieve goals they failed to obtain from legislatures.

Many courts make policy, including federal courts and state courts. As the highest federal court, the U.S. Supreme Court is the ultimate arbiter of legal controversies. The Supreme Court's preeminence should not be construed to mean that other courts play a minor role, however. In fact, the Supreme Court decides fewer than a hundred cases each year.[3] In contrast, the other courts combined handle millions of cases annually, and many of these cases have far-reaching policy implications.

CASES AND CONTROVERSIES

The issues confronted by courts are rich and diverse (see Figure 7-1). Many of them, classified as private law, involve disputes between private parties. This category comprises contracts (Is an agreement legally binding?), property (Has property been illegally damaged or confiscated?), and torts (Have people or property been directly harmed?). In public law cases, government officials are parties to legal disputes. Under this category are questions of constitutional law (Are decisions by government officials consistent with the constitution?), statutory law (What did the legislature intend when it enacted this law?), and administrative law (Are administrative decisions constitutional, legal, and consistent with past decisions?).

These categories overlap in many ways (see Figure 7-1). Antitrust actions by government officials often have public and private components. For example, government officials function as prosecutors in a case, but the charge is that one company has engaged in anticompetitive behavior against another. Torts become public when a private party sues a government official or an agency for malfeasance or nonfeasance (failure to do their job properly). Overlaps within categories are even more common. In many constitutional law

FIGURE 7-1 Branches of Law

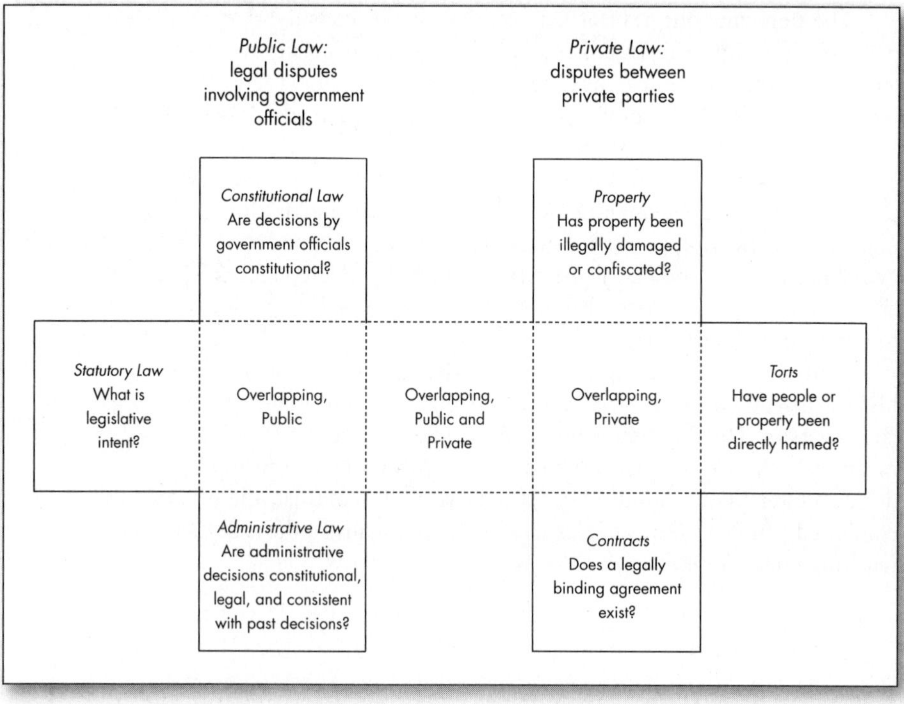

cases, the constitutionality of a statute is questioned; in many administrative law cases, the key is legislative intent; in both instances, statutory law is involved.

Because the concern here is public policy, the focus is on public law cases, which have broader implications for society than do private law cases. If one person sues a neighbor over a fallen tree, the world does not anxiously await a verdict. On the other hand, if an administrative agency proposes a change in clean air standards, the verdict may affect millions of people. Examples from administrative law and constitutional law are provided to illustrate the differences in judicial behavior when dealing with different types of law. As indicated above, although administrative law occasionally overlaps with constitutional law, each more often overlaps with statutory law. In administrative and constitutional law, questions of statutory interpretation are seldom far from view.

Constitutional Law

Constitutional law disputes raise questions about civil liberties, states' rights, interstate commerce, and other protections guaranteed by the U.S. Constitution or the constitutions of the states. The questions are enormously varied. Under what circumstances is evidence gathered by police admissible in a criminal proceeding? Under what circumstances may state governments provide financial assistance to religiously affiliated schools? What conditions or restrictions may states impose on abortions? Do abortion opponents have a right to protest in close proximity to a health clinic that performs abortions? When must an individual's right to privacy yield to freedom of the press? When must freedom of the press yield to a person's right to a fair trial? Does a state constitution guarantee same-sex couples the right to marry? Does the interstate commerce clause of the Constitution give Congress the power to penalize people who do not purchase health insurance?

As these questions illustrate, constitutional law deals with some of the most vexing and consequential issues facing society. These issues of social policy are difficult, not because they are technically complex (although some are), but because they pit one right against another—a woman's freedom of choice versus the rights of an unborn fetus, a criminal's right to a fair trial versus a newspaper's right to freedom of the press, and so forth. Obviously, the stakes are high and some interests will be adversely affected, whatever the court decides. Constitutional law is characterized by a high degree of conflict, salience, and manifest costs.

Some courts are especially likely to handle constitutional law cases. The U.S. Supreme Court deals almost exclusively with such cases, which explains the tendency among laypersons to equate judicial review with constitutional interpretation. State supreme courts also deal with constitutional issues much of the time. But the overwhelming majority of lower court decisions, at the state and federal levels, are not about constitutional issues. These cases almost always concern private law, statutory law, or administrative law. Many of these cases involve criminal defendants, whereas others involve civil litigation.

Administrative Law

Administrative law cases focus on the behavior of administrative agencies: their interpretations of statutes and their application of administrative rules, regulations, and procedures. Should automobile manufacturers be required to increase the gas mileage of the new cars they design? Should a dam be built if it poses a threat to an endangered species? When are utility rates unjustly discriminatory against low-income people? When does a nuclear power plant pose an unacceptable health risk to the public? May a hospital deny service to a poor person without forfeiting federal tax breaks? May an interstate highway be built through a public park? May a newspaper be owned by a television station or a radio station in the same city? What criteria should be applied to the location of a halfway house? These questions require courts to consider whether an administrative agency has acted in accordance with legislative standards and with provisions of the federal Administrative Procedure Act (APA) of 1946 (see chapter 4) or its state-level counterparts. These laws spell out the procedures that agencies must follow in making rules and adjudicating disputes, and the criteria for judicial review of their actions.

Administrative law cases are enormously complex. Federal courts have evaluated the adequacy of statistical experiments on foam insulation, the health effects of benzene and lead, and the capacity of the auto industry for technological breakthroughs. In passing judgment on public utility commissions, state courts must decide whether capital depreciation rates have been properly calculated, whether the utility's rate base should include plants under construction, and whether a given rate of return allows the utility to compete for capital. One judge, exasperated by such complexities, decided to narrow the focus of the case before him to a single issue, rate of return.[4] Otherwise, he argued, the court's task would be hopeless, and the case interminable.

Administrative law cases are decided initially by administrative agencies. If they are appealed, many administrative agency decisions at the federal level may go directly to the circuit courts of appeals, bypassing federal district courts. Some circuit court decisions on administrative law are appealed to the U.S. Supreme Court, but most never go that far. For all intents and purposes, circuit courts are final arbiters of most contested administrative decisions. Among circuit courts, the District of Columbia Circuit Court of Appeals handles a higher percentage of administrative law cases than do other circuit courts.[5] It has sometimes been called the second most powerful court in the land. On questions of administrative law, it is, in practice, the most powerful. At the state level, administrative law cases are handled by intermediate appeals courts and further appealed to state supreme courts.

Statutory Law

Statutory law requires judges to construe the meaning of legislative language and the nature of legislative intent. Statutory law grew in importance in the late twentieth century as scholars increasingly reached the conclusion that statutes reflected bargains struck by politicians to accommodate private interests.

This perspective encouraged closer judicial scrutiny of legislative bargains.[6] Does a law prohibiting wage discrimination on the basis of gender place the legal burden of proof on an employer, or on female employees who are alleging pay discrimination? When a statute imposes harsh penalties for the "use" of a firearm during a crime, does that apply to a situation in which someone trades an assault weapon for cocaine? Does a law that directs an environmental agency to regulate "hazardous substances" cover carbon dioxide emissions? These are the kinds of issues that statutory law raises.

Statutory interpretation is tricky even if laws contain plain language and judges believe in following legislative intent. Should judges focus on the statute itself or its legislative history, including committee reports and statements made during floor debates? Should judges seek to clarify the meaning intended by the law's authors or that commonly understood by members of society? Should they be guided by the meanings of terms as they are ordinarily used, or by their meanings as shaped by the purpose of the law? Should they focus on one or two key words or the entire text? Even "textualists," who favor judicial deference to the legislative branch, disagree on how to answer these questions.[7] Other judges, who view the textualist approach as too limiting, seek to correct defects in the legislative process by promoting fundamental values, such as the protection of disadvantaged minorities who are poorly represented in the political branches of the government.[8] Such judges reject what one scholar refers to as an "archaeological" approach to statutory interpretation in favor of a more dynamic approach.[9]

Neglected Issues

Courts seldom address issues in two important policy domains: foreign policy (responses to international crises or the use of armed forces abroad) and macroeconomic policy (taxing and spending decisions). The failure of courts to address these issues is due more to self-restraint than to a lack of plaintiffs. Many taxpayers would love to take Uncle Sam to court, if only they were permitted to do so. Although the courts have lowered barriers to standing—the right to sue—by consumer advocates and environmentalists, they have refused to facilitate taxpayer suits.[10] Taxpayers often wind up in court as defendants, with the Internal Revenue Service (IRS) or its state counterpart as the plaintiff, but they seldom appear as plaintiffs in taxation cases. In 1998, Congress made it easier for taxpayers to obtain an expedited tax court hearing without the need for a lawyer. Congress also shifted the burden of proof in civil disputes over tax bills from taxpayers to the IRS. Nevertheless, taxpayers cannot use the courts to challenge tax legislation that they regard as confiscatory, or to contest the government's use of tax revenues to carry out policies that were properly enacted.

On the rare occasions when the courts address questions of macroeconomic policy, they normally defer to elected officials, especially when elected officials are in agreement. When Congress granted President Richard Nixon the authority to impose wage and price controls in 1970, a special federal district court panel upheld the statute as a constitutional delegation of power to the president.[11] Similarly, the U.S. Supreme Court has upheld congressional delegations of authority to the president in foreign affairs.[12] Justice William H. Rehnquist wrote in *Dames & Moore v. Regan* (1981), "Presidential action taken pursuant to specific congressional authorization is supported by strongest presumptions and widest latitude of judicial interpretation, and the burden of persuasion rests heavily upon anyone who might attack it." In plain English, even the Supreme Court is reluctant to second-guess politicians in foreign policy. During George W. Bush's administration, the Supreme Court did intervene to grant prisoners held at Guantanamo Bay access to the federal court system.[13]

SELECTION OF CASES

Unlike other public policymakers, judges can address only those issues that come before them. Although courts are alike in their inability to initiate cases, they differ in their freedom to ignore them. As a general rule, supreme courts have more discretion than other courts. With the exception of a few cases, which seldom arise, the U.S. Supreme Court may decline to hear appeals from other courts (lower level federal courts or state supreme courts).[14] Although the Constitution assigns "original jurisdiction" over certain cases to the Supreme Court, that is not much of a constraint in practice. For example, the Supreme Court may satisfy its constitutional obligation to act as a trial court for cases involving disputes between states by appointing a special master to gather facts, conduct hearings, and write a report. The Supreme Court need not hold hearings on the report; it may simply ratify it. Federal district courts and circuit courts of appeals are supposed to hear all cases within their jurisdiction that come before them.[15] Since the 1990s, however, circuit courts of appeals, confronted with steadily growing caseloads, have used shortcuts to reduce the time required for individual cases. Such shortcuts include one-word rulings (affirmed or denied) and unpublished decisions, which do not establish precedents.[16]

A similar pattern prevails at the state level, although state supreme courts differ in their discretion. In some states, the supreme court must hear appeals from trial courts; in others, the supreme court is free to choose only "significant" cases if it wishes. The variations can be explained by the existence in some states, but not others, of intermediate appeals courts. In general, supreme courts have more discretion over their caseloads in states with such courts. The assumption is that one appeal from a trial court decision should be available to all parties, but that two may be excessive.

What do the U.S. Supreme Court justices look for when they are reviewing the several thousand cases before them in any given term and trying to select the 100 or fewer that the Court will hear? The importance of the issues raised in a case is one significant factor. Although the Court does not see itself as responding to public opinion in the same way that legislators or chief executives do, it does not ignore major public concerns either. Another situation that draws the Court's attention is when lower courts have issued conflicting rulings on cases involving essentially the same issues. In this circumstance, the Supreme Court is likely to step in to provide some clarity. Different circuit courts of appeals rulings on the constitutionality of the Patient Protection and Affordable Care Act of 2010 more or less forced the Supreme Court to rule on this matter in 2012. The Supreme Court is also likely to take up cases that raise new issues of law about which the Court has not ruled previously. Often these three criteria (importance, inconsistent lower court rulings, and new areas of law) intersect and overlap, making certain cases very likely to receive the Court's attention.

The federal government has a special relationship with the Supreme Court because it is a party to so many of the cases before the Court. The solicitor general, a top official in the Justice Department, works closely with the Court to identify the cases involving the government that the Court should hear. Roughly two-thirds of the cases the solicitor general recommends are heard by the Supreme Court, and the federal government is a party to close to 40 percent of the cases the Court hears in any given term.[17] Last, the policy preferences of judges often come into play. If four or more judges are interested in revisiting existing precedent in an area of law, or establishing a precedent in a new area of law, they may join together to select a case they think will enable them to act on their policy preferences.[18]

The preceding discussion introduced the concept of "standing" or standing to sue. Disputes over standing are often an important part of Supreme Court cases. The basic idea is that the plaintiff in a civil suit must be suffering some sort of real harm inflicted by the other party, which the Court can remedy by ruling on the case. If, for example, a student who was denied admission to a law school sues the school over its admission policy, but later is accepted by the school before the case reaches the Supreme Court, does he still have standing to sue? (The Supreme Court said no in *Defunis v. Odegaard*, 1974.) How much direct harm from air or water pollution must members of environmental groups experience in order to gain standing to sue government agencies or private companies? (As discussed in chapter 4, the answer has varied.) Maintaining fairly strict standards for standing enables the Court to avoid hypothetical cases, and cases that are "moot" because the parties are no longer being harmed. But determining who has standing, and who does not, is neither straightforward nor uncomplicated, and it can be key to many cases, especially those before the Supreme Court.[19]

JUDICIAL COALITIONS

It is sometimes said that the courts are more independent than other institutions of government. This is true in one sense but not in another. Judges are remarkably independent of politicians, but they are not independent of politics. Indeed, partisan politics is a significant factor in judicial recruitment and judicial behavior. Once appointed to office, however, federal judges are not subject to direct influence by the politicians who put them on the bench. Although federal judges may be impeached by the House of Representatives and convicted by the Senate for "high crimes and misdemeanors," this cumbersome machinery has been used successfully only eight times in U.S. history.

State judges are also independent of politicians, but not always of the electorate. In thirty-six states, judges may be removed from office by voters through regular elections, or through retention elections in which the judges run unopposed but may be unseated by votes of no confidence. Unpopular judges are unseated from time to time (Rose Bird, the former chief justice of the California Supreme Court, for example), but the overwhelming majority of judges who must face the voters are reelected.[20] Appointed judges at the state level may also be removed from office through a process of impeachment and conviction. Occasionally, judges step down voluntarily rather than face the embarrassment of a public trial. In 2013, Michigan Supreme Court justice Diane Hathaway resigned after she was charged with bank fraud involving a series of questionable real estate transactions.[21] In 2003, elected Alabama Supreme Court Chief Justice Roy S. Moore was removed from office (by the Alabama Court of the Judiciary) after he refused an order from a federal judge to remove a monument of the Ten Commandments from the courthouse. In 2012, he campaigned in a judicial election for his old job and won.[22]

Judges are an important part of partisan politics. Most federal judges belong to the party of the president who appointed them, and the same is true of state judges and the governors who appointed them. Furthermore, judges remain remarkably faithful to their parties while in office. Although this loyalty may vary from issue to issue, party identification is the single best predictor of judicial voting behavior.[23] Since the 1980s, the composition of the Supreme Court, and the ability of the president to affect it, has been a significant issue in presidential elections.

Diffuse Power

Many textbooks on American government portray the court system as a pyramid, with the U.S. Supreme Court at the apex. This image conveys a misleading impression, implying a hierarchical route that in reality very few cases follow. Most lower court decisions are never reviewed by higher courts. The majority of federal district court decisions are not appealed to the circuit courts; the majority of circuit court decisions are never appealed to the U.S. Supreme Court; and most circuit court decisions appealed to the Supreme Court are not accepted for review. The situation at the state level is much the same.

State supreme court decisions are usually final. Although decisions raising constitutional questions may be appealed to the U.S. Supreme Court, only 10 percent to 20 percent of the 70 to 100 cases the Supreme Court hears in any given year come from state supreme courts.[24] Even if the Court reverses a state supreme court and returns a case for further proceedings, the state supreme court may reiterate its basic conclusion while modifying some of the specifics. Although the state and federal court systems intersect, they are more independent than is commonly supposed (see Figure 7-2).

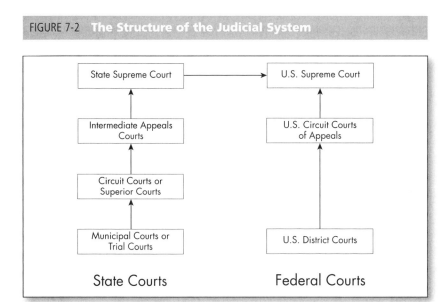

FIGURE 7-2   The Structure of the Judicial System

State Courts

- State Supreme Court
- Intermediate Appeals Courts
- Circuit Courts or Superior Courts
- Municipal Courts or Trial Courts

Federal Courts

- U.S. Supreme Court
- U.S. Circuit Courts of Appeals
- U.S. District Courts

When a higher court declines to review a lower court decision, that does not necessarily imply approval. Rather, it may mean that although the higher court would have decided the case differently, it cannot say that the lower court made a mistake. It may mean that the higher court is not prepared to address certain legal issues, or it may mean that the higher court has too many other cases to hear.

Not all cases are created equal, and the more important cases tend to be heard in the higher courts. Nevertheless, many critical decisions have been made by federal district court judges. In the 1970s, Judge Arthur Garrity desegregated Boston's public schools, and Judge Frank Johnson Jr. reformed Alabama's prisons and mental hospitals. In the 1980s, Judge Harold Greene ordered the divestiture of AT&T. In 2010, Judge Virginia A. Phillips ordered the U.S. military to stop enforcing its "don't ask, don't tell" policy regarding gay soldiers.[25] These cases illustrate the degree to which judicial power is dispersed throughout the United States.

Leadership Styles and Strategies

When a federal district court judge issues a decision, he or she acts alone. Higher courts are characterized by collective decision making. Intermediate appeals court decisions usually are made by three-judge panels, and U.S. Supreme Court decisions are made by all the members. Coalition building is essential in such courts. Before a case is decided and the opinion written, a majority of judges must agree on the outcome and on the reasoning behind it. Building such a consensus requires leadership.

Within the courts there are three forms of leadership: political, institutional, and intellectual. Political leaders are those who can build coalitions, and the task of political leadership often falls on the shoulders of the judge assigned to write the opinion. To satisfy other members of the court, the opinion writer inserts certain phrases and deletes others, with the goal of securing as many votes as possible in support of a coherent opinion. The opinion writer also seeks to discourage dissenting opinions, which convey judicial fragmentation. The late Justice William Brennan exemplified political leadership on the Supreme Court. Under chief justices as diverse as Earl Warren and William Rehnquist, Brennan parlayed his charm, persuasiveness, and gift for compromise into coalitions supportive of racial equality, gender equality, freedom of expression, welfare rights, and the rights of the accused.[26] On more than one occasion, Brennan tempered his own convictions somewhat in order to extract an elusive majority in support of a key principle. Political scientists Lee Epstein and Jack Knight refer to this as "strategic opinion writing."[27] Despite an increasingly conservative Court, Brennan used his "playmaker" skills to advance a variety of liberal principles. Law professor Kathleen Sullivan remarked, upon his death, "He was the most influential Justice of his era."[28]

Centrists or "swing voters" are strategically situated to exercise political leadership because they hold the balance of power, especially when a court is ideologically divided, which was the case with the Burger and Rehnquist Courts and is the case today with the Roberts Court. Sandra Day O'Connor seemed to relish her role as the centrist in the Rehnquist Court. She provided key votes and legal reasoning in several important policy areas such as abortion, affirmative action in colleges, church-state relations, and voting rights.[29] In the Roberts era (beginning in 2005), Justice Anthony Kennedy has replaced O'Connor as the swing vote. With Justices Scalia, Thomas, Alito, and Roberts typically on the right, and Justices Breyer, Ginsburg, Sotomayor, and Kagan on the left, Kennedy has cast the decisive vote on many of the most important cases heard in recent years.[30] In the Court's 2010 to 2011 term, for example, there were twelve cases (out of a total of eighty-five) in which the liberal bloc opposed the conservative bloc in 5-4 decisions, with Kennedy casting the deciding vote; a very similar pattern was present in the 2008 to 2009 term.[31]

Institutional leaders are those who defend the courts against various external threats and who attempt to develop the courts as institutions. When Chief Justice Charles Evans Hughes denounced President Franklin Roosevelt's attempt to "pack" the Supreme Court, he was exercising institutional leadership.[32] Chief Justice Warren Burger led the battle to add judges to the federal bench and for more discretion in case selection, which he thought would protect the Supreme Court from "overload." Chief Justice Roberts has encouraged his court to find common ground and not be defined by a simple liberal versus conservative division. He had some success in this effort in both the 2009 to

2010 and 2011 to 2012 terms.[33] His move to join the liberal group in upholding most of the Affordable Care Act in 2012 was widely viewed as motivated, at least in part, by the public's declining approval of the Court because it was perceived to be overtly partisan.[34] Various state judges also have exercised institutional leadership when they fought to modernize the courts, to reorganize the judiciary, or to reform judicial selection procedures.

Intellectual leaders are those who influence their colleagues—and subsequent generations—through the force of their reasoning and the power of their ideas. Harlan Stone's argument that "discrete and insular minorities" warrant special protection under the Constitution—an argument buried in a footnote in the 1938 case *United States v. Carolene Products*—provided the rationale for broad interpretations of the Fourteenth Amendment by subsequent courts. Hugo Black's strong views on civil liberties provided the intellectual underpinnings for many of the decisions of the Warren Court. Justice Antonin Scalia (appointed in 1986) has long been recognized as an intellectual leader among conservatives on the Supreme Court, although his opinions are sometimes so flamboyant and scathing that potential allies are reluctant to sign on to them. Judges on other courts have also exercised intellectual leadership. In the 1970s, Judge Harold Leventhal of the District of Columbia Circuit Court of Appeals articulated the "hard look" doctrine of administrative law, which justifies careful judicial scrutiny of the reasoning behind administrative decisions (chapter 4). His colleague, David Bazelon, is credited with (or blamed for) the view that the mentally ill have a right to treatment under the Constitution. The reverberations from these ideas continue.

Although courts are less hierarchical than other government institutions, the chief justice or chief judge has important powers. The chief justice of the United States presides at Court conferences and is the first to speak. If the chief justice votes with the majority, he (or she) assigns the opinion to a particular justice. Because the reasoning behind a decision matters considerably, chief justices exercise power even when they choose not to write. The chief judges of other federal courts are more constrained. The chief judge of a federal district court assigns cases to other judges, but randomly. The chief judge of a federal circuit court of appeals assigns the opinion when the court sits en banc, or all together, provided he or she is in the majority. Most circuit court of appeals cases are decided by three-judge panels, however, and the cases are assigned randomly.

At the state level, there appears to be considerable variation in the leadership potential of chief judges. In states where supreme court judges are elected, partisan conflict is often intense enough to thwart attempts at leadership. In states where supreme court judges are appointed, the opposite is true.[35]

Decision Making

If leadership is a variable that adds an element of uncertainty to the judicial process—the "wild card" in the judicial deck—there are four more predictable elements of judicial decision making. They are law, evidence, party identification and ideology, and judicial activism.

Law. In resolving constitutional disputes, judges get a good deal of guidance from the constitution itself, whether federal or state. A constitution is not a legal cookbook, but neither is it a Rorschach test. Perhaps it is best described as a document that establishes a set of presumptions or burdens of proof. The U.S. Constitution does not define phrases, such as "freedom of the press," "freedom of speech," or "freedom of religion," but these phrases are laden with meaning from years of precedents—prior decisions that command respect. Although precedents are seldom determinative, they serve as guideposts to judges as they wrestle with difficult problems that often involve more than one precedent. Although some of the most famous Supreme Court decisions stem from cases in which previous precedents were overruled, this type of action is fairly rare. Epstein and Knight found that Supreme Court decisions overruling past precedents represented fewer than 1 percent of all cases available for overruling.[36] Before 1960, it was extremely rare for the Supreme Court to overrule precedent; it became more common between 1960 and 1980, but it has become somewhat less common over the past thirty years.[37] In general, courts pay more attention to their own precedents and to those of higher courts than to the precedents of other courts.

Constitutions have less relevance for administrative law because most administrative law cases do not raise constitutional questions. Precedents are scarcer in administrative law; the "administrative state" is only about seventy years old, and higher courts offer less guidance on administrative law than on constitutional law. As judges evaluate administrative law cases, their guides are the federal APA and state administrative procedure acts. If administrative procedures are informal, the courts ask whether an agency acted "arbitrarily and capriciously." If administrative procedures are relatively formal, the courts ask whether the agency's decision is based on "substantial evidence" in the record. The latter is a more exacting form of judicial review.[38] As discussed in chapter 4, agencies face a higher burden of proof as the formality of rulemaking increases.

Evidence. Whether a case concerns constitutional law or administrative law, courts base their decisions on evidence submitted by litigants. For the most part, evidence consists of historical facts, such as who did what to whom. Courts also look at social facts, the probable consequences of decisions. Courts have been guided by empirical research on the effects of segregation on African Americans (*Brown v. Board of Education*, 1954), the effects of teacher experience on pupil performance (*Hobson v. Hansen*, 1967, 1968), and the effects of judicial procedures on the rehabilitation of juvenile offenders (*In re Gault*, 1967). Trial court judges sometimes face a quandary when experts disagree on key points relevant to the case. In one case involving experts who disagreed on whether the drug Bendectin causes human birth defects, the trial court judge dismissed expert testimony based on animal studies and unpublished research. The U.S. Supreme Court, however, overruled that decision, arguing that trial court judges must be "flexible" in their analysis of expert testimony. According to the Supreme Court, it is better to

weigh the veracity of disputed evidence through cross-examination and pre-
sentation of contrary witnesses than it is to ignore evidence that is not generally accepted.[39]

Some litigants have a distinct advantage in presenting evidence. In particular, the "haves," such as business interests, who tend to be repeat players
who know how to use the court system, usually are better at the litigation
game than the "have-nots," who tend to be one-shot participants.[40] This gap
has narrowed as a result of court decisions granting certain have-nots the
right to counsel in criminal cases (*Gideon v. Wainwright*, 1963) and the creation of legal aid societies, which represent poor individuals in civil cases.
Public interest groups draw on their experience and resources in representing
the disadvantaged or the public in court. The NAACP has filed numerous
school desegregation suits; the American Civil Liberties Union (ACLU) files
many First Amendment suits. Environmentalists have been represented in
court by the Natural Resources Defense Council, the Environmental Defense
Fund, the Sierra Club, and other groups. These public interest groups have
won a wide variety of cases securing protection of wilderness areas and wetlands, and pushing for strict enforcement of antipollution laws. In some
instances, the federal government has reimbursed them for the costs of successful lawsuits—a practice known as intervenor funding.[41]

Party identification and ideology. Few judges would cite party identification as a factor in their decisions. Indeed, many judges would take umbrage at
the implication that partisanship enters into judicial decision making.
Nevertheless, it is well established that Democratic judges and Republican
judges decide certain kinds of cases differently. Democratic state supreme
court judges are much more liberal in deciding workers' compensation cases
than are their Republican counterparts.[42] They are also more supportive of the
claims of criminal defendants, disadvantaged persons, and individuals alleging
deprivations of civil liberties.[43]

This pattern holds at all levels of the federal judiciary: Democratic judges
tend to be more liberal and Republican judges more conservative.[44] That is
especially true for cases involving the right to privacy, economic regulation,
and discrimination against racial minorities.[45] Therefore, it is a matter of some
consequence whether a Democrat or a Republican sits in the White House
because the president is able to appoint judges who share his party affiliation
and judicial outlook.[46] Following in the footsteps of his father and President
Reagan, President George W. Bush is credited with having been especially
effective in appointing conservative Republicans to the U.S. circuit courts of
appeals. As of 2009, 101 of the 177 federal appeals court judges were appointed
by Republican presidents.[47]

A president's ideology also matters, especially in the appointment of
Supreme Court nominees. President Reagan appointed staunch conservative
Antonin Scalia to the Court and elevated another staunch conservative,
William Rehnquist, to the position of chief justice. He was unable to push

through the nomination of another notable conservative, Robert Bork, and had to settle for Anthony Kennedy instead. His other successful nominee, Sandra Day O'Connor, turned out to be a bit more moderate than many conservatives would have preferred. President George H. W. Bush scored with conservative Republicans in appointing Clarence Thomas (who replaced the very liberal Thurgood Marshall), but his appointment of David Souter (to replace another liberal, William Brennan) eventually led to great disappointment among conservatives, as Souter frequently voted with the liberal wing of the Rehnquist Court. Bill Clinton solidified the liberal bloc of the Rehnquist Court with Ruth Bader Ginsburg and Steven Breyer, who replaced outgoing moderates Byron White and Harry Blackmun. President George W. Bush was able to push the Supreme Court a bit to the right by replacing Sandra Day O'Connor with Samuel Alito; his other appointment, John Roberts for William Rehnquist, had little discernible ideological effect, although Roberts may be somewhat more pragmatic than Rehnquist. In his first term, President Obama replaced liberals Souter and John Paul Stevens with liberals Sonia Sotomayor and Elena Kagan. On balance, Republican presidents have been successful in moving the Court to the right over the past thirty years; many analysts consider the Roberts Court to be the most conservative Supreme Court since the 1950s, at least in some of its terms.[48]

Judicial activism. Although ideology is an important component of each judge's political philosophy, it is by no means the only element. Felix Frankfurter, who professed to be an unswerving civil libertarian, dissented against Warren Court decisions protecting individuals against the government. Frankfurter believed the courts should defer to other branches of government under most circumstances. Oliver Wendell Holmes Jr. took a similar view. As he saw it, judges should uphold laws even though they epitomize economic mistakes or futile experiments.[49] This point of view is sometimes referred to as the doctrine of judicial restraint. Other judges have been much more willing to overturn statutes. William O. Douglas and Hugo Black, staunch civil libertarians, routinely voted to void statutes that diminished First Amendment liberties. Black and Douglas were also judicial activists who believed that the courts should not defer to other branches of government, especially when First Amendment rights are at stake. Thus, one common measure of judicial activism is the frequency with which the Court overrules legislative acts or executive actions. In constitutional law, a critical question for judges is whether to override the legislative branch; in administrative law, they must decide whether to overrule administrative agencies.

As mentioned previously, during the 1970s, the U.S. circuit courts of appeals took an increasingly "hard look" at administrative agency decisions.[50] At that same time, the Supreme Court developed a reputation for overturning state and local laws as well as acts of Congress.[51] The facts support this view, but only in a qualified way. From 1970 to 1979, the Supreme Court invalidated 195 state and local statutes, the most of any decade in its history, but the

20 federal statutes ruled unconstitutional in this period rank second to the decade of the 1990s, when the Court invalidated 24 federal statutes. Looking at the Court's full history, it is clear that the Court became much more inclined to overturn federal, state, and local laws between 1910 and 1940, and from 1960 to the present, although since 1990, the frequency with which state and local statutes (as opposed to federal ones) have been invalidated has declined significantly.[52] However, the number of statutory reversals may not be as good an indicator of judicial activism as the importance of the laws reversed. The Roberts Court essentially rewrote campaign finance law with a series of decisions culminating in *Citizens United v. Federal Election Commission* in 2010. But, as mentioned earlier, Roberts stopped short of overturning President Obama's health care law in 2012.

Another aspect of judicial activism is the willingness of the Court to fashion new interpretations of the Constitution. The Warren Court did this frequently to protect those accused of crimes, to separate church and state, and to integrate public schools. The Burger Court famously interpreted the Constitution as giving women the right to abortion in the first trimester of their pregnancies. All of these new interpretations were considered ideologically liberal. In the Rehnquist and Roberts years, however, we have seen something of a new pattern: new constitutional interpretations that are conservative in nature. There is no better example of this than the *District of Columbia v. Heller* (2008) decision, which for the first time in 220 years interpreted the Second Amendment as guaranteeing individual citizens the right to possess firearms.[53]

NEW WINE IN OLD BOTTLES

Judges, like other policymakers, are attentive to appearances, but judges are less likely than other public officials to substitute symbolic action for substantive action. Very few court decisions are purely symbolic. Unlike other public officials, judges do not avoid difficult problems or unpopular solutions. Instead, they confront many of society's most vexing problems, and having done so, they then rely on symbols to legitimate their decisions.

Two norms confirm judicial attentiveness to symbols. First, judges seek to avoid public feuding, which is viewed as unseemly and detrimental to the image of the courts. In contrast, public feuding is a popular legislative sport. Second, judges try to convey the impression that their decisions are based on an unbroken line of precedents, dating back to the Founders, whereas politicians are forever talking about new ideas, new deals, and new American revolutions. Judges care especially about two symbols: unity and continuity.

UNITY AND CONTINUITY

The school desegregation rulings of the Warren Court demonstrate the commitment to unity. Since *Brown v. Board of Education*, the Court has struggled to maintain the appearance of unity on this extraordinarily divisive issue.

During the Warren years, the justices were remarkably successful. Despite deep divisions, they managed to issue a series of unanimous decisions, which sent an important message to recalcitrant school boards, especially in the South: desegregation is the law of the land.[54]

School desegregation cases also demonstrate the commitment to continuity. The *Brown* decision reversed *Plessy v. Ferguson* (1896), a ruling that upheld the constitutionality of segregated facilities and services. In reversing *Plessy* as untenable in a modern age, the Court cited a wide variety of precedents that supported a broad interpretation of the Fourteenth Amendment. In subsequent cases, the federal courts portrayed court-ordered busing as a logical outgrowth of *Brown* and the Fourteenth Amendment. Then, in the late 1990s, federal courts applied the brakes to busing to achieve racial integration, citing the same constitutional provisions and precedents but interpreting them differently. Politicians serve old wine in new bottles, but judges prefer to serve new wine in old bottles. This modest deception legitimates policymaking by public officials, who, according to a narrow reading of the Constitution, are not supposed to be making public policy.

A commitment to unity was also evident in the Roberts Court in its 2011 to 2012 term. Breaking out of its predominately partisan mode, the Court was unanimous in making several important rulings. In one such case, the Court said that religious groups should not be subject to employment discrimination laws in the same way as nonreligious employers. The Court also ruled against the Environmental Protection Agency (EPA) in a property rights case that involved a wetlands designation that prevented owners from building a house on their property. In a potentially important search-and-seizure case, they ruled that police cannot place Global Positioning System devices on the cars of suspects without taking Fourth Amendment protections into account.[55]

Unity and continuity are two of the most important ingredients of precedents and stare decisis (meaning "to stand by things decided" and defer to precedent). Unanimous or nearly unanimous Supreme Court decisions typically provide strong guidance for the rest of the federal court system because it is unlikely that the Court's view on the legal issues decided by these margins will change in the near future. However, 5-4 majorities, with several of the justices in the majority offering concurring opinions, which modify or disagree with the reasoning used in the majority opinion, offer a much less clear precedent. Strong dissenting opinions, especially those of a unified opposition in 5-4 cases, may even provide the basis for a majority opinion in future cases.

INNOVATIVE DECISIONS

The commitment of courts to continuity may be good for the republic, but it obscures the extent to which judges are innovators in American politics. It also conveys a false impression that judicial policies differ only incrementally from earlier policies. Although most court decisions, like most decisions of other political institutions, are incremental, a remarkably high percentage of decisions made by the highest courts are innovative, especially when the issues are divisive and the decisions will have far-reaching effects.

It is widely acknowledged that the Warren Court was innovative. Its decisions on school desegregation, criminal justice, school prayer, and other matters transformed the Bill of Rights into a blueprint for economic and political equality. Other Warren Court decisions, on less visible topics, were equally revolutionary. For example, in *New York Times v. Sullivan* (1964) the Warren Court ruled that public figures must demonstrate actual malice to win libel suits against newspapers. This decision, which overruled 175 years of settled legal practice, virtually immunized the American press against libel suits.[56]

Many scholars now recognize that the Burger Court was also quite innovative.[57] In *Furman v. Georgia* (1972), the Burger Court found existing capital punishment statutes unconstitutional, which triggered changes in these statutes throughout the country that the Court later approved in *Gregg v. Georgia* (1976). In *Roe v. Wade* (1973), the Burger Court ruled that a woman's right to privacy, although not absolute, is a constitutionally protected right. The Burger Court was also innovative in a wide variety of other areas, such as commercial free speech, sex discrimination, procedural due process, and freedom of the press.

The Rehnquist Court was innovative in one area in particular—federalism. Despite numerous precedents upholding a broad interpretation of congressional authority under the commerce clause of the Constitution, the Rehnquist Court departed from those precedents in some high-profile cases. In *United States v. Lopez* (1995), the Court invalidated a federal statute prohibiting the possession of a firearm within 1,000 feet of a school. Then, in *Printz v. United States* (1997), the Court struck down the Brady bill, which required state and local officials to check the backgrounds of gun buyers. Subsequently, the Court made it difficult for parties to sue states for violations of trademark and patent rights.[58] In *Miller v. French* (2000), the Court sided with state and local governments against federal judges who issue sweeping orders governing the operation of state and local prisons and jails. In *United States v. Morrison* (2000), the Court overturned a federal law allowing rape victims to sue their attackers in federal court, and in *Board of Trustees v. Garrett* (2001), the Court limited the scope of the Americans with Disabilities Act by ruling that individuals could not sue states for monetary damages in discrimination lawsuits.[59] In these and other cases, the Rehnquist Court strengthened state discretion under the Tenth Amendment at the expense of congressional authority under the commerce clause or the Fourteenth Amendment. As Justice Rehnquist put it in *United States v. Morrison*, "The Constitution requires a distinction between what is truly national and what is truly local."[60]

The Rehnquist Court's enthusiasm for federalism left many Court watchers scratching their heads in the wake of the Bush-Gore election dispute. With the entire nation watching, the Supreme Court overturned the judgment of the Florida Supreme Court on three straight occasions. These decisions sealed a Bush victory by preventing a recount advocated by Vice President Al Gore.[61]

When the Supreme Court, or any other court, behaves with apparent inconsistency, one needs to take a closer look at the factors highlighted in this chapter: law, evidence, party identification, and ideology. However one views the *Bush v. Gore* case, the overall legacy of the Rehnquist Court was to encourage greater deference to the states.

State supreme courts have also blazed new trails in public law. In the 1970s, the New Jersey Supreme Court outlawed the use of the property tax as the sole basis for local school financing, established a right-to-die procedure for permanently comatose patients, and held hosts liable for drunk-driving accidents if they knowingly served alcohol to intoxicated persons. In *Southern Burlington County NAACP v. Township of Mt. Laurel* (1975), a landmark decision, the New Jersey Supreme Court ruled "exclusionary zoning" unconstitutional. Following New Jersey's lead, between 1973 and 2000, state supreme courts in nineteen states struck down school funding formulas that relied heavily on local property taxes as discriminatory, despite a U.S. Supreme Court ruling that such formulas are compatible with the U.S. Constitution (*San Antonio Independent School District v. Rodriguez*, 1973).[62] Reacting to rulings of the Burger and Rehnquist Courts, state supreme courts in Alaska, California, Massachusetts, Michigan, New York, and Pennsylvania went further than the U.S. Supreme Court in protecting the rights of criminal defendants.[63]

State supreme courts have taken the lead on several civil liberties questions. These courts can go beyond the U.S. Supreme Court because the federal court sets a floor, not a ceiling, on constitutional rights. If state supreme courts find that state constitutions provide stronger protection than the U.S. Constitution, they are free to follow the state constitutions, provided their conclusions are based primarily on state law (*Michigan v. Long*, 1983). According to one estimate, from 1970 through 1992, state courts handed down seven hundred decisions extending civil liberties under state constitutional law, a phenomenon known as "the new judicial federalism."[64] Among the rights state supreme courts said were protected under various state constitutions were the rights to privacy (Montana), gender equality (Hawaii), and safe schools (California).[65] The Massachusetts Supreme Judicial Court created quite a stir in 2003 when it ruled that the state's constitution guaranteed same-sex couples the right to marry.[66] Following this ruling, supreme courts in Connecticut (2008) and Iowa (2009) followed suit, and several state legislatures (Vermont, New Hampshire, and New York) passed laws granting this right.

State court procedures have also shown innovation. For example, state courts have been pioneers in allowing electronic and photographic media coverage of court proceedings, including criminal proceedings.[67] Presently, forty-eight states allow some broadcasting coverage of court proceedings, and many observers believe that state courts have managed to promote freedom of the press without infringing on constitutional rights to a fair trial.[68] Indeed, even the U.S. Supreme Court has conceded that television coverage of a criminal proceeding does not automatically violate a defendant's constitutional right to a fair trial (*Chandler v. Florida*, 1981). After experimenting with cameras in federal district courts and federal circuit courts of appeals, the Judicial Conference of the United States allowed federal appeals courts to decide whether to televise civil, but not criminal, proceedings. However, only two of the nation's thirteen federal circuit courts of appeals (the Second and the Ninth) have chosen to do so.[69] The U.S. Supreme Court has steadfastly refused to televise its proceedings, despite external pressure to do so. When CNN asked the Supreme Court to televise oral arguments for the historic Bush-Gore election dispute on December 1, 2000, the Court declined to do so. It did, however, subsequently release an audiotape of the oral arguments, and this practice is now the norm. The Roberts Court maintains a Web site where transcripts and audiotapes of oral arguments and opinions are posted.[70]

MINORITIES AS BENEFICIARIES

Because the scope of conflict in courtroom politics is more limited than in most other policymaking arenas, judges have somewhat more freedom to make rulings that protect the interests of minorities (advantaged and disadvantaged) and run against prevailing public opinion. After all, the Constitution, in particular the Bill of Rights, was written with an eye toward protecting minorities against the potential actions of democratic institutions and limiting the scope of the federal government. Thus it follows that many court decisions pertaining to constitutional law involve minority rights, and in many constitutional law cases, the government (state or federal) is being sued by minority litigants for not respecting those rights. Most administrative law cases derive from government regulation of private sector activities and focus on whether government agencies have treated minorities, such as small businesses, corporations, unions, and others, fairly and/or whether agencies have done enough to protect citizens, who are often represented in court by interest groups. A major question that scholars have debated is how disadvantaged minorities, as opposed to advantaged minorities, have fared in these two different areas of law.

Constitutional Law

Because the U.S. Supreme Court is preeminent in matters of constitutional law, scholars interested in assessing the beneficiaries of constitutional law decisions have focused on this court. Most studies of Court rulings from the mid-1950s to the 1980s found considerable support for disadvantaged minorities in its decisions.[71] Of the twenty-eight cases in which the Court overturned congressional statutes between 1958 and 1974, twenty-seven upheld minority rights, as guaranteed by the Bill of Rights or the Fourteenth Amendment.[72] The principal beneficiaries in these cases were African Americans and other disadvantaged minorities. Political scientists Reginald Sheehan, William Mishler, and Donald Songer also confirmed the influence of minority groups at the Supreme Court. In a study of Supreme Court decisions from 1953 through 1988, they found that minorities were remarkably successful in comparison with other groups, including those with more financial resources, such as unions, small businesses, and corporations. In fact, only the federal government and state governments were more successful than minorities during this time period (the other categories of litigants included in this study besides unions, small businesses, and corporations were individuals, poor individuals, and local governments). Their principal conclusion was that the ideological composition of the Court, rather than the resources of litigants, was the main determinant of judicial outcomes.[73]

Some scholars assert that these studies give too much weight to the Warren Court (1954–1969), whose strong commitment to civil liberties is universally acknowledged. Thus, it is the Burger Court (1969–1986), whose legacy is most often debated. In 1985, law professor Geoffrey Stone noted that 85 percent of the Court's "noneasy" (not unanimous) civil liberties decisions during the 1983 to 1984 term were decided against minority rights.[74] In his view, the Burger Court launched a new era of "aggressive majoritarianism." But the Burger Court's reputation as majoritarian in a conservative era can be traced mostly to its criminal procedure decisions. In this area, the Burger Court was more sensitive to public safety than to minority rights. In *Michigan v. Long*, for example, the Burger Court upheld protective searches of the passenger compartment of a car if police have a reasonable belief that the suspect is dangerous. In *New York v. Quarles* (1984), the Burger Court ruled that the police may postpone the reading of a defendant's *Miranda* warnings until they have investigated a potential threat to public safety. The Court also upheld vehicle searches by border patrol officials, provided that circumstances are suspicious and that intrusions on privacy are limited (*United States v. Brignoni-Ponce*, 1975; *United States v. Cortez*, 1981). Despite these decisions, a fairer appraisal of the Burger Court's entire record, not just its criminal procedure rulings or the decisions of a single term, is one of mixed support for the rights of disadvantaged minorities.

Even the Rehnquist Court, widely viewed as conservative, handed down a number of decisions favoring disadvantaged minorities. It voted to extend the reach of the Voting Rights Act (*City of Pleasant Grove v. United States*, 1987), to allow special job protections for pregnant workers (*California Federal Savings and Loan Assn. v. Guerra*, 1987), and to invalidate a referendum aimed at restricting the rights of homosexuals (*Romer v. Evans*, 1996). On affirmative action, the Court ruled in *United States v. Paradise* (1987) that a judge may order agencies to use promotion quotas temporarily when there is a history of "egregious" racial bias. In *Johnson v. Santa Clara County* (1987), the Court ruled that employers may give special preferences to women in hiring and promotion decisions even if no prior discrimination existed. In *United States v. Virginia* (1996), the Court held that the Virginia Military Institute must open its doors to women cadets. And in *Lawrence v. Texas* (2003), Justice Kennedy led a 6-3 majority in overturning the previous precedent (*Bowers v. Hardwick*, 1986) and establishing a right to privacy for homosexual couples.[75]

To be sure, decisions unfavorable to disadvantaged minorities can also be cited. In *Wards Cove Packing Co. v. Atonio* (1989), the Court made it more difficult for minorities to win employment discrimination cases. In *Miller v. Johnson* (1995) and *Bush v. Vera* (1996), the Court ruled against the creation of congressional districts dominated by racial minorities resulting from what Justice O'Connor described as an "impermissible racial gerrymander." In *Richmond v. Croson* (1986), the Court overturned a rigid racial quota in awarding public contracts in Richmond, Virginia. This decision cast a pall over long-standing minority preferences in local government contracts. Specifically, it required "strict scrutiny" of all race-based action by state and local governments. Later, in *Adarand Constructors, Inc. v. Pena* (1995), the Court applied the same "strict scrutiny" doctrine to federal contracts. The Court also distanced itself from strong school desegregation mandates involving school systems in Georgia (*Freeman v. Pitts*, 1992) and Missouri (*Missouri v. Jenkins*, 1995). Finally, in *Grutter v. Bollinger* (2003), Justice O'Connor led a 5-4 majority in upholding the University of Michigan Law School's admission program, which recognized race (diversity) as a factor in admission decisions, while she led a 6-3 majority in rejecting the university's undergraduate admission program, which awarded points to minority applicants (*Gratz v. Bollinger*, 2003). Clearly, the Rehnquist Court was less sympathetic to minorities, especially racial minorities, than its predecessors. Taking a wide view of the Rehnquist Court, it seems fair to conclude that its more conservative rulings in equality and civil liberties cases, along with its narrowed interpretation of the commerce clause, meant that disadvantaged minorities benefited less, and state governments and the business community (an advantaged minority) benefited more, from its decisions.[76]

The Roberts Court has, for the most part, continued down the conservative-leaning path blazed by the Rehnquist Court. With Justice Kennedy as the majority-creating vote on most of the important cases, and his record of being slightly more conservative than Justice O'Connor, that should come as no surprise. A few of the Roberts Court's most important decisions have been mentioned already; in *District of Columbia v. Heller* and *Citizens United v. Federal Election Commission*, the favored minorities were gun owners or wealthy individuals and groups that wanted an unlimited right to speak in elections. In 2007, the Roberts Court limited the ability of employees to sue their employers for pay discrimination (a ruling that was negated in 2009 when Congress passed the Lilly Ledbetter Fair Pay Act); in 2008, the Court upheld Indiana's voter identification law and Kentucky's lethal injection protocol; in 2009, it ruled that prisoners had no right to DNA testing to prove their innocence, and that the city of New Haven, Connecticut, had discriminated against white firefighters when it discarded promotional exam results; in 2011, the Court held that death row inmates could not sue prosecutors for failing to turn over exculpatory evidence, and rejected a class action suit from female employees of Wal-Mart; and in 2012, it held that police had nearly unlimited license to strip search suspected offenders before putting them in jail.[77]

Still, much like the Burger and Rehnquist Courts before it, the decisions of the Roberts Court have not always gone against the interests of disadvantaged minorities. For example, the Court has ruled that mentally ill convicts could not be put to death (*Panetti v. Quarterman*, 2007), that capital punishment could not be used as a punishment for the rape of a child (*Kennedy v. Louisiana*, 2008), that juveniles who commit crimes cannot be sentenced to life in prison without parole (*Sullivan v. Florida*, 2010, and *Graham v. Florida*, 2010), and that California had to take action to relieve the unhealthy and overcrowded conditions of its prisons (*Brown v. Plata*, 2011).[78] A comprehensive study of civil liberties cases before the Supreme Court between 1958 and 2007 found that the percentage of pro–civil liberties decisions made by the Roberts Court (2005–2007) was the second lowest on record. Only the Rehnquist Court from 1990 to 1992 had a lower percentage; however, the Rehnquist Court from 1993 to 2004 made a higher percentage of pro–civil liberties decisions than the early Roberts Court.[79] Overall, the principal beneficiaries of Roberts Court decisions would appear to be businesses, wealthy individuals and groups, and state governments.

Although there is less systematic evidence about the consequences of lower court rulings, a study of federal district court decisions on education policy in the 1970s found a strong tendency for judicial support of disadvantaged minorities. A study of sixty-five education policy decisions between 1970 and 1977, sixty-four of which concerned constitutional issues, found that minority plaintiffs were successful 71 percent of the time.[80] Plaintiffs in these cases included African Americans, Hispanics, and Native Americans; illegal immigrants; women; handicapped, poor, and elderly individuals; and nonconformists such as long-haired students. These findings were especially interesting because the authors deliberately excluded school desegregation cases from their sample. Thus, their findings did not simply reiterate the well-known conclusion that school desegregation cases were decided in favor of minorities.

In retrospect, it seems clear that the noticeable shift in the disposition of the courts favoring disadvantaged minorities in constitutional law cases that began in the mid-1950s was the result of more liberal judges on the federal bench (including women and African Americans), particularly between 1960 and 1980. Of equal or greater importance were changes outside the courtroom—in the legal and political culture—that led to the proliferation and mobilization of groups seeking justice and equality for these minorities. Groups such as the NAACP, the ACLU, and the National Organization for Women fought successfully to extend the frontiers of the First, Fourth, Fifth, and Fourteenth Amendments, and were aided greatly by a receptive Warren Court. As a result of their efforts, the Constitution was transformed to become much more of a beacon to the weak and the oppressed.

However, the many liberal rulings of the Warren Court triggered a formidable countermovement. Conservative groups (such as the Federalist Society) and politicians who shared their goals, especially Republican presidents, gradually succeeded in bringing more conservative ideas and judges to the bench.[81] This did not result in the wholesale elimination of liberal Warren Court precedents, as many of the more conservative judges believed in stare decisis and some measure of continuity in court rulings, but by the 1990s, disadvantaged minorities no longer had a clear advantage in federal courts in constitutional law cases. As our review of Roberts Court constitutional law decisions illustrates, the beneficiaries of recent Supreme Court rulings are just as likely to be advantaged minorities, such as wealthy people interested in politics and gun owners, as they are to be disadvantaged minorities, such as juveniles, prisoners, and the mentally ill.

Administrative Law

The most common result of judicial review of administrative agency actions, at either the state or the federal level, is for the court to sustain the agency.[82] This result confirms the argument made by law professor Marc Galanter in 1975 that repeat players have the advantage in civil litigation.[83] The government is the quintessential repeat player. It has greater expertise, fewer start-up costs, greater bargaining credibility, and a greater stake in shaping the rules of the game than other litigants, especially one-shot litigants. It is not surprising that the government wins most of its cases.

Nevertheless, a substantial minority of the administrative decisions reviewed by the courts are reversed or remanded, which means sent back to the agency for reconsideration. According to a 1980 study of state supreme court reviews of administrative agencies' decisions, nearly 44 percent of the court decisions did not fully support the agencies.[84] Even the more deferential U.S. Supreme Court reverses a significant percentage of federal agency decisions, and when it does, the effects of these rulings on the behavior of the agencies are often profound.[85]

The willingness of the U.S. Supreme Court to reverse a federal agency decision depends on many factors, including the ideology of the sitting justices. According to one study, the Warren Court and the Burger Court were equally likely to sustain federal agency decisions, but they handled liberal and conservative decisions differently. For example, conservative decisions by social service or regulatory agencies were sustained 63.4 percent of the time by the Warren Court, but 81.7 percent of the time by the Burger Court. As expected, liberal decisions by the same agencies were sustained more often by the Warren Court (86 percent) than by the Burger Court (69 percent). And liberal justices were more likely to sustain liberal decisions.[86]

Who benefits when the courts reverse the decision of an administrative agency? The answer depends on who the plaintiff is and what issue is under consideration.[87] When a court reverses a social welfare agency's decision, the plaintiff is almost certain to be an individual claimant—a welfare recipient or a disabled worker, for example. Typically, the beneficiaries are poor people and members of disadvantaged minority groups, and the losers are politicians seeking to cut agency spending and perhaps taxpayers. When a court reverses a regulatory agency's decision, the plaintiff is almost certain to be a business such as an insurance company or a utility company. Normally, the beneficiaries here are members of an advantaged minority, whereas the losers are citizens, in their capacity as consumers.

If this pattern looks fairly symmetrical, it seems less so when one realizes that disappointed individuals are far less likely to challenge an adverse administrative action in court than are disappointed corporations. For example, a study of the Social Security Administration (SSA) in the 1970s found that only 8 percent of all final decisions went to court, and only one-third of those resulted in the restoration of benefits for the claimants.[88] In contrast, during this same time period, about 40 percent of state public utility commission decisions in major rate cases were appealed to the courts.[89] The most frequent appellants were business groups, usually utilities, and the most frequent winners, when the public utility commissions were overruled, were also business groups, again usually utilities. This same pattern holds for many federal regulatory agencies such as the Occupational Safety and Health Administration and the EPA. These agencies face numerous "well-organized, well-resourced and litigation-prone individuals, groups and organizations."[90] Litigation is a pervasive influence in the lives of many agencies.

The previous discussion highlights an important difference between the "bias" of the judicial system and the "bias" of individual judges. As we have seen, there are many liberal judges who favor disadvantaged minority litigants and many conservative judges who tilt toward business interests. But individuals and groups with more resources are better able to defend themselves against adverse actions by administrative agencies. This illustrates an important bias in the system. It is not absolutely clear that business groups use the courts more effectively than other groups, but it is clear that business groups use the courts more often than other groups. For this reason, tough judicial scrutiny of administrative agencies tends to benefit business groups.[91]

The area of environmental policy has an especially rich history in administrative law. Some environmental statutes encourage citizen participation in administrative and judicial proceedings, and the courts generally have granted standing to these litigants. Many different environmental groups have taken the government and industry to court. Indeed, in the 1970s, the most frequent plaintiffs in federal district court cases concerning environmental disputes were environmental groups.[92] Moreover, in many instances, environmental litigants were or are well funded, experienced, and persistent. However, since the 1980s, business groups have equaled, if not surpassed, environmental groups in environmental litigation. The situation parallels the one we described regarding disadvantaged minorities and constitutional law. Although environmental groups enjoyed considerable success in court in the 1970s, business groups, aided by conservative judges, have more than leveled the playing field since then.

Who wins environmental cases in court? In one respect, the familiar pattern holds: the government is most likely to win. One reason for this is an important precedent calling for judicial deference to "reasonable" agency interpretations of legislative intent when statutory language is ambiguous, which was established in 1984 in *Chevron v. Natural Resources Defense Council*. However, the government does lose cases, and when it does, environmental groups are as likely to win these disputes as are industry groups, depending on who the judges are. The successes of environmental groups during the 1970s persisted through the 1980s, but declined in the early 1990s as judges appointed by Presidents Ronald Reagan and George H. W. Bush grew more influential. By the late 1990s, President Clinton's appointees showed themselves to be much more sympathetic to environmental causes.[93] Judicial appointments by President George W. Bush shifted the judicial balance back in a conservative direction, but a two-term Obama administration will benefit environmental groups in the second decade of the twenty-first century.[94]

A major issue in many environmental cases is how liberal courts are in granting environmental groups standing to sue. In landmark decisions such as *Sierra Club v. Morton* (1972) and *United States v. SCRAP* (1973), the Supreme Court indicated that environmental groups could secure standing to sue an administrative agency or a private firm in court by demonstrating some injury to their members. Significantly, the Court noted that an economic injury was not necessary and that an aesthetic injury would do. Throughout the 1990s, however, the Supreme Court took a tougher stance on environmental group standing. In *Lujan v. National Wildlife Federation* (1990) and *Lujan v. Defenders of Wildlife* (1992), the Supreme Court refused to grant standing to environmental groups that sought to challenge decisions by the Department of the Interior. In these and other decisions, the Supreme Court stressed the need to demonstrate a specific injury that falls within the zone of interests protected by the relevant statute. Still, the Supreme Court has shown itself to be capable of occasional surprises. In *Friends of the Earth v. Laidlaw Environmental Services* (2000), the Supreme Court granted standing to an environmental group even though evidence submitted in court suggested that the injury to group members was more imagined than real. Even more significant was *Massachusetts v. Environmental Protection Agency* in 2007. In this case, in a 5-4 majority led by Justice Kennedy and the liberal justices, the Court ruled that the state of Massachusetts had standing to sue the EPA for not acting on greenhouse gas emissions because of the potential damage to the state posed by global warming.[95]

Constitutional Law versus Administrative Law

Constitutions in the United States explicitly protect minorities. In the U.S. Constitution, these minorities are identified with some precision in various constitutional amendments (religious groups and the press in the First Amendment; gun owners in the Second Amendment; homeowners in the Fourth Amendment; those accused of crimes in the Fifth and Eighth Amendments; African Americans in the Thirteenth, Fourteenth, and Fifteenth Amendments; and women in the Nineteenth Amendment). From the mid-1950s to the 1980s, disadvantaged minorities benefited most from decisions the Supreme Court made about constitutional law, but since then, the pattern has become less distinct; minorities, both disadvantaged and nondisadvantaged, have benefited. Administrative procedure acts are more neutral than constitutions. They seek to protect affected parties from arbitrary and capricious behavior by the bureaucracy, but they do not specify which parties are to receive protection. At the time of its passage in 1946, the federal APA was expected to benefit business groups in particular, and it often has done precisely that. But the proliferation of groups interested in government actions in the 1960s and 1970s, including broad-based public interest groups that pursued litigation over agency rules and secured standing to sue in court, has transformed the APA into an instrument for protecting well-organized groups generally, whether they represent disadvantaged minorities, advantaged minorities, or the majority of citizens.

Another important difference between constitutional law and administrative law is that the Supreme Court sets more precedents in the former than in the latter. The Court, with limited room on its docket, has chosen to focus on constitutional law, and this attention has given a certain coherence to constitutional law. In contrast, administrative law is largely the province of other courts, especially state supreme courts and federal circuit courts of appeals, and they frequently disagree. Moreover, administrative agencies do not always follow administrative law precedents set by lower courts, especially when they conflict with the directives of an agency head or chief executive.[96] This practice, which has no legal basis, limits the ability of lower courts to set precedent and makes administrative law less uniform than constitutional law. This type of agency behavior illustrates another important point: a court decision is only the beginning of a lengthy process with consequences that may be either narrower or broader than anticipated.

THE LONG ROAD TO JUSTICE

A court order may seem final and definitive, but it is typically the beginning of a complex, lengthy, and often convoluted process. The ultimate impact of the court on public policy depends on a host of intermediaries, who may not be willing or able to carry out the court's order, and on social and economic conditions that are outside of the control of the courts.

Confusion and Reluctance

When they make important rulings, judges depend on other public officials to implement their policies. Implementers include bureaucrats such as regulators, police officers, and social workers; legislative bodies such as Congress, state legislatures, and city councils; quasi-legislative bodies such as school boards and zoning boards; and other judges—lower courts are expected to implement the policies of higher courts. The implementation of judicial policies, like the implementation of other policies, is not without problems, which may include unclear standards, poor communication, inadequate resources, and hostility on the part of implementers.[97]

Unclear standards. Judicial policies are sometimes vague, contradictory, or variable. This is particularly true of appellate court opinions, which must accommodate the views and sensibilities of more than one judge. As noted earlier, the judge assigned the task of writing an opinion for an appellate court often finds it necessary to yield to a colleague on an important point. A first draft that is crisp, blunt, and direct may end up as a patchwork of compromises. The Supreme Court's decision in *Swann v. Charlotte-Mecklenburg County Board of Education* (1971) illustrates this phenomenon. Divided, but anxious to issue a unanimous opinion on school busing, the Court (1) endorsed busing as a permissible remedy, but warned against busing small children; (2) established a presumption against one-race schools, but declined to prohibit them; and (3) allowed lower courts to correct for residential segregation patterns, but only if caused by school board decisions. Reflecting on *Swann*, a federal judge observed, "There is a lot of conflicting language here. It's almost as if there were two sets of views laid side by side."[98]

An ambiguous opinion is only one of several sources of confusion. Even a clear opinion, if decided by a close vote, sends conflicting signals. Astute court watchers know that a 5-4 decision about a technical aspect of whether certain kinds of evidence may be included in a criminal case may yield to a 5-4 decision the other way in a subsequent case. A flurry of concurring and dissenting opinions attached to 5-4, or even 6-3, Supreme Court decisions also generates confusion. Multiple concurrences and dissents have become more common in the modern era of the Court, and their presence adds to the difficulty of implementing judicial policies.

Poor communication. People responsible for implementation are sometimes unfamiliar with the specifics of important court decisions—especially street-level bureaucrats, who do not make a habit of reading court opinions over their morning coffee. Following *Miranda v. Arizona* (1966), police officers did not clearly understand what was required of them.[99] After *Mapp v. Ohio* (1961), in which the Court ruled that evidence obtained in violation of the Fourth Amendment could not be used in state trials, police officers could not be absolutely certain under what circumstances evidence was inadmissible in court.[100] For many years following *Engel v. Vitale* (1962) and *Abington School District v. Schempp* (1963), in which the Court ruled that organized prayers or Bible readings could not be conducted in public schools, principals and teachers failed to understand the full extent of the prohibition, and noncompliance was widespread.[101]

Typically, the mass media do little to help officials and the public understand court decisions. Media coverage of court decisions, except major U.S. Supreme Court decisions, is minimal. High-profile criminal cases get covered, sometimes at length (e.g., O.J. Simpson's 1995 murder trial), but many constitutional law rulings, and virtually all administrative law cases, receive scant attention. Limited coverage of important court decisions is the norm, and public ignorance of court rulings is, therefore, hardly surprising.

Inadequate resources. Many court orders explicitly or implicitly require the expenditure of additional funds for public purposes. School boards had to purchase buses, hire drivers, and obtain more insurance when courts required school busing as an antidote to racial segregation. When the courts order back pay for victims of employment discrimination by the government, agencies must somehow obtain the funds to carry out the order. When the courts require state bureaucracies to upgrade the services provided to individuals who are mentally ill or intellectually disabled, the states need to spend more money on psychiatrists, custodians, and physical facilities.

Lacking the power of the purse, the courts depend on legislative bodies to allocate the funds to implement court orders. But politicians have their own priorities, and minority rights are seldom high on their agendas. When Judge Frank Johnson ordered improvements in the quality of Alabama's prisons in 1976, Governor George Wallace accused him of trying to turn the state's prisons into Holiday Inns.[102] Eventually, the Alabama legislature increased appropriations to the state's prisons, but not by enough to comply with the judge's directives. The Supreme Court gave cash-strapped California two years to come up with a solution to its prison overcrowding problem as part of its 2011 *Brown v. Plata* decision. By early 2013, the state had made substantial progress in reducing the prison population in state facilities, but was still 10,000 prisoners above the level the court had prescribed in its 2011 ruling.[103]

Hostile attitudes. Judges are widely respected in American society, but their views do not automatically command deference. People charged with implementation often question the wisdom of judicial decisions, especially on matters of social policy. Many school board members strongly disapproved of busing; many teachers fervently believe in school prayer. Many police officers object to court decisions that limit their ability to put criminals behind bars. Where such hostility is present, resistance may develop.

If hostility runs deep enough, the implementers may not comply. The members of the Boston School Committee, all of whom were white, refused to draw up a desegregation plan demanded by Judge Arthur Garrity, who then directed the desegregation of the school system through the use of a judicial decree.[104] Outright noncompliance of this sort is rare, but evasion is not at all uncommon. For example, as a response to tough evidentiary requirements in *Mapp*, some police officers resorted to perjury.[105] The public sometimes refuses to comply by taking evasive action. Many whites, particularly in the South, responded to court-ordered school desegregation by sending their children to private schools.

It is clear that the implementation of judicial policies cannot be taken for granted, but we should distinguish between short-term and long-term implementation problems. Short-term problems are often formidable, but they do not necessarily doom judicial policies to failure. Most court orders are eventually implemented, and there are several reasons why this is so.

First, a single case may be ambiguous, but several interrelated cases enable the courts to establish a pattern of decisions that can guide implementers. Blockbuster opinions, such as *Brown*, *Miranda*, *Mapp*, and *Roe v. Wade*, are usually followed by a series of interpretive opinions that reduce confusion.

This clarification is strongest when the courts are reasonably consistent, as they were in the first sixteen years following *Roe v. Wade*, when they repeatedly upheld the trimester framework established by *Roe* against various state challenges.[106] Even when the courts are less consistent, as they have been in criminal cases, additional decisions usually clarify more than they obscure. Precedents are often deflected but seldom overturned. The norm of stare decisis encourages courts to render reasonably consistent opinions over time, especially in matters of constitutional law, where the brooding presence of the U.S. Supreme Court ensures a modicum of consistency. As Justice O'Connor argued in *Bush v. Vera*, the Supreme Court's legitimacy requires adherence to stare decisis, especially in highly sensitive political cases.[107]

Second, knowledge of court orders travels slowly at first, but eventually trickles down to the bureaucrats responsible for day-to-day implementation. Indeed, the mass media deserve some of the credit for this. For example, anyone who has watched a police drama on television knows about *Miranda* rights and their importance. As Justice Rehnquist noted in reaffirming the *Miranda* decision in *Dickerson v. United States* (2000), "Miranda has become embedded in routine police practice to the point where the warnings have become part of our national culture."[108] Interestingly, citizens and street-level bureaucrats may have been enlightened about court decisions more by the entertainment programming of television than by the reporting in newspapers.

Third, institutions can deal with resource shortfalls in various ways, if given sufficient time. The mass release (deinstitutionalization) of mentally ill residents from state mental hospitals was a quick and easy way of coping with court requirements for improved care in the 1970s. But soon, there was a proliferation of halfway houses and group homes and other forms of deinstitutionalized care in communities around the country. The Army Corps of Engineers responded to court orders to prepare environmental impact statements following the passage of the National Environmental Policy Act (NEPA) in 1969 by establishing environmental units in their district offices and by hiring personnel with the necessary training.[109] More recently, court decisions on sexual harassment in the workplace have caused organizations, public and private, to hire skilled personnel and create new protocols to uncover and prevent harassing behavior.

Fourth, courts can go quite far in requiring that specific steps be taken to remedy a problem. For example, in *Missouri v. Jenkins* (1990) the U.S. Supreme Court upheld a lower court ruling requiring expenditures by the state of Missouri and the Kansas City school district to remedy school segregation. The Court even upheld the lower court's decision to mandate a tax increase, although the Supreme Court stressed that the tax hike must be approved by local authorities. The Supreme Court also stressed in a later version of the same case (*Missouri v. Jenkins*, 1995) that there are constitutional limits to a federal court's ability to order additional spending in the quest for racial desegregation. Thus federal district court judges must tread carefully when they order spending increases. But judges can also levy fines, issue "cease and desist" orders, or hold individuals or organizations in contempt for failure to carry out judicial policies. An even stronger step is the use of a judicial decree, which Judge Garrity used in Boston, as did Judge Johnson in Alabama. Judicial decrees of the sort used by Garrity and Johnson give judges wide latitude to issue specific and detailed instructions to achieve full implementation of their decisions, but they also require more of a judge's time and energy than is feasible in most contexts. This explains why they are seldom used.

Finally, attitudes change over time. Police officers may not be enthusiastic about *Miranda* requirements, but they have learned to live with them. School boards may not be happy about the absence of prayers in schools, but after a long period of widespread resistance, most have adapted. Immediately following an important court ruling, the disappointed parties assume the end of civilization as they knew it. But when the world does not come to an end, acceptance often follows. Perhaps the most striking illustration of this is the sharp change in the attitudes of whites toward school desegregation. In the late 1950s, 83 percent of southern whites objected to sending their children to a school that was half black; by 1981, only 27 percent objected.[110] According to polls conducted in the 1990s, southern attitudes toward school desegregation no longer differed much from those of other regions; although southerners preferred solutions other than court-ordered busing, so too did most other Americans.[111] In the twenty-first century, support for children of all races attending the same schools is over 95 percent.[112] For years, scholars have debated whether "stateways" can change "folkways," or whether law can induce social change. Although there are limits to what courts can accomplish, it appears that they have influenced attitudes on some basic issues.

REAL SOLUTIONS AND SOLUTIONS AS PROBLEMS

Many scholars are reluctant to ascribe so much influence to the courts, instead seeing the policy impact of the courts as rather limited.[113] Political science professor Lawrence Baum writes, "In reality, the Court's impact on society is limited considerably by the context in which its policies operate."[114] Similarly, Gerald Rosenberg has argued that the Supreme Court is a "hollow hope" for advocates of social reform.[115] At first glance, these assessment appear reasonable, given the implementation problems mentioned earlier. But in our view, the long-term impacts of numerous court decisions have been very significant for society as a whole.

One area of success for the courts has been the effort to promote racial justice. In education, voting rights, employment, and housing, the courts have breathed life into constitutional requirements for due process of law and have helped ensure equal opportunity for racial minorities, especially African Americans. This has not happened overnight. For a full decade after *Brown*, Southern schools remained separate and unequal. In the mid-1960s, however, the picture began to change. By the 1972 to 1973 school year, 91 percent of black students in public schools in the South were going to school with whites.[116] Progress in Northern schools, although slower, was also noticeable by the end of the 1970s.[117] Since the 1980s, further progress toward achieving full integration of elementary and secondary schools in the United States has been slowed by the proliferation of private schools, especially in the South, the concentration of minority students in large urban schools districts nationwide, and the growing reluctance of federal judges to order forceful integration methods such as busing. Indeed, in 2007, the Supreme Court ruled that ambitious integration plans drawn up by school districts in Seattle and Louisville were unconstitutional because race figured too prominently in them (*Parents Involved v. Seattle School District No. 1*).[118]

Court decisions on voting rights produced results more quickly, in part because all three branches of government moved aggressively on this issue. The Voting Rights Act of 1965 was followed one year later by an 8-1 Supreme Court decision affirming the act in full (*South Carolina v. Katzenbach*, 1966). Over the next two years, the Justice Department sent federal examiners to some southern voting districts and appointed poll watchers in others. The effects were dramatic. From 1964 to 1968, black voter registration rates in the South jumped from 38 percent to 62 percent.[119] Increased registration led to higher black voter turnout and to the election of black local officials, which in turn generated increases in public employment and other public services for African Americans.[120] In the past two presidential elections, turnout by African Americans equaled, or nearly equaled, that of whites, both in the South and nationwide. In 2013, Chief Justice Roberts cited improved black registration and turnout statistics in striking down sections 4 and 5 of the Voting Rights Act in the case *Shelby County v. Holder.* [121]

The courts have been less aggressive in promoting equal opportunity in housing, partly because of the tradition of judicial respect for the rights of property owners and judicial deference to local zoning boards and city councils.[122] As mentioned earlier, in the 1960s and 1970s, several state supreme courts invalidated exclusionary zoning practices as violations of state constitutions. In addition, since the 1990s, the U.S. Department of Housing and Urban Development and state and local housing authorities have promoted the development of mixed-income urban neighborhoods and communities. These and other efforts to achieve affordable housing at the federal, state, and local levels have opened up opportunities for racial minorities, even in affluent, mostly white suburbs. However, the steps taken to bring about meaningful desegregation of housing have proceeded slowly and produced limited results.

Court decisions in administrative law have also had significant impact, especially in communications policy, environmental policy, and standards for institutional care. In the 1960s, television station WLBT-TV in Jackson, Mississippi, was still fanning the flames of racial discontent in its editorials against integration and its acceptance of advertisements paid for by a local racist group. A church-related citizen group, the Office of Communication of the United Church of Christ, opposed in court the renewal of the station's license on the grounds that the station had violated the fairness doctrine of the Federal Communications Commission (FCC).[123] In two important decisions, *United*

Church of Christ v. Federal Communications Commission (1966 and 1969), the U.S. Court of Appeals, District of Columbia Circuit, agreed with the church and ordered the FCC to grant the license to someone else. The immediate consequences for Jackson television viewers were that the license was awarded to another company, which promptly hired African Americans as general manager and news anchor, and improved the quantity and quality of news and public affairs programming.[124] The long-term consequences were even more significant. Using these cases as precedents, citizen groups intervened in administrative and judicial proceedings on behalf of television consumers and, in many cases, secured important concessions. In addition, these cases helped establish standing for aggrieved consumers in other issue areas.

Court decisions on environmental impact statements have also generated far-reaching changes. NEPA, mentioned previously, required all federal administrative agencies to file environmental impact statements for "major federal projects with a significant environmental effect," and the federal courts have interpreted the words "major" and "significant" rather liberally. When in doubt, they require agencies to prepare environmental impact statements, which then give environmental groups specific statements and plans to contest in court. The repercussions have been widespread. The Army Corps of Engineers, long known for its "edifice complex," began to look at nonstructural alternatives to dams and dredging projects.[125] From the 1970s to the present, the U.S. Forest Service has paid much more attention to the interests of recreational users of forest lands, and less to those of logging companies, than they had in the past.[126] The courts' interpretations of NEPA sensitized many other agencies to the importance of environmental impacts.

The consequences of judicial efforts at institutional reform have been equally profound. In 1973, a federal district court ordered the closing of Willowbrook, a New York facility for intellectually disabled individuals, where conditions were shown to be unsanitary, unsafe, and inhumane. The immediate effects of judicial intervention were disappointing. The state's Department of Mental Health at first refused to yield client records and failed to submit progress reports on time, as required by the court. Between 1976 and 1979, however, the state bureaucracy opened 100 group homes for 1,000 Willowbrook residents. Community placement was achieved without lowering property values or destroying neighborhoods. Audits revealed that group homes were properly administered and, more important, that the lives of the residents had improved. Over time, many group home residents learned how to make decisions concerning choices of food and clothing. Such choices, which most people take for granted, marked a major breakthrough and signaled a significant improvement in their quality of life.[127]

These examples demonstrate the capacity of the courts to effect changes that are in the public interest, especially over time. Many court decisions produce tangible results that benefit disadvantaged and other minorities, or the public. A problem with court decisions, however, is that they are not easily contained. They have spillover effects never imagined by judicial decision makers. Many of these unintended consequences are undesirable. At best, they detract from judicial policies; at worst, they undermine them.

The *Mapp* decision, extending the exclusionary rule to local police departments, appears to have resulted in greater reliance on plea bargaining in cases in which evidence may have been obtained through questionable methods.[128] *In re Gault*, which established formal procedures for trying juveniles accused of a crime, made it difficult for juvenile court judges to counsel and advise informally, as they had done, in cases in which no crime had been committed.[129] As discussed above, in many cities, court-ordered busing prompted whites to abandon inner-city public schools by placing their children in private schools or moving to the suburbs. For example, when Judge Garrity ordered the desegregation of Boston's public schools in 1974, 61 percent of the pupils were white; when he terminated his involvement in 1985, only 27 percent were white.[130] The goal of racial integration of the schools has receded in importance in many cities because of the paucity of white children.

Court decisions on air and water pollution have also been a mixed blessing. In some cases, the courts have supported tough EPA and state agency rules to enforce provisions of the Clean Air Act, the Clean Water Act, and other environmental laws, while in others, they have granted significant concessions to industry. Many environmental scholars believe that court decisions, which ultimately reward one side and punish the other, typically do not encourage the development of new antipollution technologies and facilities, or the building of modern plants, and thereby increase the cost of achieving cleaner air and water.[131] Making decisions that maximize economic efficiency is not one of the courts' strengths, and the unintended consequences of this weakness, though hard to quantify with precision, are no doubt considerable.

In environmental policy, as in school desegregation, the courts have accomplished much of what they intended to accomplish. School segregation and air pollution have declined appreciably, and the courts deserve at least some of the credit. The country has paid a high price for these gains, however, probably higher than necessary. Judges are not very good at calculating costs, and they are not particularly inclined to do so. Judges think in terms of rights and duties rather than economic analysis. There is, in short, an irony here. In courtroom politics, costs are often manifest, but not always relevant. The costs of judicial decisions, although unintended, are not always unforeseeable; still, most judges would maintain that they are not responsible for the adverse consequences of their actions. When the costs of unintended consequences and spillover effects are added to the manifest costs, the wisdom of many judicial decisions is open to legitimate criticism.

SUMMARY

The failures of other branches of government and the litigious character of U.S. society go a long way toward explaining the courts' prominence in making public policy. Although courts mostly avoid macroeconomic policy and foreign policy disputes, they directly address many other issues, which are characterized by a high degree of conflict and manifest costs. Issues addressed by the courts are also marked by a high level of technical complexity, a high level of moral complexity, or both. Judges rule on some of the most vexing problems society faces.

In reaching decisions on these issues, judges are guided by factors that transcend politics, such as law and evidence. But judicial decision making is also political. Judges have distinctive judicial philosophies or ideologies, and are usually affiliated with a political party. As many studies have confirmed, their voting behavior reflects their ideologies and party affiliations. Internal politicking, especially on supreme courts, where several judges must agree on the wording of an opinion, often requires coalition building and compromise. This process also opens up opportunities for judicial leadership. In the courts, as elsewhere, political leaders sometimes prefer a weak or ambiguous policy to no policy at all. In contrast, intellectual leaders adhere more steadfastly to principle.

Many court decisions are at first diluted by unclear standards, poor communication, inadequate resources, and hostile attitudes. Over time, however, most are successfully implemented and produce results that at least approximate what was intended. Unfortunately, they often have unintended consequences, some of which compromise the ultimate impacts of the decisions. However, even if judges tried to take all of the possible consequences of their decisions into account, they could not possibly foresee every result.

Courts have changed in many ways. More women and African Americans sit on the bench, lending more judicial support to minority rights in constitutional law disputes. More public interest groups litigate in court, which results in occasional triumphs for environmental and consumer interests. Finally, the choice between judicial activism and judicial restraint is resolved more frequently in favor of judicial activism. Despite talk of restraint, the modern courts are more likely to overturn statutes and administrative agency decisions, and more likely to prescribe specific ground rules and remedies, than they were a century ago.

Activism and liberalism are not one and the same. In constitutional law, activism most often ran in a liberal direction in the 1960s and 1970s, but more recently we have seen both liberal and conservative activism. In administrative law, activism ran in a conservative direction (favoring business interests) until the 1970s, when several liberal activist rulings, especially in the area of environmental protection, were made. In general, the courts have supported environmentalists on standards and business groups on some aspects of enforcement. Whatever the policy tilt of the courts, the fact remains that judges make important public policy decisions.

Living Room Politics

T he United States is a representative democracy. American grade school children are taught that government and public policy are based on the consent of the governed. President Abraham Lincoln said that American government is "of the people, by the people, and for the people," and every national leader before and after him has cited the "will of the people" to justify particular courses of action.

Debates about the proper role of citizens in guiding public policy date back to the founding of the nation. James Madison and other authors of the Constitution were strong advocates of democracy, but they did not believe that elected representatives should blindly follow mass opinion in determining public policy. Many of the Founders feared that the public could be unstable, tyrannical, and even dangerous to liberal democracy.[1] They believed that periodic elections give citizens sufficient safeguards against elected representatives who served them poorly. Between elections, leaders should govern as they saw fit. This concept of democracy was perhaps best summed up by the British political philosopher and statesman Edmund Burke. In a treatise on representative democracy, Burke wrote, "Your representative owes you, not his industry only, but his judgment; and he betrays instead of serving you if he sacrifices it to your opinion."[2]

The fact that thousands of elected officials must face the voters every so often keeps many citizens involved in government at the most basic level. But for the most part, public policy is not made and implemented by the public. Instead, elected officials, bureaucrats, judges, and corporate leaders determine public policies. They are attentive to, not ruled by, the concerns of the public— a point underscored throughout this book. Yet people's opinions influence the course of public affairs, and occasionally, when aroused, people do play a central role in politics. This chapter on living room politics explores how public opinion, the mass media, and public officials interact in the making of public policy choices.

Public opinion is a potent weapon of democracy, but it is not something one can visit, like a building, or read, like a book. There are many publics, many opinions, and many voices in American society. Public opinion is defined and channeled into the policy process by groups such as the media, public officials, bloggers, and citizen activists.[3] Elected officials gauge public opinion by scrutinizing public opinion polls and television and newspaper reports, and by talking with interest group representatives, friends and coworkers, and perhaps people at the local café or coffee shop.

The mass media—television, Web sites, radio, and newspapers—are the principal vehicles through which public opinion is expressed and manipulated.[4] Policymakers, the media, and interest groups attempt to shape the view of reality that is presented to the people. Journalists influence the public's understanding of politics and public policy and then inform public officials about what the "public" thinks. Perhaps most important, the media frame political and policy discussions, telling people what issues are important and who favors each position. When the media or public officials succeed in defining the parameters of the policy debate, they are exercising what E. E. Schattschneider called "the supreme instrument of political power."[5]

In most instances, the public does not make policy directly, but citizens *can be* more than just an audience watching contests between political elites. Citizens who are angered by government decisions or frustrated by inaction can go beyond passive forms of democratic participation and organize grassroots political movements to attempt to achieve their objectives. Citizens can choose among policy options that affect their states and communities. Through ballot initiatives and referendums—devices of direct democracy available to citizens in most states—voters can force state legislators to write new laws or to eliminate old ones.

BYSTANDERS AND ACTIVISTS

Although public opinion is involved in virtually everything that government institutions do, most citizens are typically little more than bystanders.[6] The public policy enterprise occurs in the background of their lives: they hear noise, but they seldom listen. A much smaller "attentive public," probably no more than two out of ten Americans, follows public affairs closely. They carefully read Web sites, watch cable news broadcasts, listen to radio programs, read newspapers, make comments on Web sites, and e-mail or call elected officials. They have opinions and they express them. On rare occasions, the bystanders are drawn into the fray. When large segments of the public become concerned about issues, their preferences can become a powerful force and living room politics dominates the policy process.

Real Opinions, Soft Opinions, and Nonopinions

A sizable industry is devoted to surveying the public's thoughts on every subject, from baseball players' use of performance-enhancing drugs to the morality of public figures. Television networks, newspapers, and colleges and universities regularly commission public opinion polls or report public attitudes toward political officials, government institutions, and policy issues.

Are the concerns that are measured in public opinion polls what people are really thinking about, or merely pale imitations of preferences expressed by public officials through the media? Sometimes it seems that Americans are like the hapless couple depicted in the cartoon who tell a poll taker, "We don't have any opinions today. Our television is busted."

When people have little or no personal experience or stake in the outcome of a policy debate, public attitudes are likely to reflect views expressed by public officials and political pundits as reported in the media. For people to hold real opinions, an issue must be important to them. On many policy questions, people have either no opinion or what might be called "soft" opinions, which may change rapidly in response to events or new information. When the public holds real opinions—about issues that touch basic values or arouse strong preferences or fears—media reports or the statements of public officials are far less persuasive. The public is also less malleable when the policy remedies under debate are controversial.

Opinion polls suggest that many Americans are deeply conflicted about marriage between gays and lesbians and abortion, but the polls show differences in their responses. Opposition to same-sex marriage has significantly declined since the early 2000s. In 2004, 60 percent of the public disapproved of same-sex marriage compared with only 43 percent in early 2012.[7] However, the public's shift in acceptance over the past decade took a long time to directly translate into positive votes on ballot initiatives. Voters went to the polls and rejected state ballots proposing the legalization of same-sex marriage thirty-two times between 1998 and 2012.[8] This losing streak was broken in 2012, when three states, Maine, Maryland, and Washington, approved initiatives supporting marriage between gays and lesbians.

Abortion is another matter about which people feel strongly and remain deeply divided about the proper course for public policy. For example, since 1975, Gallup has reported that the majority of the public believes abortion should be legal in "any or under certain circumstances," and in 2011, 77 percent of the public held this opinion.[9] However, the majority in favor of legal abortion disappears once the term "partial-birth abortion" is introduced into the equation. In that same year, the majority, or 64 percent, opposed legislation to legalize this type of procedure.[10] The public also overwhelmingly supports laws requiring women under eighteen years of age to obtain parental consent for any abortion, and women seeking abortions to wait twenty-four hours before undergoing the procedure.[11] The increasing political and media attention paid to late-term abortion, which opponents label "partial-birth" abortion, focused public attention on this issue and may have moved some of those who are supportive of abortions "under certain conditions" to opposition to this type of abortion. Of course, underlying these expressions of opinion is a deeply divided American public. Some believe that abortion constitutes the taking of a human life and should be outlawed. Others believe that a woman has an absolute right to determine whether to complete a pregnancy and that government should not interfere in this intensely private decision. Majorities are formed by the reaction of those in the middle to the specific circumstances surrounding abortion decisions, and the media play an important role in depicting these circumstances.

When large segments of the public have direct personal experience with a problem, pollsters are more likely to measure genuine concerns than to reveal media-manipulated sentiment. Public anxiety about unemployment is a good example. During the Great Recession economy after 2008, over 20 million American workers were unemployed, and millions more knew jobless relatives or friends.[12] Thus, the attitudes they expressed about unemployment were grounded in personal experience and not easily influenced by politicians and journalists. The Pew Research Center polled the public and asked them to list the top policy priorities for the president and Congress in 2011.[13] Eighty-seven percent viewed the economy as the top priority, 84 percent cited jobs, and only 26 percent cited global warming. The same poll broke out the party affiliations of those surveyed and listed certain issues as top priorities. Of those who cited global warming as the main concern, 10 percent were Republicans, 41 percent Democrats, and 29 percent independents. In contrast, there were only modest differences along party lines among those who listed the economy or jobs as the main concern. Eighty-seven percent of Republicans, 88 percent of Democrats, and 81 percent of independents listed "improving job situation" as a top priority, and "strengthening nation's economy" was the top priority for 90 percent of Republicans, 87 percent of Democrats, and 88 percent of independents.

Public attitudes about policies are strongly shaped by broad trends and personal experiences, and these change over time. A Pew survey in January 2007, before the Great Recession took hold, found that 38 percent of the public felt that global warming should be the president's and Congress's top priority, but as noted above, by January 2011, only 26 percent of people held this view. Consider also how Americans responded over time in Gallup polls to a question probing whether "the environment should be given priority, even at the risk of curbing economic growth [or] economic growth should be given priority, even if the environment suffers to some extent." In 1995, 62 percent said that the environment should get priority, and 32 percent cited economic growth; in 2000, the corresponding figures were 67 percent and 28 percent. But in 2012, only 41 percent indicated that the environment should get priority, and 49 percent cited economic growth.[14]

When pollsters and journalists venture into subjects that are unfamiliar to the public, they often discover, and then communicate, soft opinions or non-opinions to policymakers. Consider some of the following examples from Gallup polls that explore complicated issues about which most Americans have limited personal knowledge:

- **Cuba:** "Apart from their diplomatic relations, do you favor or oppose the U.S. Government ending its trade embargo against Cuba?" In 2009, 51 percent favored this action, 36 percent opposed it, and 13 percent had no opinion.[15]

- **Energy:** "Do you think that the U.S. is or is not likely to face a critical energy shortage during the next five years?" In 2012, 50 percent said yes, and 46 percent said no.[16]
- **The United Nations:** "Do you think the United Nations is doing a good job or a poor job in trying to solve the problems it has to face?" In 2012, 32 percent said a good job, and 61 percent said a poor job.[17]

Out of politeness, or because they do not want to appear uninformed, many people will answer pollsters' questions about policy issues even when they have no knowledge of or opinions about them. When this happens, public officials and journalists may draw misleading conclusions about what the public really wants, or if they even care, about an issue. Public opinion matters when the issue becomes sufficiently important for people to pay attention to it. Until then, public moods can swing widely. On many public issues, Americans hold ambiguous and contradictory opinions, and on such issues public officials are free to interpret poll results to fit their preconceived views.

One might assume that on important perennial issues such as taxes, spending, and the budget, the public would hold more consistent views. Yet most polls show that the public wants lower taxes, more spending, and a balanced budget too. People are unwilling to accept the logic that all three cannot be done simultaneously. The Pew Research Center conducted a survey in early 2011 that asked Americans whether they would increase, decrease, or keep federal spending the same on a host of different domestic programs. The title of the report succinctly sums up the findings: "Fewer Want Spending to Grow, but Most Cuts Remain Unpopular."[18] For over two decades, pollsters have found similarly contradictory views. In 1990, for example, 60 percent of those polled thought spending for domestic programs should increase, but 79 percent opposed raising federal income taxes (see chapter 2).[19] Elected officials and pollsters, therefore, are free to argue over what the polls mean, but they cannot ignore the results, because these kinds of bread-and-butter issues tap more than nonopinions. Even inconsistent and confusing public attitudes play a role in establishing policy options.

Polls and pollsters affect the understanding and impact of public opinion simply by asking certain questions and phrasing them in certain ways. When pollsters use the term "crisis" in seeking opinions on matters such as energy, crime, drunk driving, or the deficit, the results they report may be magnifying concerns that exist primarily in the minds of pollsters, journalists, and public officials. Or questions may be framed in ways that produce certain results. It is well known, for example, that using the word "welfare" rather than the phrase "aid for the poor" can have a large impact on favorability toward a program.[20] The framing of survey questions in ways that produce predictable results is a well-understood practice among pollsters, politicians, and political activists. Professional polling organizations such as Gallup, Pew, and university-based research groups try very hard to avoid prejudicial framing, but political groups such as the Democratic and Republican National Committees often embrace the practice.

It is one thing for the public to express concern about an issue; it is quite another for the public to agree on a policy direction that sends clear signals to policymakers. Although surveys report that the public is very concerned about the issue of crime and gun violence, public attitudes have not changed over the years about gun control. The Pew Research Center asked respondents how "closely" they were following certain gun violence stories at different points in time, and found that 48 percent were following the Colorado movie theater shooting "very closely," making it, according to Pew, "one of the most closely followed stories so far in 2012."[21] Pew's research showed that attitudes about gun control issues before and after major episodes of gun violence did not change in this case, or in other similar previous instances, including the shooting of Congresswomen Gabrielle Giffords and eighteen others in Tucson, Arizona, or the murders of thirty-two students at Virginia Tech in 2007. The public is divided over whether these shootings are "isolated acts of troubled individuals" or the result of broader problems in American society. Even after the shootings in Newtown, Connecticut, in late 2012, in which twenty school-children and six teachers were murdered, Americans remained divided over whether it is more important to control gun ownership or to protect the right of Americans to own guns to protect themselves; but after this incident, there was very strong support for background checks on all gun purchasers, and majority support for a ban on assault weapons.[22]

Another example that illustrates the point that the public may have strong views, but remain ambiguous about the best policy direction, is public attitudes about the influence of Wall Street on the Great Recession and financial crisis. A Gallup poll conducted in October 2011 found that 78 percent of Americans felt that Wall Street financial leaders deserved a great deal, or a fair amount, of the blame for the recession.[23] Yet in a poll conducted by the Pew Research Center just a few months later, in February 2012, about half of the respondents said that there was either too much regulation of banks and financial institutions (30 percent) or the right amount of regulation (20 percent).[24]

Despite their limitations, public opinion polls perform valuable functions in democracies. They are the only mechanism, outside of elections, through which the concerns of a broad cross-section of citizens are expressed to political elites. The results of public opinion polls may be more representative of public sentiment than elections because voter turnout, even for presidential elections, is usually about 60 percent (see chapter 2), and turnout for congressional elections is even lower, about 55 percent during a presidential election year and about 40 percent in off-year elections.[25] Another benefit of polls is that they can put issues on the public agenda that go beyond the demands of special interest groups.

Finally, surveys provide some feedback about public satisfaction with the direction and performance of government. One such poll is the University of Michigan's American Customer Satisfaction Index (ACSI), which provides data concerning consumer attitudes about government services. ACSI is funded by the federal government to independently measure public satisfaction with

over thirty government agencies on a 100-point scale. The Pension Benefit
Guaranty Corporation received a 90 percent satisfaction score from retirees;
the Health Resources and Services Administration of the Department of
Health and Human Services received a 78 percent satisfaction score from
Health Service Corps participants; the Internal Revenue Service (IRS) received
a 78 percent score from electronic filers, but only 57 percent from paper filers;
and the Office of Disaster Assistance received an 85 percent score from renters,
but only 78 percent from business loan recipients. Agencies with lower scores
include the Federal Aviation Administration (54 percent) from operations
managers, and the Foreign Agricultural Service at the Department of
Agriculture (60 percent) from its customers.[26]

Top-Down Public Opinion

Contrary to the civics book notion that the public will drives elected officials
to carry out the public's wishes, political elites usually decide what public opinion is, what it means, and whether to use it or ignore it. This does not mean
that the opinions of the public are unimportant, only that they are defined by
public officials. In this view, such opinions should be thought of as ammuni-
tion used by political elites to support their points of view and to advance their
policy positions.

The creation, interpretation, and use of public sentiment by public officials, the media, and interest groups in the policy process has been labeled
"top-down public opinion" by Cliff Zukin, a public policy and political science
professor at Rutgers University.[27] Political elites "construct" a notion of what
the "public" wants by listening to a variety of individuals and to reports on
public sentiment.[28] Over fifty years ago, political scientist V. O. Key Jr.
described public opinion as "private opinions which government finds it prudent to heed."[29] Nevertheless, as described in chapter 2, policy formulation and
implementation occur within the boundaries of political culture established by
public opinion. The nation's political culture comprises "the enduring beliefs,
values and behaviors that organize social communication and make common
interpretations of life experience possible."[30] Just as massive nuclear arsenals
presumably deter the United States, Russia, and China from starting a nuclear
war, public opinion constrains what government institutions can accomplish
or even propose. A "law of anticipated consequences" usually checks public
officials, preventing them from implementing policies that offend fundamental
values in the political culture. Elected officials know that if the public is
ignored or offended, it can be mobilized by political opponents.

Political elites also wield interpretations of public sentiment in day-to-
day struggles for power and policy advantage. Legislators and chief executives
cite public support as the rationale for policy innovation, such as tough new
laws against criminals. Governors and legislators also use public opinion as a
shield against modification of existing policies, such as tax rates. Even when
reliable and up-to-date public opinion polls are available, each side in a policy
debate will claim public support, as they are clearly able to do when it comes

to budgetary policies. An example of this is a question that Pew asked in 2011: "If the government makes major cuts to federal spending in an effort to reduce the budget deficit, do you think these cuts would help the job situation, would hurt the job situation, or not have much effect either way?" Twenty-six percent said the cuts would help, 27 percent that they would hurt, and 39 percent that they would not have much effect either way. So policymakers could report that 66 percent (39 percent + 27 percent) said that spending cuts would either hurt or have no effect, or that 65 percent (39 percent + 26 percent) said that cuts would either help or have no effect, depending on the policymakers' preferred stance.[31]

Chief executives are especially dependent on the mobilization of public support for their positions; they must maintain the perception that the majority stands with them. President Obama was the first president to make wide use of social media tools, such as Twitter and YouTube, to generate support for his initiatives. He set an example that future presidents are likely to follow as they try to find innovative strategies for reaching out to their supporters, and mobilizing them to persuade Congress to adopt their administrations' policies.[32] Legislators may try to read the tea leaves of public opinion to see how well the president or governor is doing before deciding whether to lend their support. If the public seems to favor the president's or a governor's policies, legislators may be reluctant to criticize.[33]

On the other hand, elected officials from the opposition party may come out against a president's policy proposal, precisely because they want to draw sharp distinctions between their party and the president's. Consider, for example, the experience of President Obama and the Patient Protection and Affordable Care Act (ACA). Against the wishes of many liberal members of the Democratic Party, Obama based his health care reform proposals on ideas supported in the past by many Republicans, including requiring people to purchase health care insurance, and using private market mechanisms more than government regulations to achieve better health care outcomes. However, shortly after he announced his proposal, Republicans came out strongly against the president's plan.

Public opinion about health care reform was also shaped by the public positions taken by the president and opponents of the law in Congress. As initially introduced, public polls showed strong support for the notion of broadening health care coverage. A Kaiser Family Foundation survey of Americans before the enactment of ACA asked whether respondents thought the "country as a whole will be better off or worse if Congress passes health care reform." In February 2009, 59 percent said that the nation would be better off, and only 12 percent said that it would be worse off. Almost a year later, in January 2010, just before the law was enacted, the corresponding figures were 42 percent and 36 percent. In January 2012, nearly two years after ACA was passed, 37 percent said that the country would be better off under the health reform law, and 37 percent said that it would be worse off.[34] Public attitudes were shaped by the partisan criticism of President Obama's proposal between its initial introduction and final passage. Although Americans supported individual components of the law, support for the legislation as a whole declined as the law's opponents questioned the requirement that individuals would be compelled to purchase health care insurance. In November 2010, 78 percent of the public supported ACA provisions to keep the "tax credits to small businesses that offer coverage to their employees," and 71 percent wanted to keep the part of the "law prohibiting insurance companies from denying coverage because of a person's medical history or health condition"; however, only 27 percent of the public wanted to keep the provision that would "require nearly all Americans to have health insurance or else pay a fine."[35]

Bottom-Up Public Opinion

The public is not always passive. Large segments of the public, marginally interested or even disinterested in politics, may be awakened gradually.[36] Salient issues, such as war, civil rights, morality, public health, or unemployment, can stir the passions of ordinary citizens, causing people to abandon their bystander status and vote on policy issues or even become active participants in movements. When this happens, public opinion may exert significant pressure on political institutions and public officials from the bottom up. Bottom-up politics is closely aligned with what is sometimes called "grassroots politics." The idea is that citizens and/or communities take direct responsibility for defining the issues that are important to them, rather than relying on politicians to perform this task.

A classic example of grassroots politics is the New England town meeting. This system of local government, present in hundreds of small communities, invites every citizen to have a say in the making of public policy. Although town meetings are often tedious and sometimes confrontational, they have maintained a niche in the political life of New England over several centuries.

Throughout the course of American history, grassroots political movements have sprung up to demand reform—sometimes with striking success, and at other times with stunning failure. For decades prior to the Civil War, for example, abolitionists sought the end of slavery, but few people or politicians listened. In the middle of the nineteenth century, suffragettes began to press for the right to vote for women, which finally was granted by ratification of the Nineteenth Amendment to the Constitution in 1920. Agrarian populists and labor unionists at the turn of the twentieth century demanded economic justice for low-income Americans, but achieved minimal success until the New Deal.

Since World War II, American politics has witnessed strong public movements to secure civil rights for African Americans and other minorities, to stop the war in Southeast Asia, to clean up the nation's air and water, to crack down on drunk drivers, and to stop abortions. More recently, conservative leaders funded and organized under the umbrella of the Tea Party, a movement for smaller government and tax cuts. This strategy helped elect more conservative Republican members of Congress by successfully challenging more moderate

Republican incumbents in primary elections.[37] A year later, the Occupy Wall Street movement captured public attention, and produced spinoff demonstrations around the country, reminding Americans of the power of mass protest.[38]

What makes citizens stop relying on the voting booth and begin attending meetings or marching in the streets? What makes people switch from watchers to active participants? Grassroots movements emerge when citizens become impatient with the pace of decision making, frustrated by the unwillingness of public officials to address their concerns, or angered by laws that infringe on basic rights or fundamental interests. When public opinion is "carried through from conversation to action [it] almost always carries with it a sense of outrage or injustice. At this point it is no longer opinion at all . . . but rather a state of emotional shock . . . a feeling of deprivation."[39] Often citizens are drawn into political conflicts when they believe their health, safety, or property is threatened by government policies. The issue could be a proposed toxic waste site, a new professional sports stadium, the introduction of charter schools, or a new condominium development that alarms people sufficiently to spur them to act. Under these conditions, a small group of citizens who normally eschew politics can be motivated to attend meetings, join protest marches, contribute money, boycott products, and become political animals. Intense local opposition to public policy decisions has come to be known as the "not in my backyard," or NIMBY, syndrome.[40] Public opinion is expressed from the bottom up when communities mobilize to protect their vital interests.

CITIZENS, POLITICIANS, AND THE MEDIA

Living room politics consists of the interaction of political leaders, who want to control and manipulate public opinion; citizens, who want to bring about changes in government policy; and the media, which serve as conduits of important political information about and to the public. On rare occasions, citizens join together to fight the White House, the Capitol, or city hall, but even "spontaneous" outbursts of public concern are unlikely to occur or succeed without the drumbeat of media and Internet coverage and strong political leadership.

The instruments of mass communication—television, the Internet, social media, radio, and newspapers—are the most important weapons in the battle for public opinion. Whether public opinion influences policies from the top down or citizens agitate from the bottom up, the mass media are involved. The media not only keep the attentive public informed, but also prominently feature and comment on stories that may eventually stir the normally apathetic mass of citizens.

Public officials and citizens can communicate face to face, but probably not on a regular basis. The media have become the principal intermediaries and, therefore, exercise enormous power.[41] The media influence people's perceptions of what is important, frame the terms of debate on many questions, and magnify the voices of a few political figures. From time to time, the media switch from an information "channel" to an information "source" to promote particular policy concerns. Coverage of the uncapped oil well that poured crude oil into the Gulf of Mexico is a powerful example of this phenomenon. One of the worst ecological and economic disasters in U.S. history, the oil spill captured the attention of both the media and the public for nearly three months after the British Petroleum (BP) Deepwater Horizon rig exploded. The nonstop news coverage of the oil spill accounted for 22 percent of the news stories aired for fourteen weeks after the April 2010 explosion, which far exceeded the next biggest news story covered by the media, the economy, which occupied only 12 percent of the stories aired.[42] The intense media coverage helped force the Obama administration to take an aggressive stance toward BP. As discussed in chapter 3, in an effort to bring accountability and financial justice to those affected by the environmental disaster, the Obama administration issued a six-month U.S. deepwater drilling moratorium and stricter safety regulations,[43] pushed for legislation funding environmental restoration projects,[44] talked BP into committing $20 billion to a victims' compensation fund,[45] and launched a criminal investigation into the oil spill, which eventually led to a guilty plea from BP.

Living room politics, like all politics, is dominated by political elites, rather than by the public or even by journalists. Journalists usually take cues on policy issues from public officials. The media seldom create policy debates on their own, but it often contributes to policy debates by tracking public attitudes. When the Pew Research Center did an analysis of the public's attitude toward the war in Iraq, it asked whether "using Military Forces in Iraq was the right thing to do" and "how well the Iraq war is going." Favorable public opinion toward the war started off high for both questions, and decreased significantly in the years when casualities were the highest (2004–2007). (From 2004 to 2007, U.S. military casualties in Iraq ranged from 800 to 900 per year, but then dropped significantly to only 314 deaths in 2008.[46]) Americans consistently believed that going to war in Iraq was a poor decision, but near the end of the war, public perception improved slightly on "how well the Iraq war is going," with 54 percent saying in 2010 that it was going very or fairly well, compared with 40 percent in 2007.[47]

Policymakers use the mass media and activists to build public support for their policy preferences. They depend on the media for feedback about policy initiatives and programs. But what officials read on the Internet or see on television is not an independent measure of public concern. Media critic Leon V. Sigal observed, "Listening to the news for the sound of public opinion, officials hear echoes of their own voices. Looking for pictures of the world outside, they see reflections of their own images."[48] What elected officials regard as public opinion is often derived from what other political actors say, rather than from systematic evidence gathered through reliable public opinion polls.

Citizen activists are also adept at using the media to pursue living room politics. They have learned that when one is losing a political battle, one "expands the scope of conflict" and tries to draw in members of the "audience who might support your cause."[49] The process goes something like this: A group is upset about an issue such as high state taxes. Its members collect signatures on petitions, hold press conferences, march to the state capitol, release public opinion polls, make speeches, publicize their cause using social media tools, appear at editorial board meetings, give interviews to newspapers, and appear on public affairs or news programs on radio and television. If they are skillful, diligent, and a little lucky, they can garner millions of dollars worth of publicity. The press and television give more exposure to their issue; the public becomes more aware and more interested; support builds; the media report that public support is building. Eventually, policymakers, sensing a groundswell of public concern, respond by cutting taxes. It should be said, however, that positive outcomes are not guaranteed. The Occupy Wall Street protests of 2011 featured groups of mostly young people who set up camps in public parks and used social media to bring more attention to the issue of income inequality in the United States. The drama of people physically occupying public spaces and clashing with police officers garnered mass media attention, but the movement was not very successful in achieving policy changes.[50]

Bringing Issues to the Living Room

The media magnify issues and promote them to the top of the agenda by their choice of what to highlight in the limited space and time available. The media may not tell people what to think, but they tell people what to think about.[51] The nation's leading newspapers—the *New York Times*, the *Wall Street Journal*, and the *Washington Post*—can each present only a small number of stories on the front page; the network news shows have time for only ten to fifteen stories in their half-hour shows.[52] Thus, at any given point in time, relatively few policy issues are receiving major media attention. Because most citizens have no personal contact with the political process, it is not surprising that they are dependent on the media for interpretations of the world around them. Over the past decade, agenda-driven media—whether cable news, social media, or Web sites—have come to play more prominent roles in shaping public attitudes about public policy and government officials. These media outlets, such as Fox News and MSNBC, not only help fragment public opinion but also often lead to divergent groups' adopting more intense positions on important issues.[53] Elected officials gravitate to issues that are salient to the public. Reports in the media help set the agenda for what is important in society. Elected officials know that issues identified by the media are likely to become priorities for the public.[54] In this way the media enhance the importance of the issues they cover and diminish the political significance of the problems they ignore.[55] Media attention also enhances or detracts from the political power of individuals. Because presidents and governors receive by far the greatest attention from the media, they have considerably more power than other political actors to set agendas, frame policy debates, and influence public sentiment. Conversely, ordinary citizens, even if they represent a widely held view, have trouble gaining access to mass media and the public airwaves.

Media surveillance of the political process helps keep issues on the agenda, especially if a president or governor addresses a policy question.[56] The public's agenda is not set in a single stroke; rather, it is built in a cycle of activity that elevates issues that are initially of interest to a few to issues that concern a broader public. The process through which the media, the government, and the citizenry influence one another has been labeled "agenda building" by scholars Gladys Engel Lang and Kurt Lang.[57] Intense media attention to issues such as tax or health care reform, or to the struggles between Congress and the president over the federal budget, transforms intramural squabbles into public controversies.

Issues ignored by the national media seldom generate sustained attention from elected officials and ranking administrative officials. Consider the case of highway traffic fatalities. In the United States, nearly 33,000 people died in motor vehicle traffic crashes in the United States in 2010.[58] Even though the number of traffic fatalities is down from previous years because of improving safety equipment on cars, they are still the leading cause of death for people aged five to twenty-four years. Yet because motor vehicle deaths are so commonplace, they are seldom covered by the national media. Contrast media reporting on motor vehicle deaths with the media's reaction to deaths caused by airplane accidents. Air traffic accidents typically result in approximately 500 deaths annually, but they receive enormous attention in the national press.[59] If the media reported cumulative statistics on automobile accidents and their causes each day or week, would they focus public attention and political debate on finding methods to reduce them?

In the 1990s, twenty-four-hour news networks, such as CNN, Fox News, MSNBC, and CNBC, among others, became more common, allowing for more extensive coverage of top stories. Such programs brought the details of the murder of moviegoers attending the premiere of the film *The Dark Knight* in Colorado; the shootings of thirty-two Virginia Tech students, staff members, and faculty members; and Hurricane Sandy, the "superstorm" that devastated communities in the Mid-Atlantic states. The proliferation of around-the-clock news shows and Web-based news coverage means that Americans now have multiple sources of information; the immediacy of much of this news means that viewers receive a lot more "unfiltered" information. On one hand, this means that people who are interested get more news than ever before; on the other hand, many of the first impressions conveyed by these programs turn out later to be incorrect and misleading. Indeed, the line between professional journalism and rumor mongering has never been more difficult to discern.

Advocates with a strong point of view may exploit these multiple media outlets to promote unsubstantiated rumors and conspiracy theories. For example, after the 9/11 attacks, there were completely unfounded claims that President George W. Bush and his administration collaborated with the terrorists to carry out the attacks on the World Trade Center and Pentagon. A loosely structured group known as the "9/11 Truthers" claimed that the Bush administration used the attacks to launch the "war on terror" and pass the

USA PATRIOT Act of 2001 (Uniting and Strengthening America by Providing Appropriate Tools Required to Intercept and Obstruct Terrorism), which gave additional authority to government agencies to conduct surveillance on Americans. Notwithstanding the lack of any credible evidence, the 9/11 Truthers are still active: a Colorado PBS television station aired a documentary in August 2012 highlighting the hidden details and evidence behind the 9/11 tragedy.[60] Over time, these arguments garnered some support despite the absence of any hard evidence to support them. In a 2006 Scripps Howard/ Ohio University poll, 36 percent of respondents said that it is "very likely" or "somewhat likely" that federal officials either participated in the attacks on the World Trade Center and the Pentagon or took no action to stop them "because they wanted the United States to go to war in the Middle East."[61]

Another unfounded assertion promoted by some extremists is that President Obama is not a natural-born citizen of the United States and is therefore prohibited by the U.S. Constitution from being president. Those who believe this idea are labeled "birthers." This notion has been promoted by some Republican elected officials and by conservative radio talk show hosts, such as Rush Limbaugh, and commentators on Fox News. In response to these accusations, President Obama released a certified copy of his Hawaii birth certificate in April 2011 to remove any doubt of his U.S. citizenship status. According to a Gallup poll, a month before the release of the president's certified birth certificate, nearly a quarter of respondents believed that President Obama was not born in the United States, including 43 percent of Republicans, 20 percent of independents, and 9 percent of Democrats. However, these numbers went down noticeably after President Obama released his certified birth certificate, dropping to 13 percent of all Americans believing in this theory, including 23 percent of Republicans, 14 percent of independents, and 5 percent of Democrats.[62]

The Myth of the Neutral Media

Just as public officials claim that they are not trying to manipulate the press, journalists perpetrate the myth that they are merely reporting what they see. Walter Cronkite, the iconic former CBS News anchorman, closed his nightly broadcast by saying, "That's the way it is," implying that he was merely letting people know what had happened that day. In fact, the media are not neutral observers of the passing scene; there is a difference between the news and the truth.[63] Newspapers, radio and television networks, and local stations shape the news and thus influence public officials and public opinion.

Journalists, Web site editors, and television producers simplify complex issues, place them in common frames of reference, and explain new policies with familiar terms.[64] When media organizations report on a public problem, an event, a speech, or a policy proposal, they not only describe it but also give the public a context within which to interpret it. According to media analyst Martin Linsky, "The way the press frames an issue is as important as whether or not it is covered at all. If the press characterizes a policy option one way early on in the decision-making process, it is very difficult for officials to turn that image around to their preferred perspective."[65]

Coverage of the debate over raising the national debt ceiling is a good case of media framing that confused many Americans. In reporting on the issue, many journalists implied that the decision to raise the national debt would authorize the federal government to spend additional money. In fact, the debt limit was established by Congress in 1917, during World War I, to enable the U.S. Treasury to borrow money to pay for government spending on laws approved by Congress.[66] Raising it does not authorize new spending. Not raising the debt limit would hinder the U.S. government in its efforts to borrow to meet its legal payment obligations, including Social Security and Medicare benefits, military salaries, interest on the national debt, tax refunds, and other payments.[67] Thus, if the debt ceiling was not raised by August 2011, the date on which the Department of Treasury warned the U.S. would run out of cash to meet its legal obligations, the nation would default on these obligations—a scenario that many economists believed would cause the credit rating agencies to downgrade the triple-A rating on U.S. Treasury bonds.[68] Media coverage of this issue tended to focus more on the political sparring between the parties, and between the president and Republicans in Congress, than on unpacking the facts behind the consequences of choosing to increase or not increase the U.S. debt ceiling.

Congress eventually reached an agreement to increase the U.S. debt limit in time to meet the August 2011 deadline. President Obama, when he signed the law, remarked, "Our economy didn't need Washington to come along with a manufactured crisis to make things worse."[69] Even with Congress's coming to an agreement on the debt ceiling issue, analysts felt that the political standoff between political parties left too much uncertainty for the United States' fiscal future: Standard & Poor's downgraded the U.S. credit rating by one notch. The agreement created the so-called fiscal cliff of tax increases and automatic spending cuts described in chapter 1.

The conventions of media reporting also influence the kinds of issues brought to the public's attention and the way they are dealt with by public officials.[70] Bureaucratic routines, organizational politics, competition, and economics distort the view of public problems mass media organizations present to the public. What reporters think may be less important than how they work. Reporters often exhibit a "herd mentality," as they take their cues about what to report from their colleagues and superiors in their organizations. Journalists and television crews position themselves where they decide news will be "made," and in so doing, they make news. In the reports themselves, extreme viewpoints are often highlighted because provocative statements and actions make more interesting reading and better television.

Complicated issues—such as the U.S. debt ceiling; mortgage-backed securities, subprime mortgages, and the housing bubble that led to the Great Recession; international trade; and health care costs—that are hard to explain and impossible to depict with pictures are frequently eschewed in favor of events that can be filmed, such as families salvaging their belongings after a flood or police beating a suspect during an arrest. News reports often convey a heightened sense of alarm about policy problems. Issues are personalized and dramatized, and a crisis atmosphere is created. In many cases, however, the "crisis is a function of publicity."[71] Public officials then feel compelled to take some action to ward off more negative stories.

After the 9/11 attacks, George W. Bush's administration coined the phrase the "war on terror." This policy framing was used as justification for the war in Iraq, and the suggestive link between these two issues created a "supportive political climate" in which Congress, the media, and the public initially stood behind the American invasion of Iraq in March 2003. The media internalized the policy framing of the war on terror through the constant reporting of the war in Iraq and Saddam Hussein's "weapons of mass destruction," without critically examining the administration's claim that these weapons did in fact exist.[72] Indeed, over 50 percent of Americans believed that "Saddam Hussein was personally involved in the September 11th terrorist attacks" in the time period leading up to the beginning of the Iraq war in 2003.[73]

As the war in Iraq continued and casualties mounted, American reporters began to cover Iraq War events in a more negative light. A former top U.S. weapons inspector, David Kay, reported to Congress in 2004 that the United States was wrong about the "prewar intelligence on Iraqi weapons of mass destruction."[74] That same year, the media covered the mutilation, caught on video, of four U.S. military contractors in Fallujah, and the abuse of Iraqi prisoners at the Abu Ghraib compound extensively. Support for the war declined, and stories about the progress of the war and conditions in Iraq received far less media attention.

A somewhat different scenario played out in 2011, when North Atlantic Treaty Organization (NATO) and U.S. airstrikes against Libyan leader Muammar al-Qadhafi's regime received prominent attention. Public opinion was mixed when U.S. warplanes first attacked Libya, with only 47 percent approving of U.S military actions in the country. This was the smallest percentage of Americans approving a U.S. military operation in the past four decades. By comparison, in 2003, 76 percent approved of the invasion of Iraq, and in 1999, 51 percent approved of the U.S. bombings in Kosovo.[75] Despite the reported success of the NATO and U.S. airstrikes in Libya, and President Obama's statement that their participation saved "countless lives," many Americans worried about the costs.[76] Approval ratings remained low six months later, with 44 percent of the public believing the airstrikes were the right decision.[77] The low ratings in the public opinion polls may have influenced President Obama's decision to keep U.S. involvement in Libya limited, remaining in a support role, while the NATO coalition played the more dominant role in the overall mission.

Media organizations also play an active role in shaping public policy when they commission public opinion polls and then report new or controversial findings. In 2012, for example, numerous polls were sponsored by news media, including ABC News/*Washington Post* polls, NBC News/*Wall Street Journal* polls, CBS News/*New York Times* polls, *Los Angeles Times* polls, *USA Today* polls, and CNN polls. The results of these polls were reported frequently and were not easily ignored by politicians who were debating policy questions and formulating policy alternatives.

Although less important than bureaucratic conventions that drive news reporting, the personal biases of journalists and media managers cannot be overlooked. Many of them are deeply suspicious of government policymakers and the ability of political institutions to solve problems. These views lead to predictable, formulaic stories about incompetence, fraud, waste, and abuse. Stories about effective programs or the achievements of dedicated civil servants are scoffed at as "not newsworthy." In the shorthand of reporters, "Good news, bad story; bad news, good story." For example, media organizations widely publicized reports that a unit of the U.S. General Services Administration held an extravagant and expensive conference near Las Vegas,[78] and that twelve Secret Service agents had paid prostitutes in Cartagena, Columbia, while doing security work in advance of President Obama's trip to Columbia.[79] Although neither of these stories is representative of the normal routines of government service, or characteristic of typical behavior of government employees, they reinforced themes of government mismanagement and the poor judgment of public officials.

Referendums and Initiatives

Citizens can select policies and structure government institutions by means of referendums and initiatives. There are no provisions in the U.S. Constitution for national referendums or initiatives, but all fifty state constitutions authorize legislative referendums, which give citizens a voice on measures approved by state legislatures.[80] Typically, referendums allow citizens to vote yes or no on amendments to state constitutions; on state capital spending projects, such as highways or new prisons; or even on major state laws, such as environmental protection and health care programs. For example, in 2011, Ohio citizens voted to repeal a new law (known as Senate Bill 5) passed by the Republican-controlled state legislature that "limited collective bargaining by public employees and required government workers to contribute more to their health care and retirement plans."[81]

Initiatives, provided for in twenty-four state constitutions, give citizens the right to petition public officials to place issues on the ballot for approval or disapproval, without waiting for the state legislature to act.[82] Before questions are put to the voters, a significant number of state residents must sign petitions, usually 5 percent to 10 percent of the number voting in the last statewide election. If the qualified initiative is then put on the ballot and receives majority support, the legislature is expected to enact a law embodying the purpose of the initiative. Initiatives have been used on a wide variety of policy questions, such as whether to raise the minimum wage, ban abortions, require photo identification to vote, prohibit government from requiring individuals or businesses to participate in the health care reform enacted in 2010, end state-run sales of liquor, allow slot machines at race tracks, or increase the maximum age for judges from seventy to seventy-five years.[83]

Giving the public a vote on policies has a long tradition in American politics. Referendums were first used in 1778, when Massachusetts voters approved the state's first constitution. The initiative grew in importance during the late nineteenth and early twentieth centuries as the Progressive political reform movement swept the country west of the Mississippi River. The influential Progressive reformer Robert M. La Follette summarized the rationale for referendums and initiatives:

> For years the American people have been engaged in a terrific struggle with the allied forces of organized wealth and political corruption. . . . The people must have in reserve new weapons for every emergency if they are to regain and preserve control of their governments. Through the initiative and referenda, people in an emergency can absolutely control. The initiative and referenda make it possible for them to demand a direct vote and repeal bad laws which have been enacted or to enact by direct vote good measures which their representatives refuse to consider.[84]

Since 1976, these instruments of "direct democracy" have been used with increasing frequency. The number of state ballot initiatives doubled between that year and 1986.[85] From 2000 to 2009, 374 initiatives were proposed by citizens and 158 were adopted.[86] In 2010, there were 160 ballot measures in thirty-eight states, including forty-two citizen-proposed initiatives.[87] Initiatives also represent a wide range of issues (see Table 8-1). In 2010, nearly 17 percent of initiatives dealt with taxes, budget, and debt issues, such as limiting property taxes or requiring voter approval for any new state tax increases; about 9 percent dealt with gambling and lottery measures; and education and health and medical issues each captured 7 percent of initiatives placed on state ballots within the first decade of the twenty-first century.[88]

To add some specifics to the categories listed in Table 8-1, voters weighed in on dozens of important, complex, and controversial ballot issues, including the following:

- Repealing the state income tax in Massachusetts (failed)
- Allowing stem cell research in Michigan (passed)
- Allowing doctor-assisted suicide in the state of Washington (passed)
- Creating a voucher system for public schools in Michigan (failed)
- Denying state services to illegal immigrants in Arizona (passed)
- Declaring English the state's official language in Arizona (passed)

TABLE 8-1   **State-Level Initiatives, 1990 to 2010**

		Approved	
Issue	Total	Number	Rate
Abortion	17	3	18.0%
Animals (hunting, farming)	40	23	58.0%
Business regulation	23	10	43.0%
Campaign, lobbying laws	36	21	58.0%
Civil rights	17	5	29.0%
Consumer, auto insurance	8	0	0.0%
Crime and punishment	13	6	46.0%
Drugs	32	17	53.0%
Education	44	12	27.0%
Elections, voting rights, registration	21	6	29.0%
English as official language (either at the state level or in public schools)	7	5	71.0%
Environment	35	10	29.0%
Government administration	23	12	52.0%
Health and medical	39	21	54.0%
Labor	31	16	52.0%
Land	19	9	47.0%
Legal, judiciary	24	11	46.0%
Lottery, gambling	64	20	31.0%
Redistricting, legislative powers	18	9	50.0%
Marriage	14	13	93.0%
Taxes, budget, debt	135	46	34.0%
Terms of office	65	47	72.0%
Tobacco, smoking	14	9	64.0%
Transportation	7	4	57.0%
Utilities	14	6	43.0%
Other	37	14	38.0%
Total	797	355	45.0%

- Awarding $1 million to a random voter each general election as a way to increase turnout in Arizona (failed)
- Requiring farmers to provide pregnant pigs and calves a certain minimal amount of living space in Arizona (passed)

- Requiring all public school instruction to be taught in English in California (passed)
- Permitting the medical use of marijuana in Alaska, Arizona, California, Colorado, Maine, Michigan, Montana, Nevada, Oregon, Washington, and the District of Columbia (all passed)[89]
- Establishing a renewable energy portfolio standard in Colorado (passed)
- Requiring proof of citizenship when registering to vote in Arizona (passed)
- Requiring photo identification to vote in Mississippi (passed)
- Banning government-sponsored affirmative action in the hiring of state workers in Washington (passed)
- Establishing public funding of political campaigns in Arizona and Massachusetts (passed)
- Banning the hunting of mourning doves in Ohio (failed)
- Legalizing the possession of small amounts of marijuana in Colorado and Washington (both passed)[90]

THE CONDUCT OF DIRECT DEMOCRACY

Most initiative and referendum campaigns rely on volunteers, but some have become costly public relations efforts requiring millions of dollars for television advertising. California's Proposition 87 made history in 2006 by becoming the most expensive campaign in the state's history, with a total of $154 million raised in support for both sides of the issue. The initiative would have placed a severance tax on oil companies, with revenue funding a $4 billion alternative energy research program in an effort to reduce the state's petroleum consumption.[91] Major oil companies, such as the Chevron Corporation, donated the majority of funds; however, Hollywood producer Stephen Bing was the single biggest donor in California, with a donation of nearly $50 million to support the oil tax for alternative energy.[92] The line between show business and politics was blurred in the controversy because of the backing of several movie stars, including Robert Redford, Julia Roberts, and Leonardo DiCaprio. With funding pouring in from both sides, the proposition was ultimately defeated in a vote of 45 percent for to 55 percent against.[93]

Initiative and referendum campaigns have spawned an industry that collects signatures and mounts public awareness advertising campaigns. These services are available for hire. They are expensive, and only groups with significant resources can afford them. In 1984, the Florida Medical Association organized an initiative drive to impose ceilings on financial awards in negligence suits. Doctors dished out $8 million to canvassers, who went door to door in "friendly" neighborhoods seeking signatures to place the question on the ballot. The canvassers assured citizens that passing the initiative would reduce medical costs, but they did not mention that their ability to sue for damages would be curtailed. The Florida Supreme Court refused to qualify the issue for the ballot because of the misleading campaign.[94] Reacting to tactics that undermine the democratic nature of the process, several states, including Montana, Nebraska, North Dakota, South Dakota, and Oregon, prohibit payment per signature, but do permit payment on a salary or hourly basis in initiative and referendum campaigns in order to prevent fraudulent activity.[95]

Governors, state legislators, and others aspiring to elected office are using ballot questions to gain political visibility and attain policy objectives. In several states, legislative and gubernatorial candidates are backing ballot initiatives, hoping that their support will bring sympathetic voters to the polls on Election Day. As David Magleby, a leading student of the initiative process, has pointed out, elected officials see referendums and initiatives as another tool in their political arsenal. If they win, initiatives allow legislators and governors to bypass the lengthy, arduous, and chancy legislative process. Even if they lose, politicians can gain political visibility through free media time.[96]

In California, more than $80 million was spent on a successful campaign in 2008 for an initiative to ban same-sex marriage known as Proposition 8.[97] Campaign spending was fairly evenly split among those for and against Proposition 8, with $44 million spent in opposition and $39 million in favor of the ban.[98] It narrowly passed, 52 percent to 48 percent.[99] Many well-known celebrities spoke out against the initiative, and actor Brad Pitt and director-producer Steven Spielberg and his wife, actress Kate Capshaw, each donated $100,000 to defeat the initiative.[100] Several other celebrities provided their support for the initiative by starring in a short online video called "Prop 8: The Musical," a lighthearted video protesting the ban against same-sex marriage.[101] Subsequently, in 2010, the ban on same-sex marriages was ruled "unconstitutional" by the California Supreme Court.

As the battle over same-sex marriage rights evolved, action in legislatures, the voting booth, and the courts expanded in dozens of states. Reacting to the 2003 legalization of same-sex marriage in Massachusetts, thirteen states approved constitutional amendments banning same-sex unions in 2004.[102] Between 2004 and 2009, thirty-four states rejected proposals to authorize same-sex marriage referendums or initiatives. In addition, twenty-nine states placed provisions in statutes or their constitutions that adopted language from the federal Defense of Marriage Act (DOMA) that defines marriage as a legal union between one man and one woman as husband and wife. On the other hand, during this same time period, the state legislatures in Washington, Maryland, New Jersey, Hawaii, New York, New Hampshire, Rhode Island, Illinois, and Delaware voted in favor of same-sex marriage or civil unions.[103] In 2009, voters in Maine and North Carolina turned down referendums permitting same-sex marriage, but in 2012, Maine, Maryland, and Washington were the first states to pass such referendums.[104]

By the summer of 2013, twelve states and the District of Columbia permitted same sex marriages. In Massachusetts, Connecticut, and Iowa, the states' highest courts had ruled that the state constitutions required that same-sex couples be accorded the same marriage rights as opposite-sex couples. In Vermont, New Hampshire, the District of Columbia, New York, Rhode Island, Delaware and Minnesota legislative bodies passed statutory changes that allow same-sex marriage. In 2012, the Washington and Maryland state legislatures passed laws allowing same-sex marriage, but opponents of these laws gathered signatures to put the issue on the ballot in November 2012; as just mentioned, in both cases (and in Maine), same-sex marriage was approved. Also, in 2012, the U.S. Ninth Circuit Court of Appeals refused to hear a case that sought to overturn a U.S. district court decision upholding the California Supreme Court ruling invalidating Proposition 8 (see above), and the U.S. Supreme Court ruled in 2013 that those appealing the district court decision lacked standing to sue and thus legalized gay marriage in California (*Hollingsworth v. Perry*).[105] In a related 2013 case (*United States v. Windsor*), the Supreme Court invalidated the provisions of DOMA that denied federal benefits (tax and income support) to legally married gay and lesbian couples.[106]

Popular Leaders

Elected officials, media elites, and large corporations play central roles in living room politics. Public officials and private business leaders attempt to manipulate public opinion to suit their specific purposes. Journalists and pollsters help shape public opinion through their work. The public, however, does not follow only elected officials and media personalities. Many leaders of initiative and referendum drives and grassroots citizen campaigns come from the ranks of ordinary citizens. These individuals, who have the power to persuade, have transformed national, state, and local politics by mobilizing citizens to take political action.

Important grassroots political movements have been led by individuals who emerged from nonpolitical roles into the limelight and became identified with their causes. Dr. Martin Luther King Jr., a charismatic preacher, developed a large, loyal following as he organized demonstrations, marches, and other efforts to secure the full rights of citizenship for black Americans in the 1960s. Ralph Nader, a shy, ascetic lawyer, raised the consciousness of the American consumer and helped secure passage of new consumer protection laws in the 1970s. His nationwide network of state and local organizations continues to monitor industry production and use of dangerous products. Phyllis Schlafly energized a large conservative movement in dozens of states to prevent passage of the Equal Rights Amendment to the Constitution, which would have expanded rights for women. More recently, Grover Norquist, a conservative tax activist, founded Americans for Tax Reform, which opposes raising taxes at all levels of government (federal, state, and local). He has demanded that political candidates and incumbents sign the "Taxpayer Protection Pledge," which vows to oppose any new tax increases.[107] By 2012, nearly all Republican lawmakers in Congress had signed Norquist's pledge.[108]

THE POWER OF PUBLIC OPINION

Living room politics has been the catalyst for significant and startling changes in government policies. Public opinion—whether it originated at the top or at the bottom—played a critical role in forcing a president from office, halting the growth of nuclear power plants, cracking down on drunk drivers, slowing the growth of government spending, and changing laws governing marriage. Citizens exert a powerful policy influence in the voting booth, on the streets of America, and, perhaps most significantly, in the minds of elected and appointed leaders.

Public Opinion and the Media

Shifts in public support for government policies, often stimulated by media coverage, have brought about important changes. Extensive television coverage of the civil rights marches in the South during the 1960s exposed racism and the use of excessive force against peaceful individuals protesting racial discrimination. Television scenes of the Vietnam War, showing bloody battles and the destruction of a country, crystallized public opposition to America's involvement.[109] Coverage of the nuclear accidents at Three Mile Island in the United States and Chernobyl in the Ukraine undermined public support for nuclear power and halted the construction of nuclear power plants for over thirty years.[110] Government funding for research to find a cure for AIDS jumped by more than 200 percent after public opinion polls revealed widespread fear about the epidemic.[111] Media coverage of Hurricane Katrina in 2005 incited citizen anger about government delays in responding to the disaster and inequity among those helped by the government (especially those in low-income New Orleans neighborhoods). The media coverage ultimately influenced President George W. Bush to fire the head of the Federal Emergency Management Agency, Michael D. Brown.[112] Media coverage of the attacks on September 11, 2001, rallied support for wars in Afghanistan and Iraq, and also helped turn public opinion against the wars when they proved to be costly in American lives and money.

Passionate public responses to issues are unusual, but they have far-reaching effects. Public policies may be changed quickly when large segments of the public rally to support or oppose issues of high salience. Politicians feel compelled to act rather than face a disgruntled, even angry, citizenry. One reason the public seldom becomes aroused is that public officials are adept at anticipating serious problems and responding to them before people get angry. For example, Congress passed and President Obama signed into law the Stop Trading on Congressional Knowledge Act in the spring of 2012, which prohibits insider trading among "lawmakers, their staffs, and some executive branch employees," in reaction to the negative press coverage surrounding insider trading laws that exclude members of Congress.[113]

Given the weight assigned to public opinion in the myth and reality of American politics, it is perhaps surprising that strongly held public preferences are sometimes ignored. Politicians are known to use public opinion polls when they support their points of view and to ignore or denounce them as unreliable when they bring unfavorable, unwanted, or inconvenient news. Public officials often believe that poll results put them in an embarrassing position. If they follow public opinion as recorded in surveys, cherished positions may have to be abandoned. If they ignore polls, their opponents or journalists may chastise them for disregarding the will of the people. Fortunately for politicians, the media are not particularly vigilant about calling attention to public officials who fail to respond to sentiment expressed in public opinion polls.

It is now common for interest groups—from AARP to the National Rifle Association—to commission polls that they then use to persuade elected officials that the public supports these groups' points of view. A good example of this phenomenon comes from polling regarding the controversial issue of drilling for oil in Alaska's Arctic National Wildlife Refuge (ANWR). One poll commissioned by the National Wildlife Foundation reported that people are against drilling in that area by a seventeen-point margin. Another poll carried out by Luntz Global (an organization known to favor Republican and energy interests) found respondents to be more in favor of drilling in that area, also by a seventeen-point margin. The main difference between the polls was that the National Wildlife–funded poll spelled out the term "Alaska's Arctic National Wildlife Refuge" in the question, whereas Luntz used only the acronym "ANWR."[114]

As intermediaries between the public and political leaders, the media influence policy choices and the evaluation of programs. Policymakers are preoccupied with managing the news because the media command public attention in a way that no elected officials or interest group possibly can. More than half of the senior federal government policymakers contacted in an independent survey in the 1980s reported that the press had substantial effects on federal policy. One official in ten believed the press to be the dominant influence on policy. To some extent, press influence has become a self-fulfilling prophecy: "If policymakers themselves believe the press is influential, then by definition it is."[115]

Managing the press and responding to it often become a surrogate for managing public opinion and responding to it. Interactions among the media, public opinion, and public officials affect public policies in subtle ways. According to Linsky, extensive press coverage oversimplifies and nationalizes stories, forces quick responses, pushes decisions up the bureaucratic chain of command, and creates supportive climates for some options and excludes others.[116] For example, in 2001, several states banned the use of cell phones while driving, in response to several widely publicized traffic fatalities in their states (the use of "hands-free" devices was not prohibited), even though research studies showed only a slight correlation between using cell phones and automobile accidents. Researchers in 1997 pointed out that cell phones were only one of many distractions that could cause accidents, and that educating drivers about these distractions might be more effective than an outright ban.[117]

Choosing Policies in the Voting Booth

Referendums and initiatives give millions of Americans a direct say on policy issues, and liberal and conservative groups have been equally successful with the voters. A study of nearly 200 initiatives approved between 1977 and 1984 revealed that 44 percent of the seventy-nine proposals backed by liberals were approved, and 45 percent of the seventy-four conservative-sponsored initiatives were approved (the remainder were classified as not having ideological content).[118] The same pattern has been evident in more recent years, as shown in Table 8-1 and described below. Liberal measures such as allowing the medical use of marijuana, support for education, and health care reform have enjoyed a good deal of success, but so have conservative measures such as banning marriage between gays and lesbians, making guns accessible, mandating that English be the official language of government and business, and requiring photo identification for voting.

Perhaps the longest and most instructive story of statewide initiatives and public policy involves tax and government spending limitations. The modern tax revolt began with California's Proposition 13, which reduced property tax revenues by 57 percent and limited future tax increases to no more than 2 percent annually in 1978. Looking back, in 1965, less than half of the electorate thought that taxes were too high, but by 1983, nearly 75 percent were complaining that taxes were excessive. And eight Americans in ten thought that government funds were often wasted.[119] Between 1976 and 1984, however, only three states of the nine that voted on Proposition 13–type initiatives approved them.

From the 1990s to the present, initiatives proposing government spending and tax limitations have met with mixed success. In 1990, voters in Colorado, Massachusetts, Montana, and Utah said no to proposals that would have required legislators to roll back or curtail taxes. Public officials, public employees and teachers, and others who would be negatively affected by budget cuts rallied enough voter support to defeat efforts to further shrink state and local governments.[120] But such propositions continued to appear on ballots in the 1990s. In 1992, Colorado voters approved a proposition that puts limits on income and property taxes and requires voter approval for state tax increases. A 1996 proposition in Oklahoma to reduce property taxes to their 1993 level was rejected by voters, whereas Montana voters approved an amendment forbidding state legislatures to increase taxes without voter approval.[121] In 1998, Nebraska voters failed to pass an initiative that cut taxes and slowed the growth of state and local government spending, and South Dakota voters denied an initiative that would prohibit taxes for school funding. In that same year, Massachusetts voters approved an initiative to cut state income taxes, and Washington voters followed Montana's lead and passed an initiative requiring public approval of legislative tax increases in 1999.[122]

In the twenty-first century, there were a few new wrinkles in tax and spending initiatives and referendums, but the mixed pattern of success for tax limitations continued. In 2004, Colorado and Montana voters passed an initiative to increase taxes on tobacco, with the revenues being used for health-related purposes. In that same year, Washington voters said no to an initiative that would have increased the sales tax by 1 percent, with revenues dedicated to education. Several states entertained propositions to limit state spending in various ways; California voters rejected one of these in 2005, as did Oregon and Nebraska voters in 2006 and Washington voters in 2009. In 2006, South Dakota voters followed Colorado and Montana with regard to cigarette taxes, but California and Missouri voters rejected such a tax.

In 2008, Massachusetts voters had a chance to eliminate their state income tax, but declined to do so; however, Arizona voters passed an initiative that prohibited state and local government from raising taxes on property sales. The year 2010 was a big one for tax initiatives, with twelve such initiatives on the ballot around the country. The mixed pattern of results continued, as half of the twelve measures were approved and half were rejected. Perhaps a fitting end to this saga of tax and spending propositions over the past forty years was the passage of an initiative in California (home of Proposition 13) to increase taxes to pay for public schools in 2012.[123]

Given the multiple opportunities for policymaking and the role of the courts in reviewing the constitutionality of state and federal laws, state initiatives, referendums, or amendments to state constitutions are not always the final word. The challenge to the national health care reform law—the ACA—of 2010 is a case in point. Within months after enactment of the law, legislators in forty-seven states introduced laws or resolutions seeking to challenge the requirement for individuals to purchase health care insurance; twenty of these laws were enacted. Some states, including Arizona and Oklahoma, approved ballot measures to prohibit the enforcement of the individual mandate provision, while Colorado voters decided to reject a similar state initiative.[124]

The initiatives and referendums adopted by state legislatures and voters set the stage for legal reviews by federal appeals courts that rendered seven decisions, with six upholding the constitutionality of the health care law, and the Eleventh Circuit Court of Appeals, based in Atlanta, ruling that the individual mandate provision in the ACA was unconstitutional.[125] The U.S. Supreme Court agreed to hear a case brought by Florida and twenty-five other states, in addition to a dispute brought on by the National Federation of Independent Business.[126] In June 2012, in a 5-4 vote, the Court's justices upheld the constitutionality of the health care mandate (see chapter 7).

According to most observers, policymaking through initiatives and referendums has reached its most advanced level in California. Indeed, many would argue that the focus of policy debate in the state has shifted from the legislature to the initiative process. During the 1980s, California citizens set major policy directions on insurance rates, the environment, and levels of spending for education. In the 1990 election, California voters were asked to weigh twenty-eight ballot issues, ranging from sweeping environmental policy changes to taxes on alcohol. In this election, Californians passed a marine resource conservation initiative, but voted down an initiative to regulate the use of pesticides. They also rejected a new surtax on alcohol. In the 1998 general election, California had twelve statewide ballot questions, ranging from raising taxes on cigarettes to animal rights. "It [the initiative] is a force that has produced occasional benefits, but at enormous cost—an erosion of responsibility in the executive and legislative branches," says Eugene C. Lee of the University of California.[127] The latest fad in California is for wealthy individuals to sponsor (pay for) initiatives of their own creation (and in some cases for their own benefit); there were four such measures on the ballot in 2012.[128]

In addition to matters of taxes and spending, public ballot proposals have also given voters a voice on issues of social policy. In recent years, voters cut abortion funding in Colorado, but similar proposals in Arkansas, Oregon, Rhode Island, and Washington were defeated. South Dakotans in 2008 banned abortions, except in cases of rape and complications with a mother's health. Other examples of direct policymaking by voters on controversial social issues include the following:

- Arkansas voters approved an initiative banning gay couples from adopting children.
- Maine and Utah voters rejected stricter regulations on the sale of pornographic materials.
- West Virginians endorsed prayer in public schools.
- Laws requiring the use of seat belts were repealed in Massachusetts.
- Maine voters threw out laws requiring large stores to close on Sunday.
- Californians voted to declare English the state's official language, rejected a proposal to quarantine victims of AIDS, and defeated a proposition to legalize physician-assisted suicide.

A POTENT WEAPON OF DEMOCRACY

Whether through the informal plebiscite of public opinion polls or through active participation, citizens can have a powerful influence on the implementation and impact of public policies. Public pressure may be brought to bear concerning the tactics and pace of program administration. The public's evaluation of government policies, institutions, and political actors, which is influenced by the media, may affect financial support for a program or cause its cancelation. Public perceptions of a specific leader's popularity may embolden or intimidate other political leaders. Finally, angry citizens can force radical changes in public policy.

Public and Media Evaluations of Government Policy

Americans are generally skeptical about government programs and institutions. Such perceptions are based partly on personal experience, such as frustration with the IRS, a state department of motor vehicles, or the local building code enforcement officer. For the most part, however, the public's understanding of politics and policy comes to it via television, newspapers, and the Internet, which not only reflect this skeptical attitude about government but also encourage it.

As messengers of public concern and guardians of the public interest, reporters often deserve high praise. Journalists criticize poorly managed government programs and inform the public about crises and conflicts, fraud, and corruption. Journalists expose corrupt public officials and call attention to insensitivity and injustice in some public institutions. Media scrutiny, followed by public anger, can spur an indifferent, cautious, or incompetent agency or legislature to positive action in the public interest.

The contributions of media organizations and journalists to policy implementation can be a mixed blessing, however. Media publicity can divert public attention from important matters and focus it on relatively trivial matters. Take, for example, the so-called sexting scandal involving Congressman Anthony Weiner from New York City, in the spring of 2011. Representative Weiner, who was married to a top assistant to Secretary of State Hillary Clinton, sent a sexually suggestive photograph of himself to a young woman who had been following him via his Twitter account. After the photo appeared on various social media and other Web sites, extensive cable television news, radio, and newspaper coverage followed. After initially denying that he had sent the photo, the congressman eventually admitted that he had "made terrible mistakes" and that he "exchanged messages and photos of an explicit nature with about six women over the last three years." He resigned a few weeks later.[129] The impact of the intense media coverage of this salacious scandal was reflected in public opinion polls. During the period that the sexting stories received widespread attention in the media, the Pew Research Center reported that it was the second most closely followed story in the news, coming in only after the national economy. But most Americans (63 percent) also said that they thought there was too much coverage of it.[130]

According to some analysts, the media's influence on elected officials and the public is pernicious. Timothy E. Cook has argued that members of Congress are less concerned with the public interest than with what will sell with the media.[131] Obsession with the way things appear in the press, he maintains, drives elected officials to search for overly simple answers to complicated questions. The need to explain one's position on television in thirty seconds encourages legislators to latch on to symbols and slogans, rather than to seek carefully crafted solutions.

Consider the symbolism attached to a major education reform bill, the No Child Left Behind Act (NCLB), enacted by Congress and President George W. Bush in 2001. Supporters of NCLB claimed that the bill increased accountability for schools and teachers and school choice. The legislation set a lofty goal of having all students proficient in reading and mathematics by 2014. Citizens and politicians from both sides of the political spectrum embraced the new legislation because few people could argue with the idea of holding schools accountable for the children they teach to ensure that "no child is left behind" (an effective slogan).

Under NCLB, federal dollars distributed to states were contingent on mandatory testing of public school students annually in reading and math from the third to the eighth grade and then publicly reporting the results. States were required to design both the curriculum and testing standards, which would be used to assess whether schools met "adequate yearly progress" (AYP) standards. The punishment for not meeting AYP was prescribed at the federal level. The consequences that schools faced accelerated each year that AYP was not met. After two years of not meeting AYP, a school was required to offer students the option to transfer to another higher performing school in the area; at three years, it was mandatory for the school to present tutoring services; and at five years, the school was forced to undergo major restructuring. The high-stakes testing used by NCLB left considerable room for unintended consequences. The legislation was criticized for being "too inflexible, too arbitrary and too punitive" (negative slogans).[132]

NCLB allowed states to design the standards students and schools would be judged against, and this scenario created a natural incentive for some schools to water down their standards in order to meet federal AYP benchmarks. This award system penalized states with rigorous testing standards and rewarded those with relaxed ones. Mississippi is a prime example of the perverse incentive system. In 2005, Mississippi had the highest percentage of proficient fourth-grade readers in the nation, with 89 percent proficiency, yet the state ranked at the bottom when its students took the more demanding National Assessment of Educational Progress test that same year, with only 18 percent of fourth graders proficient in reading.[133] Another way to bend the rules to ensure AYP in school proficiency was to simply cheat. A series of cheating scandals were uncovered during the implementation of the law, such as accounts of teachers and administrators in the Atlanta public school system changing students' test scores to inflate their testing results.

Besides lower state standards and cheating, the AYP system incentivizes teachers to focus on the middle-of-the-pack students who are on the fringe of reaching grade-level proficiency. Students at the very bottom or the very top are often ignored. Even if a poorly performing student jumps two or three reading grade levels in a single year, that progress does not pay off if the student still does not achieve his or her own grade-level proficiency. A related negative consequence was that teachers were forced to "teach to the test," and they spent more energy on getting students to pass the test than emphasizing overall progress for individual students. This high-stakes testing method also caused other subjects, such as science and social studies, to become less important because no annual testing was required for them.[134]

NCLB was scheduled for reauthorization in 2007, but no agreement on how to change the law could be reached from 2007 to 2012, despite pressure from Presidents George W. Bush and Obama. Both sides have plenty of symbols and slogans to work with: lack of educational standards versus teaching to the test, intrusive government versus local cheating, failing schools versus hard-working teachers, and so on.[135]

The pervasive role of the media in shaping the public's view of politics helps explain why it is difficult to galvanize the public to support some issues. Both the public and the media like stories with identifiable villains and/or scenes of destruction. In the mid-2000s, lax government regulations and the financial misdeeds of hundreds of banking institutions led to a near collapse of the U.S. financial system and the costliest government financial rescue in the history of this country (see chapter 2). Yet despite the enormous consequences, the mass media were very late in grasping the significance of what was going on. This seemed to be a classic example of how the media falter when a political and policy story cannot be reduced to the bare essentials and good videos. In contrast, when the media can easily sensationalize the administrative shortcomings and foibles of public officials, otherwise effective programs may be damaged and their bases of public and political support eroded.

More broadly, the media's relentless unfavorable portrayal of political institutions, public officials, and government programs fosters negative public attitudes about the public sector.[136] Media analyst Michael Robinson called these feelings about the political world "video-malaise."[137] Cynical views about government and political figures are conveyed not only by news and public affairs programs but also by prime-time drama series as well. Contempt for the political world is pervasive on entertainment television. There are very few television series in which political figures are cast in positive roles. Television regularly portrays "heroes" doing battle with evil politicians. For example, the main character of HBO's series *Boardwalk Empire* is based on Enoch L. Johnson, a New Jersey Republican politician and infamous racketeer. Another well-known HBO series, *The Wire*, explored the Baltimore drug scene through the eyes of drug dealers and law enforcement, and featured a Maryland state senator who took bribes from drug dealers, paid off the police, and smooth-talked his way out of a conviction on money-laundering charges.

Policy from the Grassroots

Grassroots political movements often grow out of the frustration citizens feel about the pace of reform or their outrage at decisions that threaten their way of life. Seeking relief from the government, citizen groups have denounced U.S. foreign policy and demanded that legislators, administrators, and judges alter policies on a host of social, moral, and environmental issues. The success of minority groups in quickening the pace of change is noteworthy. What began as an effort to secure basic rights evolved into a broad-based effort to increase economic opportunities. The ability of leaders to mobilize minorities beyond protest and get them into the voting booth had positive effects on the appointment and election of minority officeholders, expanded employment opportunities for minorities in city governments, and enlarged programs for the minority community.[138]

Since the late 1960s, hundreds of national and local environmental groups have also achieved considerable success in translating widespread public support for environmental conservation and protection into political action and policy changes. Statutes have been passed governing air and water quality, control of toxic pollution, and the disposal of industrial, agricultural, and urban wastes. Regulatory agencies have been established at the state and national levels. Billions of dollars have been allocated to environmental protection and cleanup. Environmental interest groups are represented in Washington and in state capitals. Obviously, these sweeping reforms were not stimulated entirely by ordinary citizens, but grassroots environmental organizations were powerful agents for change.[139]

For example, a broad coalition was formed among environmentalists, farmers, and businesses that effectively organized in 2004 to pass amendment 37, the nation's first-ever voter-approved renewable energy standard (RES), in Colorado. The initiative allowed citizens to shape the state's energy policy, and bypass Colorado's legislature, which had defeated similar legislation three times in the three prior years.[140] The initiative, approved by a 54-46 margin, established both a threshold and a time frame for the amount of renewable energy large utility companies must generate and sell to their customers. Environment Colorado, a statewide citizen-based advocacy organization, played a prominent role in leading the effort for passing the environmental initiative. Colorado Governor Bill Ritter commented that Matt Baker, the founder of Environment Colorado, was one of the chief "architects" of the renewable energy standard in Colorado.[141] This initiative paved the way for energy policy in Colorado, and since its passage, the legislature has voted to increase the RES threshold to 30 percent by 2020.[142]

Majority Rule and Minority Rights

Who benefits from living room politics? Who are the winners and the losers? Because living room politics concerns issues that arouse the public and galvanize ordinary citizens into action, one might glibly conclude that the public wins. Unfortunately, figuring out who benefits from living room politics is considerably more complicated than that. As we have observed in several chapters, in general, well-organized and well-financed groups are more likely to have their views heeded than are people who are economically and socially disadvantaged. Those who are better off are generally more successful in directing media and public attention to their concerns. It is no accident that many ballot initiatives are of greater interest to white, middle-class voters than they are to minorities and poor individuals.

Living room politics can be the expression of majority sentiments, and public officials are inclined to heed the will of the people when public preferences are clear and reflect a broad-based consensus. When the majority of the public supports a controversial course of action, however, policymakers may ignore it, especially if the public's wishes would infringe on minority interests. Suppose that public opinion polls showed that most people favored isolating AIDS victims from the rest of the population. It is unlikely that political institutions, especially the courts, would be guided by such opinions, because the basic rights of a disadvantaged minority would be violated in an attempt to allay the fears of the majority. Thus, a central dilemma of democracy is the clash of majority rule and minority rights. Basic issues, such as war, civil rights, morality, and public health and safety, are most likely to stimulate public concern and foster intense, divergent beliefs. Individuals with diametrically opposed positions on controversial issues, such as abortion, gay rights, and nuclear plant safety, usually do not find the alternative point of view acceptable.

When people are divided over an issue that arouses strong feelings, public officials search for compromises that might satisfy the losers as well as the winners. However, finding such answers is often impossible. When accommodation fails, the public policy process grinds to a halt because neither side is willing to compromise. Elected officials and government administrators either ignore the problem as long as they possibly can, or pass the buck to another institution—the judiciary or the president. They may even pass the buck to the voters, hoping to find an answer in the majority will expressed via referendums or initiatives.

When majority preferences are honored, the losers may be angry, feel alienated, and resort to unconventional methods, including civil disobedience and violence. Indeed, many of the most violent or potentially violent episodes in American political history took place when the losers felt the political system no longer cared about them. Riots and violence over racial segregation and injustice in the 1950s and 1960s, and widespread protests against the Vietnam War that ended in violent confrontations between marchers and police and National Guard troops, are but two vivid examples. Individuals opposed to the U.S. Supreme Court's legalization of abortion have bombed abortion clinics. Environmental activists have sabotaged chemical plants and physically blocked the construction of nuclear power plants and hazardous waste disposal facilities.

Although civil unrest in reaction to government policies has not been as widespread in the early years of the twenty-first century as it was during the civil rights movement, there are still examples of public anger reaching the boiling point. For example, riots occurred in Oakland, California, when a Los Angeles jury charged a white transit officer in the death of an unarmed black man on January 1, 2009, but said that he should be tried for involuntary manslaughter rather than murder. A video capturing the shooting of the victim while he lay unarmed and face down sparked national outrage, and many who followed the trial closely hoped for a more serious penalty for the officer.[143]

Looting and vandalism broke out that evening following the sentencing; a total of seventy-eight arrests were made for violations including "failure to disperse, vandalism, and assaulting a police offer."[144] Thousands of protestors mobilized during the 2008 Republican National Convention to protest the Iraq War and the Bush administration's policies; hundreds were arrested for vandalism and violence against police officers attempting to control the protests.[145] The Wall Street protests that began in Zuccotti Park in New York also resulted in large numbers of arrests.

Well-organized, sophisticated segments of the citizenry benefit most from living room politics, but when minority concerns are trampled on, the potential for political instability increases. It is perhaps for this reason that many politicians are fearful of greater citizen participation in the government process. Once citizens are drawn into the conflict, they demand satisfaction, and once the genie is out of the bottle, it is hard to get it back in again.

The Impacts of Initiatives and Referendums

As the preceding discussion has shown, initiatives and referendums have had profound effects on the shape of social, political, and economic change. Voters have spoken for and against same-sex marriage, placed limits on access to abortions, approved the use of medical marijuana and the sale of pornographic literature; they have brought about stronger criminal penalties for the use of certain illegal substances; and they have fostered stronger environmental protections. Citizens in Arizona, California, Florida, Oklahoma, Nebraska, New Hampshire, and Washington abolished the use of affirmative action policies in hiring state employees or selecting applicants for college (the Michigan ban was overturned by the U.S. Court of Appeals for the Sixth Circuit).[146] One-upping the eight other states that have legalized medical marijuana, Colorado and Washington legalized the possession of small quantities of marijuana in 2012. Initiatives and the political fallout generated by them have also played an important role in restraining public spending. Voters have mandated expenditure limitations and tax policies that have altered the fiscal policies of dozens of states. Resources for public institutions, poor individuals, and minority groups have been cut, while property owners have retained larger portions of their incomes. In summary, the rights, opportunities, and physical environment of citizens in most states have been directly affected by initiatives and referendums.

Like any other method of decision making, initiatives and referendums have their strengths and weaknesses.[147] On the positive side, initiatives give citizens an opportunity to raise issues that elected leaders and interest groups might prefer to ignore. Initiatives can also help overcome stalemates in the legislative process. Taking policy choices to the voters can be an effective method of legitimating controversial decisions. On the negative side, initiatives and referendums are blunt instruments. It is often not possible to reduce complicated questions to one-line statements. Ballot questions, with the choices restricted to yes or no, lack the deliberation and accommodation of legislative institutions and administrative agencies.

Moreover, initiatives and referendums may not be as sensitive to the interests or rights of minorities as the courts might be. Evidence suggests that interest groups and political officials have seized the tools of direct democracy to win victories they were unable to gain through mainstream institutions. The practice of direct democracy is becoming professionalized and costly and, therefore, may be moving beyond the reach of volunteers. Finally, the opportunity to evade difficult decisions may encourage irresponsible behavior by public officials. Rather than assume duties they were elected to perform, they may wait for voters to send a clear signal. By then it may be too late.

SUMMARY

Living room politics is a unique, important, but often misunderstood part of democratic government. High school civics books and Independence Day speeches may exaggerate citizens' control of the policy process, but many sophisticated observers also may underestimate the power the public wields in policymaking.

For many ordinary citizens, politics and public policy are another form of entertainment. They find it interesting to tune in now and then, but most do not stay tuned. From time to time, however, large segments of the public hold strong opinions on public issues, and an enraged, out-of-control public is a formidable threat to political stability. In full force, the power of public opinion and citizen participation has driven high officials from office, changed the course of American foreign and domestic policy, and stopped countless government proposals from ever getting off the ground.

The mass media are particularly important players in living room politics. Television, the Internet, radio, and newspapers are the principal sources of information about politics and government for most Americans. The power of the media derives not from a conspiracy to lead American policy in a particular direction, but from the fact that most people have no other way of conjuring up a political reality.

Legislators, chief executives, bureaucrats, corporate leaders, and even judges are sensitive to the need for public understanding and support, because without it, government can lose its legitimacy—the very foundation of governance. Public officials must not only understand, but also manage, public opinion in order to build support for their cherished programs and to maintain control of the political process.

Institutional Performance

Politicians and ordinary citizens in the United States believe that properly structured political institutions are essential to freedom, democracy, and prosperity. The Constitution reflects this view in that it prescribes certain relationships among these institutions, and between them and the citizens. Characteristic of the political culture of the United States is an unquestioning support for the election of legislatures and chief executives, an independent judiciary, and federalism. Despite the symbolic reverence for government institutions, they are continually examined and criticized by citizens and politicians alike. Explanations and evaluations of the government's performance are another political tradition. Negative evaluations of institutional performance have rarely been more widespread than in recent years.

The principal observations and conclusions offered in chapters 3 through 8 provide a useful starting point for an explanation of institutional performance.

1. Corporations focus primarily on one goal, company profits, and boardroom politics is highly centralized—dominated by top executive officers—although pressure is growing to increase the number of actors involved and for corporate boards to consider other goals. Corporate decisions, made privately, have far-reaching consequences for society.

2. Bureaucracies like to define issues so that they are compatible with standard methods of operation. Policy decisions are made at various levels in an organization by administrative officials who are subject to many outside influences, including legislative committees, interest groups, chief executives, and courts. The standards for bureaucratic decisions are often explicit, but they can be quickly and dramatically changed by outsiders.

3. Legislatures react to many issues, but are often slow to make decisions. Decision making is subject to many influences, most notably well-organized, well-financed interests. Partisan majorities can rule when they are assembled, but intense partisanship can also lead to deadlock under divided government, which is a common condition at the national level. Issue characteristics and contextual factors also have a

great impact on whether decisions are incremental, innovative, grid-locked, or symbolic, and on whether the decision-making process is slow or rapid, decentralized or centralized.

4. Chief executives address highly visible issues and dominate public perceptions about government, but the policy significance of a chief executive's term may be quite different from its image. The essence of chief executive leadership is the ability to persuade other policymakers, especially legislators, to transform the priorities of a chief executive into policy. This part of the policy process is always difficult, particularly for presidents trying to reshape domestic policy.

5. Courts consider a more restricted range of issues than legislatures or chief executives, but are capable of taking decisive policy actions that sometimes have significant effects on society. The politics of judicial policymaking is shaped by specific legal procedures and criteria, but partisan and ideological factors are also evident in judicial decisions. The independence of the courts is rarely challenged.

6. Public opinions are influential in American politics. When highly sa-lient issues are the subject of debate, the public may directly change public policy by acting through grassroots organizations and express-ing opinions via initiatives or referendums. But public opinion is also subject to manipulation by media elites and government officials. The public, therefore, can be an active agent of democracy, or a fairly weak and passive part of the policy process. Increasing partisan polarization has both shaped public opinion and limited the latitude political elites enjoy in their policy actions.

Do these disparate observations form some larger picture? The answer is that American political institutions reflect rather faithfully their historical and philosophical roots. Their performance can be explained fairly well by refer-ence to the free market and procedural democracy model of politics discussed in chapter 2. American political institutions perform different roles in striving to uphold the basic principles of the market paradigm and the ideals of proce-dural democracy. Understanding these differences is the key to explaining institutional behavior. Boardroom politics and living room politics expand the system's repertoire of policymaking processes in interesting and important ways, some of which push the political process beyond the limits of procedural democracy.

AN ANALYSIS OF CONVENTIONAL POLITICAL INSTITUTIONS

Most scholars would agree that the legislative, executive, and judicial branches of government represent core political institutions. In thinking about the executive branch, it is useful to distinguish between chief executives and the bureaucracy because the bureaucracy represents a de facto "fourth branch" of government. To gain a fuller understanding of policymaking, it is not sufficient to consider only the branches of government. As we have shown, corporations, citizens, and the media exercise considerable influence in American politics, and much of that influence finds its way into policy. Thus, our appraisal of America's political institutions encompasses both conventional and unconventional political institutions.

Courts and Legislatures

This analysis begins with a comparison of two very different political institutions: the Supreme Court and Congress. The Court acts on the basis of a philosophical view of procedural democracy; Congress understands procedural democracy on a more personal level. Why has the Court been the political institution that has often acted to secure the rights of disadvantaged minorities? The reason is that the Supreme Court justices, in their role as interpreters of the Constitution, have been forced to define in legal terms what the main principles of this document mean in specific circumstances. The nature of the judicial process—using written opinions to establish precedents that guide future decisions—induces justices to take a philosophical look at constitutional principles. The logic of the Constitution is derived from a school of thought that places importance on certain procedural values. In the case of disadvantaged minorities, the guiding principle is equality of opportunity, and the specific means to achieve equality of opportunity are the equal protection and due process clauses of the Fourteenth Amendment. The context in which the Court makes decisions, and the process used, encourage it to be decisive about the core principles of procedural democracy.

Supreme Court interpretations of constitutional principles have done a great deal for advantaged minorities as well as those that are disadvantaged. This outcome of Court decision making can be seen as another indication of the pervasiveness of the market paradigm, which discourages distinctions among market participants. An interesting example of the Court's adherence to market principles is the freedom granted to the press. The press has continually invoked the Constitution on behalf of its right to publish or display a great deal of misleading and distasteful material. Anyone who has stood in a checkout line at a grocery store can testify to the alluring, but false, headlines used by some newspapers and magazines. By defining libel and slander restrictively, the Court has allowed the press to continue printing sensational material. The courts believe there should be a marketplace of ideas in a free society, and that valid ideas persist and invalid ideas perish in such a setting. Therefore, the Court protects and promotes economic and information markets.

The Court's strength depends on its adherence to the central principles of the Constitution, and the Court is generally reluctant to increase the number, or expand the meaning, of these principles. When the Court breaks new constitutional ground, however, as it has on civil rights, abortion, and the financing of political campaigns, it is difficult for the justices to ignore subsequent cases raising related questions. Despite a tradition of deference to the political branches, the Court has consistently shown a willingness to overturn laws enacted by Congress and signed by the president. In the past twenty years alone, the Court invalidated nearly forty acts of Congress.[1] The overturned laws included gun control legislation, legislation granting the line-item veto to the president, as well as provisions of laws denying prisoners at Naval Station Guantanamo Bay access to federal courts. When the Court strikes down legislation of this magnitude, it sends a powerful message to the political branches of the federal government. In effect, that message is that the Court is the ultimate arbiter of what can and cannot be done by government.

The Court must understand the rules of procedural democracy because it is their principal guardian. To perform this guardianship well, the Court must be somewhat removed from popular passions. Citizens and politicians often fail to grasp some of the unpleasant nuances of procedural democracy—for example, that angry Americans have the right to burn their nation's flag to protest policies they oppose. The Court is not a very good vehicle for popular participation, although class action suits and other advocacy efforts have made it a forum in which some popular causes have been advanced. The Court is not likely to lead the way to radical social or economic changes such as wealth redistribution, public ownership of industry, or income guarantees, but it sometimes forces the system to live up to its ideals, as when it required that public schools admit children of all racial backgrounds.

The market paradigm fits well with cloakroom politics. Citizens register their preferences for representatives, who then try to give their constituents what they want at the lowest political cost. Those who succeed in retaining elected offices are, in most cases, effective producers of political goods. Citizen preferences can be expressed individually or through political parties or interest groups. Congressional political parties have reasserted themselves over the past twenty years, becoming major forces in the policy process as both parties became more cohesive. Since 1994, when Newt Gingrich took over as speaker of the House, the Republican and Democratic majorities in the House of Representatives have resembled the parties of Western Europe in their emphasis on orthodoxy, loyalty, and discipline. Congress remains very receptive to interest groups, but many interest groups are now closely aligned with one or the other political party. Interest groups are effective, aggressive, and persistent; they operate as if politics were a market in which each person's pursuit of self-interest is justified because it is part of a system that maximizes collective welfare. The idea that interest group competition produces policies that serve the public interest is accepted by some political scientists.[2] But some interests, it seems, will always be unrepresented or underrepresented. Those who lack resources (money) and broad, diffuse interests are less likely to be represented because they are more difficult to organize.[3]

Why does Congress specialize in policies that carry particularized benefits, created in decentralized settings where interest groups are accepted participants? Why is meaningful congressional policy action difficult to bring about on matters that do not carry clear benefits for constituents? One answer is that the legislative version of the market paradigm encourages such behavior. Like businesses in a market, legislators like to make a profit, and their profits are measured in votes. To secure comfortable electoral margins, they hand out benefits. Who gets the benefits? Those who can deliver campaign contributions or political support through the ballot box. Another part of the answer is that the very organization of Congress facilitates responsiveness to relatively narrow geographic or policy interests. Despite the increased power of party leadership organizations, the committee system remains powerful, and the decentralized policymaking it fosters provides multiple opportunities for special interests to plead their cases. If the head of one congressional subcommittee will not listen, perhaps the head of another will. Nor is strong party leadership necessarily an antidote to such behavior. Parties can advance their cause by promoting a broad partisan vision of the public interest, or by defining the public interest as the sum total of diverse special interests. When the latter happens, strong party leadership and strong interest group politics become indistinguishable in practice.

It is alleged that one of the advantages of a free market economic system is its self-correcting tendency. If producers churn out too much of a product, its price falls; then new buyers are attracted, and eventually the price stabilizes. If only a little is produced of a product people want, its high price attracts the interest of potential producers. Periods of vigorous consumer spending generate rising prices and high levels of production, which eventually result in overstocked inventories and falling prices. These self-correcting factors are not purely automatic; rather, they are linked to government monetary and fiscal policies. What about political markets? Are they self-correcting?

Recent American history suggests that congressional self-correction mechanisms do not function very well. Congress practiced dispensing benefits in exchange for votes from the 1950s through the late 1970s. Federal spending and taxes grew to the point that they became highly salient issues. Deficit spending provided a temporary refuge, but soon the deficits ballooned and threatened our nation's economy. Various reforms were tried, but most of them failed, leaving a legacy of bitterness and frustration. In 1993, President Bill Clinton persuaded Congress to take the first significant steps toward eliminating the budget deficit. Eight years later, as Clinton left office, the federal government at long last was enjoying a robust surplus, but Congress was not always a willing partner in achieving this outcome. The fiscal crises recent Congresses have faced are even more formidable than the ones Clinton confronted. The annual deficits are larger, and the fiscal policy process has been operating very poorly. The battles between Democrats and Republicans over the debt limit in 2011, and the fiscal cliff and sequester in 2012 and 2013, exposed how badly the system is working. At several junctures during these battles, falling confidence among investors about the ability of the political system to fix the debt and deficit problems resulted in visible declines in stock prices. The economic system was sending a powerful message to Congress to get its house in order.

Just as free markets do not always work as they are supposed to because entry is restricted, or because consumer knowledge is imperfect, political markets also have flaws. Voter knowledge of issues and candidates is often limited. Some groups, such as the poor, are not represented in a way that reflects their numerical significance. Some politicians engage in deceptive political campaigns and get away with it. Because elected politicians establish the rules of politics, it is not surprising that they use the rules for their own advantage and distort political markets. Political reform is always needed in a system that depends on periodic corrections of destructive tendencies.

Chief Executives and the Bureaucracy

The bureaucracy resembles the courts in some ways and the legislatures in others. It resembles the courts in having formal and specific decision-making criteria, although not so specific or complete as to eliminate discretion. The courts have laws, the Constitution, and legal precedents to guide their decisions; bureaucratic agencies have written statutes and formal rules. The agencies resemble legislatures because they are highly susceptible to politics. Agencies can be battered by interest groups, legislators, chief executives, or judges, and their vulnerability has led them to assume a defensive posture toward the outside world. Standard operating procedures, public hearings, advisory committees, and cost-benefit analyses are all forms of defense. Even innovation is usually a response to a threatening political environment.

American bureaucracies are highly political, not because they want to be but because they are forced to be in order to defend themselves against stronger political institutions. Many political scientists have confirmed the accuracy of principal-agent theory, which postulates that bureaucratic agents respond favorably to political principals.[4] Thus, bureaucratic officials are always interested in knowing where they stand with the legislature and the office of the chief executive; they know they cannot succeed if they offend powerful officials in these institutions. They are also very attentive to certain interest groups, and are increasingly conscious of their public images. But administrative policymakers cannot depend on interest group and voter satisfaction alone. They must be prepared—with defensible procedures and services—in case elected officials demand action or accountability. Even mighty agencies, such as the Federal Bureau of Investigation, are quickly humbled when political principals decide to flex their muscles.

Chief executives are the principal promoters of majoritarian rule in American politics. They are the main corrective force against the potentially harmful effects of the symbiotic relationship between powerful interest groups and legislators. Chief executives often try to define a public interest that is separate and distinguishable from the sum of the parochial interests. They set certain goals—a cleaner environment, better schools, less poverty—and try to figure out ways to achieve them. The problem is that they have limited authority to act on their own, and persuading legislators to follow a clear and consistent policy path is extremely difficult.

The nature of this difficulty should be apparent by now. Legislators have their own relationships with voters, and they do not like having them disrupted by chief executives. Legislators sometimes can be convinced that departure from their cherished mode of operation—giving subsidies to those who are organized—is necessary if a crisis is to be avoided, but they require a good deal of proof that conditions warrant such extraordinary action; they also need to be skillfully coaxed and made aware of public pressure. Some chief executives are able to provide the proof, the coaxing, and the pressure; others are not.

The strength of chief executives lies in their ability to command public attention. Their efforts to assemble ruling coalitions and resolve crises provide much of the action and drama in politics, and the mass media find action and drama irresistible. People identify with chief executives (and, for the most part, with their legislators), but not with the legislature as a whole. This interest and loyalty gives chief executives a certain amount of leverage that can be used to pursue policy objectives. The greatest weakness of chief executives is their lack of power, influence, and authority over other political elites, which stems mainly from the independence of government institutions and the power of interest groups. Although chief executives have some ability to act independently, through executive orders, in most circumstances, they must exercise their power to persuade others to enact laws, allocate funds, and implement programs.[5]

The strength of the bureaucracy lies in its staying power. Bureaucracies are essential to the operation of government, and elected officials understand this reality. Bureaucracies can be decisive, even innovative, but most show a marked preference for stability and continuity. The weakness of bureaucratic agencies is their formal and informal subservience to political institutions and interests. They can usually defend themselves against abolition, but they have to be constantly on their guard against budget and personnel cuts. The Reagan administration was unable to eliminate two cabinet-level departments it targeted (Education and Energy), but did succeed in cutting the budgets and trimming the staffs of several departments and agencies. The Clinton administration successfully reduced the size of the federal bureaucracy by 17 percent, but the government grew back by roughly the same amount during George W. Bush's and Barack Obama's administrations. Some experts, such as political scientist Donald Kettl, doubt that a leaner bureaucracy is necessarily a better bureaucracy.[6] If the size of the federal bureaucracy is reduced, the odds are that key functions will be performed by state bureaucracies and private contractors. When bureaucratic agents depend on other agents to carry out vital tasks, their performance may suffer unless they become adept at oversight and contract management.[7]

ALTERNATIVES TO CONVENTIONAL POLITICS

Politics and public policies are not produced solely by government institutions. Private institutions also shape public policy, as do individual citizens and grassroots organizations. Boardroom politics and living room politics reflect contrasting philosophical principles and cultural values.

For most corporate decision makers, the market paradigm is the world-view of utmost importance. They have no doubt about the value of the pursuit of private gain because it is accepted as an essential part of a system that maximizes social welfare by translating free market competition into overall economic efficiency and productivity. This worldview is part of what enables corporate decision makers to lay off thousands of reliable, skilled workers in Michigan, Ohio, Pennsylvania, and Texas while they commit funds to new automobile and steel plants in Mexico, Taiwan, South Korea, and China. They argue that market forces should dictate wages, plant locations, and, ultimately, living patterns. Most corporate leaders understand that markets can be cruel to human beings, and many sympathize with the plight of their workers.

Rhetoric and reality are frequently at odds in the boardroom. Government intervention is abhorred when it costs money, but eloquently defended when it protects or subsidizes. Herbert Simon's pioneering work on corporate decision making demonstrates that private sector decision making is neither simple nor automatic.[8] Economic theory holds that businesses attempt to maximize their profits. Simon showed that in practice, large corporations, with many decision makers, normally choose options that satisfy as many interests as possible, rather than seeking optimal profits in every circumstance. In this way, corporations resemble legislatures and public bureaucracies because bargaining and accommodation figure in their decision making. This kind of decision making is found particularly in large, stockholder-owned corporations, those that are subject to a great deal of government regulation, and those that are controlled by public officials. In such institutions, decision makers are sometimes forced to confront the fact that the pursuit of private gain and the enhancement of society's well-being may not be synonymous.

"We the People," the opening phrase of the Constitution, conveys an unmistakable message: government should be controlled by the citizenry. Certain Americans throughout the nation's existence have taken this message very seriously. They have attempted to make the public an active instrument of policymaking, to establish a more participatory mode of democracy. Their successes—town meetings, initiatives, referendums, recall, grassroots movements—add important elements to American politics. Clearly, many Americans believe there is an important difference between pursuing private gain and serving organized interests, and the achievement of collective well-being. Because of this belief, living room politics is very much alive.

Living room politics, in its ideal form, comprises those occasions when politicians take a backseat to citizens, when popular feelings are registered in a clear, unmistakable way. This activism is what Jean-Jacques Rousseau saw as essential to democracy, and what contemporary advocates of participatory democracy would like to see strengthened in American politics. It would be naive to think that the dominant forces could be removed from any arena of politics, however. The mass media and communication technology have shown themselves to be both friend and foe of democratic reformers and activists. The media reach people, but they also bring their own priorities, procedures, and prejudices to the information they transmit. Grassroots leaders and mainstream politicians sometimes find, to their mutual surprise, that they have much in common because they both have to deal with the media to succeed, and they often find this difficult and frustrating.

Direct democracy is easily perverted by demagoguery or captured by elite interests because symbolism and showmanship are so much a part of its practice in modern societies. Living room politics springs from the genuinely democratic impulse to allow people to determine the rules under which they will live. But we must be ever mindful of the gap between the ideal and reality in politics. Just as real markets are often woefully inadequate representations of the free market paradigm, initiatives, referendums, and grassroots movements can be a far cry from the ideals of unitary or strong democracy.[9]

PERFORMANCE APPRAISAL

The preceding brief analysis of American political institutions shows that these institutions are driven by philosophical principles, constitutional prescriptions, cultural traditions, and economic forces. Here the focus shifts to evaluation. How well do American political institutions work? Should Americans be satisfied with their performance? One way of approaching these questions is to take a broad look at society and examine how satisfied people are with it. American society has both positive and negative characteristics:

- individual freedom of thought, movement, religion, lifestyle, and consumption
- widespread prosperity, but persistent poverty
- real and symbolic violence
- great cultural, educational, residential, and aesthetic diversity
- a materialistic, pragmatic value orientation
- a pervasive belief in the importance of individual and group competition
- a tradition that people have a recognized right to participate in politics

Some positive aspects of institutional behavior were pointed out in chapters 3 through 8. Corporate boards are more representative and less incestuous than they used to be; some companies are innovative and public spirited. Modern bureaucracies are seldom completely "captured" by narrow interests, and most listen to a wide variety of interests. Chief executives can be powerful agents of change and are usually given the leeway they need to be effective in crises. Even legislatures are capable of achieving major breakthroughs when political and economic conditions are ripe. The courts address some of society's most troublesome controversies in a forthright and reasonable manner, and they can, over time, foster significant changes. Public opinion, once aroused, has played a constructive role in disputes over foreign involvement, environmental protection, and civil rights.

Those who want a society that is more cohesive, peaceful, humanistic, cooperative, and democratic would be inclined to give American political institutions a less favorable overall evaluation. But such critics would acknowledge that the dominant forces in society—legal, social, political, and economic—have been pushing in a direction that is quite different from one they advocate; that is, toward a strong private sector and a government that acts cautiously to correct the problems that private sector competition leaves behind. American political institutions were not designed to be strong enough to chart an independent course for national development because the Founders feared what unchecked political institutions might do.

Nevertheless, Americans generally impose high standards of performance on their political institutions. They expect them to be open, efficient, and caring, in part because politicians make inflated claims about what government can accomplish. When the institutions fail to live up to these expectations (as they frequently do), citizens become disappointed, cynical, and distrustful.

These attitudes are reinforced by media attention to corruption in government. Coverage of allegations, investigations, indictments, and convictions conveys the sense that corruption is widespread in American government. In the 1980s and 1990s, several top officials of the Reagan and Clinton administrations were investigated, and in some cases removed from office, for committing improprieties or illegalities. In 1996, Republican Speaker of the House Newt Gingrich was rebuked by his colleagues for improprieties involving a lucrative book contract; weakened, he later (1998) resigned. A similar episode occurred in 2004 and 2005, when House Republican majority leader Tom DeLay was indicted for laundering campaign funds, and eventually gave up his House seat. In the 2000s, corruption had a face, super-lobbyist Jack Abramoff, who was indicted and convicted of influence-peddling crimes that involved numerous prominent members of Congress.[10] Late in the decade, there was a new face of corruption, Governor Rod Blagojevich of Illinois, who tried to raise campaign money from the appointment he was about to make to replace Barack Obama in the Senate. Although there is far less corruption in the United States than in, for example, China or India, corruption persists and can have significant effects on government.

In addition to facing a demanding audience, government institutions are dealing with many complex and difficult problems. Some of these problems, such as poverty, unemployment, pollution, drug abuse, and crime, may be virtually unsolvable in a society with a dominant private sector and a rapidly changing economy. But these are matters with which government is expected to grapple. Moreover, the number of intractable problems at the top of the agenda seems to be increasing rather than decreasing. The New Deal bit off some of the "easier problems": providing a reasonable income for elderly and disabled Americans, guaranteeing workers' rights, and building a physical infrastructure for economic development. Since the 1960s, the government has directed attention and money to the more difficult problems, such as poverty, but the returns have been somewhat disappointing. The poverty rate stood at

22.2 percent when John Kennedy was elected president in 1960. It fell to below 15 percent for the first time in the post–World War II era in 1966, during the Johnson administration; from there, it reached a modern era low of 11.1 percent in 1973. Since then it has ranged from highs of just over 15 percent in 1986 and 2010 to lows of 11.3 percent to 11.8 percent between 1999 and 2001.[11] Over the past forty years, there has been a constant struggle among policymakers to find the right balance between the need to address government deficits and debt and the commitment to attack persistent social problems such as poverty, hunger, homelessness, and inadequate health care.

Americans are fixers. If something is not working properly, the American instinct is to find a cure, usually through technology. This fix-it mentality is evident in almost every aspect of American life, including government and politics. Perceived malfunctions of government generate suggestions for reform. Americans, therefore, have established a civil service to correct the evils of the spoils system, created regulatory agencies to curb private sector abuses, reorganized the executive branch to make departments more attentive to chief executive preferences, and instituted initiative and referendum procedures to make state governments more responsive to citizens. There is an obvious and natural link between performance assessments and proposals for institutional reform.

Assessing institutional performance on the basis of broad societal outcomes—how healthy, wealthy, and wise a society is—leads to endless debates about questions that are difficult to answer with any precision. For this reason, it is necessary to introduce some guidelines and standards into an evaluative discussion. Six criteria of political institutions—stability, representativeness, responsiveness, public awareness, efficiency, and competence—are identified as positive characteristics in the discussion that follows.

Stability

Government stability may be the most important standard by which to judge the success or failure of political institutions, and the American system would get high marks on anyone's stability scale. From a world perspective, the peaceful transfer of power from one regime, usually defined by its leader, to the next is still one of the most difficult problems for countries to solve. The U.S. constitutional prescriptions regarding presidential succession have passed all tests, including the Watergate crisis, with flying colors. Furthermore, when the institutions are unresponsive to strongly felt public desires, there are other mechanisms, such as living room politics, through which discontent can be expressed without threatening the stability of the system. The Founders believed that having a stable government was more important than having an enlightened one, and the performance of American institutions has generally reflected this priority.

State constitutions have also proved quite durable. For example, the Massachusetts constitution dates back to 1780, and Vermont's constitution was ratified in 1793.[12] And many newer constitutions bear a close resemblance to their predecessors. At the state level, as at the federal level, the basics of institutional design, such as three branches of government and a bicameral legislature (except in Nebraska), remain intact.

Economic markets are not expected to be stable in the same way that governments are. Indeed, the private sector is supposed to be dynamic, innovative, and ever changing. But changing private sector markets can have profoundly painful human consequences, and liberal reformers have sought to smooth the rough edges of business cycles through economic planning, joint public and private ventures, and social service programs for poor and unemployed individuals. The federal government provides modest and temporary financial assistance to individuals and communities who suffer when the economy changes. Thus workers who lost their jobs in the Great Recession started out receiving six months of unemployment insurance (partial income replacement), but coverage for unemployed workers was extended several times from 2009 to 2013, with some receiving nearly two years of payments. Workers who lose their jobs because of plant closures resulting from foreign trade agreements may also receive job training assistance in preparing for another job. Also significant is the Food Stamps program, which provides food aid for poor and unemployed Americans. In 2012, this program (now called the Supplemental Nutrition Assistance Program) served nearly 48 million Americans at a cost of almost $75 million. Such policies are also appreciated by community leaders and businesses because they have a stabilizing effect. By helping unemployed individuals and needy families buy goods and services, they encourage people to stay in their communities rather than to move elsewhere.

Stability, of course, can be a mixed blessing. The same political and cultural factors that facilitate constitutional stability can also discourage policy change. In many countries around the world, dropping constitutions, or acting outside of them, is sometimes seen as a necessary step on the road to broad policy changes. Still, most students of comparative politics would agree that the United States is fortunate to have avoided the frequent political upheavals that have wracked countries in Africa, Asia, Europe, and Latin America.

Representativeness

A simple way of approaching the representativeness of political institutions is to ask, Who gets into policymaking circles and who does not? The answer to this question has been that well-educated, white, professional men, especially lawyers and businessmen, tend to be overrepresented relative to their numbers in the population, whereas women, racial and ethnic minorities, poor people, and those with limited education are likely to be underrepresented. Despite years of effort to change the skewed demographic composition of policymaking groups, only slow and limited progress has been made. That public officials are better educated than the average citizen is not surprising, and it is not a primary concern of most critics, but other aspects of the leadership demographic profile are troubling.

Women are underrepresented in every institutional arena. In Congress, their numbers have increased steadily, but unspectacularly; in the 107th Congress (2001–2003), there were thirteen women in the Senate and sixty in the House, and by the 113th Congress (2013–2015), these numbers had reached eighty-one in the House and twenty in the Senate.[13] In 2013, only five of our nation's governors and eleven lieutenant governors were women.[14] In the private sector, women held only 16.5 percent of the seats on the boards of directors of *Fortune* 500 companies in 2012, and 3.8 percent of the CEO positions, but these represented increases over 1999, when women held only 11 percent of the board seats and fewer than 1 percent of the CEO positions.[15] This is progress, but is it enough? In Europe, several countries have passed legislation setting goals (20 percent by 2014; 40 percent by 2017) for female representation on corporate boards.[16] In politics, in addition to Congress, women have made significant gains in state legislatures and state elected executive positions (attorneys general, treasurers, secretaries of state, etc.) over a forty-year time horizon, but gains over the past decade have been modest. In 2012, 23.7 percent of the nation's state legislators were women, a small increase from 22.5 percent in 2000, but a large gain from 4 percent in 1969. In the elected executive realm, the share held by women grew from 6.6 percent in 1969 to 27.6 percent in 2000, but has actually fallen a bit (to 22.4 percent) since then.[17]

African Americans (13.5 percent of the population) and Hispanics (15 percent) have made some progress, although some glaring representation gaps persist. Nationwide, the number of African American elected officials has risen from just under 1,500 in 1970 to 10,500 in 2012; the number of Hispanic elected officials in 2011 was 5,850, up dramatically from ten years earlier.[18] Since the late 1990s, African Americans have held 7 percent to 8 percent of the seats in the House of Representatives, which is roughly double the percentage they held in the 1970s; the Hispanic percentage in 2012 was 7.1 percent (thirty-one members), up from 4 percent in 1999.[19] Like women, African Americans and Hispanics are still in short supply at the top of corporate hierarchies; in 2010, they held 9.8 percent of *Fortune* 500 board seats, which is very similar to their representation in the early 2000s; there were six African American and six Latino CEOs in the *Fortune* 500 corporate group in 2012.[20] A bright spot in minority representation is the steady election of black and Hispanic mayors. Michael Nutter of Philadelphia, Michael Coleman of Columbus (Ohio), Dave Bing of Detroit, Kasim Reed of Atlanta, Stephanie Rawlings-Blake of Baltimore, and Vincent Gray of Washington, D.C., are among the nation's black mayors. There is one African American governor, Deval Patrick of Massachusetts; one African American senator, Tim Scott of South Carolina; and three Hispanic senators, Robert Menendez of New Jersey, Marco Rubio of Florida, and Ted Cruz of Texas.

Women and ethnic minorities still face an uphill struggle in obtaining appointed policymaking positions. This situation is long standing and has improved somewhat as the pool of women and minorities with the qualifications traditionally sought for top institutional positions—advanced degrees, relevant work experience, and favorable references—has gradually expanded. Still, the preferences and commitments of those making appointments can make a big difference. The clear pattern at the federal level for judicial appointments over the past forty years is that Democratic presidents appoint higher percentages of women and minorities to federal judgeships than Republican presidents, but both groups have received an increased share of the appointments over time. Jimmy Carter made the appointment of more women and African Americans to the federal courts a priority, and 30 percent of his appointments went to these groups. Ronald Reagan did not share this commitment; fewer than 15 percent of his court appointments went to women and blacks, although he did appoint the first woman to the Supreme Court. George H. W. Bush appointed more minorities to the federal bench than did Reagan (including Clarence Thomas, whom he appointed to the Supreme Court), but fewer than Jimmy Carter, although he appointed a higher percentage of women (almost 20 percent) than Carter. Bill Clinton appointed higher percentages of women (nearly 30 percent) and minorities (nearly 25 percent) to the federal bench than any of his predecessors. George W. Bush's appointees included about 20 percent women and 18 percent minorities.[21] As of November 2012, Barack Obama's confirmed judicial appointments stood at 44 percent women and 38 percent minorities.[22] In the realm of executive branch appointments, the Clinton and Obama administrations appointed 43 percent women, which was 10 percent higher than George W. Bush's administration.[23]

The selection processes are obviously different for elected officials. A critical problem for women has been recruitment—involving women in state and local party organizations, getting some of them elected to state and local offices, and then supporting female candidacies for more visible, powerful offices. Racial prejudice seems an important reason African Americans are not elected in larger numbers. White voters have shown a reluctance to vote for black candidates at all levels of government. For the most part, African American candidates win only where nonwhites are the majority or near majority of voters, as in certain big cities. The election and reelection of President Obama is an obvious, and very significant, counterexample to this pattern.

Responsiveness

Democratic political systems are supposed to be responsive to popular needs and preferences. Critics fault the U.S. government for not being more responsive to problems such as the spread of global warming, soaring medical costs, and homelessness. Many would argue that the government has a responsibility to take the lead in diagnosing and making plans to avert potential catastrophes because the private sector cannot be relied on to do so. Judgments about which problems are the most important at any given time are difficult to make with certainty, however. Some problems turn out to be less serious than they first appeared, and government institutions are seen as justified in having given them scant attention. Moreover, small steps may eventually yield substantial returns. Still, it seems to many that major American institutions often ignore problems for which no popular and easy solution is apparent, and they do so to the detriment of society as a whole.

There is no clear consensus among political scientists on just how responsive governments have been, partly because of differences in how responsiveness is defined. If responsiveness is defined in broad ideological terms, then governments do tend to be responsive to public opinion. For example, in the early 1990s, Robert Erikson, Gerald Wright, and John McIver found that governments in states with more liberal voters tend to adopt more liberal policies; more recent analyses have come to the same conclusion.[24] Similarly, shifts in public opinion at the national level often result in changes in national policy that are roughly consistent with such shifts, and vote choices are closely linked to voter ideology and issue preferences. According to James Stimson, Michael MacKuen, and Robert Erikson, from the 1960s to the mid-1990s, national public policy shifted in a liberal direction as the electorate became more liberal, and in a conservative direction as the electorate became more conservative.[25] As Stimson and his colleagues put it, "When the public asks for a more activist or a more conservative government, politicians oblige."[26] Studies conducted more recently have shown much the same pattern; American voters follow their issue and ideological leanings in choosing the candidates for whom they vote.[27]

Still, it is easy enough to cite gross disparities between the public's policy preferences and public policy at any given point in time. For example, the public has long supported policies to address global warming, but even though many states and localities have enacted global warming policies, Congress has yet to act on this problem.[28] The public strongly opposed the 2008 Troubled Asset Relief Program legislation to bail out the financial industry, but it was enacted anyway. By 2012, Americans had soured on the war in Afghanistan, with 60 percent favoring immediate troop withdrawal, yet the war continued.[29] In most instances, limited responsiveness to public opinion means substantial responsiveness to powerful interest groups. Which is more legitimate? Although public opinion polls capture the views of all Americans, they do not take intensity of preference into account, and some political scientists and others would argue that when most people do not care about an issue, the views of those who do care (usually represented by interest groups) should shape policy responses.

Where gaps exist between public opinion and public policy, one popular explanation is our campaign finance system. Critics allege that politicians have to spend so much of their time attending to money matters—giving speeches to donor groups, attending fund-raisers, meeting with contributors, planning media promotions—that they have little time for the public's business. This problem is prevalent at the national and state levels. For most politicians, simply maintaining their positions in the highly competitive political world is almost a full-time job. In such an environment, politicians may be responsive to money, but to little else.

This argument was never more salient than in 2012, when spending by super political action committees (PACs), which were by-products of the 2010 Supreme Court decision in *Citizens United v. Federal Election Commission*, dominated many of the headlines. The received wisdom was that independent spending unleashed by the *Citizens United* ruling had propelled numerous Republican and Tea Party candidates into office in 2010, when over fifty House Democratic incumbents failed to win reelection. Could conservative super PAC spending produce a similar result in 2012? The answer was no. When all the dust had settled, despite massive spending by conservative super PACs, President Obama, who also raised and spent a great deal of money, was reelected. In addition, Democrats picked up two seats in the Senate and ten seats in the House.[30] This does not mean that spending by outside groups does not matter in American elections, but it suggests that it may not matter as much as some critics allege.

It is well known that incumbents have an advantage in raising money and getting reelected; therefore, imposing limitations on the number of terms members of Congress can serve might appear to be an attractive reform. The potential disadvantage of this reform is the possibility that Congress would be less able to compete with presidents in battles over public policy because of a lack of seasoned legislators. As we have discussed, the idea of term limits gained popularity in the early 1990s, as several states passed term limitation proposals in referendums and President George H. W. Bush publicly endorsed the idea, but the Supreme Court ruled that states cannot limit congressional terms.[31] However, eighteen states did impose term limits on state legislators, and fifteen states still have them. State legislative studies have found that states with legislative term limits do experience higher turnover among legislators (as expected), that power over policy does tend to move from the legislative to the executive branch, and that legislative staff members gain influence relative to elected legislators.[32]

Efforts to make corporations more responsive have included citizen protests and lobbying efforts by unions, churches, public interest groups, and grassroots organizations. These protests have brought to the attention of corporate managers and boards, politicians, and the public such examples of corporate abuse and social irresponsibility as the conduct of sweatshop business operations in developing countries, discrimination against African Americans and women, the exposure of workers and the public to dangerous chemicals, and the packaging and marketing of defective mortgages. Many of these efforts have stimulated changes in corporate policy and, perhaps more important, have served to politicize corporations. Once sedate stockholder meetings have been turned into forums for discussions of a wide range of political and social issues, many of which take the form of debates over shareholder or proxy resolutions.

This movement has spawned numerous corporate reform proposals, most of which aim to make managers more accountable to individual and institutional investors, and to the public. These proposals include giving all shareholders, regardless of the sizes of their investments, votes on proxy resolutions; taking the selection of directors out of the hands of management and putting it into the hands of shareholders; and requiring that corporate boards include government or other outside representatives. Although there have been a limited number of clear victories, the accountability movement has made corporate decision makers more aware of their public responsibilities. Because they are sympathetic to genuine expressions of public sentiment, some corporate managers willingly make policy changes, as long as the changes do not threaten profitability. A recent example is Apple, which announced in December 2012 that it was devoting $100 million to computer assembly plants in the United States, in an apparent response to criticism about the extent of its outsourcing. In explaining this decision, Apple CEO Timothy Cook acknowledged that his company "had a responsibility to create jobs," while also noting the improved competitiveness of American manufacturing.[33]

Public Awareness

The picture of the public's role in the political process presented thus far has not been entirely complimentary. Public opinion is often manipulated by political and media elites. Many expressions of public opinion suggest that Americans are concerned mainly about the economic well-being of their families and communities, that they are unreasonably impatient with government, and that they are ignorant of many aspects of national and international politics.

In a masterful study of what Americans knew about politics in the 1980s and early 1990s, political scientists Michael Delli Carpini and Scott Keeter found enormous holes in the public's knowledge of how the political process worked, who the country's political leaders were, and of which public policies the public approved or disapproved. Unfortunately, trivia often made more lasting impressions than facts that mattered. For example, during the early 1990s, the overwhelming majority of Americans knew that President George H. W. Bush hated broccoli, whereas only half knew that he had vetoed a plant-closing bill. Although one might hope that political knowledge would have improved over time, that did not appear to be the case; compared with the 1950s and the late 1940s, the American people in 1989 were no better informed politically.[34] As Delli Carpini and Keeter put it, "In spite of an unprecedented expansion in public education, a communications revolution that has shattered national and international boundaries, and the increasing relevance of national and international events and policies to the daily lives of Americans, citizens appear no more informed about politics."[35] However, others who have looked into the public's knowledge of politics and policy have come away with a less pessimistic view. As indicated in the previous section, it does appear that most voters can follow their partisan and ideological leanings well enough to make intelligent connections between candidates running for office and issues that matter to them.[36] Some even argue that political ignorance is rational because there are plenty of sources of cues that average citizens can use to make their voting decisions easy and consistent with their policy preferences.[37]

Another worrisome trend has been an apparent decline in what social scientists call "social capital," or the formation of social connections that can promote trust and mutual support. According to political scientist Robert Putnam, Americans are less connected to family, friends, neighbors, and other social institutions than they were a generation ago. They are also less likely to belong to organizations or groups, which, according to Putnam, means a regrettable decline in social capital.[38] An obvious cure would be for America to become once again, in Alexis de Tocqueville's famous phrase, "a nation of joiners." But political scientist Mark Warren cautions that associations differ in their ability to make a positive contribution to democratic life. For example, Warren argues, advocacy groups, consumer cooperatives, and public school organizations are more likely to develop a sense of political efficacy among members than social clubs, fraternal orders, or sports associations.[39] If Warren is right, then what matters is not just how many groups we belong to, but which groups they turn out to be.

It may also be that Putnam and others who bemoan a lack of traditional civic activities are missing some of the positive developments in society over the past forty years. Russell Dalton argues that the so-called generation X (born in the late 1960s and 1970s) and generation Y (born in the 1980s and 1990s, also known as "millennials") have been unfairly judged because they do not subscribe as strongly to some traditional values, such as the importance of obeying the law, paying taxes, and voting in elections, as do previous generations. He finds that these younger generations have a different set of civic values, which he dubs "engaged citizenship," that emphasize the importance of participating in protests and product boycotts (often through the use of social media), and feeling (as well as acting on) a sense of solidarity with poor and oppressed people around the world.[40]

Over the years, many reforms have been advanced that are aimed at increasing the quantity and quality of citizen participation in American government. Political scientist Benjamin Barber and others believe that a comprehensive system of citizen education is needed to make American democracy work. He has proposed extensive reforms that begin with institutionalized neighborhood assemblies. According to Barber, Americans have no place to meet where they can learn about and discuss issues. Therefore, all neighborhood groups ranging from 5,000 to 25,000 citizens should have facilities that can be used for regular public meetings to discuss local and national issues. Once established, these assemblies could vote on local issues and choose local officials, be tied in to a national civic education electronic network, and eventually vote on national issues through electronic referendums. Barber also would establish universal citizen service requirements, democratize the workplace, and generally reorient society to focus on communal concerns and civic responsibilities.[41]

A more modest proposal would be to encourage the development of "organizational report cards" that enable citizens to evaluate governments, government agencies, and public or private organizations that deliver social services, such as schools, hospitals, and health maintenance organizations (we discussed certain varieties of these in chapters 4 and 8).[42] By condensing and simplifying large amounts of data, report cards can shed considerable light on the performance of organizations in and around government. Armed with such information, citizens and citizens' groups would be better able to evaluate public officials and those who serve them under contractual arrangements. As William Gormley and David Weimer put it, "Report cards can be thought of as mechanisms for reducing information asymmetries between organizations and those who consume their services."[43] At their best, organizational report cards help make government more accountable to the citizenry.

Having more television coverage of court proceedings might be another means of encouraging civic education. The presence of television cameras in Congress is now accepted, and they have not disrupted or fundamentally altered the legislative process. The audience usually is small, but not insignificant. Court proceedings in Florida have been televised since the late 1970s, and almost all states now allow some television coverage of judicial proceedings; most allow full coverage of trials subject to the agreement of the trial judge. The trials of O. J. Simpson and Casey Anthony notwithstanding, the results have been generally positive—lawyers and judges do not appear to play to the camera, and witnesses and jurors are not confused or intimidated by the camera's presence.[44] The response from citizens indicates a genuine fascination in seeing how the judicial process really works, a development that advocates of participatory democracy would no doubt applaud.

Efficiency

American government is far from efficient in the way it makes and implements policies, and many of the inefficiencies stem from basic tenets of the Constitution such as the separation of powers, bicameralism, and federalism. If stability is the strongest virtue of American government, inefficiency is probably its greatest vice.

That inefficiency is demonstrated by the difficulty Congress has in making controversial policy decisions and its penchant for policies that are symbolic, vague, weakened by compromise, and internally inconsistent. When Congress cannot decide, problems are either left unresolved or settled by federal agencies, the courts, or the state governments. Bureaucratic implementation of ambiguous statutes frequently leads to new problems, and then to ongoing cycles of legislative patchwork, discretionary enforcement, public or interest group complaints, and more patchwork. Chief executives have trouble making government more efficient because legislatures often refuse to cooperate. Chief executives cannot force cooperation, because legislators have independent bases of political power and control most aspects of tax and spending policy. National and state policy is all too often a mishmash of statutory actions taken by small groups of legislators whose principal aim in formulating the statutes is to serve the interests of organized groups or of the localities they represent. Almost everyone gets something, but there is no clear policy direction, and a great deal of duplication and lack of coordination occurs.

Congressional inefficiency has never been more apparent than in recent years. As we have discussed in several previous chapters, since 2009, Congress has consistently failed to pass budget legislation in the proper way and on the prescribed timetable. This failure has resulted in a number of dramatic stand-offs between President Obama and Republicans in Congress over piecemeal, stopgap legislation that was needed to keep the government running and meeting its debt obligations. However, the last-minute deals they have made to avert disaster have fallen far short of solving the overall fiscal problems the country faces, and have produced visible negative reactions in financial markets. The public has shown a definite awareness of this malfunctioning, and has given Congress its lowest favorability ratings in modern history.

The solution? Some students of the problem have suggested greater legislative discipline and more central control, with the vehicles for discipline and central control being strong political parties, such as those found in Western Europe. As we have pointed out, particularly in chapter 5, the legislative parties in the United States have become more disciplined, and leaders do exercise more central control, particularly in the U.S. House of Representatives, but this has not fixed the problem of legislative gridlock. The frequency of divided government, and the supermajoritarian aspects of the U.S. Senate, have perpetuated stalemate even as the parties have become stronger and more cohesive. Invigorated national parties may be part of the solution to Congress's problems, but they are by no means a panacea.

Another approach to discipline is what political scientist Theodore Lowi has called "juridical democracy."[45] What Lowi had in mind was that Congress should be prevented from passing so many ambiguous laws. The Supreme Court could take the first step by resurrecting the reasoning it used in declaring unconstitutional Franklin Roosevelt's National Industrial Recovery Act of 1933, a step that would no doubt be appealing to several of the Court's current conservatives. The Court said in 1935 that policies delegating power to administrative agencies without defining the precise standards that should be used during implementation are invalid under the Constitution.[46] The problem with this remedy, however, is that it ignores both technical and political complexity. Many issues involving health care, environmental protection, telecommunications, banking, and other policy sectors have become so complex that it is difficult for Congress to specify solutions with precision. Even if Congress knew what ought to be done, it would face the political challenge of forging winning coalitions in support of policies that had clear directives and allocated resources in a definitive manner.

Another reform proposal that would complement the strengthening of parties by enhancing the power of presidents is to increase the terms of House members from two years to four, and possibly to decrease Senate terms to four years. The idea is to tie congressional electoral fortunes more directly to those of presidents, who have an obvious stake in emphasizing party loyalty. Perhaps more important, it would do away with midterm elections, which almost invariably contribute to gridlock among policymakers, because the president's party tends to lose seats. Such a change would likely instill a more national outlook among House (and perhaps Senate) members, and encourage them to tackle major national problems with more energy and a greater commitment to achieve meaningful results.

Another set of reforms would involve changing at least some of the Senate rules that have prevented majorities from being able to act. The most obvious and significant target would be the filibuster, or more accurately, the threat of a filibuster. In recent Congresses, all the minority party has had to do is threaten to filibuster a bill coming to the floor in order to force its sponsors (usually the majority leader) to hold a cloture vote, which requires sixty ayes to succeed. Many have proposed requiring those who want to use the filibuster option to actually take the floor and talk before they can force a cloture vote. Others would like to exempt executive branch and judicial nominees from filibusters. At the beginning of the 113th Congress, Senate Democrats and Republicans agreed on some modest reforms that removed the filibuster option from "motions to proceed," which will prevent one popular delaying tactic; however, many others still remain.[47]

Competence

In evaluating the competence of institutional actors, we ask whether American policymakers are knowledgeable and skilled enough to accomplish their tasks. Most elected officials are lawyers or businesspeople, which means that, on average, they are well educated. State and local politics traditionally serve as the first test of aspiring politicians' interest and ability; the more successful ones move on to Congress or state executive positions. Those who make it that far tend to stay in politics a long time. They are career politicians and policymakers.

Legislatures. The U.S. Congress stands out among the national legislatures in the world for the low turnover of its members and its preponderance of lawyers, or at least law school graduates. For several decades running, roughly 40 percent of the members of Congress have held law degrees, but most of them are better described as career politicians than practicing lawyers.[48] In most Western European countries, lawyers constitute a smaller share of the legislators, while journalists, teachers, intellectuals, and blue-collar workers are better represented; however, there is also an increasing tendency for European legislators of various backgrounds to have chosen politics as their career.[49] Low turnover among legislators would seem to earn Congress low marks for representativeness and accountability, but high marks for competence, although much depends upon what kind of competence is sought. American legislators know a good deal about policies handled by their specialized committees, but they tend to be less well informed and less able when it comes to formulating long-term answers to major national or international questions. At the state level, legislative turnover overall has remained more or less the same over the past three decades, despite the imposition of mandatory term limits in about one-third of the states. Earlier we mentioned that legislatures in term-limit states, where turnover is high, have lost power to chief executives; those in non-term-limit states show low rates of turnover and greater professionalization within the legislature.[50]

Bureaucracies. The U.S. federal bureaucracy has sometimes been criticized for inadequate competence, professionalism, and common sense.[51] That charge has been vigorously rebutted by Charles Goodsell and others.[52] Even defenders concede that civil servants in the United States lack the status and prestige of their counterparts in Great Britain, France, and Germany, where civil servants are highly regarded and extremely well paid.[53] Ever since the Reagan years, scholars have worried about the morale of the federal civil service. It is difficult to encourage young people to choose the civil service as a vocation when politicians treat bureaucrats as punching bags, and when their private sector counterparts are earning far more money.

The situation is somewhat different for the political and career executives who actually run federal and state agencies. Appointed political executives, most of whom leave for other jobs after two to three years of service, can endure challenging work conditions because such service adds luster to their resumes and they expect to depart before long. As for career executives, they must simply learn to develop thick skins. Both political and career executives take pride in being able to manage and reform important government programs that promote clean air, good health, safe roads, secure investments, and protection from discrimination. And many of them are quite good at what they do. For example, former Harvard professor John D. Graham, head of the Office of Management and Budget's Office of Information and Regulatory Affairs from 2001 to 2005, applied his academic knowledge and training in risk analysis to overseeing the numerous rules and regulations put forward by federal regulatory agencies, and received high marks from experts both inside and outside of government for the quality of the work he conducted.[54]

Several studies have documented the impressive credentials that modern (since the 1980s) state and federal agency heads bring to their jobs. The overwhelming majority have graduate and/or professional degrees and many years of relevant experience.[55] But effective bureaucratic leadership often requires more than education, professional expertise, and experience. Successful agency heads must be attuned to the political climate within and outside their agencies and make decisions that build upon their agencies' strengths, while reflecting an awareness of their weaknesses. To do this, bureaucratic leaders must take positions that are viewed as credible by both agency personnel and outside groups, including, in some cases, the media. They must know when to be bold and when to make compromises and, above all, how to avoid bringing negative public attention to their agencies.[56]

Bureaucratic reforms at the national and state levels typically revolve around similar themes: providing incentives for better performance, making it easier for managers to fire unproductive employees, establishing clear lines of authority, encouraging creative solutions to difficult problems, improving coordination within and between agencies, helping establish or cultivate productive agency networks, and bolstering the image of public employees. Unfortunately, these reforms do not always point in the same direction. For example, establishing clear lines of authority ("hierarchical" accountability) encourages bureaucrats to do what they are told, whereas creative problem solving ("professional" accountability) encourages them to think for themselves.[57]

Courts. The power and prestige of American courts are unrivaled in the world. They do far more than merely apply laws to specific cases; the courts often make policy, especially when other institutions are unwilling to do so. One way to ensure judicial competence is to improve the quality of appointments to the bench. Chief executives can appoint advisory panels—groups of citizens and legal professionals who narrow the list of potential nominees to candidates with outstanding records and abilities—to help them make nominations. The use of advisory panels does not eliminate partisan considerations, but it helps ensure that only truly competent individuals are considered. President Carter created panels of this sort to assist him in making circuit court appointments, but the panels were dropped by President Reagan. President George H. W. Bush relied on the Justice Department to help him screen nominees, and his slowness in filling vacancies was criticized by several members of the Senate Judiciary Committee.[58] Presidents Clinton, George W. Bush, and Obama have elevated the role of White House staff members in reviewing judicial candidates, and all have experienced many delays and difficulties in getting the Senate to confirm their nominees.[59] Thus Senate obstruction is now more or less a given, but in the end, most presidential nominees are confirmed, and presidents who serve two full terms can have a major impact on the ideological makeup of the federal court system (see chapter 7).

The proper connection between the law and science is increasingly of interest in modern society, and the competence of judges is tested when they confront highly technical questions. Agencies such as the Environmental Protection Agency make complex scientific assessments about what industries can and should do to comply with environmental statutes, and their assessments are often contested in court. These cases can be difficult for judges. Although they are inclined to defer to agency expertise on technical matters, they maintain a role for themselves in taking a "hard look" at the evidence and the procedures an agency used in making its assessment.[60]

The late appeals court judge Harold Leventhal, who had extensive experience with such matters, proposed that judges hire scientific experts in highly technical cases. The experts would not judge the adequacy of agency rulings, but would assist judges "in understanding problems of scientific methodology and in assessing the reliability of tests conducted by the agency in light of specific criticisms."[61] A somewhat more extensive reform would be the creation of "science courts," which would empower impartial, recognized experts to rule on the scientific and technical aspects of cases, while letting traditional judges rule on the legal issues.[62] Of course, the science-policy nexus is not just an issue in the judicial arena; it is an increasingly important concern in almost all policymaking settings.

Chief executives. If national politics are the leading edge of American politics, then presidential experiences should shed some light on the future for governors and mayors. One problem is that the public relations aspects of the job have become so dominant in the media age that competence is now what good looks used to be—a desirable quality, but not necessary. Chief executives can be, and are, packaged and sold all over the country. The more salient the politics, the more likely it is that public relations specialists will dominate. In the United States, chief executive politics is the most visible form of politics and, therefore, the most prone to deceptive appearances.

Successful chief executives must be able to perform their many difficult political and administrative tasks with the knowledge that many people are watching and waiting to exploit every stumble, both public and private. Furthermore, because they lack the authority to do everything they would like, their leadership is often more a matter of symbolism than substance. The ability to utter symbolic rhetoric convincingly in front of huge, but usually remote, audiences is rapidly becoming the primary qualification for chief executives. Although, as we have pointed out on several occasions, heavy reliance on symbolism promotes public cynicism about government and elected officials, it should be noted that all three of our most recent presidents maintained enough public credibility in their first terms to get reelected. Perhaps the critics of modern chief executive politics, ourselves included, have exaggerated this problem.

Thus far, most states and localities appear to have benefited from more visible and competitive politics. It was not all that long ago—prior to 1940— that state governments were weak and, in many cases, corrupt. Governors' powers were limited; their offices were poorly staffed and possessed little expertise; money and favor trading pervaded legislatures; and the bureaucracy was filled with patronage appointees, who did more political work than government work. A good deal of progress has been made since then. Governors have been granted broader powers, and they exercise them more vigorously. State legislatures sit longer, and legislators are better paid and less corrupt. Bureaucracies have been enlarged and revamped, with most employees governed by merit systems. Innovative policies are coming from the states: education reform, far-reaching environmental statutes and projects, welfare-to-work programs, financial incentives to encourage day care centers to improve the quality of their care, joint public and private economic development efforts, and others. Most big-city governments have also become more professional in outlook and practice, and many have become sources of innovation. Through the leadership of mayors such as Greg Nickles of Seattle and John Hickenlooper of Denver (now the governor of Colorado), many cities in the United States have launched ambitious projects in recent years to reduce automobile traffic, while promoting bicycle use and public transit options; to reduce energy use in buildings and promote alternative forms of energy production; and to use "smart planning" to encourage urban agriculture and emergence of "urban villages" and sustainable communities.[63]

Boardrooms. Private sector competence and effectiveness are difficult to characterize in general terms. The nation has experienced a steady stream of economic difficulties since the 1960s, and at least some of these problems can be attributed to private sector decisions and practices. The most important recent examples were risky, and in some cases illegal, mortgage packaging and investment practices that led to the Wall Street collapse and the Great Recession, as well as to the collapse of real estate markets in most parts of the country. These ill-advised private sector activities have cost the public, especially many individual homeowners and investors, billions of dollars. They also helped propel Barack Obama's first campaign for the presidency, and inspired economic stimulus and regulatory reform legislation in his first term. Although the country has been hurt by persistently high rates of unemployment and poverty since 2008, in comparison with most of the rest of the world Americans still enjoy a very high standard of living, and there are consistent signs of innovation and vitality in the private sector.

When the first edition of this book was written (1986), American industry was coming out of a period, dating back to World War II, during which it had depended on the high-volume manufacture of standardized products by workers who performed repetitive tasks for union-negotiated wages and benefits. There was widespread consensus that this production style could not compete effectively against Western European and Japanese systems that were more flexible and yielded higher quality products, or against low-cost systems, organized along American lines, in developing countries such as Mexico and Brazil (China had not yet emerged as a manufacturing power). The difficulties of the American steel and auto industries were attributed by most analysts to the failure of corporate leaders to modernize plants and change their product orientations soon enough to avert disaster. Problems of this sort are to be expected in market economies, however, and they can even provide valuable lessons for the future.

The experience of the steel, automobile, and other traditional American industries led to a new consensus about the importance of investment in infrastructure, research and development, and methods to improve worker productivity. When the third edition of this book was written (2001), the country had experienced many years of impressive economic growth and prosperity, driven largely by services and consumer spending, although manufacturing remained important, especially the high-tech industry. Labor productivity was high, and U.S. industry featured high-technology products, precision manufacturing, telecommunications, and high-yield farming, all areas where the United States had what economists call a "comparative advantage." The private sector had also become much more attentive to international markets, with China emerging as a major player. Our economic difficulties since the Great Recession should be sobering to those who imagined that the growth and affluence of the 1990s would continue indefinitely. China will soon surpass the United States as the largest economy in the world, and we will need many more instances of the private sector performing at its best, and many fewer of it performing at its worst, if we are to retain prosperity in a rapidly changing world economy.

SUMMARY

The competence of American policymakers is not the main issue with regard to institutional performance. The more fundamental issue is political will or the lack thereof. Overall, one of the greatest failings of American public institutions is their indecisiveness. This failing is obvious to anyone who has studied the workings of Congress, where indecision in the form of stalling, ambiguous statutory language, symbolic responsiveness, partisan deadlock, and passing the buck has been raised to an art. Former Ohio State football coach Woody Hayes always explained his reluctance to use the forward pass by saying, "There are three things that can happen when you pass—completion, incompletion, and interception—and two of them are bad." This philosophy captures the essence of legislators' attitudes: faced with the choice between taking forceful action to resolve a problem, which could be ineffective or unpopular, or using one of their polished methods of delay, obfuscation, and pacification, they almost invariably choose the latter.

Indecisiveness is not simply a product of the fear of making mistakes. It also stems from the fixation that elected officials have with public opinion and the extraordinary role played by interest groups in American politics. The socialization of conflict and increased public and group participation in decision making have produced, in a political system of fragmented power, more gridlock than direction, which is another way of saying that democratic decision making is cumbersome. Powerful groups in society often disagree about the steps that should be taken to resolve problems. The government apparatus is designed to reflect such disagreement, and it does, in the form of inaction. This inaction then becomes the target of reformers and other critics because chief executives are almost always unsuccessful in charting a clear course of government policy, bureaucrats are paranoid because they never know when elected officials are going to turn on them, and the public is confused and disillusioned.

In the twenty-first century, the effects of gridlock and indecision at the national level are placing increasing demands on the states. The inability of presidents and Congresses to chart a clear course for national policy on many issues forces states to make tough decisions about everything from social welfare and taxes to the environment. Inaction by representative institutions at all levels of government has also increased the significance of living room politics (initiatives, referendums, and grassroots movements) and courtroom politics. The growing conservatism of the U.S. Supreme Court further adds to the importance of state-level politics, particularly the importance of state supreme court decisions.

But overly harsh judgments about the performance of American political institutions may not be fully justified. In this postindustrial age, government institutions of all sorts face vastly expanded policy agendas of challenging problems. The rapidity of change in society denies policymaking institutions any opportunity to rest on their laurels. A steady stream of demands can be heard from groups who want more or less from government, as technological and social developments alter the environment within which they operate. As the government has taken on new tasks and sought to satisfy more demands, its old responsibilities have not withered away. Instead, earlier commitments usually have become permanent. The inability to shed old baggage is another reason why government institutions are reluctant to take on new problems. This reluctance to act has a positive side: it reduces the chances of making serious mistakes.

The reform impulse enjoys continuing popularity in the United States because it offers methods for overcoming governmental problems that advocates claim will not cause a great deal of pain. Americans are always searching for a "quick fix." But the reality of change is that it is almost always a slow, cumulative process rather than a single decisive act. Some of the most significant reforms, such as equal rights for women and minorities, have followed a long, painful course.

In many ways, the question is whether private sector performance is rewarding enough to justify a government that is so timid that it rarely acts in a disruptive way. Whenever such a question is posed, the answer that almost invariably comes forward is that "the people" should decide. But are the people in any position to decide? Are alternatives stated in ways that people can understand, and that allow them to make reasoned judgments about what is in society's best interest? In general, the answer to these questions is no, primarily because a good deal of what the people know has been packaged for them by people who have a vested interest in sensationalizing issues and/or keeping things much as they are. Nevertheless, history makes clear that when conditions get bad enough, decisive popular action is likely. In a free society, widespread suffering can lead to strong expressions of citizen preference, and significant changes in institutions and policies. Citizen inattentiveness to politics and government and policy gridlock are an indication of relative prosperity. Perhaps there is some wisdom in letting people's sense of economic well-being, or the lack of it, determine the government's policy.

Assessing American Public Policy

T he political struggle that yields public policies is not just a game about the exercise and maintenance of power. Whether governments and private corporations produce effective policies and programs profoundly affects the nation and its citizens. At stake are national survival, the quality of life, and the nature of justice in society.

Public policies are developed and implemented by private corporations, courts, legislatures, chief executives, administrative agencies, and citizens. In this chapter, we consider fundamental questions of governmental performance. How well do public policies serve the needs and wants of the American people? Does the United States live up to the ideals proclaimed by its elected leaders and set forth in the Constitution? Is the nation better off or worse off in the first decade of the new century than it was fifty, twenty-five, or ten years ago? What pressing problems has the nation failed to grapple with effectively? These are difficult questions to answer. A selective report card on the nation's policy accomplishments and failures is offered here; more questions are raised than answered.

CHOOSING YARDSTICKS

What criteria should be applied in an assessment of public policy? What evidence is available to measure policy performance? Against what standards can success and failure be judged? The question is not just whether the public policy "glass" is half full or half empty, but which glasses should be examined. There are many inherent difficulties in assessing public policy. Following is a discussion of a few of them and how they might be handled.

Principal Policy Goals

Before evaluating any public policy, one must decide what questions to ask, which is not as simple as it sounds. What is important to one observer may not be important to another. People in different circumstances have distinct views of the world and its problems. The inner-city resident and the suburban home-owner, whose dwellings may be less than an hour apart, have different expectations about what government should do to help them. The city dweller is more likely to be concerned about crime, public transportation, air quality, overcrowding, and housing. The suburban homeowner is more interested in the state highway system, the availability of safe drinking water, and recreational opportunities.

Public policy concerns are also shaped by the nature of the times. Some goals, such as peace and prosperity, always command attention. Issues, such as drug abuse or nuclear power plants, may seem urgent one year but less pressing the next. Circumstances change; policies change; new problems arise, or new aspects of old problems are recognized. During the late 1950s, for example, policymakers debated whether black Americans had the right to enjoy the same public facilities, schools, mass transportation, restaurants, and parks as white Americans. In the first decades of the twenty-first century, such questions are no longer debated, but disagreements still abound as to what, if anything, government should do to promote educational and economic opportunities for minority groups.

Conceptions of the proper role of government in the lives of American citizens are highly controversial and provide a framework for evaluations of public policy. Should the government encourage or even permit employers to require individuals to stop smoking, even if they smoke only when they are not on the job? Should the government reward individuals who use mass transportation, instead of driving a car to and from work, in order to curb air pollution? Should government subsidize families whose children attend private elementary and secondary schools when public schools are available? Should the United States continue to play the preeminent role in policing the world, or should other nations begin to play a larger role in defending the interests of democracies? Should governments have the right to examine a person's e-mail or text messages without a court order when law enforcement officers suspect that a crime or terrorist act is being planned by that person? Because people disagree about what government ought to do, they often disagree about what governments actually accomplish.

Despite disagreement about whether government should increase its involvement, expand its reform programs, or get out of the way, there is fundamental agreement among most Americans, but not always among policymakers, on the nation's principal public policy aspirations.[1] They are (1) to defend the nation, (2) to achieve sustained economic growth, (3) to ensure equal opportunity, (4) to provide a "safety net" for low-income and older Americans, and (5) to protect the quality of the physical environment. The stability of these central policy goals over the past several decades reflects a widespread consensus about government responsibilities in American political culture. In the United States, in contrast to some other nations, political battles usually take place over means, not ends. Public officials fight fiercely about how basic values will be expressed and defined in practice, but there is less conflict over what the core values are.

To depict American policy debates as being about means rather than core values does not mean that the differences among policymakers are trivial. In several of the preceding chapters, we have discussed the centrality of partisan and ideological disagreements in American politics, but relative to public policy goals, the differences are mostly about means rather than ends. Democrats and Republicans both consider a strong economy to be a primary public policy goal, but they have very different views about how to achieve that goal: extensive versus minimal government presence in the economy. Essentially the same difference is present with regard to protecting the environment. Similarly, both want to protect the nation from hostile outside forces (nations or terrorist groups), but Democrats see this being realized through diplomacy and world cooperation, backed up by a credible military, while Republicans believe that an overwhelming military capability is key and are skeptical about the benefits of world governance. For Republicans, equal opportunity consists of racial and ethnic blindness before the law; Democrats think the eyes of the law should be open to victims of past racial oppression. Both parties claim to want to help poor Americans, but they disagree about how much and what kind of help should be offered.

What we see in many struggles over public policy in the United States is lawmakers fighting over subtle differences in the language of a statute or a bill because they believe that their decisions may one day have profound consequences. Yet in most instances, the choices made have marginal effects. Only in rare circumstances, such as the New Deal of President Franklin Roosevelt, do major changes occur quickly. Even President Obama's major legislative achievement—the expansion of health care coverage for up to 30 million Americans—did not radically alter health care policy in the United States, because it was built upon the existing private health care delivery system, and many of the key provisions were scheduled to be phased in over time.

Weighing Evidence

How does one know whether government policies and programs are effective? Reliable, objective information is available for the evaluation of many policies. Government agencies and public and private analysts monitor unemployment, inflation, trade balances, life expectancy, race relations, the quality of the environment and education, and so on. Knowledge about the effectiveness of public policies has increased substantially over the past several decades. Policymakers can be well informed about conditions in society and the possible effects of their actions if they choose to be.[2]

Despite these gains, policymakers still may not know enough about the effectiveness of public policies to reach sound conclusions, and too often they are unwilling to use the information that is available. It is embarrassing to discover that a once ballyhooed policy does not work; therefore, many lawmakers are more likely to ask self-serving questions than to authorize careful evaluations, or listen to disconcerting evidence. Politicians are usually more concerned about who gets what, when, and how than with thorough evaluations of program performance. In divided government, they may be more concerned with making their parties or institutions look good than they are with careful evaluations of public policy outcomes.

Establishing cause-and-effect relationships between a government action and a societal consequence is difficult. If millions of Americans have heart disease and high blood pressure, is the U.S. health care system to blame, or is it because too many Americans do not exercise, eat properly, and take care of themselves? If minorities increase their membership in the professions, should credit accrue to civil rights laws, or are there simply more minority applicants who are better prepared? Because a single government policy cannot be isolated from other events, trends, or policies, the specific effects of government decisions may be difficult to detect.

Making Judgments

After evidence is gathered about the effects of a particular policy, standards must be applied to judge success or failure. For example, the unemployment rate among Americans is carefully calculated and reported each month, but the raw data do not speak for themselves. Is an 8 percent unemployment rate alarming or acceptable? Sound public policy conclusions should not be based on the optimism or pessimism of the observer, but where do analysts turn for standards that yield reasonable judgments?

The determination of standards begins with an examination of the objectives of governmental policy. One must be careful to distinguish between pronouncements and actual goals, however. Public laws, regulations, and judicial decrees state objectives, but political leaders frequently engage in hyperbole, claiming that new laws and policies will solve long-standing problems. Therefore, careful observers ignore the rhetoric and examine the realistic objectives of a policy. In addition to identifying policy objectives, proper measurements or assessments of policy outcomes and impacts are needed. As mentioned above, some such measures—unemployment rates, inflation rates, and so on—are relatively easy to obtain, but others can be more difficult to gather. The next task is connecting observed outcomes and impacts to policy objectives and the actions taken to implement a policy. To provide sound explanations of the relationship between policies and results usually requires specialized research. Fortunately, a good deal of evaluation research is conducted by government agencies and outside organizations.

A thorough evaluation of public policy also requires looking beyond contemporary policy debates. Policymakers should anticipate and address problems before they become unmanageable crises or potential catastrophes. Only governments have the broad powers to act on behalf of an entire state or nation. Scientists warn, for example, that greenhouse gases (GHGs), such as methane and carbon dioxide, are causing the earth's temperature to rise. They predict that unless the use of fuels that produce these gases is curtailed, the earth's fragile ecology may be severely damaged. Many countries around the world have made commitments to reduce their GHG emissions, through the Kyoto Protocol, but the United States has yet to join in the effort. At present, the Environmental Protection Agency (EPA) has developed regulations that take a first step toward limiting GHG emissions, and several states and localities have made commitments to reduce them. However, despite the widespread scientific evidence, significant actions to reduce GHG emissions are difficult to accomplish because they entail painful decisions today, such as raising gas taxes to deter people from driving, which will not yield a safer global environment until much later.[3]

Public perceptions should be carefully considered in judging policy performance, but it would be irresponsible to rely solely on public satisfaction. Public opinions about government policies are often based on fragmentary or unreliable information. Policies should not be judged according to whether an individual feels personally better off than before. The perspective of most citizens is narrow, usually limited to their families, jobs, and neighborhoods. What is good for one family may not be good for another family or for the community as a whole. Majority preferences may be insensitive to minority rights and needs. As we have discussed in several previous chapters, disadvantaged minorities sometimes receive benefits they would probably be denied if public policies were based exclusively on majority sentiment.

Perspectives on the effectiveness of public policy are possible when meaningful comparisons can be made to put the unfiltered evidence into perspective. Placing current policy performance in historical perspective is particularly valuable. Taken as a raw number, a 6 percent unemployment rate does not reveal much. Its significance is established only by comparison with peak levels of 10 percent in 2009. A 6 percent unemployment rate in 2013 would represent a huge improvement over 2009, but would be judged as disappointing in comparison with the 4 percent level achieved in 2000.

Comparing U.S. policy performance with experiences in other countries may also be useful, if handled with care. For instance, the fact that infant mortality rates are higher in the United States than in forty other countries even though the United States spends more per capita for health care than any other nation suggests that many Americans have inadequate access to health care.[4] Conversely, there may be little comfort from the fact that U.S. toxic waste cleanup efforts lead in comparison with those of other nations if there is ample evidence of continuing threats to human health from toxic chemicals being dumped in the United States.

Comparisons of different states, communities, and population subgroups may also yield insights. Ideally, analysts would like to know what conditions would have been like without a public policy or program. Because such knowledge is often unattainable, analysts compare states that have programs with those that do not, or compare groups in the population that have received services with those that have not. In this way, it may be possible to understand what difference the program made in people's lives. Such methods are often labeled "natural experiments," but it is important to exercise caution because there are so many important differences between states or communities and population subgroups that a straight comparison may be misleading.

In the following review of five principal policy goals, we examine how the United States measures up by comparing current performance with announced objectives, and by looking at historical and cross-national comparisons where appropriate. The effects of public policies on different groups of Americans are highlighted. In each section, we consider accomplishments, failures, and unanswered questions. The summary is a discussion of the challenges facing the nation and its leaders in the years ahead.

DEFENDING THE NATION

The U.S. Constitution declares that a primary purpose of government is to "provide for the common defense." Nothing could be more fundamental than ensuring the survival of the nation, protecting its vital economic interests, and preserving the freedom of its citizens. Americans and their leaders have had grave concerns about the nation's security since World War II. These anxieties derive from the perception that in the age of nuclear weapons and dependence on foreign oil supplies, foreign powers and terrorist organizations—"nonstate actors"—are potential or real adversaries capable of seriously threatening U.S. economic interests and national security.

Consequently, since the late 1940s, a bipartisan consensus has existed in favor of maintaining sufficient military power to deter nations from pursuing hostile intentions.[5] The American commitment extends beyond defending U.S. soil, citizens, and overseas investments. U.S. policymakers believe that military force and the threat of nuclear retaliation must be used to protect allies, and to counter attempts by hostile nations to expand their influence. American lives and military resources were spent defending Korea and Vietnam from communist regimes in the 1950s and 1960s, and in protecting Middle East oil supplies during the 1991 Persian Gulf War. In 2010, about $45 billion in U.S. foreign economic and military aid was distributed throughout the world—to Egypt, Israel, Columbia, Russia, Pakistan, and two dozen other countries.[6]

With the collapse of the Soviet Union and the spread of democracy to previously communist nations, the United States reassessed its military position. President Clinton reduced the military budget significantly during his first term, and defense spending remained relatively low throughout his presidency. However, after the attacks on the World Trade Center in New York City and the Pentagon in Washington, military spending increased significantly, rising from less than $300 billion in 2000 to nearly $700 billion in 2010.[7] Although no longer facing a threat from one large adversary, the former Soviet Union, the U.S. military has been deployed many times in the past two decades in other countries and at home.

During the 1990s, the U.S. military, in cooperation with forces of the North Atlantic Treaty Organization (NATO), was deployed to quell regional conflicts, such as the internal conflicts in Kosovo and Bosnia, and to enforce democratic elections in Haiti. The military has also been called in when the proliferation of nuclear and chemical weapons by foreign countries, such as India, Iran, North Korea, and Pakistan, has threatened the nation's interests.

In the twenty-first century, the U.S. has been deeply involved in combating terrorist organizations throughout the Middle East and the world, especially in Afghanistan and Iraq.

Soldiers and Dollars

Disputes over national security policy have often been heated. When should U.S. military forces be involved in hostile actions? American involvement in Vietnam provoked one of the most damaging internal political conflicts in the nation's history, and it has had lasting effects. How much conventional military and nuclear weaponry does the country need? Critics argue that the military establishment and many U.S. politicians have exaggerated the threats posed by the Soviet Union, China, Iran, and Iraq and that the defense budget is larger than is necessary. Supporters of a large defense budget maintain that a high price must be paid to protect U.S. interests at home and abroad. Swift military victories in Grenada, Panama, and Iraq in the 1980s and 1990s helped vindicate U.S. defense policymakers who argued that overwhelming U.S. military power could be used effectively without great cost in American lives. In stark contrast to this, during the early years of the new century, the U.S military was bogged down for over a decade in Iraq and Afghanistan. Combat operations ended in Iraq in late 2011, and a similar pull-back of troops is scheduled to occur in Afghanistan by the end of 2014.

National security policy not only affects the nation's survival and prosperity, it also influences domestic priorities and is influenced by them. The funds that remain after defense spending requirements have been met determine what else the government can do; defense spending was estimated to cost $716 billion in 2012, or 18 percent of total budget outlays that year.[8] Strong national security involves the fostering of industries to design and manufacture ships, submarines, tanks, airplanes, and nuclear weapons. For example, the cost of constructing an aircraft carrier, such as the U.S.S. *Gerald R. Ford*, under construction in 2012, was estimated to be more than $12.5 billion. Such a massive project employs thousands of workers and involves companies located in 330 of the 435 congressional districts and forty-five states.[9]

The strength and self-reliance of a nation's economy shapes the strategies that must be taken to defend it. The United States is one of the most independent and self-sustaining nations in the world; it has abundant raw materials necessary for survival and adequate food supplies for the entire population. Yet the United States depends on other nations for oil and other materials, and it sells its products and services around the world. Hence, U.S. policymakers must be concerned with the political, military, and economic situations in dozens of other nations. The U.S. use of military power to deter terrorist attacks in 2001, or to support overthrowing a repressive regime in Libya in 2011, was swift and decisive. In contrast, the United States did not intervene to aid insurgents in Egypt, Iran, or Syria from 2010 to 2012, confirming that U.S. policymakers are selective about the use of military power to deal with problems in foreign countries.

Unlike inflation, air pollution, or crime, national security problems are not "experienced" by large segments of the American public, except in times of war. Nevertheless, the defense establishment is large, with 1.4 million active-duty men and women, over 700 civilian employees, and over 1 million Reserve and National Guard troops in 2013.[10] During more than ten years of military engagement in Afghanistan and Iraq, over 2 million military personnel have been deployed to these countries. Still, this represents less than 1 percent of Americans.[11] Since the mid-1970s, U.S. armed forces personnel have been volunteers, a change that reshaped the composition of the military substantially. Soldiers in the modern volunteer army are not drafted against their will, and are more likely than in the past to come from low-income and rural areas.

The size of the defense budget is based on perceptions of risk and assumptions about the strategies that will be most effective in minimizing those risks. Unlike the planning of government entitlement programs, in which eligible populations are precisely defined and spending determined accordingly, the task of constructing defense budgets is a deadly guessing game involving serious questions. How great is the military threat posed by foreign powers? To what extent should the United States shield other nations against military attack? Under what circumstances should the United States respond to situations in which potential adversaries wield military power? When should the United States attempt to resolve ethnic and sectarian conflicts in other nations? If military power is inadequate to protect vital economic interests, the problem may not be apparent until it is too late to do anything about it.

The ups and downs of U.S. military expenditures since the end of World War II reflect changing perceptions of the threat to U.S. interests at home and abroad. From 1945 through the 1960s, military spending constituted nearly 9 percent of the gross domestic product (GDP). By the 1970s, the defense budget had dropped to 6 percent of the GDP, despite the expenses connected with the Vietnam War. By 1980, at the end of Jimmy Carter's administration, defense spending had fallen to 5.4 percent of the GDP.[12] By the end of President Clinton's second term, in 2000, defense spending had declined to about 3 percent of the GDP, but because of the long-running wars in Iraq and Afghanistan, defense spending had climbed to 5 percent of the GDP in 2010.[13] Defense spending accounted for more than 50 percent of the federal budget in 1960, 42 percent in 1970, and 23 percent in 1980.[14] As noted above, in 2012, 18 percent of the federal budget was set aside for defense spending, but the Obama administration announced plans to decrease defense spending in 2013.[15]

How Much Is Enough?

Is the United States capable of protecting itself against terrorist attacks and projecting its influence around the world? Did massive military buildups during the Reagan and George H. W. Bush administrations force the former Soviet Union to the bargaining table and bring about the first arms control agreement that resulted in the destruction of an entire class of nuclear weapons? Did U.S. military might enable the country to effectively conduct the war in the Persian

Gulf in 1991 with fewer American casualties? Have the wars in Afghanistan and Iraq, and homeland security efforts, prevented terrorist attacks on the United States since 2001?

There is little doubt that Reagan's military policies played a role in arms negotiations with the Soviets, but many would argue that the former Soviet Union was willing to bargain because of its need to reduce defense spending and to improve relations with the rest of the industrial world. After the collapse of the Soviet empire, U.S. nuclear capability on the ground, in submarines, and in bombers was unrivaled. Critics argue that the massive military buildup of the 1980s increased the likelihood that U.S. policymakers would resort to deadly force in situations in which diplomacy and economic sanctions would have worked just as effectively and without great loss of lives. Finally, as we learned after 9/11, military might does little to deter suicidal terrorist attacks on U.S. citizens and military personnel.

After the Vietnam War, American politicians were usually reluctant to engage U.S. forces in armed conflict abroad. However, U.S. intervention in the first Persian Gulf War was favorably received by the public largely because Americans perceived that a vital economic interest—the supply of oil—was at stake and because the war lasted less than two months and involved few casualties. President George H. W. Bush claimed the successful conduct of the Persian Gulf War would remove public skepticism about our ability to use the military abroad effectively. But such concerns reemerged quickly over U.S. military involvement in Somalia in 1991. President Clinton and the public were reluctant to send troops into Kosovo as part of a NATO peacekeeping force despite increasing reports of Serbian aggression against Kosovar civilians in 1998 and 1999.[16] Public opinion favored military action to hunt down terrorists and destroy their base of operations in Afghanistan. Americans were far more skeptical about invading Iraq, and when the two wars continued for more than a decade and U.S. casualties mounted, Americans were far less supportive, which suggests that public distrust of U.S. troop commitments in armed conflicts abroad will continue to shape foreign policy.

The protracted wars in Afghanistan and Iraq have been costly in many ways. By 2012, Congress had appropriated almost $1.5 trillion of funds targeted for use in these wars.[17] However, estimates of the full cost of these wars, taking into account such items as interest on the money borrowed to fight the wars, homeland security spending for the war on terror, and the social and medical costs for veterans is estimated by a Brown University study to be $3.5 trillion.[18] Casualties are another major cost. Over 30,000 American combatants were wounded, and 4,500 killed, in the Iraq War; for the ongoing war in Afghanistan, the figures as of January 2013 were 2,188 killed and 18,215 wounded.[19] In addition, there have been a disturbing number of suicides among military personnel; in fact, by 2012, more military members were dying of suicide than in combat.[20]

As these cost and casualty figures make clear, America has paid a high price for its war on terrorism. The key question, then, is, have we achieved our objectives? There have been no successful attacks on U.S. soil since 2001; one objective achieved. The al-Qaida network has been badly damaged over the past decade, with many of its leaders, including Osama bin Laden, either captured or killed. However, new al-Qaida groups have emerged, especially in Africa. Iraq's American-supported government has been relatively stable since our troop withdrawal, which is positive, but its future is by no means secure. The American-backed government in Afghanistan has been problematic for many years, and it is not at all clear that a non-Taliban government can survive in that country if American troops are withdrawn. Looking at the Middle East more broadly, our extensive efforts to encourage stable, democratic, pro-Western governments in key countries such as Afghanistan, Iran, Iraq, and Pakistan have been, at best, moderately successful.

ACHIEVING SUSTAINED ECONOMIC GROWTH

Sustained economic growth, like national security, is a central policy goal of all governments. This broad goal subsumes several specific economic objectives: rising standards of living and wealth, low levels of unemployment and inflation, increasing productivity of the workforce, and expanding exports. Policymakers of all stripes want to promote economic growth and vitality. For more than a decade, the sharpest partisan and ideological disputes have revolved around the extent to which the government can and should manage the economy. Today this partisan division on economic issues can be seen between Democrats and Republicans in Congress. Republicans favor less regulation and lower taxes, especially for upper-income taxpayers. Democrats, in contrast, support more regulation, more extensive public services, lower taxes for middle-income and working-class taxpayers, and higher taxes on upper-income Americans—families earning more than $450,000 annually.

The achievement of economic goals depends, perhaps more than any other policy objective, on the policies and financial resources of the government and the private sector. In general, government involvement in fostering a healthy economy takes two forms: *macroeconomic policy* decisions, and decisions about *investment* in human capital, research, and the nation's physical infrastructure, such as highways, ports, and airports. Macroeconomic policy encompasses matters such as the government's spending and tax policy, the supply and cost of money, and trade policies with other nations. When the economy is not expanding or is contracting (measured as a percentage of GDP from one quarter to the next), unemployment will increase, and the government may increase public and private spending through fiscal and monetary stimulation, which in turn generates greater demand for goods and services and puts more people to work. The strategy of new spending and tax cuts formed the central component of the Obama administration's response to the Great Recession, as noted in chapter 2.

The Federal Reserve Board decisions that establish the size of the money supply and the level of interest rates profoundly influence the rate of inflation in the price of goods and services, and the ability of individuals and corporations to raise capital. By setting interest rates low, as the Federal Reserve did during and after the Great Recession, the board was hoping to inject more private sector borrowing, which would lead to growth and lower levels of unemployment.

Government-sponsored education and research strategies also affect the ability of the nation to achieve its economic goals. Education and training programs translate directly into improvement in the quality and productivity of the workforce. America's colleges and universities have produced one of the most highly educated populations in the world, but the supply of qualified individuals may not be meeting the demand in some fields. For example, bachelor's degrees in computer science and electrical engineering decreased by 1 percent from 2000 to 2009.[21] According to an influential study by the McKinsey Global Institute:

> By 2008, foreign-born workers accounted for 17 percent of all employment in STEM (science, technology, engineering, and math) occupations in the United States. . . . [Advanced economies] will also need to guide more students to job-relevant training (in the United States, for example, only 14 percent of college degrees awarded are in STEM fields) . . . significantly lower than the ratio in China (42 percent), South Korea (35 percent), and Germany (28 percent).[22]

Government-sponsored research and development activities often generate new products and increase economic growth. In 2008, more than half (57 percent) of the money spent on basic research and development in the United States was supplied by the federal government.[23] Since 1962, government research in the aerospace industry has yielded numerous products and productivity improvements. For example, the demand for lightweight, reliable circuitry helped spawn the development of microchips, which eventually led to the development of the personal computer. Historically, countries with the highest rates of growth in research and development expenditures have also experienced greater gains in productivity and had higher GDPs.[24]

Finally, the quality of the nation's infrastructure is vital to a prosperous economy. The federal government spends about $120 billion per year on infrastructure construction projects, which is far short of what many experts think is needed.[25] Bridges, roads, and water systems are simply wearing out. A recent report released as part of the Renewing America project of the Council on Foreign Relations suggests that planned government spending on infrastructure should equal over $400 billion a year in order to meet the demands of our decaying roadways, water systems, public schools, and airports.[26] Most of the funds for this massive undertaking would have to be raised and spent by state governments.

Effective government policies promote a prosperous, competitive economy, but many factors are beyond government control. Private sector decisions have a direct influence on the size and health of the U.S. economy (see chapter 3).

Private businesses generate roughly 60 percent of the nation's GDP and control virtually all major industrial activities. Therefore, the cumulative impact of corporate decisions is significant. If the Ford Motor Company decides to locate a plant to manufacture automobiles for the U.S. market in Mexico, rather than in Atlanta, the decision costs Americans thousands of jobs.

Economic growth also depends on the behavior of investors, workers, and consumers. Workers' productivity and wage demands are important factors in economic expansion. The preference of American consumers for imported products, which are either of higher quality or lower cost—or sometimes both—such as Japanese or Korean automobiles, and electronic equipment or mobile devices manufactured in China, means that billions of American dollars flow to other nations.

Progress and Challenges

The United States has been the world's dominant economic power since the 1950s. American living standards have risen substantially during this period; for example, the per capita income of Americans has more than doubled since 1990.[27] Despite the economic slowdown over the past five years, by many standards the United States remains an economic powerhouse. Nevertheless, it seems proper to conclude that the record is mixed and the future is uncertain.

Despite its strong showing, the U.S. economy has not always outperformed those of other nations. From the mid-1960s to the mid-1980s, the economies of several countries, including Austria, France, Italy, Japan, Norway, and the former West Germany, grew at faster rates than the U.S. economy.[28] Japan's economy expanded at roughly twice the U.S. growth rate. This trend changed during the 1990s, with growth in the United States exceeding that in Japan and most of Europe, both of which experienced slower rates of growth than in the previous decade.[29] However, the spendable earnings of American workers have been declining since 1960.[30] By the mid-1980s, the wages of workers employed in the manufacturing sector in Belgium, the Netherlands, Sweden, and West Germany had surpassed the earnings of American workers in the same industries.[31] Using another measure, GDP per hours worked, workers in Europe did better than workers in the United States from 1979 to 2006.[32] Although the standard of living of American workers remains high in global terms, it is gradually declining relative to that of other industrial countries.

For several decades, American policymakers have faced difficult challenges in developing policies that enabled the U.S. economy to achieve sustained growth, with low unemployment and low inflation. The early years of the twenty-first century have included the worst recession in seventy years, from 2007 to 2009, which was preceded by a period of slow growth in the economy and Americans' incomes. These troubling trends in the American economy were succinctly summarized by economists Harry Holzer and Marek Hlavac:

During the 1980s, we first endured a severe recession, engineered by the Federal Reserve Bank to fight high rates of inflation, and then recovered with a lengthy period of expansion and economic growth. Another and milder recession in the early 1990s was followed by an even more robust period of expansion, often called the "Great Boom" or the "Roaring Nineties," during which high productivity and income growth returned to the U.S. economy. But in the decade of the 2000s, which once again began with a mild recession, the economic picture was more mixed; a shorter period of recovery, during which productivity growth was high but income growth was much lower, was followed by the most severe economic downturn since the 1930s, which is commonly known as the "Great Recession."[33]

As noted in chapter 2, Nobel Prize–winning economist Paul Krugman labeled the first decade of the twenty-first century, the "Big Zero . . . a decade in which nothing good happened and none of the optimistic things we were supposed to believe turned out to be true." He continued that there was "basically zero job creation . . . zero economic gains for the typical family . . . zero gains for home owners" and "zero gains for stocks."[34]

The Great Recession is the latest in a long line of recessions—periods either of no economic growth or of decline. Severe recessions, bringing high levels of unemployment, also occurred in 1954, 1958, 1975, 1979, 1982, 1991, and 2001. Life expectancy is lower in the United States than in thirty-five other nations (as of 2010). Infant mortality rates are higher in the United States than in forty other countries (as of 2011),[35] although they have declined in this country since the early 1960s as a result of the introduction of medical assistance for poor individuals. Since 1970, U.S. unemployment levels, on average (5.5 percent), have exceeded those of several other nations, including Japan (2.9 percent), South Korea (3.7 percent), the Netherlands (5.3 percent), and Sweden (4.8 percent).[36] Although the U.S. economy was very strong in the 1990s, with high rates of growth and low rates of unemployment, the high rates of unemployment from 2009 to the present suggest that it will be difficult for the United States to pull ahead of other nations in this category in the future.

Furthermore, although the sustained economic growth of the 1990s benefited many in the United States, large portions of society were left behind. There continues to be a growing bifurcation of the economic classes, with increasing disparity between the six- to seven-digit incomes of corporate executives and the minimum wage of a growing number of service workers. To compound this, capital flight from the major cities (as well as from U.S. soil altogether) has contributed to the degradation of the nation's urban centers, where large pockets of poverty have left whole communities trapped in the grip of crime and desperation.[37]

Since 2000, only 3 million net new jobs have been added to the U.S. economy, which is not sufficient to absorb the expanding workforce.[38] As discussed in chapter 2, high unemployment has been an on-again, off-again problem.

During the 1950s and 1960s, unemployment was relatively low, averaging 4.5 percent; during the 1970s, the average climbed to 6.5 percent. The average for the 1980s was 7.3 percent, accentuated by high levels in 1982 and 1983, when nearly 11 million Americans were unable to find jobs, but falling by the end of the decade. During the recession of the early 1990s, unemployment rose sharply to 7.5 percent, but then dropped to a record low (since 1970) of 4 percent in the late 1990s. It went back up during the 2001 recession and hovered in the mid-5-percent range until 2005. The few years prior to the Great Recession of 2008 marked the calm before the storm, as unemployment rates dipped back to the mid-4-percent range. In 2009, unemployment rates soared above 9 percent and remained very high through 2011.[39]

As of December 2012, there were 12.2 million unemployed persons and a 7.8 percent unemployment rate. The aggregate figures do not reveal all the underlying problems. Not counted in the official unemployment statistics are the more than 1.1 "discouraged workers"—people who have given up looking for work because they do not believe any jobs are available—and 7.9 million part-time workers who would rather be working full-time.[40] The reported unemployment figures therefore understate the magnitude of the real demand for jobs by Americans.

Older workers who have lost long-term stable jobs because of changes in the structure of the U.S. economy present another vexing problem. Although the service sector (telecommunications, insurance, banking, and restaurants) grew during the 1980s, the manufacturing sector did not. As a result, many workers have been displaced—that is, they lost their jobs permanently. It has not been uncommon for displaced workers to take positions offering lower pay, longer hours, and reduced benefits. Millions of construction, automobile, and manufacturing workers were displaced during the Great Recession.

The United States has also struggled with inflation in the prices of goods and services during several decades. From 1950 to the mid-1960s, prices increased, on average, no more than 2 percent or 3 percent annually. From 1968 to 1973, prices rose at a 4.8 percent average rate, but from 1973 to 1980, the average rate nearly doubled to 8.9 percent. Double-digit annual inflation rates were reached in 1974, 1980, and 1981. After reaching peak levels in the early 1980s, inflation rates dropped significantly in the 1990s, hovering around 3 percent for that decade and in the first decade of the 2000s. Average inflation from 2000 to 2012 was 2.5 percent; it reached a high of 3.8 percent in 2008, but once the Great Recession took hold, it dropped sharply and hit its lowest rate since 1955 of −0.4 percent in 2009.[41] In recognition of the change from great concern about inflation in the 1970s and 1980s to great concern about unemployment since the Great Recession, the Federal Reserve announced in late 2012 that it was tying its interest rate policy to the unemployment rate (not to inflation, as it had for many years); thus, it planned to keep interest rates low as long as the unemployment rate exceeded 6.5 percent.[42]

The preceding discussion suggests that the American economy performed best during the decade of the 1990s. This period featured poverty rates well below those of the 1950s and 1960s, strong economic growth rates, relatively low unemployment, and low inflation. Is there a policy dimension to this success? One important policy that was in place was federal budget discipline. The 1990 Budget and Enforcement Act required Congress to set annual caps on discretionary spending and follow the PAYGO (pay as you go) protocol for entitlement programs. The latter meant that any legislation that Congress might pass that would lead to greater deficits, such as adding a prescription drug benefit to Medicare, had to be offset by either raising more revenue (taxes) or reducing spending in another entitlement program. As we have discussed in previous chapters, PAYGO was in place throughout the decade, which ended with the government running surpluses, but was abandoned after 9/11 (another major cost of the war on terror). Income tax rates during the 1990s were higher than those in the 2000s because George W. Bush's tax cuts were not yet in place. And regulation of the financial industry was stricter—the legislation that deregulated this sector was not passed until 1999.

ENSURING EQUAL OPPORTUNITY

Since the founding of the nation, America's leaders have espoused a commitment to equality of opportunity. But when Thomas Jefferson, a slave owner himself, wrote in the Declaration of Independence that "all men are created equal," he did not include African Americans, women, or Native Americans. Over time, government policies have gradually extended political, social, and economic opportunities to groups originally denied them. The Constitution has been amended to ensure political rights for African Americans and women. Statutes prohibiting discrimination on the basis of race, gender, ethnicity, age, disability, and sexual orientation have been applied to education, employment, housing, voting, and public accommodations and the purchase of goods and services by the federal government.

The nation's moral credo rejects discrimination and advocates equal opportunity, but living up to this code and giving it practical meaning have been as difficult to accomplish as any aspect of American public policy. The battle over racial equality was marked by lynchings, bombings of black churches, and other horrible incidents. The uncomfortable chasm between American ideals and the actual distribution of opportunities and benefits has properly been called an American dilemma.[43] Americans place a high value on individual initiative and self-reliance. But there is a growing awareness that even in a democracy, prosperity that is not shared is prosperity soon disdained. Working toward and giving people a sense of fairness is the glue that holds a democratic society together. The late economist Arthur Okun commented that U.S. society awards prizes that allow the big winners to feed their pets better than the losers can feed their children. For example, in 2011, the average income of U.S. families in the top 20 percent of the income distribution was $101,583, or more than five times that of the poorest 20 percent of families, which averaged $20,262.[44] By comparison with other advanced economies that are members of the Organisation for Economic Co-operation and Development (OECD), the average income of U.S. families in the top 20 percent of the income distribution was eight times that of the poorest 20 percent of families in 2007, which meant that the United States had the fourth highest rate of income inequality and relative poverty within the OECD.[45] In 2011, American CEOs made 231 times the pay of the average worker, with an average annual salary package for a CEO, including stock options and bonuses, of more than $11 million. From 1978 to 2011, the average worker's annual compensation increased by 5.7 percent, compared with 726.7 percent for CEOs' annual compensation during this same time period.[46] Such is the double standard of a capitalist democracy, professing and pursuing an egalitarian political and social system and simultaneously generating gaping disparities in economic well-being.[47]

A policy goal of achieving equal opportunity raises four essential questions about what equal opportunity means and how the government should promote it:

1. Should government guarantees of equal opportunities encompass both the political system and the economic system?

2. To what extent is the government obligated to redress past discrimination against particular groups of Americans?

3. Should government promote greater equality in the distribution of wealth and other social benefits?

4. How do our government, business, and educational institutions ensure access to all citizens?

Unfulfilled Promises

The United States has made significant strides in the area of equal opportunity, especially since the early 1960s. Women, African Americans, and other minorities are no longer denied the right to vote or hold office. The U.S. armed forces no longer place black and white Americans in separate fighting units, and allow women to enter combat units. The Supreme Court has declared that all children in a particular community should be educated in the same schools, regardless of race. Congress has determined that Americans must not be discriminated against because of their race, gender, disabilities, ethnic origin, or sexual orientation when they apply to colleges and universities, seek employment or housing, and apply for insurance and bank loans. White Americans have become more racially tolerant (see chapter 2). An African American, Barack Obama, was elected president in 2008 and reelected in 2012.

Despite these significant accomplishments, America remains a society in which millions do not fully enjoy the nation's political, social, and economic benefits. Poverty, homelessness, and hunger remain serious problems in one of the world's most affluent nations. After dropping to 11 percent in 1973 from 22 percent in 1960, poverty gradually increased in the 1980s. In 1989, more than 31 million people, or 13 percent of the population, could not afford the basic necessities of life as defined by government standards. The poverty rate for children was even higher.[48] The overall poverty rate dropped to 12.7 percent of the population in 1998, but this still means that 34.5 million Americans were below the poverty level for that year. The number of poor children was 15.75 million in 2010, or 21.6 percent of people in the United States under the age of eighteen, which means more than one in five children in the United States lived in poverty that year.[49]

Income and wealth are unequally distributed. The bottom 20 percent of all U.S. families received only 3.3 percent of the aggregate household income in 2010; the top 20 percent received more than fifteen times that much, or 50.3 percent of the total.[50] Inequities in the distribution of income have grown sharply and consistently since the 1980s, and appear to be widening further and becoming a more salient political issue.[51] As noted above, America ranks thirtieth among the thirty-four members of the OECD in income equality, with only Israel, Mexico, and Chile being more unequal, while Australia, Canada, Ireland, the Netherlands, Germany, Switzerland, Japan, Sweden, the United Kingdom, and others are more equal.[52] The ownership of wealth is even more unevenly distributed than income; the top 1 percent of all U.S. families held 35.4 percent of the net wealth in 2010 (up from 33.4 percent in 2001), whereas the bottom 80 percent held only 11.1 percent (down from 15.6 percent in 2001).[53]

Federal, state, and local tax systems do little to redistribute income, and in some ways they increase inequities. Political scientist Benjamin Page remarked in the early 1980:

> The federal income tax is more egalitarian than other taxes. But the progressivity of the actual effective rates—as contrasted with the nominal schedule rates—is rather mild and has been eroded over time. Taxes on the rich are not very high. . . . Various exclusions and exemptions and deductions from taxable income greatly benefit the rich.[54]

The tax code revision of 1986 eliminated millions of poor and near-poor Americans from the tax rolls, but even after these major changes, tax laws remained inequitable. To address this problem, in 1993 President Clinton signed the largest expansion of the Earned Income Tax Credit (EITC) into law; it provided a refundable tax credit for 15 million working poor families. The popularity of this antipoverty policy stems from its ability to provide both "work incentives and tax relief for low-income workers and their families."[55] In 2001, President George W. Bush reformed and expanded the EITC program to include more married couples, and proposed certain EITC-related provisions to be extended permanently.[56] However, by 2004, the Bush administration had turned its attention to compliance, and funded a $100 million Internal Revenue Service venture to help find erroneous and fraudulent EITC activity.[57]

Shortly after the Great Recession of 2008, the Obama administration and Congress passed two pieces of legislation (the 2009 American Recovery and Reinvestment Act [ARRA] and the Tax Relief, Unemployment Insurance Reauthorization, and Job Creation Act of 2010) that temporarily expanded the EITC program for families who had three or more children and for married couples. The EITC program also spread to the states, and now twenty-three states and the District of Columbia have enacted their own versions of the EITC.[58] In 2011, 27 million families received nearly $60 billion from this refundable tax credit, and the policy has become one of the largest antipoverty tools in the United States.[59]

People earning the same levels of income often pay very different amounts in federal taxes. High-income Americans may pay less in taxes than people who earn a great deal less. Consider the tax situation for Warren Buffett, one of the world's wealthiest people and CEO of Berkshire Hathaway. During Obama's second-term presidential campaign, Buffett became a vocal advocate for higher taxes on top earners and millionaires after he discovered that he pays a lower percentage of his income in total federal taxes than his secretary or anyone else in his office.[60] Inequities persist because the tax code contains a host of exclusions, preferences, and deductions. For example, homeowners are permitted to deduct all of the interest they pay on mortgages for their primary residences and for vacation homes; thus, the owner of a $60,000 house and the owner of a $5 million mansion can deduct the entire amount of their interest payments from their tax liability. This tax subsidy is often thought to be regressive in nature because wealthy individuals in higher tax brackets actually earn more from the subsidy. The home mortgage deduction amounts to a direct subsidy of more than $131 billion per year, much of which goes to higher income individuals who borrow large amounts to purchase expensive homes.[61] Clearly, the distribution of those taking advantage of the mortgage and other tax deductions is uneven. In 2009, for example, a total of 49 percent of the itemized tax write-offs were housing-related: 96 percent of households earning above $200,000 itemized deductions on their tax returns, compared with only 15 percent of households below $50,000.[62] People who rent or have modest mortgage payments receive little or no tax benefits.[63]

If federal income taxes do little to redistribute income from rich to poor individuals, payroll taxes and state and local income taxes accomplish the opposite: the more money a person is paid, the lower the percentage of income paid to the government. Social Security taxes, for example, are withheld at a flat rate (6.2 percent) on earnings up to $110,100. Thus, the $500,000 per year investment banker on Wall Street pays the same amount in Social Security taxes as the $110,100 per year civil engineer.[64] State and local taxes, which rely heavily on the sales tax, are regressive. People with low incomes pay the same tax rate as those with high incomes. But a larger share of a poor person's income is used to purchase the goods and services necessary for survival.[65]

These disparities are especially difficult to justify in a society in which economic hardship is not random. Minorities are much more likely to be poor, unemployed, and otherwise disadvantaged than white Americans. In 2011, the poverty rate for African Americans was 27.6 percent and for Hispanics 25.3 percent, but only 9.8 percent for whites.[66] Unemployment rates follow a similar pattern. In December 2012, for example, the unemployment rate for white adults was 6.9 percent, but it was 14.0 percent for African Americans and 9.6 percent for Hispanics. The picture is even bleaker for young people. In December 2012, 21.6 percent of white teens were unemployed, as opposed to 40.5 percent of African American teenagers.[67]

In 2011, more than 31.2 percent of female-headed families lived below the poverty level compared with 16.1 percent of male-headed families (no wife present), continuing a trend that has been called the feminization of poverty.[68] In 2011, of all those living in poverty, 55 percent were women, and 16.3 percent of women were in poverty, compared with 13.6 percent of men.[69] This has profound effects on children living in poverty. Children living in female-headed families are four times more likely to be living in poverty compared with their peers living in married-couple families.[70] Moreover, among all children living in single female-headed families in 2011, 47.6 percent were classified as poor.[71] Many women are poor even though they work at full-time, year-round jobs. Sixty-three percent of minimum-wage earners in 2012 were women.[72] Because of inflation, the purchasing power of their minimum-wage jobs has eroded since the early 1980s. Even though the minimum wage increased to $7.25 in 2009, it is "now far below its historical level . . . by all of the most commonly used benchmarks—inflation, average wages, and productivity."[73] To remain commensurate to the peak minimum wage rate of 1968, the current minimum wage rate would have to increase to $10.52, when indexed to the official Consumer Price Index.[74]

Progress for minorities has been slow because in many ways, the United States remains a racially segregated society. Minority groups are concentrated in cities; they may be kept from living in suburban communities by discriminatory real estate sales practices, or the lack of affordable housing for moderate- and low-income individuals. Efforts to desegregate the schools have had limited success. A relatively high number of African Americans (24 percent) attended schools where African Americans made up at least one-quarter to one-half of the student body in the 2008 school year, and more than 12 percent of African Americans attended schools that were at least 75 percent African American.[75] Conversely, in that same year, only 10.4 percent of whites attended schools that were 25 percent to 49.9 percent white, while 50 percent of white children attended schools that were at least 75 percent white.[76] According to a recent report in the *New York Times*, "Across the country, 43 percent of Latinos and 38 percent of blacks attend schools where fewer than 10 percent of their classmates are white."[77] Moreover, by 2009, the typical white student attended a college where black students made up less than 10 percent of the students on campus.[78]

Women have not achieved economic and political parity with men. Women have increased their participation in the workforce from 42 percent in 1970 to over 47.2 percent in 2012, and laws guaranteeing equal pay for equal work have been passed in many states.[79] Still, in 2010, women earned on average seventy-seven cents for every dollar earned by men.[80] Women are concentrated in several occupations (teaching, nursing, child care, and clerical positions) that pay less than occupations predominantly held by men (accountants, construction workers, and physicians), even though the female-dominated jobs require similar levels of skill and training. Although women constitute more than half of the U.S. population, half of college graduates, and more than half of college students, there are relatively few women in high-ranking corporate positions and in elected positions in the United States (see chapter 9).[81]

Prospects for Change

Strategies promoting social, political, and economic equity have been highly controversial and only moderately successful. The women's movement failed to obtain ratification of the Equal Rights Amendment to the Constitution in the 1970s. Although the Supreme Court has endorsed some versions of affirmative action to promote the hiring of women and minorities, the practice is still subject to legal challenge and to resistance from many institutions. The first, and perhaps most notable, case challenging affirmative action was the landmark Supreme Court case of *Regents of the University of California v. Bakke* (1978), which imposed limitations on affirmative action in professional school admissions by ruling that the use of inflexible quotas was not a legitimate practice. This precedent was followed by *Hopwood v. University of Texas Law School* (1996), in which the U.S. Court of Appeals for the Fifth Circuit suspended the university's affirmative action program, asserting that race could not serve as a factor in admissions. The anti–affirmative action atmosphere heightened during the 1990s when two states, California and Washington, banned all affirmative action programs; several other states followed suit in the first decade of the twenty-first century.[82] In 2003, the Supreme Court found that diversity was a "compelling government interest," and upheld (in a 5-4 vote) the admission program of the University of Michigan's Law School (*Grutter v. Bollinger*), while rejecting (in a 6-3 vote) Michigan's undergraduate admissions process, which awarded points to minority applicants (*Gratz v. Bollinger*).[83] In *Grutter*, the Court ruling stated that race could be used in a public university's admissions process in a "flexible non-mechanic way," and "as one factor among many" when assembling a student body.[84] Nine years later affirmative action in higher education was challenged again at the Supreme Court level, and in the case *Fisher v. University of Texas* the Court retained the *Grutter* precedent (that race could be considered in admissions), but instructed lower courts to use more stringent standards in reviewing race-conscious university admission programs.[85]

The tax policy changes of the Reagan and George W. Bush administrations did not address inequities in the distribution of income and wealth, and the Democratic Party has not advanced any bold or promising initiatives to redistribute income in America. President Clinton enacted policies that addressed this unequal distribution by allowing working families to keep more of their income through the EITC and by modestly increasing taxes for the richest Americans; however, as discussed above, income inequality persisted throughout the 1990s. This was exacerbated by George W. Bush, who persuaded Congress to lower rates across the board—a policy that was disproportionately beneficial to upper income families. During the 2012 presidential campaign, President Obama frequently complained about the inequities of the Bush-era tax policies and vowed to return income tax rates to Clinton-era levels for individuals earning $200,000 or more and for couples earning $250,000 or more. As noted in chapter 5, after the election, the president and Republicans in Congress were able to reach an agreement to increase income taxes on individuals earning more than $400,000 and on couples earning more than $450,000. Taxes were also increased on unearned income—interest and dividends—and on estates.

A potential impetus for revising education policies to benefit low- and moderate-income earners may come from the desire of American business and industry to remain competitive in the world economy. Many business leaders, though certainly not all, believe that the nation must fully use available human resources. Even with the high unemployment rates of late 2008 to 2012, there are job openings that remain unfilled because there are not enough skilled workers in some fields. When job openings are not filled, the overall economic output of the country is diminished, and unemployed workers' standard of living falls. These two factors may combine to motivate significant changes in U.S. workforce development policy in the coming years.[86] With regard to equal opportunity, it seems clear that affirmative action, as it was practiced in the 1970s and 1980s, is dying a slow death. The Supreme Court has moved steadily toward the position that laws and programs in the United States should be blind with regard to race and gender. This raises a crucial question: can equality of opportunity advance in a society of vast wealth and income disparities with a legal environment that prohibits public and private institutions from taking race and gender into account when deciding whom to hire, whom to let in, and how to distribute benefits?

PROVIDING A SAFETY NET

The power of government has not been exercised in an attempt to achieve a radical redistribution of income and wealth, but American policymakers have erected a network of programs that provide financial support and health care to millions of citizens. These measures may not always lift poor individuals out of poverty, but they keep people from falling further into it. Initiated by liberal Democratic president Franklin D. Roosevelt in the 1930s, and expanded by Lyndon Johnson's Great Society, these social insurance and social welfare programs have been considered an essential "safety net," even by conservative Republican presidents Ronald Reagan and George W. Bush.

The vast array of programs that support elderly, poor, unemployed, and disabled Americans, including Medicare, Medicaid, Social Security, unemployment insurance, the Supplemental Nutrition Assistance Program (SNAP; formerly named Food Stamps), and others, consume the largest proportion of the federal budget. These safety net programs have grown so quickly since the 1950s that politicians are beginning to ask some very tough questions. Can Americans afford these programs? Can the country afford to be without them? How can these programs be made more efficient and equitable?

Income-Support Programs

Since the New Deal, the basic structure of the American welfare state has expanded to encompass new classes of beneficiaries and to authorize more generous benefits. Once a small fraction of the budget, income-support programs now account for approximately 37 percent of federal outlays and constitute a large portion of state and local spending.[87] Income-support programs amounted to less than 3 percent of the GDP in 1960; by 1990, they amounted to nearly three times as much, and by 2011, they constituted 10 percent of real GDP and 8 percent nominal GDP.[88] Annual federal expenditures for income-support programs increased from $240 billion in 1981 to above $1.3 trillion in 2011, or by over $1 trillion in thirty years.[89] During the 1980s, the trend of extending eligibility and expanding benefits slowed, but safety net spending continued its upward trend.[90] President George W. Bush convinced Congress to expand the safety net by adding insurance coverage for prescriptions drugs in 2003. In 2010, President Obama and Congress enacted sweeping health care reforms that sought to bring insurance coverage to up to 30 million uninsured people beginning in 2014.

The number of Americans benefiting from the safety net has grown by leaps and bounds. Social Security—which aids retirees, the children of deceased workers, and disabled workers—is the largest federal program, with expenditures of $725 billion in 2012.[91] In 2012, slightly more than one in six Americans received Social Security retirement checks, and 94 percent of the working population contributed through payroll tax deductions to the program.[92] In 2012, an average of 12.5 million Americans received unemployment compensation, with a national average benefit amount of $300 weekly, and most of the nation's more than 143 million workers are employed by companies that contribute to the federal-state unemployment insurance system.[93] Approximately 46 million people received SNAP benefits in a given month during 2012, for a total of over $86 billion in benefits that year.[94]

Income-support programs come in two forms: programs dispensed according to need and programs distributed without regard to need. As explained in chapter 1, many income-support programs are called "entitlement" programs because people receive benefits if they meet the standards specified in public laws. The largest income-support programs, including Social Security and unemployment insurance, are available to eligible recipients no matter what their income or assets may be. Therefore, most income-support programs are not subject to a means test: full benefits are extended to rich and poor Americans alike. About 75 percent of the funds reserved for older Americans do not require applicants to demonstrate financial need.[95]

Social Security and unemployment insurance replace part of the income lost because of retirement, disability, or unemployment. In 2012, retirees who made average earnings during their working years received Social Security benefits accounting for about 41 percent of their past earnings.[96] A typical unemployed worker is paid about $1,200 per month, or about a 46.2 percent replacement of his or her income.[97] Unemployment insurance typically lasts only six months, and is open only to those workers who lost their jobs through "no fault of their own"; the "insured unemployed" represented about 31 percent of the total number of unemployed workers in 2010.[98]

Social Security and unemployment insurance are based on the concept of social insurance. During their lifetime working years, average wage earners contribute about 16 percent of their incomes into the Social Security Trust Fund to help cover the cost of benefits they may eventually receive.[99] For unemployment insurance, employers pay into an insurance trust fund from which workers receive benefits during periods of unemployment. Intended as a partial supplement to private pension plans and family incomes, Social Security provides a financial base for those who could not adequately prepare for retirement. Social Security is the nation's strongest antipoverty program, along with Medicare insurance for senior citizens. These two programs have contributed substantially to reducing the number of older Americans who are poor. Once, elderly Americans were a disadvantaged group: In 1960, more than 25 percent of the nation's senior citizens lived in poverty. In 2011, 8.7 percent of elderly individuals were poor.[100] Median family incomes of elderly Americans increased by 28 percent from 1974 to 2005.[101] In fact, their incomes have increased faster than the incomes of the rest of the population. The average Social Security check for a retiree in 2012 was $1,234 per month, which by itself provides sufficient income to live above government-defined poverty levels.[102] In fact, without Social Security, almost half of elderly Americans would be poor; the program prevents 14 million elderly Americans from living in poverty.[103]

The biggest challenges for administrators of the Social Security program have been controlling growth and keeping the system solvent. The earlier retirements and longer life spans of Americans have imposed new strains on the Social Security Trust Fund. Since the mid-1970s, benefit payments have increased at regular intervals as a result of legislated cost-of-living adjustments and thus roughly keep pace with inflation. Proposals for trimming Social Security benefits nearly always are met with a firestorm of criticism from Democrats and senior citizen groups (such as AARP), which form a large, politically powerful constituency. In the 1980s, a bipartisan reform commission made several short- and long-term changes to the program, but virtually all the modifications increased the funds for distribution, rather than curtailing existing benefits.[104] There are concerns among many members of Congress about the long-term solvency of the trust fund unless future benefits are reduced and/or the age for full retirement benefits is increased. Potential revisions to Social Security benefits, and/or its tax structure, will be among the most contentious and partisan battles that Congress and the president will face in the coming years.

The balance of the federal and state income-support programs is reserved for poor Americans. Aid to Families with Dependent Children (AFDC), the welfare entitlement program that had existed for thirty years, was replaced with block grants to states through the welfare legislation called the Personal Responsibility and Work Opportunity Reconciliation Act, passed in 1996. The new welfare program institutes many changes, including the end of the entitlement status of aid to poor individuals, strict work requirements, lifetime eligibility limits, and new teen parent provisions. Temporary Assistance for Needy Families (TANF) and SNAP benefits are made available only after individuals have proved that they need assistance. A woman must have young children, and no support from her family or the father of her children, to be considered for TANF payments. States receive wide discretion in determining eligibility rules.

The TANF program is paid for by the states and the federal government and administered by states and localities. Benefit levels vary widely. For example, in 2008, the monthly payment for a single-parent family of three in Alabama was $215, whereas in New York, it was $691.[105] Benefits are below the poverty line in all fifty states, ranging from Mississippi, where benefits are $170 per month or 91 percent below the poverty line, to Alaska, where they amount to $923 a month or 49 percent below the poverty line.[106]

Welfare and SNAP consume fewer federal dollars and constitute much smaller portions of federal mandatory spending, about 6 percent, than the non-means-tested entitlement programs such as Medicare and Social Security. Family support programs and nutrition aid for poor individuals cost the federal government approximately $121 billion in fiscal year 2011—about 17 percent of the cost of Social Security alone.[107] SNAP benefits were the fastest growing component of these programs. From 1980 to 2011, the cost of SNAP increased by nearly 213 percent, or about 7 percent each year.[108] Federal spending on SNAP beneficiaries increased sharply in the latter half of the 2000s. The main drivers of this growth were the deep recession, a lagging economic recovery, and the temporary increase in average benefit levels due to the enactment of ARRA. Roughly two-thirds of the growth stemmed from the weakened economy, about one-fifth was tied to the passage of ARRA, and the remainder of the increase was driven by higher food prices and lower incomes among beneficiaries.[109]

Unlike Social Security, which is widely regarded as a successful, but expensive, program, AFDC was disliked by taxpayers and recipients alike. Even though only a small percentage of funds were spent on ineligible people, opinion polls consistently showed that the public perceived the program as awash in corruption and abuse. Welfare recipients and others complained that AFDC payments were stingy and that the system encouraged recipients to remain poor and discouraged their self-reliance. Widespread perceptions that the welfare system was "broken" led to significant welfare reform under the Personal Responsibility and Work Opportunity Reconciliation Act of 1996. As we describe above, the new programs are designed to require recipients to seek full-time employment in order to get off welfare, but they also provide extended health benefits and child care assistance for those who do find jobs, and sanction those who do not comply with the work requirements.

Health Care

America's income-support programs for elderly, poor, and unemployed persons were spawned primarily by the New Deal. The health care programs—Medicare for elderly Americans and Medicaid for poor Americans—were the offspring of Lyndon Johnson's War on Poverty. When Medicare was adopted in 1965, the Social Security Administration estimated that it would cost the federal government $8.2 billion in 1983. This estimate was extremely inaccurate; Medicare actually cost $38 billion in 1983. Federal government expenditures for Medicare were more than $479 billion in 2011; Medicaid cost the federal government another $274 billion.[110] Government health insurance (Medicare, Medicaid, and the Children's Health Insurance Program) pays about 40 percent of hospital costs and doctors' bills for the entire nation.[111] Although government support for health care in the United States still trails that of other industrial nations, the commitment was substantially increased by the passage of the Patient Protection and Affordable Care Act of 2010. When private contributions to health care spending are included, the United States leads the world in the percentage of its GDP devoted to health care (18 percent).[112]

Elderly and poor Americans are the principal beneficiaries of government health care programs, but that will change somewhat when the Affordable Care Act is fully implemented. Medicare serves all Americans over the age of sixty-five years, regardless of need. Program participants pay for part of the cost of physician visits, hospital care, and prescription drugs, but most of the tab is picked up by the government. Medicaid is reserved mostly for people below the poverty level, although eligibility varies somewhat by state. Among those categorized as "low income," which is defined as 138 percent of the federal poverty line, "41 percent of lower-income parents, 43 percent of adults without dependent children, and 16 percent of children were uninsured" in 2010.[113] The Affordable Care Act seeks to change this by eliminating varying state eligibility rules and providing Medicaid coverage to everyone with an income less than 133 percent of the federal poverty level ($31,000 for a family of three in 2012). Thus, starting in 2014, 17 million more low-income people could gain health insurance over the next decade if all states participate in the new program.[114]

Health care costs and government expenditures for health programs have skyrocketed, driven by several factors, including demographics, third-party reimbursement and the Medicare fee-for-service model, advanced technology in medical care, and new drug discoveries. Increases in the aging and poor populations have resulted in greater and greater outlays in Medicare and Medicaid. Medical consumers and medical professionals are not motivated to keep costs down, because the vast majority of medical bills are borne by third parties, namely, the government or private insurance companies.[115]

In many ways, Medicare and Medicaid meet their legislative objectives. Medicare provides financial assistance for a critical need of elderly citizens. Medicaid serves as an adjunct to TANF, SNAP, and other forms of assistance for poor and/or disabled Americans. Despite these accomplishments and burgeoning budgets, government health care programs have not substantially reduced many serious health care problems. Simply increasing health care expenditures does not necessarily lead to better health. As noted earlier in this chapter, life expectancy and infant mortality rates in the United States exceed those in many other industrial nations. Access to affordable, high-quality medical care remains a serious problem for millions of Americans, including many covered by Medicare and Medicaid. Medicare, for example, does not fund extended care in nursing homes—one of the most serious problems of elderly people. Older persons seeking nursing home care must exhaust their financial resources before they can turn to Medicaid for help.

Perhaps the most important point to make about American health insurance policies is that they are aimed primarily at treatment of diseases, rather than prevention of them. Significant public health gains were realized in the first half of the twentieth century through government-sponsored measures to improve sanitation, water quality, and immunization against communicable diseases. Government-sponsored research contributes significantly to the treatment of serious diseases, but many health policy analysts argue that government policy should be changed to encourage Americans to take more responsibility for their own health. Some of the leading causes of death— smoking, alcohol consumption, and obesity—are essentially personal choices. Significant progress has been made in the "war on tobacco" in the past fifty years. In 1965, 42.4 percent of adult Americans routinely used tobacco products; in 2011, only 18.9 percent were smokers.[116] However, smoking is still a leading cause of death and disease in this country. First lady Michelle Obama, and many states, localities, and school systems, have launched efforts to combat obesity; however, the results so far have been minimal: one-third of all Americans are obese, and the costs to the health care system from this condition are growing rapidly.[117] Our situation may be best summarized by the fact that we spend 18 percent of our GDP on health care and have no better, and in many cases worse, health outcomes than most of Europe, Japan, and Australia, where roughly 10 percent of GDP is spent on health care.[118]

PROTECTING THE ENVIRONMENT AND THE GLOBAL CLIMATE

Conserving the nation's resources, protecting its environment, and reducing GHG emissions yield both immediate and long-term tangible benefits. The immediate benefit of environmental controls is improved public health, which means lower mortality and morbidity rates and reduced medical expenses. The long-term benefits derived from protecting the environment and the global climate extend beyond the human health effects to encompass a vast array of quality-of-life issues. President Carter's Commission for a National Agenda for the Eighties posed this question: "What value can be placed on public enjoyment of purer air, cleaner water, or protected wilderness, or more importantly, on preserving the long-term integrity of natural life support systems?"[119]

During his second inaugural address, in January 2013, President Obama stated his firm view that the nation—and the world—must take strong action to combat the effects of global warming:

> We will respond to the threat of climate change, knowing that the failure to do so would betray our children and future generations. Some may still deny the overwhelming judgment of science, but none can avoid the devastating impact of raging fires, and crippling drought, and more powerful storms.
>
> The path towards sustainable energy sources will be long and sometimes difficult. But America cannot resist this transition; we must lead it. We cannot cede to other nations the technology that will power new jobs and new industries, we must claim its promise. That's how we will maintain our economic vitality and our national treasure—our forests and waterways, our crop lands and snow-capped peaks. That is how we will preserve our planet, commanded to our care by God. That's what will lend meaning to the creed our fathers once declared.[120]

Preserving and protecting the environment has been an important policy goal in the United States for a relatively short period of time. Prior to the 1960s, concern for the environment centered on preserving the natural environment. Landmark policies adopted during the early decades of the twentieth century established national parks, forests, and wilderness refuges. The federal government is the nation's largest landholder: it owns approximately 638 million acres, or 28 percent, of the entire country.[121] Although conservation goals have not been abandoned, environmental policies since the early 1960s are best viewed as reactions to the consequences of an industrialized, chemically dependent society that relies on fossil fuels, such as oil and coal, that pollute the air now and cause long-term damage to the earth's atmosphere.

For decades, American consumers and businesses took environmental quality for granted. Vast quantities of hazardous and toxic wastes and chemicals were dumped on the land and in the water and released into the air. Perhaps more than any other single event, the publication of Rachel Carson's *Silent Spring* in 1962 promoted an awareness of the fragility of the environment. Carson's book documented that the use of the chemical DDT (dichlorodiphenyltrichloroethane) in farming destroyed wildlife and threatened humans. Ten years later, the production of DDT was banned for use on American soil.

Concern over the deterioration of the environment generated widespread public support (marked by the first Earth Day in 1970) for stronger environmental laws. Americans are frequently reminded of potentially harmful substances lurking in the air and water. The poisoning of the food chain with cancer-causing PCBs (polychlorinated biphenyls), the presence of noxious fumes and smog in urban communities, and the contamination of water from leaking toxic waste dumps are the price exacted for the casual attitudes of the past. According to environmental scholar Walter Rosenbaum, "We are practically the first generation in the world's history with the certain technical capacity to alter and even to destroy the fundamental biochemical and geophysical conditions for societies living centuries after ours."[122]

More than a dozen major environmental protection laws were enacted at the federal level during the 1970s—the "environmental decade." Among the landmarks were the National Environmental Policy Act (1969), which established a process of assessing the environmental impact of federal projects; the Federal Water Pollution Control Act (the Clean Water Act, 1972); the Clean Air Act Amendments of 1970; the Federal Environmental Pesticide Control Act (1972); the Toxic Substances Control Act (1976), which regulates the production and handling of toxic waste; the Resource Conservation and Recovery Act (1976), which regulates the disposal of solid waste; and the Comprehensive Environmental Response, Compensation, and Liability Act (1980), commonly called Superfund, which established procedures for cleaning up toxic waste dumps. Hundreds of state and local laws were also adopted during this period. Standards for improving the quality of the air, water, and land were established, along with government agencies to monitor and enforce compliance. Driving this surge of government regulation was the need to correct the harmful practices of private businesses and individuals.

Several policies have been added to this list since then. The Superfund law was revised in 1986 to increase federal funding, to emphasize citizen participation in decisions concerning local toxic waste cleanup, and to strengthen state involvement in Superfund actions (chapter 4). Congress amended the Clean Air Act in 1990 to include regulations on ozone-depleting chemicals, which have been blamed for depleting the ozone layer above the earth. The new law also created a national market for sulfur dioxide emissions, allowing polluters to buy and sell pollution permits, a policy long recommended by economists (chapter 4).[123]

During George W. Bush's administration, there were many battles over air pollution policy. His Clear Skies Initiative would have amended the Clean Air Act to "cap emissions of sulfur dioxide, nitrogen oxides, and mercury" from power plants, and used market-based incentives, rather than strict regulations, to do this.[124] The Clear Skies bill, which also included the first ever national cap on mercury emissions, never passed Congress, and Bush administration efforts to pursue its objectives through regulations were stymied by the courts.[125] There were some advances in environmental policy during the Bush era, especially in the area of automobile fuel efficiency and

alternative energy (the Energy Independence and Security Act of 2007); however, the Bush administration was widely criticized by the research community, and more specifically presidential candidate Barack Obama, for
"ignoring or distorting scientific evidence when it clashed with the views of
some business supporters."[126]

The Obama administration made several efforts to strengthen environmental policies during the president's first term. President Obama proposed
more ambitious fuel economy standards, including those on trucks and buses
for the first time, which resulted in the Department of Transportation establishing higher fuel efficiency and emission standards for nearly all types of
motor vehicle models.[127] The new rules require auto makers to double mileage
standards for cars and trucks by 2025, "saving consumers $1.7 trillion at the
pump and eliminating 6 billion tons of carbon pollution."[128] Additionally, "the
Administration established the first-ever national limits for mercury and other
toxic air pollution from power plants," which they say "will prevent up to
11,000 premature deaths, 4,700 heart attacks, and 130,000 cases of childhood
asthma symptoms each year."[129] These new restrictions were projected to lead
to the closure of 68 to 231 of the "nation's oldest and dirtiest coal-fired power
plants," and the health benefits tied to these changes were claimed to be worth
$59 billion to $140 billion.[130] Following up on the Supreme Court's decision in
Massachusetts v. Environmental Protection Agency in 2007 (chapter 7), the EPA
has declared carbon dioxide to be a pollutant, allowing the agency to regulate
its emissions, but so far, it has only proposed doing so for coal-burning power
plants to be built in the future.[131]

The Obama administration also convinced Congress to enact ARRA (also
known as the economic stimulus package), which provided $90 billion in
funds to the Department of Energy (DOE) for green energy projects and
renewable energy programs.[132] Based in part on this investment, the amount
of electricity generated from wind and solar doubled (from 3 percent to 6
percent of total electricity generated) in three years.[133] The Obama administration also expanded the protection of wilderness and watershed areas. The
Omnibus Public Lands Management Act of 2009 "designated more than 2
million acres as wilderness, created thousands of miles of recreational and
historic trails, and protected more than 1,000 miles of rivers."[134] Last, the
Obama administration sought to lead by example, and issued an executive
order in 2009 that required all federal agencies to develop plans that would ease
their own environmental imprint by 2020, through steps such as "sustainability
requirements for 95 percent of all federal contracts."[135]

Of course the Obama Administration's environmental record is not flaw-
less. The President was unable to get Congress to enact legislation to control
GHG emissions and address climate change. His DOE program mentioned
above received a lot of criticism when one of the companies it subsidized
(Solyndra) defaulted on its government loans. In a well-publicized reversal,
Obama stopped regulations proposed by EPA administrator Lisa P. Jackson to
establish new standards for ambient ozone (smog) in the fall of 2011. Despite his

rhetorical efforts to get the United States back to being a world leader on climate change, we remain well behind most of Western Europe when it comes to government policies to reduce GHG emissions.[136]

A Legacy of Contempt

The laws and agencies created during America's environmental awakening set ambitious goals, but decades of indifference for the environmental consequences of human behavior are difficult and costly to rectify. Citizens and policymakers now realize that improving environmental quality requires years of sustained effort, billions of dollars, and profound changes in business practices and the way Americans live. The United States has stepped up its attack on environmental problems, but much remains to be done.

Water quality. Water quality laws enacted during the 1960s and 1970s were intended to ensure safe drinking water and to clean up polluted rivers, streams, and lakes. In 2011, the EPA reported that "approximately 93 percent of the population was served by community water systems (CWSs) with drinking water that met all applicable health-based drinking water standards."[137] This rate compares with the 79 percent of Americans who received water meeting EPA health standards in 1993.[138] However, former EPA administrator Lisa P. Jackson said that "despite many successes since the Clean Water Act was passed in 1972, today the nation's water [still] does not meet public health goals, and enforcement of water pollution laws is unacceptably low." Pollution generated by individuals and industry continues to flow into surface and ground waters, and the nearly $7 billion per year spent by the federal government on water pollution control measures has not eliminated dangerous levels of toxic chemicals, bacteria, nitrates, and phosphorus in the water supply. Although limited data on the quality of water in the nation's harbors, lakes, streams, and ponds are available, recent studies have found that over half the rivers and streams, and nearly 70 percent of lakes, ponds, and reservoirs, are "impaired," which means they are not meeting the standards for swimming, fishing, or drinking water use.[139] However, waterways are certainly cleaner than they were before clean water laws were enacted.[140]

A relatively new and controversial technology developed to extract natural gas from the earth, called "fracking" (short for "hydraulic fracturing"), may pose another threat to the U.S. water supply. This new technology enables energy companies to access previously unreachable shale deposits. According to the Energy Information Administration, the number of natural gas wells increased by 49 percent between 2000 and 2010.[141] However, independent research, such as a study conducted by Duke University in 2011, found "higher odds of natural gas contamination in water wells within 1,100 yards of fracking wells."[142] These and other studies of the fracking process have led to growing public concern, and the EPA announced in 2012 that it will conduct additional research to determine whether or not the hydraulic fracturing process is in fact contaminating drinking water supplies.[143]

Air quality. Lawmakers hoped that the standards and enforcement mechanisms established by the Clean Air Act of 1970 would significantly reduce air pollution in five years. Despite some progress, those hopes are yet to be fulfilled. On the positive side, beginning in the 1980s, dangerous lead emissions were dropping dramatically, largely as a result of a ban on the use of high-lead gasoline, and by 2008, airborne lead had been "virtually eliminated."[144] If one considers the six "criteria pollutants" under the Clean Air Act (ozone, particulate matter, lead, nitrogen dioxide, carbon monoxide, and sulfur dioxide), between 1990 and 2009, all showed substantial reductions, with lead and carbon dioxide down by 70 percent or more, while ozone and fine particulates were down by less than 30 percent.[145] According to the EPA, "nearly the entire country is meeting air quality targets set years ago for carbon monoxide, nitrogen oxides and sulfur dioxide," and the value of these improvements in air quality was estimated to reach nearly $2 trillion by 2020. However, the same report notes that GHG emissions "increased by 7% between 1990 and 2010, and global GHG emissions are increasing at an even faster rate."[146] Despite making progress in improving air quality in the United States, there are still over 100 million people living in communities where air quality, in terms of such issues as particulate pollution and ground-level ozone, is not acceptable by national standards (so-called nonattainment areas).[147]

Toxic waste. Notable success in protecting the public from the negative effects of toxic chemicals has been achieved by imposing sharp restrictions on the production and use of several cancer-causing products, including DDT, PCBs, and dioxin. Federal laws governing the handling of toxic wastes established procedures for assessing chemical hazards and disposing of them properly. Government agencies responsible for cleaning up abandoned toxic waste dumps have identified hundreds of dangerous situations, and eliminated or curtailed many threats to the environment and public health.

Unfortunately, toxic waste problems are growing in complexity and scope. Many possibly toxic chemicals are being introduced so fast that the government is unable to test them all for potential hazards. American industry generates 355 million metric tons of hazardous waste every year—about 1 ton for each citizen. Up to one-half of liquid waste or "dirty water" is flushed, untreated, deep underground.[148] In 1990, Congress passed the Pollution Prevention Act, which expanded the Toxics Release Inventory (TRI), a national database that identifies for public information the annual amount of chemicals released from manufacturing facilities. Since the TRI program began in 1987, industries have reduced their releases of chemicals by more than 45 percent, or over 3 billion pounds.[149] A key reason for this is that investors have reacted negatively to firms with higher reported toxic releases.[150]

The manufacturing, metal mining, and electric utilities sectors all saw significant reductions in the production and release of toxic pollutants and waste from 2003 to 2011, with toxic release reductions of 26 percent,

52 percent, and 43 percent, respectively.[151] Former EPA administrator Lisa P. Jackson reported:

> Since 1998, we have recorded a steady decline in the amount of TRI chemicals released into the air, and since 2009 alone, we have seen more than a 100 million pound decrease in TRI air pollutants entering our communities. This remarkable success is due in part to the TRI program and concerted efforts by industry, regulators and public interest groups to clean up the air we all depend upon.[152]

Given the extent and complexity of the problem, it is not surprising that progress in implementing the Superfund cleanup program has been somewhat slow. According to the EPA, in the mid-1980s there were over 37,000 toxic waste dumps in the United States, thousands of which posed serious health threats. At that time, the Office of Technology Assessment estimated that cleanup measures could cost more than $50 billion.[153] This estimate now seems quite low given that cleanup costs are averaging $2.1 million per site (chapter 4). In 2010, the EPA placed 1,627 hazardous waste sites on its National Priorities List for remedial action, and nearly 1,100 of these were completely, or nearly, cleaned up.[154] Thus, the EPA is still working on its hazardous waste cleanup mission, but the $13 billion available in the Superfund program will be not be adequate to complete the task.[155] Cleanups are complicated and expensive—often the health effects of toxic chemicals are impossible to detect accurately, and some of the technology for defusing toxic waste is still in development. The EPA's Superfund program received nearly $582 million in additional funds through the passage of ARRA, which allowed the agency to begin working on twenty-six additional Superfund sites and to provide additional support for twenty-five others.[156] This new funding was essential to the mission because appropriations have been modest ($1.25 billion per year) since the "polluter tax" on oil and chemical industries expired in 1995, greatly limiting the EPA's cleanup efforts.[157] Superfund projects are particularly important in the nation's urban areas, where one in four Americans are living within one mile of a Superfund site, and the pollution from these sites can have real effects on the "health, economic livelihoods, and well-being" of citizens.[158]

From react and cure to anticipate and prevent. America's policies designed to protect the environment have been marked by uneven progress and contentious politics. Much effort and billions of dollars have yielded important, but modest, improvements. The problems that have been discovered and addressed await resolution, but the environmental threats over the long term may be even more intractable. Twenty-five years ago, an EPA task force noted that "newer" environmental problems, such as "global climatic change . . . acid precipitation, and hazardous waste," would be difficult to evaluate and could "involve persistent contaminants that move from one environmental medium to another, causing further damage even after controls have been applied."[159] Policymakers in the United States and globally are just beginning to grapple with the pro-found implications of this ominous forecast.

Enormous expenditures and upheavals in industrial production practices will be needed to clean up and preserve the environment, as will serious changes in our personal behavior. Americans' "addiction to oil," as President George W. Bush called it, and our dependence on automobiles and trucks must be altered to reduce long-term environmental damage. Many of the economic and social costs must be borne today, but most of the benefits will accrue to future generations.

Thus far, private and public policymakers have been unwilling to take the necessary steps. The pressures for immediate economic growth have been too powerful to resist. The so-called greenhouse effect illustrates the trade-offs. Increased accumulation of carbon dioxide and other gases in the upper atmosphere has caused the global average temperature to rise by more than 0.74°C (1.4°F) in the past 100 years.[160] Moreover, the United Nations stated in a 2012 press release that "under current models, greenhouse gas emissions could double over the next 50 years, leading to a rise in global temperature of 3°C [5.4°F] or more by the end of the century."[161] Scientists project that similar temperature increases could occur by 2100, causing drastic changes in the earth's climate, severe flooding, drought, and famine on a scale unparalleled in human history. Reversing or slowing this trend will require reductions in the use of fossil fuels and unprecedented cooperation among the nations of the world.

Compared with many other parts of the world, the United States has an admirable environmental protection record. Although the United States performed poorly on some indicators, such as carbon dioxide emissions, it used less energy (per $1,000 of GDP) in 2009 than 64 other countries. The United States also did better than 106 countries on the proportion of land area covered by forest (as a percentage of land area).[162] By 2012, the United States had even achieved significant reductions in carbon dioxide emissions, mainly through the conversion of many utilities from coal to natural gas.[163] In contrast, China, the world's second largest economy, has a weaker environmental record. It is the world's largest producer and consumer of high sulfur coal, which can cause many environmental and health problems. Moreover, between 2001 and 2005, "about 54 percent of the seven main rivers in China contained water deemed unsafe for human consumption."[164] According to journalists Joseph Kahn and Jim Yardley, China's own Ministry of Health acknowledges that "pollution has made cancer China's leading cause of death." The authors go on to say that "ambient air pollution alone is blamed for hundreds of thousands of deaths each year. Nearly 500 million people lack access to safe drinking water. Only 1 percent of the country's 560 million city dwellers breathe air considered safe by the European Union."[165] It should also be said that China has launched a number of new programs to fight pollution, save energy, use cleaner energies, and promote clean energy vehicles, and because of the relative simplicity of its policymaking system, China may be able to move more decisively than Western democracies.[166]

Environmental degradation is widespread in developing countries, where the pressures for development to support exploding populations are intense. Thirty-two million acres of ecologically valuable forests, more than the combined areas of New England, Delaware, and New Jersey, are destroyed every year.[167] This destruction has continued despite United Nations and European Union programs to stop it. The fact that many wealthy countries are now reforesting may be contributing to the problem because reduced timber yields in those countries have increased world demand for wood products.

Clearly, public policymakers in this country and around the world must do better. In 1987, the World Commission on Environment and Development concluded:

Many present development trends leave increasing numbers of people poor and vulnerable while at the same time degrading the environment. How can such development serve next century's world of twice as many people relying on the same environment? . . . The react and cure environmental policies that governments have pursued are bankrupt. . . . Anticipate and prevent is the only realistic approach.[168]

Twenty-five years later, the United Nations Environmental Programme concluded:

The world continues to speed down an unsustainable path despite over 500 internationally agreed goals and objectives to support the sustainable management of the environment and improve human wellbeing. . . . If humanity does not urgently change its ways, several critical thresholds may be exceeded, beyond which abrupt and generally irreversible changes to the life-support functions of the planet could occur.[169]

Achieving a sustainable environment in the face of enormous worldwide development pressures will be extremely difficult, but the very survival of the planet depends on it.

SUMMARY

A fair assessment of the success of American public policy would conclude that although significant progress has been made toward fulfilling the nation's goals and values, serious problems remain. On one hand, the United States is still the world's largest economy and a powerful magnet for people who want to live in a democracy that cherishes freedom of expression and religious beliefs. The United States leads the world in science and technology, and many Americans are pretty comfortable and content with their lives. The United States is, in many ways, better off than it was fifty or twenty years ago. Some significant arms control agreements have been signed, and the prospects for farther-reaching controls among major world powers such as the United States, Europe, Russia, and China look good; however, renegade countries such as Iran and North Korea definitely pose an arms control problem. Many of the most egregious forms of discrimination on the basis of race, gender, and sexual orientation have been curtailed or at least identified. The social safety net of income support for the elderly and disadvantaged has survived attempted reductions, and health care insurance has been significantly expanded. Several important steps have been taken to preserve and protect the air, water, and land necessary for survival.

But U.S. public policies are not as effective as they should be. At the writing of this book, unemployment has remained at high levels, hovering around 8 percent to 9 percent, for nearly five years. Millions of workers have been unemployed for more than two years. The U.S. economy has not recovered all of the nearly 9 million jobs lost during the Great Recession. The incomes of most Americans have either declined or remained stable. An anemic economic recovery has failed to lift all boats. In one of the world's most affluent nations, millions are unemployed, homeless, hungry, and poor. The gaps between rich and poor, the college educated and those without college degrees, and whites and minorities have grown wider. Discrimination on the basis of race, gender, age, disability, and sexual orientation has not been extinguished. The costs of income security and health care programs have risen so rapidly that their solvency is threatened, yet benefits for poor people are barely adequate for their survival, and the health status of Americans has not improved significantly. The water and air remain dangerously polluted by automobile exhaust, industrial waste, and toxic chemicals, and the global climate is threatened for the next generation. Much, therefore, remains to be done. The problems facing U.S. policymakers and citizens are as intractable as any the nation has ever faced, yet past experience suggests that progress can be made by extraordinary leaders and when policymakers cooperate on a bipartisan basis. Among the most pressing challenges of the early twenty-first century are

- keeping America competitive in a world economy, while building a widely shared economic future;
- eliminating discrimination against minorities and women;
- expanding opportunities for low- and moderate-income people;
- protecting the nation from the ongoing threats of domestic and international terrorism;
- sustaining the social safety net of income supports and health care; and
- reducing the unprecedented threat of global warming.

CHAPTER 1

1. CQ Roll Call Staff, "Congress Narrowly Averts Cliff," *CQ Weekly*, January 7, 2013.
2. Pew Research Center for the People & the Press, "As Fiscal Cliff Nears, Democrats Have Public Opinion on Their Side: Record Number Sees Country as More Politically Divided," December 13, 2012, www.people-press.org/2012/12/13/as-fiscal-cliff-nears-democrats-have-public-opinion-on-their-side/.
3. E. E. Schattschneider, *The Semi-Sovereign People: A Realist's View of Democracy in America* (New York: Holt, Rinehart & Winston, 1960).
4. Knowledge Center, The Council of State Governments, *The Book of the States 2011*, http://knowledgecenter.csg.org/kc/view-content-type/1616.
5. Theodore Lowi, "American Business, Public Policy, Case-Studies, and Political Theory," *World Politics* 16 (1964): 677–715.
6. See National Conference of State Legislatures, www.ncsl.org; and Monica Davey, "One-Party Control Opens States to Partisan Rush," *New York Times*, November 23, 2012.
7. Samuel Kernell, Gary Jacobson, and Thad Kousser, *The Logic of American Politics*, 5th ed. (Washington, D.C.: CQ Press, 2012), 316; Chuck McCutcheon, *The Elections of 2012: Outcomes and Analysis* (Washington, D.C.: CQ Press, 2013).
8. Richard E. Neustadt, *Presidential Power: The Politics of Leadership, with Reflections on Johnson and Nixon* (New York: John Wiley, 1976), 78.
9. Samuel Kernell, *Going Public: New Strategies of Presidential Leadership*, 4th ed. (Washington, D.C.: CQ Press, 2007).
10. Kernell et al., *The Logic of American Politics*, 5th ed., 324; National Archives, "Executive Orders Disposition Tables Index," www.archives.gov/federal-register/executive-orders/disposition.html.
11. Kenneth T. Walsh, "Clinton's Campaign to End-Run Congress: He's Making Policy Changes by Executive Order," *U.S. News & World Report*, June 26, 2000.
12. Ben Protess and Benjamin Weiser, "Signal to Street in Obama's Pick for Regulators," *New York Times*, January 25, 2013. White did have connections to several banks in her earlier work as a private attorney; see Andrew Ross Sorkin, "Nominee for 'Sheriff' Has Worn Banks' Hat," *New York Times*, January, 29, 2013.
13. Charlie Savage and Steven Greenhouse, "Court Rejects Obama Move to Fill Posts," *New York Times*, January 25, 2013.
14. Richard P. Nathan, *The Administrative Presidency* (New York: John Wiley, 1983).
15. Deirdre Baker and Joseph Tannir, "Annual Survey of Public Employment and Payroll Summary Report: 2010" January 3, 2012, www2.census.gov/govs/apes/g10aspep.pdf; Harold W. Stanley and Richard G. Niemi, *Vital Statistics on American Politics 2007–2008* (Washington, D.C.: CQ Press, 2008), 318–319.
16. Lauren Smith and Melissa Attias, "An Overdue Assignment," *CQ Weekly*, September 19, 2011.
17. *Gideon v. Wainwright*, 372 U.S. 335 (1963); *Miranda v. Arizona*, 384 U.S. 436 (1966).
18. For this and other examples, see Michael W. McConnell, "Let the States Do It, Not Washington," *Wall Street Journal*, March 29, 1999.
19. Adam Liptak, "Justices, by 5-4, Uphold Health Care Law; Roberts in Majority; Victory for Obama," *New York Times*, June 29, 2012.
20. Robert Pear, "State Courts Surpass U.S. Bench in Cases on Rights of Individuals," *New York Times*, May 4, 1986.
21. Richard Neely, *How Courts Govern America* (New Haven, Conn.: Yale University Press, 1981), 7.

22. William T. Gormley Jr. and Steven J. Balla, *Bureaucracy and Democracy: Accountability and Performance*, 3rd ed. (Washington, D.C.: CQ Press, 2013), 167–177; Stanley and Niemi, *Vital Statistics*, 334.

23. See David B. Walker, *The Rebirth of Federalism: Slouching toward Washington*, 2nd ed. (Chatham, N.J.: Chatham House, 2000), 236; and Kenneth Feingold, Laura Wherry, and Stephanie Schardin, "Block Grants: Historical Overview and Lessons Learned," Urban Institute Series A, No. A-63, April 2004, www.urban.org/uploadedpdf/310991_A-63.pdf.

24. Centers for Medicare and Medicaid Services, "Medicaid Enrollment by State," www.medicaid.gov/medicaid-chip-program-information/by-state/by-state.html; Center on Budget and Policy Priorities, "United States TANF Spending Factsheet," www.npc.umich.edu/news/events/safetynet/tanf-spending-factsheet.pdf; Office of Management and Budget, "Historical Tables," www.whitehouse.gov/omb/budget/Historicals.

25. For more on subgovernments, see Randall B. Ripley and Grace A. Franklin, *Congress, the Bureaucracy, and Public Policy*, 3rd ed. (Homewood, Ill.: Dorsey Press, 1984).

26. Jack L. Walker Jr., *Mobilizing Interest Groups in America: Patrons, Professions, and Social Movements* (Ann Arbor: University of Michigan Press, 1991); Jeffrey Birnbaum, "The Road to Riches Is Called K Street," *Washington Post*, June 22, 2005, as cited in Kernell et al., *The Logic of American Politics*, 5th ed., 600.

27. Kernell et al., *The Logic of American Politics*, 5th ed., 600; Roger H. Davidson, Walter J. Oleszek, and Frances E. Lee, *Congress and Its Members*, 13th ed. (Washington, D.C.: CQ Press, 2012), 374; Center for Responsive Politics, "Lobbying: Top Spenders," www.opensecrets.org/lobby/top.php?indexType=s, January 15, 2013.

28. Davidson et al., *Congress and Its Members*, 13th ed., 377.

29. Alan J. Cigler, "Interest Group Money in the 2008 Federal Election," in *Interest Group Politics*, 8th ed., ed. Alan J. Cigler and Burdett A. Loomis (Washington, D.C.: CQ Press, 2012), 148; Center for Responsive Politics, "2012 Overview: Stats at a Glance," www.opensecrets.org/overview/index.php.

30. Kernell et al., *The Logic of American Politics*, 5th ed., 616.

31. Part of the reason for the decline in 2008 was that both Obama and John McCain made a point of saying that such groups did not speak for them. Cigler, "Interest Group Money," 158; Center for Responsive Politics, "Outside Spending," www.opensecrets.org/outsidespending/index.php?ql3. The 2012 figure includes 527 committees and an estimate for 501(c) groups, and the modest increase in 2012 over 2008 was a result of soft money moving to super PACs.

32. Center for Responsive Politics, "Outside Spending."

33. Center for Responsive Politics, "2012 Outside Spending, by Group," www.opensecrets.org/outsidespending/summ.php?disp=O.

34. See William T. Gormley Jr., "Interest Group Interventions in the Administrative Process," in *The Interest Group Connection*, ed. Paul S. Herrnson, Ronald G. Shaiko, and Clyde Wilcox (Chatham, N.J.: Chatham House, 1998), 213–223; Cornelius M. Kerwin and Scott R. Furlong, *Rulemaking: How Government Agencies Write and Make Policy*, 4th ed. (Washington, D.C.: CQ Press, 2011); and Scott R. Furlong and Cornelius M. Kerwin, "Interest Group Participation in Rule Making: A Decade of Change," *Journal of Public Administration Research and Theory*, 15 (2004): 353–370.

35. Center for Responsive Politics, "Political Parties Overview," www.opensecrets.org/parties/index.php.

36. Cassandra Tate, "Letter from 'The Atomic Capital of the Nation,'" *Columbia Journalism Review* (May–June 1982): 31–35.

37. Walter A. Rosenbaum, *Environmental Politics and Policy*, 8th ed. (Washington, D.C.: CQ Press, 2011), 306–308.

38. Zay N. Smith and Pamela Zekman, *The Mirage* (New York: Random House, 1979).

39. Kernell et al., *The Logic of American Politics*, 5th ed., 643.

40. "ACORN 2009 Undercover Videos Controversy," http://en.wikipedia.org/wiki/ACORN_2009_undercover_videos_controversy; Peter Dreier and Christopher R. Martin, "How ACORN Was Framed: Political Controversy and Media Agenda Setting," *Perspectives on Politics* 8 (2010): 761–792.

41. Stanley and Niemi, *Vital Statistics*, 174; Press Reference, "United States Press, Media, TV, Radio and Newspapers," www.pressreference.com/Sw-Ur/United-States.html.
42. Donald C. Baumer and Howard J. Gold, *Parties, Polarization, and Democracy in the United States* (Boulder, Colo.: Paradigm Publishers, 2010), 185–186.
43. Charles Edward Lindblom, *Politics and Markets: The World's Political Economic Systems* (New York: Basic Books, 1977), 170–188.
44. Lewis Solomon, "Restructuring the Corporate Board of Directors: Fond Hope—Faint Promise?" *Michigan Law Review* 76 (March 1978): 581–610; Victor Brudney, "The Independent Director—Heavenly City or Potemkin Village?" *Harvard Law Review* 95 (January 1982): 597–659; Jacob S. Hacker and Paul Pierson, *Winner-Take-All Politics: How Washington Made the Rich Richer—And Turned Its Back on the Middle Class* (New York: Simon & Schuster, 2010), 61–66.
45. Alfred Chandler Jr., *The Visible Hand: The Managerial Revolution in American Business* (Cambridge, Mass.: Harvard University Press, 1977), 1–12.
46. Stephanie Clifford, "Walmart Plans to Buy American More Often," *New York Times*, January 16, 2013; James Dao, "Wal-Mart to Announce a Five-Year Commitment to Hire 100,000 Veterans," *New York Times*, January 15, 2013.
47. Robert Dahl, *A Preface to Economic Democracy* (Berkeley: University of California Press, 1985), 162.
48. Schattschneider, *The Semi-Sovereign People*, 2–3.
49. Initiative & Referendum Institute, www.iandrinstitute.org.
50. See, for example, David S. Broder, *Democracy Derailed: Initiative Campaigns and the Power of Money* (New York: Harcourt, 2000); and Elisabeth S. Gerber, *The Populist Paradox: Interest Group Influence and the Promise of Direct Legislation* (Princeton, N.J.: Princeton University Press, 1999).

CHAPTER 2

1. Lewis Lipsitz, *American Democracy* (New York: St. Martin's, 1986), 31.
2. For a more detailed discussion of American political values and beliefs, see Linda J. Medcalf and Kenneth M. Dolbeare, *Neopolitics: American Political Ideas in the 1980s* (New York: Random House, 1985).
3. Adam Smith, *An Inquiry into the Nature and the Causes of the Wealth of Nations* (New York: Modern Library, Random House, 1937). (Originally published in 1776.)
4. The concept of procedural democracy is discussed at length in Ira Katznelson and Mark Kesselman, *The Politics of Power: A Critical Introduction to American Government*, 3rd ed. (San Diego, Calif.: Harcourt Brace Jovanovich, 1987).
5. See Alexander Hamilton, John Jay, and James Madison, *The Federalist* (Cambridge, Mass.: Belknap Press, 1966), no. 10.
6. Jean-Jacques Rousseau, *The Social Contract and Discourses*, trans. G. D. H. Cole (New York: E. P. Dutton, 1950), bk. 3, p. 94.
7. See Benjamin R. Barber, *Strong Democracy: Participatory Politics for a New Age* (Berkeley: University of California Press, 1984); Philip Green, *Retrieving Democracy* (Totowa, N.J.: Rowman & Allanheld, 1985); Benjamin R. Barber, *A Passion for Democracy* (Princeton, N.J.: Princeton University Press, 1998); and Benjamin R. Barber, *A Place for Us: How to Make Society Civil and Democracy Strong* (New York: Hill & Wang, 1998).
8. Jane J. Mansbridge, *Beyond Adversary Democracy* (Chicago: University of Chicago Press, 1983).
9. See Paul Light, *Still Artful Work: The Politics of Social Security Reform*, 2nd ed. (New York: McGraw-Hill, 1995), 56.
10. General Social Surveys, as reported in Barbara A. Bardes and Robert W. Oldendick, *Public Opinion: Measuring the American Mind* (Belmont, Calif.: Wadsworth, 2000), 124, and Robert S. Erikson and Kent L. Tedin, *American Public Opinion*, 8th ed. (New York: Pearson, 2011), 96. Much of the data presented in this section come from two major university-based survey research organizations that collect data on the political attitudes and behaviors of Americans: the Survey Research Center at the University of Michigan, which conducts the American

National Election Studies before and after all national elections, and the National Opinion Research Center at the University of Chicago, which conducts the General Social Surveys. The first American National Election Study covered the 1948 presidential election; subsequent studies have covered all presidential elections since then and all congressional elections since 1958, except 2006 and 2010. The first General Social Survey was conducted in 1972, and twenty-eight have been completed since. These two sources are used by many academic social scientists to track trends in political attitudes and behavior.

11. Pew Research Center for the People & the Press, "Did the President Score in Social Security?" April 29, 2005, www.people-press.org/2005/04/29/did-the-president-score-on-social-security/.
12. Roper Center for Public Opinion Research, *The Public Perspective* 2 (March–April 1991): 7; General Social Surveys as reported in Tom W. Smith, *Trends in National Spending Priorities, 1973–2010* (Chicago: National Opinion Research Center, 2011), 10.
13. Roper Center for Public Opinion Research, *The Public Perspective* 1 (July–August 1990): 82.
14. Pew Research Center for the People & the Press, "Fewer Want Spending to Grow, but Most Cuts Remain Unpopular," February 10, 2011, www.people-press.org/files/2011/02/702.pdf.
15. Roper Center for Public Opinion Research, iPOLL Databank, www.ropercenter.uconn.edu/data_access/ipoll/ipoll.html.
16. Ibid.
17. American National Election Studies, as reported in Bardes and Oldendick, *Public Opinion*, 112; Pew Research Center for the People & the Press, iPOLL Databank, www.ropercenter.uconn.edu/data_access/ipoll/ipoll.html.
18. General Social Surveys, as reported in Bardes and Oldendick, *Public Opinion*, 110–111; Regina A. Corso, "Confidence in Congress Stays at Lowest Point in Almost Fifty Years," *The Harris Poll*, no. 44 (May 21, 2012), www.harrisinteractive.com/NewsRoom/HarrisPolls/tabid/447/mid/1508/articleId/1068/ctl/ReadCustom%20Default/Default.aspx.
19. Harold W. Stanley and Richard G. Niemi, *Vital Statistics on American Politics 2007–2008* (Washington, D.C.: CQ Press, 2008), 14–15; Michael McDonald, "Voter Turnout," United States Election Project, http://elections.gmu.edu/voter_turnout.htm.
20. Ibid.
21. Erikson and Tedin, *American Public Opinion*, 8th ed., 111–113; Samuel Kernell, Gary Jacobson, and Thad Kousser, *The Logic of American Politics*, 5th ed. (Washington, D.C.: CQ Press, 2012), 473.
22. General Social Surveys, as reported in Bardes and Oldendick, *Public Opinion*, 147; Erikson and Tedin, *American Public Opinion*, 8th ed., 100–104.
23. Bardes and Oldendick, *Public Opinion*, 152; Erikson and Tedin, *American Public Opinion*, 8th ed., 100–104.
24. Gallup, "Death Penalty," October 6–9, 2011, www.gallup.com/poll/1606/Death-Penalty.aspx October 2011.
25. See Bardes and Oldendick, *Public Opinion*, 175.
26. American National Election Studies, as reported in Barbara A. Bardes and Richard W. Oldendick, *Public Opinion: Measuring the American Mind*, 4th ed. (Lanham, Md.: Rowman & Littlefield, 2012), 199–200.
27. General Social Survey, as reported by Erikson and Tedin, *American Public Opinion,* 8th ed., 107–108.
28. Gallup, "Religion," November 28 to December 1, 2011, www.gallup.com/poll/1690/Religion.aspx.
29. Ronald Inglehart, "Post-Materialism in an Environment of Insecurity," *American Political Science Review* 75 (December 1981): 880–900.
30. American National Election Study (2008) and General Social Survey (2008), as reported in Bardes and Oldendick, *Public Opinion*, 4th ed., 184; see also Susan A. MacManus, *Young v. Old: Generational Combat in the 21st Century* (Boulder, Colo.: Westview, 1996).
31. American National Election Studies, as reported in Bardes and Oldendick, *Public Opinion*, 4th ed., 136.

32. Ibid., 137.
33. Ibid., 140. It should be noted that depending on how the question is worded, different polling organizations come up with slightly different results regarding Americans' ideological distribution. Overall, the results of Gallup polls, the General Social Surveys, and the American National Election Studies are quite similar.
34. Donald C. Baumer and Howard J. Gold, *Parties, Polarization, and Democracy in the United States* (Boulder, Colo.: Paradigm Publishers, 2010), 25.
35. Pew Research Center for the People & the Press, "Partisan Polarization Surges in Bush, Obama Years: Trends in American Values: 1987–2012," June 4, 2012, www.people-press.org/2012/06/04/partisan-polarization-surges-in-bush-obama-years/.
36. Baumer and Gold, *Parties, Polarization*, 24–30.
37. Murat Tasci, "This Time May Not Be That Different: Labor Markets, the Great Recession and the (Not So Great) Recovery," Federal Reserve Bank of Cleveland, September 27, 2011, www.clevelandfed.org/research/commentary/2011/2011-18.cfm.
38. Unless otherwise indicated, the statistics provided in the next three sections were taken from the tables in the appendices of the *Economic Reports of the President*, 1986 and 2000, prepared by the Council of Economic Advisers and published by the U.S. Government Printing Office.
39. "The Reindustrialization of America," *Business Week*, special issue, June 30, 1980.
40. GNP was the measure of national economic output commonly used in the United States in the 1960s. It differs from GDP in that GNP includes the profits and income of American corporations and individuals who are operating abroad but does not count the profits and income of foreigners or foreign-owned corporations operating in the United States. GDP includes the latter but does not include the former. Since the mid-1980s, GDP has become the accepted measure of national economic output. Robert B. Reich, in *The Next American Frontier: A Provocative Paradigm for Economic Renewal* (New York: Penguin, 1983), 285n., cites Organisation for Economic Co-operation and Development data on this point.
41. Harrell R. Rodgers Jr., *The Cost of Human Neglect: America's Welfare Failure* (Armonk, N.Y.: M.E. Sharpe, 1982), 18.
42. Lawrence E. Lynn Jr., "A Decade of Policy Developments in the Income Maintenance System," in *A Decade of Federal Antipoverty Programs*, ed. Robert H. Haveman (New York: Academic Press, 1977), 88–95.
43. Reich, *The Next American Frontier*, 285.
44. Gregory B. Mills, "The Budget: A Failure of Discipline," in *The Reagan Record: An Assessment of America's Changing Domestic Priorities*, eds. John L. Palmer and Isabel V. Sawhill (Cambridge, Mass.: Ballinger, 1984), 111–114.
45. Frank Ackerman, Neva R. Goodwin, Laurie Dougherty, and Kevin Gallagher, eds., *The Political Economy of Inequality* (Washington, D.C.: Island Press, 2000), 2.
46. Robert Pear, "The Rich Got Richer in 80s; Others Held Even," *New York Times*, January 11, 1991.
47. Robert D. Hershey Jr., "U.S. Trade Deficit Narrows Sharply as Exports Surge," *New York Times*, January 16, 1988.
48. Carl E. Van Horn, *No One Left Behind: The Report of the Twentieth Century Fund Task Force on Retraining America's Workforce* (New York: Twentieth Century Fund Press, 1996), 64.
49. Ibid., 62.
50. William Lazonick and Mary O'Sullivan, "Maximising Shareholder Value: A New Ideology for Corporate Governance," *Economy and Society*, 29, no. 1 (2000): 13–35.
51. Organisation for Economic Co-operation and Development, *OECD Economic Outlook*, no. 66 (Paris, France: Organisation for Economic Co-operation and Development, 1999), 195.
52. Richard W. Stevenson, "Roots of Prosperity Reach Past Clinton Years," *New York Times*, October 9, 2000.
53. Ackerman et al., eds., *The Political Economy of Inequality*, 206.
54. Ibid., 7, 36.
55. David Sanger, "Senate Votes to Lift Curbs on U.S. Trade with Beijing: Strong Bipartisan Support," *New York Times*, September 20, 2000.

56. Frederic S. Pearson and Simon Payaslian, *International Political Economy* (New York: McGraw-Hill, 1999), 185.

57. Roger Cohen, "Growing Up and Getting Practical Since Seattle," *New York Times*, September 24, 2000.

58. Joseph Kahn, "Wealthy Nations Propose Doubling Poor's Debt Relief," *New York Times*, September 17, 2000; Joseph Kahn, "Congressional Leadership Agrees to Debt Relief for Poor Nations," *New York Times*, October 18, 2000.

59. Carl E. Van Horn, *Working Scared (or Not at All): The Lost Decade, Great Recession, and Restoring the Shattered American Dream* (Lanham, Md.: Rowman & Littlefield, 2013).

60. Paul Krugman, "The Big Zero," *New York Times*, December 27, 2009.

61. Eduardo Porter, "Economic Health? It's Relative," *New York Times*, October 16, 2012.

62. Binyamin Appelbaum, "Family Net Worth Drops to Level of Early '90s, Fed Says," *New York Times*, June 11, 2012; Emmanuel Saez, "Striking It Richer: The Evolution of Top Income in the United States (Updated with 2009 and 2010 Estimates)," March 2, 2012, http://elsa.berkeley .edu/~saez/saez-UStopincomes-2010.pdf.

63. Annie Lowrey, "Our Economic Pickle," *New York Times*, January 13, 2013.

64. Appelbaum, "Family Net Worth."

65. Jesse Nankin and Krista Kjellman Schmidt, "History of U.S. Gov't Bailouts," April 15, 2009, www.propublica.org/special/government-bailouts; Matthew Goldstein, "JPMorgan Buys Bear on the Cheap," *BusinessWeek*, March 16, 2008; Robin Sidel, Dennis K. Berman, and Kate Kelley "J.P. Morgan Buys Bear in Fire Sale, as Fed Widens Credit to Avert Crisis," *Wall Street Journal*, March 17, 2008.

66. Bureau of Labor Statistics, "Labor Force Statistics from the Current Population Survey, Series LNS14000000," www.data.bls.gov.

67. Paul Krugman, "On the Inadequacy of the Stimulus," *New York Times*, September 5, 2011, http://krugman.blogs.nytimes.com/2011/09/05/on-the-inadequacy-of-the-stimulus/.

68. "Quick Fact: Despite Her Previous Support, Sarah Palin Bashed TARP as 'Crony Capitalism,'" February 7, 2010, http://newscorpwatch.org/research/201002070013; Mitt Romney, *No Apology: Believe in America* (New York: St. Martin's Griffin Press, 2011).

69. CBO, Report on the Troubled Asset Relief Program, www.cbo.gov/sites/default/files/cbofiles/ ftpdocs/121xx/doc12118/03-29-tarp.pdf; Daniel W. Drezner, "The Hazards of Policymaking in a Fact-Poor, Pundit-Rich World," *Foreign Policy* blog, September 15, 2010, http://drezner .foreignpolicy.com/posts/2010/09/15/the_hazards_of_policymaking_in_a_fact_poor_ pundit_rich_world; Sewell Chan, "In Study, 2 Economists Say Intervention Helped Avert a 2nd Depression," *New York Times*, September 27, 2010; "TARP: The Successful Orphan," *The Economist*, September 25, 2010.

70. CBO, Report on the Troubled Asset Relief Program.

71. Bob Herbert, "A Different Creature," *New York Times*, April 13, 2010.

72. Romney for President, Inc., *Believe in America: Mitt Romney's Plan for Jobs and Economic Growth* (Boston, Mass.: Romney for President, Inc., 2011), 3.

73. Jessica Godofsky, Carl E. Van Horn, and Cliff Zukin, "American Workers Assess an Economic Disaster," September 2010, www.heldrich.rutgers.edu/sites/default/files/content/Work_ Trends_September_2010.pdf; Cliff Zukin, Carl E. Van Horn, and Charley Stone, "Out of Work and Losing Hope: The Misery and Bleak Expectations of American Workers," September 2011, www.heldrich.rutgers.edu/sites/default/files/content/Work_Trends_September_2011.pdf.

74. New York Times/CBS News, "Views about the Economy, Budget Deficit and Health Care," April 21, 2011, www.nytimes.com/interactive/2011/04/21/us/nat-poll.html?ref=us; ABC News/Washington Post, "ABC News/Washington Post Poll: Dissatisfaction with Washington Hits 19-Year High," July 19, 2011, http://abcnews.go.com/blogs/politics/2011/07/spurred-by-washingtons-wrangles-dissatisfaction-hits-19-year-high/; Godofsky et al., "American Workers"; Zukin et al., "Out of Work and Losing Hope."

75. Pew Research Center for the People & the Press, "Republicans Draw Even with Democrats on Most Issues: Pessimistic Public Doubts Effectiveness of Stimulus, TARP," April 28, 2010, www .people-press.org/files/legacy-pdf/608.pdf.

76. "President Exit Polls," New York Times, http://elections.nytimes.com/2012/results/president/exit-polls.
77. Rodgers, *The Cost of Human Neglect*, 104–107.
78. Ibid., 57, 103–125; Ira C. Magaziner and Robert B. Reich, *Minding America's Business: The Decline and Rise of the American Economy* (New York: Harcourt Brace Jovanovich, 1982), 11–27.
79. Norman J. Ornstein, Thomas E. Mann, and Michael J. Malbin, *Vital Statistics on Congress, 1989–1990* (Washington, D.C.: Congressional Quarterly, 1990); see also Cornelius M. Kerwin, *Rulemaking: How Government Agencies Write Law and Make Policy*, 2nd ed. (Washington, D.C.: CQ Press, 1999).
80. Susan Dudley and Melinda Warren, *Fiscal Stalemate Reflected in Regulators' Budget: An Analysis of the U.S. Budget for Fiscal Years 2011 and 2012* (St. Louis, Mo., and Washington, D.C.: George Washington University Regulatory Studies Center and the Murray Weidenbaum Center on the Economy, Government, and Public Policy, 2011), 5–8.
81. Paul L. Posner, *The Politics of Unfunded Mandates: Whither Federalism?* (Washington, D.C.: Georgetown University Press, 1998).
82. Beth Henschen and Edward Sidlow, *America at Odds: The Essentials*, 2nd ed. (Belmont, Calif.: Wadsworth, 2000), 504.
83. Barry Rabe, "Racing to the Top, the Bottom, or the Middle of the Pack? The Evolving State Government Role in Environmental Protection," in *Environmental Policy*, 8th ed., eds. Norman J. Vig and Michael E. Kraft (Washington, D.C.: CQ Press, 2013), 30–53; William T. Gormley Jr. and Steven J. Balla, *Bureaucracy and Democracy: Accountability and Performance*, 3rd ed. (Washington, D.C.: CQ Press, 2013), 167–183.
84. Steven Maguire, "State and Local Government Debt: An Analysis," Congressional Research Service, April 14, 2011, www.fas.org/sgp/crs/misc/R41735.pdf.

CHAPTER 3

1. Harold Lasswell, *Politics: Who Gets What, When, How* (Cleveland, Ohio: Meridian Books, 1958).
2. Charles E. Lindblom, *Politics and Markets: The World's Political Economic Systems* (New York: Basic Books, 1977), 171–172.
3. Joe Weisenthal, "Guess Which Country Has the Highest Percentage of Workers Employed by the Government," *Business Insider*, November 28, 2011, http://articles.businessinsider.com/2011-11-28/markets/30449203_1_guess-sector-government-sector.
4. Harvey Feigenbaum, Jeffrey Henig, and Chris Hamnett, *Shrinking the State: The Political Underpinnings of Privatization* (Cambridge, UK: Cambridge University Press, 1999), 59–86.
5. E. S. Savas, *Privatization and Public-Private Partnerships* (New York: Chatham House, 2000), 72; E. S. Savas, *Privatization: The Key to Better Government* (Chatham, N.J.: Chatham House, 1987), 131.
6. Mark Schlesinger, Robert A. Dotwart, and Richard T. Pulice, "Competitive Bidding and States' Purchase of Services: The Case of Mental Health Care in Massachusetts," *Journal of Policy Analysis and Management* (Winter 1986): 245–259.
7. Council of State Governments, *Book of the States, 1997–98* (Lexington, Ky.: Council of State Governments, 1998), 32:485; Keon S. Chi, Kelley A. Arnold, and Heather M. Perkins, "Privatization in State Government: Trends and Issues," *Spectrum: The Journal of State Government* (Fall 2003), www.csg.org/knowledgecenter/docs/spec_fa03Privatization.pdf.
8. Leonard Gilroy and Lisa Snell, "Annual Privatization Report 2011: State Government Privatization," April 2012, http://reason.org/files/state_annual_privatization_report_2011.pdf.
9. Paul Chassy and Scott H. Amey, "Bad Business: Billions of Taxpayer Dollars Wasted on Hiring Contractors," September 13, 2011, www.pogo.org/our-work/reports/2011/co-gp-20110913.html.
10. Ibid.

11. David Masci, "Telecom's Unfinished Business," *CQ Outlook*, March 8, 1999.
12. Daniel J. Parks, "Financial Services Bill in the Final Stretch," *CQ Weekly*, October 23, 1999; William D. Cohan, *House of Cards: A Tale of Hubris and Wretched Excess on Wall Street* (New York: Doubleday, 2009).
13. Keith Perine, "Bush Signs Corporate Fraud Bill, but Many Wonder about Its Impact," *CQ Weekly*, August 3, 2002.
14. Jan Austin, ed., *CQ Almanac 2010* (Washington, D.C.: CQ Roll Call, 2011), chap. 3, 3–9.
15. Aaron Bernstein, "Too Much Corporate Power?" *Business Week*, September 11, 2000.
16. Pew Research Center for the People & the Press, "Distrust, Discontent, Anger and Partisan Rancor: The People and Their Government," April 18, 2010, www.people-press.org/2010/04/18/distrust-discontent-anger-and-partisan-rancor/.
17. Maggie McComas, "Atop the *Fortune* 500: A Survey of C.E.O.s," *Fortune*, April 28, 1986. The *Fortune* 500 is a list compiled annually of the 500 publicly held U.S. industrial companies with the largest sales.
18. John Portz, "Politics, Plant Closings, and Public Policy: The Steel Valley Authority in Pittsburgh" (paper presented at the annual meeting of the Midwest Political Science Association, Chicago, April 9–11, 1987); Terence Bell, "The 10 Biggest Steel Producers," http://metals.about.com/od/suppliersbyname/tp/The-Ten-Biggest-Steel-Producers.htm.
19. Yochi J. Dreazen, "Labor Unions Turn to Mergers in Pursuit of Growth," *Wall Street Journal*, September 1, 2000; Bureau of Labor Statistics, "Union Members Summary," January 27, 2012, www.bls.gov/news.release/union2.nr0.htm.
20. Cohan, *House of Cards*, 404–416.
21. See Bro Uttal, "Behind the Fall of Steve Jobs," *Fortune*, August 5, 1985; and Peter Burrows, "Apple," *Business Week*, July 31, 2000.
22. Walter Isaacson, "American Icon," *Time*, October 17, 2011.
23. Lev Grossman and Harry McCracken, "The Inventor of the Future," *Time*, October 17, 2011.
24. Keith Bradsher, "General Motors Raises Stakes in Fuel Economy War with Ford," *New York Times*, August 3, 2000.
25. Katie Thomas and Michael S. Schmidt, "Drug Firm Guilty in Criminal Case," *New York Times*, July, 3, 2012.
26. "Mergers and Acquisitions," http://en.wikipedia.org/wiki/Mergers_and_acquisitions; Mary DiMaggio, "The Top 10 Best (and Worst) Corporate Mergers of All Time . . . or, the Good, the Bad, and the Ugly," September 15, 2009, http://rasmussen.edu/degrees/business/blog/best-and-worst-corporate-mergers.
27. James Glanz, "Contractors Outnumber U.S. Troops in Afghanistan," *New York Times*, September 2, 2009.
28. David Streitfeld and Edward Wyatt, "U.S. Is Escalating Inquiry Studying Google's Power," *New York Times*, April 27, 2012; Edward Wyatt, "U.S. Ends Inquiry onto Way Google Sets Up Searches," *New York Times*, January 4, 2013.
29. Proxy resolutions are proposals introduced by shareholders and voted on by shareholders. If adopted, they become corporate policy.
30. Ben Protess and Katherine Reynolds Lewis, "From Reticence to Joining the Revolt," *New York Times*, June 8, 2012.
31. Stephanie Clifford, "Wal-Mart Vote Shows Rise in Shareholder Unrest," *New York Times*, June 5, 2012.
32. *Munn v. Illinois*, 94 U.S. 118 (1877).
33. Mary H. Cooper, "Critics Question National Energy Policy," *CQ Outlook*, April 22, 2000; RAP Energy Solutions, "Electricity Regulation in the U.S.: A Guide," www.reponline.org/document/download/id/645.
34. Jack Walker, "The Origins and Maintenance of Interest Groups in America," *American Political Science Review* 77 (June 1983): 390–406.
35. Quoted on the MacNeil/Lehrer NewsHour, April 16, 1987.
36. Jackie Calmes, "For 'Party of Business,' Allegiances Are Shifting," *New York Times*, January 16, 2013.

37. Robert A. G. Monks, *The Emperor's Nightingale: Restoring the Integrity of the Corporation in the Age of Shareholder Activism* (Reading, Mass.: Addison-Wesley, 1998), 68; Marshall E. Blume and Donald B. Keim, "Trends in Institutional Stock Ownership and Some Implications," March 12, 2008, www.q-group.org/archives_folder/pdf/spring2008/Keim-InstitutionalOwnership.pdf.

38. Alex Berenson, "Buccaneer, or the Shareholder's Best Friend?" *New York Times*, September 24, 2000; Protess and Lewis, "From Reticence to Joining the Revolt."

39. Arthur O'Sullivan and Steven M. Sheffrin, *Microeconomics: Principles and Tools*, 2d ed. (Upper Saddle River, N.J.: Prentice Hall, 2001), 250–251; Andrea Alegria, Agata Kaczanowska, and Lauren Setar, "Highly Concentrated: Companies That Dominate Their Industries," IBISWorld, February 2012, www.ibisworld.com/Common/MediaCenter/Highly%20Concentrated%20 Industries.pdf.

40. Michael Lewis, *The New New Thing: A Silicon Valley Story* (New York: W. W. Norton, 2000).

41. Lisa Mesdag, "The 50 Largest Private Industrial Companies," *Fortune*, May 31, 1982.

42. See Jared Sandberg, "Microsoft's Six Fatal Errors," *Newsweek*, June 19, 2000.

43. Michael J. de la Merced, "Once Remote, Goldman Sachs Puts on a Friendly Public Face," *New York Times*, May 4, 2012; Jessica Silver-Greenberg and Ben Protess, "JPMorgan Chief Expected to Play Down Trade Risks," *New York Times*, June 13, 2012.

44. Jessica Silver-Greenberg, "Morgan's Board Uses a Pay Cut as a Message," *New York Times*, January 17, 2013.

45. Nick Wingfield, "H.P. Board Selects Whitman as New Chief," *New York Times*, September 23, 2011; Quentin Hardy and Nick Wingfield, "Ouster of Hewlett-Packard C.E.O. Is Expected," *New York Times*, September 22, 2011.

46. Catalyst, "1998 Catalyst Census: Women Board Directors of the *Fortune* 500," www.catalyst. org/knowledge/1998-catalyst-census-women-board-directors-fortune-500; Alliance for Board Diversity, "Missing Piece: Women and Minorities on *Fortune* 500 Boards," http:// theabd.org/Missing_Pieces_Women_and_Minorities_on_Fortune_500_Boards.pdf.

47. Victor Brudney, "The Independent Director—Heavenly City or Potemkin Village?" *Harvard Law Review* 95 (January 1982): 597–659.

48. David Halberstam, *The Reckoning* (New York: Morrow, 1986), 462.

49. Clea Benson, Rachel Bloom, John Cranford, Benton Ives, and Phil Mattingly, "Sorting Out the Bailout," *CQ Weekly*, February 23, 2009; John Schatz, "President Signs 'Cash for Clunkers' Law; Program Coffers Are Refilled with $2 billion," *CQ Weekly*, August 10, 2009.

50. Bill Vlasic, "A Weight Hobbling G.M.," *New York Times*, May 3, 2012. By the end of 2012, the government had sold 40 percent of its remaining GM stock; Bill Vlasic, "G.M. Chief Expects to Regain Market Share," *New York Times*, January 10, 2013.

51. Bill Vlasic, "Two-Tier Pay Now the Way Detroit Works," *New York Times*, September 13, 2011.

52. Bill Vlasic, "Sign of a Comeback: U.S. Carmakers Are Hiring," *New York Times*, February 22, 2013.

53. "America's Most Admired Companies," *Fortune*, February 21, 2000.

54. See Monks, *The Emperor's Nightingale*, 96–97.

55. Bill Vlasic, "Bluntly and Impatiently, Chief Upends G.M.'s Staid Tradition," *New York Times*, December 11, 2011.

56. Walter Adams and James Brock, *The Bigness Complex: Industry, Labor, and Government in the American Economy*, 2nd ed. (New York: Pantheon, 1986).

57. Claudia H. Deutsch, "The Fading Copier King," *New York Times*, October 19, 2000.

58. Xerox Corporation, "Xerox At a Glance," www.xerox.com/about-xerox/company-facts/enus .html.

59. Martha Derthick, *Up in Smoke: From Legislation to Litigation in Tobacco Politics*, 2nd ed. (Washington, D.C.: CQ Press, 2005).

60. Reed Abelson, "Can Respect Be Mandated? Maybe Not Here," *New York Times*, September 10, 2000.

61. Eric Dash, "An Ousted Chief's Exit-Pay Package Is Seen by Many as Typically Excessive," *New York Times*, January 4, 2007.

62. Ben Protess, "In Split Vote, S.E.C. Adopts Rules on Corporate Pay," *New York Times*, January 26, 2011.

63. Jessica Silver-Greenberg and Nelson D. Schwartz, "Citigroup's Chief Rebuffed on Pay by Shareholders," *New York Times*, April 18, 2012; Jessica Silver-Greenberg and Susanne Craig, "Citi Chairman Is Said to Have Planned Chief's Exit over Months," *New York Times*, October 26, 2012.

64. Nelson D. Schwartz, "Bank of America Investors Complain, but Approve Chief's Pay," *New York Times*, May 9, 2012.

65. Annie Lowrey, "Facing Down the Bankers," *New York Times*, May 30, 2012; Leslie Wayne, "Seeking to Stay Out of Proxy Battles," *New York Times*, April 8, 1991.

66. Frank Ackerman, Neva R. Goodwin, Laurie Dougherty, and Kevin Gallagher, eds., *The Political Economy of Inequality* (Washington, D.C.: Island Press, 2000), 64.

67. Christina Rexrode and Bernard Condon, "Typical CEO Made $9.6M Last Year, AP Study Finds," Associated Press, May 26, 2012, http://article.wn.com/view/2012/05/28/Typical_CEO_made_96M_last_year_AP_study_finds/; Nathaniel Popper, "CEO Pay, Rising Despite the Din," *New York Times*, June 17, 2012.

68. Katie Thomas, "Glaxo Opens Door to Data on Research," *New York Times*, October 11, 2012.

69. Arthur Louis, "Lessons from the Firestone Fracas," *Fortune*, August 28, 1978; Stuart Feldstein, "How Not to React to a Safety Controversy," *Business Week*, November 6, 1978.

70. Katie Thomas, "In Documents on Pain Drug, Signs of Doubt and Deception," *New York Times*, June 24, 2012.

71. Mark Leibovich, "Child Prodigy, Online Pioneer," *Washington Post*, September 3, 2000; "Can Amazon Make It?" *Business Week*, July 10, 2000.

72. Nick Wingfield, "Amazon's Profit Drops 35% but Tops Expectations," *New York Times*, April 27, 2012; *Fortune*, December 3, 2012.

73. Allison Enright, "E-Commerce Sales Jump 16% in 2011," Internet Retailer, www.internetretailer.com/2012/02/16/e-commerce-sales-jump-16-2011.

74. Google did acquire Motorola Mobility in May 2012. Evelyn M. Rusli, "$12 Billion Deal Will Put Google in Mobile Market," *New York Times*, August 16, 2011.

75. *Pacific Gas & Electric Co. v. State Energy Resources Conservation and Development Commission*, 461 U.S. 190 (1983).

76. Matthew L. Wald, "Federal Regulators Approve Two Nuclear Reactors in Georgia," *New York Times*, February, 9, 2012.

77. Illinois Government News Network, "Governor Quinn Launches Production of Mitsubishi Outlander Sport in Normal," July 17, 2012, www3.illinois.gov/PressReleases/ShowPressRelease.cfm?SubjectID=1&RecNum=10400; Abelson, "Can Respect Be Mandated?"

78. Francesca Levy, "America's Most Livable Cities," April 29, 2010, www.forbes.com/2010/04/29/cities-livable-pittsburgh-lifestyle-real-estate-top-ten-jobs-crime-income.html.

79. Jon Gertner, "True Innovation," *New York Times*, February 26, 2012; John Brooks, *Telephone: The First Hundred Years* (New York: Harper & Row, 1976), 12–16; Dale Russakoff, "A High-Tech, High-Stakes Race Begins," *Washington Post*, June 15, 1987.

80. Randall E. Stross and Alicia Hills, "Mr. Gates Builds His Brain Trust," *Fortune*, December 8, 1997, http://money.cnn.com/magazines/fortune/fortune_archive/1997/12/08/234912/index.htm; Microsoft Research, http://research.microsoft.com/en-us.

81. Adriel Bettelheim, "Policing the Internet Boom," *CQ Outlook*, February 20, 1999.

82. Committee Encouraging Corporate Philanthropy, "Giving in Numbers: 2011 Edition," www.corporatephilanthropy.org/pdfs/giving_in_numbers/GivingNumbers2011.pdf; William Ouchi, *The M-Form Society: How American Teamwork Can Capture the Competitive Edge* (Reading, Mass.: Addison-Wesley, 1984), 16–31, 192–193.

83. Kate Zernike, "Pupils Prosper from an Investment," *New York Times*, August 2, 2000.

84. Stephanie Strom, "Billionaires' Pledge to Give Away Half Gains Followers," *New York Times*, August 5, 2010.

85. Look to the Stars: The World of Celebrity Giving, "Warren Buffett: Charity Work, Events and Causes," www.looktothestars.org/celebrity/183-warren-buffett.

86. Reed Abelson, "New Philanthropists Put Donations to Work," *New York Times*, July 6, 2000; Gates Foundation, www.gatesfoundation.org; Hewlett Foundation, www.hewlett.org.

87. Carl E. Van Horn, *Working Scared (or Not at All): The Lost Decade, Great Recession, and Restoring the Shattered American Dream* (Lanham, Md.: Rowman & Littlefield, 2013).

88. *Economic Report of the President* (Washington, D.C.: U.S. Government Printing Office, 2000), 355, Table B-41; Frank Ahrens, "Black Teen Unemployment Rises to Nearly 50%," *Washington Post*, December 7, 2009.

89. Mark C. Rom, *Public Spirit in the Thrift Tragedy* (Pittsburgh, Pa.: University of Pittsburgh Press, 1996).

90. Timothy Curry and Lynn Shibut, "The Cost of the Savings and Loan Crisis: Truth and Consequences," FDIC Banking Review, www.fdic.gov/bank/analytical/banking/2000dec/brv13n2_2.pdf.

91. Congressional Budget Office, "CBO's Latest Estimate of the Cost of the TARP: $24 billion," www.cbo.gov/publication/43663.

92. For more, see the Project on Government Oversight, www.pogo.org.

93. Gardiner Harris, "Minerals Management Service Director Resigns over Spill," *New York Times*, May 27, 2010.

94. John M. Broder, "Companies Knew of Cement Flaws before Rig Blast," *New York Times*, October 29, 2010.

95. John M. Broder, "Panel Points to Errors in Gulf Spill," *New York Times*, January 6, 2011; John M. Broder, "Panel Finds No Evidence That Safety Shortcuts Led to BP Explosion," *New York Times*, November 9, 2010.

96. John Schwartz, "BP Says Spill Settlement Terms Are Too Generous," *New York Times*, February 18, 2011.

97. John Schwartz, "Man with $20 Billion to Disburse Finds No Shortage of Claims or Critics," *New York Times*, April 18, 2011.

98. John M. Broder and Clifford Krauss, "Oil Drilling to Resume in the Gulf's Deep Waters," *New York Times*, March 1, 2011.

99. Clifford Krauss, "In BP Indictments, U.S. Shifts to Hold Individuals Accountable," *New York Times*, November 16, 2012; see also Clifford Krauss, "Judge Accepts BP's $4 Billion Criminal Settlement over Gulf Oil Spill," *New York Times*, January 30, 2013.

100. John M. Broder and Stanley Reed, "BP Is Barred from Taking Government Contracts," *New York Times*, November 28, 2012; John Schwartz, "Oil Rig's Owner Settles Gulf Spill Case for $1.4 Billion," *New York Times*, January 4, 2013; see also Geof Koss, "From the Coast to the Courts," *CQ Weekly*, December 10, 2012.

101. Clifford Krauss and Barry Meier, "As Trial Opens, Deal Effort Continues," *New York Times*, February 26, 2013.

102. Daniel Press and Daniel A. Mazmanian, "Toward Sustainable Production," in *Environmental Policy: New Directions for the 21st Century*, 8th ed., eds. Norman J. Vig and Michael E. Kraft (Washington, D.C.: CQ Press, 2013), 230–254.

103. Nelson D. Schwartz, "Banks Look to Burnish Their Images by Backing Green Technology Firms," *New York Times*, June 11, 2012.

104. James Dao, "Wal-Mart to Announce a Five-Year Commitment to Hire 100,000 Veterans," *New York Times*, January 15, 2013; Stephanie Clifford, "Walmart Plans to Buy American More Often," *New York Times*, January 16, 2013.

105. Jack Walker, "The Diffusion of Innovations in the American States," *American Political Science Review* 63 (September 1969): 880–889.

106. See Andrea Gabor, *The Man Who Discovered Quality: How W. Edwards Deming Brought the Quality Revolution to America—The Stories of Ford, Xerox, and GM* (New York: Random House, 1990).

107. Steven Greenhouse, "More Lockouts as Companies Battle Unions," *New York Times*, January 23, 2012.

108. See Paul S. Grogan and Tony Proscio, *Comeback Cities: A Blueprint for Urban Neighborhood Revival* (Boulder, Colo.: Westview, 2000); Enterprise, "About Us," www.enterprisecommunity.com/about/mission-and-strategic-plan; LISC, "Building Sustainable Communities: By the Numbers," www.lisc.org/accomplishments/LISC_By_Numbers_2011.pdf.

109. E. E. Schattschneider, *The Semi-Sovereign People: A Realist's View of Democracy in America* (New York: Holt, Rinehart & Winston, 1960), 1–19.

110. Binyamin Appelbaum, "For U.S. Families, Net Worth Falls to 1990s Levels," *New York Times*, June 11, 2012; Malia Wollan, "Years of Unraveling, Then Bankruptcy for a City," *New York Times*, July 19, 2012.

CHAPTER 4

1. U.S. Census Bureau, "Government Employment & Payroll: Historical Data: 2010," www.census.gov/govs/apes/historical_data_2010.html.

2. Emmette S. Redford, *Democracy in the Administrative State* (New York: Oxford University Press, 1969).

3. U.S. Department of Transportation, Federal Motor Carrier Safety Administration, "No Texting Rule Fact Sheet," www.fmcsa.dot.gov/rules-regulations/topics/distracted-driving/texting-factsheet.aspx.

4. On the statutory language for these and other independent regulatory commissions, see Marver Bernstein, *Regulating Business by Independent Commission* (Princeton, N.J.: Princeton University Press, 1955); Theodore Lowi, *The End of Liberalism: The Second Republic of the United States*, 2nd ed. (New York: W. W. Norton, 1979); and Benjamin Taylor and Fred Whitney, *Labor Relations Law*, 4th ed. (Englewood Cliffs, N.J.: Prentice Hall, 1983).

5. Steven J. Balla, "Political and Organizational Determinants of Bureaucratic Responsiveness," *American Politics Quarterly* 28 (April 2000): 163–193.

6. William T. Gormley Jr. and Steven J. Balla, *Bureaucracy and Democracy: Accountability and Performance*, 3rd ed. (Washington, D.C.: CQ Press, 2013).

7. See Theda Skocpol, *Protecting Soldiers and Mothers: The Political Origins of Social Policy in the United States* (Cambridge, Mass.: Harvard University Press, 1992); Christopher Howard, *The Hidden Welfare State: Tax Expenditures and Social Policy in the United States* (Princeton, N.J.: Princeton University Press, 1997); and Rebecca Blank, *It Takes a Nation: A New Agenda for Fighting Poverty* (Princeton, N.J.: Princeton University Press, 1997).

8. Paul M. Krawzak and Kerry Young, "President's Budget: Primer, and Harbinger of Fray," *CQ Weekly*, February 20, 2012; Office of Management and Budget, "Historical Tables," www.whitehouse.gov/omb/budget/Historicals; also see Suzanne Mettler, *The Submerged State: How Invisible Government Policies Undermine American Democracy* (Chicago: University of Chicago Press, 2011).

9. Laurence E. Lynn, *Managing Public Policy* (Boston: Little, Brown, 1987), 64.

10. Philip Shenon, "U.S. Acts to Stop Quotas in Hiring It Backed in the Past," *New York Times*, April 30, 1985; John L. Palmer and Isabel V. Sawhill, eds., *The Reagan Record: An Assessment of America's Changing Domestic Priorities* (Cambridge, Mass.: Ballinger, 1984), 204–208.

11. Executive Office of the President, Office of Management and Budget, *Budget of the United States Government: Government-Wide Performance Plan* (Washington, D.C.: U.S. Government Printing Office, 2000), 140; Phillip Cooper, Linda P. Brady, Olivia Hidalgo Hardeman, Albert Hyde, Katherine C. Naff, J. Steven Ott, and Harvey White, *Public Administration for the Twenty-First Century* (Fort Worth, Tex.: Harcourt Brace, 1998), 276.

12. Charlie Savage, "In Shift, Justice Dept. Hiring Lawyers with Civil Rights Backgrounds," *New York Times*, June 1, 2011.

13. John W. Kingdon, *Agendas, Alternatives, and Public Policies*, 2nd ed. (New York: HarperCollins College, 1995), 87.

14. Ibid., chap. 7.

15. For an extensive discussion of this trend and its implications, see William T. Gormley Jr., *Taming the Bureaucracy: Muscles, Prayers, and Other Strategies* (Princeton, N.J.: Princeton University Press, 1989); and Gormley and Balla, *Bureaucracy and Democracy*, 3rd ed.

16. Francis Rourke, *Bureaucracy, Politics, and Public Policy*, 3rd ed. (Boston: Little, Brown, 1984), chap. 3.

17. Ibid., chap. 4.
18. See Lance DeHaven-Smith and Carl E. Van Horn, "Subgovernment Conflict in Public Policy," *Policy Studies Journal* 12 (Summer 1984): 627–642.
19. Gormley and Balla, *Bureaucracy and Democracy*, 3rd ed., 92–95, 185–186; Robert Gilmour, "Policy Formulation in the Executive Branch: Central Legislative Clearance," in *Cases in Public Policy-Making*, ed. James Anderson (New York: Praeger, 1976), 80–96.
20. Charles Lindblom, *The Intelligence of Democracy: Decision Making through Mutual Adjustment* (New York: Free Press, 1965).
21. Linda L. Fisher, "Fifty Years of Presidential Appointments," in *The In-and-Outers: Presidential Appointees and Transient Government in Washington*, ed. G. Calvin Mackenzie (Baltimore, Md.: Johns Hopkins University Press, 1987), as cited in Gormley and Balla, *Bureaucracy and Democracy*, 3rd ed., 87.
22. See Norman J. Vig and Michael E. Kraft, eds., *Environmental Policy in the 1980s: Reagan's New Agenda* (Washington, D.C.: Congressional Quarterly, 1984), chaps. 5, 7, 8, and 17; and Palmer and Sawhill, eds., *The Reagan Record*, 146–151.
23. Anne Marie Cammisa, *From Rhetoric to Reform? Welfare Policy in American Politics* (Boulder, Colo.: Westview, 1998), 131.
24. Norman J. Vig, "Presidential Powers and Environmental Policy," in *Environmental Policy*, 8th ed., eds. Norman J. Vig and Michael E. Kraft (Washington, D.C.: CQ Press, 2013), 94.
25. See Eugene Lewis, *Public Entrepreneurship: Toward a Theory of Bureaucratic Political Power* (Bloomington: Indiana University Press, 1980); Robert Caro, *The Power Broker: Robert Moses and the Fall of New York* (New York: Knopf, 1974).
26. Gormley and Balla, *Bureaucracy and Democracy*, 3rd ed., 215. The quotation is attributed to Senator Fritz Hollings, D-S.C.
27. Anthony Downs, *Inside Bureaucracy* (Boston: Little, Brown, 1967), 88–89.
28. John Brehm and Scott Gates, *Working, Shirking, and Sabotage: Bureaucratic Response to a Democratic Public* (Ann Arbor: University of Michigan Press, 1997).
29. Lewis, *Public Entrepreneurship*, 214–215; Caro, *The Power Broker*.
30. Rourke, *Bureaucracy, Politics, and Public Policy*, 118–119.
31. William Claiborne, "Tribes and Tribulations: BIA Seeks to Lose a Duty," *Washington Post*, June 2, 2000.
32. Lynn, *Managing Public Policy*, 119–125.
33. Gormley and Balla, *Bureaucracy and Democracy*, 3rd ed., 281–285.
34. Daniel Lewis, "The Trailblazer," *New York Times Magazine*, June 13, 1999.
35. William T. Gormley Jr., *Family Day Care Regulation in Wisconsin: The Bureaucracy Heals Itself* (Madison: La Follette Institute of Public Affairs, University of Wisconsin, 1990).
36. See Herbert Simon, *Administrative Behavior: A Study of Decision-Making Processes in Administrative Organizations* (New York: Macmillan, 1957); James March and Herbert Simon, *Organizations* (New York: John Wiley, 1964); Aaron Wildavsky, *The Politics of the Budgetary Process*, 3rd ed. (Boston: Little, Brown, 1979); and Charles Lindblom, "The Science of 'Muddling Through,'" *Public Administration Review* 19 (Spring 1959): 79–88.
37. Lindblom, "The Science of 'Muddling Through,'" 79–88.
38. Rourke, *Bureaucracy, Politics, and Public Policy*, 29–35.
39. Morton Halperin, "Shaping the Flow of Information," in *Bureaucratic Power in National Politics*, 3rd ed., ed. Francis Rourke (Boston: Little, Brown, 1978), 102–115.
40. Ibid., 102–110.
41. Michael Lipsky, "Toward a Theory of Street-Level Bureaucracy," in *Bureaucratic Power in National Politics*, 3rd ed., ed. Rourke, 135–157.
42. For an excellent description of the rational perspective, see Edith Stokey and Richard Zeckhouser, *A Primer for Policy Analysis* (New York: W. W. Norton, 1978), or E. S. Quade, *Analysis for Public Decisions* (New York: Elsevier, 1975).
43. See William T. Gormley Jr. and David L. Weimer, *Organizational Report Cards* (Cambridge, Mass.: Harvard University Press, 1999), 1–19; Gormley and Balla, *Bureaucracy and Democracy*, 3rd ed., chap. 7.

44. A more complete discussion of this example can be found in B. Guy Peters, *American Public Policy: Promise and Performance*, 2nd ed. (Chatham, N.J.: Chatham House, 1986), 297–309.
45. Walter A. Rosenbaum, *Environmental Politics and Policy*, 8th ed. (Washington, D.C.: CQ Press, 2011), 172–174.
46. Sheila M. Olmstead, "Applying Market Principles to Environmental Policy," in *Environmental Policy*, 8th ed., eds. Vig and Kraft, 211.
47. U.S. General Accounting Office, *The Government Performance and Results Act: 1997 Governmentwide Implementation Will Be Uneven* (GGD-97-109) (Washington, D.C.: U.S. General Accounting Office, 1997); Stephen Barr, "GOP Sees No Results in Results Act," *Washington Post*, June 9, 1998; Stephen Barr, "'Performance Reports' Faulted," *Washington Post*, May 4, 2000.
48. Gormley and Balla, *Bureaucracy and Democracy*, 3rd ed., 19–21.
49. Ibid., 21–23.
50. Richard Zerbe Jr., "Is Cost-Benefit Analysis Legal? Three Rules," *Journal of Policy Analysis and Management* 17 (Summer 1998): 421.
51. Lynn, *Managing Public Policy*, 187; Michael E. Kraft and Scott R. Furlong, *Public Policy: Politics, Analysis, and Alternatives* (Washington, D.C.: CQ Press, 2004), chap. 4.
52. See Cornelius M. Kerwin and Scott R. Furlong, *Rulemaking: How Government Agencies Write and Make Policy*, 4th ed. (Washington, D.C.: CQ Press, 2011), 51–52.
53. Ibid., 202–210.
54. See Kenneth Culp Davis, *Administrative Law of the Seventies*, supplement to *Davis's Administrative Law Treatise* (Rochester, N.Y.: Lawyers Cooperative Publishing, 1976), chap. 8.
55. See A. Lee Fritschler, *Smoking and Politics: Bureaucracy Centered Policymaking*, 5th ed. (Upper Saddle River, N.J.: Prentice Hall, 1996), 138–140.
56. Board of Governors of the Federal Reserve System, "Federal Banking Agencies Issue Policy Statement on Funding and Liquidity Risk Management," March 17, 2010, www.federalreserve.gov/newsevents/press/bcreg/20100317a.htm.
57. Lipsky, "Toward a Theory of Street-Level Bureaucracy."
58. See Davis, *Administrative Law of the Seventies*, chap. 4.
59. Murray Edelman, *The Symbolic Uses of Politics* (Urbana: University of Illinois Press, 1964), chap. 3.
60. See Frances Fox Piven and Richard Cloward, *Regulating the Poor: The Functions of Public Welfare* (New York: Vintage Books, 1971), or Frances Fox Piven and Richard Cloward, *Poor People's Movements: Why They Succeed, How They Fail* (New York: Vintage Books, 1979).
61. William Gormley Jr., Joan Hoadley, and Charles Williams, "Potential Responsiveness in the Bureaucracy: Views of Public Utility Regulation," *American Political Science Review* 77 (September 1983): 704–717; William Gormley Jr., *The Politics of Public Utility Regulation* (Pittsburgh, Pa.: University of Pittsburgh Press, 1983), 113–130.
62. See Andrew McFarland, *Public Interest Lobbies: Decision Making on Energy* (Washington, D.C.: American Enterprise Institute, 1976), or Jeffrey Berry, *Lobbying for the People: The Political Behavior of Public Interest Groups* (Princeton, N.J.: Princeton University Press, 1977).
63. See Mark Nadel, *The Politics of Consumer Protection* (Indianapolis, Ind.: Bobbs-Merrill, 1971); Kenneth Meier, *Regulation: Politics, Bureaucracy and Economics* (New York: St. Martin's, 1985), 96–97.
64. Gormley, *The Politics of Public Utility Regulation*; Douglas Anderson, "State Regulation of Electric Utilities," in *The Politics of Regulation*, ed. James Q. Wilson (New York: Basic Books, 1980), 3–41.
65. On the FTC, see Meier, *Regulation*, 106–113; on the Army Corps of Engineers, see Daniel Mazmanian and Jeanne Nienaber, *Can Organizations Change? Environmental Protection, Citizen Participation, and the Corps of Engineers* (Washington, D.C.: Brookings Institution, 1979).
66. Gormley, *Taming the Bureaucracy*, chap. 6.
67. David Osborne and Ted Gaebler, *Reinventing Government: How the Entrepreneurial Spirit Is Transforming the Public Sector* (New York: Penguin, 1993); Donald Kettl, "Building Lasting Reform: Enduring Questions, Missing Answers," in *Inside the Reinvention Machine: Appraising Governmental Reform*, eds. Donald Kettl and John DiIulio Jr. (Washington, D.C.: Brookings Institution, 1995), 9–83.

68. A good example is the National Environmental Performance Partnership System inaugurated by the EPA in 1995. See National Academy of Public Administration, *Resolving the Paradox of Environmental Protection* (Washington, D.C.: National Academy of Public Administration, 1997), 143–169; Barry G. Rabe, "Racing to the Top, the Bottom, or the Middle of the Pack? The Evolving State Government Role in Environmental Protection," in *Environmental Policy*, 8th ed., eds. Vig and Kraft.

69. For an interesting discussion of state-level reforms, see Maria Aristigueta, *Managing for Results in State Government* (Westport, Conn.: Quorum Books, 1999); Rabe, "Racing to the Top."

70. Ben Protess and Jessica Silver-Greenberg, "In Its First Action, Consumer Bureau Takes Aim at Capital One," *New York Times*, July 19, 2012.

71. Edward Wyatt, "U.S. Consumer Watchdog to Issue Mortgage Rules," *New York Times*, January 10, 2013.

72. Jessica Silver-Greenberg, "Bank Deal Ends Flawed Reviews of Foreclosures," *New York Times*, January 11, 2013.

73. Binyamin Appelbaum, "A Bold Dissenter at the Fed, Hoping His Doubts Are Wrong," *New York Times*, January 9, 2013.

74. See Bernstein, *Regulating Business*; Lowi, *The End of Liberalism*, 2nd ed.; Grant McConnell, *Private Power and American Democracy* (New York: Knopf, 1966); and George Stigler, "The Theory of Economic Regulation," *Bell Journal of Economic and Management Sciences* 2 (Spring 1971): 3–21.

75. See Bernstein, *Regulating Business*; Bradley Behrman, "The Civil Aeronautics Board," in *The Politics of Regulation*, ed. Wilson, 57–120; David Howard Davis, *Energy Politics*, 3rd ed. (New York: St. Martin's, 1982), 130–165; and Jonathan Macey, "Organizational Design and Political Control of Administrative Agencies," *Journal of Law, Economics, and Organization* 8 (March 1992): 93–110.

76. Stigler, "The Theory of Economic Regulation."

77. Macey, "Organizational Design," 99.

78. Gormley, *The Politics of Public Utility Regulation*, 152–159.

79. Kerwin and Furlong, *Rulemaking*, 4th ed., chap. 3.

80. Gormley and Balla, *Bureaucracy and Democracy*, 3rd ed., chap. 4.

81. For evaluations of American social welfare programs by authors with contrasting ideological perspectives, see Piven and Cloward, *Regulating the Poor*; Charles Murray, *Losing Ground: American Social Policy, 1950–1980* (New York: Basic Books, 1984).

82. See Robert Haveman, ed., *A Decade of Federal Antipoverty Programs: Achievements, Failures and Lessons* (New York: Academic Press, 1977); John Schwarz, *America's Hidden Success: A Reassessment of Public Policy from Kennedy to Reagan*, revised ed. (New York: W. W. Norton, 1988); Karen Davis and Kathy Schoen, *Health and the War on Poverty: A Ten-Year Appraisal* (Washington, D.C.: Brookings Institution, 1978); Robert Taggart, *A Fisherman's Guide: An Assessment of Training and Remediation Strategies* (Kalamazoo, Mich.: W. E. Upjohn Institute for Employment Research, 1981); Lisbeth B. Schorr, *Within Our Reach: Breaking the Cycle of Disadvantage* (New York: Anchor Books, 1989); Gormley and Balla, *Bureaucracy and Democracy*, 3rd ed., 195–197.

83. House Committee on Ways and Means, *1998 Green Book* (Washington, D.C.: U.S. Government Printing Office, 1998), 1413.

84. Office of Management and Budget, "Historical Tables," 5-1, 8-5, www.whitehouse.gov/omb/budget/Historicals.

85. Rosenbaum, *Environmental Politics and Policy*, 8th ed., 98–105; Walter Rosenbaum, "Science Politics and Policy at EPA," in *Environmental Policy*, 8th ed., eds. Vig and Kraft, 158–184.

86. Michael E. Kraft and Norman J. Vig, "Environmental Policy over Four Decades: Achievements and New Directions," in *Environmental Policy*, 8th ed., eds. Vig and Kraft, 19–25.

87. Environmental Protection Agency, "Superfund National Accomplishments Summary," August 10, 2012, www.epa.gov/superfund/accomp/pdfs/FY%2011%20Summary%20FINAL.pdf.

88. Ibid; Rosenbaum, *Environmental Policy*, 8th ed., 267.
89. Ibid.; Jonathan L. Ramseur and Mark Reisch, "Superfund: Overview and Selected Issues," May 17, 2006, http://digital.library.unt.edu/ark:/67531/metacrs9266/m1/1/high_res_d/ RL33426_2006May17.pdf.
90. Ibid.
91. Ibid; EPA, "Superfund National Accomplishments Summary."
92. Ramseur and Reisch, "Superfund," 13.
93. Rosenbaum, *Environmental Politics and Policy*, 8th ed., 267.
94. Harold Seidman, *Politics, Position and Power: The Dynamics of Federal Organization*, 3rd ed. (New York: Oxford University Press, 1975), 255.
95. Nye Stevens, "Postal Reform," August 14, 2003, http://digital.library.unt.edu/ark:/67531/ metacrs4563/m1/1/high_res_d/IB10104_2003Aug14.pdf.
96. Jan Austin, ed., *The CQ Almanac Plus, 2006* (Washington, D.C.: CQ Press, 2007), 11-3-4.
97. Kevin R. Kosar, "The U.S. Postal Service's Financial Condition: Overview and Issues for Congress," January 27, 2012, http://digital.library.unt.edu/ark:/67531/metadc83934/m1/1/ high_res_d/R41024_2012Jan27.pdf.
98. Ibid., 4.
99. Steven Greenhouse, "Losing Billions, Postal Service Is Near Default," *New York Times*, September 4, 2011.
100. Rachel Bade, "Postal Overhaul Defers Cuts," *CQ Weekly*, April 30, 2012.
101. Ron Nixon, "As Default Looms, Postal Service Sees Deeper Woes," *New York Times*, August 1, 2012; Ron Nixon, "Distress Deepening, Postal Service Defaults on $5.6 Billion Benefits Payment," *New York Times*, October 2, 2012.
102. John Cranford, "2012 Legislative Summary," *CQ Weekly*, January 14, 2013; Ron Nixon, "Trying to Stem Losses, Post Office Seeks to End Saturday Letter Delivery," *New York Times*, February 7, 2013.
103. Ben Weyl, "Remodeling Fannie and Freddie," *CQ Weekly*, January 31, 2011.
104. Kraft and Vig, "Environmental Policy over Four Decades," 20–24.
105. U.S. Energy Information Administration, "U.S. Energy-Related CO_2 Emissions in Early 2012 Lowest Since 1992," August 1, 2012, http://eia.gov/todayinenergy/detail.cfm?id=7350#tabs_ co2emissions-1.
106. Geof Koss and Pam Radtke Russell, "Running Low on Power," *CQ Weekly*, July 16, 2012.
107. Rosenbaum, *Environmental Politics and Policy*, 8th ed., 188–190.
108. Daniel Press and Daniel A. Mazmanian, "Toward Sustainable Production," in *Environmental Policy*, 8th ed., eds. Vig and Kraft, 235; Olmstead, "Applying Market Principles," 215.
109. Norman J. Vig and Michael E. Kraft, "Conclusion," in *Environmental Policy*, 8th ed., eds. Vig and Kraft, 385–388.
110. Gormley and Balla, *Bureaucracy and Democracy*, 3rd ed., 269.
111. Ibid., 286–287. The other agencies rated were the FBI (58 percent approval), NASA (58 percent), the CIA (47 percent), Homeland Security (46 percent), the IRS (40 percent), and the FDA (38 percent).
112. American Customer Satisfaction Index, "ACSI Scores for U.S. Federal Government 2011," January 19, 2012, www.theacsi.org/acsi-results/acsi-benchmarks-for-us-federal-government-2011.

CHAPTER 5

1. Alexis de Tocqueville, *Democracy in America* (New York: McGraw-Hill: 1981), 141. (Originally published in 1835 and 1840.)
2. As cited in Kathleen Hunter, "Telemarketers Get Higher Approval Rating Than U.S. Congress," August 16, 2012, www.bloomberg.com/news/2012-08-15/telemarketers-get-higher-approval-rating-than-u-s-congress.html.
3. Roger H. Davidson, Walter J. Oleszek, and Frances E. Lee, *Congress and Its Members*, 13th ed. (Washington, D.C.: CQ Press, 2011), chap. 7.

4. Jack L. Walker, "Setting the Agenda in the U.S. Senate: A Theory of Problem Selection," *British Journal of Political Science* 7 (1977): 423–445.

5. Miles A. Pomper, Chuck McCutcheon, and Pat Towell, "GOP Leaders Refuse to Close Ranks with Clinton on Bombing Iraq," *CQ Weekly*, December 22, 1998.

6. Miles A. Pomper and Vanita Gowda, "Congress Weighs Next Kosovo Move with a Tight Hold on Purse Strings," *CQ Weekly*, June 12, 1999.

7. Alan Rosenthal, *The Decline of Representative Democracy: Process, Participation, and Power in State Legislatures* (Washington, D.C.: CQ Press, 1998), 16; see also Richard C. Elling, "The Utility of State Legislative Casework as a Means of Oversight," in *Legislative Studies Quarterly* 4 (August 1979): 353–379.

8. Davidson et al., *Congress and Its Members*, 13th ed., 125; Thomas Mann, *Unsafe at Any Margin: Interpreting Congressional Elections* (Washington, D.C.: American Enterprise Institute, 1978).

9. See Gary C. Jacobson, *The Politics of Congressional Elections*, 8th ed. (New York: Pearson, 2012).

10. Davidson et al., *Congress and Its Members*, 13th ed., 95–98.

11. Randy Wynn, "For the Record," *CQ Weekly*, November 27, 1999.

12. Chuck McCutcheon, "Hill Takes a Hands-On Approach to Tightening Nuclear Security," *CQ Weekly*, July 1, 2000.

13. The Campaign Finance Institute, "Table 3-1: The Cost of Winning an Election, 1986-2010 (in Nominal and 2010 Dollars)," www.cfinst.org/data/pdf/VitalStats_t1.pdf.

14. On the relationship between congressional committees and campaign contributions, see Richard L. Hall and Frank W. Wayman, "Buying Time: Moneyed Interests and the Mobilization of Bias in Congressional Committees," *American Political Science Review* 84 (September 1990): 797–820; Vincent G. Moscardelli, Raymond J. La Raja, and Nathaniel B. Kraft, "Buying Time in the Connecticut Legislature before Clean Elections" (paper presented at the 8th Annual Conference on State Politics and Policy, Temple Institute for Public Affairs, Philadelphia, Pa., May 30–31, 2008).

15. See Thomas E. Mann and Norman J. Ornstein, *The Broken Branch: How Congress Is Failing America and How to Get It Back on Track* (New York: Oxford University Press, 2006).

16. James G. Gimpel, *Fulfilling the Contract: The First 100 Days* (Boston: Allyn & Bacon, 1996); John Healey, "Clinton Success Rate Declined to a Record Low in 1995," *Congressional Quarterly Weekly Report*, January 27, 1996.

17. Donald C. Baumer and Howard J. Gold, *Politics, Polarization, and Democracy in the United States* (Boulder, Colo.: Paradigm Publishers, 2010), 193.

18. Congressional Research Service, *Congressional Staff: Duties and Functions* (Washington, D.C., U.S. Government Printing Office, 2003).

19. U.S. Government Accountability Office, "GAO at a Glance," www.gao.gov/about/gglance .html; Ida A. Brundnick, *The Congressional Research Service and the American Legislative Process* (Washington, D.C.: U.S. Government Printing Office, 2011), 2; Lisa Rein, "U.S. Printing Office Shrinks with Round of Buyouts," *Washington Post*, January 25, 2012.

20. National Conference of State Legislatures, "Legislative Staff Services," www.ncsl.org/legislative-staff.aspx.

21. For a summary of the law and the timeline to its enactment, see The White House, "A More Secure Future: What the New Health Law Means for You and Your Family," www.whitehouse .gov/healthreform/.

22. Woodrow Wilson, *Congressional Government* (New York: Meridian Books, 1956).

23. Davidson et al., *Congress and Its Members*, 13th ed., 180.

24. Hugh Heclo, "Issue Networks and the Executive Establishment," in *The New American Political System*, ed. Anthony King (Washington, D.C.: American Enterprise Institute, 1978), chap. 3.

25. John Cranford and John Schatz, "Rearguing the Contract," *CQ Weekly*, April 11, 2011.

26. Seth Stern, "Under the Gun, ATF's Weakness Exposed," *CQ Weekly*, July 4, 2011; Jonathan Broder, "Getting the Diplomatic Security You Pay For," *CQ Weekly*, October 15, 2012.

27. See Steven S. Smith, *Call to Order: Floor Politics in the House and Senate* (Washington, D.C.: Brookings Institution, 1990).

28. Barbara Sinclair, *Unorthodox Lawmaking: New Legislative Processes in the U.S. Congress*, 3rd ed. (Washington, D.C.: CQ Press, 2007), 131–134.

29. Davidson et al., *Congress and Its Members*, 13th ed., 242–248; Steven Smith, "Parties and Leadership in the U.S. Senate," in *The Legislative Branch*, eds. Paul J. Quirk and Sarah A. Binder (New York: Oxford University Press, 2005), 255–278.

30. U.S. Senate, "Senate Action on Cloture Motions," www.senate.gov/pagelayout/reference/cloture_motions/clotureCounts.htm.

31. David Stockman, *The Triumph of Politics: Why the Reagan Revolution Failed* (New York: Harper & Row, 1986), 250–251.

32. Interview by the authors, Washington, D.C., December 10, 1984.

33. Andrew Taylor, "Congress Wraps Up and Heads Home on a Trail of Broken Budget Caps," *CQ Weekly*, October 24, 1998.

34. "5 Significant Achievements from Lame-Duck Congress," *San Francisco Chronicle*, December 24, 2010, www.sfgate.com/opinion/editorials/article/5-significant-achievements-from-lame-duck-Congress-2452352.php; "Landmark Health Care Law and Late Flurry of Bills Mark Session," in *CQ Almanac 2010*, ed. Jan Austin (Washington, D.C.: CQ Roll Call, 2011), 1-3–1-8.

35. Legislative leaders are elected by their respective party memberships in the House and Senate. In Congress, the leadership is the speaker of the House, the majority and minority leaders of the House and Senate, assistant leaders (sometimes called party whips), and the party caucus officers in the House and Senate.

36. Randall B. Ripley, *Congress: Process and Policy*, 4th ed. (New York: W. W. Norton, 1998), 210–212.

37. Davidson et al., *Congress and Its Members*, 13th ed., 263–267; Barbara Sinclair, *Majority Leadership in the U.S. House* (Baltimore, Md.: Johns Hopkins University Press, 1983); Randall B. Ripley, *Majority Party Leadership in Congress* (Boston: Little, Brown, 1969).

38. Sinclair, *Unorthodox Lawmaking*, 3rd ed., 131–134, chap. 11; Gimpel, *Fulfilling the Contract*.

39. Sinclair, *Unorthodox Lawmaking*, 3rd ed., 132.

40. Davidson et al., *Congress and Its Members*, 13th ed., 146–152.

41. Alan Rosenthal, *Legislative Life: People, Process, and Performance in the States* (New York: Harper & Row, 1981), 167–168.

42. Rosenthal, *The Decline of Representative Democracy*, 72–80, chap. 7.

43. Rosenthal, *Legislative Life*, 266.

44. Interview by the authors, Washington, D.C., May 29, 1985.

45. Murray Edelman, *The Symbolic Uses of Politics* (Urbana: University of Illinois Press, 1964).

46. Randall B. Ripley and Grace Franklin, *Congress, the Bureaucracy, and Public Policy*, 5th ed. (Pacific Grove, Calif.: Brooks/Cole, 1991); see also Frances Fox Piven and Richard Cloward, *Poor People's Movements: Why They Succeed, How They Fail* (New York: Vintage Books, 1979).

47. Sharon Parrot, "2008 Omnibus Appropriations Bill Cuts Funding for Head Start," Center on Budget and Policy Priorities, February 6, 2008, www.cbpp.org/cms/index.cfm?fa=view&id=1151.

48. Aaron Wildavsky, *The Politics of the Budgetary Process*, 3rd ed. (Boston: Little, Brown, 1979).

49. Austin, ed., *CQ Almanac 2010*, 1–5; *CQ Weekly*, December 22, 2011; *CQ Weekly*, December 31, 2012.

50. David Mayhew, *Congress: The Electoral Connection* (New Haven, Conn.: Yale University Press, 1974); Theodore Lowi, *The End of Liberalism: The Second Republic of the United States*, 2nd ed. (New York: W. W. Norton, 1979).

51. Rosenthal, *The Decline of Representative Government*, 316–317.

52. Jeff Plungis, "The Driving Force of Bud Shuster," *CQ Weekly*, August 7, 1999, 914–919.

53. Costas Panagopolous and Joshua Schank, *All Roads Lead to Congress: The $300 Billion Fight over Highway Funding* (Washington, D.C.: CQ Press, 2008), 11–14.

54. Office of Management and Budget, "FY 2010 Earmarks by Appropriations Subcommittee," http://earmarks.omb.gov/earmarks-public/2010-appropriations-by-spendcom/summary.html.

55. Paul M. Krawzak and Kerry Young, "Bracing for a Budget Battle," *CQ Weekly*, February 7, 2011.

56. Charles O. Jones, "Speculative Augmentation in Federal Air Pollution Policy-Making," *Journal of Politics* 36 (May 1974): 438–464; see also Paul Light, *Government's Greatest Achievements: From Civil Rights to Homeland Security* (Washington, D.C.: Brookings Institution, 2002).

57. Lawrence Brown, *New Policies, New Politics: Government's Response to Government's Growth* (Washington, D.C.: Brookings Institution, 1983).

58. See Donald C. Baumer and Carl E. Van Horn, *The Politics of Unemployment* (Washington, D.C.: Congressional Quarterly, 1985); and Carl E. Van Horn, *Working Scared (Or Not at All)*, (Lanham, Md: Rowman & Littlefield, 2013).

59. Figures derived from *Economic Report of the President* (Washington, D.C.: U.S. Government Printing Office, 2000), 357, Table B-43, and Tami Luhby, "Jobless Benefits Cost so Far: $319 Billion," CNNMoney, November 17, 2010, http://money.cnn.com/2010/11/17/news/economy/unemployment_benefits_cost/index.htm.

60. David Harrison, "Extended Benefits: Extended Jousting," *CQ Weekly*, November 28, 2011.

61. John Cranford, "2012 Legislative Summary," *CQ Weekly*, January 14, 2013.

62. Baumer and Van Horn, *The Politics of Unemployment*, 168–172.

63. David E. Price, "Congressional Committees in the Policy Process," in *Congress Reconsidered*, 3rd ed., eds. Lawrence C. Dodd and Bruce I. Oppenheimer (Washington, D.C.: Congressional Quarterly, 1985), 211–222.

64. Allen Schick, "The Distributive Congress," in *Making Economic Policy in Congress*, ed. Allen Schick (Washington, D.C.: American Enterprise Institute, 1983), 258.

65. Congressional Budget Office, "The Budget and Economic Outlook: Fiscal Years 2012 to 2022," www.cbo.gov/publication/42911.

66. "Done Deal," *CQ Weekly*, Special Report, August 8, 2011.

67. Jonathan Weisman, "Tentative Accord Reached to Raise Taxes on Wealthy," *New York Times*, January 1, 2013; Cranford, "2012 Legislative Summary," 82–84.

68. "Vote Studies," *Congressional Quarterly Weekly Report*, December 19, 1992; Humberto Sanchez, "Fight for Control Shows in Votes," *CQ Weekly*, January 21, 2013, 132–136.

69. Lowi, *The End of Liberalism*, 2nd ed.

70. Morris Fiorina, *Congress: Keystone of the Washington Establishment* (New Haven, Conn.: Yale University Press, 1977), chaps. 7 and 8.

71. Barry Rabe, *Beyond NIMBY: Hazardous Waste Siting in Canada and the U.S.* (Washington, D.C.: Brookings Institution, 1994); Walter A. Rosenbaum, *Environmental Politics and Policy*, 8th ed. (Washington, D.C.: CQ Press, 2011), 269–272.

72. Charles O. Jones, *Clean Air: The Policies and Politics of Pollution Control* (Pittsburgh, Pa.: University of Pittsburgh Press, 1975).

73. Michael E. Kraft and Norman J. Vig, "Environmental Policy over Four Decades: Achievements and New Directions," in *Environmental Policy*, 8th ed., eds. Norman J. Vig and Michael E. Kraft (Washington, D.C.: CQ Press, 2013), 2–29.

74. Richard Scher and James Button, "Voting Rights Act: Implementation and Impact," in *Implementation of Civil Rights Policy*, eds. Charles S. Bullock III and Charles V. Lamb (Monterey, Calif.: Brooks/Cole, 1984), 20–54.

75. M. V. Hood III, Quentin Kidd, and Irwin L. Morris, *The Rational Southerner: Black Mobilization, Republican Growth, and the Partisan Transformation of the American South* (New York: Oxford Press, 2012), 39–45.

76. Michael Kirst and Richard Jung, "The Utility of a Longitudinal Approach in Assessing Implementation: A Thirteen-Year View of Title I, ESEA," in *Studying Implementation: Methodological and Administrative Issues*, ed. Walter Williams (Chatham, N.J.: Chatham House, 1982), 119–148; David Nather, "Dozens of Amendments Make for Slow Progress on Senate's ESEA Bill," *CQ Weekly*, May 6, 2000.

77. Baumer and Van Horn, *The Politics of Unemployment*, 53.

78. See Beryl A. Radin, *Beyond Machiavelli: Policy Analysis Comes of Age* (Washington, D.C.: Georgetown University Press, 2000), 39; Deborah Stone, *Policy Paradox: The Art of Political Decision Making*, 3rd ed. (New York: W. W. Norton, 2012).

79. John Burghardt, Peter Z. Schochet, Sheena McConnell, Terry Johnson, R. Mark Gritz, Steven Glazerman, John Homrighausen, and Russell Jackson, "Does Job Corps Work? Summary of the National Job Corps Study," Mathematica Policy Research, Inc., June 2001, http://wdr .doleta.gov/opr/fulltext/01-jcsummary.pdf; Peter Z. Schochet, John Burghardt, and Sheena McConnell, "Does Job Corps Work? Impact Findings from the National Job Corps Study," *American Economic Review* 98, no. 5 (2008): 1864–1886.

80. U.S. General Accounting Office, "GAO at a Glance."

81. See Joel D. Aberbach, *Keeping a Watchful Eye: The Politics of Congressional Oversight* (Washington, D.C.: Brookings Institution, 1990).

82. See Mathew McCubbins and Thomas Schwartz, "Congressional Oversight Overlooked: Police Patrols versus Fire Alarms," *American Journal of Political Science* 28 (February 1984): 180–202; Davidson et al., *Congress and Its Members*, 13th ed., 340–343.

83. Rosenbaum, *Environmental Politics and Policy*, 8th ed., 261–262.

84. See Jones, *Clean Air*, and Jones, "Speculative Augmentation."

85. Jacob S. Hacker and Paul Pierson, *Winner-Take-All Politics: How Washington Made the Rich Richer—and Turned Its Back on the Middle Class* (New York: Simon & Schuster, 2010).

CHAPTER 6

1. Most governors have formal powers that are similar to those of presidents. They serve four-year terms and can run for reelection at least once. Often they can appoint many high-ranking state officials, although some state legislatures share this power. Most states also have other high-ranking state officials, such as attorneys general, who are elected statewide. Governors have considerable control over the budget process and many have a line-item veto over legislative actions. For more details, see Alan Rosenthal, *The Best Job in Politics: Exploring How Governors Succeed as Policy Leaders* (Washington, D.C.: CQ Press, 2012); Thad C. Beyle, "Being Governor," in *The State of the States*, 4th ed., ed. Carl E. Van Horn (Washington, D.C.: CQ Press, 2006); and Larry Sabato, *Goodbye to Good-Time Charlie: The American Governorship Transformed*, 2nd ed. (Washington, D.C.: Congressional Quarterly, 1983).

2. See John W. Kingdon, *Agendas, Alternatives, and Public Policies*, 2nd ed. (New York: Longman, 2003).

3. James K. Oliver, "Presidents as National Security Policy Makers," in *Rethinking the Presidency*, ed. Thomas E. Cronin (Boston: Little, Brown, 1982), 396–397.

4. See Sabato, *Goodbye to Good-Time Charlie*, 105–110, 115–116, and Beyle, "Being Governor," 74.

5. Jeffrey L. Barnett and Phillip M. Vidal, "State and Local Government Finances Summary: 2010," September 2012, www2.census.gov/govs/estimate/summary_report.pdf.

6. Paul Light, "Presidents as Domestic Policy Makers," in *Rethinking the Presidency*, ed. Cronin, 361.

7. Ibid., 362–364.

8. Jeff Fishel, *Presidents and Promises: From Campaign Pledge to Presidential Performance* (Washington, D.C.: Congressional Quarterly, 1985).

9. Theodore J. Lowi, "Ronald Reagan—Revolutionary?" in *The Reagan Presidency and the Governing of America*, eds. Michael S. Lund and Lester M. Salamon (Washington, D.C.: Urban Institute Press, 1984), 29–56; Stephen Skowronek discusses the intellectual, ideological, and practical aspects of several efforts to build and then reform national government in *Building a New American State: The Expansion of National Administrative Capacity* (New York: Cambridge University Press, 1982), 1877–1920.

10. See Thomas Cronin, "On the Separation of Brain and State: Implications for the President," in *Modern Presidents and the Presidency*, ed. Marc Landy (Lexington, Mass.: Lexington Books, 1985), 54–58.

11. Kingdon, *Agendas, Alternatives, and Public Policies*, 2nd ed.

12. Light, "Presidents as Domestic Policy Makers," 365.

13. Fishel, *Presidents and Promises*, 26.

14. Chuck McCutcheon, *The Election of 2012: Outcomes and Analysis* (Washington, D.C.: CQ Press, 2013), 6.

15. Fishel, *President and Promises*, 20–22. For more general treatments of this subject, see E. E. Schattschneider, *The Semi-Sovereign People: A Realist's View of Democracy in America* (New York: Holt, Rinehart & Winston, 1960; rev. ed., 1975), and Peter Bachrach and Morton S. Baratz, *Power and Poverty: Theory and Practice* (New York: Oxford University Press, 1970).

16. Ilene Rosenthal, "The Clinton-Gore Digital Divide Proposal," *Technology and Learning*, May 2000.

17. Theda Skocpol, *Boomerang: Clinton's Health Security Effort and the Turn against Government in U.S. Politics* (New York: W. W. Norton, 1996); Margaret Carlson, "Another Dose of Harry and Louise," *Time*, November 24, 1997.

18. Jennie Jacobs Kronenfeld, *The Changing Federal Role in U.S. Health Care Policy* (Westport, Conn.: Greenwood Publishing, 1997), 15.

19. Richard E. Neustadt, *Presidential Power: The Politics of Leadership from FDR to Carter* (New York: John Wiley, 1980).

20. Rosenthal, *The Best Job in Politics*.

21. Andrew Taylor, "Few on Congress Grieve as Justices Give Line-Item Veto the Ax," *CQ Weekly*, June 27, 1998.

22. See Duane Lockard, *The Politics of State and Local Government*, 3rd ed. (New York: Macmillan, 1983), chaps. 7 and 8; Thad Beyle and Margaret Ferguson, "Governors and the Executive Branch," in *Politics in the American States: A Comparative Analysis*, eds. Virginia Gray and Russell L. Hanson (Washington, D.C.: CQ Press, 2008), 192–228.

23. See Bert A. Rockman, *The Leadership Question: The Presidency and the American System* (New York: Praeger, 1984).

24. This argument is presented more fully by Samuel Kernell in *Going Public: New Strategies of Presidential Leadership*, 4th ed. (Washington, D.C.: CQ Press, 2007).

25. Ibid., chap. 2.

26. William J. Clinton, "Remarks at a Democratic National Committee Luncheon in New York City," *Weekly Compilation of Presidential Documents*, April 3, 2000.

27. See, for example, Daniel J. Palazzolo, *Done Deal: The Politics of the 1997 Budget Agreement* (Chatham, N.J.: Chatham House, 1999).

28. Kernell, *Going Public*, 4th ed., chap. 5.

29. See Rockman, *The Leadership Question*; James MacGregor Burns, *Leadership* (New York: Harper & Row, 1978); and Neustadt, *Presidential Power*.

30. Rockman, *The Leadership Question*, chap. 2.

31. See James David Barber, *The Presidential Character: Predicting Performance in the White House*, 2nd ed. (Englewood Cliffs, N.J.: Prentice Hall, 1977).

32. Executive Office of President, "Fiscal Year 2012 Congressional Budget Submission," www .whitehouse.gov/sites/default/files/2012-eop-budget.pdf.

33. Arthur M. Schlesinger Jr., *The Imperial Presidency* (Boston: Houghton Mifflin, 1973).

34. James P. Pfiffner, *The Strategic Presidency: Hitting the Ground Running* (Lawrence: University Press of Kansas, 1996), 151–153.

35. Bob Woodward, *The Agenda: Inside the Clinton White House* (New York: Simon & Schuster, 1994); Bob Woodward, *The Price of Politics* (New York: Simon & Schuster, 2012).

36. Annie Lowrey, "Obama's Remade Inner Circle Has an All-Male Look, so Far," *New York Times*, January 2013; David Rothkopf, "Managing the Oval Office," *New York Times*, January 20, 2013; also Stephen J. Wayne, *Personality and Politics: Obama for and against Himself* (Washington, D.C.: CQ Press, 2012).

37. Knowledge Center, The Council of State Governments, "Table 4.1: The Governors' Compensation, Staff, Travel and Residence," in *The Book of the States 2012* (Lexington, Ky.: The Council of State Governments, 2012), 217–218.

38. Coleman B. Ransone Jr., *The American Governorship* (Westport, Conn.: Greenwood Press, 1982), 109–111.

39. Ibid., 114; and Rosenthal, *The Best Jobs in Politics*.
40. Personal interview with author, March 1990.
41. Michael Cooper and Dalia Sussman, "Massacre at School Sways Public in Way Earlier Shootings Didn't," *New York Times*, January 18, 2013.
42. These categories are a slightly modified version of those used by Thomas Cronin in *The State of the Presidency*, 2nd ed. (Boston: Little, Brown, 1980), 145–153.
43. Ibid.
44. Beyle, "Being Governor."
45. National Governors Association and National Association of State Budget Officers, *The Fiscal Survey of States*, December 2009 (Washington, D.C.: National Governors Association, 2009).
46. Ibid.
47. See Harrell H. Hodgers Jr. and Charles S. Bullock III, *Law and Social Change* (New York: McGraw-Hill, 1972), chaps. 2 and 5, and Phyllis Wallace, "A Decade of Policy Developments in Equal Opportunities in Employment and Housing," in *A Decade of Federal Antipoverty Programs: Achievements, Failures and Lessons*, ed. Robert H. Haveman (New York: Academic Press, 1977).
48. James W. Ceaser, "The Rhetorical Presidency Revisited," in *Modern Presidents and the Presidency*, ed. Landy, 33.
49. See Frances Fox Piven and Richard A. Cloward, *Regulating the Poor: The Functions of Public Welfare* (New York: Vintage Books, 1971).
50. McCutcheon, *The Election of 2012*, 6; Donald C. Baumer and Howard J. Gold, *Parties, Polarization, and Democracy in the United States* (Boulder, Colo.: Paradigm Publishers, 2010), 81; Herbert B. Asher, *Presidential Elections and American Politics: Voters, Candidates, and Campaigns Since 1952*, 3rd ed. (Homewood, Ill.: Dorsey Press, 1984).
51. See Fishel, *Presidents and Promises*, 93.
52. Martha Derthick, *New Towns In-Town* (Washington, D.C.: Urban Institute Press, 1972).
53. Ibid., 82–102.
54. Morton H. Halperin, "Implementing Presidential Foreign Policy Decisions: Limitations and Resistance," in *Cases in Public Policy Making*, ed. James E. Anderson (New York: Praeger, 1976), 208–236.
55. Graham T. Allison, *Essence of Decision: Explaining the Cuban Missile Crisis* (Boston: Little, Brown, 1971), 132.
56. Donald S. Van Meter and Carl E. Van Horn "The Policy Implementation Process: A Conceptual Framework," *Administration and Society* 6, no. 4 (1975): 445–488.
57. Lester M. Salamon, "Follow-ups, Letdowns, and Sleepers: The Time Dimension in Policy Evaluation," in *Public Policymaking in a Federal System*, eds. Charles O. Jones and Robert D. Thomas (Beverly Hills, Calif.: Sage, 1976), 257–283.
58. Ibid., 267.
59. Ibid., 263.
60. The original Head Start evaluation was done by the Westinghouse Learning Corporation and Ohio University; see *The Impact of Head Start: An Evaluation of the Effects of Head Start on Children's Cognitive and Affective Development*, report to the Office of Economic Opportunity (Washington, D.C.: U.S. Government Printing Office, 1969). For subsequent research, see Irving Lazar, *Summary: The Persistence of Preschool Effects* (Ithaca: Community Service Laboratory, New York State College of Human Ecology at Cornell University, 1977). For a more recent study, see Steven W. Barnett and Greg Camilli, "Definite Results from Loose Data: A Response to 'Does Head Start Make a Difference?'" (New Brunswick, N.J.: Rutgers University Press, 1996). For numerous studies, see Office of Planning, Research and Evaluation, Administration for Children and Families, Department of Health and Human Services, "Head Start Impact Study: Final Report: Executive Summary," January 15, 2010, www.acf.hhs.gov/sites/default/files/opre/executive_summary_final.pdf.
61. On the impact of federal job-training programs, see Carl. E. Van Horn, Christopher T. King, and Tara Smith, *Identifying Gaps and Setting Priorities for Employment and Training Research* (prepared for the U.S. Department of Labor, Employment and Training Administration), July 2011, www.heldrich.rutgers.edu/sites/default/files/content/ETA_Research_Gaps_Priorities.pdf.

On the impact of the Supplemental Nutritional Assistance Program, see U.S. Department of Agriculture, "The Benefits of Increasing the Supplemental Nutrition Assistance Program (SNAP) Participation in Your State," www.fns.usda.gov/snap/outreach/pdfs/bc_facts.pdf.

62. Kenneth K. Wong, "The Politics of Education," in *Politics in the American States*, eds. Gray and Hanson; Egon G. Guba, "The Failure of Educational Evaluation," in *Evaluating Action Programs*, ed. Carol H. Weiss (Boston: Allyn & Bacon, 1972), 250–266; James S. Coleman, "Problems of Conceptualization and Measurement in Studying Policy Impacts," in *Public Policy Evaluation*, ed. Kenneth M. Dolbeare (Beverly Hills, Calif.: Sage, 1975), 19–40.
63. William T. Gormley Jr. and Steven J. Balla, *Bureaucracy and Democracy: Accountability and Performance*, 3rd ed. (Washington, D.C.: CQ Press, 2013), 287–289.
64. For an excellent example, see Laurence E. Lynn Jr., "A Decade of Policy Developments in the Income Maintenance System," in *A Decade of Federal Antipoverty Programs*, ed. Haveman, 55–117.
65. For a discussion of presidential reorganization efforts, see Erwin E. Hargrove and Michael Nelson, *Presidents, Politics, and Policy* (New York: Knopf, 1984), 249–265, and Joel D. Aberbach and Mark A. Peterson, eds., *The Executive Branch* (New York: Oxford University Press, 2005).
66. Pfiffner, *The Strategic Presidency*, 154.
67. Congressional Budget Office, "Comparing the Compensation of Federal and Private-Sector Employees," January 2012, www.cbo.gov/sites/default/files/cbofiles/attachments/01-30-FedPay.pdf.
68. Paul C. Light, "The New True Size of Government," August 2006, http://wagner.nyu.edu/performance/files/True_Size.pdf.
69. Curtis W. Copeland, "The Federal Workforce: Characteristics and Trends," April 19, 2012, www.digital.library.unt.edu/ark:/67531/metadc40238/m1/1/high_res_d/RL34685_2011Apr19.pdf.
70. Beyle, "Being Governor," 38.

CHAPTER 7

1. Martin Shapiro, *Courts: A Comparative and Political Analysis* (Chicago: University of Chicago Press, 1981), 105–124; Richard Posner, *The Federal Courts: Crisis and Reform* (Cambridge, Mass.: Harvard University Press, 1985).
2. Donald Horowitz, *The Courts and Social Policy* (Washington, D.C.: Brookings Institution, 1977), 9.
3. In the 2010 to 2011 term, the Supreme Court decided eighty-five cases; in the 2011 to 2012 term, the Court heard only seventy-eight cases. Supreme Court of the United States, "Opinions," www.supremecourt.gov/opinions/opinions.aspx.
4. Richard Neely, *How Courts Govern America* (New Haven, Conn.: Yale University Press, 1981), 212.
5. J. Woodford Howard Jr., *Courts of Appeals in the Federal Judicial System: A Study of the 2nd, 5th, and D.C. Circuits* (Princeton, N.J.: Princeton University Press, 1981), 25–33; Christopher Banks, *Judicial Politics in the D.C. Circuit Court* (Baltimore, Md.: Johns Hopkins University Press, 1999), 36; G. Alan Tarr, *Judicial Process and Judicial Policymaking*, 5th ed. (Boston: Wadsworth, 2010), 36.
6. William Popkin, *Statutes in Court: The History and Theory of Statutory Interpretation* (Durham, N.C.: Duke University Press, 1999), 152.
7. Ibid., 184.
8. Ibid., 189–194.
9. William Eskridge, *Dynamic Statutory Interpretation* (Cambridge, Mass.: Harvard University Press, 1994), 13.
10. See *United States v. Richardson*, 418 U.S. 166 (1974); *Valley Forge Christian College v. Americans United for Separation of Church and State*, 454 U.S. 464 (1982).
11. *Amalgamated Meat Cutters v. Connally*, 337 F. Supp. 737 (1971).
12. *United States v. Curtiss-Wright Export Corp.*, 299 U.S. 304 (1936); *Dames & Moore v. Regan*, 453 U.S. 654 (1981).

13. The cases were *Hamdan v. Rumsfeld* (2006) and *Boumediene v. Bush* (2008). Lawrence Baum, *The Supreme Court*, 10th ed. (Washington, D.C.: CQ Press, 2010), 24.

14. By statute, the U.S. Supreme Court is required to hear appeals stemming from decisions by special three-judge federal district courts. Some voting rights cases have traveled to the Supreme Court's docket via that route. Ibid., 7–9.

15. Federal judges are not entirely powerless in these matters. District court judges can—and do—encourage parties to settle a case without going to trial. Also, judges may refuse to hear a case on the grounds that a party lacks standing, that the issue is not ripe, or for other reasons.

16. William Glaberson, "Caseload Forcing Two-Level System for U.S. Appeals," *New York Times*, March 14, 1999.

17. Baum, *The Supreme Court*, 10th ed., 94, 157.

18. Ibid., 90–96.

19. Ibid., 91.

20. Melinda Gann Hall, "State Courts: Politics and the Judicial Process," in *Politics in the American States: A Comparative Analysis*, 9th ed., eds. Virginia Gray and Russell L. Hanson (Washington, D.C.: CQ Press, 2008), 248–249.

21. The Associated Press, "Judge's Property Transaction Leads to a Charge of Fraud," *New York Times*, January 20, 2013.

22. Campbell Robertson, "In South, Republicans Find That Dominance Does Not Ensure Solidarity," *New York Times*, October 21, 2012.

23. Tarr, *Judicial Process*, 5th ed., 243.

24. Baum, *The Supreme Court*, 10th ed., 10.

25. Although Phillips's decision was later overturned by the Ninth Circuit Court of Appeals, her ruling was part of a process that led to congressional action two months later, and the elimination of the policy in July 2011. John Schwartz, "U.S. Judge Halts 'Don't Ask' Policy," *New York Times*, October 12, 2010.

26. Edward Lazarus, *Closed Chambers: The Rise, Fall, and Future of the Modern Supreme Court* (New York: Times Books, 1998), 196–197; Linda Greenhouse, "William Brennan, 91, Dies," *New York Times*, July 25, 1997.

27. Lee Epstein and Jack Knight, *The Choices Justices Make* (Washington, D.C.: CQ Press, 1997), 95–107.

28. Kathleen Sullivan, "A Thousand Opinions, One Voice," *New York Times*, July 25, 1997.

29. O'Connor's center leadership is described at length by Jeffrey Toobin in *The Nine: Inside the Secret World of the Supreme Court* (New York: Anchor Books, 2008).

30. Ibid.; Baum, *The Supreme Court*, 10th ed., 135.

31. Adam Liptak, "A Significant Term, with Bigger Cases Ahead," *New York Times*, June 29, 2011; Adam Liptak, "Roberts Court Shifts Right, Tipped by Kennedy," New York Times, July 1, 2009.

32. Hughes denounced Roosevelt's plan in a calm but forceful letter to Senator Burton Wheeler, D-MT. The letter is credited with weakening congressional support for the court-packing plan.

33. Adam Liptak, "The Roberts Court Comes of Age," *New York Times*, June 30, 2010; Adam Liptak, "Supreme Court Moving beyond Its Old Divides," *New York Times*, July 1, 2012; David Von Drehle, "Roberts Rules," *Time*, July 16, 2012.

34. Adam Liptak and Allison Kopicki, "Approval Rating for Justices Hits Just 44% in Poll," *New York Times*, June 8, 2012.

35. Henry Glick, *Supreme Courts in State Politics* (New York: Basic Books, 1971); Hall, "State Courts."

36. Epstein and Knight, *The Choices Justices Make*, 176.

37. Baum, *The Supreme Court*, 10th ed., 120.

38. Rosemary O'Leary, "Environmental Policy in the Courts," in *Environmental Policy*, 8th ed., eds. Norman J. Vig and Michael E. Kraft (Washington, D.C.: CQ Press, 2013), 138–139.

39. *Daubert et al. v. Merrell Dow Pharmaceuticals, Inc.*, 509 U.S. 579 (1993).

40. Marc Galanter, "Why the 'Haves' Come Out Ahead: Speculations on the Limits of Legal Change," *Law and Society Review* 9 (Fall 1974): 95–160.

41. Paul S. Weiland, "Business and Environmental Policy in the Federal Courts," in *Business and Environmental Policy: Corporate Interests in the American Political System*, eds. Michael E. Kraft and Sheldon Kamieniecki (Cambridge, Mass.: MIT Press, 2007), 218–219.

42. Glendon Schubert, *Quantitative Analysis of Judicial Behavior* (Glencoe, Ill.: Free Press, 1959); Malcolm Feeley, "Another Look at the 'Party Variable' in Judicial Decision-Making: An Analysis of the Michigan Supreme Court," *Polity* 4 (Fall 1971): 91–104; Harold J. Spaeth, *Supreme Court Policy Making: Explanation and Prediction* (San Francisco, Calif.: W. H. Freeman, 1979); Tarr, *Judicial Process*, 5th ed., 243.

43. Philip Dubois, *From Ballot to Bench: Judicial Elections and the Quest for Accountability* (Austin: University of Texas Press, 1980), 231; Lawrence Baum, *The Supreme Court*, 8th ed. (Washington, D.C.: CQ Press, 2004), 128; Baum, *The Supreme Court*, 10th ed., 128.

44. C. Neal Tate, "Personal Attribute Models of the Voting Behavior of U.S. Supreme Court Justices: Liberalism in Civil Liberties and Economics Decisions, 1946–1978," *American Political Science Review* 75 (June 1981): 355–367; Sheldon Goldman, "Voting Behavior on the U.S. Court of Appeals Revisited," *American Political Science Review* 69 (June 1975): 491–506; Robert Carp and C. K. Rowland, *Policymaking and Politics in the Federal District Courts* (Knoxville: University of Tennessee Press, 1983); Baum, *The Supreme Court*, 10th ed., 124.

45. Robert Carp and Ronald Stidham, *The Federal Courts*, 3rd ed. (Washington, D.C.: CQ Press, 1998), 126–127; Baum, *The Supreme Court*, 10th ed., 123–125.

46. Peter Baker, "Liberal in Moderation," *New York Times*, May 11, 2012.

47. Charlie Savage, "Appeals Court Pushed to Right by Bush Choices," *New York Times*, October 29, 2008.

48. Adam Liptak, "The Most Conservative Court in Decades," *New York Times*, July 25, 2010.

49. Bernard Schwartz, *Super Chief: Earl Warren and the Supreme Court* (New York: New York University Press, 1983), 40–44.

50. Martin Schapiro, "On Predicting the Future of Administrative Law," *Regulation* 6 (May–June, 1982): 18–25; R. Shep Melnick, *Regulation and the Courts: The Case of the Clean Air Act* (Washington, D.C.: Brookings Institution, 1983); William T. Gormley Jr., *Taming the Bureaucracy: Muscles, Prayers, and Other Strategies* (Princeton, N.J.: Princeton University Press, 1989), chap. 4.

51. Lawrence Baum, *The Supreme Court* (Washington, D.C.: Congressional Quarterly, 1981), 156–162; Baum, *The Supreme Court*, 10th ed., 165.

52. Ibid., 162–169.

53. The *Heller* case pertained to federal (District of Columbia) law, but the right of individuals to bear arms in the face of state and local statutes was established in the 2010 case *McDonald v. Chicago*. Both decisions involved 5-4 votes, with Kennedy joining the conservatives to form a majority. Adam Liptak, "Justices Extend Firearm Rights in 5-4 Ruling," *New York Times*, June 29, 2010.

54. Much of the credit for the unanimous decisions goes to Earl Warren, a remarkably adroit political leader. Warren's handling of the *Brown* decision is a good case in point. When Warren took over as chief justice, the *Brown* case had already been argued, and the Court was prepared to vote 5-4 in favor of desegregation. In a clever ploy, Warren suggested that the justices postpone the vote. Instead, Warren led a freewheeling discussion that ultimately revealed some common ground on which they could agree. The process was not easy. Three separate conferences and numerous private conversations between Warren and individual justices were required before Warren's efforts were successful. In 1954, the Supreme Court issued a unanimous opinion in a case that is doubtless one of the most important in U.S. history. See Schwartz, *Super Chief*, 72–127.

55. Adam Liptak, "Supreme Court Moving beyond Its Old Divides."

56. Archibald Cox, *The Role of the Supreme Court in American Government* (New York: Oxford University Press, 1976), 38–39.

57. Vincent Blasi, "The Rootless Activism of the Burger Court," in *The Burger Court: The Counter-Revolution That Wasn't*, ed. Vincent Blasi (New Haven, Conn.: Yale University Press, 1983), 198–217; Baum, *The Supreme Court*, 10th ed., 175–177.

58. Robert Greenberger, "Firms Had Mixed Success in High Court," *Wall Street Journal*, June 25, 1999.

59. Baum, *The Supreme Court*, 10th ed., 165–166.

60. *United States v. Morrison*, 529 U.S. 598 (2000).

61. Toobin, *The Nine*, chaps. 11–13.

62. For an excellent discussion of leading cases, see Douglas Reed, *On Equal Terms: The Constitutional Politics of Educational Opportunity* (Princeton, N.J.: Princeton University Press, 2001); Tarr, *Judicial Process*, 5th ed., 312–321.

63. A. E. "Dick" Howard, "State Courts and Constitutional Rights in the Days of the Burger Court," *Virginia Law Review* 62 (June 1976): 873–944; Mary Porter, "State Supreme Courts and the Legacy of the Warren Court: Some Old Inquiries for a New Situation," in *State Supreme Courts: Policymakers in the Federal System*, eds. Mary Porter and G. Alan Tarr (Westport, Conn.: Greenwood Press, 1982), 3–21; Robert Pear, "State Courts Surpass U.S. Bench in Cases on Rights of Individuals," *New York Times*, May 4, 1986.

64. John Kincaid and Robert Williams, cited in Staci Beavers and Jeffrey Walz, "Modeling Judicial Federalism: Predictors of State Court Protections of Defendants' Rights under State Constitutions, 1969–1989," *Publius* 28 (Spring 1998): 45; Tarr, *Judicial Process*, 5th ed., 319.

65. Ibid., 320.

66. Ibid., 318; Hall, "State Courts and the Judicial Process," 229–230.

67. Charlotte Carter, *Media in the Courts* (Williamsburg, Va.: National Center for State Courts, 1981).

68. Michael Fletcher, "Court Camera Measure Rolls," *Washington Post*, June 1, 2000; Norman Davis, "Television in Our Courts: The Proven Advantages, the Unproven Dangers," *Judicature* 64 (August 1980): 85–92; Marjorie Cohn and David Dow, *Cameras in the Courtroom: Television and the Pursuit of Justice* (Jefferson, N.C.: McFarland & Company, 2011), 60.

69. Fletcher, "Court Camera Measure Rolls," 23; Lorraine H. Tong, "Televising Supreme Court and Other Federal Court Proceedings: Legislation and Issues," CRS Report for Congress, November 8, 2006, www.fas.org/sgp/crs/secrecy/RL33706.pdf.

70. Tong, "Televising Supreme Court," 2–3; Cohn and Dow, *Cameras in the Courtroom*, chap. 8. The Supreme Court's Web site is at www.supremecourt.gov.

71. Jonathan Casper, "The Supreme Court and National Policy Making," *American Political Science Review* 70 (March 1976): 50–63; Baum, *The Supreme Court*, 169–170; Harold Spaeth, "Burger Court Review of State Court Civil Liberties Decisions," *Judicature* 68 (February–March 1985): 285–291.

72. Casper, "The Supreme Court and National Policy Making."

73. Reginald Sheehan, William Mishler, and Donald Songer, "Ideology, Status, and the Differential Success of Direct Parties before the Supreme Court," *American Political Science Review* 86 (June 1992): 464–471.

74. Geoffrey Stone, *Individual Rights and Majoritarianism: The Supreme Court in Transition* (Washington, D.C.: Cato Institute, 1985).

75. Toobin, *The Nine*, 219–226.

76. Baum, *The Supreme Court*, 10th ed., 177.

77. Linda Greenhouse, "In Steps Big and Small, Supreme Court Moved Right," *New York Times*, July 1, 2007; Linda Greenhouse, "On Court That Defied Labeling, Kennedy Made the Boldest Mark," *New York Times*, June 29, 2008; Liptak, "Roberts Court Shifts Right"; Liptak, "A Significant Term"; Liptak, "Supreme Court Moving beyond Its Old Divides."

78. Greenhouse, "In Steps Big and Small"; Greenhouse, "On Court That Defied Labeling"; Liptak, "The Roberts Court Comes of Age"; Liptak, "A Significant Term."

79. Baum, *The Supreme Court*, 10th ed., 128.

80. Michael Rebell and Arthur Block, *Educational Policy Making and the Courts: An Empirical Study of Judicial Activism* (Chicago: University of Chicago Press, 1982), 36.

81. Toobin, *The Nine*, chaps. 1–2.

82. Martin Shapiro, *The Supreme Court and Administrative Agencies* (New York: Free Press, 1968); Jerry L. Mashaw, Charles Goetz, Frank Goodman, Warren Schwartz, and Paul Verkuil, *Social Security Hearings and Appeals: A Study of the Social Security Hearing System* (Lexington, Mass.: D. C. Heath, 1978), 125–150; Craig Wanner, "The Public Ordering of Private Relations, Part Two: Winning Civil Court Cases," *Law and Society Review* 9 (Winter 1975): 293–306;

Stephen Frank, "The Oversight of Administrative Agencies by State Supreme Courts: Some Macro Findings," *Administrative Law Review* 32 (Summer 1980): 477–499; Donald Crowley, "Judicial Review of Administrative Agencies: Does the Type of Agency Matter?" *Western Political Quarterly* 40 (June 1987): 265–284.

83. Galanter, "Why the 'Haves' Come Out Ahead."

84. Frank, "The Oversight of Administrative Agencies."

85. Reginald Sheehan, "Administrative Agencies and the Court: A Reexamination of the Impact of Agency Type on Decisional Outcomes," *Western Political Quarterly* 43 (December 1990): 875–886; William T. Gormley Jr. and Steven J. Balla, *Bureaucracy and Democracy: Accountability and Performance*, 3rd ed. (Washington, D.C.: CQ Press, 2013), 104.

86. Sheehan, "Administrative Agencies and the Court," 875–886; Gormley and Balla, *Bureaucracy and Democracy*, 3rd ed., 107.

87. It also depends on the court. For example, during the 1970s, the District of Columbia Circuit Court of Appeals was much more supportive of environmental protection than other circuit courts of appeals. See Lettie M. Wenner, *The Environmental Decade in Court* (Bloomington: Indiana University Press, 1982), 35–63. This same court was less likely to affirm federal agency decisions throughout the 1970s and 1980s; Gormley and Balla, *Bureaucracy and Democracy*, 3rd ed., 105.

88. Mashaw et al., *Social Security Hearings and Appeals*, 125–150.

80. William Gormley Jr., *The Politics of Public Utility Regulation* (Pittsburgh: University of Pittsburgh Press, 1983), 94.

90. Cornelius M. Kerwin and Scott R. Furlong, *Rulemaking: How Government Agencies Write and Make Policy*, 4th ed. (Washington, D.C.: CQ Press, 2011), 261.

91. Weiland, "Business and Environmental Policy"; Lettie McSpadden, "Industry's Use of the Courts," in *Business and Environmental Policy*, eds. Kraft and Kamieniecki.

92. Wenner, *The Environmental Decade in Court*, 35–63.

93. Lettie McSpadden, "Environmental Policy in the Courts," in *Environmental Policy*, 4th ed., eds. Vig and Kraft (Washington, D.C.: CQ Press, 2000), 154.

94. O'Leary, "Environmental Policy in the Courts."

95. Ibid.

96. According to Mashaw, this was the practice of the SSA, the National Labor Relations Board, and the IRS, as well as other agencies in the 1970s. See Jerry L. Mashaw, *Bureaucratic Justice: Managing Social Security Disability Claims* (New Haven, Conn.: Yale University Press, 1983), 186. The SSA's refusal to follow precedents set by lower federal courts aroused considerable controversy during the Reagan years, when the agency cut financial awards to disabled workers.

97. Donald Van Meter and Carl Van Horn, "The Policy Implementation Process: A Conceptual Framework," *Administration and Society* 6 (February 1975): 445–488; Carl Van Horn, *Policy Implementation in the Federal System: National Goals and Local Implementors* (Lexington, Mass.: D. C. Heath, 1979); and George C. Edwards III, *Implementing Public Policy* (Washington, D.C.: Congressional Quarterly, 1980).

98. Bob Woodward and Scott Armstrong, *The Brethren: Inside the Supreme Court* (New York: Simon & Schuster, 1979), 112.

99. Neal Milner, *The Court and Local Law Enforcement: The Impact of Miranda* (Beverly Hills, Calif.: Sage, 1971), 225.

100. Horowitz, *The Courts and Social Policy*, 226.

101. Kenneth M. Dolbeare and Phillip E. Hammond, *The School Prayer Decisions: From Court Policy to Local Practice* (Chicago: University of Chicago Press, 1971).

102. Tinsley E. Yarbrough, *Judge Frank Johnson and Human Rights in Alabama* (University: University of Alabama Press, 1981).

103. Jennifer Medina, "California Sheds Prisoners but Grapples with Courts," *New York Times*, January 22, 2013.

104. J. Anthony Lukas, *Common Ground: A Turbulent Decade in the Lives of Three American Families* (New York: Knopf, 1985).

105. Horowitz, *The Courts and Social Policy*, 234.

106. This consistency changed with the *Webster v. Reproductive Health Services* decision in 1989 and the *Planned Parenthood of Southeastern PA v. Casey* decision in 1992, as Justice O'Connor developed her "undue burden" standard that allowed states to place some restrictions on first-trimester abortions. See Lawrence Tribe, *Abortion: The Clash of Absolutes* (New York: W. W. Norton, 1992), and Melody Rose, *Safe, Legal and Unavailable? Abortion Politics in the United States* (Washington, D.C.: CQ Press, 2007).

107. *Bush v. Vera*, 517 U.S. 985 (1996); the case involved congressional districting in Texas.

108. Edward Walsh, "High Court Upholds Miranda Rights, 7–2," *Washington Post*, June 27, 2000.

109. Daniel A. Mazmanian and Jeanne Nienaber, *Can Organizations Change? Environmental Protection, Citizen Participation, and the Corps of Engineers* (Washington, D.C.: Brookings Institution, 1979), 37–60.

110. Jennifer Hochschild, *The New American Dilemma: Liberal Democracy and School Desegregation* (New Haven, Conn.: Yale University Press, 1984), 180.

111. Leslie McAneny and Lydia Saad, "America's Public Schools: Still Separate? Still Unequal?" *Gallup Poll Monthly*, no. 344, May 1994.

112. Robert S. Erikson and Kent L. Tedin, *American Public Opinion: Its Origins, Content, and Impact*, 8th ed. (New York: Pearson, 2011), 100–104.

113. Dolbeare and Hammond, *The School Prayer Decisions*; Milner, *The Court and Local Law Enforcement*; Baum, *The Supreme Court*; Charles Johnson and Bradley Canon, *Judicial Policies: Implementation and Impact* (Washington, D.C.: Congressional Quarterly, 1984); Gerald Rosenberg, *The Hollow Hope: Can Courts Bring About Social Change?* (Chicago: University of Chicago Press, 1991).

114. Baum, *The Supreme Court*, 10th ed., 216.

115. Rosenberg, *The Hollow Hope*.

116. Ibid., 187.

117. Charles Bullock III, "Equal Education Opportunity," in *Implementation of Civil Rights Policy*, eds. Charles Bullock III and Charles Lamb (Monterey, Calif.: Brooks/Cole, 1984), 68–69.

118. Baum, *The Supreme Court*, 10th ed., 193.

119. Richard Scher and James Button, "Voting Rights Act: Implementation and Impact," in *Implementation of Civil Rights Policy*, eds. Bullock and Lamb, 40.

120. Albert Karnig and Susan Welch, *Black Representation and Urban Policy* (Chicago: University of Chicago Press, 1980); Peter Eisinger, "Black Employment in Municipal Jobs: The Impact of Black Political Power," *American Political Science Review* 76 (June 1982): 380–392.

121. David Lauter, "Black Voter Turnout May Have Surpassed Whites for the First Time," *LA Times*, December 26, 2012 and Adam Liptak, "Supreme Court Voids Oversight of States In Voting Rights Act," *New York Times*, June 26, 2013, A1, A16.

122. Michael Danielson, *The Politics of Exclusion* (New York: Columbia University Press, 1976).

123. The fairness doctrine, abolished by the in 1987, required broadcasters to devote a reasonable amount of time to the discussion of issues of public importance. When covering such issues, broadcasters did not need to provide equal time to all points of view, but their coverage had to be balanced and fair.

124. Fred W. Friendly, *The Good Guys, the Bad Guys, and the First Amendment: Free Speech vs. Fairness in Broadcasting* (New York: Random House, 1975), 89–102.

125. Mazmanian and Nienaber, *Can Organizations Change?*

126. Walter A. Rosenbaum, *Environmental Politics and Policy*, 8th ed. (Washington, D.C.: CQ Press, 2011), chap. 9.

127. David J. Rothman and Sheila M. Rothman, *The Willowbrook Wars: Bringing the Mentally Disabled into the Community* (New York: Harper & Row, 1984).

128. Horowitz, *The Courts and Social Policy*.

129. Ibid.

130. Matthew Wald, "After Years of Turmoil, Judge Is Yielding Job of Integrating Boston Schools," *New York Times*, August 22, 1985.

131. Melnick, *Regulation and the Courts*.

CHAPTER 8

1. Alexander Hamilton, John Jay, and James Madison, *The Federalist* (New York: Random House, 1982); W. Lance Bennett, *Public Opinion in American Politics* (New York: Harcourt Brace Jovanovich, 1980).
2. As quoted in Leo Bogart, *Polls and the Awareness of Public Opinion*, 2nd ed. (New Brunswick, N.J.: Transaction Books, 1985), 3.
3. See, for example, W. Russell Neuman, *The Paradox of Mass Politics: Knowledge and Opinion in the American Electorate* (Cambridge, Mass.: Harvard University Press, 1986); and Benjamin Ginsberg, *The Captive Public: How Mass Opinion Promotes State Power* (New York: Basic Books, 1986).
4. Martin Linsky, *Impact: How the Press Affects Federal Policymaking* (New York: W. W. Norton, 1986), 36–37.
5. E. E. Schattschneider, *The Semi-Sovereign People: A Realist's View of Democracy in America* (New York: Holt, Rinehart & Winston, 1960).
6. Neuman, *The Paradox of Mass Politics*.
7. Pew Research Center for the People & the Press, "More Support for Gun Rights, Gay Marriage than in 2008 or 2004," April 25, 2012, www.people-press.org/2012/04/25/more-support-for-gun-rights-gay-marriage-than-in-2008-or-2004/?src=prc-headline.
8. Rachel Weiner, "Why Does Gay Marriage Keep Losing at the Ballot Box?" *Washington Post*, May 9, 2012.
9. Gallup Organization, "Abortion," July 15–17, 2011, www.gallup.com/poll/1576/Abortion.aspx.
10. Ibid.
11. Ibid.
12. Carl E. Van Horn, *Working Scared (or Not at All): The Lost Decade, Great Recession, and Restoring the Shattered American Dream* (Lanham, Md.: Rowman & Littlefield, 2013).
13. Pew Research Center for the People & the Press, "Economy Dominates Public's Agenda, Dims Hopes for the Future: Less Optimism about America's Long-Term Prospects," January 20, 2011, www.people-press.org/2011/01/20/economy-dominates-publics-agenda-dims-hopes-for-the-future/.
14. Gallup Organization, "Environment," 2012, www.gallup.com/poll/1615/Environment.aspx#2.
15. Gallup Organization, "Cuba," April 20–21, 2009, www.gallup.com/poll/1630/Cuba.aspx.
16. Gallup Organization, "Energy," March 8–11, 2012, www.gallup.com/poll/2167/Energy.aspx.
17. Gallup Organization, "United Nations," February 2–5, 2012, www.gallup.com/poll/116347/United-Nations.aspx.
18. Pew Research Center for the People & the Press, "Fewer Want Spending to Grow, but Most Cuts Remain Unpopular: Changing Views of Federal Spending," February 10, 2011, www.people-press.org/2011/02/10/fewer-want-spending-to-grow-but-most-cuts-remain-unpopular/.
19. Roper Center for Public Opinion Research, *The Public Perspective* 1 (July–August 1990), 82.
20. Samuel Kernell, Gary Jacobson, and Thad Kousser, *The Logic of American Politics*, 5th ed. (Washington, D.C.: CQ Press, 2012), 271.
21. Pew Research Center for the People & the Press, "Views on Gun Laws Unchanged after Aurora Shooting," July 30, 2012, www.people-press.org/files/legacy-pdf/7-30-12%20Gun%20Control%20Release.pdf.
22. Pew Research Center for the People & the Press, "After Newtown, Modest Change in Opinion about Gun Control: Most Say Assault Weapons Make Nation More Dangerous," December 20, 2012, www.people-press.org/2012/12/20/after-newtown-modest-change-in-opinion-about-gun-control/; Pew Research Center for the People & the Press, "In Gun Control Debate Several Options Draw Majority Support: Gun Rights Proponents More Politically Active," January 14, 2013, www.people-press.org/2013/01/14/in-gun-control-debate-several-options-draw-majority-support.
23. Roper Center for Public Opinion Research, iPOLL Databank, www.ropercenter.uconn.edu/data_access/ipoll/ipoll.html.
24. Ibid.

25. Michael McDonald, "Voter Turnout," United States Election Project, http://elections.gmu.edu/voter_turnout.htm.
26. American Customer Satisfaction Index, "ACSI Benchmarks for U.S. Federal Government 2011," January 19, 2012, www.theacsi.org/acsi-results/acsi-benchmarks-for-us-federal-government-2011.
27. The concepts of top-down and bottom-up public opinion are based on the work of Cliff Zukin, "Comment on Davis: Yes, but . . . Public Opinion Is a *Top-Down* Process," *Public Opinion Quarterly*, 56 (Autumn 1992): 311–314.
28. Bennett, *Public Opinion in American Politics*.
29. V. O. Key Jr., *Public Opinion and American Democracy* (New York: Knopf, 1961), 14.
30. Bennett, *Public Opinion in American Politics*, 367.
31. Roper Center for Public Opinion Research, iPOLL Databank, www.ropercenter.uconn.edu/data_access/ipoll/ipoll.html.
32. Chris Snyder, "Government Agencies Make Friends with New Media," March 25, 2009, www.wired.com/business/2009/03/government-agen.
33. See, for example, George C. Edwards, Andrew Barrett, and Jeffrey Peake, "The Legislative Impact of Divided Government," *American Journal of Political Science* 41 (April 1997): 545.
34. The Henry J. Kaiser Family Foundation, "Kaiser Health Tracking Poll: Public Opinion on Health Care Issues," January 2010, www.kff.org/kaiserpolls/upload/8042-F.pdf.
35. The Henry J. Kaiser Family Foundation, "Kaiser Health Tracking Poll: Public Opinion on Health Care Issues," November 2010, www.kff.org/kaiserpolls/upload/8120-F.pdf.
36. Neuman, *The Paradox of Mass Politics*.
37. "Tea Party Movement," *New York Times*, updated October 4, 2012, http://topics.nytimes.com/top/reference/timestopics/subjects/t/tea_party_movement/index.html.
38. Michael Kimmelman, "The Power of Place in Protest," *New York Times*, October 16, 2011.
39. Bogart, *Polls and the Awareness of Public Opinion*.
40. See Barry George Rabe, *Beyond NIMBY: Hazardous Waste Siting in Canada and the United States* (Washington, D.C.: Brookings Institution, 1994).
41. See, for example, Linsky, *Impact*; Stephen Hess, *The Ultimate Insiders: U.S. Senators and the National Media* (Washington, D.C.: Brookings Institution, 1986); and Austin Ranney, *Channels of Power: The Impact of Television on American Politics* (New York: Basic Books, 1985).
42. Pew Research Center's Project for Excellence in Journalism, "100 Days of Gushing Oil—Media Analysis and Quiz: Eight Things to Know about How the Media Covered the Gulf Disaster," August 25, 2010, www.journalism.org/node/21828.
43. "Offshore Drilling and Exploration," *New York Times*, March, 5, 2012, http://topics.nytimes.com/top/reference/timestopics/subjects/o/offshore_drilling_and_exploration/index.html.
44. Chris Mann, "Congress Must Help Restore Coastal Communities," The Pew Charitable Trusts, April 30, 2012, www.pewtrusts.org/news_room_detail.aspx?id=85899384142.
45. Shannon L. Sole, "BP's Compensation Fund: A Buoy for Both Claimants and BP," *Journal of Corporation Law* 34 (2011): 246.
46. Iraq Coalition Causality Count, /www.icasualties.org.
47. Pew Research Center for the People & the Press, "Public Attitudes toward the War in Iraq: 2003–2008," March 19, 2008, www.pewresearch.org/2008/03/19/public-attitudes-toward-the-war-in-iraq-20032008/; Roper Center for Public Opinion Research, iPOLL Databank, www.ropercenter.uconn.edu/data_access/ipoll/ipoll.html.
48. Leon V. Sigal, *Reporters and Officials: The Organization and Politics of Newsmaking* (Lexington, Mass.: D. C. Heath, 1973), 186.
49. Schattschneider, *The Semi-Sovereign People*, 2–3.
50. "Occupy Movement (Occupy Wall Street)," *New York Times*, updated September 17, 2012, http://topics.nytimes.com/top/reference/timestopics/organizations/o/occupy_wall_street/index.html.
51. Donald L. Shaw and Maxwell E. McCombs, *The Emergence of American Political Issues: The Agenda-Setting Function of the Press* (St. Paul, Minn.: West Publishing, 1977).
52. Sigal, *Reporters and Officials*, 12.

53. Erik Wemple, "The Dumbing Effect of Cable News," *Washington Post*, May 23, 2012, www.washingtonpost.com/blogs/erik-wemple/post/the-dumbing-effect-of-cable-news/2012/05/23/gJQAEa4IlU_blog.html.

54. Linsky, *Impact*, 90.

55. Sigal, *Reporters and Officials*; Shaw and McCombs, *The Emergence of American Political Issues*.

56. Timothy E. Cook, "P.R. on the Hill: The Evolution of Congressional Press Operations," in *Congressional Politics*, ed. Christopher J. Deering (Homewood, Ill.: Dorsey Press, 1989).

57. Gladys Engel Lang and Kurt Lang, *The Battle for Public Opinion: The President, the Press, and the Polls during Watergate* (New York: Columbia University Press, 1983), 58–61.

58. U.S. Department of Transportation, National Highway Traffic Safety Administration, "2010 Motor Vehicle Crashes: Overview," February 2012, www-nrd.nhtsa.dot.gov/Pubs/811552.pdf.

59. U.S. Department of Transportation, Research and Innovative Technology Administration, "Table 2-1: Transportation Fatalities by Mode," www.bts.gov/sites/rita.dot.gov.bts/files/publications/national_transportation_statistics/html/table_02_01.html. The last year covered by these data was 2010.

60. 911Truth.org, www.911truth.org.

61. Thomas Hargrove, "Third of Americans Suspect 9-11 Government Conspiracy," Scripps Howard News Service, August 1, 2006, http://www.jonesreport.com/articles/020806_third_suspect.html.

62. Lymari Morales, "Obama's Birth Certificate Convinces Some, but Not All, Skeptics," Gallup Organization, May 13, 2011, www.gallup.com/poll/147530/obama-birth-certificate-convinces-not-skeptics.aspx.

63. Edward Jay Epstein, *Between Fact and Fiction: The Problem of Journalism* (New York: Vintage Books, 1975).

64. Linsky, *Impact*; Sigal, *Reporters and Officials*.

65. Linsky, *Impact*, 94.

66. Mindy R. Levit, Clinton T. Brass, Thomas J. Nicola, Dawn Nuschler, and Alison M. Shelton, "Reaching the Debt Limit: Background and Potential Effects on Government Operations," Congressional Research Service, April 27, 2011, http://assets.opencrs.com/rpts/R41633_20110427.pdf.

67. U.S. Department of the Treasury, "Debt Limit: Myth v. Fact," www.treasury.gov/initiatives/Documents/Debt%20Limit%20Myth%20v%20Fact%20FINAL.pdf.

68. Glenn Kessler, "Explaining the Debt Ceiling Debate," *The Washington Post*, June 29, 2011, www.washingtonpost.com/blogs/fact-checker/post/explaining-the-debt-ceiling-debate/2011/06/28/AGVM80pH_blog.html.

69. "The Debt-Ceiling Deal, No Thanks to Anyone," *The Economist*, August 6, 2011.

70. See, for example, Edward Jay Epstein, *News from Nowhere: Television and the News* (New York: Vintage Books, 1983); W. Lance Bennett, *News: The Politics of Illusion* (New York: Longman, 1983); and Sigal, *Reporters and Officials*.

71. Sigal, *Reporters and Officials*, 186.

72. Stephen D. Reese and Seth C. Lewis, "Framing the War on Terror," *Journalism* 10, no. 6 (2009): 777–797.

73. Gallup Organization, "War on Terrorism," August 19–21, 2002, www.gallup.com/poll/5257/war-terrorism.aspx#2; John Mueller, "The Iraq Syndrome," in *American Politics: Classic and Contemporary Readings*, 7th ed., eds. Alan J. Cigler and Burdett A. Loomis (Boston: Houghton Mifflin, 2008), 144–153.

74. Council on Foreign Relations, "Timeline: The Iraq War," www.cfr.org/iraq/timeline-iraq-war/p18876?gclid=CJKctJm977ECFYNM4AodaGoADQ.

75. Jeffrey M. Jones, "Americans Approve of Military Action against Libya, 47% to 37%: Support Is Lower than for Other Recent U.S. Military Actions," Gallup Organization, March 22, 2011, www.gallup.com/poll/146738/americans-approve-military-action-against-libya.aspx.

76. "Libya: Obama Says US Intervention Will Be Limited," BBC News, March 29, 2011, www.bbc .co.uk/news/world-africa-12888826.

77. Pew Research Center for the People & the Press, "Libya: Steady Views, Declining Interest," September 8, 2011, www.people-press.org/2011/09/08/libya-steady-views-declining-interest/1/.

78. U.S. General Services Administration, Office of Inspector General, *Management Deficiency Report: General Services Administration Public Buildings Service* (Washington, D.C.: U.S. Government Printing Office, 2012), 4.

79. Pierre Thomas and Jason Ryan, "Colombia Secret Service Prostitution Scandal Spreads to the DEA," ABC News, May 21, 2012, http://abcnews.go.com/US/colombia-secret-service-prostitution-scandal-spreads-dea/story?id=16399758.

80. National Conference of State Legislatures, "Initiative, Referendum and Recall," www.ncsl.org/legislatures-elections/elections/initiative-referendum-and-recall-overview.aspx.

81. Initiative & Referendum Institute, "Election Results 2011," www.iandrinstitute.org/BW%20 2011-2%20Election%20Results.pdf.

82. National Conference of State Legislatures, "Initiative, Referendum and Recall."

83. Initiative & Referendum Institute, "Election Results 2011."

84. Ellen Torelle, comp., *The Political Philosophy of Robert M. La Follette* (Westport, Conn.: Hyperion, 1975), 173–174.

85. Michael Nelson, "Power to the People: The Crusade for Direct Democracy," in *The Clash of Issues: Readings and Problems in American Government*, 7th ed., eds. James Burkhart, Samuel Krislov, and Raymond L. Lee (Englewood Cliffs, N.J.: Prentice Hall, 1981), 25–28.

86. Initiative & Referendum Institute, "Overview of Initiative Use, 1904–2009," www.iandrinstitute .org/IRI%20Initiative%20Use%20(2010-1).pdf.

87. National Conference of State Legislatures, "2010 Ballot Measures: Pre-Election Overview," www.ncsl.org/legislatures-elections/elections/ballot-measures-2010-an-overview.aspx.

88. Initiative & Referendum Institute, "Data," www.iandrinstitute.org/data.htm. Unless otherwise indicated, all the initiative and referendum data presented in this section come from this source.

89. National Conference of State Legislatures, "State Medical Marijuana Laws," updated August 2012, www.ncsl.org/issues-research/health/state-medical-marijuana-laws.aspx.

90. Charlie Savage, "Administration Weighs Legal Action Against States That Legalized Marijuana Use," *New York Times*, December 7, 2012.

91. Margot Roosevelt, "California's Big-Bucks Battle over Clean Energy," *Time*, October 23, 2006.

92. Carla Hall, "High-Profile Goals, Low-Profile Donor," *Los Angeles Times*, November 9, 2006.

93. University of California, Berkeley, Institute of Governmental Studies, "Proposition 87," http:// igs.berkeley.edu/library/elections/proposition-87.

94. Manning J. Dauer and Mark Sievers, "The Constitutional Initiative: Problems in Florida Politics," in *State Government: CQ's Guide to Current Issues and Activities, 1986–1987*, ed. Thad Beyle (Washington, D.C.: Congressional Quarterly, 1986), 29–82.

95. National Conference of State Legislatures, "Paid vs. Volunteer Petitioners," updated June 17, 2010, www.ncsl.org/legislatures-elections/elections/paid-vs-volunteer-petitioners .aspx.

96. David B. Magleby, *Direct Legislation: Voting on Ballot Propositions in the United States* (Baltimore, Md.: Johns Hopkins University Press, 1984).

97. Gregory B. Lewis and Charles W. Gossett, "Why Did Californians Pass Proposition 8? Stability and Change in Public Support for Same-Sex Marriage," *California Journal of Politics & Policy* 3, no. 1 (2011), www.degruyter.com/view/j/cjpp.2011.3.issue-1/cjpp.2011.3.1.1130/ cjpp.2011.3.1.1130.xml?format=INT.

98. "Proposition 8: Tracking the Money: Final Numbers," *Los Angeles Times*, updated February 3, 2009, www.latimes.com/news/local/la-moneymap,0,2198220.htmlstory.

99. Dan Morain and Jessica Garrison, "Focused beyond Marriage," *Los Angeles Times*, November 6, 2008.

100. Andrew Malcolm, "Steven Spielberg and Kate Capshaw Donate Big to Stop California's Marriage Initiative," *Los Angeles Times*, September 22, 2008.

101. "Prop 8—The Musical," Funny or Die, www.funnyordie.com/videos/c0cf508ff8/prop-8-the-musical-starring-jack-black-john-c-reilly-and-many-more-from-fod-team-jack-black-craig-robinson-john-c-reilly-and-rashida-jones.

102. The Pew Forum on Religion & Public Life, "States with Voter-Approved Constitutional Bans on Same-Sex Marriage, 1998–2008," November 13, 2008, www.pewforum.org/Gay-Marriage-and-Homosexuality/States-With-Voter-Approved-Constitutional-Bans-on-Same-Sex-Marriage-1998-2008.aspx.

103. "Polls on Gay Marriage Not Yet Reflected in Votes," CBS News, May 27, 2012, www.cbsnews.com/8301-250_162-57442311/polls-on-gay-marriage-not-yet-reflected-in-votes/.

104. Erik Eckholm, "Push Expands for Legalizing Gay Marriage," *New York Times*, November 13, 2012.

105. Adam Liptak, "Two 5-4 Decisions Bolster Same-Sex Marriage," *New York Times*, June 27, 2013, A1, A18.

106. Ibid.

107. Americans for Tax Reform, "What Is the Taxpayer Protection Pledge?" http://atr.org/taxpayer-protection-pledge.

108. Felicia Sonmez, "Boehner Calls Grover Norquist 'Some Random Person,'" *Washington Post*, November 3, 2011, www.washingtonpost.com/blogs/2chambers/post/boehner-calls-grover-norquist-some-random-person/2011/11/03/gIQAidcviM_blog.html.

109. David Halberstam, *The Powers That Be* (New York: Knopf, 1979); Peter Braestrup, *The Big Story* (New York: Doubleday Anchor, 1978).

110. Peter M. Sandman and Mary Paden, "At Three Mile Island," in *Media Power in Politics*, ed. Doris Graber (Washington, D.C.: Congressional Quarterly, 1984), 267; Christopher Flavin, "Reassessing Nuclear Power," in *State of the World 1987*, eds. Lester R. Brown, William U. Chandler, Christopher Flavin, Jodi Jacobson, Cynthia Pollock, Sandra Postel, Linda Starke, and Edward C. Wolfe (New York: W. W. Norton, 1987), 57–80.

111. Victor Cohn, "Fear of AIDS Is Spreading Faster than the Disease," *Washington Post*, September 16, 1985.

112. "Hurricane Katrina," *New York Times*, updated April 4, 2012, http://topics.nytimes.com/top/reference/timestopics/subjects/h/hurricane_katrina/index.html.

113. Bloomberg News, "Hill Insider Trading Bill Signed," *Washington Post*, April 2, 2012.

114. David W. Moore, "Conflicting Polls Show an Uncertain Public on ANWR," Gallup Organization, March 8, 2005, www.gallup.com/poll/15178/conflicting-polls-show-uncertain-public-anwr.aspx. This is another illustration of the importance of question framing, discussed earlier in the chapter.

115. Linsky, *Impact*, 84; see also David L. Protess, Fay Lomax Cook, Thomas R. Curtin, Margaret T. Gordon, Donna R. Leff, Maxwell E. McCombs, and Peter Miller, "The Impact of Investigative Reporting on Public Opinion and Policymaking Targeting Toxic Waste," *Public Opinion Quarterly* 51 (Summer 1987): 166–185.

116. Linsky, *Impact*, 86.

117. National Highway Traffic and Safety Administration, "An Investigation of the Safety Implications of Wireless Communications in Vehicles," November 1997, www.nhtsa.gov/people/injury/research/wireless/.

118. "Liberals, Conservatives Share Initiative Success," *Public Administration Times*, February 15, 1985.

119. Susan Hansen, "Extraction: The Politics of State Taxation," in *Politics in the American States: A Comparative Analysis*, eds. Virginia Gray, Herbert Jacob, and Kenneth N. Vines (Boston: Little, Brown, 1983), 441–442.

120. Carol Matlack, "Where the Big Winner Was the Status Quo," *National Journal*, November 10, 1990.

121. Joseph F. Zimmerman, *The Initiative: Citizen Law-Making* (Westport, Conn.: Praeger, 1999), 105–106.
122. Initiative & Referendum Institute, "Data," www.iandrinstitute.org/data.htm. Unless otherwise indicated, all the specific information in the remainder of this section comes from this source.
123. Norimitsu Onishi, "Californians Endorse Tax Initiative to Avoid Education Cuts," *New York Times*, November 8, 2012.
124. National Conference of State Legislatures, "State Legislation and Actions Challenging Certain Health Reforms," updated January 2013, www.ncsl.org/issues-research/health/state-laws-and-actions-challenging-ppaca.aspx.
125. T. R. Goldman, "Legal Challenges to Health Reform," *Health Affairs*, October 11, 2011, www.healthaffairs.org/healthpolicybriefs/brief.php?brief_id=54.
126. Robert Barnes, "Supreme Court Upholds Obama's Health-Care Law," *Washington Post*, June 28, 2012.
127. As quoted in James A. Barnes, "Losing the Initiative," *National Journal*, September 1, 1990.
128. Norimitsu Onishi, "California Ballot Initiatives, Born in Populism, Now Come from Billionaires," *New York Times*, October 17, 2012,
129. "Weiner Apologizes for Lying, 'Terrible Mistakes,' Refuses to Resign," CNN, June 6, 2011, http://articles.cnn.com/2011-06-06/politics/new.york.weiner_1_anthony-weiner-twitter-account-lewd-photo?_s=PM:POLITICS.
130. Roper Center for Public Opinion Research, iPOLL Databank, www.ropercenter.uconn.edu/data_access/ipoll/ipoll.html.
131. Cook, "P.R. on the Hill."
132. Alex Teharani, "How to Fix No Child Left Behind," *Time*, May 24, 2007.
133. Ibid.
134. Ibid.
135. See John Cranford, "2012 Legislative Summary," *CQ Weekly*, January 14, 2013.
136. Linsky, *Impact*, 146–147.
137. Michael J. Robinson, "Public Affairs Television and the Growth of Political Malaise: The Case of the 'Selling of the Pentagon,'" *American Political Science Review* 70 (June 1976): 409–432.
138. See, for example, Rufus P. Browning, Dale Rogers Marshall, and David H. Tabb, *Protest Is Not Enough: The Struggle of Blacks and Hispanics for Equality in Urban Politics* (Berkeley: University of California Press, 1984).
139. Michael E. Kraft and Norman J. Vig, "Environmental Policy over Four Decades: Achievements and New Directions," in *Environmental Policy*, 8th ed., eds. Norman J. Vig and Michael E. Kraft (Washington, D.C.: CQ Press, 2013), 2–29; Daniel Mazmanian and Jeanne Nienaber, *Can Organizations Change? Environmental Protection, Citizen Participation, and the Corps of Engineers* (Washington, D.C.: Brookings Institution, 1979); Lynton Caldwell, Lynton R. Hayes, and Isabel M. MacWhirter, *Citizens and the Environment: Case Studies in Popular Action* (Bloomington: Indiana University Press, 1976).
140. Kirk Johnson, "Coloradans Vote to Embrace Alternative Sources of Energy," *New York Times*, November 24, 2004.
141. Andy Vuong, "Ritter Appoints Environmentalist to PUC," *Denver Post*, January 15, 2008.
142. Colorado State Senate, Majority Office, "Senate Passes New Renewable Energy Standard," March 4, 2010, http://coloradosenate.org/home/press/senate-passes-new-renewable-energy-standard-on-2nd-reading.
143. Demian Bulwa, "Mehserle Convicted of Involuntary Manslaughter," *San Francisco Chronicle*, July 9, 2010.
144. "Next Stage in Transit Killing Case: The Sentence," MSNBC News, July 9, 2010, www.msnbc.msn.com/id/38156983/ns/us_news-crime_and_courts/t/next-stage-transit-killing-case-sentence/.

145. Lindsey Ellerson, "Violence Breaks Out at Anti-War Protest in St. Paul," ABC News, September 1, 2008, http://abcnews.go.com/blogs/politics/2008/09/violence-breaks/.

146. Tamar Lewin, "Affirmative Action Ban in Michigan Is Rejected," *New York Times*, November 16, 2012.

147. Magleby, *Direct Legislation*.

CHAPTER 9

1. Lawrence Baum, *The Supreme Court*, 10th ed. (Washington, D.C.: CQ Press, 2010), 165.

2. For the classic statements of pluralist theory, see Robert A. Dahl, *Who Governs? Democracy and Power in an American City* (New Haven, Conn.: Yale University Press, 1961), and David Truman, *The Governmental Process: Political Interests and Public Opinion*, 2nd ed. (New York: Knopf, 1971). For the classic critiques of the pluralist position, see Peter Bachrach and Morton S. Baratz, "Two Faces of Power," *American Political Science Review* 56 (December 1962), and Theodore J. Lowi, *The End of Liberalism: The Second Republic of the United States*, 2nd ed. (New York: W. W. Norton, 1979).

3. Mancur Olson, *The Logic of Collective Action: Public Goods and the Theory of Groups* (Cambridge, Mass.: Harvard University Press, 1971).

4. Terry Moe, "Regulatory Performance and Presidential Administration," *American Journal of Political Science* 26 (May 1982): 197–224; B. Dan Wood and Richard Waterman, "The Dynamics of Political Control of the Bureaucracy," *American Political Science Review* 85 (September 1991): 801–828; William T. Gormley Jr. and Steven J. Balla, *Bureaucracy and Democracy: Accountability and Performance*, 3rd ed. (Washington, D.C.: CQ Press, 2013).

5. Kenneth Mayer, "Executive Orders and Presidential Power," *Journal of Politics* 61 (May 1999): 445–466.

6. Donald Kettl, "Building Lasting Reform: Enduring Questions, Missing Answers," in *Inside the Reinvention Machine: Appraising Governmental Reform*, eds. Donald F. Kettl and John J. DiIulio Jr. (Washington, D.C.: Brookings Institution, 1995), 9–83.

7. Donald Kettl, *Sharing Power: Public Governance and Private Markets* (Washington, D.C.: Brookings Institution, 1993); Project on Government Oversight, "Bad Business: Billions of Taxpayer Dollars Wasted on Hiring Contractors," http://pogoarchives.org/m/co/igf/bad-business-report-only-2011.pdf.

8. See Herbert A. Simon, *Administrative Behavior: A Study of Decision Making Processes in Administrative Organizations* (New York: Macmillan, 1957), or James G. March and Herbert A. Simon, *Organizations* (New York: John Wiley, 1964).

9. Jane Mansbridge, *Beyond Adversary Democracy* (Chicago: University of Chicago Press, 1983); Benjamin R. Barber, *Strong Democracy: Participatory Politics for a New Age* (Berkeley: University of California Press, 1984).

10. Donald C. Baumer and Howard J. Gold, *Parties, Polarization, and Democracy in the United States* (Boulder, Colo.: Paradigm Publishers, 2010), 101.

11. U.S. Census Bureau, "Historical Poverty Tables—People," http://www.census.gov/hhes/www/poverty/data/historical/people.html.

12. Christopher Hammons, "Was James Madison Wrong? Rethinking the American Preference for Short, Framework-Oriented Constitutions," *American Political Science Review* 93 (December 1999): 847–848.

13. Ashley Parker, "Day of Records and Firsts as 113th Congress Opens," *New York Times*, January 4, 2013; Center for American Women and Politics, "Facts on Women in Congress 2011," www.cawp.rutgers.edu/fast_facts/levels_of_office/Congress-CurrentFacts.php.

14. Center for American Women and Politics, "Facts on Women Officeholders, Candidates and Voters," www.cawp.rutgers.edu/fast_facts/index.php.

15. Catalyst, "Catalyst 2012 Census of Fortune 500: No Change for Women in Top Leadership," www.catalyst.org/media/catalyst-2012-census-fortune-500-no-change-women-top-leadership.

16. James Kanter, "Push for Gender Balance on Boards Gains Steam," *New York Times*, January, 25, 2013.

17. Center for American Women and Politics, "Facts on Women Officeholders, Candidates and Voters."

18. Figures were taken from the Joint Center for Political and Economic Studies, "National Roster of Black Elected Officials: Fact Sheet," November 2011, www.jointcenter.org/research/national-roster-of-black-elected-officials/, and the National Association of Latino Elected Officials, "2011 Directory of Latino Elected Officials," www.naleo.org/directory.html.

19. Roger H. Davidson, Walter J. Oleszek, and Frances E. Lee, *Congress and Its Members*, 13th ed. (Washington, D.C.: CQ Press, 2012), 112; Rodney Hero et al., "Latino Participation, Partisanship, and Office Holding," *PS: Political Science and Politics* 33 (September 2000): 533.

20. Alliance for Board Diversity, "Missing Pieces: Women and Minorities on *Fortune* 500 Boards," http://theabd.org/Missing_Pieces_Women_and_Minorities_on_Fortune_500_Boards.pdf; Diversity Inc. "Where's the Diversity in *Fortune* 500 CEOs?" January 7, 2013, http://www.diversityinc.com/diversity-facts/wheres-the-diversity-in-fortune-500-ceos/.

21. Harold W. Stanley and Richard G. Niemi, *Vital Statistics on American Politics 2007–2008* (Washington, D.C.: CQ Press, 2008), 290–292; Sheldon Goldman and Thomas Jahnige, *The Federal Courts as a Political System*, 3rd ed. (New York: W. W. Norton, 1987), 55.

22. Richard Wolf, "Obama Determined to Fill Federal Judgeships," *USA Today*, November 29, 2012.

23. Annie Lowrey, "Obama's Remade Inner Circle Has an All-Male Look, so Far," *New York Times*, January 8, 2013.

24. Robert Erikson, Gerald Wright, and John McIver, *Statehouse Democracy: Public Opinion and Policy in the American States* (Cambridge, UK: Cambridge University Press, 1993); Virginia Gray, "The Socioeconomic and Political Context of States," in *Politics in the American States: A Comparative Analysis*, 9th ed., eds. Virginia Gray and Russell L. Hanson (Washington, D.C.: CQ Press, 2008), 2–5.

25. James Stimson, Michael MacKuen, and Robert Erikson, "Dynamic Representation," *American Political Science Review* 89 (September 1995): 543–565.

26. Ibid., 559.

27. Baumer and Gold, *Parties, Polarization, and Democracy*, chap. 3; Robert S. Erikson and Kent L. Tedin, *American Public Opinion*, 8th ed. (New York: Pearson, 2011), chaps. 9–11.

28. Deborah Lynn Guber and Christopher J. Bosso, "High Hopes and Bitter Disappointment: Public Discourse and the Limits of the Environmental Movement in Climate Change Politics," in *Environmental Policy*, 8th ed., eds. Norman J. Vig and Michael E. Kraft (Washington, D.C.: CQ Press, 2013), 54–82.

29. Pew Research Center for the People & the Press, "Most Swing Voters Favor Afghan Troop Withdrawal: Support for U.S. Troop Presence Hits New Low," April 18, 2012, www.people-press.org/2012/04/18/most-swing-voters-favor-afghan-troop-withdrawal/.

30. Chuck McCutcheon, *The Elections of 2012: Outcomes and Analysis* (Washington, D.C.: CQ Press, 2013).

31. *U.S. Term Limits, Inc. v. Thornton*, 515 U.S. 779 (1995).

32. Keith A. Ham and Gary P. Moncrief, "Legislative Politics in the States," in *Politics in the American States*, 9th ed., eds. Gray and Hanson, 170–171.

33. Catherine Rampell and Nick Wingfield, "In Shift of Jobs, Apple Will Make Some Macs in U.S.," *New York Times*, December 7, 2012.

34. Michael Delli Carpini and Scott Keeter, *What Americans Know about Politics and Why It Matters* (New Haven, Conn.: Yale University Press, 1996), 62–134.

35. Ibid., 133.

36. Baumer and Gold, *Parties, Polarization, and Democracy*; Erikson and Tedin, *Public Opinion*, 8th ed., chap. 11.

37. Samuel Kernell, Gary Jacobson, and Thad Kousser, *The Logic of American Politics*, 5th ed. (Washington, D.C.: CQ Press, 2012), 462–464.

38. Robert Putnam, *Bowling Alone: The Collapse and Revival of American Community* (New York: Simon & Schuster, 2000).

39. Mark E. Warren, *Democracy and Association* (Princeton, N.J.: Princeton University Press, 2000), 142–162; see also Matthew Baggetta, Chaeyoon Lim, Kenneth T. Andrews, Marshall Ganz, and Hahrie C. Hahn, "Learning Civic Leadership: Leader Skill Development in the Sierra Club," in *Interest Group Politics*, 8th ed., eds. Allen J. Cigler and Burdett A. Loomis (Washington, D.C.: CQ Press, 2012), 110–138.

40. Russell J. Dalton, *The Good Citizen: How a Younger Generation Is Reshaping American Politics*, rev. ed. (Washington, D.C.: CQ Press, 2009).

41. Benjamin R. Barber, *Strong Democracy: Participatory Politics for a New Age* (Berkeley: University of California Press, 1984), chap. 10; Benjamin R. Barber, *A Place for Us: How to Make Society Civil and Democracy Strong* (New York: Hill & Wang, 1998), 75.

42. William T. Gormley Jr. and David L. Weimer, *Organizational Report Cards* (Cambridge, Mass.: Harvard University Press, 1999).

43. Ibid., 24.

44. See Marjorie Cohn and David Dow, *Cameras in the Courtroom: Television and the Pursuit of Justice* (Jefferson, N.C.: McFarland and Company, 2011); Norman Davis, "Television in Our Courts: The Proven Advantages, the Unproven Disadvantages," *Judicature* 64 (August 1980): 85–92.

45. Lowi, *The End of Liberalism*, 2nd ed., 298.

46. *Schechter Poultry Co. v. United States*, 295 U.S. 495 (1935).

47. Jeremy W. Peters, "New Senate Rules to Curtail the Excesses of a Filibuster," *New York Times*, January 25, 2013.

48. Davidson et al., *Congress and Its Members*, 13th ed., 111–112.

49. Gabriel A. Almond, Russell J. Dalton, and G. Bingham Powell Jr., *European Politics Today*, 2nd ed. (New York: Longman, 2002).

50. Keith Hamm and Gary Moncrief, "Legislative Politics in the States," in *Politics in the American States*, eds. Gray and Hanson, 170.

51. See, for example, E. S. Savas, *Privatization and Public-Private Partnerships* (Chatham, N.J.: Chatham House, 2000); Philip Howard, *The Death of Common Sense: How Law Is Suffocating America* (New York: Random House, 1994).

52. Charles Goodsell, *The Case for Bureaucracy: A Public Administration Polemic*, 3rd ed. (Chatham, N.J.: Chatham House, 1994).

53. B. Guy Peters, *The Politics of Bureaucracy*, 4th ed. (White Plains, N.Y.: Longman, 1995), 109.

54. Gormley and Balla, *Bureaucracy and Democracy*, 3rd ed., 282.

55. Cynthia Bowling and Deil Wright, "Change and Continuity in State Administration," *Public Administration Review* (September/October 1998): 431; Joel Aberbach and Bert Rockman, *In the Web of Politics: Three Decades of the U.S. Federal Executive* (Washington, D.C.: Brookings Institution, 2000).

56. Gormley and Balla, *Bureaucracy and Democracy*, 3rd ed., 281–285.

57. Barbara Romzek, "Where the Buck Stops: Accountability in Reformed Public Organizations," in *Transforming Government: Lessons from the Reinvention Laboratories*, eds. Patricia Ingraham, James Thompson, and Ronald Sanders (San Francisco, Calif.: Jossey-Bass Publishers, 1998), 193–219.

58. See Joan Biskupic, "Bush Lags in Appointments to the Federal Judiciary," *Congressional Quarterly Weekly Report*, January 6, 1990.

59. Baum, *The Supreme Court*, 10th ed., 25–36.

60. Harold Leventhal, "Environmental Decision-Making and the Role of the Courts," *University of Pennsylvania Law Review* 122 (January 1974): 514.

61. Ibid., 550.

62. Walter A. Rosenbaum, *Environmental Politics and Policy*, 8th ed. (Washington, D.C.: CQ Press, 2011), 114.

63. Robert C. Paehlke, "Sustainable Development and Urban Life in North America," in *Environmental Policy*, 8th ed., eds. Vig and Kraft, 255–276.

CHAPTER 10

1. See, for example, President's Commission for a National Agenda for the Eighties, *A National Agenda for the Eighties* (Englewood Cliffs, N.J.: Prentice Hall, 1980); The White House, "Remarks by the President in State of the Union Address," January 24, 2012, www.whitehouse.gov/the-press-office/2012/01/24/remarks-president-state-union-address.

2. See, for example, Carol Weiss, *Evaluation Research: Methods for Assessing Program Effectiveness* (Englewood Cliffs, N.J.: Prentice Hall, 1972); Frank Fischer, *Evaluating Public Policy* (Chicago: Nelson-Hall, 1995); Peter Rossi and Howard E. Freeman, *Evaluation: A Systematic Approach*, 8th ed. (Thousand Oaks, Calif.: Sage, 1999); and Michael C. Munger, *Analyzing Policy: Choices, Conflicts, and Practice* (New York: W. W. Norton, 2000).

3. Environmental Protection Agency, "Climate Change," www.epa.gov/climatechange/.

4. World Bank, "Mortality Rate, Infant (per 1,000 Live Births)," http://data.worldbank.org/indicator/SP.DYN.IMRT.IN.

5. Alice R. Buchalter, *Military Support to Civil Authorities: The Role of the Department of Defense in Support of Homeland Defense* (Washington, D.C.: U.S. Government Printing Office, 2007).

6. Jan Austin, ed., *CQ Almanac 2010* (Washington, D.C.: CQ Roll Call, 2011), 2–14.

7. Megan Scully, "A Change in Course for Some Significant Programs," *CQ Weekly*, February 20, 2012.

8. Office of Management and Budget, "Historical Tables," www.whitehouse.gov/omb/budget/Historicals.

9. Roxana Tiron, "U.S. Navy Bets $42 Billion on Carriers in China's Sights," Bloomberg News, June 19, 2012, www.bloomberg.com/news/2012-06-19/u-s-navy-bets-42-billion-on-carriers-in-china-s-sights.html.

10. U.S. Department of Defense, "About the Department of Defense (DOD)," www.defense.gov/about/.

11. Luis Martinez and Amy Bingham, "U.S. Veterans: By the Numbers," ABC News, November 11, 2011, http://abcnews.go.com/Politics/us-veterans-numbers/story?id=14928136#; Rand Corporation, "After Nearly a Decade of War, Servicemembers and Families Report Stress, Resilience," 2011, www.rand.org/content/dam/rand/pubs/corporate_pubs/2011/RAND_CP22-2011-09.centerpiece.pdf.

12. Office of Management and Budget, "Historical Tables."

13. Ibid.

14. *Economic Report of the President* (Washington, D.C.: U.S. Government Printing Office, 1985); John L. Palmer and Isabel V. Sawhill, *The Reagan Record: An Assessment of Changing Domestic Priorities* (Cambridge, Mass.: Ballinger, 1984), 8.

15. Megan Scully, "A Change in Course."

16. Pat Towell, "Congress Set to Provide Money, but No Guidance, for War in Kosovo," *CQ Weekly*, May 1, 1999.

17. Amy Belasco, "The Cost of Iraq, Afghanistan, and Other Global War on Terror Operations Since 9/11," CRS Report for Congress, March 29, 2011, www.digital.library.unt.edu/ark:/67531/metadc99090/?q=%20defense%20economics%22.

18. Watson Institute, "Costs of War," http://costsofwar.org.

19. U.S. Department of Defense, www.defense.gov/news/casualty.pdf.

20. Ed Clifton, "Suicide Rate in Military at Highest Level in Ten Years," June 8, 2012, http://thinkprogress.org/security/2012/06/08/496604/military-suicide/?mobile=nc.

21. National Science Foundation, National Center for Science and Engineering Statistics, "Chapter 2. Higher Education in Science and Engineering," www.nsf.gov/statistics/seind12/c2/c2s2.htm.

22. Richard Dobbs, Anu Madgavkar, Dominic Barton, Eric Labaye, James Manyika, Charles Roxburgh, Susan Lund, and Siddarth Madhav, "The World at Work: Jobs, Pay, and Skills for 3.5 Billion People," McKinsey Global Institute, June 2012, www.mckinsey.com/insights/mgi/research/labor_markets/the_world_at_work.

23. U.S. Congress, Joint Economic Committee, *The Pivotal Role of Government Investment in Basic Research* (Washington, D.C.: U.S. Government Printing Office, 2010).

24. Office of Management and Budget, *Budget of the United States Government, Fiscal Year 1992* (Washington, D.C.: U.S. Government Printing Office, 1991), 35; Congressional Budget Office, "R&D and Productivity Growth" (Washington, D.C.: U.S. Government Printing Office, 2005).

25. Associated General Contractors of America, "Infrastructure Investment: Federal Budget," www.agc.org/cs/federal_budget.

26. Scott Thomasson, "Encouraging U.S. Infrastructure Investment," www.cfr.org/infrastructure/encouraging-us-infrastructure-investment/p27771.

27. Bureau of Business and Economic Research, University of New Mexico, "Per Capita Personal Income by State," http://bber.unm.edu/econ/us-pci.htm.

28. Bruce R. Scott, "U.S. Competitiveness: Concepts, Performance, and Implications," in *U.S. Competitiveness in the World Economy*, eds. Bruce R. Scott and George C. Lodge (Boston: Harvard Business School Press, 1985), 36–37; Robert Kuttner, *The Economic Illusion: False Choices between Prosperity and Social Justice* (Boston: Houghton Mifflin, 1984), 291.

29. Organisation for Economic Co-operation and Development, *Is There a New Economy? First Report on the OECD Growth Project* (Paris, France: OECD Publications, 2000), 4–5.

30. Scott, "U.S. Competitiveness," 35–36.

31. Ibid., 39; Robert B. Reich, *The Next American Frontier: A Provocative Program for Economic Renewal* (New York: Times Books, 1983), 118.

32. Jacob S. Hacker and Paul Pierson, *Winner-Take-All Politics: How Washington Made the Rich Richer—And Turned Its Back on the Middle Class* (New York: Simon & Schuster, 2010), 27.

33. Harry J. Holzer and Marek Hlavac, "A Very Uneven Road: U.S. Labor Markets in the Past 30 Years," March 2010, www.s4.brown.edu/us2010/Data/Report/report03082012.pdf.

34. Paul Krugman, "The Big Zero," *New York Times*, December 27, 2009.

35. World Bank, "Mortality Rate, Infant (per 1,000 Live Births)."

36. U.S. Department of Labor, Bureau of Labor Statistics, "International Comparisons of Annual Labor Force Statistics, Adjusted to U.S. Concepts, 16 Countries, 1970–2011," www.bls.gov/fls/flscomparelf/tables.htm#table01_ur.

37. See William Julius Wilson, *When Work Disappears: The World of the New Urban Poor* (New York: Knopf, 1996).

38. U.S. Department of Labor, Bureau of Labor Statistics, "Databases, Tables & Calculators by Subject," http://data.bls.gov/pdq/SurveyOutputServlet.

39. U.S. Department of Labor, Bureau of Labor Statistics, "Labor Force Statistics from the Current Population Survey," http://stats.bls.gov/cps/cpsaat01.htm.

40. U.S. Department of Labor, Bureau of Labor Statistics, "The Employment Situation: December 2012," www.bls.gov/news.release/archives/empsit_01042013.pdf.

41. CoinNews Media Group, "Historical Inflation Rates: 1914–2013," US Inflation Calculator, www.usinflationcalculator.com/inflation/historical-inflation-rates/.

42. Binyamin Appelbaum, "Fed Ties Rates to Joblessness; 6.5% Is Target," *New York Times*, December 12, 2012; Binyamin Appelbaum, "Fed to Maintain Stimulus Efforts Despite Jobs Growth," *New York Times*, March 20, 2013.

43. Gunnar Myrdal, *An American Dilemma: The Negro Problem and Modern Democracy* (New York: Harper & Row, 1944).

44. Carmen De Navas-Walt, Bernadette D. Proctor, and Jessica C. Smith, "Income, Poverty and Health Insurance Coverage in the United States: 2011," U.S Census Bureau, September 2012, www.census.gov/prod/2012pubs/p60-243.pdf.

45. Organisation for Economic Co-operation and Development, "United States: Income Key Findings," OECD Better Life Index, www.oecdbetterlifeindex.org/countries/united-states/; Organisation for Economic Co-operation and Development, "Society at a Glance—OECD Social Indicators," December 4, 2011, www.oecd.org/social/socialpoliciesanddata/47573390.pdf.

46. Lawrence Mishel and Natalie Sabadish, "CEO Pay and the Top 1%: How Executive Compensation and Financial Sector Pay Have Fueled Income Inequality," Economic Policy Institute, May 2, 2012, www.epi.org/files/2012/ib331-ceo-pay-top-1-percent.pdf.

47. Arthur M. Okun, *Equality and Efficiency: The Big Tradeoff* (Washington, D.C.: Brookings Institution, 1975), 1.

48. *Economic Report of the President*, 320.
49. Suzanne Macartney, "Child Poverty in the United States 2009 and 2010: Selected Race Groups and Hispanic Origin," U.S. Census Bureau, November 2011, www.census.gov/prod/2011pubs/acsbr10-05.pdf.
50. De Navas-Walt et al., "Income, Poverty and Health Insurance Coverage in the United States."
51. Organisation for Economic Co-operation and Development, "Growing Income Inequality in OECD Countries: What Drives It and How Can Policy Tackle It?" May 2, 2011, www.oecd.org/els/socialpoliciesanddata/47723414.pdf; Emmanuel Saez, "Striking It Richer: The Evolution of Top Incomes in the Unites States (Updated with 2009 and 2010 Estimates)," March 2, 2012, http://elsa.berkley.edu/~saez-UStopincomes-2010.pdf.
52. Organisation for Economic Co-operation and Development, "Reducing Income Inequality While Boosting Economic Growth: Can It Be Done?" in *Economic Policy Reforms 2012: Going for Growth*, 2012, chap. 5, www.oecd.org/eco/labourmarketshumancapitalandinequality/49421421.pdf.
53. Edward N. Wolff, "The Asset Price Meltdown and the Wealth of the Middle Class," National Bureau of Economic Research, November 2012, www.nber.org/papers/w18559.pdf.
54. Benjamin I. Page, *Who Gets What from Government* (Berkley: University of California Press, 1983), 22–23.
55. Daniel P. Gitterman, Lucy S. Gorham, and Jessica L. Dorrance, "Expanding the EITC for Single Workers and Couples with*out* Children (aka Tax Relief for Low-Wage Workers)," University of North Carolina, January 2007, www.law.unc.edu/documents/poverty/publications/gitterman policybrief.pdf.
56. Ibid.
57. Ibid.
58. Steve Holt, "Ten Years of the EITC Movement: Making Work Pay Then and Now," Brookings Institution, February 2011, www.brookings.edu/~/media/research/files/papers/2011/4/18%20eitc%20holt/0418_eitc_holt.pdf.
59. Blake Ellis, "Don't Overlook This $6,000 Tax Credit," CNNMoney, April 12, 2012, http://money.cnn.com/2012/04/12/pf/taxes/earned-income-tax-credit/index.htm.
60. "Warren E. Buffet," *New York Times*, updated January 4, 2013, http://topics.nytimes.com/top/reference/timestopics/people/b/warren_e_buffett/index.html.
61. Eric Toder, Margery Austin Turner, Katherine Lim, and Liza Getsinger, "Reforming the Mortgage Interest Deduction," Tax Policy Center, Urban Institute and Brookings Institution, April 2010, www.taxpolicycenter.org/UploadedPDF/412099-mortgage-deduction-reform.pdf.
62. Kenneth R. Harney, "Limit on Mortgage Interest Deduction Would Penalize Only a Minority of Taxpayers," *Washington Post*, October 26, 2012.
63. Joseph A. Pechman, *Federal Tax Policy*, 4th ed. (Washington, D.C.: Brookings Institution, 1983), 60–128.
64. Social Security Administration, "Update 2013," SSA Publication No. 05-10003, www.ssa.gov/pubs/10003.pdf.
65. Page, *Who Gets What from Government*, 35–41.
66. U.S. Census Bureau, "Income, Poverty and Health Insurance Coverage in the United States: 2011," September 12, 2012, www.census.gov/newsroom/releases/archives/income_wealth/cb12-172.html.
67. Bureau of Labor Statistics, "Economic News Release: Table A-3. Employment Status of the Hispanic or Latino Population by Sex and Age," www.bls.gov/news.release/empsit.t03.htm; Bureau of Labor Statistics, "Economic News Release: Table A-2. Employment Status of the Civilian Population by Race, Sex, and Age," www.bls.gov/news.release/empsit.t02.htm.
68. U.S. Census Bureau, "Income, Poverty and Health Insurance Coverage in the United States."
69. Ibid.
70. Thomas Gabe, "Poverty in the United States: 2011," Congressional Research Service (Washington, D.C.: U.S. Government Printing Office, 2012).
71. Ibid.

72. Bureau of Labor Statistics, "Characteristics of Minimum Wage Workers: 2011," www.bls.gov/cps/minwage2011tbls.html.
73. John Schmitt, "The Minimum Wage Is Too Damn Low," Center for Economic and Policy Research, March 2012, www.cepr.net/documents/publications/min-wage1-2012-03.pdf.
74. Ibid.
75. National Center for Education Statistics, "Characteristics of Postsecondary Students: Table A-39-2. Percentage Distribution of Fall Enrollment of Each Racial/Ethnic Group in Degree-Granting Institutions, by Control of Institution and Concentration of Racial/Ethnic Group: Fall 2008," http://nces.ed.gov/programs/coe/tables/table-hec-2.asp.
76. Ibid.
77. Motoko Rich, "Segregation Prominent in Schools, Study Finds," *New York Times*, September 19, 2012.
78. Scott Jaschik, "Measures of Segregation," *Inside Higher Ed*, January 4, 2013, www.insidehighered.com/news/2013/01/04/data-presented-economics-meeting-show-extent-desegregation-higher-education.
79. U.S. Census Bureau, "Census Bureau Releases Equal Employment Opportunity Tabulation That Provides a Profile of America's Workforce," November 29, 2012, www.census.gov/newsroom/releases/archives/employment_occupations/cb12-225.html.
80. De Navas-Walt et al., "Income, Poverty, and Health Insurance Coverage in the United States."
81. Richard Perez-Pena, "U.S. Bachelor Degree Rate Passes Milestone," *New York Times*, February 23, 2012.
82. Borgna Brunner, "Timeline of Affirmative Action Milestones," http://infoplease.com/spot/affirmativetimeline1.html.
83. Ariane de Vogue, "Affirmative Action: Supreme Court Justices Skeptical of University of Texas Plan," ABC News, October 10, 2012, http://abcnews.go.com/blogs/politics/2012/10/affirmative-action-supreme-court-justices-skeptical-of-university-of-texas-plan/.
84. Ibid.
85. Adam Liptak, "Justices Weigh Race as Factor at Universities," *New York Times*, October 10, 2012 and Adam Liptak, "Justices Step Up Scrutiny of Race in College Entry," *New York Times*, June 25, 2013, A1, A12.
86. Carl E. Van Horn, *Working Scared (or Not at All): The Lost Decade, Great Recession, and Restoring the Shattered American Dream* (Lanham, Md.: Rowman & Littlefield, 2013).
87. Office of Management and Budget, "Historical Tables," Table 3-2.
88. Ibid; Bureau of Economic Analysis, U.S. Department of Commerce, "National Income and Product Accounts: Gross Domestic Product for Third Quarter 2012," www.bea.gov/newsreleases/national/gdp/gdpnewsrelease.htm.
89. Office of Management and Budget, "Fiscal Year 2013: Historical Tables," (Washington, D.C.: U.S. Government Printing Office, 2012).
90. R. Kent Weaver, "Controlling Entitlements," in *The New Direction in American Politics*, eds. John E. Chubb and Paul E. Peterson (Washington, D.C.: Brookings Institution, 1985), 308.
91. Congressional Budget Office, "The Budget and Economic Outlook: Fiscal Years 2012 to 2022," January 2012 (Washington, D.C.: U.S. Government Printing Office, 2012).
92. U.S. Social Security Administration, "Social Security Basic Facts," July 30, 2012, www.ssa.gov/pressoffice/basicfact.htm.
93. Bureau of Labor Statistics, "Economic News Release: Table B. Employment Status of the Civilian Population by Race, Sex, and Age, Seasonally Adjusted," www.bls.gov/news.release/empsit.nr0.htm; Hannah Shaw and Chad Stone, "Introduction to Unemployment Insurance," Center on Budget and Policy Priorities, www.cbpp.org/files/12-19-02ui.pdf.
94. U.S. Department of Agriculture, Food and Nutrition Service, "Supplemental Nutrition Assistance Program (SNAP)," www.fns.usda.gov/cga/FactSheets/SNAP_Quick_Facts.htm.
95. Arloc Sherman, Robert Greenstein, and Kathy Ruffing, "Contrary to 'Entitlement Society' Rhetoric, over Nine-Tenths of Entitlement Benefits go to Elderly, Disabled, or Working Households," Center on Budget and Policy Priorities, February 10, 2012, www.cbpp.org/files/2-10-12pov.pdf.

96. Center on Budget and Policy Priorities, "Top Ten Facts about Social Security," November 6, 2012, www.cbpp.org/files/PolicyBasics_SocSec-TopTen.pdf.

97. Shaw and Stone, "Introduction to Unemployment Insurance."

98. U.S. Census Bureau, "Labor Force, Employment, and Earnings," 2011, www.census.gov/prod/2011pubs/12statab/labor.pdf, p. 405.

99. C. Eugene Steuerle and Stephanie Rennane, "Social Security and Medicare Taxes and Benefits over a Lifetime," Urban Institute, updated June 2011, www.urban.org/UploadedPDF/social-security-medicare-benefits-over-lifetime.pdf.

100. U.S. Census Bureau, "Poverty: Highlights," www.census.gov/hhes/www/poverty/about/overview/.

101. Employee Benefit Research Institute, "Income of the Elderly Population Age 65 and Over, 2005," *EBRI Notes*, May 2007.

102. Center on Budget and Policy Priorities, "Top Ten Facts about Social Security."

103. Ibid.

104. Weaver, "Controlling Entitlements," 320.

105. Liz Schott and Zachary Levinson, "TANF Benefits Are Low and Have Not Kept Pace with Inflation," Center on Budget and Policy Priorities, November 24, 2008, www.cbpp.org/pdf/11-24-08tanf.pdf.

106. Ibid.

107. D. Andrew Austin and Mindy R. Levit, "Mandatory Spending Since 1962," Congressional Research Service, March 23, 2012, www.fas.org/sgp/crs/misc/RL33074.pdf.

108. Ron Haskins, "Reflecting on SNAP: Purposes, Spending, and Potential Savings," Brookings Institute, May 8, 2012, www.brookings.edu/research/testimony/2012/05/08-snap-haskins. The figures cited are not adjusted for inflation.

109. Congressional Budget Office, "An Overview of the Supplemental Nutrition Assistance Program," April 19, 2012, www.cbo.gov/publication/43175.

110. Office of Management and Budget, "Historical Tables."

111. Federal spending for Medicare, Medicaid, and the Children's Health Insurance Program came to $790 billion in 2011; adding an estimated $170 billion from the states for Medicaid brings the public spending total very close to $1 trillion, which is almost 40 percent of the $2.7 trillion in health care spending overall. Office of Management and Budget, "Historical Tables"; Robert Pear, "Growth of Health Spending Stays Low," *New York Times*, January 8, 2013.

112. Ibid., Eduardo Porter, "Health Care and Profits, a Poor Mix," *New York Times*, January 9, 2013.

113. Fredic Blavin, John Holahan, Genevieve Kenney, and Vicki Chen, "A Decade of Coverage Losses: Implication for the Affordable Care Act," Urban Institute, 2011, www.urban.org/UploadedPDF/412514-Implications-for-the-Affordable-Care-Act.pdf.

114. Phil Galewitz, "How Will the Election Change Medicaid?" Kaiser Health News, October 3, 2012, www.kaiserhealthnews.org/stories/2012/october/04/medicaid-obama-romney-election.aspx.

115. Weaver, "Controlling Entitlements," 328.

116. Centers for Disease Control and Prevention, "Trends in Current Cigarette Smoking among High School Students and Adults, United States, 1965–2011," www.cdc.gov/tobacco/data_statistics/tables/trends/cig_smoking/index.htm.

117. Jessica Dimmock, "Pounding Away at America's Obesity Epidemic," National Public Radio, May 12, 2012, www.npr.org/2012/05/14/152667325/pounding-away-at-americas-obesity-epidemic.

118. Porter, "Health Care and Profits, a Poor Mix."

119. President's Commission for a National Agenda for the Eighties, *A National Agenda for the Eighties*, 49.

120. Barack Obama, "Inaugural Address by President Barack Obama," The White House, January 21, 2013, www.whitehouse.gov/the-press-office/2013/01/21/inaugural-address-president-barack-obama.

121. Ross W. Gorte, Carol Hardy Vincent, Laura A. Hanson, and Marc R. Rosenblum, "Federal Land Ownership: Overview and Data," Congressional Research Service, February 8, 2012, www.fas.org/sgp/crs/misc/R42346.pdf.

122. Walter A. Rosenbaum, *Environmental Politics and Policy* (Washington, D.C.: Congressional Quarterly, 1985), 100.

123. Richard Andrews, *Managing the Environment, Managing Ourselves: A History of American Environmental Policy* (New Haven, Conn.: Yale University Press, 1999), 271; Sheila M. Olmstead, "Applying Market Principles to Environmental Policy," in *Environmental Policy*, 8th ed., eds. Norman J. Vig and Michael E. Kraft (Washington, D.C.: CQ Press, 2013), 206–229.

124. Environmental Protection Agency, "Clear Skies Act of 2003," www.epa.gov/clearskies/fact2003.html.

125. Michael E. Kraft, "Environmental Policy in Congress," in *Environmental Policy*, 8th ed., eds. Vig and Kraft, 109–134.

126. Chris Mooney, "After Bush, Restoring Science to Environmental Policy," *Yale Environment 360*, June 25, 2008, http://e360.yale.edu/feature/after_bush_restoring_science_to_environmental_policy/2033/.

127. The White House, "Energy, Climate Change and Our Environment," www.whitehouse.gov/energy/our-environment#energy-menu.

128. Ibid.

129. Ibid.

130. Paul Glastris, Ryan Cooper, and Siyu Hu, "Obama's Top 50 Accomplishments," *Washington Monthly*, March/April 2012.

131. Ibid.

132. John M. Broder, "After Federal Jolt, Clean Energy Seeks New Spark," *New York Times*, October 23, 2012.

133. Ibid.

134. Glastris et al., "Obama's Top 50 Accomplishments," 2.

135. Ibid.

136. Norman J. Vig and Michael E. Kraft, "Toward Sustainable Development?" in *Environmental Policy*, 8th ed., eds. Vig and Kraft, 370–394.

137. Environmental Protection Agency, "National Water Program: Best Practices and End of Year Performance Report—Executive Summary: Fiscal Year 2011," April 2012, http://water.epa.gov/resource_performance/performance/upload/Executive_Summary_-OW_EOY_Report.pdf.

138. Environmental Protection Agency, "40 Years of Achievements, 1970–2010," www.epa.gov/40th/achieve.html.

139. Michael E. Kraft and Norman J. Vig, "Environmental Policy over Four Decades," in *Environmental Policy*, 8th ed., eds. Vig and Kraft, 22.

140. Environmental Protection Agency, "40 Years of Achievements."

141. Dan Vergano, "Natural Gas Gold Rush: Is Your State Next?" *USA Today*, July 2, 2012.

142. Ibid.

143. Daniel Gilber and Russell Gold, "EPA Backpedals on Fracking Contamination," *Wall Street Journal*, April 1, 2012, http://online.wsj.com/article/SB10001424052702303404704577313741463447670.html.

144. Walter A. Rosenbaum, *Environmental Politics and Policy*, 8th ed. (Washington, D.C.: CQ Press, 2011), 201.

145. Kraft and Vig, "Environmental Policy over Four Decades," 20.

146. Environmental Protection Agency, "Our Nation's Air: Status and Trends through 2010," Report EPA-454/R-12-001, February 2012, www.epa.gov/airtrends/2011/report/fullreport.pdf.

147. Ibid.

148. Rosenbaum, *Environmental Politics and Policy*, 8th ed., 251.

149. Ibid., 247–248; Environmental Protection Agency, "Toxics Release Inventory: Summary of Key Findings, 2007," www.epa.gov/tri/NationalAnalysis/archive/2007_National_Analysis_ Overview_Brochure.pdf.

150. James Hamilton, "Pollution as News: Media and Stock Market Reactions to the Toxic Release Inventory Data," *Journal of Environmental Economics and Management* 28 (1995): 98–113.

151. Environmental Protection Agency, "2011 TRI National Analysis: Briefing Slides," January 9, 2012, www.epa.gov/tri/tridata/tri11/nationalanalysis/briefingslides/2011_TRI_National_ Analysis_Briefing_Slides.pdf.

152. Environmental Protection Agency, "EPA's 2011 Toxics Release Inventory Shows Air Pollutants Continue to Decline/Total Toxic Chemicals Increase as a Result of Mining," January 16, 2013, http://yosemite.epa.gov/opa/admpress.nsf/0c0affede4f840bc85257 81f00436213/c50e11354ba76aae85257af500581f24!OpenDocument.

153. Office of Technology Assessment, *Technologies and Management Strategies for Hazardous Waste Control* (Washington, D.C.: U.S. Government Printing Office, 1983), 7n1.

154. Kraft and Vig, "Environmental Policy over Four Decades," 23.

155. Environmental Protection Agency, "EPA Announces Superfund Cleanup Progress for FY 2009," March 4, 2010, http://yosemite.epa.gov/opa/admpress.nsf/652d9edd5cf71a258525735 9003f5343/41cc05cbd62cd7f7852576dc005c76eb!OpenDocument.

156. Ibid.

157. Braunson Virjee, "Stimulating the Future of Superfund: Why the American Recovery and Reinvestment Act Calls for a Reinvestment of the Superfund Tax to Polluted Sites in Urban Environments," *Sustainable Development Law & Policy* 11, no. 1 (2011): 27–65.

158. Ibid.

159. Environmental Protection Agency, "Unfinished Business: A Comparative Assessment of Environmental Problems" (Washington, D.C.: Environmental Protection Agency, February 1987), xiii.

160. National Research Council, "America's Climate Choices: Final Report" (Washington, D.C.: National Academies Press, 2011); United Nations, "The Earth's Changing Climate," www .un.org/wcm/content/site/climatechange/pages/gateway/the-science/the-earths-changing-climate.

161. United Nations Environment Programme, "World Remains on Unsustainable Track Despite Hundreds of Internationally Agreed Goals and Objectives," June 6, 2012, www.unep.org/geo/ pdfs/geo5/GEO5-Global_PR_EN.pdf.

162. United Nations Statistics Division, "Millennium Development Goals Indicators," http:// unstats.un.org/unsd/mdg/Default.aspx.

163. Eduardo Porter, "A Model for Reducing Emissions," *New York Times*, March 20, 2013.

164. The World Bank, "Cost of Pollution in China: Economic Estimates of Physical Damages," February 2007, http://siteresources.worldbank.org/INTEAPREGTOPENVIRONMENT/ Resources/China_Cost_of_Pollution.pdf.

165. Joseph Kahn and Jim Yardley, "As China Roars, Pollution Reaches Deadly Extremes," *New York Times*, August, 25, 2007.

166. Kelly Sims Gallagher and Johanna I. Lewis, "China's Quest for a Greener Economy," in *Environmental Policy*, 8th ed., eds. Vig and Kraft, 325.

167. Stanford Report, "Developing Countries Often Outsource Deforestation, Study Finds," Stanford News, November 24, 2010, http://news.stanford.edu/news/2010/november/woods-outsource-deforestation-112410.html.

168. World Commission on Environment and Development, *Our Common Future: From One Earth to One World* (New York: Oxford University Press, 1987), 4.

169. United Nations Environment Programme, "World Remains on Unsustainable Track."

Donald C. Baumer is professor of government at Smith College. Past research and publication projects have covered employment and training policy, Senate leadership, and public images of political parties. His most recent book, co-authored with Howard J. Gold, is *Parties, Polarization, and Democracy in the United States* (Paradigm Publishers, 2010).

Carl E. Van Horn is professor of public policy and the director of the John J. Heldrich Center for Workforce Development at Rutgers University's Edward J. Bloustein School of Planning and Public Policy. He is also the author of *Working Scared (Or Not at All): The Lost Decade, Great Recession, and Restoring the Shattered American Dream* (Rowman & Lttlefield, 2013).

CQ Press, an imprint of SAGE, is the leading publisher of books, periodicals, and electronic products on American government and international affairs. CQ Press consistently ranks among the top commercial publishers in terms of quality, as evidenced by the numerous awards its products have won over the years. CQ Press owes its existence to Nelson Poynter, former publisher of the *St. Petersburg Times,* and his wife Henrietta, with whom he founded Congressional Quarterly in 1945. Poynter established CQ with the mission of promoting democracy through education and in 1975 founded the Modern Media Institute, renamed The Poynter Institute for Media Studies after his death. The Poynter Institute (*www.poynter.org*) is a nonprofit organization dedicated to training journalists and media leaders.

In 2008, CQ Press was acquired by SAGE, a leading international publisher of journals, books, and electronic media for academic, educational, and professional markets. Since 1965, SAGE has helped inform and educate a global community of scholars, practitioners, researchers, and students spanning a wide range of subject areas, including business, humanities, social sciences, and science, technology, and medicine. A privately owned corporation, SAGE has offices in Los Angeles, London, New Delhi, and Singapore, in addition to the Washington DC office of CQ Press.